SCHOOLING AROUND THE WORLD

SCHOOLING AROUND THE WORLD

Debates, Challenges, and Practices

KAS MAZUREK

The University of Lethbridge

MARGRET A. WINZER

The University of Lethbridge

PEARSON

Boston ■ New York ■ San Francisco ■ Mexico City ■ Montreal
Toronto ■ London ■ Madrid ■ Munich ■ Paris ■ Hong Kong
Singapore ■ Tokyo ■ Cape Town ■ Sydney

Executive Editor and Publisher: *Stephen D. Dragin*
Editorial Assistant: *Meaghan Minnick*
Marketing Manager: *Tara Kelly*
Production Editor: *Greg Erb*
Editorial Production Service: *Walsh & Associates, Inc.*
Composition and Manufacturing Buyer: *Andrew Turso*
Electronic Composition: *Publishers' Design and Production Services, Inc.*
Cover Administrator: *Joel Gendron*

For related titles and support materials, visit our online catalog at www.ablongman.com.

Between the time website information is gathered and then published, it is not unusual for some sites to have closed. Also, the transcription of URLs can result in typographical errors. The publisher would appreciate notification where these errors occur so that they may be corrected in subsequent editions.

Library of Congress Cataloging-in-Publication Data

Mazurek, Kas.
Schooling around the world : debates, challenges, and practices / Kas Mazurek, Margret A. Winzer.—1st ed.
p. cm.
Includes bibliographical references and index.
ISBN 0-205-45459-3
1. Comparative education. 2. Education—Cross-cultural studies. 3. Educational change—Cross-cultural studies. I. Winzer, M. A. (Margret A.), 1940- II. Title.

LB43.M324 2005
370'.9—dc22 2005050809

Printed in the United States of America

10 9 8 7 6 5 4 3 2 1 RRD-VA 09 08 07 06 05

In memory of Professor Czeslaw Majorek. Dear friend and colleague; internationally acclaimed scholar. You are deeply missed.

CONTENTS

Preface xv

PART I ABOUT THIS BOOK 1

CHAPTER ONE
An Introduction, Overview, and Guide for Students 3
KAS MAZUREK AND MARGRET A. WINZER

COMPARATIVE STUDIES AS A COMPONENT OF TEACHER EDUCATION 4
VARIETIES OF COMPARATIVE STUDIES IN EDUCATION 4
THE VALUE AND UTILITY OF COMPARATIVE STUDIES IN EDUCATION 4
APPROACHES TO COMPARATIVE STUDIES IN EDUCATION 7
THE NEED FOR THIS TEXTBOOK 8
A NOTE ON CONTRIBUTING AUTHORS 9
THE STRUCTURE OF CONTRIBUTORS' CHAPTERS 10
WHY BOTHER? 12
A BLUEPRINT TO ASSIST YOU 13
MAJOR THEMES 14
OPTIMISM: A CONCLUDING COMMENT 27

PART II THE PACIFIC RIM: A LANDSCAPE OF DIVERSITY 29

CHAPTER TWO
Japanese Schooling: Tradition and Modernization 31
HIROYUKI NUMATA

THE SOCIAL FABRIC 32
SCHOOLING 34

SUCCESSES, CHALLENGES, AND DEBATES 40

CONCLUSION 50

REFERENCES 51

CHAPTER THREE

Education in South Korea: Changes and Challenges 52

DAEYOUNG JUNG

HISTORY AND CULTURE 53

SOCIETY AND ECONOMY 54

SCHOOLING IN SOUTH KOREA 54

SUCCESSES, CHALLENGES, AND DEBATES 60

CONCLUSION 66

REFERENCES 67

CHAPTER FOUR

Education Reform for National Competitiveness in a Global Age: The Experience and Struggle of China 68

WING-WAH LAW

THE BROAD CONTEXT 69

STRUCTURE OF THE EDUCATION SYSTEM 72

RATIONALE AND OBJECTIVES: REFORMING EDUCATION 74

IMPLEMENTATION: REFORMING SCHOOLING AND CURRICULA 75

HIGHER EDUCATION REFORMS: THE PURSUIT OF EXPANSION AND EFFICIENCY 79

CONTENTIOUS ISSUES CREATED BY EDUCATION REFORMS 81

CONCLUSIONS: POLICY IMPLICATIONS FOR EDUCATION AND DEVELOPMENT IN A GLOBAL AGE 96

REFERENCES 99

CHAPTER FIVE

Schooling in Australia: The Interplay of Education, Politics, and Culture 104

CYNTHIA JOSEPH, MARGRET A. WINZER, AND VIKKI POLLARD

THE SOCIAL AND POLITICAL FABRIC OF CONTEMPORARY AUSTRALIAN SOCIETY 105

THE SCHOOLING SYSTEM IN AUSTRALIA 108

ISSUES IN AUSTRALIAN EDUCATION 113

CONCLUSION 118

REFERENCES 118

PART III THE MIDDLE EAST AND SOUTHWEST ASIA: PROGRESS IN THE FACE OF UNRESOLVED STRUGGLES 121

CHAPTER SIX

Palestine's Education System: Challenges, Trends, and Issues 123

SAMIR J. DUKMAK

NOTES ON TERMINOLOGY 123

THE SOCIAL FABRIC 124

THE SOCIAL AND HISTORICAL CONTEXT OF PALESTINIAN SCHOOLING 126

SCHOOLING 128

SUCCESSES 133

CHALLENGES 135

CHALLENGES ARISING FROM THE FIRST INTIFADA 137

DEBATES AND CONTROVERSIES 142

CONCLUDING COMMENTS: CREATING A VISION OF A FUTURE PALESTINIAN EDUCATION SYSTEM 146

REFERENCES 147

CHAPTER SEVEN

The Israeli Education System: Blending Dreams with Constraints 149

THOMAS P. GUMPEL AND ADAM E. NIR

A HISTORICAL AND POLITICAL PRIMER 150

SCHOOLING 156

LOOKING FORWARD: PROBLEMS AND CHALLENGES 160

CONCLUSION 165

REFERENCES 165

CHAPTER EIGHT

Education Systems in an Ideological State: Major Issues and Concerns in Pakistan 168

MAHNAZIR RIAZ

THE SOCIAL FABRIC 168

SCHOOLING 172

SUCCESSES, CHALLENGES, AND DEBATES 187

REFERENCES 190

CHAPTER NINE

Education in India: Progress and Promise in a Land of Paradox 192

JOHN P. ANCHAN

THE SOCIAL FABRIC 192

SCHOOLING 197

PROMISES AND POSSIBILITIES 202

CONCLUSION 203

REFERENCES 203

PART IV THE NEW EUROPE: SUSTAINING THE WEST; REINVENTING THE EAST 205

CHAPTER TEN

French Education's Dilemma in the Globalization Process: How to Accommodate Simultaneously the Objectives of Equality and Excellence? 207

ESTELLE ORIVEL AND FRANÇOIS ORIVEL

SOCIOECONOMIC CONTEXT 208

SCHOOLING 211

MAJOR ISSUES, CONTROVERSIES, AND PROBLEMS 217

THE FUTURE OF SOCIETY AND SCHOOLING 226

POSTSCRIPT 227

REFERENCES 228

CHAPTER ELEVEN

England: New Labour, New Schooling? 229

PHILIP GARNER

THE SOCIAL FABRIC 230

SCHOOLING IN ENGLAND 233

SUCCESSES 237

KEY DEBATES AND CHALLENGES 241

CONCLUDING OBSERVATIONS 244

REFERENCES 244

CHAPTER TWELVE

Schooling, Education Reforms, and Policy Shifts in the Russian Federation 246

JOSEPH ZAJDA

THE HISTORICAL AND SOCIAL FABRIC 247

SCHOOLING 249

EDUCATION REFORM AND POLICY SHIFTS 254

SUCCESSES IN EDUCATION REFORMS 256

EDUCATION REFORMS AND CHALLENGES 257

CONCLUSION 261

REFERENCES 262

CHAPTER THIRTEEN

Poland: Transformations in Society and Schooling 264

KAS MAZUREK AND CZESLAW MAJOREK

THE SOCIAL FABRIC 265

SCHOOLING 267

SUCCESSES, CHALLENGES, AND DEBATES 277

CONCLUDING COMMENTS 282

REFERENCES 282

PART V NORTH AMERICAN NEIGHBORS: WORLDS APART 285

CHAPTER FOURTEEN

Mexican Education: A Melding of History, Cultural Roots, and Reform 287

ALINA GAMBOA AND CAROLINE LINSE

THE SOCIAL FABRIC 287

SCHOOLING SYSTEM IN MEXICO 291

SUCCESSES IN MEXICAN EDUCATION 298

CHALLENGES FACING MEXICAN EDUCATION 300

CONCLUSION 302

REFERENCES 302

CHAPTER FIFTEEN
Schooling in the United States: Democratic and Market-Based Approaches 304
TIMOTHY E. JESTER

THE SOCIAL FABRIC: SCHOOLS' SOCIOCULTURAL CONTEXT 305
SCHOOLING IN THE UNITED STATES 309
MULTICULTURAL EDUCATION 311
STANDARDS-BASED EDUCATION 314
SUCCESSES, CHALLENGES, AND DEBATES 318
CONCLUSION 321
REFERENCES 322

PART VI SNAPSHOTS FROM TWO SOUTHERN CONTINENTS: REPAIR AND RECONSTRUCTION; LEARNING FROM EXPERIENCE 325

CHAPTER SIXTEEN
Post-Apartheid Policy and Practice: Education Reform in South Africa 327
DAVID GILMOUR, CRAIN SOUDIEN, AND DAVID DONALD

THE SOCIAL FABRIC 328
SCHOOLING 329
MAJOR ISSUES, CONTROVERSIES, AND PROBLEMS 332
THE FUTURE OF SOCIETY AND SCHOOLING 338
REFERENCES 338

CHAPTER SEVENTEEN
Brazil: The Quest for Quality 340
CANDIDO ALBERTO GOMES, CLÉLIA CAPANEMA, AND JACIRA CÂMARA

THE SOCIAL FABRIC 340
SCHOOLING 342

SUCCESSES 346

CHALLENGES 350

DEBATES AND CONTROVERSIES 353

POSTSCRIPT 356

REFERENCES 357

Author Index 359

Subject Index 363

PREFACE

Schooling Around the World follows on the success of *Education in a Global Society: A Comparative Perspective* (Allyn and Bacon, 2000). However, while the two share many commonalities, it is not a second, updated edition; it is a new and significantly different textbook. While some material from the former has been included herein, *Schooling Around the World* differs from its predecessor in six major ways.

First, it is a markedly shorter book. The number of case studies has been reduced from twenty-seven to sixteen. This change was made to assist students and instructors. *Schooling Around the World* was written to make it ideal for the thirteen-week course cycle found in most colleges and universities.

Second, selection of case studies was made on the criterion of highlighting "high-interest" nations. That is, nations that are both geopolitically significant and illustrative of important perspectives and lessons for understanding education principles and practices were chosen.

Third, while each chapter still opens with a description of the social milieu of the country, that description is briefer and more focused. The unique characteristics of each country and its major political, cultural, religious, ideological, and other traits are nonetheless still clearly identified. This is essential in order to provide the social context necessary for understanding each nation's education system. However, there is less detail given to the historical evolution of the country than was provided by the previous textbook. The focus herein is upon succinctly identifying key social forces and factors that characterize the country and shape its education system.

Fourth, the education systems of each nation are described, but concisely and without undue specificity and detail. While the reader is acquainted with the essential structure of each national school system, its curricula, pedagogical practices employed, evaluation modes, teacher training, and so on, *Schooling Around the World* does not go into the detail that its predecessor provided. Both the above-noted outline of the social milieu of each nation and this sketch of the education system serve the function of providing readers with a contextual framework for understanding the next component.

Fifth, the editors' guiding principle behind *Schooling Around the World* is to provide future teachers with a clear understanding of the realities of their chosen profession: the debates, controversies, and challenges they will face as professional educators. Relevance for the practicing teacher is emphasized in the issues brought to light.

Accordingly, the heart of each chapter is a spirited discussion of the successes, challenges, issues, debates, and controversies facing educators in their nations. Each contributing author has identified the strongest, most significant, and most desirable aspects of education in his or her nation. (Essentially telling us: "*Here is what we are doing right!*") Next, authors identify the major challenges that schools and educators face in the effort to improve education in their nations. (Essentially, "*This is what is most weak and in need of attention and remedy!*") Finally, each author identifies the issues and debates that are currently taking place in her or his nation's schools, teachers' professional organizations, ministries of education, the media, and so on. (Essentially, "*Here is what we are arguing about in education!*")

Sixth and finally, the preceding point leads us to the essence of the differences between this textbook and its predecessor. On one hand, *Schooling Around the World* is a very practical book. In addition to gaining basic knowledge of other societies and education systems, future teachers learn what the strengths of those systems are. More importantly, learning the successes other countries are experiencing (i.e., the "*Here is what we are doing right*" component of each case study) immediately invites a critically important question: What lessons may be learned from this to improve schooling in *my* country? Similarly, understanding the challenges facing educators in other nations and then drawing parallels to our own situations (the "*This is what is most weak and in need of attention and remedy*" element) illuminates avenues for finding solutions. What can we learn from each other? What can we borrow from each other? What can we teach each other? These are the questions that should frame student inquiry as each chapter is read.

Accordingly, *Schooling Around the World* is written in a spirited tone; the human element is not lost. In examining national issues and debates (the "*Here is what we are arguing about in education*" part of each chapter) we invite students to be drawn into the controversies—often raging ones—that characterize the highly ideological and politicized profession of teaching in every country. The issues future teachers face are profound and contentious. In each chapter, the authors take a stand; lines are drawn in the sand. In consequence, readers are invited to comprehend, confront, and take positions on the debates that will engulf them when they enter the teaching profession. The controversies are clearly illuminated in each chapter; how these battles are resolved will define the professional lives of the next generation of teachers.

Indeed, everything else can be considered as background to this. The ultimate value and use of the information and analyses provided is to give students a basis upon which to engage in the debates and dialogues of the profession they are entering. That is the focus of *Schooling Around the World.*

Part I

ABOUT THIS BOOK

AN INTRODUCTION, OVERVIEW, AND GUIDE FOR STUDENTS

KAS MAZUREK

MARGRET A. WINZER

This Introduction is written for you, the student. Please take the time to read it carefully; we have written it to help you get the most out of working with this textbook. We also strongly encourage you to read the Preface. It contains additional information that will greatly help you get the most out of your textbook.

In this Introduction we, the editors, will explain why we took the time and effort to compile this book, why we went about things in the manner we did, why comparative studies courses are important for future teachers, what comparative education is, how this book is organized, what the main findings of the investigations are, and how you can read and study this book for your maximum benefit.

On behalf of our contributing authors, we also warmly invite you to an exciting and informative journey around the world. A total of twenty-six distinguished teacher educators and scholars, representing sixteen nations, have willingly donated their time and expertise to make this book possible. They did so because they want to share their worlds with you.

Think of each chapter as an invitation to glimpse into their societies and their education systems. The authors want to help you better understand the realities, successes, problems, and aspirations of teachers, students, parents, and citizens in their countries and education systems. There are some surprises in store for you. Sometimes these are strikingly different from, sometimes unexpectedly similar to, your own experiences and to the future that awaits you as a member of the teaching profession.

Kas Mazurek is Professor of Education at the University of Lethbridge, Canada. His research interests overlap the fields of comparative education, multiculturalism and minority group relations, the social contexts of educational ideas, policies and practices, and the logic of inquiry in education.

Margret A. Winzer is a professor at the University of Lethbridge, where she teaches in the areas of early childhood education and special education. She has researched and written extensively in these fields, with one stress on comparative studies in special education. Her scholarly achievements are internationally recognized. Most recently, she was awarded her university's Medal for Distinguished Research and Scholarship, and the Division of International Special Education Services of the Council for Exceptional Children honored her with a Lifetime Achievement Award.

COMPARATIVE STUDIES AS A COMPONENT OF TEACHER EDUCATION

Much of current education planning is focused on preparing teachers-in-training for the increasingly interdependent (economically, technologically, politically, ecologically, and so on) world and the diverse (culturally, racially, and so on) societies they will graduate into. This places an obligation on our profession. The need for teachers to have a sound awareness of other nations—their social milieus, cultures, customs, political and economic processes, education systems, and so on—is now well understood by professional educators and policy makers. Accordingly, teacher education programs in colleges and universities across North America, Europe, the Commonwealth Nations, and indeed the world, have responded by increasingly introducing courses of study and program components to help meet this need.

VARIETIES OF COMPARATIVE STUDIES IN EDUCATION

Such courses and programs fall under the generic heading of *comparative education.* However, they appear under different labels in different institutions. The most common—but not exclusive—designations are *comparative studies in education, international education,* and *development education.* While we do not wish to gloss over important differences in these varieties of comparative education, this is not the time or place to digress into an extended discussion on terminology. Suffice it to say that all courses in comparative education have at least two characteristics. First, they describe education systems in different nations. Second, the role of the education system within a society is examined—i.e., how the education system as a whole works within society, how it interacts with other components of the social structure.

These two components constitute the minimal content of all comparative education courses, and the core knowledge of comparative education programs (i.e., majors, minors, specializations, and so on) in undergraduate and graduate teacher education degrees and diplomas. The editors prefer the term *comparative studies in education,* will treat it as synonymous with comparative education, and will use the two terms interchangeably in this *Introduction.*

THE VALUE AND UTILITY OF COMPARATIVE STUDIES IN EDUCATION

There are many specific reasons why a particular course in comparative studies may be offered, and different programs emphasize some elements over others. But, a general rationale for all such courses is likely to include the following.

First, to expand on what has been noted above, there is a sense (especially in the so-called "developed" nations) that current events are such that all societies and their citizens must become very knowledgeable about the world beyond their national borders. Most commonly, this imperative is cast in economic terms. Business and political leaders constantly warn us that the world's economies and financial systems are incredibly interdependent, and our material well-being is dependent upon professionals and workers who have a sophisticated knowledge of this new global economy.

But this perspective goes beyond a merely selfish desire to maintain a competitive edge to protect one's standard of living. It is part of a more inclusive belief that the world is becoming infinitely more complex in that events in one nation or one part of the world have impacts that are global. Sometimes these are negative. For example, terrorism, political unrest, economic instability, and environmental degradation are not merely local events; they inevitably impact upon all nations, and they cause problems for citizens of all lands. Sometimes they are positive. For example, mobilization of nations to come to the aid of people in need because of famine or natural catastrophes, the sharing of research and technology to eradicate diseases, and coordination of economic policies for mutual benefit—these are also international in their impact and consequences.

However, whether we speak of triumphs or tragedies, the same conclusion holds. The inescapable reality of the third millennium is that individuals, institutions, and countries simply cannot afford the luxury of parochialism. There is no place to hide. The world is such that our professional, political, economic, social, cultural, and moral decisions and actions are intimately tied into new global realities. We must possess the knowledge and skills to act wisely and prudently. Unless people are able to grasp issues and events well beyond their homes and national borders, they will not be able to anticipate, understand, and intelligently respond to such events. The twenty-first century demands sophisticated citizens who are competent to deal with rapidly changing realities.

In the above senses, it is fair to say that the need for comparative studies has been forced upon us all. The world has changed; we have little choice other than to understand the changes if we are to have any hope of intelligently managing our affairs. And, we are not talking about a pressing need for comparative studies in education alone. The same argument is valid in the realms of economics, technological studies, politics, medicine, and so on. Our concern here, however, is limited to our chosen careers as professional educators. For us, the consequences are clear. It is our responsibility to educate a knowledgeable next generation that can positively and constructively meet the challenges of rapidly evolving new social, cultural, economic, political, and demographic realities.

The second major rationale for comparative studies switches our focus from the global to the local. That is, as teachers you will want to be the most competent professionals you possibly can be. To accomplish this, individual teachers and teachers' professional associations cannot limit themselves only to the knowledge and experience that local practitioners and education systems possess and generate.

Schooling in all its aspects—teaching strategies, curricular content, evaluation, classroom management, organization and administration, and so on—is conducted in fundamentally different ways around the world. Research into how children learn, what constitutes best practices, how schools serve social and class interests, as well as many other topics, is undertaken by many societies and in many different national and cultural contexts. All around the world teachers, departments of education, education research institutes, professors of education, and others are working conscientiously to produce pedagogy, curricula, diagnostic tools, and so on, to better serve students, parents, society, and the teaching profession.

Without drawing upon this collective wisdom, without benefiting from the experiences of our colleagues in other countries, without becoming informed of each other's experiments, successes, and failures, our individual professional practices are doomed to be parochial and myopic. We can only know how competent we are, how "good" our professional choices and practices are, if we know the full range of options available and have a fully documented story of the successes and failures of all alternatives. Individual teachers, schools, and education systems can get this information only by consciously reflecting on their practices and theories in the light of information and insights gathered from around the world—and then testing these in the crucible of their own schools. In this sense, comparative studies are an essential tool for the improvement of local practices.

The third major rationale complements the second, but it is more expansive. Improving local practices is a concrete benefit that is a result of enhanced technical knowledge possessed by educators. However, the educator who is informed about education theory, practice, and research around the world gains more than technical knowledge. Also gained are valuable insights that might be labeled professional knowledge. That is, comparative studies do more than merely provide educators with strategies for becoming more effective teachers.

Let us recall our earlier discussion on the content of comparative education courses and programs. There it was emphasized that such courses and programs always did more than merely describe the education systems of different nations. They also provided analyses of the role of education systems within societies, how the education system as a whole works, and how it interacts with other components of a nation's social structure. Such insights allow educators to appreciate the larger social context of the education enterprise. That is, we become aware of the pressing issues of our time—not just in our profession, but also in our society and around the world.

Such understanding is very important because it is a foundation for fulfilling one of our most general, but very critical, responsibilities as members of a profession. That responsibility, as privileged members of society, is to work toward a better world, to be positively and constructively proactive in public debates about the evolution of schools and societies. This is a great and sometimes ignored responsibility. However, we (the editors) want you to know that we are using the phrase "privileged members of society" very consciously in describing professional educators.

As future teachers, you will be just that. You will be members of a profession; you will be granted a protected and powerful position by the state; you will have autonomy; you will have authority and control over your society's most cherished possession, its children; you will have the responsibility of evaluating and certifying your students, and your professional judgment will greatly influence their future lives. But there is an even greater, more general, responsibility you will have.

You will be, by definition and by virtue of your credentials, a molder of public opinion and a leader in the debate of public issues. Your years of advanced education, your position of trust, the power you exercise in your classroom, the respect you command in your community, and the political influence and moral authority your professional associations wield make it inevitable that yours will be a respected voice in the public domain. It is a burden, responsibility, and great privilege that comes with the career you have chosen.

There is a word for this role, responsibility, and privilege—one that has sadly been out of vogue recently. Your education, and social and professional status, make you a member of the *intelligentsia.* You, and the professional associations you will be a member of, are expected to take a leadership role in the social debates—be they political, economic, cultural, or other—of your time. This is not an elitist concept. It is simply recognition that you, as a professional educator, are rather blessed: You have the benefit of advanced education; you occupy a position of trust and authority in your community; you have accepted an inherent duty of ongoing professional development; your career is one of public service; and you are charged with educating the next generation of workers, parents, and leaders.

That is simply the way it is; it is the fundamental difference between a job and a profession. A job demands technical competence. A profession demands technical competence and something more: an avocational element. The educator who forgets this crucial distinction loses the privilege of calling her- or himself a "teacher" and a "professional." Comparative studies serve our profession well here; they give us a global perspective on the issues and challenges that face us—and the choices and options available to us as we embark, with great uncertainty, into a new century.

APPROACHES TO COMPARATIVE STUDIES IN EDUCATION

Courses in comparative education tend to fall into two general categories. On the one hand, there are survey courses. Survey courses have three basic objectives. First, they introduce students to the field of comparative studies in education. Students learn what the nature of this interdisciplinary field is; come to appreciate its value, significance, and relevance; and understand how comparative studies are pursued. Second, examinations of selected countries are undertaken as case studies. The case studies provide the database and substantive content for the third learning objective: comparing national systems of schooling, discerning common themes and trends, appreciating differences, understanding problems and controversies, and drawing conclusions, insights, and lessons for application to the student's own school system and professional practice.

A second category of courses focuses on specific issues in contemporary schooling, examined in an international context. In such courses, pressing issues in education are illuminated through an examination of how they are manifested in and grappled with in different societies and different national contexts. The scope of issues that the current literature addresses is quite remarkable. For example: equality of educational opportunity; educational achievement; globalization; evaluation and examinations; the treatment of minority groups; women in education; formal, nonformal, and informal education; delivery modes; teacher training, certification, and supply; citizenship education; politics, ideology, and schooling; language and literacy; schooling and the economy; education, modernization, and development; education reform; education accountability; effective schooling; and school administration and governance; to name a representative example.

THE NEED FOR THIS TEXTBOOK

Virtually all of the current textbooks in comparative education are tailored to the second category of courses. Many of the texts are excellent and are wholly appropriate for comparative education courses dealing with specific topics and issues in education. However, they are not well suited to the first category of courses in comparative education. This is because books taking an "issues" approach assume students possess a great deal of background knowledge about individual countries and national systems of education. That is not always the case. As students, you know very well the plethora of demands on your time and energy that makes it difficult to keep abreast of local, let alone national and international, developments in education systems and societies. Consequently, texts taking the issues approach cannot stand alone as assigned course texts in survey courses.

For two decades now, research in comparative education has exhibited a trend toward ever-increasing specialization. The consequences of this have been both positive and negative. On the positive side, specialization has brought remarkable progress in extending the depth of investigation in narrow and precisely defined subfields. Those subfields are the issues that have been noted in our above discussion on the second category of comparative education courses. As has been acknowledged, there are many suitable texts available that address, in detail, the plethora of issues that have been identified.

On the other hand, this concentration on in-depth studies of specific aspects of education in an international context has resulted in a marked lack of survey textbooks detailing school systems and societies. For students in comparative education courses, the results have been unfortunate. Lacking a choice of texts offering a concise overview of many societies and national school systems, it becomes necessary to access a wide variety of books, journals, encyclopedias, and government reports—physically and over the Internet—in order to piece together a coherent overview of both schooling and the national social context within which schooling is defined and practiced in other nations.

This is the editors' motivation for compiling *Schooling Around the World.* We want to provide you with a comprehensive cultural/social/political/demographic/etc. overview of a good number of countries around the world—*and* an in-depth look at their education systems—*and* an insight into the issues, challenges, and debates that are taking place among educators in those countries.

As you can readily see from the Table of Contents, the nations and education systems represented encompass a sizable percentage of the world's population. In fact, the sixteen countries presented in this book are home to about 4.7 billion people. That is a staggering number; indeed, it is 70 percent of the total world population as it currently stands (at just over 6.4 billion).

However, much more important than the absolute number of people that our selected nations encompass is why the countries in this book were selected. One criterion, as was emphasized in the Preface, is to profile "high-interest" nations. That is, we chose nations that are both geopolitically significant *and* illustrative of important principles and lessons for understanding education principles and practices. You will also notice a balance between "dominant" nations—in terms of economic and military power, population, and other parameters—and less prominent nations. But, above all, one overriding consideration compelled us in our selection and organization of nations represented here—providing you, within the limited space a textbook can reasonably allow, with a sampling of the diversity and complexity of the world's nations and education systems.

Finally, nations have been grouped under five sections on the basis of regions. They could have been grouped in a number of ways, but our experience is that people tend to think regionally, that is, mentally to group nations geographically. Therefore, we felt you would be more comfortable working with this structure.

Before going on to the next section in this Introduction, we again ask you please to remember that we encourage you to look well beyond the sixteen nations represented. The analyses in each chapter and in this Introduction are a beginning, a foundation, for your continued study of education systems worldwide. Each chapter provides an overview of education structures, practices, and so on, as well as a clear picture of the social climate within which each national school system exists, and most importantly, the debates, challenges, and controversial issues facing educators in those nations. But, that is not the full extent of the book or each contributing chapter. *Schooling Around the World* hopes to assist you in interpreting the cultural forces and social milieus that shape the nature and direction of schooling around the world; understanding the major current international debates on the objectives, practices, structures, and functions of education; and discerning the directions in which education around the world is evolving.

Thus *Schooling Around the World* is designed to serve simultaneously as an encyclopedic resource (describing sixteen national systems, curricula, programs, and so on); an analytical treatise (defining and interpreting the social forces shaping national school systems); a book of lessons on both the successes nations have experienced in their education systems and the challenges they have not been able to overcome; and a vehicle for future teachers to participate in the vigorous and profound debates educators around the world are engulfed in.

To ensure that your journey begins with the best possible preparation, we invited extraordinarily talented and accomplished scholars and educators to contribute to this book of readings.

A NOTE ON CONTRIBUTING AUTHORS

In that our contributing authors literally speak for the nations represented, the question of who shall have that voice is a central consideration. Our strategy was to invite scholars who are themselves residents of the nations they write about and are active professionals within the education systems of their nations. Only a few exceptions to this rule were made. However, even in those cases the contributors are scholars who have extensive professional experience in the nations they write about.

This is important. It allows the cultural uniqueness of the nations and their education systems to come through to readers. This is because contributors are speaking as cultural and education "insiders" of the nations represented. Our quest is to obtain and convey a truly intimate knowledge of societies and schools, one that only an insider can adequately capture. The contributor, by definition, will not be observing and interpreting the nation's culture and schooling system from the ethnocentric worldview of another cultural perspective.

We therefore consider any unevenness in tone and expression between chapters to be a strength of this book. We have edited only for continuity of structure between chapters, length of manuscript and, because English is a second or third language for many of our contributing scholars, clarity of expression. We always tried to avoid editorial changes that might affect cultural nuances. We did not want to homogenize the distinct voices of sixteen nations into an even monotone.

THE STRUCTURE OF CONTRIBUTORS' CHAPTERS

However, to assist you in comparing the societies and education systems presented, drawing out common themes and identifying areas of difference, we felt it important that all sixteen chapters have a consistent format. Accordingly, authors were asked to write their chapters within the following framework.

The first section of each chapter begins with the heading *The Social Fabric*. In this section, authors were first asked to describe and then to explain the major and most significant social realities that constitute the distinguishing features of their nations. Included are elements such as a basic demographic, economic, political, cultural, and religious profile; identification of the major forces and events that shape the contemporary social milieu of the nation; and insights into the unique cultural and social realities of the nation.

It is important to understand why we asked our contributors to begin here, why the social context within which educational objectives, practices, and structures exist should be the opening focus of each essay. A basic premise of this textbook is that a nation's education system cannot be understood in isolation from the social milieu that defines and nurtures it. It is the demographic, economic, political, cultural, religious, and historical peculiarities of a nation that determine the unique manifestations of public schooling in that society. To understand schooling requires that the social context that shapes education must first be made clear.

Contributing authors then turn their attention to their nation's education system, and the nature, contents, processes, and structures of schooling are described and explained. In this second section of each chapter, *Schooling*, guiding educational philosophies, educational objectives, formal legislation and policies, pedagogical practices, student characteristics, curricula, evaluation, teacher education programs, the professional responsibilities of practicing teachers, bureaucratic and administrative structures of education, and the organization and governance of schooling are among the topics elaborated.

A primary objective of the second section is to provide a clear description of the education system in each nation. However, there is more to it than that. As was emphasized above, an education system cannot be understood without reference to the social milieu that defines and nurtures it. Accordingly, the authors take care to make this link, and they show us the degree to which their nations' education systems are a reflection of the broader social milieu outlined in the first section (The Social Fabric).

By this point in each chapter, you will have a very good knowledge base on both the nation and its education system. However, you will develop something even more important; you will begin to have a good sense of why things are as they are in that nation. The social forces that have shaped and continue to shape the nation, the characteristics of the education system, why that system is as it is rather than having evolved in another direction, the professional preparation and working lives of teachers, the contents and processes of schooling, as well as other realities, will be clear. This is because you will have taken a critical step in trying to "get inside" the cultural and social reality of that nation. This is very important. It begins to allow you to see that society a bit more from the perspective of one who lives there. You begin to feel less of a clinical, detached, "outside" observer.

Of course, this is a very difficult task to accomplish without prolonged immersion in a culture. It is too much to ask that this be done through reading, thinking, and discussion alone. Certainly, a claim is not being made that you are now able to empathize with and understand that society in a way that its citizens do. But, you have gone some distance in that direction. That is important—in fact, very important, because you are now in a better position to appreciate the complexities brought out in the third section of each chapter: *Successes, Challenges, and Debates.*

In this third section you will grapple with the pressing issues facing each nation represented in the text. This section is divided into three subsections: First, the authors start off on a positive note; they identify and discuss the strongest/most significant/desirable aspects of education in their nations. Essentially, they are telling you "*Here is what we are doing right when it comes to schooling! These are our successes!*" Next, authors identify the major challenges that schools and educators face in the effort to improve education in their nations. Essentially, they are telling you "*Here is where we are not succeeding! These are the things that are most weak and in need of attention and remedy!*" Finally, the authors turn their attention to the major debates and controversies that are consuming the time and energy of educators in their nations. Identified are the education debates, controversies, and issues that are currently taking place in their nation's schools, professional organizations, ministries of education, political circles, and media. Essentially, they are telling you "*Here is what we are arguing about in education!*"

We (the editors) consider the Successes, Challenges, and Debates section of each chapter to be the most significant section. It is the section that will stay with you—you will remember it long after the details of demography, history, structure of the education system, teacher training programs, education policies, and so on begin to fade from your memory. This is because the objective of this section is to draw you into the debates—often raging ones—that characterize the highly ideological and politicized profession of teaching in every nation. In this section the authors take a stand on the debates and controversies they bring up. This is to encourage you to formulate and articulate your own positions on the issues that they illuminate for you. They invite you to engage in dialogue and debate.

Indeed, everything else in each chapter can fairly be considered as background to the Successes, Challenges, and Debates section. The ultimate value and use of the background information and analyses the contributing authors provide is to give you a solid basis upon which to engage in the debates and dialogues of the profession you will be entering soon. This section is the real focus of *Schooling Around the World.*

It is at this point that you will most fully realize one of the important reasons why comparative education courses and programs exist as a component of your professional training. You recall that, earlier in this Introduction and in the Preface, we highlighted the point that one of the major rationales for comparative studies is to offer educators a global perspective on the issues education systems face, and the choices that have to be made, as we walk into the future. We emphasized that comparative studies courses and programs always aim to do more than merely describe different societies and the educational systems of different nations. They seek to provide educators with insights and analyses that will yield an awareness of the pressing issues of our time—not just in their profession, but also in their country and around the world.

In reading the Successes, Challenges, and Debates section of each chapter, you will develop this broader perspective. Some of the education and social issues, debates, and problems, even the successes, will be alien to you—concerns of places and peoples unlike the society you live in and the education profession you recognize and plan to enter. But, we promise you, that will be the exception. More often, much more often, the education and social issues, debates, challenges, problems, and successes you read about will be eerily familiar. They will invoke a sense of *déjà vu.* You will be struck by how educators practicing in distant nations, living in remarkably different cultures, are struggling with the same professional and social issues that concern you as a professional and a person. You will see how much common cause you have with your fellow educators around the world. As teachers we are more bonded by similarities than alienated by differences.

WHY BOTHER?

You will recall that, near the beginning of this Introduction, we brought up the idea of educators as members of the *intelligentsia.* We emphasized that you, and the professional associations you will be a member of, are expected to take a leadership role in debates about education. You will also be looked to for leadership in larger social debates—be they political, economic, cultural, or other—of your time. Society expects this of you and your professional associations. Quite simply, teachers' voices and opinions matter.

In speaking to the education and social issues of your time, and by helping frame outlines for courses of future action, as educators you fulfill your professional and public service duties. And you must, because some things are certain: Social, economic, cultural, and political events and changes will continue to put intense pressure on your profession. Schools, ministries of education, teachers' associations, and teacher training institutions will be pushed, prodded, cajoled, bribed, and threatened to go in certain directions and to make certain changes. Changes in curricula, teacher education and certification, evaluation, management, and all facets of education will continue. Our profession, like our society, is in a constant state of change; this always has been and always will be.

But change in which direction? Who will decide which changes in curricula, teacher education and certification, evaluation, management, and so on, are of benefit to children, parents, our profession, and society? Who will decide which forces for change are negative and should be resisted and which are positive and should be embraced and facilitated? Educators must have a strong voice in these debates, and we must be at the table when plans for change are drawn up.

However, we can only make sound arguments and put forward sound proposals if our views are based on sound information. What are all the options? How unique are our circumstances? Have others encountered similar situations? What approaches are our colleagues around the world taking? What has worked? What has failed?

It is here that comparative studies help us greatly. Comparative studies provide a rich database and broad international perspective on professional issues and pressing questions. While each contributing chapter provides information and insights in the context of a specific nation and its education system, the cumulative effect of reading the chapters is the development of a scope of understanding that will help you address the issues relevant to your professional life from a knowledge base that is global in its breadth.

A BLUEPRINT TO ASSIST YOU

We stress that it is ultimately you, the reader, who will integrate for yourself the data, analyses, and lessons from your reading of the separate chapters into a coherent, meaningful, whole. However, we would like to facilitate that process a bit for you. Indeed, we already have—by ensuring that there is structural consistency between each of the sixteen contributing chapters.

We have already noted that all contributors are writing within a common format to make this textbook easier to use. You will not find it difficult to make comparisons and draw out similarities and differences between nations. We are sure that the structural continuity between chapters will allow you to identify thematic coherences between essays, giving you a basis for understanding both similarities and differences between the individual nations represented in this textbook. Your own framework for comprehending the range of similarities and variations in schooling and society around the globe will emerge—that is ultimately what is most important and what you will remember long after finishing this book.

However, we do not want to put all the responsibility on you and let you do all the work. So, to help prepare you for your reading of *Schooling Around the World,* we would like to share with you some of the major common themes we have identified from our reading of these chapters.

But, please understand that what follows is not offered as a definitive summary of what is in this book. Quite the opposite. It is merely a general blueprint to assist you initially in reading and finding meaning in the sixteen case studies that follow. We wish only to summarize and share with you some of the themes that struck us. Our hope is that, in sharing these with you, we will prepare you to read the chapters and assist you in interpreting and integrating the material.

Furthermore, the purpose of the following listing is neither to prioritize nor to analyze. Therefore, the themes we identify below are listed in alphabetical order and are not greatly elaborated upon. They are merely presented. We simply wish to draw them to your attention; something for you to keep in mind as you read the chapters. By major themes we mean elements common to the majority of chapters. These are factors, issues, and problems that the majority of contributing authors feel are important and address in their chapters. Indeed, you may be surprised by how many remarkably similar discussions take place in countries that are very distant from each other and culturally distinct. Some common things, in fact, were seen to be very important in virtually every one of our sixteen countries—across the globe, educators share many common issues, debates, challenges, and successes. We encourage you to look for, and think about, these common themes as you read this book.

MAJOR THEMES

Listed *alphabetically* (not in order of significance or number of chapters that address them), and *with minimal elaboration,* the following are the issues, forces, and developments the majority of our contributing authors feel are very significant in their nations. These constitute themes—a total of thirty-eight—that are reflected in the majority (in many instances all) of the sixteen case studies. As is to be expected, the themes overlap. For your convenience and easy reference, major areas of overlap are cross-referenced for each theme.

Academic versus Vocational/Technical Focus

Here the debate is whether schools and postsecondary institutions should be primarily academic institutions, or whether a vocational/technical emphasis should dominate. The unfolding of this issue is particularly evident in many nations' dramatic attempts to link secondary education to the labor force by increasingly linking vocational high schools to vocational colleges/universities. (See also *Brain Drain, Global Economic Competition, Globalization, Human Capital, Market Economy Model, Technology,* and *Uncertainty.*)

Accountability

Education systems, at all levels, are increasingly being held to rigorous scrutiny by governments, parents, and other stakeholders. This phenomenon is a result of several economic and political factors, which are touched on below. Accountability is also transcending national boundaries through international comparisons of student achievement and "quality" rankings of education institutions. (See also *Administration, Policies, and Regulations; Decentralization; Downsizing Education Bureaucracies; Financial Constraints; Global Economic Competition; Globalization; Human Capital; Market Economy Model; Privatization; Reforms; Structural Changes;* and *Teacher Training and Certification.*)

Administration, Policies, and Regulations

For education systems, there is little bureaucratic or legislative stability in the world today. Fundamental revisions in the structures, rules, regulations, policies, and laws under which schooling is carried out seem to be the norm. Sometimes these changes are dramatic attempts to revamp virtually the entire education system of a nation. Other times, we see incremental changes. Regardless of what the case is in any particular nation, the results—to greater or lesser degrees—are the same: administrative reconstitution of schools and redefinition of educators' duties. As in the case of so many of the other themes identified herein, the justification for such changes is usually the argument that social, economic, technological, and many other changes make these administrative, policy, and legal changes necessary and desirable. (See also *Accountability, Decentralization, Downsizing Education Bureaucracies, Expansion of Education, Financial Constraints, Global Economic Competition, Globalization, Human Capital, Market Economy Model, Privatization, Reforms, Structural Changes,* and *Teacher Training and Certification.*)

Brain Drain

In response to a highly mobile world, many countries are simultaneously trying to do three things: teach much-needed technical expertise, use this expertise to remain competitive in a brutally competitive international economic environment, and retain the best graduates of their colleges and universities in their national labor force. For many, it is a losing battle. The "brain drain" is a critical problem for all but the most prosperous nations. (See also *Academic versus Vocational/Technical Focus, Global Economic Competition, Globalization, Human Capital, Market Economy Model, Technology,* and *Uncertainty.*)

Change

One thing that all authors address, yet have perhaps the greatest difficulty in conveying precisely, is the notion that each of our sixteen nations is caught up in a tide of incredibly rapid social and education change. This change is not localized; it is ubiquitous. The sense the editors get from the case studies in this regard is that educators around the world are overwhelmed. It seems that change is so pervasive, so fundamental, and so rapid that the education community does not know how to cope or keep up with it. Indeed, if you look at the chapter titles in the Table of Contents, you will be struck by how often the word "change," or a synonym for it, appears.

However, this is only to be expected. Societies around the world are in a state of flux. The world is in an era of incredibly rapid social change, and national systems of education are simply undergoing changes as profound as any other component of society. (See also *Curricular Changes, Decentralization, Downsizing Education Bureaucracies, Expansion of Education, Inclusion, Reforms, Structural Changes,* and *Uncertainty.*)

Children at Risk

A very welcome international development is the increasing attention being paid to meeting the needs of at-risk children. Massive and innovative intervention programs are being put in place across the globe to reach street children, trauma victims, special needs populations, migrant children, isolated children, and other such populations. On the negative side of the coin, however, is the pressing issue of how to cope with the social, economic, and political conditions that are exposing increasing numbers of children to risk factors. (See also *Equality of Access, Equality of Opportunity, Financial Constraints, Gender Inequalities, Globalization, Inclusion, Inequalities, Inequality of Educational Opportunity,* and *Rural–Urban Inequalities.*)

Culture

The degree to which culture—history, social norms, religion, and other factors—influences the philosophy, principles, and practices of schooling cannot be overstated. Culture also provides a pervasive counterbalance to the overwhelming intrusions of globalization. This has both negative and positive manifestations—sometimes giving rise to incomprehensible social injustices, sometimes nurturing highly desirable local perspectives and practices from an increasingly homogenized world. (See also *Gender Inequalities, Globalization, Inequalities, Inequality of Educational Opportunity, Literacy, Nationalism, Religion,* and *Social and Ideological Conflicts.*)

Curricular Changes

Curriculum is one of the front lines in the battle to implement changes in schooling. It is also a front line in the preservation of traditions in schooling in the face of sweeping social transformations. However, in the great majority of nations, curriculum is bending in the winds of global change. It seems that virtually all education systems are embarking upon almost wholesale revisions of their curricula. This is placing an enormous strain on the profession. Teachers are at a loss to keep pace with fundamental changes in this area.

Accordingly, contributors consistently speak to the vital role of curriculum in advancing educational, social, political, and economic ideologies and ends through public schooling. Furthermore, flexibility in curriculum design at regional and local levels is increasingly being introduced. (See also *Academic versus Technical Focus, Change, Decentralization, Downsizing Education Bureaucracies, Expansion of Education, Reforms, Structural Changes,* and *Uncertainty.*)

Decentralization

Even in the most centralized governments and societies, there is a clear trend toward decentralizing responsibilities at all levels of education. What may be called varieties of "site-based management reforms" are being implemented internationally. On one hand, this is rationalized as a desirable innovation in that it allows on-site decision making by experts who know the communities they serve. It is also argued to be cost effective and responsive to community/local/regional needs. Cynics, on the other hand, view this development as an international trend by governments bent on evading their responsibilities for providing education services by "downloading" the costs of schooling to local levels—which often can ill afford the costs of providing quality education. (See also *Accountability; Administration, Policies, and Regulations; Change; Curricular Changes; Decentralization; Downsizing Education Bureaucracies; Expansion of Education; Financial Constraints; Globalization; Market Economy Model; Privatization; Reforms;* and *Structural Changes.*)

Demographic Transformations

Nations around the world are witnessing a redrawing of their population profiles. This has tremendous consequences for not just schools, but for the entire social system. Everything from the economy to social security is being affected.

In some nations, the issue takes the form of an aging population. As the ratios of youth to elderly, and workers to retired, increase, the social welfare systems of many nations are reaching a crisis point. Other nations have the exact opposite problem: a burgeoning population of children and young people who require quite different services. The consequences for education are dramatic.

In societies with aging populations, the expansion of post-secondary education and nonformal education is redefining traditional notions of education and schooling as people become lifelong learners. Societies with youthful populations—overwhelmingly, these are relatively poor countries—worry about how so many children can be accommodated in school systems that are already stretched to the limit in terms of resources. And, once these children graduate, will there be jobs for them in the volatile global economy?

Additionally, the global demographic landscape is changing in ways other than redistribution on the basis of age. (See *Multiculturalism.*)

Downsizing Education Bureaucracies

Virtually all countries are concerned about and are addressing bloated and inefficient education bureaucracies. It is an international trend that has yet to crest. Advocates argue that downsizing increases efficiency, directs funding from administration to classrooms, and allows for more decision making at the community and regional levels. Critics argue that such supposed savings never do find their way into local schools, and downsizing is merely a smoke screen for cutbacks in education budgets. (See also *Accountability; Administration, Policies, and Regulations; Decentralization; Financial Constraints; Market Economy Model; Privatization; Reforms;* and *Structural Changes.*)

Equality of Access

Even where a relatively high level of equality of opportunity to attend education institutions exists (certainly it never does fully), there is no guarantee that there is equality of access for children. Accessing schooling is mitigated by many factors: number of spaces available; suitability/relevance of programs offered; the existence of services and resources for special needs students; and the overall quality and resources of available schools. Thus, equality of access is not to be equated with equality of opportunity. Even on a "level playing field," mitigating circumstances make it inevitable that not all children are able to afford themselves of an optimal school placement. (See also *Children at Risk, Equality of Opportunity, Expansion of Education, Financial Constraints, Gender Inequalities, Equality of Opportunity, Inequalities, Inequality of Educational Opportunity,* and *Rural-Urban Inequalities.*)

Equality of Opportunity

This is the great dividing line between parents and children who are able to maximize use of available educational opportunities and resources and those who are less successful. Authors discuss, in detail, the degree to which the benefits of schooling are appropriated by dominant groups in the sixteen nations studied. (See also *Children at Risk, Equality of Access, Financial Constraints, Gender Inequalities, Globalization, Inequalities, Inequality of Educational Opportunity, Market Economy Model, Privatization,* and *Rural-Urban Inequalities.*)

Expansion of Education

A very positive international development is the concerted effort by governments to make education more widely available. This takes several forms. First, there is a focus on higher national averages for years of schooling completed. Second, there is investment in making more classroom spaces available. Finally, there is an effort to make school services available to marginalized populations such as those in remote areas, migrant children, children with special needs, at-risk children, and children who are socially, economically, or otherwise disadvantaged. (See also *Decentralization, Downsizing Education Bureaucracies, Financial Constraints, Human Capital, Inclusion, Privatization, Reforms, Structural Changes,* and *Teacher Training and Certification.*)

Financial Constraints

If it is clear that education systems around the world are not sure of how to cope with the changes buffeting them, it is equally clear that they will not get adequate financial resources even if they agree on what should be done. A financial crisis has gripped the world's school systems. In some cases, it has crippled them. In virtually all of our sixteen nations, the financing of education is a major concern and issue.

In all cases, the underfunding of education is linked to broader economic concerns: the general state of the global economy and the particular state of the national economy. Needs are seen to be outstripping available resources, and there is little indication the situation will improve in the near future. In many countries, the situation has reached a crisis point.

This is an interesting phenomenon, in view of our preceding discussion on change. The important roles assigned to schools in meeting the challenges facing the next generation imposed by a rapidly changing world, the increasing demands placed on the education community, and the number of structural, bureaucratic, legal, curricular, and program changes taking place in the world's education systems all point to the conclusion that education should receive financial priority. This is not the case. Within each contributing chapter, you will find documentation on how education is unable to meet its objectives because of a lack of adequate financial support. While there is much lip service from virtually all aspects of society on the importance of education and promises for adequate funding are routinely made, it is usually the case that sufficient resources are not allocated.

In consequence, difficult decisions have to be made about which education projects, programs, and initiatives should receive priority over others. This is a debate that is consuming educators all over the world and causing much tension, dissention, and frustration. (See also *Accountability; Administration, Policies, and Regulations; Decentralization; Downsizing Education Bureaucracies; Children at Risk; Equality of Opportunity; Expansion of Education; Gender Inequalities; Inequality of Educational Opportunity; Globalization; Human Capital; Market Economy Model; Privatization; Reforms;* and *Rural-Urban Inequalities.*)

Gender Inequalities

One of the most discussed issues in this book is gender inequality. In virtually every nation, the education of girls is compared to the education levels of boys. Clearly, in many ways, girls are disadvantaged. The optimistic aspect of this is that at least the problem is well-documented and internationally recognized, and conscious intervention measures are being undertaken. The efforts are most pronounced and ambitious in relatively poor countries. (See also *Children at Risk, Culture, Equality of Access, Equality of Opportunity, Financial Constraints, Inequalities, Literacy,* and *Rural-Urban Inequalities.*)

Global Economic Competition

The effects upon national systems of education from an increasingly interdependent and brutally competitive global economy are reflected in every chapter. Economic imperatives are virtually impossible to separate from education decision making today. Intimately tied to the factor of globalization, education systems are responding to intense global economic competition by increasingly viewing schools as vehicles for technical and scientific training matched to the realities of the labor market and long-term national economic strategies. (See also *Academic versus Vocational/Technical Focus, Brain Drain, Globalization, Human Capital, Market Economy Model, Technology,* and *Uncertainty.*)

Globalization

Perhaps there is no single word in education discourse today that is more often used than *globalization.* A catchall word, it seems to have as many nuances of meaning as the number of people who use it. However, the core of each use is constant. Globalization speaks to the modern phenomenon of an incredibly shrinking world where powerful cultural, economic, political, and technological forces ignore national and cultural boundaries. Events in one part of the world ripple through the whole. However, this does not imply equilibrium, a balance of forces, or genuinely multilateral influence. Most often, globalization is equated to cultural, political, social, and economic imperialism.

At the heart of the matter is a global expansion of the capitalist economic model and Western social values and practices. In this view, a specific form of hegemony (centralized in the Western, industrialized, capitalistic, and democratic nations, most notably the United States and Western Europe) is taking root around the world. Depending on how one looks at this—i.e., from which ethnocentric perspective—this can be a very good thing or evil incarnate. Some chapters take the former view; some the latter.

However, regardless of value judgments passed, it is clear that globalization is a force to be reckoned with. The most pronounced effect is that all nations now have to, in one way or another, incorporate elements of the free market into their economies and social institutions. The second most pronounced effect is that societal values of cultures incompatible with what is usually called a Eurocentric perspective are being undermined across the world. (See also *Academic versus Vocational/Technical Focus; Accountability; Administration, Policies, and Regulations; Brain Drain; Culture; Decentralization; Downsizing Education Bureaucracies; Financial Constraints; Global Economic Competition; Human Capital; Market Economy Model; Privatization; Reforms; Structural Changes; Technology;* and *Uncertainty.)*

Human Capital

Virtually all countries today subscribe to the "human capital" view of financing the education systems of their citizens. Here, schools are seen as an investment in the long-term economic development of a country. Like investment in infrastructure, technology, or manufacturing, money spent on education institutions is calculated on a cost-benefit basis. That is, money spent on educating children and postsecondary students will pay off in the form of an economically more productive labor force, lower unemployment, increased economic competitiveness in the global economy, higher gross domestic product, and lower future expenditures in the areas of crime prevention and punishment, poverty alleviation, and so on. Clearly, economic considerations are the essence of this view and drive education reforms. (See also *Academic versus Vocational/Technical Focus, Brain Drain, Decentralization, Downsizing Education Bureaucracies, Financial Constraints, Global Economic Competition, Globalization, Market Economy Model, Reforms, Structural Changes, Teacher Training and Certification, Technology,* and *Uncertainty.)*

Inclusion

A marked change in the way nations see students with special needs is sweeping the globe. First, students with special needs are now being recognized and acknowledged as a hitherto marginalized population. Second, it is recognized that equality of access to schools is their entitlement as citizens. Finally, provision of education services to such students is increasingly being provided by public schools, rather than specialized institutions.

However, this does not imply that full inclusion and the eradication of specialized institutions is being practiced everywhere. Indeed, it is both logical and sensible that full inclusion cannot serve the needs of all students requiring special education services. Furthermore, the inclusion movement is encountering resistance in many cultures. However, it is clear that this once marginalized and segregated population is recognized and being attended to by public education institutions to an extent unprecedented in history. (See also *Change, Children at Risk, Curricular Changes, Decentralization, Equality of Access, Equality of Opportunity, Expansion of Education, Reforms, Structural Changes,* and *Uncertainty.)*

Inequalities—Social, Economic, Racial, Ethnic, and Cultural

The degree to which social inequalities exist in every nation, and how myriad the forms of inequality are, is addressed in detail by our authors. Readers will find ample detail, illustration, and explanation in each chapter. The bottom line is that the quest for a society not riddled with inequalities remains a utopian dream. However, great progress is noted in lessening at least the most irrational and destructive inequalities—based on racial, ethnic, cultural, and so on, discriminatory treatment. However, the battle is far from over; indeed, it is likely more correct to say that it has just begun in earnest. (See also *Children at Risk, Culture, Equality of Access, Equality of Opportunity, Financial Constraints, Gender Inequalities, Inequality of Educational Opportunity, Privatization,* and *Rural-Urban Inequalities.)*

Inequality of Educational Opportunity

Obviously, this topic falls directly under the umbrella of the preceding theme. However, for equally obvious reasons, our authors pay particular attention to this form of inequality, so we will discuss it in a separate strand.

In a world of rapid change and inadequate resources for education, perhaps it is to be expected that there will be winners and losers in the race to access "better" schools, teachers, programs, and so on. Indeed, that is the case. The most disturbing theme running through all sixteen of our national studies is the huge and depressing lack of equality in education opportunities for all children.

The particular form such inequality of opportunity assumes varies. Sometimes there is outright discrimination on the basis of race, ethnicity, gender, or religion. Sometimes the problem takes the form of regional inequalities, as in the case of urban versus rural communities and prosperous jurisdictions versus impoverished areas. Then there are more subtle manifestations, such as bias on the basis of social class or cultural background. These become particularly evident as public education systems become increasingly replaced with private schools catering to selective clientele.

Different as these forms of inequality are, the general phenomenon is pervasive. All nations seem to be struggling with how to provide all children equal access to, and services within, the educational arena. Unfortunately, solutions are more elusive than ever and some societies have literally abandoned the ideal of equality of educational opportunity for all. Perhaps this is understandable in light of the preceding discussion on financial constraints.

Nevertheless, educators continue to resist this trend and work toward innovative, if partial, solutions. Carrying on the battle is becoming increasingly difficult, however. Schools are becoming institutions where, for some, forwarding specific agendas and gaining competitive advantages are the real goals. (See also *Children at Risk, Culture, Equality of Access, Equality of Opportunity, Financial Constraints, Gender Inequalities, Inequalities, Privatization, Rural-Urban Inequalities, Teacher Shortages,* and *Teacher Attrition.)*

Literacy

Regardless of the wealth of a nation, there is a continued concern and focus upon increasing literacy rates. In countries with high literacy rates, the fixation is on raising literacy levels ever higher. Literacy is seen as the base from which all progress in increasing national levels of education must be made. Most of our authors, especially those reporting on relatively poor nations, emphasize the issue of literacy. On this front, great progress is being made. However, for many countries, it is a case of running hard to remain in the same place. Nations with a surging population of young people are making great progress, but their high fertility and population growth rates make it an uphill battle. (See also *Demographic Transformations, Equality of Access, Equality of Opportunity, Expansion of Education, Financial Constraints, Gender Inequalities, Inequalities, Inequality of Educational Opportunity,* and *Rural-Urban Inequalities.)*

Market Economy Model

As our above discussions indicate, a business orientation is now well established in most nations' administration and funding of education. For schools and postsecondary institutions, this has resulted in a change of orientation from an equality of access and equality of educational opportunity mode of operation to a market economy model. That is, education institutions are now expected to operate on and be accountable to the same criteria that business is—cost efficiency, client satisfaction, and so on. This has resulted in a fundamental change from schools being regarded as essential social services that are exempt from market forces.

Today, with concerns about limited finances, governments are very willing to engage in experimentation with alternative education delivery services and modes. Accordingly, there is an explosion of private schools and universities around the world, accountability for schools is in place, decentralization of administration is continuing, bureaucracy is being reduced, and many reforms in education center around economic considerations. In some countries this has resulted in a near dismantling of free, universal, publicly funded education systems built on the social principles of equality of access and equality of educational opportunity. In the face of dwindling resources, public schools, critics argue, are fast becoming dumping grounds for those without social and economic advantages who are unable or who cannot afford to shop for the best education delivery services. Rather than facilitating the improvement of public schools, the market model is slowly dooming them because they are underfunded, must accept all who knock on their doors, have increasing societal and government expectations placed on them, have fixed and high expenses such as salaries of certified teachers, yet must still operate on the principles of "business." (See also *Academic versus Vocational/Technical Focus, Accountability, Brain Drain, Decentralization, Downsizing Education Bureaucracies, Financial Constraints, Global Economic Competition, Globalization, Human Capital, Privatization, Reforms,* and *Structural Changes.)*

Multiculturalism

All nations are becoming increasingly diverse in terms of culture, race, ethnicity, religion, and social ideologies. Even traditionally homogenous national populations are feeling the impact of minority populations and alternative political, social, cultural, and other views. The result is that school systems, and nations, around the world are grappling with how to accommodate the minority populations increasingly found in their classrooms and the increasingly diverse worldviews emerging within their societies.

Responses to the forces of pluralism range from exclusion to assimilation to embracing cultural pluralism. However, regardless of dominant groups' attitudes and responses, a new reality is literally being forced upon all societies. In the long run, it may not matter that some embrace their new pluralism, while others resist. What is clear is that as countries become increasingly diverse in terms of culture, race, social ideas, and other parameters, their very characters are becoming redefined by this new demographic reality. (See also *Demographic Transformations, Gender Inequalities, Globalization, Inequalities, Inequality of Educational Opportunity, Literacy, Nationalism, Religion,* and *Social and Ideological Conflicts.)*

Privatization

In line with the shifting, primarily economic, priorities in education is a large and increasing trend toward allowing the establishment of private schools and postsecondary institutions. In many countries where private education institutions were virtually nonexistent but a decade or two ago, the private education sector is literally booming. Where private education was long allowed, the trend is one of accelerated growth. (See also *Decentralization, Downsizing Education Bureaucracies, Financial Constraints, Globalization, Human Capital, Market Economy Model, Reforms,* and *Structural Changes.)*

Reforms

It is important to realize that all the above-noted shifts in education principles and practice did not happen overnight. Schooling around the world has indeed entered a new era, but the seeds for this transformation were planted in the late 1980s and 1990s. Major reforms in national education systems were proposed, drafted, initiated, and slowly realized for over two decades. Only today do we see them fully manifested. The education (and other economic and social) reforms that nations undertook were indeed staggering in their scope, depth, and complexity. Our chapter authors are careful to clearly trace the genesis of the "new" social and education realities we are just coming to understand and cope with. (See also *Academic versus Vocational/Technical Focus, Change, Curricular Changes, Decentralization, Demographic Transformations, Downsizing Education Bureaucracies, Expansion of Education, Financial Constraints, Global Economic Competition, Globalization, Human Capital, Inclusion, Market Economy Model, Privatization, Structural Changes,* and *Uncertainty.)*

Religion

An interesting and potent counterbalance to the forces of globalization outlined above is a prominent resurgence of religious ideologies across the globe. Religion is a strong force in almost all the countries studied. Indeed, in some nations, it is the defining element of the social milieu. (See also *Culture, Demographic Transformations, Inequalities, Multiculturalism, Nationalism,* and *Social and Ideological Conflict.)*

Rural-Urban Inequalities

Yet another form of inequality that warrants more than generic mention is the great disparity between rural and urban regions. Particularly in relatively poor nations, the chasm between the affluence and opportunities of urban centers and the realities of basic subsistence and minimal schooling has yet to be bridged. The situation in some countries is clearly one where there is still very much work to be done. Ameliorating the problem of regional disparities is a priority for many governments, and schooling is regarded as a key weapon in that difficult battle. (See also *Children at Risk, Decentralization, Equality of Access, Equality of Opportunity, Financial Constraints, Gender Inequalities, Globalization, Inequalities, Inequality of Educational Opportunity,* and *Technology.)*

Social and Ideological Conflict

Even as changes accelerate and financial hardships grip societies and their schools, one constant remains. Schooling, in the form of credentials earned, continues to correlate significantly with economic success and social status. Indeed, the instability resulting from profound social and economic change has made this increasingly, rather than less, the case.

The result is predictable. Dominant groups—identified by economic status, race, gender, and so on—consciously attempt to "use" schools for the advantage of their children.

This, of course, heightens inequalities in educational opportunities. The groups with the greatest resources and strongest political will secure access to the most prestigious institutions; their children enjoy greater academic success; and upon graduation the returns on their education are largest. However, education is a contested arena in more ways than a simple cost-benefit formula equating better schooling with getting a better job.

Some of the bitterest battles in education are being fought over issues that at first glance have little to do with economics. Because schools are value-transmitting and consciousness-shaping institutions, political, religious, cultural, and all manner of socioeconomic/ideological groups aspire to have their views legitimized and propagated through the sanction of public and private schools. In this quest, some groups and their viewpoints prevail; others are marginalized.

Sometimes the dominant values are nationalistic or cultural; sometimes they are religious or secular; sometimes they reflect political values or social philosophies; usually they are a potent mixture of all these and more. In some countries one set of values dominates; in others diverse orientations coexist. However, it is always the case that the situation is dynamic and fluid. Competing viewpoints emerge, and education institutions are arenas in which they clash and vie for supremacy. This affects all aspects of schooling—the curriculum, pedagogy, authority relations, and so on. To borrow a phrase, schools are a microcosm of society's culture wars.

Our contributing authors recognize that the schools in their societies stand for something—they are not value-free institutions. Indeed, they are not meant to be. If you think about it, a value-free school system is an education system without a purpose, without a vision. But, with this acknowledged, a problem immediately emerges.

If schools were institutions somehow closed to external influences, then perhaps they might be able to implement a consistent vision or reify a particular ideology. But they are not; schools are part of a larger social milieu. And, in today's world, no society is completely isolated from external influences.

That is why schools are necessarily arenas of social conflict. Inevitably, different groups in today's increasingly pluralistic world will hold different ideological visions. All want to build a better world through an enlightened education system—but sometimes their visions clash. When that happens, a contest between social factions begins, as each wants the education system to recognize, respect, disseminate, and ultimately, to legitimize its particular orientation.

In reading the case studies in this book, you may be struck by how the values promulgated by some school systems challenge your own cultural, political, social, economic, and religious views. We encourage you to wrestle with these issues. As individual teachers, you will bring your values into the classroom; as an education system, your schools have an identifiable value base. What values does your school system embrace and promote? Why do you hold the values you do? Should all viewpoints be explicitly included in schools or should some perspectives take precedence over others? On what bases can the acceptance of some values over others be justified? What is the responsibility of teachers when it comes to shaping the values of students? (See also *Change, Culture, Demographic Transformations, Gender Inequalities, Globalization, Inequalities, Inequality of Educational Opportunity, Multiculturalism, Nationalism, Religion,* and *Uncertainty.)*

Structural Changes

At every level, the above-noted shifts in the meaning, purpose, and implementation of schooling require complementary structural changes to education systems. Such changes have indeed been effected—and they are massive. Our authors take great care to outline how dramatically the institutional framework of education has been transformed in nations.

Interestingly, the most affected levels are postsecondary education and secondary level schools. Postsecondary education has seen a tremendous—and not always successful—merging of colleges and universities and the creation of new institutions, as a reaction to the above-mentioned economic, social, political, and ideological changes. In consequence, secondary schools have been realigned to complement the new structural and functional realities of the postsecondary institutions they feed into. (See also *Academic versus Vocational/Technical Focus; Accountability; Administration, Policies, and Regulations; Decentralization; Downsizing Education Bureaucracies; Expansion of Education; Financial Constraints; Global Economic Competition; Globalization; Human Capital; Market Economy Model; Privatization;* and *Reforms.)*

Teacher Shortages and Teacher Attrition

Virtually all countries have major problems attracting good candidates into the teaching profession, retaining qualified personnel, and enticing good teachers to teach in schools where students need the most help—rural areas, impoverished areas, schools with disproportionate numbers of special needs students, and so on. The scope of factors that make these perennial problems is well addressed in many chapters. (See also *Children at Risk, Curricular Changes, Decentralization, Financial Constraints, Inclusion, Market Economy Model, Privatization, Rural-Urban Inequalities, Social and Ideological Conflict, Teacher Stress,* and *Teacher Training and Qualifications.)*

Teacher Stress

Following from the preceding point, it seems that educators everywhere are experiencing increased demands on their services. Whether this takes the form of more students per classroom, increased teaching hours, extracurricular duties, or others, the demand for teachers and administrators to do more seems to be universal. The justification for this is often an economic argument. Declining resources are said to dictate such necessities. (See also *Children at Risk, Curricular Changes, Decentralization, Financial Constraints, Inclusion, Market Economy Model, Privatization, Rural-Urban Inequalities, Social and Ideological Conflict, Teacher Shortages and Teacher Attrition,* and *Teacher Training and Qualifications.)*

Teacher Training and Qualifications

In light of the themes discussed above and following, it is obvious that great demands are made on today's teachers, and important social responsibilities weigh on their shoulders. Therefore, it should not come as a surprise that all contributors addressed the issue of teacher education and certification. Virtually all of our sixteen nations have made substantive changes in both areas recently.

Two things are clear: Training is becoming increasingly rigorous, and the time of study for certification is increasing. As measured by certification requirements, there seems to be a rapid professionalization of teaching. There is also great diversity; teachers are educated and certified in a myriad of ways around the world. Much can be learned from this diversity as teacher training institutions continue to experiment and refine their programs and approaches. (See also *Accountability; Administration, Policies, and Regulations; Curricular Changes; Decentralization; Downsizing Education Bureaucracies; Financial Constraints; Inclusion; Teacher Shortages and Teacher Attrition; Teacher Stress; Teaching Strategies; Technology;* and *Uncertainty.)*

Teaching Strategies

It is not the content of schooling alone that is changing. School systems across the world are debating pedagogy, and experimentation in instructional strategies is rampant. Some nations are experimenting with what might be called "progressive" approaches, including elements such as student-centered teaching, group work, individualized assessment and progress, and so on. Other nations complement progressive practices with a "traditional" approach rooted in teacher-centered instruction, uniform curricula, standardized evaluations, and so on. And, beyond and between these poles, a myriad of alternative and hybrid approaches can be identified in specific nations.

The common thread, however, is that the nations of the world seem to be turning away from monolithic, systemwide, pedagogical strategies. To greater or lesser degrees, depending upon the individual nation, an increased diversity in pedagogical strategies is becoming manifested in schools. (See also *Children at Risk, Curricular Changes, Inclusion, Multiculturalism, Reforms, Social and Ideological Conflict,* and *Structural Changes.)*

Technology

Technological changes are affecting classrooms around the globe. The need to make both teachers and students aware of technological advances and competent in using new technologies is universally acknowledged. However, there is not a consensus on which technologies are most crucial or how to teach technological awareness. Thus, while coping with technological change is a demand made on both teachers and students, what needs to be done and how it should be done is far from clear.

However, in some areas—such as delivering education services to rural populations and using technology to enhance the marketable skills of students—remarkable progress is evident. (See also *Academic versus Vocational/Technical Focus, Brain Drain, Global Economic Competition, Globalization, Human Capital, Market Economy Model,* and *Uncertainty.)*

Uncertainty

This is quite remarkable, and unsettling, for educators. We are charged with inculcating the next generation with academic and cultural knowledge; with instilling attitudes, habits, and skills that will serve students well in the world of work; and with preparing them to cope with their responsibilities as members of society. Yet there is a crisis in the profession because the future is uncertain: What knowledge is of most value? What skills will the economy demand? What values will be appropriate in the new social order students will graduate into? All of our contributing authors wrestle with these dilemmas, as do nations, ministries of education, local school authorities, teacher associations, and teachers.

In other words, educators are in a state of uncertainty because their job is to teach, but as a professional community, we are not confident of what we should be teaching. We are not sure how the content of schooling can keep up with the rapid changes in the society around us. Very often, this crisis is framed in the language of vocational training, that is, what job skills are needed by today's students so that they may succeed tomorrow in a rapidly changing economy. One institutional response to this has been an emphasis upon vocational education. Another is a proliferation of comprehensive schools. (See also *Academic versus Vocational/Technical Focus, Change, Curricular Changes, Global Economic Competition, Globalization, Human Capital, Market Economy Model, Reforms,* and *Structural Changes.)*

OPTIMISM: A CONCLUDING COMMENT

We close this Introduction with reference to what really belongs in our listing of themes above. However, it is such an important theme—one permeating every single chapter in the book—that we wish to highlight it separately. It is interesting to note that so many of the above themes focus on issues, problems, and areas of contention. One can be forgiven for coming to the conclusion that our contributing authors have painted an overall bleak picture of education around the world.

That is not at all the case. In fact, quite the opposite is true. In spite of all the issues, dilemmas, and problems facing nations and schools around the globe, and in spite of the fact that educational institutions and professional educators have been at best only partially successful in meeting those challenges, societies continue to have faith that their schools and the education community have made great progress and will continue to make progress. In other words, there is a worldwide enduring faith in schools and an equally enduring faith in the future. And, that faith is justified. Each contributor, under the Successes section of her or his section, speaks eloquently to the remarkable progress and accomplishments that educators have achieved. Even if most of the battles have not been fully won, there clearly is progress and improvement. Besides, in the quest to fashion a "perfect world," our goals will necessarily and inevitably be set higher and higher.

This validates the principal belief upon which schools are founded: the belief that a better society can be built if we succeed in providing an appropriate and enlightened education—as best we can—for the next, and successive, generations. Each successive generation picks up the torch and continues a little farther down the road to enlightenment. But it is a moving goal; it cannot and will not ultimately ever be reached—and that is as it should be. What really matters is that the journey continues in a positive direction; what really matters is that schools and educators are facilitating that positive thrust. Such is the faith that unites educators, parents, policymakers, and citizens in a common cause. It is inspiring to see that optimism reflected in each and every one of our contributed chapters.

Welcome, now, to *Schooling Around the World: Debates, Challenges, and Practices.* We wish you an informative and enjoyable read.

Part II

THE PACIFIC RIM

A Landscape of Diversity

CHAPTER TWO

JAPANESE SCHOOLING

Tradition and Modernization

HIROYUKI NUMATA

Japan is an island country situated in Far East Asia, consisting of four main islands and about 3,000 smaller islands. Japan's neighboring countries on the west are Korea and China, but they are separated by a natural border, the Sea of Japan. On the east are such countries as the Philippines, the United States of America, and Australia, but they are also separated by the huge Pacific Ocean. In pre-modern ages, the seas were almost insurmountable. This geographical situation gave the Japanese people a characteristic of insular narrowness but also a strong curiosity to know, to learn, and to import what the rest of the world was doing.

Japan belongs to the Asia-monsoon temperate climate with four mild seasons. The main industry has long been agriculture, which requires diligence and work. Even if earthquakes, typhoons, and other natural disasters are frequent, the Japanese people are comfortable with the natural environment and do not feel any antagonistic sentiments toward the surrounding world. Or, more precisely, the ambivalent character of the climate—friendly, but sometimes cruel—has given the Japanese a similarly ambivalent character. A history of more than 2,000 years of agriculture in this climate has determined the Japanese ethos to live with nature harmoniously and to work industriously. But there is simultaneously a strong sense of *mujokan* (emptiness of life on the earth) that persuades people not to cling too much to earthly life.

Japan has a population of more than 126 million people. Today about 49 percent of the population are Shintoists. Another 45 percent are Buddhists. Christians are less than 1 percent.

In relation to per capita national income among OECD countries, the average Japanese earned US$24,038 in 2001. This is lower than Denmark (US$24,866) but higher than Iceland (US$22,753) (Asahi Shimbun, 2004).

Dr. Hiroyuki Numata started his academic career at Ueno Gakuen College in Tokyo in 1964 and moved to Tohoku University in 1982. He is now Professor Emeritus at Tohoku University and Professor at Kamakura Women's University. He is also President of the Tohoku Philosophy and History of Education Society.

THE SOCIAL FABRIC

Tradition and Modernity

Before entering into the modernization of the country and the successes and tensions in the educational system, it is useful to look back briefly to the traditional religious and cultural background of modern Japan.

From the beginning of the seventeenth century, and lasting for about 260 years, Japan had a policy of seclusion. Isolated from the world, the people of Japan lived naively, following the Shintoist simple way of living that rested on the belief that a pure and clean mind was fundamental to the achievement of human beings on the earth.

Of course, people were also eager to learn from abroad. Confucianism and Buddhism came to Japan around the sixth century, from China, via Korea. In the beginning, it was difficult for the Japanese to understand the sophisticated Confucian five cardinal virtues: benevolence, justice, politeness, wisdom, and fidelity. The fourteenth century, however, is known in Japanese history as the age of the popularization of Buddhism and Buddhist teachings such as *Gedatsu* (emancipation from earthly desires) and *Mujo* (emptiness of life).

Over the centuries, the borrowings from Chinese culture became gradually Japanized, including the Japanization of Chinese characters into the Japanese language, known as *Kanji.* As well, the most refined aspects of Japanese culture such as *Chanoyu* (tea ceremony), *Ikebana* (flower arrangement), and *No* (No-theater) flourished in those days under the influence of the indigenous sensitivity to the simple way of life and the religious feelings of Shintoism, Buddhism, and the Confucian ethos to live simply, honestly, and diligently on the earth.

One of the keys to understanding the educational situation today in Japan is to remember that Japan has always been, very generally speaking, eager to learn everything, starting from the essential minimum knowledge such as the 3Rs right up to Confucian teachings. In fact, Confucianism was a kind of general education for all people in the premodern era. It is estimated that in the late Edo Era (seventeenth century to the late nineteenth century; Edo is the ancient name of Tokyo) the literacy rate was already very high and a large portion of the population frequented *Juku* (small private teaching facilities), although the exact attendance rate is unknown.

The other critical key to understanding Japanese education today, together with all the cultural aspects of the country, is to recognize the importance of the Meiji Restoration in the late 1860s. *Meiji* is the name of the age under the Emperor Meiji (1852–1912). In Japanese history, the renovation process from the feudal period (seventeenth century to the 1860s) to the establishment of the new modern government in the late 1860s is called the *Meiji Restoration.*

The feudal system, based mainly on the strict hereditary hierarchy of *Samurai* (warriors), farmers, artisans, and tradesmen, ended in 1867 when Shogun Yoshinobu Tokugawa (1837–1913) transferred the reins of government to the emperor in 1867. This occurred after a decade of conflicts between the British, French, Dutch, and new American states that required Japan to open the country, thus suspending the isolation policy that the Tokugawa government wanted to keep.

With the Meiji Restoration, Japan opened its doors to the world and began to modernize the country, especially its industry. "Wealth and Military Strength" together with

"Civilization and Enlightenment" were the slogans of late nineteenth-century Japan. The country did not want to be colonized by the Western Powers and simultaneously wanted to catch up with the modernization process of the rest of the world.

However, the discontinuity of traditional cultural ways and the sudden arrival of Western modern values around this period were the origin for most of the serious problems of Japanese culture today. This aspect—the traditional ethos versus modern imported values—forms a crux as this chapter analyzes modern Japanese education.

Political and Institutional Life

Japan has been a constitutional country with the Tennoism (Emperor System) since 1889. But, as declared in the Constitution of Japan promulgated in 1946 that came into effect in 1947, the Emperor is now "the symbol of the State and the unity of the people" (Article 1) and has no political power. Therefore, since World War II, Japan has been a democratic constitutional country based on the division of the three powers—administrative, legislative, and judiciary.

The Diet, the highest organ of state power, is composed of two Houses—the House of Representatives and the House of Councilors (Article 41). Executive power is vested in the Cabinet, which consists of the Prime Minister and other Ministers of State. All judicial power is vested in the Supreme Court and in inferior courts.

Politically, the Japanese are generally conservative and realistic. They have a tendency to behave, not with the aim at any future political ideal, but rather following realistic present interests. Rightly or wrongly, the Japanese do not usually want to initiate any drastic political changes but prefer to approve of the political status quo around them. In fact, it is remarkable that in the period from World War II up to 2004—more than half a century—the party in power has always been conservative except for two years of the Socialist Party regime from 1947 to 1949. It should be noted, however, that this realistic and conservative attitude in political life contrasts starkly with the innovative spirit in the field of industrial technology.

During the Meiji Restoration, it was mainly the pressure of world powers that pushed Japan to open its doors to the world, although certainly the time was ripe to abandon the feudal system of the Edo Era and to modernize the country. In the case of World War II, it was the GHQ of the U.S. occupation army, again a pressure from outside, that pushed the Japanese government to abandon forever ultra-militarism and ultra-nationalism, to adopt the democratic regime in every domain of social life, and to create a new democratic education system.

From this, we can give a recent example of how conservatism and realism function sometimes unexpectedly in political life. None of the articles of the Constitution have been amended since promulgation in 1946. Article 9 of the Constitution declares that "Aspiring sincerely to an international peace based on justice and order, the Japanese people forever renounce war as a sovereign right of the nation or use of forces as means of settling international disputes. . . . The right of belligerency of the state will not be recognized."

Yet, this is one of the hottest political issues in Japan today. Japanese conservatism persuades the people that it is good to keep what was decided sixty years ago. However, realism says that the world today is not so peaceful that we can survive without military power. Under these conditions, interestingly, it is the conservative parties now that insist on the necessity to amend Article 9. They are realistic. On the other hand, it is the intellectual progressives who do not want to amend the article. They are in a sense idealistic and want to conserve what the people decided sixty years ago.

Economy and Industry

The Meiji Restoration in the late 1860s brought modernization and industrialization. By the beginning of the twentieth century, Japan was a power capable of fighting with the Russian fleet. Then Japan rushed into the so-called fifteen-year-war period from 1931 to 1945. In 1931, Japan occupied Manchuria, after the Mukden incident. In 1937 Japan invaded China and then attacked Pearl Harbor in 1941. All of this led to Japan's unconditional surrender in 1945. After 1945, however, the country again began to walk its path to become an economic and industrial power in the world.

The rapid development of economics and the renovation of technology inevitably caused changes in the industrial structure. Beginning in about 1960, for example, the farming population drastically diminished. In 1960, farm workers were 26.8 percent of the total working population; they were only 4.4 percent in 2001. In 1960, agricultural production accounted for 9.0 percent of the total gross domestic product (GDP); in 2000, only 1.0 percent. Moreover, the farmers are becoming older; in the fiscal year 2002, those aged 65 or more constituted 47.1 percent of all farm workers. The ratio of workers in the primary, secondary, and third industries was 4.7 percent, 29.1 percent, and 65.3 percent respectively in 2002 (Asahi Shimbun, 2004).

As well, the industrial structure is changing. Today, Japan's flourishing industrial products are machinery and equipment, automobiles, and electrical and electronic product machine tools (in 2002, 72 percent of all products). But note that Japan had to import more than 80 percent of primary energy from abroad in 2002 (Asahi Shimbun, 2004).

Japan has been the world's biggest creditor nation since 1985. It is also confronted with many serious financial problems such as the huge amount of long-term debt of the national and local governments—130 percent of the country's annual GDP—and a high-cost economic structure.

In spite of financial and economic difficulties, including the rise of the unemployment rate up to 5.4 percent in 2002, the Japanese are enjoying a decent life today, at least materially. Most feel that they belong to the middle class of society. Most enjoy long life. For women, life expectancy was the longest in the world in 2002 (85.23 years old; the second, Hong Kong, 84.7; the third, Switzerland, 82.6 [1999–2000]). As for men, the top is Hong Kong, 78.7; with Japan at 78.32 years (Asahi Shimbun, 2004).

SCHOOLING

People Who Love Education

The Japanese have always been fond of learning. Since pre-modern ages, people have frequented small private institutes (*Juku*) to learn basic knowledge such as the 3Rs and discipline. The main reasons for this were first of all the agricultural way of life, which required people to work diligently and led them naturally to learn. Second, Confucianism insisted on the necessity of learning in order to live honestly on the earth.

The modern school system that evolved after the Meiji Restoration fitted with the traditional national ethos of learning. Until the 1980s, school was a wonderland that enabled people to realize a happy life in the future. That myth is rapidly disappearing. Today, educational problems such as violence, bullying, and students not attending schools have become serious.

Aims of School Education before World War II

A new modern educational system was introduced in 1872 after the Meiji Restoration. From the outset, there were intense struggles between progressive leaders, who wanted to introduce Western humanistic values such as individualism and liberalism, and conservative politicians, who wanted to maintain Confucian values such as loyalty and filial piety.

When the Imperial Rescript on Education was promulgated in 1890, the aims of education represented a compromise. In part, the document declared:

> . . . pursue learning and cultivate arts, and thereby develop intellectual faculties and perfect moral powers; furthermore advance public good and promote common interests; always respect the Constitution and observe the laws; should emergency arise, offer yourselves courageously to the State; and thus guard and maintain the prosperity of Our Imperial Throne coeval with heaven and earth. So shall ye not only be Our good and faithful subjects, but render illustrious the best traditions of your forefathers. (English translation authorized by the Department of Education, Japan, 1907)

This Rescript largely determined the aims of school education from 1890 until the end of the war in 1945. In the Rescript, several elements appear: imperial virtues such as loyalty to the Emperor; family virtues such as filial piety to parents and harmony between husband and wife; perfection of individual morality—modesty, moderation, benevolence, learning, and the cultivation of intellectual faculties; and public morals such as the promotion of common interests and respect for the laws. There is also the problematic recommendation that, if emergency should arise, the people should offer themselves courageously to the state.

During these years, Japanese education was, except for a short period at the beginning of the twentieth century, imperialistic. It was based on the principles of loyalty and patriotism; these were concretized in school education through ceremonies and moral training. Moreover, the final idea in the above Rescript was interpreted to justify the imperialistic, chauvinistic, and militaristic education designed to build a nation for the state at the last stage of World War II.

Aims of Education after World War II

The end of the war brought drastic changes to all of Japanese society. Education was no exception. The Fundamental Law of Education promulgated in 1947 shows totally different principles and aims for education and illustrates the new spirit. The preamble states:

> Having established the Constitution of Japan, we have shown our resolution to contribute to the peace of the world and welfare of humanity of building a democratic and cultural state. The realization of this ideal shall depend fundamentally on the power of education. We shall

> esteem individual dignity and endeavour to bring up the people who love truth and peace, while education which aims at the creation of culture general and rich in individuality shall be spread far and wide.

Article 1, the Aim of Education, goes on to say that:

> Education shall aim at the full development of personality, striving for the rearing of the people, sound in mind and body, who shall love truth and peace, esteem individual value, respect labour and have a deep sense of responsibility, and be imbued with the independent spirit, as builders of the peaceful state and society.

These sentences show the resolution of the Japanese people after the defeat of the war. It shows how deeply they wanted to change completely the pre-war imperialistic ideology into a new democratic way of looking at the rearing of future young generations.

Critiques from the conservative side have argued that the law stressed individualistic values and neglected the importance of patriotism. In spite of this, the law has been supported by most Japanese over for the past half century. Very recently, however, amending the Fundamental Law of Education has become a hot political issue in proportion to the general tendency toward conservatism seen in Japanese society in recent years.

School System

Under the School Education Law of 1947, *school* means primary school, junior and senior high school, university and technical college, and schools for those who are blind, deaf, physically disabled, mentally retarded, and others.

Schools are categorized according to who establishes them: national schools by the national government, municipal schools by municipal or local government, and private schools by school corporations. However, schools for the blind, for the deaf, special schools, and kindergartens can be established by individuals other than school corporations. On the compulsory education level, most of the schools are public, whereas in the field of kindergartens, universities, and junior colleges, there are many private schools.

Preschool. Preschool institutions include infant education, nursery services, day-care centers, and kindergartens. Some of these exist for mothers who work. Daily nurture hours are usually more than eight hours.

Primary School. Japanese children enter primary school at 6 years of age. From 6 to 15 years of age, up to junior high school, education is compulsory. In Japan, compulsory means compulsory school attendance, compulsory school establishment, compulsory assistance to school attendance, and compulsory prohibition of learning obstruction. At this stage of compulsory education, all students follow the same curriculum.

The compulsory school enrollment rate is almost 100 percent. The percentage of students who went on to senior high school was 96 percent in 2003. So, even though senior high school education is not compulsory, almost all young people in Japan up to the age of 18 years old go to school today.

The enforcement Regulations for the School Education Law prescribes the variety of subjects and the standard class hours in a year. In primary schools the total school hours are the following: first grade, 850 hours; second, 910; third, 980; fourth, 1,015; fifth, 1,015; and sixth, 1,015. The curriculum is composed of Japanese language, social studies, arithmetic, life environment studies, science, music, drawing and handicraft, homemaking, physical education, moral education, and special activities.

In junior high school, the total school hours are first grade, 1,050 hours; second, 1,050; and third, 1,050. The curriculum is composed of compulsory subjects, elective subjects, moral education, and special activities. Subjects include Japanese language, social studies, mathematics, science, music, fine arts, health and physical education, foreign language, industrial arts, and homemaking.

International comparison shows that class hours in Japan are not overlong when compared to some other countries. For example, at the primary school level Italy has 5,780 hours; India, 5,760; France, 5,094; Canada (Quebec), 5,076; the United States (Washington, DC), 4,968; and Japan, 3,872. At junior high a sample of school hours shows Hong Kong, 2,754; France, 2,735; Canada (Quebec), 2,700; Taiwan, 2,580; Germany (Berlin), 2,509; and Japan, 2,361 (Asahi Shimbun, 2004).

Japanese class sizes are among the biggest in the world. For example, Korea has 36.3 children in primary levels, and 37.7 students in lower secondary school; Japan has 28.8 children in primary and 34.5 in lower secondary school (OECD, 2003).

Secondary Schools. The revision of the School Education Law in 1988 enabled the creation of six-year secondary education, which combines junior and senior high schools. In 1962, technical colleges came into existence following the demand from the industrial world to supply middle-level technicians.

At the high school level, the curriculum and types of courses vary. Subjects are counted on the basis of credit. The subject areas are Japanese language, geography and history, civics, mathematics, science, health and physical education, arts, foreign languages, and home economics. Specialized vocational courses include commerce, industry, agriculture, fishery, English, science, and mathematics. Students also take part in special activities such as homeroom activities, student council activities, club activities, and school events.

Formal and Nonformal Schooling. Schools and learning institutes have existed in Japan for at least 1,000 years. They served not only children of the leading Samurai class but also the common people, who acquired fundamental knowledge such as calligraphy, abacus, and reading from a private master.

This tradition still exists in Japanese society where large numbers of children attend *juku* outside the framework of formal school life. For example, for the primary school fifth and sixth grades, 42.4 percent of the girls and 37.1 percent of the boys were learning in *juku.* Of these, 72.9 percent of the girls and 42.9 percent of the boys were doing *keikogoto* (literally learning and practice such as piano, painting, and ballet). When junior high school and senior high school students are included, in total 28.2 percent of the girls and 33.6 percent of the boys learn in *juku;* 38.5 percent of the girls and 21.4 percent of the boys do *keikogoto* (Kodomo Katei Sogo-Kenkyusho, 2001).

Higher Education. The percentage of students who went to universities, including junior colleges, was only 16.9 percent in 1965, but 49.0 percent (total of male and female) in 2003. The rate of those who went on to graduate school was 11.8 percent in 2004 (Asahi Shimbun, 2004).

To enter university, students have to pass entrance examinations after twelve years of school education. Those who have passed the Qualifying Certificate Examination or the International Baccalaureate can also enter universities.

School Administration. Japanese educational administration is based on five principles. These are the Principle of Legalism, the Principle of Democratic Administration, the Principle of Neutralism, the Principle of Adjustment and Establishment of Educational Conditions, and the Principle of Decentralization.

On the national level, education is managed by the Ministry of Education, Science and Culture, which administers educational administration as a whole; school education; local educational administration; international educational administration; and organization of the internal subdivisions. At the same time, various councils act to solve actual daily problems of education. At the local, prefectural, and municipal level, there are assemblies composed of elected members, the boards of education, and the superintendents that administrate education of local communities.

These two levels have no vertical connection. However, they must cooperate closely in order to solve educational problems that relate to every aspect of society (see Takakura & Murata, 1998).

Curricula

In a formal sense, curricula are the responsibility of the Ministry of Education, Science and Culture, the board of education, and each school. But in reality it is the schools that are responsible for the planning of the contents of education of each school.

Evaluation

For long time—before the War, and even after the War—in spite of the introduction of American system that insisted on the importance of practical activities for every student, the result of students' learning was evaluated only on knowledge obtained through text reading and skills measurable objectively and quantitatively. As a result, the harsh competitive university entrance examination was sustained on the premise that an objective learning evaluation system can distinguish those who are intelligent and those who are not. It was only in 1991, when the *Gakushu-Shido-Yoryo* (Authorized Guideline for Curriculum) was reviewed that such human affective faculties as will, interest, attitude, thinking, judgment, and expression began to be evaluated as indicators of performance.

International comparison of learning achievement indicates that the level of knowledge attained by Japanese students is relatively high. For example, in 2000 Japanese students at the age of 15 earned 557 points in the mathematical field to make them the top performers. (South Korea was number 2 with 547 points; number 3 was New Zealand with 537 points). In the scientific field, Korea was at the top with 552 points. Japan followed with 550 points; third was Finland, 538 points (Asahi Shimbun, 2004).

Student Characteristics

Japanese schools are well-organized small communities. The school calendar begins in April with an entrance ceremony where new pupils are welcomed by teachers and senior pupils. The senior pupils take care of the newcomers in every activity, such as cleaning of classrooms, extracurricular activities, and all kinds of ceremonies. At graduation, graduates give thanks to their teachers, to the school, and to the pupils still remaining at school. Parents come often to volunteer.

One remarkable point in Japanese school life is the cleaning of the school by students right up to the end of senior high school. After classes are over, students clean not only their own classrooms but also common places such as toilets, gyms, entrance halls, corridors, and sports grounds. The idea is that humans have to clean what they have made dirty.

Some pupils detest cleaning. But this habit was established long ago and the idea itself is worthy of revaluating in modern society where people have a tendency to think only of themselves, not caring about what they have done themselves and the environmental problems around them.

Part of in-school cooperation arises from the sophisticated notion of group-oriented life. In all of school life, from primary school up to senior high school, the spirit of the group is highly respected. In every aspect, teachers teach pupils how to behave in group life. Through ceremonies, school excursions, athletic meetings, and extracurricular activities, students are taught ways of greeting each other, the polite way to behave in the corridors of school, and the ways to encourage one's team in interschool sport matches.

The strength of the group naturally leads to another facet of Japanese education. That is, Japanese schools have never been just institutes for the learning of knowledge. The hidden curriculum consists of preparing young students for their lives as adults. Therefore, knowledge of subjects such as mathematics, language, and natural sciences join music, drawing, handicrafts, and gymnastics as centers of school activities. After classes, the pupils sometimes play with their teachers in the sports ground and talk about personal problems such as their families and what they want to be in the future. During the high economic growth period, because of the so-called entrance examination hell, the latter aspect was somewhat neglected. Recently, however, there is a new tendency to reconsider it.

Teaching Force

Teachers' Status in Japanese Society. Japanese culture, particularly under the strong influence of Confucianism, respected teachers, who were considered as sacred. In premodern society, teachers in small communities played the role not only of people who transmitted knowledge to children but also of consultants to every familial and communal problem.

With the modernization of the country, a new view of teacher, specifically teacher as laborer and specialist, was introduced. Especially after World War II, the conflict between these two views became popular. Following the Recommendation concerning the Status of Teachers (ILO, 1966), the concept of teaching as a profession began to be established, at least in public discussion. However, Japanese society has not yet reached any conclusion concerning the meaning of *profession* for teachers.

Even today, Japanese teachers in all school levels have functions that extend beyond subject teaching to encompass familial discipline or school and environmental duties. Included are lunch programs, traffic safety programs, safety programs in general, school cleaning programs, medical checkup programs, sex education, and so on. Teachers should work from 8:00 to 17:00. But in order to fulfill all these functions, most teachers have to work after 17:00.

The ethos that saw teachers as respected persons whom people consulted about their own private problems still exists under the modern schooling system. When, for example, delinquency or discipline problems occur in a family, it is very usual that parents talk to the teachers. It is also a long-established habit for Japanese teachers to make a round of calls at his or her pupils' homes, irrespective of whether the pupils have any problems. These visits provide good opportunities for parents to talk about problems of the family or the community. Through this intimate personal relationship between families and schools, schools have been deeply integrated into the communities.

This process causes much annoyance and trouble to some teachers; others are tired of the severe work. A survey done by the Japan Teachers Union, for example, indicates that in a district where the schools are disastrous, one-third of classroom teachers want to quit their jobs (Ogi, 2001).

Teacher Training System. Since the modernization of the country in the late nineteenth century and right up to the educational reform after World War II, normal schools trained teachers. The present teacher training system, which was established after 1949, requires universities and colleges to train teachers in national teacher training colleges or in the departments of education of universities. But any university or college, even one lacking a department of teacher training, can train teachers if authorized by the Minister of Education, Culture, Sports, Science, and Technology.

A teacher certificate is earned by students who have accomplished the prescribed basic qualifications and credits in teaching subjects, professional subjects, and teaching practice. Once qualified, novice teachers have to spend one year in an initial probationary period. Moreover, as teachers are required to always improve their knowledge and skills, there is a system of in-service training offered by both educational administration and universities.

SUCCESSES, CHALLENGES, AND DEBATES

There are many positive aspects of Japanese schooling, particularly seen before the 1980s. After that, however, serious school problems became noticeable. Most prominent are bullying, violence, loss of will to study, and not attending school.

Successes

The Modernization Process from the Meiji Restoration up to the End of World War II (1868–1945). The history of modern Japanese schooling from the Meiji Restoration until the late twentieth century is, in general, a success story. After the abolishment of the old political and administrative system, one of the urgent programs of the government was to organize an education system for all the people. A common understanding of political leaders at the time was that to modernize the country, education had to bring up modern citizens.

The new government established *gakusei* (new system of education) in 1872. The fundamental principles of the new education laws were to deny feudalistic and Confucian teaching as empty doctrines and to adopt a new modern educational system based on the principle of utilitarian pragmatism.

With the underlying assumption that in order to build a powerful and independent modern country, Japan had to educate its young people with the spirit of independence born in Western civilization, models were taken from countries such as Britain, France, Holland, and the United States. Textbooks provided by the Ministry of Education were filled with fables and moral stories from these countries, used to teach young Japanese students Western individualistic morals that included hard work, thrift, tolerance, patience, and honesty, as well as social morals such as rights, obligations, justice, and patriotism.

The *gakusei* also sought to build an ideal single-track schooling system modeled after the centralized schooling system of France joined to pragmatic American educational ideals. That is, a four-year junior primary school, a four-year senior primary school, a three-year junior secondary school, and a three-year senior secondary school and university.

But because it did not fit the reality of Japanese society at that time, the revised system was poorly accepted. The new system was alien to the Japanese traditional way of understanding human relations that were based on the sovereign-subject hierarchy. As well, the cost of education was too expensive for the farmers who formed more than 80 percent of the population in those days. Most of them did not understand why they had to send their children to school during the busiest farming seasons.

After a period of trial and error, the Primary School Law was enacted in 1886. This marked the beginning of compulsory education in Japan; it was now obligatory for parents to send their children to the six-year primary school. By 1907, the percentage of pupils going to primary school reached 90 percent.

Following the firm establishment of primary schools, the 1899 Junior High School Law decided the pre-war junior high school framework of Japan. Laws promulgated between 1894 and 1903 also laid down the structure of college education. The economic prosperity after World War I made it possible to enact the 1919 University Law that allowed the establishment of both national and private universities.

The schooling system from the Meiji Restoration up to the end of World War II was efficient enough to produce people who could respond to the national catch-up-and-pass policy. Japan became powerful enough to make war with the United States of America for four years, even if the end was miserable.

But was it really a success? It is true that the Japanese educational system had been able to furnish excellent government officials, businessmen, intellectuals, and workers who could respond to demands from the industrial world and to the popular ambition of society. However, these excellent people could not, or did not, resist either the imperial ultranationalism or the ultra-militarism that characterized the fifteen-year-war period. People displayed their talents in their own small special fields but were not, generally speaking, all-round players who had broader perspectives.

After World War II. After World War II, the Japanese educational system tended to repeat its pre-war history concerning the types of persons educated by the school system. Despite the failure of such a policy before the war, educational systems followed principally the national demand for industrial and economic recovery from the damage of the war.

In 1946, the United States Education Mission came to Japan. It insisted on the necessity of reform to embrace a system based not on imperialism and militarism, but on democracy and liberalism. The commission's recommendations quickly materialized, first as the Fundamental Law of Education in 1947 and then by the introduction of the single-track 6-3-3-4 school system. As well, the Board of Education on the basis of a decentralized system was introduced.

While it was assumed that democratic principles would lead Japanese education in the future, criticisms about the new democratic education modeled after American pragmatism and the new experimental learning methods surfaced rapidly. Specifically, it was said that although the method was effective in taking into consideration each pupil's individual interest, it was inappropriate in teaching systematic knowledge such as mathematics and natural sciences.

The direction of education changed with the outbreak of the Korean War (1950–1953). The Korean crisis, together with the revival of conservatism, gave some advantage to advocates who insisted on the necessity of rearmament and also the need to make changes in the democratic tendency in schooling.

Under these circumstances, education reform changed in the 1950s. The control and regulation of school administration by the Ministry of Education was strengthened, and demands for the establishment of schooling appropriate to the economic growth of the late 1950s became loud. And, with the disastrous chaos that followed the war, people began to insist on the importance of systematic learning methods.

At the same time, based on high economic growth and under the slogan of "Structural Change of Industry," the industrial world demanded that the educational world renovate the schooling system in order to provide competent and talented leaders who could promote technical innovation, as well as workers.

As a result, schooling extended quantitatively in the 1960s and 1970s. Growth rates corresponded approximately to the economic growth of Japan after World War II. In this sense, the "catch-up policy" to make Japan a major power in the world through universal education that leaders visualized in the late 1860s was realized about one century later.

Challenges

It is ironic that the Japanese schooling system began to dysfunction in the 1980s, exactly at the moment when the original plan of the modern schooling system, made at the beginning of the Meiji Restoration, was almost completely achieved. Nevertheless, it was in the 1980s that people began to talk about school violence, domestic violence, bullying, not attending school, the collapse of classes, the collapse of school, and the disappearance of the will to study.

School Dropouts. In the 1970s, Japanese economic growth was amazing. But behind this economic power there was a strong competitive habit in school life that extended from primary school up to university and served to support the economic structure. Sometimes, even small children went to cram school in order to get into a famous primary school. University entrance examinations were brutal. It is true, however, that once a student entered a well-known university, he or she was guaranteed a good salary in good companies and the promise of a beautiful rosy life in the future.

It was in this climate that the problem of *ochikobore* (dropouts) occurred. As a serious educational problem, dropouts attracted interest in the 1970s.

In the Japanese view, dropouts are those students who cannot follow the required lessons. For example, a survey on learning ability in 1976 revealed that less than 44 percent of the primary school students in the fifth grade could write correctly half of the Chinese characters they were supposed to know. Also, one-third of the students of the first-grade lower secondary school could not calculate when asked to divide 29,866 by 36 (Numata & Masubuchi, 1997).

There is also the problem of students not attending school (thirty or more days a year). However, new data from the Ministry of Education (Asahi Shimbun, 2004) shows that today the number of the students who do not attend school, both at primary schools and junior high schools, is diminishing. For primary schools, the 2002 number of 25,869 dropped to 24,086 in 2004. In junior high schools, the 2002 number of 105,342 was lowered to 102,126 in 2004. Still, about 130,000 students of primary and junior high schools do not attend schools. This translates into 1 among 300 students of primary schools and 1 among 37 students in junior high schools.

School Violence and Bullying. Teacher–student relations today are, very generally speaking, not so bad; they arise mainly and psychologically from the atmosphere in society that respects teachers. Based on this culture of respect, teachers in training in normal schools are taught not only to be good instructors of different subjects but also to be good friends of the students. This tradition is still alive in spite of the rational modernization of schooling that insists on the importance of teachers as subject specialists.

Nevertheless, the recent deplorable phenomenon of school problems such as violence against teachers cannot be ignored. Acts of violence in schools are increasing. From a 1994 total of 2,100 cases both in primary and junior high schools, there were 5,100 cases in 2002 (Asahi Shimbun, 2004).

Another serious issue that has grown since about 1997 is what is called the collapse of classes. It is estimated that in about 7 or 8 percent of classes of all the primary and junior high schools in Japan, teachers cannot control their students. During lessons students talk loudly, walk around in the classrooms, and throw papers and trash (Ogi, 2001).

On the other hand, cases of bullying are diminishing. In 1994, there were a total of 52,000 cases in both primary and junior high schools; in 2002, there were about 20,000 cases.

Lack of Interest. Japanese adults have been working for the economic growth of the country and for the beautiful future of individual lives. But their children have begun to understand that, even if they work hard in school and pass the entrance examinations, their futures are not guaranteed at all.

In the 1980s, the Japanese economy went into a recession phase. Under the name of restructuring of companies, many elite employees were laid off. Therefore, what motive then did young students have to work to get jobs in good companies?

If one does not aim too high, one can at least live today in Japan. The nation is now rich enough, and part-time jobs can guarantee decent lives. For example, if a university student works part-time in a convenience store for a month during summer vacation, he or she can take a tour abroad with the earned money.

Outsiders have traditionally believed that Japanese students learn well and study hard. However, recent research indicates that this may not be the case, because students from primary school up to university cannot find any strong motives to learn in school. For example, one study compared questionnaires from about 1,000 Japanese senior high school students and 1,000 in China, Korea, and the United States. When asked, "When in school do you feel yourself satisfied and happy?" Korean students answered, "When I get good marks." Chinese students said, "When I am in an interesting class, or when I get good marks." American students said "When I am with good friends, . . . get good marks, . . . am in an interesting class." But the Japanese students answered, "Only when I am with good friends." Summarizing these findings with other indices, the researchers commented that the low interest of Japanese students in their studies is conspicuous among the four countries. Japanese senior high school students do not have much interest in their future lives: They do not want to be famous, do not want to be leaders in their classes, and do not want to have their own commercial companies in the future. They have a general tendency to think only of their own present enjoyment.

Of course, this tendency should not be exaggerated. An ethos of a culture that rests on a long history does not change quickly. Generally speaking, Japanese students show enough interest in learning at every level of the school system from kindergarten up to university. At the same time, this recent symptom must be examined seriously. School has lost its magic power as a sacred place that promises a ticket for a wonderland of gorgeous things: a beautiful house, beautiful cars, and a beautiful life. Many students are not expecting anything from schools and are abandoning the schooling system.

Teacher Workload. Japanese society is changing. It seems that it is becoming more controlled. Businessmen are controlled by time cards and their managers; policemen are watching the citizens' behavior. Because every action of an individual is more or less controlled, there is little room for free behavior, and for some, daily life is full of frustration.

An old Japanese proverb says *Kurushii tokino kamidanomi,* which translates as "Once in danger, we pray God." The Japanese today are in a state of lethargy. They have lost the economic energy of the 1960s and the 1970s that propelled them into being a power in the world. In this situation, school is a good target to complain about and encompass all the frustrating problems of community and daily life.

Onoda (2004) explains this interesting new tendency concerning the role of a school in a community that manifests as illogical complaints of people about schools. One example happened like this. A schoolboy went to a convenience store to buy food because he forgot his lunchbox at home. When the boy developed a stomachache, his mother called the manager of the son's school, not the manager of the convenience store, and complained and protested to the school manager. "Why," she asked, "did you allow my son to go to a shop to buy rotten food?" (p. 27).

The result is a generally recognized tendency among teachers, especially conscientious teachers, to be tired of their jobs. In addition to the normal work of classes and subjects, teachers also have to deal with community problems, and overtime work is a general phenomenon among school teachers in Japan.

Crisis of Childhood. School, as an institution where pupils and teachers meet, presupposes the differences between teachers and pupils. Simply, teachers are usually older, more mature, and possess more experience than young, immature, and inexperienced students. Schools will function smoothly as long as the young generation recognizes itself as young and immature but wants to develop to be adults like the teachers. While teachers have always taught what they know to the coming generation, this changed, especially from the middle of the twentieth century when TV began to invade all phases of our lives. Our present information-oriented society has abolished the boundary between the world of children and that of adults.

Some scholars (e.g., Numata 2003, 2004; Postman, 1982) observe that the popularization of TV since the 1950s has abolished the difference of the world of children and that of adults, in particular in industrialized countries. Japan is not an exception. About 73 percent of primary and junior high school students watched TV for more than two hours in a day in 1999. This compares to Korea, 59 percent; the USA, 55 percent; UK, 64 percent; and Germany, 52 percent (Kodomo Katei Sogo-Kenkyusho, 2001). Moreover, a survey undertaken by the Japan PTA Confederation in 1999 showed that 32.2 percent of fifth-grade primary school students and 39.4 percent of second-grade junior high school students have their own private televisions in their own private rooms (Ogi, 2001).

Television does not select its viewers. Children can watch every kind of adult program—sex, violence, and crime—without being scolded by their parents. Add to this the influence of the Internet, and it becomes easy to imagine how children's worlds are strongly influenced by adult culture. Moreover, today young people can talk on mobile telephones without having to worry about any attention from their parents. Indeed, children can enjoy their lives without any interference from an adult.

Following on this, another deplorable phenomenon has appeared concerning Japanese children—that is, *Koshoku* (solitary breakfast or a child taking breakfast alone). One 1982 survey found 22.7 percent of primary school students taking breakfast alone; numbers rose to 27.8 percent in 1988 and 31.4 percent in 1994. A second survey discovered that 38.4 percent of fifth- and sixth-grade students took breakfast alone or only with other children of their family in 1982. By 1999, it was 50.9 percent (Ogi, 2001).

Adults today seem to have forgotten the habit of carefully protecting the world of children. Another manifestation is the terrible increase in child abuse cases, which puzzles conscientious people. In 1990, there were 1,101 cases of child abuse handled by Child Consultation Centers; the number increased to 23,274 in 2001 (Asahi Shimbun, 2004).

University as a Leisure Land. About half the school-age population in Japan proceeded to university in 2004. By the year 2007, all students who want to study at the university level can do so, unless they want a particularly famous university. Wider openings in higher education are the result of the decline of newborn babies.

Certainly, it is a good thing that so many young people can attend higher education institutes. Yet serious negative aspects are emerging in proportion to the popularization of higher education.

A major problem is that many students enter universities without any clear and positive motivation except to enjoy the last two or four years of their youth. These students have little intellectual curiosity: They come to university only to get licenses for a job, or only because their friends go to universities. This brings a dilemma to the universities.

Lack of student direction translates into a deplorable phenomena, particularly in private and not well-known universities. Such students do not seriously listen when the professors are talking; they chatter with their comrades and use mobile phones in the classroom.

It also brings a dilemma to the universities. They do not want dull students, and they do not want to give licenses to these students. But these students are welcomed because universities, in particular private universities, need all these students to generate fees and ensure their finances. Otherwise, they cannot maintain themselves.

Further, this dilemma begs the question of how the universities can bring up elite researchers for tomorrow under such conditions. That is, how can they maintain the intellectual levels of higher education and create the mechanisms to get good students for graduate schools?

Debates

Tradition and Modernization. When in a stream, you have to swim. If not, you will be drowned. Japan plunged into a strong stream of modernization around the 1870s and has swum with the stream desperately, not caring how it looks. After 100 years, it attained the goal set by the leaders of the Meiji Restoration. But while Japan has succeeded in modernizing the country and is now a big economic power, success has been accompanied by many sacrifices.

As it followed the route toward modernization, Japan could not afford to look back on what it had been doing. However, it is now time to consider what Japan has gained and lost by the modernization of the country or, more specifically, by the establishment of a modern schooling system.

In discussing the conditions of education, Numata (2002) argued that it is difficult to transplant a complex system such as schooling from one culture into another, especially when each culture has long-established traditions. The Japanese models of modernization were Western industrialized countries. From Britain, France, Germany, the Netherlands, and the United States of America, Japanese policymakers learned the administrative and structural aspects of the schooling system. But the leaders of the time did not understand that Western culture, including industrial civilization, was based upon a strong ethos of traditions, such as Greek and Judeo-Christian.

In Japan, industrialization was the supreme order. The political leaders and the intellectuals made frantic efforts to catch up to the Western level of civilization, mainly looking at material aspects of it. They built the schooling system for that purpose. After 100 years of effort, the Japanese schooling system was perfect, at least for the purpose of bringing up excellent leaders and workers to promote modern industry. In this sense, Japan succeeded.

The Difference of Time Consciousness That Sustains Education. Education is a humanistic activity deeply rooted both in the conscious and unconscious phases of a culture.

A schooling system is built up consciously and can be observed objectively from the outside. At the beginning of the modernization period, the Japanese learned about this objective aspect of schooling and implanted it, naturally with modifications, in Japan.

Examining the unconscious level of a culture is not an easy task. For example, the argument here centers on the concept of time. Education cannot exist without setting its aims toward the future. In the Judeo-Christian tradition, it is a self-evident truth that education is carried out in the framework of time axes—past, present, and future—and that these three moments of time have equal values. The present is as important as the past and the future. Man cannot exist without having a past and without thinking of a future. Life has its history and also its plan in the future. Education is an intentionally well-planned human activity, based unconsciously on this time conception, at least in the Greek and Judeo-Christian tradition.

However, in the Shintoist and Buddhist ethos, the present, the past, and the future do not have equal values. The present is always at the center of consciousness and not as strongly connected with the past and the future, either in an individual's mind or in mass psychology. This time consciousness did not change in Japan, even after the arrival of Western cultures in the nineteenth century.

On the positive side, this time consciousness enables the Japanese to enjoy every precious moment, not bothering about the past or about the future. For example, hospitality is highly appreciated in Japanese culture. People offer all possible measures to welcome their guests: good food, invitation to a gorgeous hotel or to guide them around the town, and so on, without thinking of their true daily lives in which they must live modestly. It is easy to see that in this psychology the hearty welcome of a guest at the present moment is more important than the future life of the host. This present moment might never come back again, so he or she thinks.

On the negative side, Japanese people can easily forget what they have done in the past. Neighboring Asian countries, for example, are irritated by the fact that Japanese conservative politicians do not want to apologize for what Japan did during the War. As well, the Japanese are not good at planning for future life, individually as well as publicly. For example, Japanese cities sometimes look chaotic because of the lack of planning. Next to an ultramodern skyscraper one can see a traditional wooden two-floor house.

The modern Western schooling system was introduced in this time culture. Consequently, under a seemingly similar schooling system, the Japanese have not behaved, and do not yet behave, like Western people. A survey (cited in Asahi Shimbun, 1994) illustrates this through a comparison of the life consciousness of high school students in several countries. Randomly selected for the study were groups of second-grade junior high school students (14 years old) and second-grade senior high school students (17 years old) from Japan, Taiwan, and the United States of America (each about 1,000 students). Students were asked, among other things, about their lifestyles. To the question, "Do you enjoy this moment without thinking of your future?" 22.3 percent of U.S. students and 13.0 percent of the Taiwanese answered, "Yes." But 51.7 percent of the Japanese students said, "Yes." Another question was, "Do you think you should study now for your own future?" To this, 76.9 percent of Taiwanese and 65.2 percent U.S. students responded "Yes." Only 47.3 percent of Japanese students agreed. Responses led to conclusions that Japanese students belong to a type of those who enjoy only the present moment.

This appears to be a continuing tendency. The same survey was undertaken in 2001, this time taking samples from Japan, Korea, France, and the United States.

To the question, "Do you live in order to enjoy your life?" 34.7 percent of Korean, 4.0 percent of U.S., and 6.3 percent of French students affirmed that this was so. However, 61.5 percent of Japanese students answered, "Yes." When asked, "Do you think the culture of your country will become important in the world in the future?" 73.0 percent of Korean, 43.5 percent of French, and 78.8 percent of U.S. students answered affirmatively. Only 33.3 percent of Japanese students so answered. Finally, to the question, "Do you think you will make progress in the future?" responses in the affirmative were 94.5 percent Korean, 75.6 percent U.S., 67.6 French, and 59.0 percent Japanese students (Kyoiku Gakujutsu, 2001).

This tendency to enjoy the present moment, thinking neither of the future nor of the past, is not only characteristic of today's high school students, but of almost all the Japanese people. It is embedded in the deep stratum of their ethos from historical times, unaltered by modernization of industry and the economic system.

As long as the country held to the concrete aim of catching up with Western countries and enriching Japan, this aspect of the unconscious ethos remained hidden. Now that modernization has been accomplished, the concrete objectives have disappeared. Now, too, the Japanese must confront the fact that the deep stratum of the Western tradition of *Paideia* (general education) originated in the Greek and Judeo-Christian culture based on a different time consciousness. *Paideia* is an aspect of human beings that does not change in accordance with progress of time—past, present, and future.

If the Japanese sought to understand the spirit of the schooling system in the Western context, then they should have also made the effort to learn the ways of thinking of Western people—for example, living at this moment but also taking into account the ideals in the future and reflecting on the past. But in reality, this did not happen. After more than 100 years of desperate efforts to modernize the country, it is becoming clear that the Japanese have not learned some important aspects of Western culture.

Fundamental Law of Education Cannot Have Real Power. The aims of education were prescribed beautifully in the Fundamental Law of Education promulgated in 1947. But the noble and elegant phrases of the Fundamental Law have had so far no real power; they were just ornamental. Few teachers have taken this educational aim seriously into consideration. For example, the sentence, "Education shall aim at the full development of personality" presupposes at least that those who are engaged in education should have future aims in mind. In reality, it is practical aims that have almost always been used to organize the school system. One example is the entrance examination, a very concrete near-future aim.

Transferring Cultures. It is an obligation of those engaged in Japanese education today to consider the reasons for the serious problems seen in today's schools. At the same time, they should address carefully what the Japanese had been practicing before the modernization process and consider what Japan has lost and gained by modernization. Ultimately, if Japan could establish a desirable new institution—a new school system—by keeping the good traditions of the old, then the new model would fit the culture more smoothly.

An example from Japanese history illustrates this point. In the Edo period (1600–1867), before the Meiji Restoration, there existed in Japan *Tenaraijuku.* This is a kind of school, although not designed solely to impart knowledge. Rather, it was a training room in a private house where housewives, priests, or intellectuals transmitted skills or fundamental knowledge such as the 3Rs. They did this, not by teaching, but by guiding calligraphy for small children of the neighborhood.

After a simple contract made between the parent of a disciple (student) and a *sensei* (master), the child frequented the *Tenaraijuku.* Time was not fixed but flexible and each child followed his or her own schedule. Each disciple had his or her own small desk, not lined up in order as they are today in most of the classes in school, but piled in a corner of the room so that the child bring it and set it up wherever he or she wanted.

A class system did not exist. The way of training was fundamentally based on the idea that each disciple should learn things, mainly calligraphy, by imitating texts or the behavior of the master. There was no competition among the disciples. Each did what he or she should do, such as writing down the texts given by the master. In this way, each disciple competed with himself or herself because he or she was praised or encouraged by comparing the present task with what was accomplished yesterday.

This story clearly shows the way of thinking that underlies the Japanese traditional way of learning and provides a contrast concerning the methods of learning language in a Western tradition based on the priority on speaking and the Japanese tradition based on writing. Even in today's Japanese educational system, to write beautifully is more respected than to speak eloquently. This may be why the Japanese are not as good as others at expressing their opinions in public, such as in international meetings. Another simple example is how people learn greeting behavior. By molding the form of bowing, children understand the importance of bowing; that is, lowering the head implies modesty toward other people. Therefore, children should acquire *kata* (form) in the way of bowing when they meet their acquaintances. Another simple example comes from the traditional Kabuki Theater. Here the most important thing for the actors is to express their roles and the corresponding sentiments by showing correct *kata* (form) for the scene.

Ambivalent Attitude toward Human Life. It is better not to simplify a complicated thing like the ethos of a culture too much. Everywhere and at every time, there existed—and still exists—in the Japanese mind both elements. One element wants to be successful in the world; the other recognizes that life on the earth is nothing.

Before the beginning of modernization, it was the pessimistic aspect that predominated the Japanese mind. However, people in the Meiji Era switched their interest to the worldly directions encouraged by the leaders and the government. Such directions persuaded them that in order to survive in a modern imperial age, individuals had to make the effort to be number one both individually and socially.

The traditional pessimistic way of looking at life and the world is still strongly embedded in the mentality of Japanese people. In a sense, this tendency was suffocated during the modernization process, especially when the economy was growing. But when the pressure of the "catch-up policy" came to an end, the residue floated to the surface.

It may not be enough to describe this tendency as merely pessimistic. This is because it comes also from the teachings of Buddhism and Confucianism that recommend that people live and be satisfied with what they are now. They should be content with their present status quo, need not be ambitious, and do not need to become successful people and be famous. In other words, people should be content with themselves.

Is It Possible to Revive the Japanese Schooling System? The problem is that those who are involved in education today do not seem to recognize these new, but old, tendencies. Generally speaking, the Japanese schooling system does not function today. It is heading for a collapse. But this observation is from the perspective of the modern schooling system. It might be more true to say that the Japanese schooling system is coming to an end *if it is taken as a modern institution of education.* The following three symptoms need to be seriously considered.

First, many students are now taking lessons outside of the formal school system. These include piano, abacus, ballet, painting, dance, and flower arrangement. When compared with students of other countries such as China and Korea, the eagerness of Japanese students to study is lower. Yet, it appears that Japanese students want to learn things that are not offered by the modern schooling system. Harking back to *Tenaraijuku* education, students could go whenever they wanted and could learn calligraphy helped by their masters and without competition with other friends. Perhaps today's trend is a sign that young students want to learn not in the framework of modern schooling but in something similar to *Tenaraijuku.*

Second, people around the school communities make complaints about illogical issues to teachers. This seems to be a hidden request by the people to expect teachers not to be modern specialists who teach only their special subjects but to be all-round consultants as they were in the pre-modern period. However, school teachers are now so busy that they cannot fulfill such severe tasks. But if such requests are overwhelming, perhaps it is time to reconsider the responsibility of school teachers, not only in the framework of modern education, but also taking into consideration the traditional roles in the community.

Third, that many young students of high school or college level do not want to be "number one" is significant. In the year 2003, one song gained tremendous popularity among the young in Japan. The title of the song was "The Only One Flower in the World." The lyrics said: "There are small flowers and big flowers in the world/ Each flower is different/ You need not to be Number 1/ I am a special only one." Perhaps part of the song's popularity arises from the protest of young students against the presupposition of the modern schooling system in Japan that they should study competitively in order to be number one in every field of human activities, as an individual and also as a member of the nation.

CONCLUSION

This chapter demonstrated how Japan has succeeded in modernizing the country, including the schooling system. But, ironically and tragically, school problems have erupted just at the moment when the modernization of the schooling system was accomplished.

Students today seem to be bored with their schooling. They concentrate their interests in the present moment, not in the future. It is suggested that Japanese students are tired of the hard work needed to survive the harsh competition to enter good schools and good companies and to ultimately get a better life. Japan is not poor, and people can manage to live without having good positions in good companies. It is also suggested that the ennui represents at least some of the residue of a pre-modern ethos that has been hidden for more than a century under the national slogan of modernization. Traditionally, the Japanese had strong affinities with Buddhist pessimistic sensibility, which is called *Mujokan* (belief in uncertainty and nothingness of earthly things, including human life). Today, when Japan is materially rich, students show a pessimistic view.

Japan's modern schooling system is now at a turning point. The key words are *traditional values in the modern context.* This chapter has argued that it is better to revaluate the old system of education that Japan abandoned more than 130 years ago. Such a reevaluation does not mean that Japan should return to the pre-modern, feudalistic Edo Era. This is both impossible and a simple anachronism. But it is true that Japan lost irretrievably good educational traditions by adopting the modern schooling system, even if, on the plus side, modernity brought to Japan precious values that had not existed in pre-modern Japanese culture.

REFERENCES

Asahi Shimbun. (2004). *Asahi Shimbun Japan almanac 2004.* Tokyo: Asahi Shimbun Publishing Company [in English and Japanese].

Department of Education, Japan. (1907).

ILO. (1966).

Kodomo Katei Sogo-Kenkyusho. (2001). *Nihon Kodomo Shiryo Nenkan* (Japanese Children Almanac). Nagoya: KTC Chuo-Shuppan [in Japanese].

Kyoiku Gakujutsu Shimbun. (2001, September 19).

Numata, H. (2002). *The conditions of education: Human being, time and language.* Sendai: Tohoku University Press [in Japanese].

Numata, H. (2003). What children have lost by the modernization of education: A comparison of experiences in Western Europe and Eastern Asia. *International Review of Education, 49,* 241–264.

Numata, H. (2004). Discovery and disappearance of childhood. Kyoiku Shiso *Educational Thoughts, 31,* 3–36.

Numata, H., & Masubuchi, Y. (Eds.). (1997). *A science of education.* Tokyo: Fukumura Publishing Company [in Japanese].

Ogi, N. (2001). *How can you understand the crisis of childhood?* Tokyo: Iwanami Publishing Company [in Japanese].

Onoda, M. (2004). *Schools are screaming* (Booklet). Osaka: Osaka University [in Japanese].

Organization for Cultural and Economic Development (OECD). (2003). *OECD indicators: Education at a glance.* Geneva: Author.

Postman, N. (1982). *The disappearance of childhood.* New York: Dell Publishing Company. Translated into Japanese by Nakamura, Masanao.

Takakura, S., & Murata, Y., (1998). *A bilingual text: Education in Japan.* Tokyo: Gakushu Kenkyusha [in Japanese and English].

CHAPTER THREE

EDUCATION IN SOUTH KOREA

Changes and Challenges

DAEYOUNG JUNG

The Korean peninsula is divided into two parts. One is communist North Korea; the other is South Korea, which holds to democracy and a market economy.

South Korea is located at the southern part of the Korean peninsula in the southeastern region of Asia. Toward the north, the Korean peninsula is connected to Iberia and the Northeastern region of China. To the south, Korea faces the islets of Japan. Climatewise, there are very distinct seasons in South Korea with great differences in temperature; in winter, the continental climate is very cold and dry; in summer, the weather is very sultry due to the monsoon climate.

Korea's geographic location has historically made it prone to conflict and tension with the neighboring nations of China, Russia, and Japan. In the past, Korea was ceaselessly invaded by those nations. The end of World War II brought about liberation from the oppressive Japanese colonial rule over Korea. However, Korea soon faced national division along the 38th parallel. Military occupation by foreign powers ensued in both the northern half and the southern half of the peninsula, under the Soviet Union and the United States respectively.

The United Nations General Assembly adopted a resolution calling for a general election in Korea, which took place on May 10, 1948, in the area south of the 38th parallel. The Government of the Republic of Korea was inaugurated on August 15, 1948. But on Sunday, June 25, 1950, without warning of war, North Korean troops invaded the unprepared South across the 38th parallel. Thus, the Korean War broke out. It ended with the 1953 armistice. But the two hostile forces are still deployed along the 155-mile demilitarized zone (DMZ), which as a boundary replaced the 38th parallel.

Daeyoung Jung is Associate Professor in the Department of Special Education at Changwon National University. He is author or co-author of seven books in diverse areas of special education, including functional assessment of problem behaviors, music therapy, teaching programs for children with ADHD, early education of children with special needs, and vocational rehabilitation. *Education of Students with Learning Disabilities* is his latest (2002) book, co-authored with K. Wiyoung. He sits on the editorial boards of several major journals in the field of special education.

At present, China and Japan are pursuing a military and diplomatic expansionist policy, and North Korea is resorting to a self-reliant survival strategy depending on its military might, which simply means ongoing tension and conflict. However, South Korea has recently made serious attempts at opening a dialogue with North Korea.

The area of South Korea is 996,000 square meters, and it is home to around 47.9 million people as of July 1, 2003. Seoul, the capital city of South Korea, has a population of around 10 million. South Korea's population density is 471 persons per square kilometer, one of the highest rates in the world. Yet the birth rate has plummeted as a result of a population control policy over the past three decades, recording below 0.57 persons as of 2003. Therefore, South Korea is becoming a "silver society" due to the lengthened lifespan of the population joined to the falling birth rate.

HISTORY AND CULTURE

According to Korean history, the earliest state was founded by Dangun, the mythical father of Korea. This tribal state, called Ancient Joseon, ended around 100 B.C. with the advent of the "Three Kingdoms": Goguryeo in the north, Baekje and Silla in the south.

Ethnically, Koreans are one family of the Mongolian race; they speak one common language and share a strong cultural identity. Their language, which belongs to the Ural-Altaic family, is distinct from Chinese and Japanese. Koreans use a unique phonetic alphabet called *Hangeul,* which is characterized by a scientifically designed system that is easy to understand.

What is unique about Korean culture is the way in which it developed through its interactions with diverse exogenous cultures that formed the intricate web of foreign and intrinsic values seen today. In ancient times, for example, typical Korean folk customs of shamanism and ancestor worship blended harmoniously with the Buddhism, Confucianism, and Taoism originating from China and, in doing so, developed unique rituals and norms that became an integral part of the Korean way of life. Today, Buddhism, Roman Catholicism, Protestantism, Cheondogyo (a modernized religion based on Dong Hak), and so forth, coexist in Korea. In the absence of a state religion, every Korean is free to engage in the religious life of his and her choice.

The second feature of Korean culture is the advanced science and technology that has existed since ancient times. Wood block printing, as an instance, was developed during the Silla Kingdom. It was perfected during the Goryeo Dynasty when Koreans carried out the incredible feat of publishing the voluminous Tripitaka in its entirety, using over 80,000 wood block printing plates. Indeed, the Koreans were the first to invent the art of movable metal type printing, preceding Gutenberg by 200 years.

The creativity of Koreans is demonstrated further by masterpieces of painting and sculpture, which can be considered as the third unique aspect of their culture. Paintings on the walls of ancient tombs provide a vivid display of the lifestyles in the Three Kingdoms period. The Hangeul phonetic alphabet is another source of pride for Koreans. Before Hangeul was invented, Korean intellectuals used Chinese characters, but the difficulty of learning the characters left the masses illiterate. Deploring mass illiteracy, King Sejong the Great commissioned royal scholars to invent Hangeul. This movement made folklore and folk novels flourish while enhancing the literacy of the populace.

SOCIETY AND ECONOMY

South Korea remained a predominantly agricultural society until the first half of the twentieth century. After that, the country achieved rapid socioeconomic development and change that has hardly been matched in any other place around the world. South Korea was able to join the leading group among developing countries despite its poor natural resources thanks to the five government-led five-year economic development plans implemented from the early 1960s on. Too, the *Semaeul* (new village) movement launched in 1972 provided the country with the prime fuel to ignite modernization in the rural region based on the spirit of diligence, self-help, and cooperation.

As of 2002, the per capita GNI of Korea was US$10,013 (a provisional GNI). The amount of trade made Korea the thirteenth largest trading country in the world. Recently, the government of Korea has pressed for the development of heavy and chemical industries, high technology, and the expansion of exports.

Growing national power enabled South Korea to engage successfully on the international stage. For example, it staged the Asian Games in 1986. The Olympics were hosted in 1988; 160 countries took part and sent 1,300 athletes. Five years later, the global festival Daejeon EXPO '93 attracted 108 nations and 33 international organizations.

Of course, rapid development brings its own set of problems. For example, there is conflict among the classes and regions. Recently, some undesirable phenomena have arisen from the widening gap and ensuing conflict among generations. Another problem is urban density. As traditional family systems, in which many generations lived together, changed into nuclear families, the housing shortage became serious in urban areas. To cope with the problem, many apartments have been and are being built in many large metropolitan areas across the country. There are also many newly built cities around Seoul where modern apartments and other convenient facilities can be found.

SCHOOLING IN SOUTH KOREA

Educational Philosophies

The ideology underlying education in South Korea pursues *Hong-Ik human,* which means essentially an image of an ideological citizen who has a high degree of independence and who can contribute to the development of the nation's democracy and the well-being of humankind. This ideology forms a concrete goal of education: that is, education to foster the type of human being consistent with Hong-Ik ideology.

This is most clearly seen in the curriculum at the nationwide level, which has been revised seven times since it was first developed in 1955. With each revision, the image of the human to be formed by education was characterized somewhat differently depending on the demand and the spirit of each period, but always remaining within the fundamental ideology of the Hong-Ik human being.

The first curriculum had the goal of fostering a human with integrity, with the ability to maintain democratic life, and with the qualifications to be a citizen who could contribute to the development of the nation's democracy and to the welfare of humankind. The second curriculum emphasized aspects of life and experience: It aimed to meld the traditional culture with modern culture, strengthen the anticommunism of the people, and foster a human who could choose his or her own occupation on the foundation of sound character and moral judgment. The third curriculum intended to rear a human being with the spirit of the ethnic commonwealth and with intelligence and morality based on both good mental and physical health. The fourth one was directed toward fostering a human being with the spirit of the ethnic commonwealth, with mental and physical health, and with intelligence and morality. The fifth curriculum intended to raise a human being who was healthy, independent, creative, and moral. The aim of the sixth curriculum was to raise a human being who could catch up with and respond to developing and changing international trends. The seventh curriculum, in place from 1997 onwards, intends to realize a human being who can create new cultures and make contributions to society as a democratic citizen.

Budget for Local Education

In 2000, Korea spent 2.3 times as much as Japan, 2.0 times as much as the USA, 3.5 times as much as England, 7.0 times as much as Germany, and 8.2 times as much as France on education in comparison with the member nations of OECD. This revenue is earmarked for personnel expenses, including the subsidiary funds for private schools, management expense, facilities, and contingency funds.

Organization and Structure of the Education System

The macro-organization of the educational system in South Korea includes the Ministry of Education and Human Resource Development at the national level and Regional Offices of Education at the metropolitan or provincial level. The national Ministry of Education and Human Resource Development is responsible for the formulation and implementation of polices related to academic activities, sciences, and public education. The Ministry plans and coordinates educational policies; works out ideas for the elementary, secondary, and higher educational support for all levels of schools; supports local educational agencies and national universities; operates the teacher training system; and is responsible for lifelong education and developing human resource policy.

Regional or local administrative offices make decisions regarding education, art, and science pertaining to each local area. Each local office has a board of members, a reviewing and decision-making organ, and the Superintendent of Education as an independent executive organ.

The school ladder system, the backbone of the school education system, is a unified structure connecting the different school levels, as shown in Figure 3.1. South Korea has a single-track 6-3-3-4 system that maintains a single line of school levels in order to ensure that every citizen can receive elementary, secondary, and tertiary education without discrimination and according to her and his abilities.

The main track of the system includes six years of elementary school, three years of middle school, three years of high school, and four years of university education. The higher education institutions consist of graduate schools, four-year universities, and two- or three-year junior colleges.

Curriculum and Textbooks

The School Education Law articulates the goals and the objectives of education for each school level, which are indicative of the contents to be organized by schools and teachers. The Ministry of Education and Human Resources Development, under Article 23 of the Elementary and Secondary School Education Law, promulgates the national school curriculum, prescribes the curriculum for each school level, and lays out the criteria for the development of textbooks and instructional materials.

The national curriculum ensures a standard quality of education, maintains the quality of education, and guarantees equal education opportunity for all. The national curriculum works with regional guidelines, however, to afford flexibility for individual schools to apply them in pursuit of the characteristics and objectives of each school.

As mentioned earlier in this chapter, the national curriculum has been revised on a periodic basis to reflect the newly rising demands for education, the emerging needs of a changing society, and the new frontiers of academic disciplines. It was revised in 1997 around the philosophical ideals and under the principles of enriching elementary and basic education; increasing self-directed ability; practicing learner-centered education; and increasing autonomy at the local and school level. The 1997 revision defined the desired image of an educated person as one who seeks individuality as the basis for the growth of the whole personality; exhibits fundamental creative capacity; pioneers a career path within a wide spectrum of culture; creates new values on the basis of understanding the national culture; and contributes to the development of community on the basis of democratic civil consciousness (Ministry of Education and Human Resources Development, 1997).

The seventh curriculum introduced ten basic common subjects, autonomous activities, and special activities that cover the ten years from the first year of elementary school through the first year of high school. For the final two years of high school, elective subjects are designed to provide student choice with regard to individual differences in career desire and aptitude.

The seventh curriculum presented the desired image of human beings, the direction of curricular organization, and educational goals for different school levels. Based upon these principles, textbooks have been developed that emphasize raising students' self-directed learning capacity and creativity; address different levels of student achievement; and are fun, kind, and easy to use. The textbooks for mathematics and English have been structured hierarchically for different learning stages, while the textbooks for Korean language, social studies, and science have incorporated enrichment and supplementary contents from which students can choose.

In total, 2,296 new textbooks have been published according to the Seventh Curriculum for use in kindergartens, elementary schools, middle schools, high schools, and special schools. One manifestation of the multiple textbooks is that the elementary school curriculum has changed from the one-textbook-per-subject rule of the past to the present practice of permitting multiple textbooks per subject.

Preschool Education

Kindergarten education is carried out in national, public, and private kindergartens for children age 3 to 5 years. As of April 1, 2003, 29.1 percent of the kindergarten-age children (or

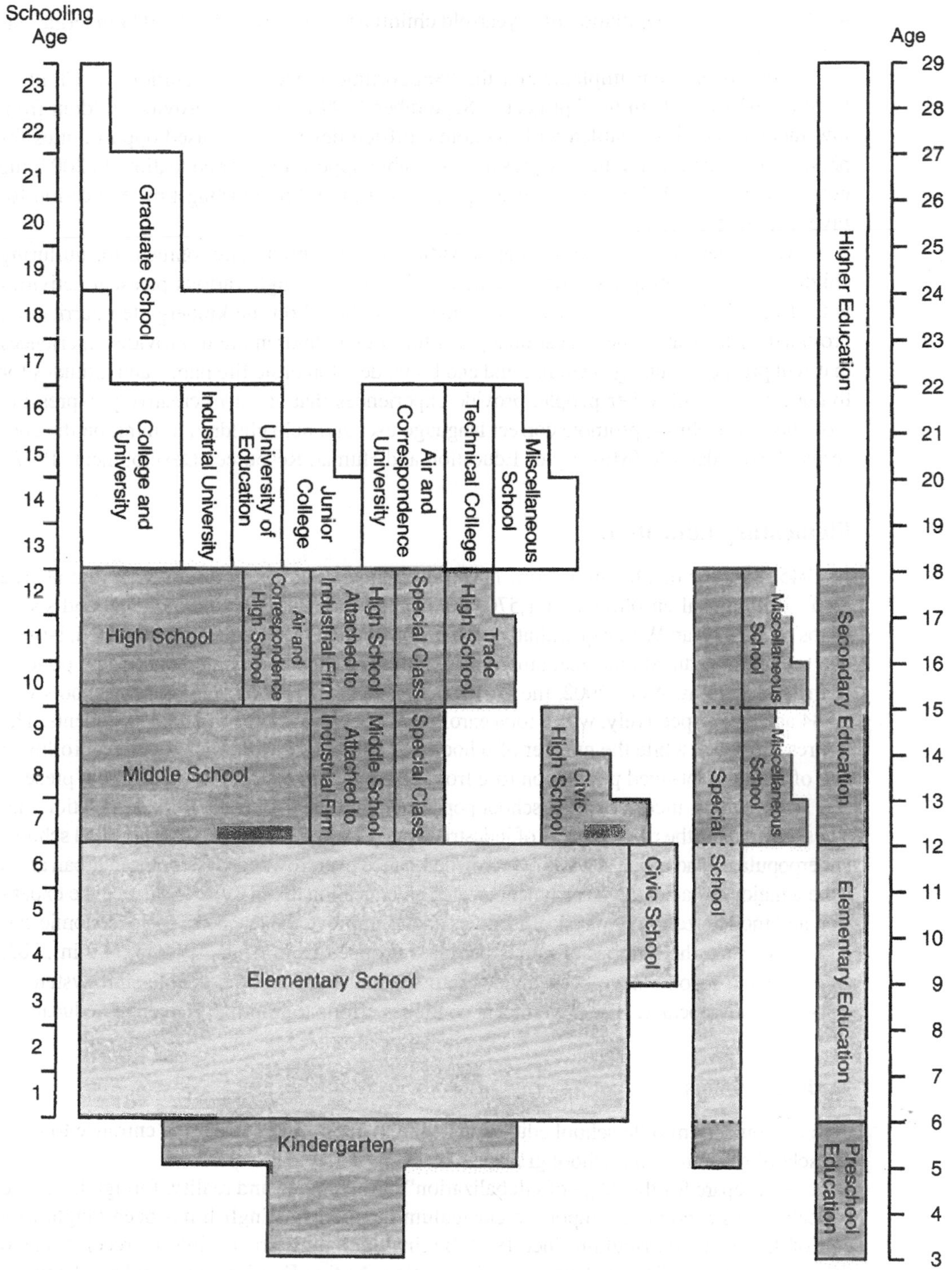
Schooling Age
Age
Graduate School
College and University
Industrial University
University of Education
Junior College
Air and Correspondence University
Technical College
Miscellaneous School
Higher Education
High School
Air and Correspondence High School
High School Attached to Industrial Firm
Special Class
Trade High School
Miscellaneous School
Secondary Education
Middle School
Middle School Attached to Industrial Firm
Special Class
Civic High School
Special School
Miscellaneous School
Elementary School
Civic School
Elementary Education
Kindergarten
Preschool Education

FIGURE 3.1

46.9 percent of the population of 5-year-old children) were enrolled in 8,292 kindergartens nationwide.

The government implemented the "Supporting Kindergarten Tuition for Children from Low-Income Families" project in September 1999 in order to provide children from low-income families troubled with economic difficulties with increased opportunities for preschool education and thereby preserve equitable opportunity for education. In 2002, the government expanded the scope of the project, calling it "Supporting Free Education for Five Year Old Children."

Kindergarten education aims at providing an appropriate environment for nurturing children and promoting their wholesome development through various pleasant activities with diversified content and methods of instruction based on the kindergarten curriculum provided by the state. The educational goals for young children are to provide experiences that will promote sound growth in mind and body, develop basic life habits and attitudes for living together with other people, provide experiences that assist in creatively expressing thoughts and feelings, promote correct language use, and help children to think on the concerns of everyday life (Ministry of Education and Human Resources Development, 1997).

Elementary Education

In 1945, the year of liberation from Japan, elementary schools in South Korea numbered 2,807, with a total enrollment of 1,570,000. In the years following the political and social chaos of the Korean War, a quantitative expansion of elementary education occurred, largely due to the high educational zeal among the public and the appropriate educational policies of the government. As of 2002, the number of elementary schools and branch schools was 5,384 and 603 respectively, with a total enrollment of approximately 4,138,000 students. The figures show that while the number of schools registered a 2.6-fold increase, the enrollment rate of the relevant-aged population rose from 64 percent in 1945 to 98.5 percent at present.

The sudden increase of the school population and the drift of the rural population into cities attendant to the rapid process of industrialization in the 1970s and 1980s left rural schools underpopulated and urban schools overcrowded. Since overcrowded classrooms in urban areas were a major obstacle, the government created an education tax in 1982 to finance the expansion and modernization of physical facilities and to improve the teachers' socioeconomic status. As a result, the number of pupils per class dropped from 65 in 1965 to 34.9 in 2002. Overcrowded schools have been divided into smaller ones, and the double-shift system of classes has disappeared. The government continues efforts to improve elementary education.

Middle Schools

Free compulsory middle school education began in 1985. As of 2002, the entrance to middle school of elementary school graduates reached more than 99 percent.

To prepare for the "Age of Globalization" both in name and reality, foreign language education has become an important curriculum component. English has been taught as a part of the regular curriculum since 1997. Beginning in third grade, children receive one to two hours a week of English language instruction. Native English speakers have been assigned to middle schools since 1995.

High Schools

High school education is mainly aimed at raising the students' ability to pioneer their own career paths in ways that fit individual aptitudes and talents but based upon the outcomes of education and the need to develop as global citizens. More specifically, the goals for high school are to form a balanced character supported by a sound mind and body and a mature sense of self; acquire the ability to think and develop attitudes that are logical, critical, and creative in preparation for the world of learning and living; be trained in the knowledge and skills in various fields; develop the ability to pioneer one's career path in a way that fits individual aptitudes and talents; seek the development of Korea's tradition and culture in the context of the world; and work for development of the national community through awareness and the attitude of a global citizen (Ministry of Education and Human Resources Development, 1997).

Higher Education

Institutions of higher education in Korea are divided into seven categories. These are colleges and universities, industrial universities, universities of education, junior colleges, Air and Correspondence University, technical colleges, and other miscellaneous institutions.

The number of the universities has soared over the last decade due to the combined factors of more university students and a larger number of people being admitted to the universities. One offshoot is worsening quality in the high schools. To alleviate this problem, the Ministry of Education and Human Resources Development recently adopted innovative multifaceted efforts such as Brain Korea 21 (BK 21), the New University for Regional Innovation (NURI), and projects for the reconstruction of the university under the slogans of choice and concentration.

Special Education

Special education offers school instruction, therapeutic education, and vocational training through curriculum, instructional methods, and educational media to meet the unique needs of students with visual, auditory, mental, physical, emotional, linguistic, or other impairments. There are 137 special schools with a total enrollment of 24,192 children with severe disabilities. In the case of mild disabilities, 26,868 children are given education in 4,102 special classes and 19,399 in general classes within regular schools.

Special school teachers are recruited from the graduates of the special education departments in universities, graduate schools of education (with a major in special education), and the graduate schools designated by the Minister of Education and Human Resources Development (with a major in special education). Special school teachers are educated according to the level of education they are expected to teach. Those who want to be elementary school teachers take courses suitable for elementary education; secondary school teachers pursue courses aimed at improving their teaching at that level.

Special education is based on the Elementary and Secondary School Education Law and the Special Education Promotion Act, which was enacted in 1977 and completely revised and repromulgated in 1994. It emphasizes the introduction of a variety of teaching methods, student selection and admission methods, and inclusive education.

The National Institute for Special Education, which opened in 1994, serves to improve the quality of special education. It is responsible for research and experimentation, providing information on special education, developing and supplying teaching and learning materials, and training teachers for the handicapped.

Teacher Education and Training

Teacher education is offered by universities of education, colleges of education, departments of education, those with teaching certificate programs in general colleges and universities, the Korea National University of Education, junior colleges, the Korea National Open University, and graduate schools of education. Together, these institutions train approximately 25,000 teachers every year.

In-service training is aimed at helping to improve educational expertise and quality, to enhance the quality of teaching, to establish a desirable view of the teaching profession, and to encourage a sense of commitment for teachers to carry out educational activities faithfully. It is offered in three categories: training for certificates, general training, and special training.

Certificate training is tied to promotion to a higher level. Participants in the programs, which last thirty days (180 hours) or longer, may be first-grade and second-grade teachers, vice principals, principals, librarians, and professional counselors.

General training is designed to nourish the abilities and capacities needed in various areas of school life, including curricular instruction, student guidance, and administrative tasks. Overseas training, a part of general training, consists of hands-on experience training and field training (for teachers who majored in science and industrial subjects). Field training has been offered since 1978 in either foreign universities or training institutions for the duration of four to eight weeks for the purpose of acquiring the advanced knowledge, educational methods, and scientific technology of foreign countries. Recently, the number of participating trainees was approximately 180 a year.

Special training consists of long-term programs (two years maximum) offered by the teacher training institutes for the enhancement of special fields, at home and abroad. Special training is sponsored or arranged by the Ministry of Education and Human Resources Development.

SUCCESSES, CHALLENGES, AND DEBATES

Successes and Landmarks in South Korean Education

South Korea has shown such rapid socioeconomic development over the short period of the last three decades that it has emerged as a leader among the developing nations. Education is the driving force behind this rapid and sustained development.

The success of education in South Korea comes not only from public education, but also from the great contributions of private education that are founded on the unique traditions of Korea and the people's consciousness of citizenship. Most particularly, the establishment of obligatory education accelerated the expansion of education on the quality side, greatly reduced illiteracy, and contributed to the production of skilled workers. Furthermore, compulsory education promoted an improved sense of citizenship because it produced people with high educational backgrounds who played a pivotal role in moving the country ahead to democratization.

South Korea is proud of its educational successes. Some of the major areas are summarized below.

- *Opportunities for education have conspicuously expanded.* In 2001, 98 percent of children went to primary schools compared with 10.7 percent in 1970; 98 percent of students entered middle school compared with 50.9 percent in 1970; and 95.3 percent of students attended high school in 2001 compared with 27.9 percent in 1970. Higher education in 2001 saw 83.7 percent benefiting as compared to 8.8 percent in 1970. For example, doctors in liberal arts accounted for 0.05 among 10,000 people in 1970, which increased to 4.02 in 2001. Doctors in natural science numbered 0.08 in 1970 but 4.03 in 2001.

- *Education has made many qualitative changes.* For example, the number of the children in a primary school class in 1970 was 62.1, which declined to 35.6 in 2001. Middle school classes had 62.1 students in 1970; 37.7 in 2001. High schools had 60.1 in 1970, which was reduced to 41.6 in 2001. This means that teachers deal with fewer children.

- *Illiteracy has dropped to 2 percent,* helped by the expansion of both quality and quantity in schooling. As people's basic educational levels rose, their social and cultural consciousness improved. As a result, the sense and understanding about democracy have been enhanced. In particular, the entrance of the people with high educational levels into the workplace has elevated everyone's assertiveness about their rights in a democracy and about the labor movement within the workplace.

- *Education has contributed to political development.* Following on the above point, education has played a major role in laying the foundations upon which democratic principles and democratic institutions are based. Specifically, education has served as a means of political socialization through promotion of knowledge, changing behavior patterns, and shaping attitudes toward values, the nation, and the world. It has created public awareness of political participation.

- *Education has contributed to economic development.* Education has been the major source of trained manpower in various fields, has provided the skills needed for economic development, and is credited with contributing to improvements in productivity, the enhancement of the industrial structure, and the total increase of the GNP. Education is also closely related to improvements in living standards and the promotion of the nation's welfare due to an increase in opportunities for employment and more disposable income.

- *Education has contributed to social and cultural development* such as the internalization of new values by the Korean people. This provides people with an orientation toward the future and instills a sense of commitment to modernization and citizenship.

- *Education relates to an increase in social mobility.* The hierarchical social structure of Korea has changed as a result of increased educational opportunities so that the middle class has expanded and upward social mobility has increased.

■ *From a cultural perspective, education has played its role in the rediscovery and appreciation of traditional values* as the people confront new waves of foreign cultures. Education's aim is to establish a new synthesis of Korean culture that will contribute to national development and the advance of human civilization.

Challenges and Controversies

Education in South Korea has both light and shadow. There are many successes, but today there are also many discussions about the collapse of public education in South Korea (Back, 1998). It is argued that schools are losing control because of a matrix of factors. These include the indulgence of parents toward their children, excessive enthusiasm about education, unsound individualism, a breakage in the tradition emphasizing strict instruction and training, and the limits on teachers' ability to influence students' lives.

In particular, the trend that emphasizes educational level so much is raising concerns about the nation's future. This is manifested clearly in the university admission system, which places achievement above the development of traits such as creativity and the ability to solve problems.

The major tasks for South Korea's education system in the twenty-first century include schools that are enlivened with the joy of learning, a teaching profession full of pride in teaching, an education welfare society that provides all people with necessary education, universities with world-class competitiveness as a foundation for a knowledge-rich country, and vocational education that meets industrial demand. The system must also try to establish a lifelong learning society that increases the quality of life, an educational environment that enables creative learning and humane life, networking and globalization of education that offers learning in cyberspace and in the global village, the realization of a decentralized educational administration, and stable educational finances.

Concrete strategies to actualize these tasks include the construction of the human resource development system, the shift toward an education system that seeks recovery of the essence of education, competition in pursuit of educational excellence, dramatic improvement in educational conditions, and the formation of a body constituted mainly of teachers to spearhead education reform. Some of these challenges are discussed in greater detail below. We move from broad issues to those that are more school based.

■ *Strengthening education in preparation for national unification.* Since it is possible that the two Koreas will be unified in the near future, it is necessary to come up with various tactics to prepare for the unification at the national level. Because of weakened awareness of youth about the need for unification, it is urgent to provide them with education stressing the imperative of unification, means of unification, and life after unification.

As well, despite the high increase in the number of North Korean defectors, including youngsters, South Korea has not yet been able to offer systematic and adequate programs for their adaptation to society. In the long run, educational contents that help recover national identity should be created and the elementary building blocks for constructing the post-unification curriculum should be prepared in advance.

■ *Constructing the base for a lifelong learning society.* As an important institution, the school has the potential to become the educational site for the local community in terms of its facilities, educational equipment, and manpower. Thus, the school has to be open to local residents as the most important place for learning so that it can satisfy the diverse educational demands of the local residents in future society (Han, 2003).

There must also be increases in opportunities for adult education through implementation of various lifelong education institutions. As people's demand for lifelong education becomes concrete and diverse in the pluralistic society of the twenty-first century, the need for implementing lifelong education that meets such a demand is rising. Especially, the increase in the size of the elderly population gives rise to the call for more diversified education than ever before to help the elderly fit into society and to promote human resource development.

Although a variety of lifelong learning activities are taking place in South Korea, there is not yet a well-organized system for conferring social recognition on the outcomes of such learning nor are there networks and channels for information exchange among institutions of lifelong education. South Korea could perhaps follow the lead of EU countries, the United Kingdom, and Japan and stress the importance of lifelong learning. It could undertake a variety of activities designed to motivate citizens to participate in lifelong learning, such as declaring adult education week and opening festivals for lifelong learning.

■ *Vocational education that responds to industrial demand.* To meet the manpower structure of high industrialization, measures to reform the education system of vocational high schools must be established and implemented. This initiative includes strengthening cooperation between school and industry.

■ *Invigorating the teaching profession.* It is necessary to quickly seek stability in the teaching profession in order to realize excellent education and continue the current education reform drive. While South Korea needs to establish a new long-term teacher supply policy to meet implementation of the Seventh Curriculum, there is a temporary difficulty in supplying the appropriate number of teachers due to a lowering of the teacher retirement age and voluntary "honorary" retirement.

Simultaneously, there is a need to reorganize the teacher training system and improve the qualitative level of teacher training institutions. Teachers should play a central role in education reform. Insofar as the ultimate goal of education reform lies in helping learners develop abilities, character, and a worldview necessary for leading self-directed lives, it is hardly an exaggeration to say that the accomplishment of such a goal depends on the dedicated participation of the teachers (Han, 2003; Kang, 2002).

■ *Correction of the distorted purpose of education.* In South Korea, equality and excellence has been a focus of education. However, excellence has outstripped quality in the minds of many.

The 31st Article of the Constitution states that "all people are entitled to the adequate education in accordance to their ability." But with current education in South Korea, there are, for instance, limits on the right of the choice for the high school admission; there exist neglect and lack of attention to the education for the physically and mentally challenged; and there are a soaring number of students who are lagging behind.

To ensure equity, the fulfillment of democratic education, and to maximize harmony, the recognition and acceptance of diversity must be in place. That is, equality will have to be newly interpreted and approached (Jung, 2002, 2003).

■ *Diversity must be recognized and accepted.* Korean society is divided into various groups and is loaded with conflict among the regions, classes, and generations. Discrimination prevails, manifested as exclusion and isolation of the disabled or isolation of a colleague for reasons of difference.

To create harmony and end discrimination, the focus has to be on fostering a citizenry that knows how to cooperate beyond the bounds of ethnicity, generation, religion, and region for mutual benefits. For example, schools must accept various students within a community as they are and offer educational services that suit their demands and characters.

■ *Emphasizing education for learning to live together.* Korean youths appear to be troubled by such problems as the lack of the sense of community, the lack of an awareness of how to live together with others, and a lack of democratic citizenship, all of which have led to a dramatic increase in juvenile delinquency (Jung, 2002, 2003). Meanwhile, the generation gap between students and teachers is getting wider and the "school collapse," or "classroom collapse" is getting more serious, threatening the basic order of formal schooling.

These problems have been caused in part by the knowledge-centered, entrance-examination nature of Korea's present education, plus the prevalent negligence of character and moral education (Han, 2003). To overcome these problems, it is important to continue to seek character education stressing the practical dimension so that students can nourish the capacity for living together with neighbors as members of a community.

■ *Disseminating an educational ideal of gender equality.* The twenty-first century is characterized by a knowledge-based society in which the ability to create and utilize knowledge determines social and economic affluence. Such a society demands a new image of human beings as creative persons who can think autonomously, solve problems, and constantly develop personally, on the one hand, and as persons with an equal attitude toward both sexes, who can live with the opposite sex as equal members of a community, on the other.

Gender-equal education is necessary so that both men and women can develop their own talents and potential and grow to become creative human beings appropriate for the new society (Kang, 2004). Accordingly, it is necessary to create an educational environment in each school in which both male and female students can be freed from a framework stereotyped by sex and express their own talents and interests without restriction.

■ *The focus on education level and the dependence on private education in Korea must change.* In its development, education has centered on the pivots of both public and private education. This was often leverage in speeding up development, but it also generated adverse effects by distorting the function of education.

In recent years, scholastic attainment has become an instrument for obtaining social authority. Indeed, there is a prevailing view and belief among people in Korea that education is the only way to success. Scholastic attainment has also become the powerful basis not only for economic discrimination but also for wide-ranging discrimination based on social status.

Because scholastic attainment functions as an important commodity or cultural capital, there exists invisible social and cultural discrimination. Those with low attainment are prone to be humiliated and discriminated against in such things as marriage.

In the past, a university diploma was an index that guaranteed movement in social status; now it is relegated to the minimum certificate for joining the competition (although it is still believed as an index of the potential to reach the highest social status). Still, a good major at a good university is the greatest goal of the school years. To achieve this goal, more than 50 percent of primary school children and 86.9 percent of middle school students receive intensive private lessons in major subjects such Korean, English, and math. As well, a number of people are taking the extreme measure of migrating for the education of their offspring.

▪ *Creating a curriculum that accurately reflects social change and student demand.* At the beginning of the new century, society faces unprecedented changes in terms of both speed and quality. In order to cope with such sociocultural changes, education should respond with a qualitatively new content and system (Back, 1998). Especially in consideration of the mounting criticism of the closed nature of school education and ever-increasing demands for diversification of education, it should be recognized that the present Korean school model no longer fits the twenty-first century society. There is a rising call for a shift to education that is equipped with a flexible system suitable for the knowledge-based society.

In order to raise creative human beings suitable for the knowledge-based society of the twenty-first century and also to enhance national competitiveness, the school curriculum should be totally revamped using educational content that can help develop the new abilities demanded by the information society of the future. Curricula should be organized in a way that stresses acquiring the knowledge and skills needed in the future society, such as information processing ability, communication ability, and creativity.

In efforts to cope with rapidly changing society and culture, the timing of curricular revision should avoid the current uniform practice and be managed flexibly so that, depending on the nature of the subject, the curricula of some subjects could be revised quite often, while the curricula of others remain untouched for a rather long period.

▪ *Realization of educational welfare and reducing overcrowdedness in the classrooms of elementary and secondary schools.* In urban areas, the number of students per class is rising rapidly, particularly in newly developed regions filled with high-rise apartments. In rural areas it is plummeting, accurately reflecting the intensification of regional imbalance.

Overcrowded classrooms cause many educational problems such as difficulty in practicing classroom discussion, level-specific curricular management problems, and the need for improving the quality of school education. Because of the excessive number of students per classroom, individualized education does not occur, resulting in serious alienation among the students.

▪ *Education for gifted students.* With the arrival of the knowledge-based society, the need for education for gifted students is increasing. However, Korea does not have a sufficient physical and institutional base to support education for the gifted (Jung, 2004). It is necessary to make education for gifted students happen in ordinary school education offering various types of programs.

▪ *Increasing the opportunity for early childhood education and improving its quality.* An urgent need exists to establish various support systems for qualitatively elevating early childhood education. Another urgent call is emerging with respect to incorporating early childhood education into the public education system and making it compulsory within the national framework of education. At the same time, the training system for the teachers of early childhood education needs reorganizing, and the teacher training system should be reviewed based on a long-term vision for securing a high quality teaching force (Jung, 2002, 2003).

■ *Strengthening the base of special education and enriching its substance.* Societal interest in special education involving handicapped children is increasing, and national support is being called for. In order to systematically promote such development, it is necessary to build a comprehensive education system to improve the welfare and social integration of individuals with disabilities. A more concrete policy direction is to increase educational opportunity for all handicapped children in both integrated education in ordinary schools and special education in educational institutions that offer appropriate instruction for different types of handicaps of varying degrees.

Continued support will be needed for the disabled population, which is susceptible to public negligence. This can be done by constructing a support system for the lifelong education welfare of the handicapped population, securing a stable budget for special education, increasing both organizations and personnel for special education, and establishing an evaluative system of the entire support program for handicapped children (Jung, 2002, 2003).

CONCLUSION

South Korea is a unique nation that has maintained a 5,000-year-long history even while being surrounded by powerful neighbors. It made a quantum leap during the 1960s amid the invasion, tension, and the conflict involving China, Russia, and Japan. Education made a tremendous contribution to the nation's emergence from absolute poverty to one with a thriving political and socioeconomic policy. South Korean education has made steady progress. The rate of the admission not only to primary schools, middle schools, and high schools, but also to universities and above, has dramatically soared. Illiteracy is very low. The 1997 Seventh Curriculum forms the standard for the contents of education for all school levels and the basis for developing textbooks.

In some ways, however, the values and the goals of education have been distorted due to the ups and downs of Korean politics. Currently, education in South Korea has been put on the backburner. There are various other priorities in the nation, in particular, investment.

There are many successes, but also multiple tasks with which education in South Korea is faced. These include the distortion of the purpose of the education, the conflicting values of education, Koreans' perspectives toward education levels, and their reliance on private education. These manifest as the "first-class syndrome" (the trend to stick to the top-class universities), excessive private lessons (the dependency on the private education to enter a good university), and students who failed in the previous entrance exam (in worst cases, some students retry the exam three times or four times). In the twenty-first century, South Korea has a lot of work ahead in order to reestablish the purpose and the instrument of education, develop the contents and methods of it, and mobilize the resources required for its realization, so that it can adapt to accelerating globalization and an information society.

REFERENCES

Back, H. K. (1998). *The future and challenges of Korean education.* Seoul: Hakzisa.

Han, K. U. (2003). *The pedagogy of 21c Korea.* Seoul: Korea Academic Information.

Jung, D. Y. (2002). *The prospect and tasks of Korean special education.* The 2nd UN ESCAP Asian-Pacific 10 year survey on the prospect and tasks of Korean Disabled Persons. In the 10th Rehabilitation International Korea conference.

Jung, D. Y. (2003). A study on the educational structure and practical direction supporting inclusive education. *Journal of Emotional and Behavioral Disorders, 19,* 139–165.

Jung, D. Y. (2004). *Education of children with gift/talent and/or disabilities.* Kyungnam: Changwon National University Press.

Kang, C. D. (2002). *The history of Korean educational culture.* Seoul: Moonumsa.

Kang, M. S. (2004). School culture in Korea. In I. H. Kim, *Educational history and the lecture of educational philosophy.* Seoul: Moonumsa.

Ministry of Education and Hunan Resource Development. (1997).

CHAPTER FOUR

EDUCATION REFORM FOR NATIONAL COMPETITIVENESS IN A GLOBAL AGE

The Experience and Struggle of China

WING-WAH LAW

Many developed and developing countries have a phobia about lagging behind, or being superseded, by other countries in international trade. In this era of globalization, nations feel driven to reform their education systems, with a view toward enhancing their competitive edge. Their common objective is improving the quality of their human capital—i.e,. a well-educated citizenry to serve as a vital resource of knowledge and skills for the international pursuit of global capital (Stewart, 1996). China is no exception.

This chapter explores modern education reforms that are intended to enhance China's competitiveness in the global economy. Implementing these reforms is not a straightforward or uncomplicated task. The reforms are confronting long-standing and deeply seated cultural perceptions of education. They are also causing difficulties in balancing global and national/local tensions. This chapter first identifies some broad social, political, and economic changes that have implications for education reform in China. Next, the structure of the education system is explained. This is followed by a discussion of education reforms intended to prepare China for the challenges of economic globalization. The chapter ends with a discussion of contentious issues arising from these reforms and outlines policy implications for development and education.

Wing-Wah Law is Associate Professor in the Faculty of Education, The University of Hong Kong. His recent publications include "Globalization and Citizenship Education in Hong Kong and Taiwan," *Comparative Education Review* (2004); "Globalization, Localization and Education Reform in a New Democracy: Taiwan's Experience" in *Globalization and Education Re-Structuring in the Asia Pacific Region* (2003); and "Legislation, Education Reform and Social Transformation: The People's Republic of China's Experience," *International Journal of Educational Development* (2002). His research interests include education and development, higher education, citizenship education, values education and curriculum, and education in Chinese societies including Mainland China, Hong Kong, and Taiwan.

THE BROAD CONTEXT

Demography

Since the disintegration of the USSR in 1991, China is one of the very few countries that continue to claim to be communist. It is a vast and populous country. Its territory encompasses 9,600,000 square kilometers (slightly smaller than the United States), thirty-two administrative divisions (including four municipalities, twenty-three provinces, and five autonomous regions), and two Special Administrative Regions (Hong Kong and Macao, whose sovereignty was returned from the European powers in the late 1990s, and which are allowed to retain their capitalist systems under the principle of "one country two systems"). As for Taiwan, it is claimed as an inalienable part of China.

China (hereafter understood as excluding Hong Kong, Macao, and Taiwan) is the most populous country in the world. Its 1.3 billion people constitute about one-fifth of the world's total population. Ninety-two percent of Chinese are Hans, while the rest are comprised of fifty-five minority nationalities. The percentage of rural dwellers in China decreased from about 90 percent in 1950 to 67 percent in 2000, but this figure is still higher than in developed countries, which have agricultural populations below 10 percent (National Bureau of Statistics, 2003).

The Overriding Importance of Political Stability

The principle of a "people's democratic dictatorship" is institutionalized in such a way that the National People's Congress and the local peoples' congresses at different levels (whose members are mainly indirectly elected) are law-making bodies that have the power to create and supervise executive, judicial, and procuratorial state organs (National People's Congress, 2004). The Communist Party of China (CPC) has been the ruling party since 1949. Eight other political parties are recognized, but on the precondition that they accept the CPC's leadership.

In 2002, the CPC had 67 million members (over 5 percent of the population). It has overwhelmingly dominated the state leadership. The CPC Central Committee determines the top echelon of the state leadership—including the President, Premier of the State Council, the Chairman of the National People's Congress, and the Chairman of the Military Commission. CPC party organs are established in virtually all levels of the government, including schools and universities. It is not uncommon that the head of a government organ is also the secretary of the respective CPC party organ; for example, the Education Minister, Zhou Ji (2003–) is the party secretary of the Ministry of Education.

Since the turmoil of the Cultural Revolution (1966–1976), political stability has been a prime concern of the Chinese state. Deng Xiaoping and his successors have reiterated this repeatedly for decades. To stave off a recurrence of an event like the disastrous Cultural Revolution and civil war, the clear focus at the very top of the CPC leadership has been on political and social stability (Deng, 1994). This priority has many profound manifestations. For example, it has led to economic reforms, including the attraction of foreign investment. Stability is also cited as the reason for rejecting the introduction of multiparty elections similar to those of Western countries such as the USA and UK.

Economic Transformation: From Socialist to Socialist Market Orientation

Unlike the political structure, which emphasizes stability, the economy of China has experienced drastic change since its opening to Western countries and the former socialist bloc in the late 1970s. This is a result of changing strategies for economic development. The first such change was a drastic reutilization of market and private forces to vitalize the declining socialist economy. A free market economy was formerly condemned as a feature of capitalism, and so the private sector and private ownership were banned. However, since the introduction of market forces in the late 1970s, China has gradually changed from a centrally planned economy to a socialist market economy under the state's macro supervision and regulation.

Despite strong ideological debate, particularly in the 1980s, about the use of capitalist means in a socialist society, the nonstate sector, comprising individual businesses and private enterprises, is now recognized and accounts for about half of the gross domestic product (GDP). In some industrial areas, such as Dongguan and Wenzhou in eastern China, the private sector reportedly accounts for over 95 percent of the local economy (Fang, 2004). Moreover, in 2004 the Constitution was amended to protect citizens' rights to legal private property and its inheritance (National People's Congress, 2004).

The second strategy for economic development was a deliberate but gradual shift of the economic structure from the primary to the secondary and tertiary sectors. The percentages of GDP in the respective sectors changed from 28, 48 and 24 percent in 1978 to 21, 47, and 32 percent in 2001 (National Bureau of Statistics, 2002). In the same period, the distribution of labor in the respective sectors gradually changed from 71, 17, and 12 percent to 50, 22, and 28 percent. The growth of the service subsector is most conspicuous in the tertiary sector (Liu, Lu, Zhang, & Li, 2003).

The third strategy for economic development was to let some areas and people prosper ahead of others. As the population and territory of China is so vast, it is very difficult to develop all areas at the same pace and at the same time. In the 1980s, China began to develop the economic and cultural advantages of the eastern part. Dozens of high technology parks and special industrial and economic zones were established, particularly in coastal areas. At the turn of the millennium, China launched a large-scale development program for the western region by supporting its science, technology, and education and by improving its communications, energy, and water conservancy facilities (Zhu, 2001).

The fourth strategy for economic development has been to diversify economic activity by actively participating in the pursuit of global capital, rather than continuing to practice economic protectionism. After opening up to the world in the late 1970s, China diversified its economic ties to include capitalist countries. In 1986, China applied for membership in the General Agreement on Tariffs and Trade (GATT, predecessor of the World Trade Organization, WTO). After a series of negotiations lasting nearly fifteen years, China successfully joined the WTO in 2002. To accomplish this, China had to lift many restrictions on the importation of foreign goods and services.

As a result of the above changes, China has made significant economic gains. In the course of twenty-five years, between 1978 and 2003, the GDP of China increased nearly ten-fold: from US$147 billion to about US$1,400 billion, bringing it within the top ten largest economies in the world (Xinhua News Agency, 2004, 24 April). Meanwhile, its per capita GDP rose slightly slower; five-fold from US$225 to US$1,090. While this ranks China below 100th place in the world, this figure is still higher than what is recognized internationally as a fairly well-off standard, US$800 (Sun, 2004). China intends to quadruple its 2000 GDP to US$4 trillion, and its per capita GDP to US$3,000 by the year 2020. Even today, China is one of the largest economies and traders in the global economy. Imports and exports increased from US$21 billion in 1978 to US$850 billion in 2003. The actual amount of direct foreign investment increased from less than US$2 billion in 1985 to US$54 billion in 2003 (National Bureau of Statistics, 2002; State Council, 2004).

Challenges Facing the Redefinition of the Needs of Manpower and Human Capital

Despite these economic achievements, domestic economic change and pressure from economic globalization have redefined China's manpower and human capital needs. This is creating problems that may negatively affect the development of China. First, the gradual economic shift from labor- to capital- and technology-intensive industries, alongside a downsizing, streamlining, and upgrading of existing industries, has given rise to a serious redundancy problem. In both urban and rural areas, unemployment is increasing, particularly among those with low qualifications and poor vocational skills. The size of the labor pool far exceeds the availability of jobs. For example, in 2002, newly created vacancies amounted to 8.4 million. But there were about 8 million people entering the labor market, an additional 6 million unemployed people, and a further 6 million redundant workers from state-owned enterprises (Liu et al., 2003).

Second, the change from a socialist to a socialist market economy has sped up the pace of urbanization. This has widened the disparity between rich and poor within, and between, administrative divisions. The ratio of per capita GDP of the eastern, central, and western parts increased, respectively, from 1:0.64:0.55 in 1990, to 1:0.52:0.40 in 2002 (Lian, 2004). The per capita GDP of China ranged, for example, from less than RMB¥3,000 in Guizhou Province to over RMB¥37,000 in Shanghai in 2001 (National Bureau of Statistics, 2002). Between 1978 and 2000, the Gini coefficient for income inequality increased from 0.16 to 0.32 in urban areas and from 0.21 to 0.33 in rural areas (United Nations Country Team in China, 2004).

Third, the problems of redundancy and regional economic disparities have led to migrations of people from less developing areas (e.g., villages and townships) to more developed areas (e.g., towns and cities) in search of job opportunities and higher incomes. This can occur within the same province or between provinces. According to the national population census of 2000, migrant workers amounted to 93 million people: 67 million from rural to urban areas and 26 million from urban to rural areas (State Council, 2002). In early 2004, the migrant working population rose to over 130 million (almost half of the population of the United States) and is increasing at a rate of 5 million a year (Xinhua News Agency, 2004, 17 April). In some cities, there are more migrant than local workers in the labor market.

Fourth, the more China engages in competition for global capital, the more it needs to enhance its national competitiveness. This means it constantly has to improve the quality of its labor force. It needs to enhance its people's capacity for innovation in response to an increasingly global competition between knowledge-based economies. It also needs to prepare different types of workforces—ranging from frontline workers to top management personnel—in order to meet the demands of the production bases of international enterprises established in China as a result of the global division of production and labor. Furthermore, China needs to prepare its people for the intensification of interactions with people who have different ideas, cultures, traditions, and habits. This is challenging because, up to now, China has had long-standing and acute problems such as a weak economic foundation and underdeveloped productivity; thus, it lacks a quality labor force capable of rising to new global challenges.

The above concerns, in turn, create other socioeconomic problems—such as security and social problems—that might challenge the political stability of the regime. They also have implications for education, including urgency in reforming the whole education system to meet new needs imposed by domestic development and economic globalization, meeting the education needs of children of migrant workers, closing the digital and linguistic (knowledge of English) divides among students arising from regional disparities between urban and rural areas, and training and keeping local talent.

STRUCTURE OF THE EDUCATION SYSTEM

China has the largest education system in the world—a total of over 240 million students and 12 million full-time teachers in 2003. The education structure consists of four major tiers: primary, junior secondary, senior secondary, and higher education. The first two tiers constitute the nine compulsory years of basic education. The great majority of graduates from the common primary school system go on to general junior secondary schools. However, some students go to vocational junior schools. The three years of senior secondary education are also divided into academic and vocational tracks. The former refers to general senior secondary education, which prepares students mainly for higher education; the latter includes specialized secondary schools, vocational senior secondary schools, and skilled worker schools that train mid-level technicians and personnel for specific occupations. Higher education consists of degree and nondegree programs, mainly four years in duration, that train professionals in various areas. Beyond this, there are highly academic masters and doctoral programs (see Figure 4.1).

Public examinations are used as the major mechanism to screen and select students for the next level of education. These include the junior secondary education examination and the senior secondary entrance examination at the local level, and the national college entrance examination. In many local areas, the scores in junior graduation examinations are used for the allocation of places in senior secondary schools. As can be seen in Figure 4.1, a great deal of progress in increasing promotion rates has been made in recent years. However, the public expenditure on education in China remains low: 3.41 percent of GDP in 2003, which is higher than the average of low-income countries (3.1 percent), but less than both the international average (4.1%) and the average of high-income countries (5.2%) in 2001 (UNESCO Institute for Statistics, 2004).

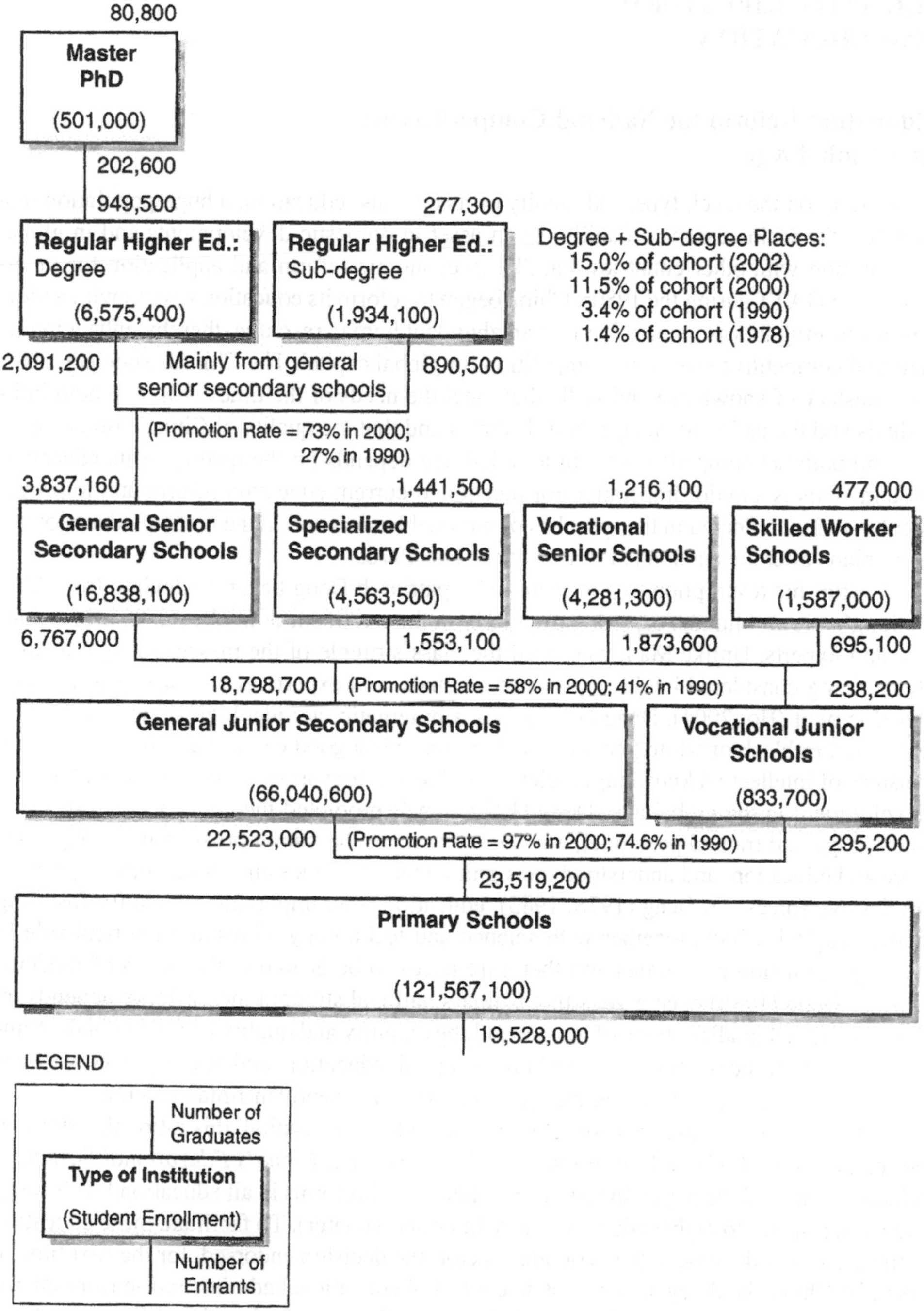

FIGURE 4.1 Educational structures with enrollment sizes and numbers of entrants as well as graduates at various levels in China, 2002–2003.

Source: Figures taken from Ministry of Education (2003, 13 May).

RATIONALE AND OBJECTIVES: REFORMING EDUCATION

Education Reform for National Competitiveness in a Global Age

Depending on the level, type, and quality of its citizens' education, a huge population in a country like China can be a liability or an asset in domestic developments and in global competition with other countries. Parallel to economic reform and application for membership in GATT during the 1980s, China began to reform its education system with a view toward turning its vast population into an abundant human resource, thereby enhancing its national competitiveness in the competition for global capital. The Chinese state perceives that mastery of knowledge and skills that meet the needs of the times will help both individuals and the nation to change their destinies and that the quality of China's human capital and national competitiveness in a global age depends on the quality of its education system. This is a major imperative for recent and current education reform and improvement—a view reflected in the speeches of national leaders and in the texts of education reform plans after the economic reforms of the late 1970s.

After his resumption to power in 1976, patriarch Deng began to deviate from Mao Zedong's view of human capital, particularly in the treatment of intellectuals, professionals, and experts. Unlike Mao, who used the class struggle of the masses to fight against them, Deng considered intellectuals, professionals, and experts as vital assets to China's development (Ho, 2004). Deng (1962) took a pragmatic, not ideological, approach: Any cat, whether black or white, that can catch a mouse is a good cat. In particular, Deng saw mastery of intellectual knowledge, science, and technology as being important for China's development in the global age. Deng (1977, 1988) promoted the concepts of respecting knowledge and trained personnel, envisioned making the nation prosperous through science and education, and understood the significance of science and technology as primary productive forces. To Deng (1978, 1983), education is an important vehicle for fostering human capital, which, together with science and technology, plays an important role in making the nation prosperous and therefore needs to be geared to the needs of modernization. Deng (1985) even argues that China's national strength increasingly depends on the educational qualifications of people and the quantity and quality of intellectuals. Similar concepts of the relation between human capital, education, and development were expressed by his successors, including Jiang Zemin (1997) and Hu Jintao (2003).

In line with this understanding of the value of human capital, this rationalization can be seen in the CPC Central Committee's (1985) *Reform of China's Educational Structure,* which established the major directions of fundamental reforms in all education levels ranging from primary to higher education (as will be shown later). To facilitate these education reforms, as was the case in the economic sector, the decision endorsed, for the first time in socialist China, the deregulation of state control of educational administration from micro-management to macro-supervision, and the diversification of educational financing from state sources to include nonstate sources.

In the *Scheme for the Reform and Development of Education in China,* the CPC Central Committee and State Council (1993) further rationalized the reform of the education system for the challenges of the twenty-first century. Education reform was key to developing a strategic leading position in international competition. The argument was that national competition in the global economy is really a competition between the quality of nations' peoples, science, and technology.

The *Action Plan for Invigorating Education for the 21st Century* reiterates this position, with special reference to drastic changes brought forth by economic globalization and progress in information technology (Ministry of Education, 1999). In a followup action plan for the specific period between 2003 and 2007, the Ministry of Education (2004a) expresses the state's determination to use education to turn China's huge population into an abundant human resource for fostering domestic developments and international competition in the knowledge economy—particularly for inculcating strong abilities for innovation in hundreds of millions of high-quality workers, millions of professionals, and a batch of top-notch talents.

IMPLEMENTATION: REFORMING SCHOOLING AND CURRICULA

Accordingly, since the 1980s, China has launched many reform initiatives to enhance the quality of its labor force for economic modernization at the lower, middle, and top occupational strata. Common to all these education reforms was a focus on the principle: quantity first, quality later. It should be noted here that China is still concerned with the issue of quality as it continues to expand education under severe constraints of limited resources. It should also be added that, in response to domestic changes and globalization, citizenship education in China is also being reformed (see Lee & Gu, 2004), but this requires a separate examination and is not the focus of this chapter.

Eradication of Illiteracy and the Universalization of Basic Education

Fundamental education reform began in the mid-1980s, starting with programs aimed at people in the lower, and largest, stratum of the labor force. Initiatives were launched to inculcate basic literacy and numeracy skills. To accomplish this, China emphasized two goals. The first was the eradication of illiteracy among people aged 15 and above. Although many ethnic Chinese are proud of their long-standing civilization, over 80 percent of the population was illiterate in 1949. This was a great barrier to nation building. As a result of numerous literacy classes, the illiteracy rate was reduced from 35 percent (230 million) of the national population in 1982 to 9 percent (87 million) in 2000 (China's Education and Human Resource Development Project Team, 2003). At the end of 2004, the Ministry of Education announced that the illiteracy rate was less than 4 percent (China Daily, 2005). It is fair to say that progress on the front of eradicating illiteracy in China has been remarkable.

The second goal was to avoid the emergence of new illiterates through the universalization of basic education for children aged 6 to 15. In 1986 (the same year in which it applied for membership in GATT), China enacted the Basic Education Law to reinforce nine-year compulsory schooling. In 1991, child labor was forbidden. Similar to the principle of letting some people prosper economically first, the universalization of basic education started with the eastern coastal region in the 1980s and was extended to the western region in the late 1990s.

As a result, between 1985 and 2003, the net admission rates of primary and junior secondary education rose dramatically. According to the most recent national population census, in 2000 the average schooling of people aged above 15 was 7.85 years (increased from 5.3 years in 1982), and over 80 percent of the Chinese labor force had education qualifications below grade nine (National Bureau of Statistics, 2003). However, the former figure is similar to that of the United States 100 years ago, and much less than that of present-day United States (13.4 years average schooling) and South Korea (11.5 years). Furthermore, the latter figure is below that of many developed economies—for example, those OECD countries in which 80 percent of the labor force has senior secondary education qualifications or above (Hu, 2004).

Rapid Vocationalization of Senior Secondary Education

To improve the quality of the labor force at the middle stratum, in the 1980s China expanded the vocational track of senior secondary education and reduced the academic track correspondingly. During the Cultural Revolution (1966–1976), the vocational track (as well as the academic track and other levels of education) was almost destroyed. The coexistence of general senior secondary schools and vocational schools was criticized as a replica of the dual curriculum of capitalist countries. Apart from schools for training teachers, all vocational and technical schools were closed down, and many were turned into factories, at the beginning of the Cultural Revolution. It is estimated that China lost the chance to train over 6 million technical workers over the ten years of the revolution; this disastrously lowered the vocational and technical level of the labor force.

Recognizing the magnitude of the problem, in the early 1980s the State Council began to reform the secondary educational structure on a national scale in order to give millions of junior and mid-level management staff, technicians, and subprofessionals more diversified skills to cope with the newly emerging socialist market economy. In particular, three measures of rapid vocationalization were introduced. The first was a sudden expansion of student enrollment through conversions of hundreds of general senior secondary schools into vocational ones. Many teachers were simply redeployed to teach vocational subjects. The second measure was the 1981 introduction of positive discrimination in employment. That is, employers were asked to give preference to candidates with certificates of relevant vocational training. The third measure was enactment of the Vocational Education Law in 1996, which provided legal protection for the development of vocational and technical education. The last two measures were also expected to fight against social prejudices that favored the academic curriculum and to enhance the social image of vocational and technical education.

As a result, the percentage of student enrollment in the vocational curriculum increased from 19 percent in 1980 to 57 percent in 1996. However, such rapid vocationalization reinforced, rather than eradicated, social discrimination against vocational education. This is largely because of poor facilities and low teacher qualifications in vocational schools, a consequence of the rapid pace of expansion (Law, 2000). Moreover, vocationalization is gradually being defeated because of parents' and students' deep-seated preference for academic education. Furthermore, because of the expansion of higher education since the late 1990s, there are simply more opportunities for securing coveted seats in higher education institutions. Accordingly, in spite of the government's efforts, the share of student enrollment in the vocational track actually dropped to 37 percent in 2003 (Ministry of Education, 2004, 27 May).

School Curriculum Reform

Having expanded and readjusted school education, in the 1990s China began to pay more attention to the issue of the quality of its school graduates. This was in response to several criticisms of the school curriculum: It was too subject based and had too many subjects. The subject contents were considered outdated, repetitive, and too difficult for students. An examination-oriented culture, spoon-feeding, memorization, and mechanical drilling marked the teaching and learning processes. A criticism specific to the senior secondary curriculum was its early streaming of students into grammar and vocational curricula and into arts and science tracks. To tackle these problems, the state reformed its school curriculum and issued two sets of new curriculum standards for basic education in 2001, and for general senior secondary education in 2003 (Ministry of Education, 2001a, 2003b). The first set involved eighteen subjects and affected the learning of about 200 million primary and junior secondary students; the second set covered fifteen subjects and affected about 17 million students.

The two new curricula share four commonalities. First is the expansion of the goals of the socialist school curriculum to incorporate global imperatives on education. In addition to the old goals, such as the production of students who love socialism, the nation, and the CPC, the new goals include helping students to develop a global outlook and to master lifelong learning skills to cope with a changing society and world. To ensure this, and to guard against irrelevance in the school curriculum, China adopted three major guiding principles in the selection of the content of the school curriculum: its relevance to students' lives, its relationship to modern society, and its connection to the development of science and technology. These three elements were and are seen by the Chinese leadership as vital means to make China prosperous.

The second commonality is a shift in focus from emphasizing content learning to making the development of students' generic skills and introducing comprehensive practical activities as compulsory components of the curriculum from primary to senior secondary levels. The generic skills include active participation and practicing, critical thinking, collaborative exploration, searching and processing information, acquisition of new knowledge, problem solving, communication, and collaboration. The practical activities include the use of information technology (IT), project learning, community service, and labor skills and technologies. All these are expected to develop students' basic knowledge and skills for lifelong learning and survival in a changing world.

The third commonality is the gradual move from a subject-based to an integrated curriculum, with a view to equipping students with a broad knowledge base. At the level of compulsory schooling, seven subjects were amalgamated into four. Music and art in primary and junior secondary schools became "arts." At the junior secondary level, physics, chemistry and biology in junior secondary schools have been combined to become "integrated science"; and history and geography will become "history and social studies."

At the general senior secondary level, the integrated curriculum is more conspicuous, and more complicated, because of the use of a credit system and a three-tier arrangement: key learning area (KLA), subject, and module. The senior curriculum is specifically divided into eight compulsory KLAs for all students. Under each KLA is a combination of certain subjects. Every subject is made up of both compulsory and elective modules (see Figure 4.2.)

The KLAs include language and literature (comprising Chinese and one foreign language from either English, Japanese, or Russian); mathematics; humanities and social studies (including ideology and political thought, and history); sciences (comprising physics, chemistry, and biology); technology (with focus on IT and general technology); arts (in which

FIGURE 4.2 The structure of the general senior secondary school curriculum.

KEY LEARNING AREA	SUBJECT	COMPULSORY COMPONENT (116 CREDITS)	ELECTIVE I (55 CREDITS)	ELECTIVE II (18 CREDITS)
Language & literature	Chinese language	10	Each subject can provide a certain number of elective modules for students to choose according to their interests and needs of future development	School can offer electives according to (a) local society, economy, science and technology, culture, and (b) specific conditions for students to choose
	Foreign language	10		
Mathematics	Mathematics	10		
Humanities & social studies	Ideology and political thought	8		
	History	8		
	Geography	6		
Sciences				
	Physics	6		
	Chemistry	6		
	Biology	6		
Technology	Information technology	4		
	General technology	4		
Art	Art or Art and music	6		
Physical education and health	Physical education and health	11		
Practical activities	Project learning	15		
	Community services	6		
	Social practices	2		

Source: Translated by the writer from Ministry of Education (2003b) and Guo (2003).

schools choose from either art and music, or just music); physical education and health; and practical activities (including project learning, community services, and social practices). Geography commonly belongs to two KLAs: humanities and social studies and sciences.

The fourth commonality is a shifting from centralized curriculum management to partial decentralization as a means to give more autonomy to schools and students. Formerly, the Ministry of Education designed and issued curriculum and teaching plans, local educational authorities redirected them to schools, and schools closely followed them (Cui, Ke, & Lin, 2003). This resulted in some irrelevancy of the school curriculum for local school conditions. To balance the national needs of China, the contextual realities of local areas, and the characteristics of individual schools, the new curriculum of the nine-year compulsory schooling is divided into three components: national, local, and school-specific. The first component accounts for 70 to 80 percent of total class hours, and the last two 20 to 30 percent.

The senior school curriculum has a similar type of division, but the local and school-specific components account for less than 10 percent. Unlike their counterparts in basic education, students in the new general senior secondary curriculum are given the opportunity to choose elective modules. This is facilitated by the use of a credit system. Any module that has thirty-six hours in nine teaching weeks (and one week for revision and examination) is equivalent to 2 credits. The maximum number of credits is 189: 116 (61.4%) for compulsory KLA modules; 55 (29.1%) for Elective I (from different subjects of the eight KLAs); and 18 (9.5%) for Elective II, offered according to local and school characteristics (Guo, 2003). The minimum number of credits for graduation is 144, including 116 credits for compulsory modules and at least 6 for Elective II (and 22 for Elective I). In other words, the proportion of electives can vary from 19.4 percent for those taking the minimalist approach to 38.6 percent for those taking maximum advantage of options.

HIGHER EDUCATION REFORMS: THE PURSUIT OF EXPANSION AND EFFICIENCY

Parallel to the above school education reforms, the Chinese state initiated a series of reforms in higher education. These were adopted to rectify the problems inherited from the model adapted from the former Soviet Union in the 1950s and to enhance the efficiency and quality of higher education. Higher education institutions are crucially important; they train high-level personnel capable of competing with the educated elites of other countries.

The Legacy of Chinese Higher Education Adapted from the Former Soviet Union

In the 1950s, China restructured its higher education according to the model of the former Soviet Union (Law, 1995). In the 1980s, this created many problems for changing from a centrally planned to a socialist market economy and for competition in the global economy. These problems included the overdominance of the state, exclusion of market forces in the adjustment of relations between higher education and the labor market, lack of autonomy and flexibility of individual universities and colleges in response to the needs of students and the labor market, low institutional efficiency because of small enrollment size, repetition of specializations and courses as a result of small enrollment size, and a weak research capacity of higher education institutes as a result of separating research from higher education.

Large-Scale Structural Realignment of Higher Education

In the 1990s, the Chinese state began to realign universities and colleges on a large scale to enhance their efficiency. In 1980, fewer than 3 percent of universities and colleges had over 5,000 students—most had fewer than 2,000, and were overstaffed. Under the pressure of a tight government budget and the pursuit of efficiency and cost-effectiveness, small is no longer beautiful or affordable in higher education institutions in many modern societies; China is no exception. In the 1990s, China improved the efficiency of its higher education system through the co-administration of colleges by local governments; transfer of administrative power and ownership of some ministry-run universities and colleges to lower units of governance; cooperation of universities and colleagues under a single administration responsible for the employment of teachers, development of courses, and research; and amalgamation of higher education institutes (D.Y. Chen, 2002; Law, 1995).

By 2000, authority and ownership of nearly 160 higher education institutes had been transferred to lower units of governance. Between 1992 and early 2003, over 310 amalgamated higher education institutes were formed by mergers (Ministry of Education, 2003a). The average enrollment size in higher education institutions increased from 2,070 in 1992 to 3,100 in 1997, and to over 7,100 in 2003 (Ministry of Education, 2004, 27 May). The number of institutions with over 5,000 students increased from 14 in 1980 to 253 in 1999. However, despite this effort, the number of general higher education institutes unfortunately increased from 1,022 in 1998 to 1,552 in 2004 because of a growth of short-term, sub-degree-awarding colleges. This kind of structural realignment can facilitate attraction of more funding by central and local governments, reduce repetition of specializations and human resources, further strengthen top universities by expanding disciplines through the absorption of small but prestigious specialist institutions (such as the merger in 2001 of Peking University, which focused on humanities and social sciences, and Peking Medical University), allow medium-sized institutions to become conglomerates in competition with top national universities by converting specialized universities into multidisciplinary universities, fertilize disciplines and form cross-interdisciplinary specializations, and broaden students' knowledge base through the provision of multidisciplinary learning environments.

Whether such realignment helps make universities and colleges more efficient remains to be seen. Mergers, particularly, have created new issues and problems. As with many university and college mergers in other countries (such as Australia, Britain, New Zealand, South Africa, and Vietnam) (Harman & Meek, 2002), one subtle challenge to realigned institutes, particularly those formed by bringing culturally different institutions together, is how to minimize their cultural conflicts over traditions and practices in the areas of teaching, research, and administration, and how to develop new loyalty and high morale among colleagues from different institutes.

The Drastic Expansion of Higher Education

To produce more highly trained personnel for the high end of the labor market, China has drastically expanded undergraduate and postgraduate student enrollment. Between 1998 and 2003, new places in first-degree and sub-degree programs in universities and colleges increased from 1 million to 3.8 million (Ministry of Education, 1999, 2004, 27 May). Postgraduate education was also expanded by increasing the admission quota of master and doctoral programs from 73,000 to 270,000. All these expansions increased the total student enrollment from 3.6 million to 12 million, turning the Chinese higher education system into the largest one in the world. It also moved Chinese higher education from an elite system (below 15 percent of 18-year-olds in higher education) to a mass system (between 15 and 50 percent), according to the classification of Trow (1969, 1970). Despite this, the percentage of people accessing higher education is still low compared with that of other developed countries in the West (such as over 50 percent in Canada, New Zealand, and United States) and Asia (such as 49 percent in Japan in 1999) (Arimoto, 2002). In 2002, the Ministry of Education proposed bringing 23 percent into higher education by 2010.

Unfortunately, the quality of higher education has been compromised by expansion because the growth of public education expenditure on higher education has not caught up to increased enrollments. The overall public education expenditure in 2003 of 3.4 percent of GDP is essentially the same as the mid-1980s level. Also, as is the case in the drastic expansion of higher education in many modern societies (Trow, 2003), many Chinese higher education institutes were not designed for such rapid change and consequently faced great strain. Many expanded involuntarily under pressure from local governments, the officials of which used increased admission rates as an indicator of performance. Some, particularly small and less competitive institutes that lacked revenue, expanded by lowering the threshold score of admission in order to get extra subsidies allocated by the state in accordance with student numbers. As a result, many did not have enough classrooms, teachers, teaching and library facilities, and dormitories. The interests of students as consumers of education, to some extent, were sacrificed at the expense of expansion.

CONTENTIOUS ISSUES CREATED BY EDUCATION REFORMS

The reforms in school education and higher education for national competitiveness in China have given rise to many contentious issues. These include a tension between proficiency in IT and English language arising from subnational socioeconomic disparities, a dilemma between curriculum reform and students' heavy study loads as a result of examinations, problems of education for domestic migrant children, concerns about the "brain drain" and "brain gain" in the global exchange of human capital, and struggles in the pursuit of excellence and the creation of world-class universities. In this section, these five issues will be examined in turn. As will be seen, two elements are common to all five issues: a phobia about "lagging behind" and belief in the function of education as an important vehicle for social mobility within and across national borders.

The Pursuit and Divide of Proficiency in IT and English Language

The first contentious issue in the Chinese education system is the tension between the national pursuit of proficiency in IT and English and the widening of the technological and linguistic divides between students in urban and rural areas. Of the skills highlighted in the curriculum reforms, the learning of IT and English has received the most attention. The combination of learning IT and English is considered almost a must for all students who do not wish to lag behind and be unable to communicate with other peoples as China actively engages in the international economy and other international arenas.

At the turn of the century, the Ministry of Education (2000b) began a national plan to popularize IT education in primary and secondary schools within five to ten years, starting from 2001. Specifically: Compulsory IT courses were required to be offered in all senior secondary schools nationwide and in junior secondary schools in big and medium cities by 2001; in all junior secondary schools in the nation, and primary schools in relatively developed areas, by 2005; and in over 90 percent of schools nationwide as early as possible. These courses are expected to equip students with basic knowledge and skills in IT; develop the ability to search for, transfer, and process information; and lay an important foundation for learning, working, and life in the future knowledge society (Ministry of Education, 2000d). The length of IT courses is not less than 68 class hours in primary and junior secondary education, and between about 70 and 140 hours in senior secondary education. The Ministry of Education (2000c) also introduced the IT network project for schools (*xiao xiao tong*). It is expected that 90 percent of schools nationwide will be connected to the Internet before 2010. The national student–computer ratio has already been reduced from 121:1 in 1999 to 51:1 in 2001 (Z. L. Chen, 2002). By September 2001, the percentages of senior secondary and junior secondary schools (in big and small cities) offering IT lessons were, respectively, 90 percent and 70 percent.

In addition to, and complementing, IT proficiency, the demand for bilingual manpower in areas such as finance, management, and communications is increasing in China. Bilingual manpower refers to competence in the mother tongue and a foreign language. Formerly, Russian was the first and dominant foreign language to be studied. But, since the opening up of China to Western countries in the late 1970s, it was demoted in favor of English, which students began to learn from junior secondary level. English language was and continues to be designated as a compulsory subject for admission to first degree or postgraduate programs and is a compulsory undergraduate course. It has received even greater attention in education at all levels after the accession of China to the WTO in 2002 and after China won the bid to host the Olympic Games in Beijing in 2008 and the World Exposition in Shanghai in 2010.

In 2001 the Chinese state began to extend the learning of English from junior secondary school level down to primary level three (Ministry of Education, 2001b). Primary schools in cities and counties were required to gradually introduce English from 2001 to 2002, and those in towns and villages from 2002 to 2003. Schools have to arrange at least four learning activities (classes) per week. To achieve this, they are permitted to cut one lesson of Chinese language and use classes allocated to the local curriculum.

The focus of learning English is on the development of students' interests and their ability to communicate, rather than on phonetics and grammar. Assessment is required to be formative, rather than summative. Schools are not allowed to use students' results in English language for the purposes of competition and selection, but many schools do not strictly observe this. Moreover, many schools in developed areas go beyond the national policy by extending the learning of English down to primary one. For example, in 2001 the Shanghai Municipal Commission of Education requested both primary schools and secondary schools to offer one English class per day, and primary schools to start offering English from primary one. In Beijing, the municipal education authority requested its primary schools to offer English at primary one from September 2004, starting with listening and speaking rather than with grammar.

In higher education, special attention is paid to the English proficiency of non-English major students. In 2004, the Ministry of Education (2004b) began to pilot a new English language curriculum in 180 higher education institutes. It aims at equipping university students with comprehensive English proficiency, particularly in listening and speaking, so that they can use English effectively in oral and written communication in international exchanges at home or abroad. The weight of this English curriculum is quite heavy, at 10 percent of the undergraduate program. Clear standards are set for students to reach, covering five dimensions: ability to listen to and understand broadcast programs of English-speaking countries; ability to use oral English in discussion and presentation in class and engage in daily conversation with English-speaking people; ability to read and comprehend teaching materials and journal articles written in English; ability to write short articles and papers in English; and ability to translate from English to Chinese and vice versa. Universities and colleges are encouraged to help students learn English with the use of IT in and outside the classroom. However, the quality of the learning of English in higher education is hampered by teachers' weak professional training in the subject, a poor understanding of English-speaking cultures, and poor IT facilities for teaching and learning English in classrooms and student hostels (Zhang & Zhang, 2004).

Unfortunately, the national promotion of learning IT and the English language has widened, rather than reduced, the digital and linguistic divides between students in urban and rural areas and could lead to social stratification and exclusion. For example, total education expenditure is heavily tilted towards urban areas. In 2002, 77 percent of expenditures, amounting to RMB¥580 billion (US$70 billion), was spent in cities and towns for less than 40 percent of the population, and 23 percent in rural areas where over 60 percent of the population lived (China Daily Reporter, 2004). Because of such disparity in education financing, students in urban areas have better teachers, resources, and more exposure to IT and English environments than their counterparts in rural areas.

Some schools in poor counties or villages in Jiangxi Province (that the writer visited in 2004) were struggling to have toilets and a main gate, rather than IT facilities or teaching aids for learning English. They also lack qualified teachers, let alone teachers who are good at English or the use of IT. It is sad that some schools were given computer workstations, but did not have money to pay for electricity for lighting; therefore, administrators did not encourage their teachers and students to use these workstations. Such divides at the school level affect students' learning in higher education. The teaching of English in universities is seriously affected by big variations in the proficiency of students in English and the use of IT to learn English (Zhang & Zhang, 2004).

Heavy Study Load: A Backlash of Assessment

The second contentious issue in the Chinese education system is the problem of heavy study loads. Heavy study loads have been a national concern of the state, schools, and parents for decades. Since the Cultural Revolution (1966–1976) examinations are a major assessment mechanism to select students for the next level of education and have caused excessive study loads.

Forms and Consequences of Overloading. There are many forms of overloading, such as supplementary reading materials, drilling exercises, tests and examinations, longer school time, supplementary lessons or training courses after school or in holidays, and public competitions outside school. Broadly speaking, the study pressure on students is greater in secondary schools than primary schools, in prestigious schools than ordinary ones, in graduating classes than others, and in examination subjects than non-examination subjects. The Ministry of Education has publicly and repeatedly condemned widespread heavy study load, asking schools to ease the problem and even issuing instructions to lower units of governance.

At the turn of the millennium, the Ministry of Education (2000a) issued an urgent circular concerning the reduction of study loads in primary schools. There were seven major regulations: use only one approved textbook for each major subject; no buying of supplementary materials and newspapers; no extra school activities, including supplementary lessons on weekends or holidays; no homework for primary one pupils, and the limitation of homework time for pupils of other primary levels to within one hour; no examinations of any subjects except Chinese language and mathematics; no examinations for admission to junior secondary school; and no competitive learning activities in any educational institution without the approval of the relevant education commission. Parallel to this measure was the promotion of a reduction in study load in order to enhance the quality and effectiveness of learning (Wang, 2002). There are good examples of how some schools readjusted teaching contents, homework, and modes of assessment, thereby creating more time and space for students to think, learn, and enjoy extracurricular activities (Cheng & Liang, 2000).

But, in spite of the above, heavy study continues to worsen. Public and underground supplementary lessons keep on blooming in different forms such as interest, elite, and remedial classes (Li, 2004). Many schools that had tried reducing study loads returned to drilling. In explanation, there are two heart-breaking sayings: those students who reduce their study load lose at the start line, and those schools or teachers who reduce study load are sinners. A widely discussed example of the latter was the public apology of a primary three class teacher in Wuhan to parents for reducing homework, her pledge of not to do so again, and her remark that if her students had studied until 11:00 P.M. every night as other students did, she and her students' parents might not have sad feelings after the examination (Wu, 2002). In the past, pupils of her class usually got good academic results but when, in the first semester of 2001–2002, her class piloted a reduction of study load in response to the city government's instruction of September 2000, the overall academic results of her students in the term examination ranked second from the bottom in the primary three league table. Students of other classes that did not reduce homework got better results. To remedy the drop in students' academic performance, she asked her students to do a lot of homework during the spring vacation (holidays between the first and second terms).

After the widespread public reporting of this case, many school principals in Wuhan also remarked that teachers and schools that piloted the reduction in study load initiative also did not fare well in examinations while those that did not participate "won"—i.e., their students did better on examinations. Thus, while reducing unnecessary pressure on students is publicly praised (at least with lip-service), the reality is that different forms of heavy study continue to openly prevail.

Causes of Overloading. Teachers are often the first to be blamed by the public because they are the ones who give homework and examine students. But then, why do they sacrifice their weekends and holidays to offer supplementary lessons and why do they publicly dare to defy the instructions of the state and their local government? It is difficult to point a finger at any single individual or entity for imposing heavy study loads on students; many complicated and intertwined factors and differing vested interests of different stakeholders are involved.

The fundamental cause seems to be the combination of a scarcity of places at higher levels of education and the reliance on examinations as the major means of screening and selection. In particular, the national college entrance examination has, for decades, had a deleterious effect on students' learning and teachers' teaching in schools. The expansion of higher education does not necessarily reduce students' study pressure. In some areas that have higher gross admission criteria than the national average, such as Beijing (52 percent in 2003) and Shanghai (53 percent) (Shanghai Municipal Education Commission, 2004), heavy study pressure still prevails; indeed, it is even heavier. Because of inevitable disparities in quality and prestige between schools and universities, it is natural for parents and students to choose ones with a record of good student performance in public examinations. Their concern is not so much about getting a place somewhere in the higher education system, but which specific very good school or university they can get into. For entrance into elite and prestigious institutions, there is always intense competition.

Second, overburdening students can be seen as a manifestation of the Chinese mass psychology of not letting children lag behind at the start line, complemented by the cultural perception of diligence as reflected by the Chinese saying: One's inadequacy can be made up by diligence (*jiang qin bu chu*). Drilling is often seen as an important indicator of diligence, is used as a vital means to help students remedy inadequate academic ability, and is thought to give them a head start in the academic race. Commonly, teachers, parents, and students believe in the dictums: More drilling may lead to better examination scores, thus a better chance of proceeding to the next level of education and a choice of better schools or universities, and, ultimately and hopefully, a better career.

Third, from the socioeconomic perspective, heavy study loads are a result of the increasing importance of diplomas and qualifications. This is particularly the case today, as more people are entering the labor market and competing for fewer jobs than were available as recently as the turn of the millennium. The one-child policy (limiting couples to one child), which has been implemented since 1979, further reinforces parents' wishes to help their only child become a "dragon" or a "phoenix" who will earn a better living than theirs. Many parents are willing to spend money and time on buying supplementary academic materials, finding private tutors, engaging "crammer schools," and arranging different types of activities (such as special talent classes) after school or during holidays. Several principals in Shanghai, whom the writer interviewed in 2004, said that their schools and teachers readjusted homework amounts after complaints by parents about giving less homework than other schools in the same vicinity, or teachers in other classes at the same school.

Fourth, as pointed out by Education Minister Chen (2000), publishers and schools profit from parents' desires to provide their children with a better education. They profit by producing and selling reading and reference materials. In a working conference in mid-2004, the Shanghai Municipal Education Commissioner reportedly urged publishers not to overpromote these materials (Chen, 2004). Teachers (particularly of the most prestigious "special rank") can gain extra money from writing study materials, model examination papers, and guidelines for preparing and tackling examinations at both national and local levels. Meanwhile, schools can raise additional revenue by running supplementary lessons or by renting school premises to other educational organizations for operating tutorial classes.

From another perspective, and more importantly, public examinations and competitions have a backlash not only on teaching and learning, but also on educational administration and personnel management. This is because the academic performance of students, particularly in examinations and competitions, is a convenient and important indicator of "performance." It is a criterion for assessment that is used in a simplistic manner by both consumers and providers of education to serve different purposes.

At the consumer level, parents and students often use a school's performance in public examinations as a major consideration for choosing a school. This in turn affects the school's prestige, social status, intake, and revenue from nongovernment sources such as sponsorships. At the providers of education services level, is not rare for governments and education authorities at higher levels to use the overall local performance of students in public examinations, particularly national college entrance examinations, as a means to evaluate the achievements of lower units and appraise individual government officials. In order to demonstrate their achievements, local governments and education authorities are in turn using their schools' performance in public examinations to judge and rank the performance of individual schools, to determine their input to individual schools in terms of finance, personnel, and other resources, and even to praise or blame school principals and teachers.

To compete with other schools for student intake and for funds from the local government, school administrators put pressure on their teachers. School principals use student performance in both public and internal examinations and competitions as an important consideration in many areas: assessing teachers' performances in annual appraisals, awarding professional titles and promotions, and allocating classes. Examination scores are therefore instrumental in teachers' professional lives. They even influence contract renewal—particularly under the system of dismissing teachers who are ranked near the bottom (e.g., bottom 5 percent) in staff appraisal.

As a result, the demand and pressure for good student performance on examinations is distributed from the top of the education hierarchy down to schools and teachers, and finally ends up in students. On the "food chain" of heavy study loads, students are victims, publishers and cram schools are predators, and all other parties are both predators and victims.

Unequal Education for Domestic Migrant Workers' Children

The third controversial issue is related to the urbanization of China and concerns education for internal migrant workers' children. The issue emerged in the early 1990s, became acute in early 2000, and continues unabated today. Domestic migration is a double-edged sword. On the one hand, migrant workers contribute to the local development of both their places of destination and origin. They constitute a major industrial force, provide cheap labor, and reduce production costs in the destination places. Because a majority of migrants come from the lower classes of society (such as peasants and rural workers) and do not have high educational qualifications, they are willing to take up low-status, low-income jobs that their local counterparts do not wish to take, as hawkers, construction workers, and garbage collectors in Fujian Province (Xiao & Wu, 2004). They also contribute to the development of their villages of origin by sending money back or returning home to invest in small local businesses. This transfer of capital helps improve the living conditions of their left-behind family members, blurs the dualistic economic distinction between urban and rural areas, and increases the pace and scale of urbanization. In order to ease the alienation of migrant workers (particularly those who bring their children), some local governments and schools run migrant workers' schools in destination places and employ migrant teachers.

On the other hand, domestic migration brings new social problems in destination places. One is the provision of basic education for migrant children. The migrant working population comprises both single and married people. A national census showed that, in 2000, over three-quarters of the 67 million migrants who moved from rural to urban areas were aged below 35 and the proportions of males and females were approximately the same (Wu, c. 2002). After settling in new areas for some time, many men marry and have children, whereas many of the women, particularly those in couples, bring their children with them. The number of migrant workers' children (*dagong zinu*) aged below 18 in destination places increased from 2 million in 2000 to 20 million in early 2004 (Liu, 2004). According to a survey in twelve cities, the majority (85 to 90 percent) of migrant workers' children were of the age for primary schooling (Cui & Pan, 2003).

Although there are public and legal private schools, migrant workers prefer to send their children to illegal schools exclusively for migrant children (*dagong zidi xuexiao*). Before the early 2000s, the majority of migrant children studied in these illegal schools. The reasons are multiple and complex. First and most importantly, the tuition fees in migrant schools are relatively low; many migrant workers cannot afford the high tuition and other miscellaneous fees of public and legal private schools. Despite the national reinforcement of free nine-year compulsory schooling, children of migrant workers, unlike their local counterparts, are not entitled to "free" access to public schools. This is a result of local policies of admission to basic education, the decentralization of education financing to local governments, and domicile registration.

According to the Basic Education Law, all children are entitled to nine years of compulsory schooling in nearby schools (National People's Congress, 1986). Local governments are responsible for financing this schooling for local students, but not for non-local students. The policy of domicile registration does not allow migrant workers from other areas to have permanent local residence; this prevents them from enjoying the social benefits (including education subsidies to their children) provided by local governments. If local public schools admit non-local students, they do not receive a subsidy from their local governments and have to make up the "loss" by charging them a school-place borrowing fee (*jie du fei,* sometimes known as supplementary or donation charges). For example, in Beijing in 2001 the school-place borrowing fees per semester in public primary and public secondary schools for anyone who did not have permanent local residence were respectively RMB¥600 and RMB¥1,000, whereas the average fee in migrant schools was only RMB¥300 per semester. The standard fee in public primary and secondary schools was far beyond the ability of many migrant worker families (Cui & Pan, 2003). A survey in Beijing suggests that, in 2003, the average annual overall school fees for migrant children studying in public schools was over RMB¥3,000, and that this accounted for 15.5 percent of the household family expenditure, which was double that of their local counterparts (Shen, 2004).

Second, although some migrant workers are willing to pay school-place borrowing fees, many public schools, particularly those that are famous in parents' eyes, are not willing to admit migrant workers' children. A major reason for this is that public schools do not want to have their academic standards lowered by migrant children, who are often deemed capable of only lower academic performance. Third, some migrant workers' children do not want to study in public schools with local students because they are afraid of being discriminated against because of two major aspects: the low-status occupation of their parents and their rural identity betrayed by their Putonghua accent. Fourth, migrant workers do not want their children to repeat their low-income career paths and see education as a major means of social mobility. They prefer their children to become urban residents rather than farmers, or white-collar rather than blue-collar workers. Despite poor learning conditions (as discussed below), to send their children to receive education in illegal migrant schools is better than their having no education at all.

The existence of migrant schools brings forth a tension in the process of urbanization in China. On the one hand, migrant schools play an important part in urbanization by keeping and stabilizing migrant workers (who are highly mobile) in order to contribute to local economic development. These schools also help ease the great needs of migrant children for education and prevent the mass emergence of "little migrant illiterates" roaming the streets. On the other hand, many migrant schools are inadequate.

First, they are illegal, and therefore face closure by local governments. Second, their buildings are dangerous because they are built with very crude materials near markets or rubbish dumps; they sometimes operate in deserted factories. Hygiene in canteens and toilets is a serious problem. Third, teaching facilities are poor and teachers' qualifications are very low. For example, in 2004 only 13 of 299 migrant schools in Beijing were up to minimum standards and approved as legal private schools by the municipal government (Wang & Yan, 2004). One reason for low standards is that many migrant schools do not have a stable income because they have to rely on fees from students whose parents often move from one place to another in search of work. Another reason is that many migrant schools are oriented toward profit making and try to reduce expenditures while diverting funds to personal pockets. As a result, the great majority of migrant schools do not have enough money to employ qualified teachers or to improve school conditions, such as the provision of classrooms with standard facilities, not to mention information technology.

Many measures are taken to curb the phenomenon of illegal migrant schools. Often the schools are closed and their students transferred to regular ones. For example, in 2000 a district of Beijing closed down fifty illegal schools. Second, some local governments force local schools to admit migrants' children if their parents can produce evidence including an identity card, provisional residence, and work permit. Third, some provincial and local governments have reduced or even abolished school-place borrowing fees. For example, in 2002–2003 the Beijing Municipal Commission of Education (2002) reduced the school-place borrowing fees for primary and junior secondary schools from RMB¥500 and RMB¥1,000 to RMB$200 and RMB¥500 per term, respectively. In 2003, the State Council issued a national circular asking related government departments (including public security, planning, finance, personnel, and social security) to take necessary measures and action to facilitate the flow of migrant rural workers into cities with a view to maintaining social stability and demanded that schools treat migrant children as their local counterparts as of 2004. This is expected to remove all legal grounds for fee differentiation between local and non-local students.

With the introduction of measures to curb illegal schools, more migrant children can study in public ones. For example, in mid-2004, Beijing reportedly had 290,000 migrant children; about one-third studied in about 300 schools run by migrant workers for migrant children, and two-thirds in public schools (Wang & Yan, 2004). However, as a result of increasing urbanization in China, illegal schools for migrant children are still blooming, as shown in the case of Beijing above. A survey of 7,800 migrant children and 12,000 parents or guardians of migrant children in nine cities, including Beijing and Shenzhen, shows that nearly 50 percent of 6-year-old migrant children who were supposed to enter grade one had not done so, and that nearly 60 percent of migrant children aged between 12 and 14 who were supposed to receive junior secondary education had begun to work (Xiao & Wu, 2004). Although many local governments and schools declare the abolition of school-place borrowing fees, there are many other fees that many local parents, not to mention migrant workers, cannot afford, such as miscellaneous fees.

Moreover, migrant children's chances of entering post-compulsory education in destination places is greatly limited by the policy of domicile registration. After graduation in destination places, migrant children can only get a certificate of study through place borrowing and not an official graduation diploma. In many destination cities (including Beijing, Guangzhou, Tianjian, and Xiamen), migrant workers' children who graduate from local junior secondary education are not allowed to apply to local general (grammar) senior secondary schools and universities, but only to vocational and technical schools and institutes (Cui & Pan, 2003). This, together with high school-place borrowing fees in junior secondary schools in destination places, drives many migrant graduates to return to their home areas for junior or senior secondary education. However, when they return to their places of origin, they face the problem of different textbooks and teaching materials, which can reduce their performance, particularly in local examinations for admission to senior secondary schools.

Domestic migration in China also creates education problems for children who are left behind by their migrant parents (*liushou zinu*). It was estimated in early 2004 that there were nearly 10 million stay-behind children aged below 16 (Xu, 2004, 5 June). Unlike their counterparts in destination places, stay-behind children do not face problems of admission to public schools. On the contrary, they can enjoy several benefits as a result of staying behind—such as an improvement of living conditions, provision of new toys, an increase in their family's financial ability for education, and information about city life from their migrant parents. Despite this, many of these children have problems. In a recent survey in major cities including Beijing, Guangzhou, and Shenzhen, 19 percent of 402 migrant parents brought their children with them; 47 percent left them to the care of their grandparents, 27 percent to other relatives, and 7 percent to schools in their places of origin (Wang & Zhou, 2004). Many of these stay-behind children became quasi-orphans or as if from single-parent families. Furthermore, it is not uncommon that, after working away for a long period, migrant workers divorce their spouses, leaving their children with just one parent.

This in turn gives rise to four major problems related to the provision of holistic family education for stay-behind children. First, many lack parental love and care, simply because the parents are elsewhere. For example, 60 percent of migrant parents communicated with their children once or twice a month and 10 percent rarely communicated, only returning home in the New Year or for long holidays (Wang & Zhou, 2004). This minimal communication cannot help migrant parents understand the concerns and needs of their stay-behind children. In order to allay their sense of guilt, many migrant parents give their stay-behind children more than enough pocket money, which spoils them.

Second, many children in the care of their grandparents have a bigger generation gap with their grandparents than with their parents. Over 80 percent of old people are illiterate, and many grandparents do not have enough knowledge to help their grandchildren with homework and to cope with new social values or behavior arising from the modernizing economy (such as consumerism). They often use materialist means, such as giving the children more pocket money and more freedom to make friends and play outside. In these ways, such stay-behind children are spoiled more by their grandparents than their parents.

Third, these two problems may affect the personal and social development of stay-behind children. Many become introverted, with eccentric and unsociable characters and weak social skills, while others are short-tempered and attention seeking (Wu & Yu, 2004). Fourth, the problems of stay-behind children are refracted into society and school. Juvenile delinquency (such as stealing) among stay-behind children is increasing, and the academic performance of many stay-behind students is often poor (Xu, 2004, 15 August), while some do not behave well in class and break school regulations.

Public schools in places of origin are also suffering from large-scale domestic migration. The enrollment reduction in public schools, particularly those with poor conditions in poor rural areas, is further intensified by the competition of private schools for teachers, students, and promotion rates. In urban areas, it is very difficult for private schools to compete with public schools, particularly "keypoint" ones. In contrast, public schools in poor areas face strong challenges from private schools. The principal of a public primary school in a poor village in Jiangxi Province told the author in 2004 that private schools can pay higher salaries to attract good teachers from public schools. This in turn enhances the attraction of private schools to students, including stay-behind ones who can pay for higher fees for better education, and improve the overall performance of private schools in public examinations, thereby raising the rates of promotion of their students to junior or senior secondary education. Besides the help of commercial advertisement, private schools in poor areas are very attractive to parents who can afford a better education with a higher chance of promotion to the next level and a university place. As a result, domestic migration increases the extraction of students from public schools and provides private schools with the precious opportunity to compete with public schools in poor areas.

Brain Drain and Brain Gain in the International Community

The fourth controversial issue is related to the unequal exchange of human capital across the international community. To narrow the science and technology gap, China has bought technology directly from Western countries since the late 1970s. Another way of narrowing the gap is for China to send and support scholars and students to study overseas as a quick means to access foreign knowledge and advanced. Initially, China suffered a "brain drain" because of its less favorable studying and working conditions. But, from the late 1990s, China began to taste "brain gain" because of the rise in returning foreign-trained Chinese students.

China is the largest "exporter" of students for overseas studies. In 2000, China accounted for about 25 percent (over 1.6 million) of overseas students throughout the world—an astonishing statistic. The number of Chinese students and academic personnel who wanted to upgrade their qualifications overseas increased from 3,000 in 1978 to 117,300 (including 8,100 dispatched by the government and enterprises) in 2003, and the accumulated total in this period was 700,000 in over 100 countries (People's Daily Reporter, 2004). The preferred destinations are industrialized countries such as the United States, Germany, Japan, and Canada, and the most popular fields of study are science and technology.

About half of these students are sponsored by the Chinese government; the rest are self-financed. Studying abroad in developed countries, such as the United States, is often seen as a symbol of elite socioeconomic status. Furthermore, overseas qualifications from universities in developed countries are often perceived as better than those from Chinese universities of similar rank or even above. This is a strong incentive for Chinese students who cannot enter brand-name Chinese universities but can afford to opt for overseas study and for foreign-trained Chinese students to return.

China has suffered from a significant loss of human capital because of the imbalance between brain drain and brain gain, which is to say between the outflow into and inflow from other countries. Between 1978 and 2003, only 172,000 (25 percent) of Chinese students and academic personnel returned to work in China, while 524,000 (75 percent) stayed overseas (Ministry of Education, 2004c). In contrast, although China can attract overseas students (for example, 78,000 in 2003) to study Chinese language and sinology, mainly on a short-term basis, nearly all of them do not stay long after their study for various reasons, such as difficulty in working and living in a predominantly Chinese-speaking environment and low salaries.

To tackle the brain drain problem, both the central and regional governments developed policies to attract foreign-trained Chinese students to return. In 1992, the central government adopted three principles for overseas studies, which can be summarized in twelve

Chinese words: *zhi chi liu xue, gu li hui guo, lai qu zi you* (to support overseas studies, to encourage the return of overseas Chinese students, and to lift restrictions on their coming and going). The Ministry of Education set up Project Spring Ray to sponsor overseas students with PhD degrees and distinguished achievements to return to China to work. Meanwhile, the Chinese Academy of Sciences offers senior visiting fellowships to distinguished Chinese scientists overseas. Between the mid-1980s and 2001, the Ministry of Personnel allotted about RMB¥200 million to support the scientific research of 4,000 returnees and to sponsor short-term visits of 3,000 returnees in China. Across the nation, there are over sixty start-up business parks for returned students. At the regional level, some provincial or municipal governments of China, such as Shanghai and Jiangsu, sent teams to different countries to encourage Chinese scholars to return to work for their regions by giving them travel allowances and improved living conditions in China. From June 2002, the Shanghai Municipal Government has allowed returnees (and overseas experts) to take up residence in Shanghai without giving up their foreign passports.

As a result, in the late 1990s China began to experience brain gain as the return rate of foreign-trained Chinese nationals from overseas studies (*haiguipai*) began to rise. In 2003 the number of returnees increased by 13 percent, from less than 18,000 in 2002 to over 20,000. Foreign-trained returnees, particularly those who emigrated in the late 1970s and mid-1990s, have enhanced the quality of human resources in China. In particular, they play an important role in developing domestic teaching and research teams. In addition, many returnees took up senior management and academic posts. For example, in early 2004, returnees took up 78 percent of university vice chancellor and president posts, 62 percent of PhD supervisory posts, 81 percent of fellowships in the Chinese Academy of Science, and 54 percent of posts in the Chinese Academic of Engineering (Liu, 2004). Many returnees also engaged in business. By the end of 2003, China had designated twenty-one special zones for returned students to run businesses and had established 5,000 companies with a total production value of RMB$30 billion (about US$3.7 billion) (People's Daily Reporter, 2004). But, still more efforts are needed to explore, attract, and recruit not only not-yet-returned Chinese nationals but also overseas nationals to serve the development of China in the twenty-first century.

The rise in the return of foreign-trained Chinese nationals, however, creates two new problems. First, it further widens regional disparities in the distribution of academic talent. It is natural that a majority of returnees prefer to work in the major cities of the eastern and coastal areas of China; for example, up to 2003, over 40 percent of 172,000 returnees worked in Beijing. Thus, less developed areas benefit less from brain gain. The uneven geographical distribution of human capital presents a challenge to national leaders as they strive for more balanced regional development (Cheng, 2004).

Second, the phenomenon of unemployed returnees, particularly those aged below 25, has recently become an acute problem. Since the drastic expansion of higher education from the late 1990s, their employment prospects have been reduced by the surge of locally trained graduates—who are willing to accept lower remuneration. Many returnees cannot easily find jobs; they expect too high remuneration, which many enterprises are not able or willing to offer, unless locally trained graduates cannot easily substitute their expertise. Many returnees are very reluctant to accept posts of lower rank, and many do not want to work in less competitive cities in central or western China.

The Pursuit of Excellence and the Creation of World-Class Universities

The fifth contentious issue in China's education reforms is the pursuit of world-class universities. In the early 1990s, the Chinese state exhibited a strong desire to build up its own world-class universities for competition in the international academic community. It was a very hot topic of discussion at the second Chinese-Foreign University Presidents' Forum in Beijing in 2004. Chinese leaders deem top-notch universities to be an indication of the strength of education; a key to revitalizing the nation through science and education; a sign of comprehensive national strength; a milestone of scientific, social, and cultural progress; and a mark of the international success of China as a socialist country (Jiang, 1998, 2001; Yuan, 2002). At a more practical level, China, as suggested by Deputy Education Minister Zhou (2001), needs to create universities that have the ability to compete for knowledge creation with their global counterparts and to be hubs for fostering, attracting, utilizing, and exchanging talents.

The Chinese state accepted, and still recognizes, that its universities have not reached world-class standards. However, since the late 1980s, great efforts have been made to improve their quality, particularly in research. These efforts include "buying" foreign-trained human capital, boosting domestic research capacity, and launching specific research projects.

As has been discussed earlier, foreign-trained Chinese nationals have been recruited to return to China to work on a short- or long-term basis. However, to avoid overreliance on overseas resources, China used two major strategies to boost the research capacity of higher education. First, the state improved the infrastructure of research. By 1988, 1,715 research units were established in the higher education system (Zhu, 1998): 15.7 percent of these units were for national sciences, 42 percent for engineering and technology, 13.1 percent for agriculture, 25.9 percent for medical sciences, and 3.3 percent for interdisciplinary research. Up to early 1998, 100 national laboratories and 27 national engineering research centers had been established. Second, in addition to the expansion of postgraduate education, a strong research team is being built up. The percentages of professors and associate professors increased from 7.1 percent and 25.8 percent respectively in 1994, to 9.7 percent and 29.8 percent (of 730,000 academic and teaching staff) in 2003 (Ministry of Education, 2004, 1 September). It has become a common activity of academic life to develop research projects and seek research grants at national and subnational levels, and publication has become a major criterion for recruitment and promotion.

To help Chinese universities develop cutting-edge research, the state has introduced several significant programs since the 1980s. The 863 Programme of March 1986 aimed to make breakthroughs in sophisticated fields of science and technology to narrow the gap with other high-tech powers. Project 211, which was launched in the mid-1990s by the Ministry of Education, was expected to enhance the quality of higher education by selecting and pushing a small proportion of higher education institutes to reach international standards within a short period. The Project has two specific goals: (1) the construction of about 100 key higher education institutes, with some of them being designed to reach the standards of first-class universities in other parts of the world, some developing their own areas of excellence and taking the lead, and others serving local needs and acting as the mainstay;

and (2) the development of about 800 key disciplines, most of which fall into agriculture, basic industries, high or new technology, basic science, economy, administration and jurisdiction, resources and environment, medicine and health, liberal arts, and social sciences (Ministry of Education, 2001c). Between 1996 and 2002, the central government allocated an unprecedented sum of RMB¥18.4 billion as incentive money to facilitate the project (Cheng, 2004). By early 2001, the number of officially approved Project 211 universities increased to 98. These began to develop 602 key items covering seven major disciplines: humanities and social sciences, 62 (10 percent); economics, law, and political sciences, 57 (9.4 percent); basic sciences, 89 (15 percent); environment and resources, 42 (7 percent); foundation industries and high technologies, 255 (42 percent); medicine and health, 66 (11 percent); and agriculture, 31 (5 percent) (Wei, 2001). To accelerate some Project 211 universities to world-class status, the Ministry of Education launched Project 985 (initiated by Jiang Zemin in May 1998), which gave generous funding to nine top research universities. Peking University and Tsinghua University each received RMB¥1.8 billion, and Shanghai Jiaotong University and Nanjing University each got RMB¥1.2 billion (Feng, 2004).

These attempts to pursue excellence have had both positive and negative impacts on the development of higher education in China. On the one hand, Project 211 demonstrates a model of state-university collaboration in pushing universities to excel. Universities had to develop feasibility plans, apply for assessment, raise some of their own funds, and demonstrate their capacity to meet requirements for infrastructure and quality in both teaching and research. Meanwhile, central and local governments provided funds to Project 211 universities to improve their infrastructure and monitored their development with the help of experts from peer universities. Moreover, unlike the designation of keypoint universities by national and regional governments in the past, the process of selection and accreditation for Project 211 universities is more "transparent" and is conducted on a more competitive basis. They serve as a model of excellence for other institutes, and to some extent constitute the Chinese version of the United States' Ivy League universities.

By strengthening infrastructure and human resources, China's higher education is gradually increasing its contribution to world knowledge. The influence of China in major disciplines, at the international level, has increased gradually since the 1980s. To some extent, the number of publications reflects the research performance of a country or an institution, and the number of its articles cited by others reflects its influence. For example, the record of the three major databases of international publications on science and technology (Science Citation Index, Index to Scientific and Technological Index, and Engineering Index) shows that between 1996 and 2002 China increased publications on science and technology from 27,569 to 77,395 (5.4 percent of the world total), and its global ranking rose from 11th to 5th (after the USA, Japan, the UK, and Germany) (Ministry of Science and Technology, 1998, 2004). Meanwhile, the number of Chinese articles cited by others in the international community increased from 8,826 to 24,154. Despite these remarkable achievements over a short period, the quantitative contribution of China to the international academic community is still relatively small when compared with leading countries such as the United States.

On the other hand, these attempts to pursue excellence reinforce the stratification of Chinese universities at home and the dominance of Western academic culture in the international arena. Project 211 is arguably a consolidation of the stratification among Chinese higher education institutes that began with the keypoint universities of the 1950s. The majority of Project 211 universities, such as Peking University (established in 1898), Tsinghua University (1911) and Fudan University (1905), already had a long history and enjoyed strong governmental support. Now, the titles "Project 211 University" and "Project 211 Discipline" have become alternative marks of good university or discipline. The Project has also widened the gap between Project 211 universities (fewer than 10 percent of over 1,000 higher education institutes) and non-Project 211 universities and colleges. Project 211 universities take the lion's share of the national higher education budget. For example, in 2000 they took 72 percent of total research grants, 54 percent of the total value of equipment and facilities, 31 percent of the total volume of books and journals, 96 percent of national laboratories, and 88 percent of key disciplines (Wei, 2001). They are also in a better position to compete for teachers and, particularly, postgraduate students. By 2001, they employed 87 percent of all teachers with PhD degrees, and enrolled 84 percent of all PhD students, 69 percent of master students, and 32 percent of undergraduates. Consequently, many non-Project 211 institutes worry about whether resources from central and regional governments and non-state sources will be further lopsided to Project 211 universities (Gong, 1997).

The pursuit of excellence in Chinese higher education leads to two other, intimately related, contentious issues. How far away are Chinese universities from world-class standards? More importantly, what are these standards, and who defines them? In 2001, a research team at Shanghai Jiaotong University attempted to compare leading Chinese universities with world-renowned universities in the United States, Britain, Germany, France, and Japan in three major areas: history and achievements, the quality of human resources, and the availability of financial resources (Liu, Cheng, Liu, & Zhao, 2004). The team used these criteria for this comparison: long history; clear vision and mission; clear positioning in their own higher education systems; strong academic prestige with excellent achievements in research, particularly in science and technology; production of Nobel laureates; top-notch programs that attract excellent students from the nation and the world; brilliant vice-chancellors or presidents who are renowned specialists in their own fields and are good educators; a staff of top-quality scholars with doctoral degrees from world-class universities and recruited through highly competitive exercises; a high proportion of research students (between 30 percent and 60 percent of the total enrollment); an international student population with over 20 percent overseas students; a large annual budget ranging between several hundred million to 1 billion US dollars; a strong ability to attract large contributions from society and alumni; and significant research funding secured through national and international competitions.

The survey concluded that, in the league of world-class universities, only Peking and Tsinghua Universities could be ranked between 200th and 300th, while Nanjing, Fudan, and Shanghai Jiaotong Universities were between 300th and 500th. The survey predicted that by 2025 the former two could reach the top 100, and the latter three could reach the top 200 list of world-class universities.

However, the criteria used by the Shanghai research team are not unquestionable. First, the concept of world-class universities is not absolute; it is relative. The fundamental question is: By what and whose standards is a university judged as world class? The criteria for comparing and ranking universities within the same higher education system are often highly selective and cannot give a comprehensive picture of the inputs, operation processes, and outputs of individual universities. Criteria for the global ranking of universities are even more controversial. They are very much complicated by differences in macro contexts such as socioeconomic, political, cultural, and educational conditions, and variation in micro contexts such as institutional history and characteristics of the universities concerned.

Second, it is dangerous to deify some world-renowned universities (such as Harvard, Yale, Cambridge, and Oxford). Like Rome, they were not built in one day, but over several centuries. Chinese universities have a relatively short history—Peking University, which is one of the oldest, has a history of only just over one century. Also, world-class universities are not necessarily excellent in all disciplines and require not only the support of strong infrastructure and financial and human resources, but also backing by an excellent academic culture and traditions, and excellent strategies for development. All these often take a very long time to accumulate and develop.

Third, the pursuit of creating world-class universities in China can easily fall into the chicken-and-egg trap: Do elite students make universities world class, or do world-class universities produce elite students? Foreign world-renowned universities are ensembles of elites that can attract top students (particularly in research programs) and academic talents from not only their own nations but also from the rest of the world. Over a dozen leading universities in China attract top students from all over the country, but very few of them, if any, attract elite students from the rest of the world. On the contrary, they lose their bright students to other countries. For example, in 2003 over half of 4,000 Beijing applicants for overseas study, who held tertiary qualifications or above, were year-four students of Peking University and Tsinghua University (Zhou, 2004). There is a saying in China: Schools in different areas convey their talents to Peking University and Tsinghua University in Beijing, which in turn convey their graduates to universities of other countries, particularly the United States. The saying may be an exaggeration, but it does indeed reflect the domestic and international flow of educated Chinese human capital—particularly the inability of top Chinese universities to keep their best graduates for postgraduate education.

CONCLUSIONS: POLICY IMPLICATIONS FOR EDUCATION AND DEVELOPMENT IN A GLOBAL AGE

Since the late 1970s, China has made remarkable progress in economic and social development and in the pursuit of global capital. This is a result of adopting appropriate strategies of education reform. This reform is gradually helping to turn China's huge population from a liability to an asset for development; it is also helping to enhance China's national competitiveness in the accumulation of global capital. However, the reform is confronted with deep-seated cultural perceptions of education, long-standing educational problems, practical constraints, and difficulties in balancing national and global tensions and national and local needs. The experience and struggle of China has five major policy implications for education and development in an increasingly globalized environment.

First, although global imperatives can be translated into education reform, the success of such reform often hinges on corresponding cultural shifts. Reform can indeed restructure education and curriculum. However, reform will not necessarily change the culture that underpins the daily practices of students, teachers, and education officials. For example, the issue of heavy study loads in China shows that, no matter how convincing the curriculum reform initiatives and changes promoted by policymakers or reformers, many stakeholders simply do not believe that a reduction in drilling will enhance the quality of learning. Instead, they stubbornly continue to believe in the power and value of drilling. Students are more likely to keep on suffering from the vicious cycle of heavy study burdens if there is no matching change in the culture and perceptions of different stakeholders concerning the relations between drilling, performance, and future careers.

Second, policy and law must be dynamic, particularly in times of rapid change. They may need to be revisited regularly, and even revised, in light of new developments. This is illustrated in the case of the unequal pace of development in China. The rapid pace of urbanization and the easier domestic flow of people increasingly blur the economic dichotomy between urban and rural areas. The problems of rural areas can become that of urban areas and vice versa.

For example, this chapter has discussed the case of education for migrant children, particularly in destination places. Their problems could be eased by an increase in financial resources for migrant workers, willingness of local public schools to admit migrant workers' children, and upgrading learning conditions in migrant workers' schools to reach the standards required by the local governments concerned. To facilitate mobility within China, the policy of domicile registration, which was launched in the old planned economy, needs to be changed to eliminate differentiation between local and non-local people. The selection of children by schools in accordance with local catchment areas needs to be deregulated to allow migrant students to be legally entitled to a nine-year compulsory schooling at their destinations. This can be done by amending the Basic Education Law that was enacted in 1986, when the National People's Congress could not foresee the massive flow of peasants into cities in response to the economic developments of today. Migrant students should also be allowed to sit for entrance examinations to senior secondary or higher education in destination places. The migration and education of migrant children in China can be seen, to some extent, as a microcosm of the international flow of students and workers that is subject to visa control and responded to by differential social welfare and tuition fees for local and non-local students. These differentials reinforce the concepts of national borders and distinctions in residence and citizenship between nations and discourage students who are less socioeconomically advantaged to win scholarships abroad.

Third, it is important in policymaking and curriculum development to balance carefully between the translation of global imperatives for education and the actual needs of local people at different stages of development. For example, as has been discussed, because of the pressure of economic globalization, the learning of English receives unprecedented attention across China. However, because of different rates of urbanization, it would be more advantageous to China if the level of required English proficiency were different in different areas, rather than the same set of standards and requirements being imposed across the nation. Moreover, an important barrier to the learning and use of English in China, as in many non-English-speaking societies, is the lack of an English environment for students to practice speaking and communication outside classrooms in urban, not to mention poor and remote rural, areas. For the majority of Chinese students, English remains a second language used mainly in English lessons in schools and in limited courses in universities across the nation. In the workplace, the majority of workers probably only need simple vocational English, rather than fluency. Perhaps, they will need higher levels of English proficiency later when their areas have more communication with the outside world.

Fourth, the opening up of the Chinese academy to the Western world is a two-edged sword. On the one hand, it has created many opportunities for Chinese higher education to expand partnerships with Western countries, to broaden its horizon of academic research, and to enhance its representation in the international academic community. On the other hand, it has resulted in a substantial influence on Chinese scholarship by foreign academics. China's scholars have to accept the rules of a game that is dominated by the Western academic community, and they are increasingly orienting their academic culture to the West. Moreover, the legitimization of innovation and academic output becomes increasingly reliant on sources outside China. It includes the invitation of Western scholars to participate in journals and conferences held in China, and the adoption of Western conventions in both domestic and international publications.

Accordingly, as has been discussed above, the creation of first-class universities in China should be conducted with extreme caution. The pursuit of so-called world-class-university status is used rhetorically, but strategically, by the state to force universities to catch up with international standards and by the university leadership to force staff to contribute to the international academic community. Comparison with internationally renowned universities abroad may help China locate the achievement of its higher education in the international context, reflect on its strengths and weaknesses for further enhancement, and give a direction for and an impetus to the development of individual institutions. For example, Peking University, as revealed by its President Xu (2004), planned to take ten years to reach world-class status by 2015.

However, the Chinese state and Chinese universities should not underestimate themselves. Whether Chinese universities are world class can be an important concern. But what matters more is whether they can ultimately contribute to the specific national and local developments of China, and later to the development of the world; and whether more Chinese nationals, who are trained in world-class universities overseas, can return to contribute, together with locally trained counterparts, to cutting-edge research. The latter may have been helped in August 2004 with the lifting of the cap on granting permanent residence to high-level foreign personnel, including academics (Ministry of Public Security & Ministry of Foreign Affairs, 2003). Unlike Chinese nationals, who are restricted by domicile registration (as discussed earlier), foreigners who are granted permanent residence in China are allowed to work and live anywhere.

Fifth, the case of China suggests an urgent need to respect the principles of plurality and equality among peoples, economies, and international communities in an increasingly globalized environment. Inequalities in academic relationships can be improved, first by recognizing them and then by creating "a world that ameliorates these inequalities" (Altbach, 2004). Altbach argues that in bilateral (for example) exchanges, ameliorations are bidirectional, rather than unidirectional, accommodations of one party to the other.

Genuine cultural and academic exchanges are mutual accommodations, but the domination of a single language (namely English) on the Internet mitigates against the promise of globalization to facilitate more communication and interconnectivity among peoples in different parts of the world. English-speaking students and scholars could learn at least one foreign language (for example, Japanese or Chinese) and publish in non-English journals. Perhaps the time is not yet ripe and a critical mass has not been developed, but this would be a positive step forward. The greatest contribution of English-speaking societies to the alleviation of inequalities would be to ease the pressure on students in non-English-speaking societies to learn English. On the part of non-English-language societies (such as China), the problem could be ameliorated by encouraging students and scholars to learn English and to publish in English journals. Non-English-language societies could also enhance the quality and status of domestic journals in different fields so as to attract foreign scholars.

The recognition of publications at the local, national, and international levels should be judged on their quality, rather than where and in what language they are published. If globalization transcends geo-territorial borders of world knowledge, there is no point insisting on the superiority of overseas publications over national or local ones (or vice versa). There is a Chinese saying: Those who hold themselves in contempt invite contempt by others (*ren ruo zi wu ren bi wu zhi*). If a nation does not treasure its own national/local publications and academic achievements as much as international ones, who will?

REFERENCES

Altbach, P. G. (2004). Globalisation and the university: Myths and realities in an unequal world. *Tertiary Education and Management, 10*(1), 3–25.

Arimoto, A. (2002). *Trends in higher education and academic reforms from 1994 onwards in Japan* (commissioned as support material for the book, *Transformation in higher education: Global pressures and local realities in South Africa*). Cape Town: Centre for Higher Education Transformation.

Beijing Municipal Commission of Education. (2002). *Guanyu duiliudong renkouzhong shiling ertong xiaonian shishi yiwu jiaoyude zhanxing banfa (A circular concerning the temporary measure for providing basic education for migrant children of relevant age).* Beijing: Beijing Municipal Commission of Education.

Chen, D. Y. (2002). A study on the amalgamation of Chinese higher educational institutions. *Asia Pacific Education Review, 3*(1), 48–55.

Chen, Z. L. (2000). Qieshi jianqing xuesheng guozhong fudan quanmian tuijin suzhi jiaoyu (To reduce students' study load and promote quality education). *Renmin Jiaoyu (People's Education), 2*, 6–7.

Chen, Z. L. (2002, 17 September). Shisanjie sizhong guanhui yilai woguo jiaoyu gaige yu fazhan de lishi chengjiu (The historical achievements of education reform and developments in China since the 4th Congress of 13th Plenary Session). *Zhongguo Jiaoyubao (China Education Daily)*, 1–2.

Cheng, L. (2004). Bringing China's best and brightest back home: Regional disparities and political tensions. *China Leadership Monitor, 11*, 1–9.

Cheng, S. H., & Liang, W. G. (2000). Xinqiannian xiangxuesheng guozhong fudan xuanzhan (A challenge to the overloading of students in the new millennium). *Renmin Jiaoyu (People's Education), 2*, 9–14.

China Daily. (2005, 2 March). China sees progress in education. Retreived 3 September 2005, from http://www.chinadaily.com.cn/english/doc/2005-03/02/content_421023.htm

China Daily Reporter. (2004, 1 September). Leveling school playing field. *China Daily.*

China's Education and Human Resource Development Project Team. (Ed.). (2003). *Zongrenkou daguo maixiang renli ziyuan qiangguo (Stride from a country of tremendous population to a country of profound human resources).* Beijing: Higher Education Press.

Communist Party of China Central Committee. (1985). *Reform of China's educational structure.* Beijing: Foreign Languages Press.

Communist Party of China Central Committee and State Council. (1993). Zhongguo jiaoyu gaige he fazhan gangyao (The scheme for the reform and development of education in China). In *Zhonghua renmin gongheguo jiaoyufa, yiwu jiaoyufa, jiaoshifa (The education law, basic education law and teachers law of the People's Republic of China)* (pp. 35–57). Beijing: China Law Publishing House.

Cui, C. Y., & Pan, Y. G. (2003). Duijincheng mingong zinu jieshou yiwu jiaoyu zhuangkuangde diaocha (a survey on compulsory education for the children of farmers working in urban areas). In H. Ma & M. K. Wang (Eds.), *Zhongguo fazhan yanjiu guowuyuan zhongxin yanjiu baoguoxuan (China development studies: Selected research reports of the development research center of the State Council)* (pp. 603–611). Beijing: Zhongguo Fazhan Publishing House.

Cui, Y. H., Ke, Z., & Lin, Y. G. (2003). Putong gaozhong kecheng de lishi yanbian (The development of curriculum planning in general senior secondary education). In Q. Q. Zhong, Y. H. Cui, & G. P. Wu (Eds.), *Putong gaozhong xinkecheng fangan daodou (Introduction to the new curriculum of general senior secondary education)* (pp. 29–40). Shanghai: East China Normal University Press.

Deng, X. P. (1962). Zenyang huifu nongye shengchan (Restore agricultural production). In Central Committee of Communist Party of China Document Editorial Commission (Ed.), *Deng Xiaoping wenxuan, 1938–1965 (Selected work of Deng Xiaoping, 1938–1965)*. Beijing: Renmin Publication House.

Deng, X. P. (1977). Zunzhong zhizhi zhuzhong rencai (Respect knowledge, respect trained personnel). In Central Committee of Communist Party of China Document Editorial Commission (Ed.), *Deng Xiaoping wenxuan, 1975–1982 (Selected work of Deng Xiaoping, 1975–1982)* (pp. 37–38). Beijing: Renmin Publication House.

Deng, X. P. (1978). Zaiquanguo kexue dahui kaimushi shang de jianghua (Speech at the opening ceremony of the national conference on science). In Central Committee of Communist Party of China Document Editorial Commission (Ed.), *Deng Xiaoping wenxuan, 1975–1982 (Selected work of Deng Xiaoping, 1975–1982)* (pp. 82–97). Beijing: Renmin Publication House.

Deng, X. P. (1983). Wei jianshan xuexiao tici (Message written for Jingshan School). In Central Committee of Communist Party of China Document Editorial Commission (Ed.), *Deng Xiaoping wenxuan, 1983–1992 (Selected work of Deng Xiaoping, 1983–1992)* (p. 35). Beijing: Renmin Publication House.

Deng, X. P. (1985). Ba jiaoyu gongzuo renzhen zhuaqilai (Devote special efforts to education). In Central Committee of Communist Party of China Document Editorial Commission (Ed.), *Deng Xiaoping wenxuan, 1983–1992 (Selected work of Deng Xiaoping, 1983–1992)* (pp. 120–122). Beijing: Renmin Publication House.

Deng, X. P. (1988). Kexue jishu shi diyi shengchanli (Science and technology constitute a primary productive force). In Central Committee of Communist Party of China Document Editorial Commission (Ed.), *Deng Xiaoping wenxuan, 1983–1992 (Selected work of Deng Xiaoping, 1983–1992)* (pp. 274–276). Beijing: Renmin Publication House.

Deng, X. P. (1994). Yadao yiqiedeshi wending (The overriding need is for stability). In Central Committee of Communist Party of China Document Editorial Commission (Ed.), *Deng Xiaoping wenxuan, 1982–1992 (Selected work of Deng Xiaoping, 1982–1992)* (pp. 284–285). Beijing: Renmin Publication House.

Fang, D. (2004, 21 June). 40 million private investors by 2010. *South China Morning Post.*

Feng, D. H. (2004). The four corners agreement between Shanghai Jiao Tong University and University of Texas at Dallas: An educational alliance building toward shared technology and skilled labor (a prepared statement for the panel on business opportunities and challenges of China), *Greater Dallas Chamber of Commerce and Haynes and Boone LLP*. Dallas: The University of Texas at Dallas.

Gong, F. (1997). Eryiyi gongcheng (Project 211: A strategic decision to develop higher education in China). *Zhongguo Gaodeng Jiaoyu Yanjiu (China Higher Education Research), 1*, 41–51.

Guo, X. M. (2003). Kecheng jiegou ji qi gazhi quxiang (The structure and value orientation of the curriculum). In Q. Q. Zhong, Y. H. Cui, & G. P. Wu (Eds.), *Putong gaozhong xinkecheng fangan daodou (Introduction to the new curriculum of general senior secondary education)* (pp. 87–100). Shanghai: East China Normal University Press.

Harman, K., & Meek, V. L. (2002). Introduction to special issue: "Merger revisited: International perspectives on mergers in higher education." *Higher Education, 44*(1), 1–4.

Ho, A. K. (2004). *China's reform and reformers*. Westport, CT: Praeger.

Hu, J. T. (2003). Zai sange daibiao yantaohui shangde jianghua (speech at the symposium on the "three represents"). In D. Y. Shen & L. S. Cheng (Eds.), *Hu jintao tongzhi qiyi zhongyao jianghua xueji duben (A study guide for the speech of Hu Jiantao at the symposium on the "three represents")* (pp. 1–18). Beijing: Communist Party of China Central Committee Party School Press.

Hu, R. W. (2004). Gaodeng jiaoyu yingjianchi shidu chaoqian he kechixu fazhan (To persist in keeping reasonably quick and sustainable development of higher education). *Zhongguo Gaodeng Jiaoyu (China Higher Education), 25*(13–14), 5–7.

Jiang, Z. M. (1997). *Gaoju deng Xiaoping lilun weida qizhi ba jianshe yao zhongguo tuse shehui zhuyi shiye guanmian tuixiang 21 shiji (To raise the flag of Deng Xiaoping's theory and to push the construction of the socialist business with Chinese characteristics into the 21st century)*. Beijing: Renmin Press.

Jiang, Z. M. (1998). Zai qingzhu beijing daxue jianxiao yibai zhounian dahuishang de jianghua (The speech at the centenary anniversary of Peking University). Retrieved 11 August 2004, from http://www.moe.edu.cn/zhuanti/1stdaxue/1.htm

Jiang, Z. M. (2001, 29 April). Zai qingzhu qinghua daxue jianxiao jiushi zhounian dahuishang de jianghua (The speech at the 90th anniversary of Tsinghua University). Retrieved 11 August 2004, from http://news.tsinghua.edu.cn/new/news.php?id=880

Law, W. W. (1995). The role of state in higher education reform: Mainland China and Taiwan. *Comparative Education Review, 39*(3), 322–355.

Law, W. W. (2000). Schooling and society in the People's Republic of China. In K. Mazurek, M. Winzer, & C. Majorek (Eds.), *Education in a global society: A comparative perspective* (pp. 355–370). Boston: Allyn and Bacon.

Lee, W. O., & Gu, R. F. (Eds.). (2004). *Guoji shiye yu gongmin jiaoyu: Xianggang ji shanghai zhongxue zhuankuang diaocha (International outlook and citizenship education: A survey on secondary schools in Hong Kong and Shanghai).* Shanghai: Shanghai Academy of Social Sciences Press.

Li, X. L. (2004, 9 July). Jiaoyubumen sanlingwushen xuexiao jigou bianzhefaer shujia buke heshi nengjinzhu (Schools find ways to defeat the repeated instructions of the ministry of education. When can supplementary lessons be stopped?). *Wen Hui Bao,* 6.

Lian, Y. M. (Ed.). (2004). *Zhongguo shuzi baogao (A report on the statistics of China).* Beijing: Zhongguo Shidai Jingji Publishing House.

Liu, N. (2004, 1 March). Liuxue renyuan huiguo chuangye chengjiuzhan chuangsanzui (Three new records of the exhibition on the achievements of returness from abroad after study overseas). *Zhongguo Jiaoyubao (China Education Daily),* 1.

Liu, N. C., Cheng, Y., Liu, L., & Zhao, W. H. (2004). Woguo mingbai daixue li shijie yiliu youdouyuan (How far away are China's famous universities from world class standards?). In Shanghai Jiaotong University Institute of Higher Education (Ed.), *Jianshe shijie yiliu daxue xilie yanjiu baogao huibian (A collection of research reports on constructing world class universities)* (pp. 1–16). Shanghai: Shanghai Jiaotong University Institute of Higher Education.

Liu, S. J., Lu, Z. Y., Zhang, L. Q., & Li, J. W. (2003). 2002–2003 nian jingji xingshi fenxi yu zhengce jianyi (An analysis of the economic situation of 2002–2003 and policy suggestions). In H. Ma & M. K. Wang (Eds.), *Zhongguo fazhan yanjiu guowuyuan zhongxin yanjiu baoguoxuan (China development studies: Selected research reports of the development research center of the State Council)* (pp. 9–19). Beijing: Zhongguo Fazhan Publishing House.

Liu, X. Q. (2004, 17 February). Shibasui yixia liudong renkou shoujiaoyu kanyou (The worrying situations of migrant children aged below 18). *Renmin Ribao (People's Daily),* p. 1.

Ministry of Education. (1999). Mianxiang 21 shiji jiaoyu zhenxing xingdong jihua (action plan for invigorating education for the 21st century). In *2003–2007 nian jiaoyu zhenxing xingdong jihua (2003–2007 action plan for invigorating education)* (pp. 22–39). Beijing: China Law Publishing House.

Ministry of Education. (2000a). Guanyu zaixiaoxue jianqing xuesheng guozhong fudan de jinji tongzhi (An urgent circular concerning the reduction of study load of primary school students). *Renmin Jiaoyu (People's Education), 2,* 8.

Ministry of Education. (2000b). *Zai zhongxioaxue puji xinxi jishu jiaoyu de tongzhi (A circular concerning the popularization of information technology education in primary and secondary schools).* Beijing: Ministry of Education.

Ministry of Education. (2000c). *Zai zhongxioaxue shishi xiaoxiaotong de tongzhi (A circular concerning the implementation of the information technology network project in primary and secondary schools)* (No. Jiaoji [2000] 34). Beijing: Ministry of Education.

Ministry of Education. (2000d). *Zhongxioaxue xinxi jishu jiaoyu kecheng zhidao gangyao (zhanxing) (Provisional syllabus for information technology education in primary and secondary schools).* Beijing: Ministry of Education.

Ministry of Education. (2001a). *Jichu jiaoyu kecheng gaige gangyao shixing (Guidelines on the curriculum reform of basic education)* (No. Basic Education, 2001–17). Beijing: Ministry of Education.

Ministry of Education. (2001b). *Jiji tuijin xiaoxue kaishe yingyu kecheng de zhidao yijian (Guidelines on the provision of English language subject in primary schools)* (No. Jijiao, 2001–2). Beijing: Ministry of Education.

Ministry of Education. (2001c). Project 211: An introduction. Retrieved 16 July 2004, from http://www.edu.cn/HomePage/english/education/highedu/211/index.shtml

Ministry of Education. (2003, 13 May). 2002 nian quanguo jiaoyu shiye fazhan tongji gongbao (Statistical report on educational achievements and developments in China in 2002). *Zhongguo Jiaoyubao (China Education Daily),* p. 2.

Ministry of Education. (2003a). 92 nian yilai gaoxioa hebing qingkuang (The development of realignment of higher education institutes in China). Retrieved 9 August 2004, from http://www.moe.edu.cn/highedu/gxtz/gxhb_20030417.xls

Ministry of Education. (2003b). *Kaizhan putong gaozhong xinkecheng shiyan gongzuo de tongzhi (A circular concerning the pilot of the new curriculum of general senior secondary education)* (No. Jiaoji 2003–6). Beijing: Ministry of Education.

Ministry of Education. (2004, 27 May). 2003 nian guanguo jiaoyu shiye fazhan tongji gongbao (Statistical report on educational achievements and developments in China in 2003). *Zhongguo Jiaoyubao (China Education Daily)*, p. 2.

Ministry of Education. (2004, 1 September). Guanguo putong xuexiao jiaoshi duiwu xianzhuang (The status quo of teachers in regular schools in China). *Zhongguo Jiaoyubao (China Education Daily)*, p. 3.

Ministry of Education. (2004a). 2003–2007 nian jiaoyu zhenxing xingdong jihua (2003–2007 action plan for invigorating education). In *2003–2007 nian jiaoyu zhenxing xingdong jihua (2003–2007 action plan for invigorating education)* (pp. 1–21). Beijing: China Law Publishing House.

Ministry of Education. (2004b). *Guanyu yinfa daxue yingyu kecheng jiaoxue yaoqiu de tongzhi, shixing (Circular concerning the demand on the provisional curriculum of Engllish language in higher education)* (No. Jiaogaoting 2004–1). Beijing: Ministry of Education.

Ministry of Education. (2004c). *Zhongguo liuxue renyuan huiguo chuangye chengjiuzhan xinwengao (Exhibition on the achievements of returned overseas Chinese students: Press release)*. Beijing: Ministry of Education.

Ministry of Public Security and Ministry of Foreign Affairs. (2003). *Weiguoren zaizhongguo yongjiu juliu shenpi guanli banfa (Regulations on examination and approval of permanent residence of aliens)*. Beijing: Ministry of Public Security and Ministry of Foreign Affairs.

Ministry of Science and Technology. (1998). *1996 nian zhongguo keji lunwen de tongji yu fengxi (Statistics and analysis of China's publications in science and technology, 1996)*. Beijing: Ministry of Science and Technology.

Ministry of Science and Technology. (2004). *2002 nian woguo guoji keji lunwen chanchu zhuangkuang (Statistics on China's international publications in science and technology, 2002)*. Beijing: Ministry of Science and Technology.

National Bureau of Statistics. (2002). *Zhongguo tongji nianjian, 2002 (China statistical yearbook, 2002)*. Beijing: China Statistical Publishing House.

National Bureau of Statistics. (2003). *Zhongguo renkou tongji nianjian 2003 (China population statistics yearbook 2003)*. Beijing: China Statistics Press.

National People's Congress. (1986). Zhonghua renmin gongheguo yiwu jiaoyufa (The basic education law of the People's Republic of China). In *Zhonghua renmin gongheguo jiaoyufa, yiwu jiaoyufa, jiaoshifa (The education law, basic education law and teachers law of the People's Republic of China)* (pp. 1–13). Beijing: China Law Publishing House.

National People's Congress. (2004). *Zhonghua renimin gongheguo xianfa (The constitution of the People's Republic of China)*. Beijing: China Law Publishing House.

Pan, S. Y. (2004). *How higher educational institutions cope with social change: The case of Tsinghua University, China.* Unpublished Ph.D., The University of Hong Kong, Hong Kong.

People's Daily Reporter. (2004, 16 February). Record 20,100 Chinese students return home in 2003. *People's Daily.*

Shanghai Municipal Education Commission. (2004). *Qieshe jianqing zhongxiaoxuesheng guozhong keye fudan de regan yijian (Opinions about how to reduce students' heavy study load)*. Shanghai: Shanghai Municipal Education Commission.

Shen, J. L. (2004, 13 August). Liudong ertong zaijing shangxue meinian 3129 yuan (It is difficult for migrant children to go to school because the annual tuition fee is RMB¥3,129). *Xinjing Bao (Beijing News).*

State Council. (2002). *Zhongguo renkou pucha ziliao 2000 (National population census, 2000)*. Beijing: National Statistics Bureau.

State Council. (2003). *Guanyu jinyibu zuohao jincheng wugongjiuye nongmin zinu yiwu jiaoyu gongzuode yijian (An opinion concerning the further improvement in the compulsory schooling for children whose parents move from rural to urban areas to work)*. Beijing: Government Document.

State Council. (2004). *Report on the work of the government.* Beijing: Second Session of the Tenth National People's Congress.

Stewart, F. (1996). Globalisation and education. *International Journal of Educational Development, 16*(4), 327–333.

Sun, X. W. (2004). Chengshiren pinfu chaju you duoda (How large is the disparity between rich and poor in urban areas?). *Zhongguo Guoqing Guoli (National Situations and Strengths of China), 5.*

Trow, M. (1969). Elite and popular functions in American higher education. In W. R. Niblett (Ed.), *Higher education: Demand and response* (pp. 181–201). London: Tavistock Publications.

Trow, M. (1970). Reflections on the transition from mass to universal higher education. In S. R. Graubard & G. A. Ballotti (Eds.), *The embattled university* (pp. 1–42). New York: George Braziller.

Trow, M. (2003, 8 April). *On mass higher education and institutional diversity.* Paper presented at the Israeli Higher Education Conference, Tel Aviv.

UNESCO Institute for Statistics. (2004). Edstats. Retrieved 18 August 2004, from http://devdata.worldbank.org/edstats/cd.asp

United Nations Country Team in China. (2004). *Millennium development goals (MDGS): China's progress.* Beijing: Office of the United Nations Resident Coordinator in China.

Wang, S. H., & Yan, K. (2004, 16 August). Beijing caiqu duozhong cuoshi baozhang liudong ertong shaonian jieshou yiwu jiaoyu (Beijing adopts different measures to ensure the provision of the basic education for migrant workers' children). Retrieved 18 August 2004, from http://news.xinhuanet.com/edu/2004-08/16/content_1797939.htm

Wang, X., & Zhou, Y. (2004, 18 May). Nongcun liushou ertong: Sixiang daode jiaoyu zhuangkuang kanyou (Stay-behind children in rural areas: Worries about their ideological and moral education). *People's Daily,* p. 5.

Wang, X. X. (Ed.). (2002). *Zhongguo jiaoyu mianlin de jinyao wenti (Urgent problems confronting education of China).* Beijing: Jingji Ribao Press.

Wei, Y. (2001, 8 February). Eryiyi gongcheng shi kejiao xingguo zhanlu de jichu gongcheng (Project 211 as the fundamental project of the strategy of making the nation prosperous with science and education). *Guangming Daily.*

Wu, B. W. (2002, 27 February). Jianfude laoshi weiheyao tonggai qianfei (Why a teacher regrets for reduction in students' study load). *Zhongguo Qingnianbao (China Youth Daily).*

Wu, Y. S., & Yu, B. Y. (2004, 13 May). Fumu lilexiang haizi zenmoban (How to help children whose parents have left villages for earning living in urban areas). *Guangming Daily,* p. B1.

Wu, Y. W. (c. 2002). Zongwupu shuju kan wuguo loadong liudong (The labour mobility as reflected from the fifth national population census). Retrieved 24 June 2004, from http://www.cpirc.org.cn/yjwx/yjwx_detail.asp?id=2182

Xiao, Y. B., & Wu, D. S. (2004, 17 February). Heihu xuexiao yuanhe chixiang (Why are illegal schools popular?). *Workers' Daily,* p. 6.

Xinhua News Agency. (2004, 17 April). Migrant workers: Urban underclass. Retrieved 17 April 2004, from http://news.xinhuanet.com/english/2004-04/17/content_1424934.htm

Xinhua News Agency. (2004, 24 April). China's per capita GDP to hit US$3,000 in 2020. *China Daily.*

Xu, M. (2004, 5 June). 1000 wan liushou ertong qidai guanai (10 millions stay-behind children waiting for love and care). *Zhongguo Jiaoyubao (China Education Daily),* p. 1.

Xu, M. (2004, 15 August). Wunaide liushou rangtamen shiqu duoshao guanai (How much love and care have the migrant workers' children who stay behind at home place). *Zhongguo Jiaoyubao (China Education Daily),* p. 1.

Xu, Z. H. (2004, 6 August). *Beijing daxue chuangjian shijie yiliu daxue de fazhan zhanlue yu shijian (The strategy and implementation of developing Peking University into a world-class university).* Paper presented at the Second Chinese-Foreign University Presidents' Forum, Beijing.

Yuan, G. R. (2002, 29 April). Jianshe shehui zhuyi gaoshuiping daxue de dongyuanling (The mobilization order to construct high-level socialist universities). Retrieved 11 August 2004, from http://www.moe.edu.cn/zhuanti/1stdaxue/2.htm

Zhang, Y., & Zhang, Z. M. (2004). Chuangxin jiaoxue moshi shenhua daxue yingyu jiaoxue gaige (Innovating teaching pattern to deepen the reform of English teaching in the university). *Zhongguo Gaodeng Jiaoyu (China Higher Education), 25*(13–14), 21–22.

Zhou, T. (2004, 18 August). Zhongguo muqian you 52 wan liuxue renyuan beijing cheng haiguipai shouxuande (China has had 0.5 million people studying overseas and Beijing is the first choice of returnees). Retrieved 19 August 2004, from http://www.Chinanews.com.cn/news/2004year/2004-08-18/26/473341.shtml

Zhou, Y. Q. (2001, 16 January). Ershiyi shji: Jianshe yege shemoyang de gaodeng jiaoyu (Twenty-first century: What higher education should be developed?) *Zhongguo Jiaoyubao (China Education Daily),* p. 1.

Zhu, K. X. (1998, 11 February). Zaiguojiajiaowei 1998 nian jiaoyugongzuo huiyishang de jianghua (A speech of the commissioner in the working conference of state education commission in 1998). *Zhongguo Jiaoyubao (China Education Daily),* pp. 1–2.

Zhu, R. J. (2001). *Report on the implementation of the 2000 plan for national economic and social development and on the draft 2001 plan for national economic and social development.* Beijing: National People's Congress.

CHAPTER FIVE

SCHOOLING IN AUSTRALIA

The Interplay of Education, Politics, and Culture

CYNTHIA JOSEPH

MARGRET A. WINZER

VIKKI POLLARD

Cynthia Joseph is a Lecturer in the Faculty of Education at Monash University, Australia. She teaches in the areas of Educational Research Methodology, Sociology of Education, and International Education. Her research specialization is postcolonial feminism of difference. She uses this theoretical lens to research gender, ethnicity, and education, as well as cultural difference and globalization. Cynthia has taught in the schools and in the higher education sector in Malaysia.

Margret Winzer is a professor at the University of Lethbridge, where she teaches in the areas of early childhood education and special education. She has researched and written extensively in these fields, with one stress on comparative studies in special education. Her scholarly achievements are internationally recognized. Most recently, she was awarded her university's Medal for Distinguished Research and Scholarship, and the Division of International Special Education Services of the Council for Exceptional Children honored her with a Lifetime Achievement Award.

Vikki Pollard is currently a Masters of Education student at Monash University. Her thesis, "We Are Women You Know and We Talk Free: Rhizomatic ESL Education with Southern Sudanese Women Living in Melbourne," is an ethics for English as a Second Language teaching. The philosophy of Deleuze and Guattari is put to work to create problems for ESL teaching. The empirical work for this project was an ESL class for women born in Southern Sudan and now residents/citizens of Australia.

Acknowledgements

The authors wish to acknowledge the contributions of Dr. Gaell Hildebrand and Dr. Jane Mitchell of the Faculty of Education, Monash University, in the writing of this chapter.

THE SOCIAL AND POLITICAL FABRIC OF CONTEMPORARY AUSTRALIAN SOCIETY

Australia, the largest island in the world, is also ranked among the largest countries. In land area, it is the sixth largest, following Russia, Canada, China, the United States of America, and Brazil. Geographically, Australia is a relatively isolated nation. About 1,300 miles to the east, across the Pacific Ocean and the Tasman Sea, lies New Zealand. To the north is Papua-New Guinea and West Irian. South from the Australian island state of Tasmania is Antarctica. The closest country to Australia is in the west—the closest point of the Indonesian archipelago is only 90 miles away.

Although the land mass is vast, Australia's population is small. Statistics from the 2001 and 2002 census estimate the current Australian population at 20 million (Australian Bureau of Statistics, 2004). The population tends to cluster on the eastern and southern seaboards. In fact, the 2002 statistics indicated that 63.7 percent of Australians lived in capital cities. More than half of the Australian population is located in the states of New South Wales and Victoria.

The urbanization of the population owes much to the geography of Australia. The entire center is desert, popularly referred to as the "Red Centre," the "outback" or, in Australian jargon, "the back of Burke." The outback's aridity means that cattle ranches are isolated, often hundreds of miles in area.

Because of its geographical location, many people consider Australia to be a part of Asia. Certainly, the country maintains friendly relations with its Asian neighbors (although interactions with Indonesia can be rather strained). Australia also has close ties with the United Kingdom, the source of most immigrants until the 1940s. Trade, defense, and cooperative pacts and treaties with the United States are critically important.

Together with geographical determinants, various historical and current events have shaped the social, cultural, and political aspects of life in Australia. As well, issues to do with globalisation, transnational mobility, migration issues and refugees, and other global, regional, and national events have an impact on the politics and culture of Australian society. Education and schooling, as important social and political institutions, are influenced by the prevailing dominant social ideology. In turn, the tensions and contradictions within the social and political systems impact on Australian schooling and on the education system.

In this chapter, we provide an overview and analysis of contemporary Australian education. We outline the structure of the system; discuss some of the successes, particularly the innovative curricula emerging across the country; and analyse some of the challenges facing Australian education today.

The Political System

Australia is a relatively new country. It was not until 1901 that the founding colonies federated to become the Commonwealth of Australia. January 26 is now celebrated as Australia Day.

The Australian federation consists of six states—New South Wales, Victoria, Queensland, Western Australia, South Australia, and Tasmania. There are also two territories—the

Australian Capital Territory, which is Canberra, the Australian capital and seat of the federal (Commonwealth) government, and the Northern Territory.

Four divisions exist in the system of government: commonwealth, state, territory, and local government. Explicit and far-reaching responsibilities accrue to the commonwealth government. According to the Australian constitution, Canberra holds power in areas of national importance; that is, matters relating to trade and commerce, taxation, postal services, foreign relations, defence, immigration, naturalization, quarantine, currency and coinage, weights and measures, copyright, patents, and trademarks. Even though the states and territories guard their rights jealousy, the commonwealth also has pervasive influence on matters to do with industrial relations, financial regulation, companies and securities, and health and welfare. Of particular salience to the issues addressed in this chapter are the dual responsibilities of states and the federal government in education, from preschool to tertiary.

While the primary responsibility for school education and vocational training lies with the state and territorial governments, Canberra retains responsibilities for the education and training of Aboriginal and Torres Straits Islander peoples, for migrant education, for international partnerships in education, and for assistance for students. At the same time, commonwealth research, mandates, and initiatives are highly influential in diverse areas: for example, innovative curricula, national assessment standards, and proposals for a uniform national school beginning age. Funding for private and Catholic schools is increasingly being assumed by Canberra (although funds for tertiary education are declining dramatically).

Two major Australian federal government departments—the Department of Education, Training, and Youth Affairs (DETYA) and the national Ministerial Council for Education, Employment, Training, and Youth Affairs (MCEETYA)—are responsible for education policy from a national perspective. DETYA ensures that there is national consistency and coherence in the provision of education and training across Australia. Within the structure of MCEETYA, federal and state education ministers for education meet regularly to ensure that the common educational interests of the nation are met through the educational policies and practices in each state.

Australia has two major political parties, Labor and Liberal, and a number of small and generally noninfluential parties. Historically, and at the present, the political climate has been dominated by the contest between the Labor and Liberal parties. The swings in power between these two parties and the discourse of politics exert a major influence on goals, objectives, and reforms in the schooling system.

Ideologically, the Labor party is constructed as a social democratic left-wing party that adopts a critical view to education—it advocates education for the masses and democratic approaches to schooling. In recent years, the Labor party has hearkened to the global discourse on education, which emphasizes economic rationalism and corporate managerialism. It has taken on some of these markers of the managerialist concern for efficiency and effectiveness while holding onto its older agenda about equity (Lingard, Porter, Bartlett, & Knight, 1995; Marginson, 1997). Philosophically, the Liberal party is a right-wing party with a corporate managerialist approach to education. In 2004, the Liberals were returned to power for an unprecedented fourth term.

Each of the six states is governed by a ministry headed by a premier. Each state also has a formal Opposition, with the same role as at the Commonwealth, headed by an Opposition leader. The Australian Capital Territory and the Northern Territory have powers similar to the states.

The People of Australia

Australia began as a penal colony when Britain was forced to establish new convict settlements to replace the north Atlantic colonies after the American War of Independence. Following Captain James Cook's discovery of Australia in 1770, the First Fleet of eleven ships arrived at Botany Bay in January 1788. Half of those on board were convicts.

Convicts were sent to Australia until 1842. But the discovery of economic opportunities and resources such as land and wool, and especially the discovery of gold in Victoria in the 1850s, soon changed the nation. Australia began to develop as a settler society, part of the expansion of the British Empire and Europe.

As a British colony, the United Kingdom was Australia's major and preferred source of immigrants; most settlers were from a British or Irish background (Jupp, 2001). But the gold rushes affected patterns of early migration to Australia and heralded the arrival of many groups.

By the close of the nineteenth century, a combination of factors that included (but were not restricted to) colonial conditions, government policy, impatience with British domination, severe economic depression in the 1890s, a growing sense of Australian identity, the rise of trade unionism, and unease about non-white settlers led to immigration quotas and the eventual White Australia policy. Although Australia was very much a settler society, prior to 1947 its restrictive immigration policies translated into a population that was 89 percent Anglo-Celtic. Only 8.6 percent came from other parts of Europe or were Aboriginal people (Jupp, 2001).

After the Second World War, Australia desperately needed migration. For one thing, compared to the population at the time, large numbers of young Australian men were killed in the war. For another, there existed the need to fill jobs in industry and create an infrastructure.

A formal migration program initiated by the Australian government after the war aimed to bring in over 40,000 new immigrants, preferably from the United Kingdom. However, there were simply not enough British individuals wishing to emigrate, and the original goal of the mass migration program expanded. Of the 6 million migrants, most came from southern Europe, an influx that altered dramatically the cultural and ethnic makeup of the population of Australia. Quotas on immigration were completely abandoned by 1972. It is not then surprising that by 1996 there was a major shift from source countries in Europe to those in Asia (Jupp, 2001).

Nowhere else in the world have the sources of immigrants been so diverse as in Australia (Castles, Kalantzis, Cope, & Morrissey, 1992). In recent years, people from some 200 different countries have made Australia their home. The 2001 statistics estimate that 23.6 percent are overseas-born population: 6.1 percent were born in United Kingdom and Ireland; 12.1 percent come from Europe, including the former USSR; and 5.5 percent were born in East and Southern Asia. That is, almost one in four of Australia's population was born overseas, and 43 percent have one or both parents born overseas. Over 200 languages are spoken in Australia today. English was stated as the only language spoken at home by 80 percent of people in the 2001 census. The three most common languages spoken at home other than English were Chinese languages (2.1 percent), Italian (1.9 percent), and Greek (1.4 percent).

More than 60,000 years before the arrival of European settlers, Aboriginal peoples inhabited most areas of Australia. They lived in distinct groups, each with its own territory, traditions, beliefs, and language. Torres Strait Islander peoples were in Australia and on the islands to the north. Currently, only 2.2 percent of the population are indigenous.

THE SCHOOLING SYSTEM IN AUSTRALIA

Schools emerged quickly after the first white settlement of Australia in 1788. History traces the first schools to the 1820s, established in response to the vast number of children in the colony "going about the streets in a most neglected manner" (Austin, 1963, p. 3). By the middle of the nineteenth century, primary schooling was well established. Comprehensive secondary schooling began in the early 1900s, although it was not consolidated until half a century later (Green, 2003).

When it came to school and who should teach young children and under what religion, divisiveness abounded. Many British colonists believed that "the Church of England was the established Church in that colony" (Austin, 1963, p. 1). Such an assertion was promptly objected to by the Presbyterians, the Roman Catholics, and the Emancipist Party; thus the Anglicans lost their hope for a monopoly in education.

The bickering and animosity between religious groups so prominent throughout the nineteenth century left its mark. In fact, it is not possible to understand current Australian education without acknowledging the deep commitment that religious groups have had, both historically and in the present, toward education, as well as the way in which private and religious agencies have advanced and supplemented (or sometimes hindered) the government system.

With the formation of the federation of Australia in 1901, a full-scale educational infrastructure and its processes developed. Schooling became a state responsibility with state and territorial governments providing most education and training, including the administration and substantial funding of primary and secondary education, and the administration and major funding for vocational education and training. In 2004, the country's six states and two territories provided about 83 percent of the $20.9 billion (Australian) spent in state (public) schools.

The Structure of the System

Australian schooling consists of one or two years of optional preschool, six or seven years of primary schooling, and five or six years of secondary schooling. Years 11 and 12 are the final two years of secondary schooling. The Year 12 qualification is competitive and recognized by all Australian tertiary institutions. The structure of schooling in Australia is shown in Figure 5.1.

School attendance is compulsory for students between the ages of 6 and 15 (or 16 in South Australia and Tasmania). Students who live in remote areas far away from a school have the option of the School of the Air, a correspondence program delivered over short-wave radio and administered by the relevant authorities.

Indigenous students who live in remote communities generally do not have the option to attend government schools. However, in 2003 there were 125,892 indigenous full-time school students, a 3.5 percent increase since 2002. Just over 57 percent of indigenous students attended schools in New South Wales or Queensland (Australian Bureau of Statistics, 2004).

Government and Private Schools

In essence, a dual system of schooling exists in each Australian state—government and nongovernment schools. But the situation is exceedingly complex; in Australia there are actually eight different educational systems.

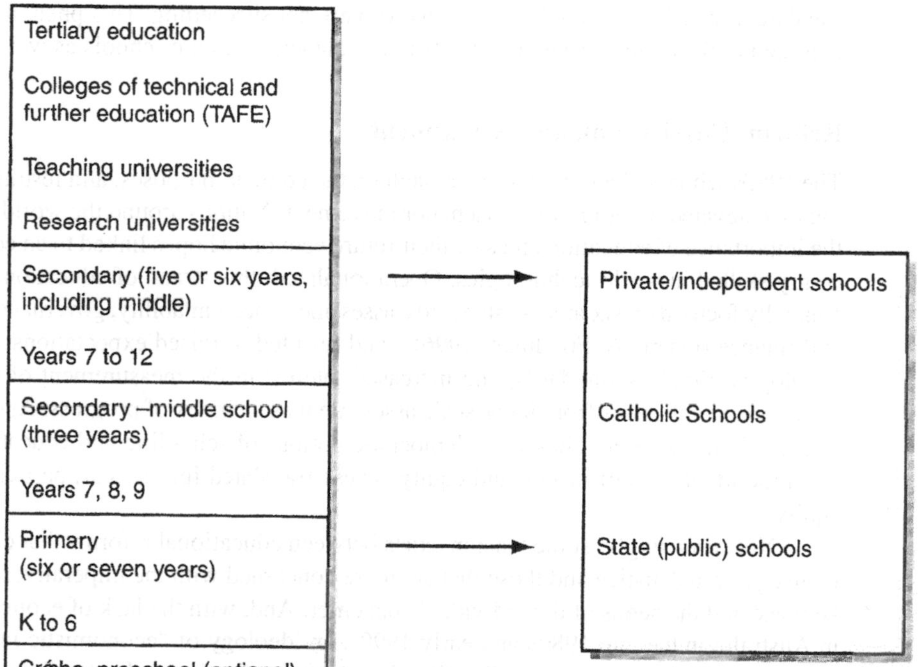

FIGURE 5.1 Structure of the Australian system.

Government schools (state schools) operate as the responsibility of each state government. Each state also has a complex of nongovernment schools that are essentially in two overlapping categories—independent/private schools and Catholic schools. The overlap occurs because some independent schools are elite boarding schools; others are managed by religious denominations and are rooted in religious education.

The Australian Bureau of Statistics (2004) indicated that in August 2003 there were 3,318,620 full-time and 25,858 part-time students attending 9,607 schools in Australia with 225,000 teachers. Of schools, 6,930 (72.1 percent) were government schools and 2,677 (27.9 percent) were nongovernment schools.

By far the largest group of nongovernment schools are operated by the Catholic Church, which has its own school system in each state and territory. The Catholic system of education has 1,600 schools serving 607,000 students, about 18 percent of the country's total, and representing two-thirds of all private schools nationwide.

Both government and nongovernment schools provide a similar education that ensures a uniformity of curriculum in each state (Meadmore, 1999). Research evidence is compelling, however, that private school pupils outperform their peers in government schools. Moreover, even as Catholic schools are financially disadvantaged, their academic performance is not correspondingly poor. They attain better entrance for students to tertiary programs than do government schools.

According to the OECD, Australian schools are performing well by international standards, save for a long tail of students who are not succeeding. This phenomenon is not confined to the public systems; it exists in private and Catholic schools as well.

Reform, Curriculum, and Assessment

The 1980s witnessed an unrelenting assault on the content, purposes, and results of schooling that elevated school reform to a major movement. Nations around the world focused on the importance of education and saw their future economic hopes linked to an educated citizenry skilled in world technologies. Operationalized, this strand of education reform has generally focused on six areas—standards, assessment, accountability, governance, teachers, and finance (Goertz & Friedman, 1996)—and resulted in raised expectations, attempts to develop world-class standards, and increased interest in the measurement of school outcomes using indicators from large-scale assessment as an index of progress. Another strand of the reform movement based on democratic notions of schooling and education emphasized the ideologies of justice and equity. These translated into access, participation, and equity.

Not surprisingly, some tension exists between educational reforms that claim to promote equity and justice and those that are more concerned with the imperatives of the marketplace and the needs of the individual consumer. And, with the lack of economic growth in Australia in the late 1980s and early 1990s, an ideology of "economistic impulse" and "technical efficiency and control" rather than "communicative understanding and emancipation" drove the education system (Lovat & Smith, 2003, p. 223).

Australia has leaned toward the marketing and consumerism of education. It has raised the bar on accountability and excellence based on concerns that declining standards and decreased functional literacy will lead to national vulnerability (see, e.g., Taylor, Rizvi, Lingard, & Henry, 1997).

In recent years, some significant curriculum reforms have emerged in the Australian education system at both state and federal levels. Various parties drive education reform: policymakers, academics and researchers, teachers, parents, and global trends in education reform and educational theory. The curricular reforms, therefore, can be interpreted as different perspectives on the meaning of education and the role of schools.

According to the federal government, the main objectives for Australian schooling in the twenty-first century are "to see a strengthening in the educational foundations of Australia's democratic society, and to ensure that school education does all it can to prepare young Australians for a satisfying life and for careers in a challenging and competitive world environment" (DETYA & DETE, 2001, p.33). In pursuit of these goals, Canberra has endorsed two official discourses—the *National Goals for Schooling in the Twenty-First Century* and the *National Literacy and Numeracy Plan*—both of which bring on new curriculum priorities, namely information technology, vocational education, literacy and numeracy, and civics and citizenship (Smith, 1998). The state governments have funded a significant number of initiatives as well. For example, the states have provided hundreds of millions of dollars in efforts to inspire young Australians to pursue futures in science and thereby boost the nation's capacity for innovation and leading-edge technology.

The goals for schooling in the new century are manifested clearly in the current futures-oriented curriculum reforms that have been developed as most states and territories revise their curriculum frameworks.

In approaching curriculum reform, there was a high level of agreement among stakeholders about the general approach needed. Consensus existed that values should become explicit; that education must better equip students for a world of great change, rapid technological development, and globalization; that students need to be given more chances to increase the depth of their learning, even if that means reducing the content; that more attention needs to be paid to such things as individual learning styles and ability to access information; and that the widespread problem of year 9 and 10 "disengagement" needs to be addressed.

Victoria, Queensland, South Australia, the Northern Territory, and Tasmania have led the way in rethinking the curriculum and have introduced their own "essential learnings." For example, beginning in 2005, the Victorian school curriculum will adopt a new approach to what students learn, how they are assessed, the standards they must meet, and how their progress is reported. Traditional subjects such as math and English will not disappear; nor will they dominate. The new essential learnings framework will group these subjects as core areas but give equal importance to social and personal development and to skills with wide application, such as reasoning and problem solving.

In Queensland, the New Basics Project, considered as one of the most radical examples of systemic curriculum reforms in Australia, not only prepares people to learn with and learn through new technologies but also prepares them to deal with the cultural and community changes that flow from their use (Luke, Matters, Herschell, Grace, Barrett, & Land, 2000). The curriculum seeks to address broad-brush social and technological change; to reduce and revamp the number of subjects in the curriculum through interdisciplinary study; to focus on content that is intellectually engaging and connected to students' lives; and to align curriculum content with pedagogy and assessment (Luke et al., 2000; Mitchell & Murray, 2004).

Important elements of the political and educational discourses in Australia are concerned with the development of accountable systems, taken in terms of both cost effectiveness and learning outcomes. It is inevitable, then, that curricular reform is linked to assessment and standards. Today's system is characterized by the assessment of students and schools, formal testing in basic skills, and reporting programs such as the league tables in the state of Victoria.

This is seen every August when classrooms full of 8- and 9-year-old pupils Australia-wide sit down to a literacy and numeracy examination set by their own state. Designed to monitor children's reading progress, the year 3 literary test varies only slightly between states and territories, with spelling, grammar, and comprehension questions similar to an IQ test. And, although the questions are harder, a similar process is repeated in years 5 and 7.

Middle Years Schooling

In the Australian context, the *middle years* refer to students in grades 6 through 9 (aged 10 to 15 years); that is, the upper years of primary school and the lower years of high school. *Middle schooling* refers to sets of school practices perceived as relevant to students in these grade levels (Mitchell, Kapitzke, Mayer, Carrington, Stevens, Bahr, Pendergast, & Hunter, 2003).

Current research indicates that many students in the Australian middle years of schooling of upper primary and secondary schools are disengaged and achieving below their potential (Carrington, 2004). These findings have stimulated various initiatives at systemic and school levels in both government and nongovernment sectors (Mitchell et al., 2003).

For example, Victoria has the Middle Years Pedagogy Research and Development (MYPRAD) project in collaboration with Deakin University, which aims to analyse current pedagogical practices within middle years classrooms and develop a process to assist teachers to critically reflect on their classroom practices (Department of Education and Training, Victoria, 2003). The state of Queensland is in the process of developing a Middle Years of Schooling policy along with the New Basics Curriculum (Mitchell et al., 2003).

As well, there is a national trend to raise the school leaving age and develop programs to keep young students in some form of flexible education for as long as possible. In 2006 in Queensland and by 2008 in Tasmania, students will stay in school until age 17. Western Australia is considering similar legislation.

Special Education

In late 1972, Australia's Labor government introduced a raft of social legislation and adopted integration as its preferred way of meeting the educational needs of children with disabilities. Today, Australian national and state education authorities advocate the inclusion of students with special needs into general classrooms (Campbell, Gilmore, & Cuskally, 2003).

Australia's special education policies reflect the experiences of North American and European nations (see Jung, Park, Ashman, Givner, & Ochiai, 1997). But while Australian scholars and educational practitioners have responded quickly to international initiatives, Ashman (1997) points out that "Special education in Australia has a national character that has developed independently of overseas innovations" (p. 14). However, inclusion policies do not follow singular or consistently agreed-upon frameworks, and each Australian state approaches implementation differently.

Australian and international anti-discrimination legislation together with the policies of various state governments on social justice, anti-discrimination, and equity have had significant influence on educational provisions for students with special needs (Westwood, 2001). But despite an abundance of political and educational discourses, a plethora of state reports and recommendations, and a wealth of general education law, Forlin and Forlin (1998) point out that there is still no legal mandate to ensure that integration or inclusive education occurs. Support for integration is expressed in all states' education policies, with varying degrees of enforceability (Dempsey, Land, & Foreman, 1995).

The language used in the field of special education has changed dramatically in the last half century, with terms referring to students' school addresses moving from *integration* to *mainstreaming* to *inclusion.* In general in Australia, inclusive philosophy and contemporary lexicon mirrors the state of Victoria's Meyer report (2001), which defined *inclusion* as "the term used to articulate the rights of students with disabilities, impairments and learning difficulties to participate in the full range of programs and services and to use any facilities provided by the education system" (p. 7). Under this definition, advocates have not argued for the elimination of special settings. It is not proposed that children with disabilities be automatically integrated in general classrooms, but rather that a range of options should be available to them in order to ensure that they are in "the most advantageous environment" (Gow, Ward, Balla, & Snow, 1988, p. 7). A complex of special schools thrives alongside inclusive programs. In Victoria, for example, 88 special schools are in operation.

ISSUES IN AUSTRALIAN EDUCATION

As in any system, many important issues challenge contemporary Australian education. Who pays, for whom, and how much form a fundamental crux of controversy.

From 1995 to 2000 (the most recent figures) public and private spending on schools increased as a proportion of gross domestic product. Australia now ranks third of OECD countries, spending well above the average. That represents a substantial increase in real spending, including a dramatic increase in government spending per school student. Nevertheless, funding spills over to affect many issues, some discussed briefly below.

Marketing Education

As we pointed out, reform efforts have shown two major threads. On the one side is knowledge, competition, schools as training grounds for excellence, and responsiveness to social and economic mandates. On the other is commitment to democratic principles of diversity, inclusiveness, and personal development. In many nations today, however, when efforts in school reform are operationalized, often a conservative fiscal reasoning dominates. For example, international agencies such as the OECD have been important in proselytizing a microeconomic version of human capital theory, new managerialism, and spreading a new rationalization through the development of global educational performance indicators (see Lingard, 2001).

In the early 1990s, a free market economic agenda for public education was introduced within the education system in Australia (Meadmore, 1999). While curriculum decisions and testing programs became more centralized, schools became more autonomous in relation to personnel and budgeting and more responsible for generating their own funding to supplement government funding. Hence, as Lingard (2001) writes, "schooling systems have been restructured along managerialist lines and schools have become more competitive with each other in a quasi-market environment" (p. 13). And, as schools witness a shift from liberal or progressive values to a more conservative marketplace approach, raising achievement has emerged as the leitmotif of educational discourse. Meadmore (1999) observed that "The major benefits which education is seen to provide for society are those which can be measured by calculable outputs" (p. 93).

Government and Private Schools

Government schooling is usually construed as free schooling. However, Meadmore (1999) points out that in Australia "Even the fundamental issue of free instruction in government schools has been redefined as schools struggle to balance their budgets as a result of reduced government funding" (p. 95). Today, fees must be charged for some elective subjects in schools and parents may have to assume the costs of computer use, school visits, and sports equipment.

Catholic schools educate about one in five children in Australia. As nongovernment schools, they are mainly commonwealth funded, but this differs from independent nongovernment schools. Catholic schools are not funded individually but through a lump sum to the state and territory Catholic Education Commissions, which then distribute the money to individual schools as they see fit. At the most general level, Catholic schools are funded at about 56 percent of government-school student-funding levels. The remainder is gathered from fees and fund raising.

But Catholic schools may be at a critical point. The overall demands on schools to provide high-quality education, the rise of mass secondary education, the decline in religious orders, and the limited ability of Catholic communities to support schools financially have placed huge pressures on the Catholic system. For low-income families, access to Catholic schools has declined due to the rising costs of attendance (Pascoe, 2004).

There has always been considerable debate in Australia about private schooling. This occurs in part because private schools are usually religious schools, in part because such schools are seen to reproduce unequal social relations, and in part because many hold that "It is not the responsibility of governments to fund private schools or persons using private schools" (Cobbold, 2004).

For nongovernment schools, both Catholic and private, Canberra is adopting a policy by which it increasingly takes the lead in funding; it provides about 35 percent of nongovernmental school funding. This type of government funding emerged in the 1970s (Meadmore, 1999). The initial policy was designed to assist needy schools; however, subsequent programs provide funding to all nongovernment schools, including wealthy and privileged elite schools. In fact, funding to the nongovernment school sector has doubled since the budget of 1996–1997, although the proportion of children it represents has increased by only 10 percent. The arguments are that government is underwriting the costs of educating students who might otherwise be attending government schools and has provided parents with greater choice by making private schools affordable to a wider range of families.

Criticisms of government funding abound. One argument holds that nongovernment (and some government) schools are in a position to choose parents and students and can adopt selection criteria to determine which students are accepted. Most government schools are less prestigious than nongovernment schools and are at the mercy of the marketplace.

Others adopt a more philosophical stance and contend that the school split enhances differentiation on the basis of social class and confirms the hierarchical nature of Australian education. Meadmore (1999), for example, claims that an "under class" of schools is being created through the economic policies currently being implemented and that "it appears that this approach will further open the gap between the 'haves' and others in Australia, placing the most vulnerable students (working class, Indigenous, migrant) at further risk in an education system which is becoming more inequitable" (p. 96). On a like theme, Gronn (2000) argues that a meritocratic elite in Australia is reproduced and groomed through a small number of prestigious schools. He produced statistical analyses to show that those who hold positions of relative power in Australia have come from a handful of elite schools. Similarly, Western (2000) contends that "educational institutions continue to play a central role in processes of class formation and the distribution of social inequality" (p. 91). As one route for gaining access to the middle class is through university education, as university is more accessible for those from middle-class backgrounds who attended private schools, and as the economic changes to fees structure at universities also privilege those already wealthy, Western concludes that higher education reproduces class inequality.

Tertiary Education

Scholars, policymakers, and media commentators tend to agree that higher education has been undergoing significant transformations over the past two or three decades. These transformations are usually attributed to the intermingling of sociocultural, political, and economic processes that have global as well as local scope. Australia is not immune and has witnessed vast changes in terms of attendance and privatization, among other factors.

On the Australian landscape, mounting numbers are becoming involved in higher education. Year 12 retention rates have improved, aspirations for tertiary training have increased, and the growth in the population of university-aged persons has increased. The time to earn a degree has lengthened, research and graduate work enrollments have increased much more than undergraduate enrollments, and double degrees have become common for undergraduates (Davis, 2004).

But as aspirations soar, Canberra's share of university funding has declined. Public income for universities is already below average levels of the United Kingdom and Canada and approaching U.S. public universities in the low proportion of university funding from government appropriations (Davis, 2004).

Commonwealth support now accounts for only 40 percent or less of university income (Davis, 2004). Domestic students pay most of the costs of their education—up to 85 percent in law and 74 percent in business. A recent survey found that one in five students was forced to pull out of courses or fail as the demand to earn money through part-time work took a heavy toll on study time (Cassidy, 2004).

As universities seek new sources of income, there is a gradual privatization of public universities from within and a reliance on entrepreneurial activity. One route is to establish teaching-only universities within Australia and offshore. The more familiar way is through international students. Currently, nearly one in four undergraduates is drawn from overseas. If the trend continues, by 2025 more than 1 million international students will study at Australian universities either on- or offshore. Education exports will rise to $38 billion Australian a year (Davis, 2004).

The Teaching Force

About 225,000 teachers are employed in Australian schools. Australian teachers are very highly unionized. Contracts are negotiated by the state so that income levels do not vary greatly across the country or between government and nongovernment schools.

At the moment, a major national debate rages over the "crisis of masculinity" in schools. Over the past two decades, the overall number and percentage of male primary teachers has decreased steadily. Between 1984 and 2002, the overall number of male primary teachers fell from 26,949 to 23,885 (from 29.68 percent to 20.87 percent). At the same time, the number of men enrolling in primary teacher courses has increased, but the number of men completing their courses has significantly declined. Moreover, while the percentage of male teachers employed in Australian government schools has declined, the number and percentage in non-Catholic private schools has increased.

In the belief that the quality of teachers is the most important feature of the education system affecting student outcomes, increasing the incentives has become a key policy initiative in Australia. Innovative approaches are in place to induce men into the elementary teaching force.

In Australia, 50 percent of teachers leave in their first five years. School-based factors included teachers being forced to teach outside their area of expertise, lack of support and sometimes alienation from school leaders and colleagues, and insufficient information about the teaching and learning plans used by previous teachers.

Indigenous People

For Indigenous Australians, the founding of the modern Australian nation disrupted their traditional way of life; it led to death, disease, and dispossession (Jupp, 2001). The Aboriginal people, perceived by European colonist settlers as primitive, less intelligent, and culturally and genetically inferior, were dispossessed of their lands. Many were massacred, and many died of introduced disease and starvation (Malin, 1998).

Moreton-Robinson (1999) argues that "the relationship between the white center and Indigenous people at the margins of Australian society has been a feature of colonialism since its appearance at Botany Bay in 1788 to the present" (p. 34). To some extent, the power relations between the indigenous people and the majority have changed over time, but this group remains still the most marginalized, unfairly disadvantaged, and at risk.

There is still a great need to address the wide gap between Indigenous Australians and mainstream Anglo-Celtic Australians in education, health, and employment. There is also the necessity to address the roots of social dysfunction through continued support for alcohol management plans, engaging families in money management, and continuing to tackle passive welfare, a process sometimes called *practical reconciliation* in the Australian lexicon.

Not much was done for the education of Aboriginal children during the period from 1788 to 1950. In general, these children were not allowed to attend public schools. Some Aboriginal children were removed from their families and civilized by exposure to English, basic literacy, and Christianity (Malin, 1998, p. 343). Children of mixed descent were assimilated into European ways through orphanages or missionaries.

During the 1950s and 1960s, Aboriginal children were assimilated into mainstream schools that adopted an Anglo-Celtic culture and schooling system that nevertheless failed to accommodate to the languages, cultures, and ways of Aboriginal peoples. It was not until 1972 that Aboriginal affairs were given significant attention and funding through various programs and initiatives such as the state Aboriginal Education Consultative Committee and the National Aboriginal Education Committee. About seventeen small, independent, Aboriginal-controlled community schools around Australia then developed (Malin, 1998).

Pearson (2004) describes indigenous education as a "massive disaster." Another report (Ministerial Council on Education, Employment, Training, and Youth Affairs, 2000) observed that the scale of educational inequality remains vast for Australia's Aboriginal and Torres Straits Islander peoples and continues, despite considerable work particularly over the last decade by all governments.

For Indigenous Australian children, both the federal and state governments give importance to education in terms of funding, access to schooling and higher education, literacy levels and skills, languages, improving school attendance rates and retention rates, and improving resources. There is also a call from Indigenous Australians and other educators for the integration of Australian Indigenous contributions and experiences in Australia's past, present, and future into the mainstream curriculum.

Multiculturalism

Contemporary Australian society is usually depicted as a melting pot of different cultures. Into the 1960s, the official discourse of migrant settlement was assimilation, based on the nation's supposedly shared British roots and the concept of an Australian national identity.

Ideas about integration emerged in the 1970s (Jupp, 2001). These led to a policy of multiculturalism that favored an inclusionary, pluralist, and equitable recognition of the diverse ethnic groups living within the boundaries of the nation. It presumed that migrant communities were able to create and preserve their own way of life and heritage, while partaking in the general life of the nation, which was predominantly Anglo-Celtic (Jupp, 2001).

Where this multicultural policy would seem to be a response to the failure of the policy of assimilation, there was still a dominant Anglo-Celtic culture in the various government, political, and social machineries and institutions. Although policies and reports such as the *National Agenda for a Multicultural Australia* (OMA, 1989), the *Native Title Act* (1993), and the *Report of the National Inquiry into Racist Violence* (Human Rights and Equal Opportunities Commission, 1991) provided an official discourse in addressing the cultural and social differences within Australian society, there was a backlash against multiculturalism in the late-1990s. Again, assimilation is seen as the most desirable approach to cultural difference.

CONCLUSION

Australians cannot but be aware that they live in changing times. Politically, the Liberal Party, led by John Howard, has won four elections in a row. Socially, Australia remains a settler country for large numbers of immigrants from many countries. Within the education system, global and national objectives have resulted in broad reforms that include innovative curriculum designs, standards testing, and locating schools within a competitive, market-oriented environment.

In general, Australian educators and legislators seek to ensure that students grow up to be happy and productive citizens in an increasingly globalized, multicultural, and technological society. Many tensions exist in the school system, perhaps the most lasting and prominent are the public–government school split and the concerns about social class and mobility that link to pragmatic problems regarding school funding.

REFERENCES

Ashman, A. (1997). Australia. In D. Y. Jung, H. C. Park, A. F. Ashman, C. C., Givner, & T. Ochiai (Eds.), *Integration of students with disabilities into regular schools in Korea, Australia, Japan, and the United States* (pp. 96–157). Korea: Korean Institute for Special Education.

Austin, A. G. (1963). *Select documents in Australian Education 1788–1900.* Melbourne: Pittman Publishing.

Australian Bureau of Statistics (2004). *Australian Year Book 2004.* Accessed October 20, 2004, from http://www.abs.gov.au

Campbell, J., Gilmore, L., & Cuskally, M. (2003). Changing student teachers' attitudes towards disability and inclusion. *Journal of Intellectual and Developmental Disability, 28,* 369–380.

Carrington, V. (2004). Mid-term review: The middle years of schooling. *Curriculum Perspectives, 24,* 30–41.

Cassidy, F. (2004, September 8). High costs force students to abandon university. *The Canberra Times.*

Castles, S., Kalantzis, M., Cope, W., & Morrissey, M. (1992). *Mistaken identity: Multiculturalism and the demise of nationalism in Australia.* Sydney: Pluto Press.

Cobbold, T. (2004). http://www.acsso.org.au/ACSSOis.htm, accessed October 20, 2004; http://www.acsso.org.au/hot3.htm, accessed October 20, 2004; http://www.acsso.org.au/elect04.htm#facts, accessed October 20, 2004.

Davis, G. (2004, November 22). *Tiers or tears? The regulation of Australian higher education.* The inaugural Melbourne political lecture, University of Melbourne.

Dempsey, L., Land, J., & Foreman, P. (1995). Trends and influences in the integration of students with disabilities in Australia. *The Australasian Journal of Special Education, 19,* 47–53.

Department of Education and Training, State Government Victoria. (2003). *Blueprint for government schools: Future directions for education in the Victorian government school system.* Melbourne: Author.

Department of Education, Training and Youth Affairs (DETYA) and the South Australian Department of Education, Training and Employment (DETE). (2001). *The development of education: National report of Australia.* Canberra: Author.

Forlin, P., & Forlin, C. (1998). Constitutional and legislative framework for inclusive education in Australia. *Australian Journal of Education, 42,* 204–217.

Goertz, M., & Friedman, D. (1996) *State education reform and students with disabilities: A preliminary analysis.* New Brunswick, NJ: Rutgers University Consortium on Policy Research in Education and Center for Policy Research on the Impact of General and Special Education Reform.

Gow, L., Ward, J., Balla J., & Snow, D. (1988). Directions for integration in Australia: Overview of a report to the Commonwealth Schools Commission. Part 2. *The Exceptional Child, 35,* 5–22.

Green, W. (2003). Curriculum inquiry in Australia: Toward a local genealogy of the curriculum field. In W. Pinar (Ed., *International handbook of curriculum research.* Mahevah, NJ: Erlbaum.

Gronn, P. (2000). From lucky country to clever country: Leadership, schooling and the formation of Australian elites. In T. Seddon & L. Angus (Eds.), *Beyond nostalgia: Reshaping Australian education.* Melbourne: Australian Council of Educational Research.

Jung, D. V., Park, H. C., Ashman, A. F., Givner, C. C., & Ochiai, T. (1997). *Integration of students with disabilities with regular schools in Korea, Australia, Japan, and the United States.* Korea: Korea Institute for Special Education.

Jupp, J. (Ed). (2001). *The Australian people: An encyclopedia of the nation, its people and their origins.* Cambridge, UK: Cambridge University Press.

Lingard, B. (2001). Some lessons for educational researchers: Repositioning research in education and education in research. *Australian Educational Researcher, 28*(3), 1–46.

Lingard, B., Porter, P., Bartlett, L., & Knight, J. (1995). Federal/state mediations in the Australian national education Agenda: From the AEC to MCEETYA 1987–1993. *Australian Journal of Education, 39*(1), 41–66.

Lovat, T. J., & Smith, D. L. (2003). *Curriculum: Action on reflection.* Sydney: Social Science Press.

Luke, A., Matters, G., Herschell, P., Grace, N., Barrett, R., & Land, R. (2000). *New Basics Project: Technical paper.* Brisbane, Australia: Education Queensland.

Malin, M. (1998). Aboriginal education, policy and teaching. In E. Hatton (Ed.), *Understanding teaching.* Sydney: Harcourt-Brace.

Marginson, S. (1997). *Educating Australia: Government, economy and citizen since 1960.* Cambridge, UK: Cambridge University Press.

Meadmore, P. (1999). Education at what price? In D. Meadmore, B. Burnett, & P. O'Brien (Eds.), *Understanding education: Contexts and agendas for the new millennium.* Sydney: Prentice-Hall.

Meyer, L. H. (2001, February). *Victoria Department of Education: Employment and training review of the program for students with disabilities and impairments.* Report submitted to the Director, Office of School Education.

Ministerial Council on Education, Employment, Training and Youth Affairs (2000). *Achieving educational equality for Australia's Aboriginal and Torres Strait Islander peoples: A discussion paper.* Canberra: Author.

Mitchell, J., Kapitzke, C., Mayer, D., Carrington, V., Stevens, L., Bahr, N., Pendergast, D., & Hunter, L. (2003). Aligning school reform and teacher education reform in the middle years: An Australian case study. *Teacher education, 14*(1), 69–82.

Mitchell, J., & Murray, S. (2004). *Connecting educational research, policy and practice: Reform in Queensland state schools.* Seminar presented to the Faculty of Education Research Seminars, Monash University, Australia.

Moreton-Robinson, A. (1999). Unmasking whiteness: A. Goor Jondal's look at Duggai business. In B. McKay (Ed.), *Unmasking whiteness: Race relations and reconciliation.* Queensland: Griffith University.

Pascoe, S. (2004, August 30). Critical time for Catholic education. *The Australian.*

Pearson, N. (2004, September 13). Urgent need to raise quality bar. *The Australian.*

Smith, C. (1998, July). Not so common goals. *The AEU News,* p. 17.

Taylor, S., Rizvi, F., Lingard, B., & Henry, M. (1997). Educational policy and the politics of change. London: Routledge.

Western, M. (2000). Competition, education and class formation. In T. Seddon, & L. Angus (Eds.), *Beyond nostalgia: Reshaping Australian education.* Melbourne: Australian Council of Educational Research.

Westwood, P. (2001). *Integration of handicapped children in South Australia.* Magill: SACAE.

Part III

THE MIDDLE EAST AND SOUTHWEST ASIA

Progress in the Face of Unresolved Struggles

CHAPTER SIX

PALESTINE'S EDUCATION SYSTEM

Challenges, Trends, and Issues

SAMIR J. DUKMAK

Palestine is a small country in the Middle East. Its boundaries are Lebanon and Syria to the north, Jordan to the east, the Mediterranean Sea to the west, and the Red Sea in the south. However, in spite of its size and small population, it is a very well-known country. The long-standing, and continuing, struggles of Palestinians for dignity and freedom have saturated international media coverage, and held the attention of national and international bodies, for generations. This chapter discusses contemporary education in Palestine within the context of these struggles.

NOTES ON TERMINOLOGY

Given the ongoing political problems in Palestine, it makes sense to provide some explanations regarding terms and concepts that appear before proceeding further into this chapter. The terms *Palestine, West Bank, Gaza Strip,* and *East Jerusalem* are used in this chapter

Samir Dukmak has worked in the Bethlehem Arab Society for Rehabilitation (BASR) in Bethlehem city of Palestine as a community projects coordinator for almost ten years. His work in this period entailed the setup and development of community special education centers in the greater Bethlehem region. The training and supervision of special education teachers was one of his major duties during these years. He completed his undergraduate studies in psychology and sociology at the University of Bethlehem in Palestine and received his Ph.D. from the University of Manchester in England. He is now an Assistant Professor in the Special Education Department at the United Arab Emirates University. His major research interests are in integration and inclusive education, comparative studies in education and special education, teacher education, intellectual disabilities, policy and practice in special education, assessment in special education, and attitudes toward people with special needs. His current research topics include the teaching effectiveness of special education teachers in the United Arab Emirates, styles of teaching among special education teachers in the United Arab Emirates, and social problems among children with reading disabilities in the United Arab Emirates.

to indicate the Palestinian land that has been occupied by the Israelis since 1967. The land that has been occupied since 1948, that is called *Israel* nowadays, is also referred to in this chapter. The Palestinians who live in Israel are herein referred to as *Palestinian Israelis, Arab Israelis,* or *Palestinian Arabs.* (Other Palestinians, who are scattered across Middle-Eastern countries and internationally, are not the subject of this chapter.)

The word *Intifada* in this chapter means the "Uprising," and there are references to two uprisings—the "the first Intifada" and "the new Intifada." The first Intifada indicates the uprising that was started against Israeli occupation in December 1987 and ended in 1993. The new Intifada indicates the uprising that has been going on against Israeli occupation since September 2000.

THE SOCIAL FABRIC

Life under Occupation

Palestinians have never had a national government, as they have been occupied for hundreds of years. Palestine was under Turkish rule for four centuries (1517–1917). Then, immediately after World War I (and as a consequence of it), Palestine, along with other Arab countries, was subjected to the British Mandate. At the same time, Arabs and Jews in Palestine were involved in a continuous war that started on a semi-organized basis in the 1920s and escalated after that. The most noticeable fighting periods were the late 1930s and the late 1940s.

Arabs were the majority in Palestine until 1948, when they suddenly became a dominated minority in their own land. The British Mandate over Palestine, which lasted for three decades, ended in 1948. In May of that year, Israel was established as a Jewish state on the major portion of Palestinian land. The remainder belonged to Egypt (Gaza Strip) and to Jordan (the West Bank).

When the British evacuated Palestine, Israel was declared a Jewish state. However, 156,000 Arabs remained within the boundaries of the newly created state (the Israeli-Arab part). And, although war had ended or, at least, seemed to have ended, mutual mistrust continued.

One of the consequences of Jewish mistrust was the subjection of the Arab minority to military administration, which lasted until 1966. Military administration meant, among other things, curfews and special permits for most Arabs to be able to leave their villages and towns to look for jobs, education, and trade (Maari, 1978). Later, during the first Intifada that started in 1987, the Palestinians suffered more than six years of conflicts, confrontations, and torture, which led many Palestinians to be detained, injured, disabled, and/or killed.

In 1994, the Palestinian people had to accept the Oslo Agreement. The terms of the agreement greatly favored the Israelis; however, the Palestinians hoped that this agreement would finally bring an end to their suffering. Unfortunately, it merely exposed them to a different form of suffering. Palestinians were virtually locked up in their cities (so called "self-ruled areas"); they were denied the freedom to move freely between cities and villages. On many occasions, the Palestinians were not even allowed to move between those cities ruled by the Palestinian Authority. Furthermore, all Palestinian people who lived outside Jerusalem were not allowed to go to Jerusalem, or any other place ruled by the Israelis, unless they had a special permit from the Israeli authorities. Since the first Intifada, success in obtaining such a permit constitutes a miracle—the vast majority of Palestinians (more than 95 percent) cannot get one.

Today, unemployment is a major problem caused by the permanent closing of the self-ruled areas. For example, unemployment is currently over 50 percent; two-thirds of the population is below the poverty line and lives on less than US$2 per day, and in the West Bank and Gaza Strip commodities as basic as food are beyond many families. The inevitable result is rising malnutrition rates, particularly among children (Islamic Relief, 2005). Thus, contemporary Palestinian society is a very low-income society in terms of its social and economic characteristics. Indeed, present-day Palestine could be viewed as a member of the Third World countries, because it shares similar problems.

The most recent, and morally incomprehensible, manifestation of Israeli occupation is the ongoing construction of "The Wall." In June 2002, Israel began erecting a formidable physical barrier to physically seal off Palestinians in the West Bank, East Jerusalem, and Gaza once and for all. Appropriately, it is often referred to as "Israel's Apartheid Wall." When finished, the wall could extend 750 kilometers. It consists of a series of 25-foot high concrete walls, trenches, barbed wire, and electrified fencing. The design includes numerous watchtowers, electronic sensors, thermal imaging and video cameras, unmanned aerial vehicles, sniper towers, and roads for patrol vehicles (Palestine Monitor, 2005).

Significantly, the path of the wall does not follow the so-called "Green Line"—the internationally recognized border that existed between Israel and the West Bank until the war of 1967. In some places the wall will cut deep into the West Bank—as much as six kilometers inside the Green Line. The ongoing destruction of homes, confiscation of land, isolation of families, restrictions on free movement, and so on, is having a disastrous effect on Palestinians (Palestine Monitor, 2005). Yet, incredibly, this latest, massive, and cruel manifestation of the severity of Israeli occupation and oppression receives little media attention in the West.

Demography

The current population of Palestine is estimated to be about 3.7 million. It is estimated that about 2.3 million people live in the West Bank and 1.4 million in the Gaza Strip. Importantly, there is an additional Palestinian population of approximately 1 million living within Israel (Arabic News, 2005).

Religion

The present-day religious culture of Palestine is largely Islamic. Christians, who formed the majority in the land before the advent of Islam in the seventh century, have contributed significantly to the historical development of Palestinian society. However, after the Crusade period (which began in the twelveth century), Christians became a minority in Palestine—mainly living in Galilee, Ramleh, Ramallah, Jerusalem, and Bethlehem.

During the twentieth century, as a result of migration, the number of Christians rapidly declined. For example, before the Israeli invasion of Palestine in 1967, the number of Christians in the Bethlehem area was about 100,000; today, it is about 40,000. Many hundreds of thousands of Christian Palestinians presently live abroad, primarily in the Americas. Currently, about 2 percent of the Palestinians living in the West Bank, East Jerusalem, and Gaza Strip are Christians. They belong to different churches, including Roman Catholic, Greek Orthodox, and Greek Catholic communities, and to a lesser extent, various Protestant, Syriac, and Armenian churches (Freres School, 2000).

Social Services

Abu-Shokor (1990) argues that poverty in Palestine during the decades of occupation has been roughly in line with other developing countries. Health conditions provide a good indicator. During the period of the Israeli occupation that started in 1948 and continued until 1994, there was no infrastructure to provide people with health services. The Israeli occupying powers were instrumental in keeping health services for all Palestinian people in a very poor condition, and they did not provide Palestinians with any social security benefits. This was reflected in a neglect of primary health care, a lack of adequate health insurance plans, and insufficient and unequal distribution of health services (Ballantyne, 1988). Moreover, many health agencies and institutions in the West Bank and Gaza Strip agree that the quality and quantity of health and social services that were provided by the Israeli government before the Palestinian Authority took over these responsibilities deteriorated after 1980.

In summary, Palestinians were served (until 1994) either through the Israeli Health System at a minimal level, or through private charitable health institutions. For registered refugees, the United Nations Relief and Works Agency (UNRWA) administered the refugee camps and provided all refugees with health, education, and welfare services (UNRWA, 1990). In contrast to the Israeli system, UNRWA was reported as offering significantly better services, although these were still far from adequate (Benevenisti, 1984).

The Palestinian Authority is not yet a government and has not yet managed to improve health and social services for Palestinians. The Palestinian National Authority (PNA), together with some private charitable health institutions, has been serving people since 1994. But, following the new Intifada that has been continuing since September 2000, the situation is far worse, and poverty has greatly increased.

THE SOCIAL AND HISTORICAL CONTEXT OF PALESTINIAN SCHOOLING

The historical, political, socioeconomic, sociocultural, and demographic background information must be considered as important factors to understanding any education system. When Palestine is addressed, the education system must be seen as functioning in a society that belongs to two conflicting entities at the same time—to Israel and to the Palestinians (Maari, 1978). Therefore, the Palestinian educational system in any region of Palestine has to operate within this fragmented sociocultural and psychological situation.

Before moving on to discuss current legislation and policies in education (which are not many), it is very important to give a clear historical description of the legislation and policies that were carried out by several occupying powers in the country over the past century.

British Mandate

A long time before the British Mandate, Ibrahim Basha, a Palestinian leader, initiated an education policy in Palestine that included widespread development of education in the country. However, when the British occupied Palestine in 1917, the educational movement that had been started was greatly affected. The establishment of new schools in Palestinian villages was forbidden and, in many instances, schools were closed because they did not cooperate with the British authorities.

Ironically, this suppression elevated education to a central point in Palestinian thought and behavior and led the Palestinians to establish their own schools and provide them with teachers. This was willingly done by the Palestinians, even though the costs for a poor people were formidable. For example, the cost to the Palestinians to establish schools between 1941 and 1945 was about half a million dollars; the British government contributed less than $100,000 toward the establishment of new schools in the country in the same period.

At this time, the attitude toward education in Palestinian society was the most positive one among Arabs in the Arab world. For example, in 1945/1946, 10 percent of the Palestinian people attended schools, while 3.4 percent, 5 percent, and 2.4 percent of the population in Iraq, Syria, and Jordan, respectively, attended schools in that year. In 1946/1947, the percentage of Palestinians who attended schools reached 15.7 percent; this was the highest percentage in the Arab world, second only to Lebanon (Al-Nimer, 1993).

Israeli Occupation

After the Israeli occupation of the larger part of Palestine in 1948, education became more and more important for the Palestinians, especially for those who became refugees. However, and unfortunately, Palestinians further lost control of their education system because many educated Palestinians emigrated. That is, the Israeli intrusions fragmented the Palestinian people and led many Palestinians to leave to search for jobs in other countries. In Saudi Arabia alone, educated Palestinians formed 90 percent of teachers in Saudi schools (Al-Nimer, 1993).

Responsibility for education was handed to various bodies, so that a number of authorities supervised education. Most important were the Israeli authorities and the United Nations Relief and Work Agencies (UNRWA) (which was considered as an international relief agency by face, and an American agency by heart).

In order to control the Palestinians easily, the Israelis tried hard to create educational policies toward that end. But, the Israeli authorities soon realized that the best thing they could do was *not* to form a clear policy (Maari, 1978). In fact, the lack of policy on education in Palestinian schools, in the whole country in general, and in the Israeli part in particular became a policy in itself. The Israelis neglected education among the Palestinians according to a plan aimed at converting the greater part of Palestinian students to ignorant people, thereby decreasing their national and political consciousness. They did not emphasize the basics of primary education for Palestinians, in order to keep them in the elementary stage with a minimum education (although, of course, primary education was strongly emphasized for Israeli students).

The Israeli occupation policies greatly affected the curriculum used in the country—it made it a lot worse. For example, the education system in the West Bank was affiliated with the Jordanian system (the curriculum that was used in the West Bank was introduced during the Jordanian rule of the country before 1967). The Israelis refused to carry out any modifications on the curriculum, although it was reviewed, modified, and changed many times in Jordan after 1967. In the Gaza Strip, the education system was affiliated with Egypt.

In 1994/1995 there was a transfer of responsibility for education in the West Bank and the Gaza Strip from the Israeli government to the newly established Palestinian Authority. However, while the Palestinian Authority now has responsibility for education in the West Bank and Gaza Strip, little legislation and few policies have been established. But, there is some progress. The Palestinian Authority is working on setting up a compulsory education policy and supportive education programs for children with low achievement in schools. Furthermore, the Ministry of Education has implemented an inclusive education program that emphasizes including children with disabilities in the mainstream system of education (a brief description of this program is highlighted later in this chapter). Changing the curriculum, increasing the number of schools, upgrading the skills of existing teachers, and creating more newly qualified ones are other elements that the Palestinian Ministry of Education is currently working on. But, progress is painfully slow. The reality is that the deteriorating political situation, and the ongoing unrest, make it inevitable that all of these modifications and changes will go very slowly.

SCHOOLING

A Cautionary Note on Data

One of the many frustrations in trying to accurately depict the state of education in any region of the world that is subject to tremendous poverty, instability, political turmoil, and military conflict is the lack of reliable and current data. Statistics on any aspect of education are simply not available in turbulent regions; they are not routinely gathered because authorities do not have the financial and human resources to meet basic education needs—let alone compile documentary information on schools and schooling. Palestine falls precisely into this category.

Certainly, the level of chaos for educators and students in Palestine is overwhelming. (It must be remembered that—as noted at the beginning of this chapter—the first Intifada ended in 1993, and a new Intifada against the Israeli occupation has been going since September 2000.) To western educators, the situation described by the Palestinian Minister of Education and Higher Education in 2002 is likely incomprehensible. In his "Appeal . . . in the Occasion of Opening the New School Year (02/03)," he notes how the "experience from the last school year is not encouraging at all." Why? He recounts: 216 students and 17 teachers killed; 2,514 students injured; 1,289 schools closed for three weeks; half of Palestinian students and 87,000 university students were not able to reach their schools; the Final Secondary Examination (*Tiwjihi*) took over a month to administer because of disruptions; inability to finance resources as basic as textbooks and furniture; inability to repair schools damaged by the fighting in Palestine; and families so poor that they cannot afford to send their children to school (Hommous, 2002). "Not encouraging" indeed!

The Palestinian situation is further complicated by the fact that the Palestinian Authority took over responsibility for education in the West Bank and Gaza Strip in 1994. Not only did this have immediate consequences for funding and personnel, but the economic and political situation since 1994 has deteriorated sharply and government priorities quickly became, of necessity, focused elsewhere. Simply providing adequate education services, let alone gathering statistical information on schools and schooling, became impossible.

The Palestinian Central Bureau of Statistics readily acknowledges this. In August 2003, it reported on the state of gathering statistical data in Palestine. The analysis is not encouraging. But a few major points were made: Most institutions do not even have strategic plans for gathering data, and there is a lack of coordination among institutions, a chronic lack of adequate funding, continuing political turmoil, and lack of technology and trained personnel (Palestinian Central Bureau of Statistics, 2003, pp. 4–5).

Accordingly, since 1994, there really is no database; there are only estimates and insights by people knowledgeable about the situation in Palestine. Accordingly, what follows relies on a data baseline dating back to the mid-1990s, with an extrapolation of trends into today based on the author's experience and knowledge.

Administration

Administratively, the current directorates of education are divided into two types—governmental and UNRWA. The governmental directorates directly supervise government schools in the West Bank and Gaza Strip, follow up on private education, issue permissions needed for the inauguration of private kindergartens and schools, and control curriculum and the extent to which schools meet the required conditions and the circumstances of the educational process (Abu-Libdeh, 1995). In each of the government directorates, there is an office of the Ministry of Education that is responsible for carrying out various activities locally, including directly supervising schools, student enrollment, appointments and transfer of teachers, and school budgets.

The main task of UNRWA directorates of education is to supervise UNRWA schools directly. Although UNRWA schools have their own administration system that can fire and hire teachers independently, these schools follow ministerial directives. The main UNRWA office is located in Jerusalem; there are five subsidiary offices in five administration districts.

Most UNRWA schools are located in refugee camps. Many of them have one to five or six grades but the largest ones have one to nine grades. Their students transfer to government schools after they successfully complete the ninth grade.

Structure

The number and types of schools in Palestine differs from place to place. For example, the number of schools in the rural West Bank and Gaza Strip in 1993/1994 was 1,357—992 of which were governmental schools, 111 were private, and 254 were UNRWA schools. Of these, 1,057 were in the West Bank, 300 in the Gaza Strip. The number of Palestinian schools in East Jerusalem in the year 1986/87 was 91. These schools were governmental, private, and UNRWA, distributed at 30, 48, and 13 respectively (Abu-Libdeh, 1995).

According to the Palestinian Central Bureau of Statistics (1996), the number of students attending schools (basic and secondary) in the West Bank and Gaza Strip, including East Jerusalem, in the year 1995/1996, was 662,427 (340,390 males and 322,035 females). The number of teachers in the same year was 21,563 (11,641 male teachers and 9,922 female).

Preschool education (kindergarten) is popular in Palestinian society. The kindergartens in the West Bank and Gaza Strip are distributed between two supervisory authorities, private and UNRWA. However, most kindergartens belong to the private sector. The number of private kindergartens in 1993/1994 in the West Bank was 453; the number of UNRWA kindergartens was 13 in the same year (that is, 97 and 3 percent respectively). In the Gaza Strip, the number of private and UNRWA kindergartens in the year 1993/1994 was 76 and 113 respectively.

Children in Palestine begin their preschool education at the age of 4. The legal attendance age (attending first elementary class) is almost the same in all Palestinian schools—6 years, which means that the child's age must be 6 years at the beginning of September so as to attend school (Abu-Libdeh, 1995).

After nine years of so-called "basic level," there are two years of secondary education either in scientific or literary streams. The choice between the two streams depends on the student's interests and his or her achievement in math and science. Other students do two years of vocational schooling in the secondary level. At the end of the second secondary year, all students sit for the General Secondary Examination (*Tawjihi*), which is administered by the Ministry of Education (Abu-Libdeh, 1995; Shalabi, 2000).

In terms of university education, the West Bank, Gaza Strip, and East Jerusalem have twelve universities. According to Anabtawi (1986), the number of universities in the West Bank and Gaza Strip are more than in any single Arab state, except for Egypt and Saudi Arabia. The number of universities in the West Bank and Gaza Strip equals half that of Egypt, a country with approximately forty times the population of Palestine.

With regard to the number of students at Palestinian universities, this is different from year to year, depending on political and economic conditions and the level of conflict. In the year 1995/1996, the number of students was 37,094 (21,190 males and 15,904 females). The number of graduates in the same year was 3,032. The number of teachers in the same year was 1,369 (Palestinian Central Bureau of Statistics, 1996).

In addition to public education, there are other types of education programs in Palestine (Abu-Libdeh, 1995). These are:

- *Literacy and adult education.* This is provided for those who are above 15 years of age and who never attended schools, received education for a short period, or lost the skills they acquired through time.
- *Private education.* This is provided for talented children or any other special needs students.
- *Irregular education.* These are short courses in computer, languages, secretarial work, and the like.
- *Vocational training centers.* These centers are used to graduate technical workers over a period of one or two years.

Fees

Students' fees depend on the type of school attended. For example, in government schools (before the Israelis handed over the West Bank and Gaza Strip to the Palestinians) the Israeli Civil Administration was responsible for covering expenses, and students only paid small fees to cover the costs of materials and equipment. In UNRWA schools students do not pay any fees at all. In private schools, some schools charge students relatively high fees; some others charge little or no fees. This depends on whether these schools are aiming for financial profit or are schools organized by charitable societies or foreign and local organizations (Abu-Libdeh, 1995).

Curriculum

According to The Palestinian Curriculum Development Centre, the academic curricula in the West Bank and Gaza Strip reflect foreign national histories, traditions, and educational philosophies that are incongruent with a Palestinian heritage (Ghali, 1997).

Schools in the West Bank were required to follow the Jordanian curriculum, and Jordan supplied the textbooks. School in the Gaza Strip followed the Egyptian curriculum, and the textbooks were supplied by Egypt. Both the Jordanian and Egyptian curricula were outdated and inappropriately sequenced in terms of academic level, both across subjects and grade level. Worse, Palestinian students were taught things related to the history, culture, and literature of Jordan or Egypt, not Palestine.

In addition, Israeli administration had to approve the educational materials because it reserved the right to ban or censor any textbook or any educational material. Any reference to Palestine or Palestinian people was removed by the Israeli authorities from school textbooks and educational materials. In fact, from 1967 until the year 1992, the Israeli authorities banned 103 textbooks from schools.

Examinations

As for the official exams such as the General Secondary School Exams (*Tawjihi*), students in the West Bank took the Jordanian exam; those in the Gaza Strip wrote the Egyptian exam. Failure to sit and pass any of the examinations resulted in failure to matriculate, and the student had to wait another year before trying again. This meant that students prevented from sitting the exams because of arrest, curfews, school closure, or some other reason in effect lost a year's schooling.

Currently, the *Tawjihi* is a general examination that is held at the end of the secondary stage by special committees. One examination is held for all twelfth-class students in the West Bank and another for Gaza Strip students. Successful students get the General Secondary Certificate.

Special Education

McConkey (2000) argues that disability and poverty are often "first cousins" throughout the world, but more especially in poorer countries where there are no social security benefits. According to Oliver and Barnes (1998), living with impairment is generally associated with poverty, social isolation, stigmatization, and second-class citizenship. They add that "to become 'disabled' is to be assigned a new identity indicating membership of a separate tribe or species" (p. 66). Because of negative attitudes, people with special needs in Palestine are either ignored or confined out of sight in institutions (Giacaman & Deibes, 1989).

In spite of this social attitude, there is nonetheless a good number of institutions and programs in the country that provide rehabilitation services for people with disabilities. In 1993 there were 62 centers, 46 in the West Bank and 16 in the Gaza Strip. Among these centers, 10 were providing services for people with physical handicaps; 15 for people with visual impairments, 8 for people with hearing impairment, 15 for people with mental handicaps, 7 for persons with drug addiction, in addition to 7 advisory centers (Abu-Libdeh, 1995).

However, there are very few qualified people in this field, and there is no statistical information on this type of education. It may very well be that there are now more institutions and programs that provide rehabilitation services for people with special needs. However, while there are a good number of institutions, the reality is that institutions that provide effective special education services are very few (not exceeding four or five institutions and/or programs).

According to the Palestinian Central Bureau of Statistics (1997), 55.1 percent of people with special needs (aged 5 to 24) are enrolled in regular education; 48.3 percent (aged 10 years and over) are illiterate. In addition, children with specific learning difficulties in regular schools who make inadequate progress are excluded more often than helped (Saunders, 1985).

With regard to policy in special education, special education services for school-age children with special needs in the country are underdeveloped due to the fact that there is no policy in place within the general education legislation to emphasize education for such a group of children. The absence of a well-developed national education system and a national curriculum, as well as financial constraints, limited resources, and limited teaching materials are other factors leading to undeveloped special education. The negative attitudes of parents as well as the attitudes of staff and administrators and lack of advisory and support services are also important factors that impede rapid development in this field.

Teacher Training

Two types of academic institutions train school teachers—teacher training colleges and universities. The former award undergraduate diplomas that qualify participants to be teachers; the latter award diplomas and bachelor degrees in education in various areas.

Postgraduate diplomas and master's degrees are also offered by some universities in the country. The higher colleges and universities require students to successfully complete the General Secondary Certificate Examination (*Tawjihi*) in order to apply for admission at these universities. The majority of these universities are modeled on the North American system of course credits, which requires students to take a certain number of credit hours from a range of course credits in order to graduate.

Female Teachers

Many years ago, employment opportunities in the field of education were only available for men. Palestinian women only started working as teachers a few decades ago, and this was at the Palestinian schools in the Israeli parts of the country. They started as teachers in kindergartens or in the lower grades of elementary schools (Maari, 1978). Currently, many women work as teachers in the Palestinian schools that exist either in the Israeli parts or in the West Bank and Gaza Strip in all grades. This encourages many parents to send their daughters to school.

SUCCESSES

Palestinian society has been exposed to various major issues, controversies, and problems. These can be dated to the beginning of the Turkish occupation many centuries ago, followed by the British Mandate, and then the Israeli occupation of the country in two stages—the 1948 war that was ended by occupying two-thirds of Palestine and the 1967 war that ended by occupying the remaining one-third of Palestinian land. Both prior to 1948 and afterwards, Palestinians have encountered a series of traumatic experiences. Nonetheless, and inspiring in view of the incredible hardships, there are a number of areas in which remarkable successes in Palestinian schooling have been effected. These are to be found in the areas of curriculum, educational attainment, literacy, and special education. Each is discussed in turn below.

Curriculum

One of the major successes for Palestinian education in the past decades was the opportunity to have its own, independent curriculum. This opportunity, however, had both a bright and a dark side. On the bright side, the Palestinian Ministry of Education announced, back in September of 1994, that its work on a Palestinian curriculum was completed. The new curriculum was to consist of thirteen subjects from the Jordanian curriculum, plus two subjects dealing with civics and Palestinian society.

Unfortunately, introduction of the curriculum immediately ran into obstacles. The Palestinian National Authority (PNA) was unable to introduce a new unified curriculum because the transfer of authority took place on September 1, 1994, and the school year commenced just two days later. It was an impossible deadline to meet, and so delays in implementation were encountered. Furthermore, the extreme economic and political hardships discussed above make it obvious that financial obstacles continue to hamper implementation. As well, the curriculum is in need of ongoing reform, resources must be supplied to facilitate its teaching, and teacher training very much needs to be improved. In summary, a national curriculum exists but has yet to be successfully and fully implemented.

Levels of Education and Educational Attainment among Palestinians

There is a comparatively high level of education among the Palestinian population, and this can be considered a great success. Interestingly, studies show that the educational level of the refugee camps' population is higher than the educational level of the population of the cities. A study carried out by Heiberg and Ovenson (1993), cited in Abu-Libdeh (1995), shows that 21 percent of camps' populations in the West Bank and Gaza Strip (excluding old people) had gained education higher than General Secondary Certificate Examination, in comparison with 9 percent in the rural West Bank and 7 percent in East Jerusalem. The study also showed that 45 percent of the refugees in the West Bank and Gaza Strip completed at least ten years of education in comparison with 36 percent of the rural West Bank and Gaza Strip population. There was also an increase in the number of those who completed nine to twelve scholastic years since 1985. The number of students who completed these scholastic years in 1985 was 30 percent, while this number increased to 41 percent in 1993 (Abu-Libdeh, 1995).

Regarding differences in educational attainment between girls and boys, a few studies show that the level of education attainment among Palestinian males is higher than among females for all age groups. The rate of males who completed thirteen scholastic years in 1993, for example, was 13 percent, while the rate for females was 6 percent; the rate of males who completed nine to twelve scholastic years reached 45 percent, while the rate of females reached 37 percent. The percents of males and females who never attended schools in 1993 were 9 percent and 25 percent respectively (Abu-Libdeh, 1995).

Literacy

Various studies show that illiteracy among both males and females in Palestinian society has been reduced over the years. The level of illiteracy among females in the Gaza Strip decreased from 75.6 percent in 1970 to 31.7 percent in 1990. In the rural West Bank, the rate has also decreased from 84 percent in 1970 to 31.7 percent in 1990. Male literacy rates are reported to be 91.5 percent (Palestinian Central Bureau of State, 1998).

Special Education

Children with special needs, wherever they are, have the right to be included and taught in mainstream schools. The Palestinian Authority acknowledges the principles of the Salamanca Statement, which states that the inclusion of pupils with special needs into mainstream schools benefits both pupils and their families (Soboh & Maas, 1997). According to the Palestinian Central Bureau of Statistics (1997), 55.1 percent of people with special needs (aged 5 to 24) are enrolled in regular education, while 48.3 percent (aged 10 years and over) are illiterate.

In Palestine, a three-year pilot project of inclusive education was started three years after the Palestinian Ministry of Education became operational in 1994. The Ministry of Education adopted the inclusive education approach as part of the strategy for reaching the goal of "Education for All" according to the Jomtien Declaration of 1990. The project was piloted in different parts of Palestine (Bethlehem, Ramallah, Nablus, and Hebron) in order to establish the groundwork needed to adopt the philosophy of inclusion in the country as a whole. The ultimate goal of this program is to improve the quality of education by investing in teachers and by bringing about changes in attitudes and classroom practices in order to facilitate learning for all children and, in particular, by including those with special educational needs. As part of the three-year plan, the Ministry identified a core team consisting of thirty-one resource staff across twelve directorates specifically to work with students with special educational needs enrolled in government schools.

Today, it is well understood that inclusive education is a viable and effective means of working toward achieving "Education for All." Collaboration has been established among school authorities, school communities, and parents. The first practical experiences of including children with special needs in regular classrooms are being undertaken in thirty pilot elementary schools in the West Bank and Gaza. Some 350 teachers in these schools received training from the Core Resource Team using the *UNESCO Teacher Training Resource Pack: Special Needs in the Classrooms*. These initial experiences have already led to changing attitudes on the part of teachers and students toward students with special needs (UNESCO, 1997).

CHALLENGES

While Palestinian society has not disintegrated, it has been severely undermined by drastic socioeconomic and political transformations. For example, many Palestinians have become refugees; of these, many live in deplorable conditions. What was formerly a stable, functional, and self-sufficient social structure has been destroyed. Also important here is today's relative lack of farmers, a result of the fact that much of Palestine's cultivable land has been lost to Israel. The occupation adversely affected the economics of the country through controlling employment opportunities, which led people to be exposed to poor and limited medical and health services. It also created different social classes; the vast majority of people now belong to the lower class, with only a small minority distributed among the middle and higher classes. The traditional political leadership has vanished; a new, nontraditional leadership has emerged, both at the local and the national levels. As a result, the Palestinian people have become divided into about ten conflicting political groups.

It is within the above contexts that severe challenges for the provision of education inevitably arose. This section will address major challenges for the education system in the West Bank, Gaza Strip, East Jerusalem (the areas occupied in 1967), and the Israeli side (the areas occupied in 1948). Difficulties and problems will be discussed within the following framework: challenges related to schools and the school system of Palestinian Israelis; challenges in relation to teacher training; challenges related to curriculum; challenges arising from the first Intifada; challenges related to teaching and learning practices; challenges in relation to students' academic achievements; and lesser strategic problems. These seven issues are discussed in turn below. This section of the chapter will conclude with a cursory sketch of some possible solutions to these challenges.

Challenges Related to Schools and the School System of Palestinian Israelis

We will first turn to a discussion of the conditions of schooling for Palestinians living in Israel. In 1948, Israel passed a law to separate the Jewish and the Arab education systems. This law is one of the most important characteristics of the Israeli education system. Different goals were set for different curricula, and separate budgets were assigned. This division laid the groundwork for discrimination between the Arab and Jewish schools. In about forty years, this led to the obsolescence and underdevelopment of the Arab education system—to this day a huge gap exists between the Arab and Israeli schools.

In terms of different goals, the function of Israeli schools is to engender national pride in Jewish boys and girls, to convey Zionist ideology, and to integrate students into society. On the other hand, the function of the Arab schools is to separate Arab boys and girls from their people and from their Arab and Palestinian heritage and to make them forget their past and the history of their people. Arab schools teach children to accept the fact that they are second-class citizens in Israeli society. These schools have become a tool for perpetuating the gap between the Jewish and Arab societies, rather than being agents for change and social progress (Human Rights Watch, 2001; Lahav, 1995).

In terms of budget and fiscal resources, discrimination against the Palestinian Arab schools is also clearly evident. The budget allocated for Jewish schools is much higher that that allocated for the Palestinian Arab schools. This was admitted long ago in a 1991 Israeli state report: The Israeli Ministry of Education allocated 308 shekels (Israeli currency) per Jewish child and only 168 shekels per Palestinian Arab child (Lahav, 1995).

The long-standing discrimination against Palestinian Arab students in Israeli schools as a result of inadequate funding is shown in all aspects of schooling and at all levels of the education system. For example, Palestinian children are in classes with a much higher student–teacher ratio than Israeli children. Palestinian Arab schools, unlike Israeli schools, lack learning facilities such as libraries, computers, science laboratories, recreation space, film editing studios, theater rooms, and so on. As for Palestinian Arab children with special needs, they are marginalized, with no provision of special education teachers or any other special education facilities. There is no suitable infrastructure existing in the field of special education, and there are no professionals who can deal with the diagnosed special educational needs. The Israeli Ministry of Education spends proportionately less on integration or mainstreaming, special education services, and special schools for Palestinian Arab children than it does for Jewish children (Human Rights Watch, 2001).

On the other hand, the Israeli school system has highly developed special education programs. With regard to kindergarten, Palestinian Arab kindergartens are inadequately constructed compared to the Jewish ones. Thirty-five percent of classrooms are rented, and many do not meet minimum requirements for classrooms. Poor school facilities and schools requiring travel over long distances result in children dropping out of the education system altogether at a very high rate (Human Rights Watch, 2001). The dropout rate in Arab schools is 20 percent at the compulsory education level (kindergarten to tenth grade) and 55 percent by the end of high school (Lahav, 1997). There is little indication that an amelioration of this situation can be expected.

Challenges in Relation to Teachers' Training

Continuing our focus on Palestinians living in Israel, there are serious concerns about the state of the training of teachers in Arab Israeli schools. The Israeli education system gives a low priority for teacher training in Palestinian Arab schools and only provides "in-service" training to the Palestinian Arab teachers. These teachers also have lower qualifications and receive lower salaries than their counterparts in the Israeli schools. Training in special education for Palestinian Arab teachers has been largely insufficient. According to Lahav (1995), in the entire Arab sector there is not even one institution that specializes in diagnosing learning disabilities.

Challenges Related to Curriculum

The discrimination against Palestinian Arabs in Israel is also shown in curricular content—which alienates students and teachers alike. For example, in Hebrew language classes, Jewish religious texts and the works of Jewish Talmudic scholars are imposed on Palestinian Arab students. Palestinian Arab teachers and students cannot refuse to use these curricular materials—they are included in the mandatory subjects in the matriculation exams (*bagrut*) taken at the end of high school.

The curriculum used in Israeli schools includes very important subjects—Hebrew to the mastery level, the Bible, old Israeli history, modern Israeli history, general history, Israeli geography, general geography, and arithmetic. On the other hand, the curriculum used in Israeli Arab schools never emphasizes elements that deal with the land of Palestine, the history of Palestine, the Palestinian personality, and the like. The Israelis also changed the names of almost all areas, villages, and cities in Palestine, and they even omitted the name of Palestine in all books used (Al-Nimer, 1993). The natural result of this policy is to reduce the number of students at the Palestinians schools year after year and to reduce the success of Palestinian students in the general examinations (Al-Nimer, 1993).

Discrimination at every level of the education system winnows out a progressively larger proportion of Palestinian Arab students as they go through the school system, or it channels those who persevere away from the opportunities of higher education. At each stage, the education system filters out a higher proportion of Palestinian Arab students than Jewish students (Human Rights Watch, 2001), and this denies Palestinian Arab students an equal opportunity to get into higher education. Israeli universities, who reject a higher number of Palestinian Arab students than Jewish students, also show this attitude.

CHALLENGES ARISING FROM THE FIRST INTIFADA

We now turn to some major challenges found in the West Bank and Gaza Strip. Palestinians, both in the Diaspora and living under occupation, place a particularly high value upon formal educational attainment. In uncertain circumstances, educational qualifications take on an even more enhanced significance. They are seen as a form of investment for the future, a passport to greater economic security and enhanced life chances (Badran, 1979; Maari, 1978). More importantly, education can be a major outlet for coping with the lack of a political identity as a result of a lack of statehood. Furthermore, and equally importantly, it is a vehicle for learning how to effect deep structural and social transformations in Palestine. It is therefore not surprising that Israel targeted educational institutions in the power struggle that lay at the heart of the Intifada. During the first Intifada (1987–1993), the education system in the occupied territories was subjected to an unprecedented assault by Israeli authorities.

At the postsecondary level, Israeli authorities harassed, arrested, and deported troublesome students and teachers. They also closed down educational institutions for varying periods of time as a form of collective punishment aimed at subduing unrest. This was in retaliation for demonstrations and protests against Israeli rule that had taken place on college and university campuses. However, demonstrations and protests were and are not limited to secondary education institutions. Since the beginning of the Israeli occupation of Palestine, schools, colleges, and universities have been sites of demonstrations, protests, strikes, and confrontations with the Israelis. For example, each time a confrontation started, students typically blocked the road, set fire to tires, and threw stones at advancing soldiers—who usually responded by shooting tear gas and rubber and live bullets at the students. After that, schooling would be interrupted through closure by military order until further notice.

In the West Bank and Gaza Strip, schools were closed for lengthy periods of time. This was part of a conscious Israeli strategy of collective punishment aimed at undermining the active resistance of the population. It is estimated that Palestinian children lost between 35 and 50 percent of school days during the first four years of the first Intifada.

The closure of schools was very sudden—there was no official advance notification of the closure, and there was no opportunity for teachers to meet collectively in school to prepare contingency plans. Furthermore, teachers did not know how long schools would remain closed. Certainly it appeared that the closure would be lengthy: Many government schools were taken over by the military for use as barracks, temporary detention centers, and storage bases.

Many teachers frustrated the closure orders by preparing self-study packs for pupils, meeting with them on an individual basis at regular intervals to discuss their work and giving and marking assignments. However, "teaching from a distance" was hard for teachers because they were not trained for such a task and did not have any experience or expertise in this mode of education service. Furthermore, after the first set of packs was distributed, the Israeli authorities ordered schools to stop such activity (Rigby, 1995). The Israelis went even further by declaring all "popular committees" (i.e., neighborhood associations) illegal. This meant that anyone involved with organizing any kind of educational or cultural activity risked prosecution and imprisonment for up to ten years.

Accordingly, a new plan was developed. In spite of being banned, neighborhood committees persisted and began to organize alternative education classes for students in private homes. The result was that, in the first four years of the first Intifada, Palestinians developed an alternative system of schooling represented by neighborhood-based "popular schools." The significance of these schools goes beyond the realm of providing schooling; they were also a form of unarmed civilian resistance to occupation. Accordingly, the development of popular schools was heralded as a significant move in the strategy of resistance through progressive disengagement from the Israeli occupation authorities. It was also depicted as a first tentative step toward the development of a truly indigenous Palestinian educational process.

However, popular education varied from one neighborhood to another, and serious problems were encountered. One major problem is that there were few people with appropriate experience to take on the role of a teacher. Furthermore, there was no central coordination of what to teach and how to go about it, and there were no backup services to assist the in experienced. As well, there was a common problem of motivating students.

Despite the problems encountered by this new community-based education system, it was nonetheless seen by many people as a significant challenge to the occupiers' ability to control the process and contents of Palestinian education. This seems to have been recognized by the Israeli authorities. It is worth mentioning here that, in one stage when schools were closed and the Palestinian system of community-based education was running, the Israeli authorities allowed the schools to reopen for a few weeks in order to disrupt the development of the community-based education. However, the popular committees made a decision that, despite the reopening of schools, the popular neighborhood schools would continue, operating in the afternoon after the end of the school day.

During the Intifada, schools closed and reopened several times, but when the occupiers allowed the schools to be reopened, as a result of the continued confrontations with the Israelis, the school day was shortened. The attempt to cover the ground in examinable subjects during the restricted day was very demanding of both staff and students, particularly when events outside the classroom intruded. One of the students in a school in Ramallah said, "Lots of time while we are in class we smell tires burning and hear shots in Ramallah. Our minds are outside so we cannot do anything in class." Another student admitted, "Sometimes I feel bad in school. Everyone outside is in the Intifada and we are stuck in school." Such is the world Palestinian school children lived, and continue to live, in.

Challenges Related to Teaching and Learning Practices

The teaching methods used in the majority of schools in the West Bank and Gaza Strip continue to be fairly traditional, although there have been sporadic initiatives to effect changes in teaching methods. Teaching methods are based on rote learning and on inappropriate practices such as insisting that students sit quietly and not talk to other students, teachers overwhelmingly monopolizing classroom discourse at the expense of student input/discussion, the expectation that students need only respond to direct questions asked by the teacher rather than initiating inquiry, students being assigned only individual classwork, and so on. Teachers adopt a "chalk and talk" approach, while students are expected to adopt a "paper and pencil" approach. Students sit at their desks the whole day long listening to their teacher; small group activities are not employed; there is a complete absence of a constructivist approach; and science experiments are not experiential—the teacher simply demonstrates them. Outside curriculum activities are forbidden; parents are not involved much in the educational process of their children; not much emphasis on music and art is to be found; and so on. In these schools great emphasis is placed on exams, which are considered the only valid method of assessing students' progress and understanding of the subject (Bredekamp, 1993).

Since the Palestinian Authority took over the education system in the country (except in Jerusalem and other Israeli Arab areas), it was hoped that various measures would be implemented and that modern pedagogical theories and practices in the field of education would be introduced. However, there is little indication that child-centered activity or inquiry-based pedagogical innovations will soon characterize the Palestinian school system.

Challenges in Relation to Students' Academic Achievements

In general, Palestinian society and Palestinian schools place a great emphasis on competition and academic achievement. Hence, most teachers are intent on the inculcation of academic knowledge and skills, and pupils are constantly under pressure to achieve academic success at school. This causes a great deal of stress for students.

However, teachers are also under stress from a variety of factors. These include high student–teacher ratios, coping with students who have behavioral problems, operating within a confined timetable, and having only a quite restricted period of time within which the curriculum must be covered. Furthermore, teachers lack the knowledge and experience needed to cope socially and academically with pupils who have learning problems, of which there are a significant number. Hence, the needs of such pupils at schools are great—for example, low achievers are almost ignored by their regular classroom teachers. This can complicate their problems and can lead to delinquency and truancy. Furthermore, such pupils are often nicknamed and stigmatized as idiots, slow, and the like, although many of them have good potential to learn. They just need more attention from the teacher and, through remedial work, can catch up with the other pupils in the regular classroom. However, classroom conditions make such individual attention unlikely.

Beyond the individual classroom, there are structural factors that hinder quality special education provision for pupils with low achievement in the West Bank and Gaza Strip. These include the absence of a well-developed national education system, lack of a national curriculum, lack of policy for a "whole-school" approach to special needs, financial constraints, limited resources and teaching materials, negative attitudes of parents toward children with special needs, negative attitudes of staff and administrators toward these children, lack of advisory and support services, and a lack of well-qualified professionals.

These concerns are merely another manifestation of how negatively and greatly the Palestinian education system has been affected by the Israelis (Dukmak & Kanawati, 1995). Indeed, the number of pupils experiencing learning problems that are not detected has been constantly increasing, especially during the first Palestinian Intifada, which lasted for six years. Constant curfews and closures of schools during the Uprising resulted in the deterioration of the quality of education and had negative impacts on pupils' academic performance.

Lesser Strategic Problems

Joining the above, there are other strategic problems in education. These may be summarized as:

- *Supervision.* The education system in Palestine suffers from the existence of too many supervisory bodies over schools—that is, the Israeli authorities for twenty-seven years, together with UNRWA and private organizations. These contributed to cutting the body of Palestinian society into parts and preventing it from facing difficult challenges with one united bureaucracy. Today, with the existence of the Palestinian Authority as a result of the peace treaty, Israeli authorities do not have control of any type over Palestinian schools in the West Bank and Gaza Strip. This bodes well for the creation of coordinated initiatives to address problems. However, Jerusalem currently is still under the control of the Israeli authorities, and the educational system is greatly affected by the Israeli occupation. And, of course, Arab Israelis are fully under the control of Israel.

■ *Leadership.* There is an absence of high-level educational leadership for all the private schools in Palestinian society. Thus, in the sector of private schools, much remains to be done.

■ *Collaboration.* There is a lack of cooperation between schools and the community in general, and between schools and parents in particular. This could be due to a lack of people's confidence in schools because of the administrative and financial problems that these schools suffer from, and the high frustration level that Palestinian society suffers from as a result of worsening economic, social, and security conditions. Too, the poor financial situation makes parents work very hard for long hours, with no time remaining to follow up on their children's progress in school.

■ *Support problems.* As mentioned, there is a weak school infrastructure that includes a lack of classrooms, activity halls, labs, playgrounds, and the like; a lack of qualified school teachers and directors; a lack of support activity for the learning process, including equipment, aids, and material needed for the learning process such as videos, TVs, computers, photocopiers, and the like; a lack of student support services such as health, psychology, social, counseling, and vocational services; and a lack of extracurricular activities (Kamal & Zughby, 1996).

Solutions

Solutions to Palestine's educational problems stretch far wider than just the schools. However, educational solutions—as opposed to political and social ones—would have to include the following:

- Providing enough, and ongoing, financial support to academic institutions to allow them to provide effective educational services. Financial support is also needed to establish new academic institutions and reinvigorate old ones.
- Strengthening the existing Palestinian educational system that took over education in the West Bank and Gaza Strip.
- Working on changing the curriculum to a purely Palestinian curriculum that emphasizes modern educational aspects.
- Effecting coordination and cooperation between all schools—government, private, and UNRWA schools.

DEBATES AND CONTROVERSIES

There are seven major areas of fundamental debate and controversy in Palestine today: education levels of Palestinians, curriculum, the education of women and the hidden curriculum, fear for the future, teachers' training and pedagogy, special education, and research.

Education Levels of Palestinians

As emphasized earlier, the Palestinian educational system has been greatly and negatively affected by the Israelis, including closure of schools, making it impossible to undertake positive curricular reforms (Dukmak & Kanawati, 1995). Despite these impositions and the poverty that has been created by the Israeli occupation, the Palestinians challenged the situation through education. This is because Palestinians consistently regard education as a means of maintaining identity and as a source of power, and they believe that education is a significant contributory factor in the achievement of political goals. Palestinians consider education as their only means of survival after losing most of their lands and means of living in 1948. As Henderson (1988) puts it: "Education had become the only wealth of the Palestinian people, their passport and the only way they could hope to keep their cultural identity" (p. 11). In this sense, the Palestinian response to occupation validates Freire's (1985) dictum that "Education is always a political event. It serves either to domesticate people or liberate them" (p. 12).

It is heartening that, although the Palestinian education system has been so negatively affected by the Israeli occupation, resulting in lower academic achievement for many Palestinians, Palestinians are still committed to education. Soboh and Maas (1997) argue that, despite occupation and associated poverty, many Palestinians are considered to have a high level of education. Palestinians are credited with having one of the highest proportions of any Arab group in completing higher education.

However, it is worth noting here that the literacy rates of men and women in the country, according to the Palestinian Central Bureau of Statistics (1998), are 91.5 percent for men and 77 percent for women. With respect to enrollment in higher education, it was found that 43 percent of those who were enrolled in higher education in 1996/1997 were women and 57 percent were men.

Curriculum

In general, religion is much more rooted in Arab society than in societies in the West (Freres School, 2000). And it is here that, in a country that is largely religious and where many of students' motives, concerns, and wishes are couched in terms of religion, we should not neglect cultural-religious experiences in education.

With reference to education and religion in Palestine, a question arises: Do government and UNRWA curricula deal with Christianity or Moslem Christian relations? Not really. First, in government schools there is no such subject as religious studies, but there is Islamic studies. In other words, there is no explicit focus upon religions other than Islam. Second, Christianity enters the picture largely as a rival religion. For instance, students do not learn about the pre-Islamic Christian (Byzantine) period in Palestine, nor about the historical contribution of Christian Palestinians to the development of Palestinian nationalism; rather they are told about the challenge the Crusades constituted to Islam. (A few years ago, the local Christian churches called for a critical study of the representation of Christianity in the public Palestinian curricula. But, due to internal Christian divisions, the study never took off [Freres School, 2000]).

In private schools the situation is different, because such schools enroll both Christian and Moslem students. Religious studies at these schools involve separate lessons for Moslem and Christian students. Similar to government schools, the Islamic lessons in the higher classes deal with matriculation requirements. In contrast, religious lessons for Christians do not prepare them for the matriculation exam. As in government schools, religious studies teachers at private schools are usually not qualified. Many are educated in other subjects and teach religious studies lessons in addition to, or instead of, their primary subject (Freres School, 2000).

The Education of Women and the Hidden Curriculum

The hidden curriculum refers to "those aspects of learning in schools that are unofficial, unintentional, or undeclared consequences of the way teaching and learning are organized and performed" (Skelton, 1994, p. 333, cited in Ghali, 1997, p. 22). The hidden curriculum is evident in gender discrimination in Palestinian school textbooks, teacher–pupil interaction, informal education, and the devaluation of the arts stream. For example, according to Abu Nahleh (1996, as cited in Ghali, 1997), many teachers perceive arts students as "slow," "dumb," "retarded," or "illiterate." Since the number of female students is much higher than the number of male students enrolled in the arts stream, this makes female students doubly disadvantaged—being females and arts stream students.

In the West Bank, the ratio of female literary students to female science students is 2.6 to 1 as compared with a ratio 1.6 to 1 for males. According to some people, this is due to the fact that the demand for female science schools is low, but other people argue that this is due to the supply-side. Furthermore, a girl living in a rural area may have to travel to a nearby town to attend a science school, and this may make her parents discontinue her schooling—especially if her academic achievement is low. The Palestinian Ministry of Education finds it easier and less costly to open extra literary schools than science schools, especially in the remote areas, because science schools require laboratories and need very qualified teachers.

Fear for the Future

According to Hugh Carnegy (cited in Rigby, 1995), many Palestinians in the West Bank and Gaza Strip regard the long-term consequences of the continued closure of schools during the Intifada as a policy of "cultural massacre." There were always worries about older students not completing their *Tawjihi* examinations, and also fear that younger students would lose their basic foundation in literacy and numeracy. There was also a fear that the young were beginning to lose their study skills in general, and the fear that they were developing problems in coping with the return to "normal" schooling. All of these problems were linked to worries about problems of motivation and discipline among the student body.

During school closures, students had a considerable amount of spare time. Although they should have been studying, most students found that almost impossible. As one student put it: "I spend my time switching from one radio station to another, trying to find out what is happening around. When Palestinians of my age are being killed, I cannot just sit and study." All these factors add up to uncertainty of the Palestinian people about the future of their children.

Teachers' Training and Pedagogy

The availability of quality teachers is critical for improving the quality of education in the West Bank and Gaza Strip. In recent years, as a result of the Intifada, teachers in Palestine have faced a moral crisis related to the continued interruption of the school year, poor working conditions, and inadequate rates of pay. In addition, many teachers are poorly qualified and schools have great difficulty in recruiting and retaining well-qualified staff. According to a study carried out by UNESCO (cited in Rigby, 1995), it was found that less than one-third of teachers have been educated to the level of holding a degree, two-thirds had diplomas, and the rest had only secondary schooling. During the Intifada, government schools teachers were prevented from attending training courses and workshops carried out at Palestinian universities, and new methods of teaching were not encouraged or allowed by the Israeli authorities.

The learning process during the years of the Israeli occupation was based on lectures, testing, and punishment. Teachers today still lecture students and make them copy from the blackboard, memorize texts, and recall content in examinations. The dominant teaching methodology is authoritarian and teacher centered; education in Palestine is about control and power vested in the teacher, with the student a passive vessel (Ghali, 1997). Teachers still try to discipline using physical punishment—even though Instruction no. 4 of 1981 on School Discipline explicitly prohibits the use of corporal punishment for disciplinary purposes, and the Ministry of Education has ruled that teachers charged with corporal punishment are subject to immediate expulsion. According to Abu-Hein (cited in Ghali, 1997, p. 23) 19 percent of students (8 to 15 years of age) who dropped out of schools did so due to physical punishment that they received from their teachers.

Obviously, there is an urgent need to develop and upgrade the teachers' teaching skills. This can be carried out through closer cooperation between the Palestinian Ministry of Education and universities.

Special Education

As mentioned earlier, there are some programs and centers in the country that provide children with special needs with special education, but the most debatable issue here is whether these programs provide an effective special education. For one thing, the effectiveness of special education differs from one place to another, and from one center to another, in the

West Bank and the Gaza Strip. Although special education centers have existed in the country for several years, in the author's view the majority of these centers do not provide effective special education. Many teachers in these centers simply teach in exactly the same way as teachers teach in regular schools.

According to Mittler (2000), teachers of pupils with special needs should receive specific training and professional development, and McConkey and colleagues (1999) argue that these teachers should receive ongoing support and specialist provision. Oliver (1994, 1995), on the other hand, argues that "teaching is teaching" regardless of the range of needs of pupils; the only thing that teachers need is a commitment to teach these children as this commitment is an essential prerequisite of inclusion (Oliver, 1994). This author firmly believes that, in order to effectively teach pupils with special needs, special education teachers should receive specific training, especially when teaching pupils with learning disabilities, because these pupils, by the nature of their special needs, are extremely difficult to teach. McConkey (1998), however, argues that our knowledge about the impact of schooling on the lives of young people with intellectual disabilities is very limited. He also argues that, in spite of the fact that millions of sterling pounds have been spent each year in the past two decades on special needs education in England, there is still little empirical evidence to indicate what aspects of special needs education are of proven value and what needs to be reformed.

According to Dukmak (1994), qualified special educators in Palestine usually assess pupils with special needs and then plan individual educational programs for them. Teachers whose work is supervised by such qualified special educators implement individual educational programs because there are few qualified special educators in the country. The majority of individual educational programs are implemented using the behavioral approach, which is based on task analysis and behavioral targets.

In terms of psychoeducational assessment of children with special needs, the author believes that few tests are used in the country for this purpose, as the only available ones are the Wechsler (WISC-R or WISC-III) and Stanford-Binet Intelligence Scales (Dukmak, 1994). However, even when administered, the results of these tests are not accurate because the tests are not standardized for use with Palestinians in the West Bank and Gaza. The assessment methods that are used for children with special needs are restricted to a very few, including the Portage and the Denver Screening Tests. There are no tests for those who are experiencing specific learning difficulties. Psychological services for children with special needs in the country are very limited and provided by only a few organizations, such as the Gaza Community Mental Health Program, the Young Men's Christian Association, the Bethlehem Arab Society for Rehabilitation, mental hospitals, and some individual psychologists who work independently in their own clinics (Dukmak, 1994).

Research

Publication output is relatively low in Palestine. A study carried out by the Science and Technology Planning Unit at the Ministry of Planning and International Cooperation (MOPIC) found that the ranking of Palestinian research output as an average number of publications per researcher per year is 0.7 compared to .05 in the Arab countries, 1.6 in Turkey, and 6.3 in Israel. Obstacles to progress in individual academics' research productivity may be attributed to factors that include intellectual isolation, no freedom of choice of research topics, lack of access to information bases, and lack of incentives to do research. Hindrances to research at the work environment level may be ascribed to lack of university support staff, lack of facilities, demanding teaching loads, and institutional instability. It is recommended that national research objectives be defined and identified within the wider context of a national policy. It is also recommended that clear, achievable, national research goals be set and ways to achieve them identified (MOPIC, 1999).

CONCLUDING COMMENTS: CREATING A VISION OF A FUTURE PALESTINIAN EDUCATION SYSTEM

Creating a concept of what the Palestinian education system should be like in the near future would serve as a major catalyst for improving the human, and social conditions of the Palestinian people. Such a vision needs to focus on developing an education system that is capable of transforming current conditions for the better. This system would require the articulation of goals that are consistent with Palestine's legitimate right to self-determination. Goals and procedures must be authentic, genuine, and dynamic as much as universal and practical, because they must complement Arab cultural values and their commitment to human rights (Nasru, 1993).

Such a vision should also avoid utopian rhetoric—in a very practical and realistic manner, it must build on the natural, human, and cultural resources of the Palestinian people. For example, Rigby (1995) argues that student progress in the Palestinian education system depends on the acquisition of appropriate skills and concepts upon which further development can be based. Many educationalists express their concerns about young students who failed to achieve basic levels in literacy and numeracy during the years of occupation and who are still affected by the current prevailing political situation. One of the methods to overcome children's academic problems is to establish remedial learning programs to be targeted at elementary, preparatory, and secondary school pupils to make them acquire the foundational skills and capabilities needed to progress satisfactorily through the formal education system. Without such a firm base, education plans for the future would be built on sand.

However, a base is just that—a base. It is not the end; it is rather but a steppingstone on the journey toward much loftier things. As Rigby (1995) suggests, the future Palestinian education system should ultimately be related to a democratic political system that rests on a democratic and open political culture. In such a culture, people claim the right to voice their own opinions, while respecting the rights of their opponents to do likewise. Such a culture respects differences and appreciates diversity; the formal education system reflects this culture and serves as a prime agency in the socialization of youth and the inculcation of these fundamental cultural values. Such an education system must clearly start with the promotion of a sense of self-worth within students themselves. This means that the old patterns of Palestinian education need to be eradicated. In contemporary Palestine, such patterns (of authority) within classrooms are merely reflections of authoritarian and patriarchal relationships that permeate the Palestinian family and the wider community.

REFERENCES

Abu-Libdeh, H. (1995). *Education statistics in the West Bank and Gaza Strip.* Current Status Report Series (No. 5). Ramallah-West Bank, Palestine: Palestinian Central Bureau of Statistics.

Abu-Shokor, A. (1990). Income distribution and its social impact on the Occupied Territories. In K. Abu Jaber, M. Buhbe, & M. Smadi (Eds.), *Income distribution in Jordan.* Boulder, CO: Westview Press.

Al-Nimer, K. (1993). *The ordeal of education in Palestine.* Jeddah, Saudi Arabia: (Arabic version) Dar Al-Mujtama' for Publication and Distribution.

Anabtawi, S. (1986). *Palestinian higher education in the West Bank and Gaza Strip: A critical assessment.* London, UK: KPI Ltd.

Arabic News. (2005) *Israel's population tolls 6.8 million.* Accessed March 15, 2005, from http://www.arabicnews.com/ansub/Daily/Day/041231/2004123117.html

Badran, N.S.A. (1979). *Education and modernization in the Palestinian Arab society* (2nd ed., Arabic version). Beirut, Lebanon: Palestine Liberation Organization.

Ballantyne, S. (1988, December). *Physiotherapy—Fact finding visit to the West Bank and Gaza Strip.* A final evaluation report written to evaluate the physiotherapy services in the West Bank and Gaza strip for the purpose of developing this field in the country.

Benevenisti, M. (1984). *U.S.A. governmental funded projects in the West Bank and Gaza Strip (1977–1983) (Palestinian Sector).* Working paper no. 13. The West Bank Data Base Project.

Bredekamp, S. (Ed.). (1993). *Developmentally appropriate practice in early childhood programs serving children from birth through age 8.* Washington, DC, USA: National Association for the Education of Young Children.

Dukmak, S. J. (1994). The West Bank and Gaza Strip. In K. Mazurek & M. A. Winzer (Eds.), *Comparative studies in special education.* Washington, DC, USA: Gallaudet University Press.

Dukmak, S., & Kanawati, R. (1995). *Special education provision: Establishing a special class for low achievers in three main-stream schools in Greater Bethlehem area.* Project proposal. Bethlehem, Palestine: Bethlehem Arab Society for Rehabilitation.

Freire, P. (1985). *The politics of education, culture, power and liberation.* Houndmills, UK: Macmillan.

Freres School. (2000). *Palestinian education across religious borders: An inventory.* Bethlehem: Palestine RAI House of Art.

Ghali, M. (1997). *Palestinian women: A status report.* Palestine: Women's Studies Program, Birzeit University.

Giacaman, R., & Deibes, I. (1989). *Towards the formulation of a rehabilitation policy: Disability in the West Bank.* Birzeit, Palestine: Birzeit University.

Henderson, E. (1988, November 4). UNESCO stress Arab plight. *Times Higher Educational Supplement, 835,* p. 11.

Hommous, N. A. (2002, August 28). *Appeal from the Palestinian Ministry of Education and Higher Education in the Occasion of Opening the New School Year (02–03).* The Palestinian Monitor. Accessed March 13, 2005, from http://www.palestinemonitor.org/updates/appeal_from_ministry_of_education.htm

Human Rights Watch. (2001). *Second class: Discrimination against Palestinian Arab children in Israel's schools.* New York: Human Rights Watch.

Islamic Relief. (2005). *The struggle for Palestinians continues.* Accessed March 13, 2005 from http://www.irw.org/wherewework/palestine/

JMCC. (1989). *Palestinian education: A threat to Israeli security.* East Jerusalem, Palestine: JMCC.

Jomtien Declaration (1990, March 5–9). *World Declaration on Education for All and Framework for Action to Meet Basic Learning Needs* (World Conference on Education for All). Jomtien, Thailand.

Kamal, S., & Zughby, S. (1996). *The needs of Jerusalem in the Year 2000 in the field of education and teaching* (Arabic version). Jerusalem: Arab Studies Society.

Lahav, H. (1995). *The additional factor: The role of the community in confronting the crisis of the Arab education system in Israel. The case of the Mother's School in Majd al-Krum.* Jerusalem: Hanitzots A-Sharara Publishing House (HPH).

Maari, S. K. (1978). *Arab education in Israel.* Syracuse, New York, USA: Syracuse University Press.

McConkey, R. (1998). Education for life. *British Journal of Special Education, 25*(2), 55–59.

McConkey, R. (2000). *A bundle of sticks: Family based organisations in developing countries.* Unpublished paper. Newtown Abbey, Northern Ireland, UK: School of Health Sciences, University of Ulster.

McConkey, R., O'Toole, B., & Mariga, L. (1999). Educating teachers in developing countries about disabilities. *Exceptionality Education Canada, 9,* 15–38.

Ministry of Planning and International Cooperation (MOPIC). (1999). *Current status of scientific research at Palestinian universities.* Palestine: Ministry of Planning and International Cooperation.

Mittler, P. (2000). *Working towards inclusive education: Social context.* London, UK: David Fulton Publishers.

Nasru, F. (1993). *Preliminary vision of a Palestinian education system in light of the declaration of Palestinian independence.* Palestine: Birzeit University, Centre for Research and Documentation of Palestinian Society.

Oliver, M. (1994). *To be or not to be? Special education in the twenty-first century.* Extract from a paper presented at the 1994 Irish Association of Teachers in Special Education Conference, London.

Oliver, M. (1995). Does special education have a role to play in the twenty-first century? *Journal of Special Needs Education in Ireland, 8*(2), 67–76.

Oliver, M., & Barnes, C. (1998). *Disabled people and social policy: From exclusion to inclusion.* London: Longman.

Palestine Monitor. (2005). *Fact sheet–apartheid wall.* Accessed March 13, 2005, from.http://www.palestinemonitor.org/factsheet/wall_fact_sheet.htm

Palestinian Central Bureau of Statistics. (1996). *Palestinian territories—statistical brief.* Ramallah, West Bank, Palestine.

Palestinian Central Bureau of Statistics. (1997). *Population, housing and establishment census: Summary of census results.* Ramallah, West Bank, Palestine.

Palestinian Central Bureau of Statistics. (1998). *Women and men in Palestine: Trends and statistics.* Ramallah, West Bank, Palestine.

Palestinian Central Bureau of Statistics. (2003, August). *The statistical system in Palestine: Gaps, obstacles, challenges and needs: A country report submitted to Regional Forum on Strengthening Statistical Capacity of the Arab States.* Amman, Jordan, September 8–10, 2003.

Palestinian Central Bureau of Statistics. (2005, June). *Figures at a glance: Projected population (September 2004).* Accessed June 14, 2005, from http://www.pcbs.org/

Rigby, A. (1995). *Palestinian education: The future challenge.* Palestine: Palestinian Academic Society for the Study of International Affairs (PASIA).

Saunders, C. A. (1985). *Prevalence of handicapping conditions affecting children and a case finding intervention in the refugee camp population of Gaza Strip.* Gaza Strip: The Society for the Care of Handicapped Children.

Shalabi, F. (2000). *Effective schooling in the West Bank.* Ph.D. thesis. Netherlands: Twentw University Press.

Soboh, N., & Maas, L. (1997). *Promoting inclusive education through child-to-child activities.* A pilot project at Jerusalem Centre for Disabled Children-Palestine.

UNESCO. (1997). *Inclusive schools and community support programmes: Pilot project 1997–1999.* A report written by UNESCO about inclusive education program in Palestine.

UNRWA. (1990). *Report on the Commissioner-General of the United Nations Relief and Works Agency for Palestine refugees in the Near East: 1 July 1989–30 June 1990.* General Assembly. Official Records: Forty-Fifth Session, Supplement No. 13 (A/45/13). New York: UN.

CHAPTER SEVEN

THE ISRAELI EDUCATION SYSTEM

Blending Dreams with Constraints

THOMAS P. GUMPEL

ADAM E. NIR

National systems of public education develop through the interplay between larger sociohistorical trends and bureaucratic requirements. Accordingly, to fully understand a country's bureaucratic system and in order to be able to conduct both inter- and intranational analyses, comparative studies must initially describe both "deep structures" (the sociohistorical milieu) and how they impact on the system's everyday functioning, or "surface structures" (Gumpel & Awartani, 2003). Such analyses must examine the salient events shaping the nation's varying identities and scrutinize how these different realities shape the educational system.

Understanding the development of the Israeli public educational system is no exception to this rule. In this chapter we present and attempt to answer four questions. First, what are the underlying sociohistorical trends that inform the Israeli educational system? Second, how does the system embrace some social trends while attempting to neutralize others? Then, how does such a system attempt to provide a culturally and nationally accepted

Thomas P. Gumpel is a Senior Lecturer and former Chair of the Special Education Program at the Hebrew University of Jerusalem, Israel, and an Associate Professor in the Department of Special Education and Disability Policy at Virginia Commonwealth University. His primary research interests focus on social justice and the distribution of equity and how they influence special educational policy as well as the study of school violence and severe emotional disturbance, specifically regarding the study of victims and their victimizers.

Adam Nir is a Senior Lecturer and Head of Educational Administration and Planning Program at the Hebrew University of Jerusalem, Israel. His current interests and research are in decentralization and school-based management, educational planning, and human resource management. Among his most recent works are "The Impact of School-Based Management on Public Schools in Israel," *Curriculum and Teaching*, and "School–Parent Relationships in the Era of School-Based Management: Harmony or Conflict?" *Leadership and Policy in Schools.*

educational system for all its citizens? Finally, how can the system attempt this gargantuan task while so much of its national resources are invested in other vital arenas? Overarching all of these questions is one fundamental dilemma—that is, how can a small nation such as Israel deal with each of these challenges, where failure is not an option because it would lead to the state's military, economic, and cultural demise?

In order to best understand these issues and the complex system of Israeli public education, we must first develop an understanding of the political and cultural milieu from which the system sprang and in which it continues to develop. Understanding these differing exigencies from a sociohistorical point of view is a necessary precondition for understanding current debates and dilemmas in the Israeli school system. These competing histories are complex, as anyone who follows the news from the Middle East will appreciate. We hope to simplify, yet not trivialize, these issues and show how they have impacted in the past and will continue in the future to impact upon the Israeli educational system.

To do this, we first offer a historical and political primer on Israeli history in which we present, in the broadest possible strokes, the salient aspects of the Israeli experience and how it is related to the Israeli educational system. Before we begin, a disclaimer is in order. It is nigh impossible to discuss anything about Israel, Arabs, Palestinians, or the Middle East without taking and expressing a political view. We have no such desire or intention here; indeed, we have labored to "walk between the raindrops" and present a politically free discussion of Israel (if such a thing is, indeed, possible). We do so unabashedly, as Jewish Israelis.

A HISTORICAL AND POLITICAL PRIMER

The state of Israel is a small country (20,770 square kilometers) with a primarily industrial- and service-oriented economy (96.5 percent). Within this relatively small, yet densely populated, country one can find a veritable mosaic of demographies, ideologies, and histories.

The population of 6.8 million is composed of two primary ethnic groups: 81.5 percent Jewish and 18.5 percent Israeli Arabs who hold Israeli citizenship and are either Muslims or Christians (Bassok, 2004). Druze and Bedouins are two additional ethnic groups affiliated with the Arab sector. (It is important to note that in this chapter the term Israeli Arab does not refer to those Palestinians living in the Occupied Territories or Gaza Strip—areas captured by Israel in the 1967 war, also known as the Six-Day War—who do not hold Israeli citizenship.)

There are four primary religions represented in the country. These are Jewish (81.5 percent), Muslim (14.6 percent; predominantly Sunni Muslim), Christian (2.1 percent), and Druze (1.8 percent).

Israeli Arabs are dispersed in four primary geographical areas: Israeli Arab cities, mixed Jewish and Israeli Arab cities, villages, and unrecognized settlements. Different demographic groups inhabit different types of settlements. The majority of the Arab population in Israel lives either in Israeli Arab or mixed cities or villages. The Druze population lives almost exclusively in villages in the northern part of the country. The once nomadic Bedouin population lives primarily in unofficial villages in the southern part of the country.

Becoming a Jewish State

The state of Israel was founded in 1948 based on the Zionist movement founded by Theodor Herzl (1860–1904), which called for the establishment of a Jewish national and religious homeland in the biblical land of Israel. Disheartened by continuing European anti-Semitism, Herzl wrote that despite their attempts at assimilation into the fabric of nineteenth-century European culture, Jews would always be outsiders and subjected to continuing anti-Semitism. Only in their own land could Jews ever hope of being free from the 2,000-year-old yoke of European anti-Semitism.

Herzl's views on the imperative for a Jewish State in Palestine took hold; Zionist policy became part of British foreign policy intent on dismantling the ailing Ottoman Empire. Following the Armistice of 1918, Palestine was ceded to the United Kingdom, and an active period of settlement of Palestine by European Jews began.

With many stops and starts and by overcoming political and military attempts by the indigenous Arab population to thwart their mass migration, the colonial hold in Palestine grew steadily from 1918 until 1948. In fact, the migration was massive. In 1882, the population in Ottoman-occupied Palestine consisted of a small group of religious Jews (24,000 or 4.8 percent) in the midst of an Arab population of 500,000. By 1948, the year the state of Israel was founded, the population of Palestine was 1.9 million with 31 percent of the population Jewish (Farsoun & Zacharia, 1977).

As envisioned initially by the early Zionists, the Jewish state would be the national and secular homeland of the Jewish people scattered throughout the Jewish Diaspora. Bridging the language and cultural gaps between Jews around the world involved creating a common *lingua franca.* Hebrew, the ancient language known only from prayers, had lain dormant for over 2,000 years. In order to create a common identity, a brilliant Jewish scholar named Eliezer Ben Yehuda modernized, restructured, and began to speak modern Hebrew—now the cornerstone of Israeli identity.

Since Israel, by definition, is a Jewish state, one major challenge in becoming a viable and stable country was the need to create a Jewish majority in Palestine where none had existed for 2,000 years. Therefore, within minutes of declaring independence from the United Kingdom in 1948, the first act enacted by the *Knesset* (the unicameral parliament) was the opening of all borders to unrestricted Jewish immigration.

Because immigration is the cornerstone of the Israeli experience, the issue is critical in understanding Israel and the Israeli psyche. The Hebrew word for immigration is *aliyah,* or alighting. People do not *immigrate* to Israel; rather, they make *aliyah*—that is, "they alight to a higher spiritual plane."

Therefore, the new state did not only open its borders: It made a timeless and unbreakable commitment that any Jew, anywhere, with whatever resources, could freely immigrate to Israel. Any Jew who could not immigrate because of lack of resources or oppressive laws or restrictions would be brought to a safe haven in Israel, no matter the expense or hardship. Once in Israel, they would be given as a starting point a special status as an *oleh* (Hebrew: one who alights).

"The gathering of the exiles" (migration of Jews from all over the Jewish Diaspora) along with *aliyah* was, and still is, seen by many Jews as a moral, national, and religious imperative no matter what the cost. The picture has played itself out repeatedly over the last fifty-five years. It can be seen in the rescuing of Jews from refugee camps in war-torn Europe following the Second World War; airlifting Yemeni Jews from Yemen in "Operation Magic Carpet" in 1949–1950; providing a safe haven for Argentinean Jews fleeing military juntas in the 1970s or economic collapse in the 1990s; bringing in massive numbers of immigrants with the breakdown of the former Soviet Union; and in the surreptitious airlifting of Falasha Jews from Ethiopia in the 1980s and 1990s.

Responsibility for the cultural and linguistic assimilation of immigrants has historically been under the purveyance of the educational system. For example, between 1989 and 1991, Israel was deluged with waves of immigrating Soviet Jews. During these years, the educational and social support systems were called upon to acculturate approximately 376,000 new citizens (an increase in the population of about 7.8 percent in two years) (Israel Ministry of Foreign Affairs, 1998).

Another smaller, yet equally challenging immigrant group is that from Ethiopia, which posed unique problems for the absorbing society. Today, there are approximately 56,000 Ethiopian Jews in Israel (Israel Ministry of Foreign Affairs, 1996).

Ethiopian or Falasha Jews arrived in Israel in two primary waves: "Operation Moses" lasted from the early and mid-1980s and included 8,000 immigrants over a five-year span. "Operation Solomon" (1991) included 14,000 immigrants; most arrived during one weekend. This was a time when Israel was reeling from the mass immigration of Jews from the former Soviet Union, along with high unemployment (11 percent) and high inflation (18 percent) (Jewish Virtual Library, 2003).

The absorption of this small, yet culturally distinct group also brought with it many unique challenges in housing and social integration, employment, and education. Educational challenges were extreme, since access to education was limited in Ethiopia, with most adults receiving little or no formal education (Israel Ministry of Foreign Affairs, 1996).

Dilemmas in Israeli Society

No other modern nation has seen its population grow more than threefold in fifty years. However, such unbridled growth implies a heavy price. The challenge is extreme: to mold such different groups into a cohesive nation.

The seeds of the primary and basic dilemmas of modern Israeli society were sown early. For example, the Zionist movement began as a secular movement primarily among European Jews whose source of ethnic identity over the two millennia of European coexistence and anti-Semitism was based primarily on their maintaining both separate and distinct religious and cultural identities. Viewing Zionism as a secular movement instantly created tension between the religious orthodoxy and their Zionist secular co-religionists (Shafir & Peled, 2003)—tensions that are still visible today.

A second set of problems concerns the very nature of these European émigrés. European Zionists were predominately of Jewish-*Ashkenazi* backgrounds (Hebrew, in plural: *Ashkenazim*) from the occident (that is, Western and Eastern Europe) and brought with them to the land of Palestine the formal and informal cultural institutions of their European homelands.

With the first immigration wave of 1948–1951, the number of Jews in Israel increased rapidly (Israel Ministry of Foreign Affairs, 1998), with the majority of immigrants coming from the remnants of European Jewry following the Holocaust, or from the tremendous influx of Jews of primarily oriental backgrounds (that is, Jews of Middle Eastern descent), referred to as *mizrachim* (Hebrew translation of "easterners"). As *mizrachim* immigrated to, and were absorbed by, the predominately Europeanized Jewish state, intraethnic tensions mounted as *mizrachim* were predominantly delegated to a lower socioeconomic status and were politically and culturally disenfranchised.

The different demographic trajectories of *Ashkenizim* and *mizrachim* can be illustrated through the examination of geographical residency within Israel. As Shafir and Peled (2003) point out, the common *Ashkenazi–mizrachi* distinction disguises important differences among the *mizrachim* themselves. This ethnic group is primarily bimodal, with its members originating in two different cultural areas: the Middle East (primarily Iraq and Yemen) and North Africa (primarily Morocco).

This differentiation is visible in the absorption of immigrants from these two geographical areas. Middle Eastern Jews arrived in Israel in the early 1950s and were primarily settled in the center of the country in towns, villages, and neighborhoods left vacant by fleeing Palestinian refugees during the War of Independence in 1948 (Shafir & Peled, 2003). North African Jews, however, arriving primarily in the late 1950s and early 1960s, were settled in "developmental towns" located in the periphery in outlying areas (Yiftachel & Tzfadia, 1999). Middle-Eastern Jews, therefore, became owners of prime real estate in the country's center, and North African Jews were shunted to "development towns" (a designation for newly formed towns founded to aid in the economic and Jewish development of a geographical area). This differential settlement process brought with it economic, social, and educational by-products. Today, a majority of Israeli Jews live in the country's center (Shafir & Peled, 2003), which remains the powerhouse of the Israeli economy, establishment, and culture.

Despite being a Jewish ethnic minority within an *Ashkenazi* hegemony, *mizrachi* birth rates are traditionally higher than their *Ashkenazi* counterparts and have led, over the years, to the gradual realignment of the Jewish electoral and economic base of the country. Having been the culturally and socially disenfranchised group for the first thirty years, today *mizrachim* constitute a significant and politically powerful part of the country's Jewish electorate.

Disparities still exist, however. For example, within the Jewish majority, unemployment among second-generation *Ashkenazim* in 1993 was 4.9 percent and among *mizrachim* 13.2 percent. In 1988, the average *mizrachi* head of a household earned only 80 percent of the income of his *Ashkenazi* counterpart, but only 64 percent per capita (Shafir & Peled, 2003). Further, whereas in 1975 the income of an Israel-born *mizrachi* employee with a college degree was equal to that of a similarly qualified *Ashkenazi*, in 1995, the former's income was only 78 percent of the latter's (Shafir & Peled, 2003, p. 84).

Taking another focus, it can be seen that massive immigration, along with the United Nations declaration, changed Palestine forever. It went from an unimportant backwater province of the Ottoman empire, consisting only of a handful of impoverished groups of Jews in the late nineteenth and early twentieth centuries to a fledgling modern nation with a clear Europeanized majority. The creation of the Jewish state meant demographic transformation, land acquisition, the development of a separate Jewish economy, and the development of separate social, political, and economic, and educational institutions (Farsoun & Zacharia, 1977).

Dramatic alterations in the balance of power between the different ethnic and religious groups in Israel meant the delegation of the Israeli Arab population into the status of a permanent minority with questionable political power. Wherever the Arab population lives, incomes and educational levels remain below those of their Jewish compatriots. (Note that similar income and education-level gaps may also be found in the Jewish sector when comparing central cities with peripheral towns and between orthodox religious and nonreligious Jews.)

Poverty remains endemic in the Israeli Arab population, as exemplified by infant mortality rates. For instance, in 1993 the mortality rate for the Jewish majority was 5.7 deaths per 1,000 births. For the Muslim minority, this number was 13.5 per 1,000 births, and for the Druze and Bedouins, it was 14.2 per 1,000 births (Israel Ministry of Foreign Affairs, 1998).

Early Educational Efforts

Before independence, during the *yeshuv* (Hebrew for "settlement," used to describe Jewish settlers in pre-independence Israel) period, all types of Jewish educational institutions from kindergarten to teacher-training colleges were divided into three primary ideological trends, which differed from each other in their educational aims, curricula, and methods of instruction. Each trend received its own funding and advocated for its own educational and political agendas through the school system and through affiliated youth movements (Zameret, 1998). Hence, pre-independence Israel saw each trend competing for resources and power, which manifested itself in the competition for more schools and more students.

More than half of the students attended the "General Trend," associated with Jewish secularism, modernity, and scientific and cultural enlightenment coupled with general Zionist values. These schools steered a middle course between Jewish religion and culture and secular nationalism and emphasized ideals of a national revival movement, focusing on the study of the Bible, Hebrew literature, and language and knowledge of Palestine (Kleinberger, 1969).

The schools of the Labor trend emphasized manual work, agriculture, and the principles of the Zionist Labor movement. It focused on the development of a secular-socialist and Zionist youth and was closely aligned with the *Kibbutz* (collective farm) movement. About 20 percent of enrolled children attended schools associated with the Labor trend. The third trend, the *Mizrachi* trend, espoused primarily a religious-Zionist philosophy through an integration of religious studies and Zionist culture and placed special emphasis on study of the Torah and the Talmud—the primary sources of religious Jewish doctrine—at the expense of scientific, technical, and cultural subjects (Zameret, 1998).

After 1948, Israel was a highly splintered nation with massive immigration, few resources, and many real and existential enemies who presented a clear and present danger for the new nation's existence. The small economic, agricultural, and industrial base present in pre-independence Israel had been destroyed by the War of Independence and subsequent waves of immigration. During its initial years, due to dire economic conditions, the government imposed emergency rationing for food, clothing, fuel, and other necessities. The challenge to integrate society and to build a nation out of an assortment of widely differing ethnic groups, customs, and languages was a daunting task for the new and impoverished country. The founders quickly realized that the nation's viability was dependent on its cohesiveness, and they saw the unification of the educational system as the primary vehicle for achieving national unity, cohesiveness, and strength.

Education Post-1948

As stressed, a common thread throughout the Israeli experience is the effects of the absorption of waves of Jewish immigration. Then, when the Jewish majority took hold, it created a European hegemony in all cultural and national institutions that was, of course, reflected in the educational system of the time.

The ethos of equality and unity was a main driving force. Approximately forty years of successive governments controlled by the Labor party espoused a clear socialist and welfare state ideology, in which the school system was always the primary agent of change and a major device for mobility and integration for new immigrants.

The Compulsory Education Law of 1949 saw the massive entrance of children into public education. It also saw a shift in the emphasis from the pedagogical and politically oriented educational subsystems that characterized the administration of schools before 1948 to a more centralized and homogenous orientation. In an attempt to promote equality and to ensure uniformity, the emerging national educational system featured a high degree of central control.

However, the educational challenges facing the nation between 1948 and 1973 were massive. During that period, Israel's gross domestic product (GDP) rose by more than 10 percent per annum. This exponential and sustained increase in GDP continued while Israel absorbed waves of immigrants, built a modern economic and military infrastructure, fought four wars where each presented a clear existential threat to the state's survival, and maintained internal public security in the face of continued terrorist attacks on Israelis (Israel Ministry of Foreign Affairs, 2003). Education faced the challenges of a young country with a market economy heavily burdened by defense expenditures. Until the 1967 war (also called the Six-Day War), defense spending ranged between 10 and 16 percent of GDP; from 1970 to 1972, this outlay increased to over 25 percent. It has since leveled out again at between 10 to 16 percent.

As with most industrialized countries, between 1973 and 1979 GDP fell, only to jump again in the 1990s to an annual growth rate of 6.4 percent. Also, since the late 1970s, the Israeli body politic has become more capitalistic, and with it have come the typical social-welfare problems of other western capitalist states. During the immigration waves of the last decade, GDP per capita grew by more than 60 percent, despite a change in the civilian labor force from 1.65 million workers in 1990 to 2.52 million in 2001 (Israel Ministry of Foreign Affairs, 2003).

In 2003, only 41.16 percent the national budget was allocated to all of the nation's social services. Despite this, the Ministry of Education (MOE) received approximately 31 percent of that allocation. This only constitutes approximately 13 percent of the entire national budget, compared to 21.62 percent for defense spending and 17.29 percent for debt reduction.

Nevertheless, national expenditure on education places Israel among the highest investing countries in public education in comparison with other OECD (Organization for Economic Co-operation and Development) countries.

SCHOOLING

The educational system during the Mandate period and following the creation of the state reflects the successes, challenges, and internal debates facing the Israeli education system for the opening decades of the twenty-first century. The continuing economic, social, and political gaps between the Jewish and non-Jewish sectors of Israeli society, as well as within the different sectors of the Jewish population (for example, *Ashkenazim* versus *mizrachim;* Israeli-born, known as old-timers or *sabras,* versus immigrants or newcomers; secular versus religious) creates major cultural, political, ethnic, and economic realities as the educational system attempts to mold these competing identities into a unified nation. Also remaining is the question of how to deal with security versus social equity. Waves of immigration add new layers of complexity. And, looming over this, and all other processes in the country, is the tremendous burden of the cost of defense and debt reduction.

The Educational System

The educational system has always been charged as the primary vehicle for diminishing the differences among immigrants and between immigrants and the *vatikim* (Hebrew: old-timers) and ensuring social, political, cultural, and economic mobility for all. The system is controlled by a strong central bureaucracy located in Jerusalem and run by the Minister of Education (MOE) and a Director General.

The MOE is judicially and politically responsible for the enactment of laws and the operation of the educational system. It sets national goals, tightly controls inputs and the allocation of budgets, monitors and controls student achievements through national performance evaluation tests, determines the national curriculum, and is responsible for employing teachers and the construction of new schools (Glasman, 1986).

As shown in Figure 7.1, the educational system is divided geographically into six districts (the Jerusalem district is divided into the periphery of Jerusalem and the city of Jerusalem). These supervise and monitor the educational processes conducted by schools to ensure the compatibility of these processes with central policies (Zucker, 1985).

The official state school system consists of two trends in accordance with the Law of State Education enacted in 1953 recognizing each religious sector's right to autonomy regarding separate institutions, teachers, inspectors, and curricula (Gaziel, 1996). State schools serve the nonreligious sector; state-religious schools serve those seeking greater emphasis on religious Judaism in the curriculum. The ratio of enrollment in the two trends is about 75 percent in the state system and 25 percent in the state-religious system.

Two additional sectors whose schools belong to the official school system are Israeli Arabs and Druze (Ministry of Education, Culture and Sport, 1988). Both groups regard themselves as part of the Arab world by virtue of shared culture and language, which manifests itself in the existence of separate institutions, teachers, and curricula.

The structure of these schools and the curricula studied are analogous to those in the Jewish sector, with necessary changes to accommodate the different language and cultural needs; teaching is almost exclusively conducted in Arabic, for example. These schools are centrally supervised and controlled by the Directorate of the Arabic Education and Culture

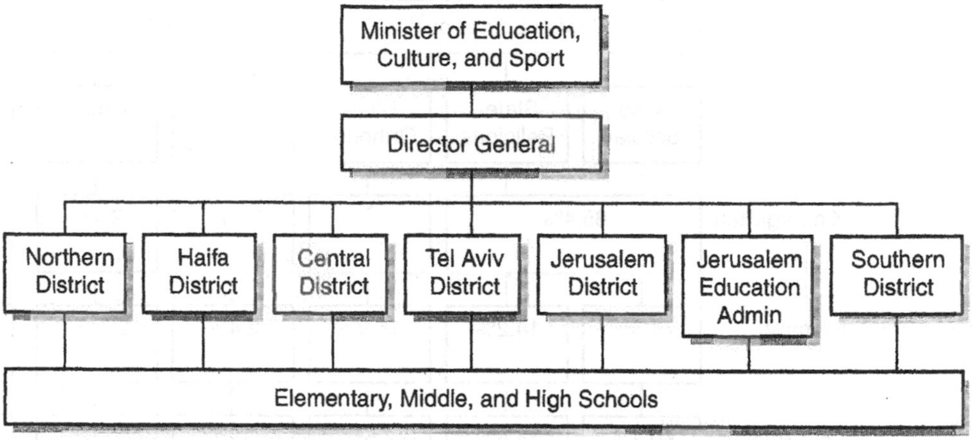

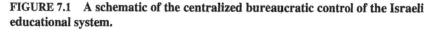

FIGURE 7.1 A schematic of the centralized bureaucratic control of the Israeli educational system.

Department at the Ministry, and all structural and thematic changes introduced in Hebrew education are also implemented in Arab and Druze schools.

A relatively new trend, although rather heterogeneous, consists of schools serving various social groups seeking educational services characterized by a particular educational, ideological, and/or pedagogical emphasis. These groups are served mostly by nonformal and recognized schools, which are supervised by the MOE.

Finally, Christian Arabs and Ultra-Orthodox Jews are two additional sectors receiving educational services in exempted schools outside the state school system. This group of schools consists of Arab Mission schools supervised and controlled by the Catholic Church and Jewish traditional Talmud-Torahs supervised by Ultra-Orthodox political parties and the rabbis of the Ultra-Orthodox community. A breakdown of the different systems is summarized in Figure 7.2.

Variations exist in the number of teaching hours in the curriculum for various issues by each trend or sector. However, there are several core issues that are studied in all Israeli elementary schools.

The system sees constant growth. For example, the number of pupils enrolled increased more than sixteen-fold over a period of fifty years, from 108,131 pupils in 1948 to 1,804,410 pupils in 1998. The number of immigrant pupils is also continually increasing (about 1.5 percent in 1991 to approximately 11 percent in 1996) (Ministry of Education, Culture and Sport, 1996), as is the number of immigrant teachers (1,950 teachers in 1992 to 5,150 in 1996).

In the school year 2001, the Israeli educational system included 3,652 schools (including schools for children with special needs) (Central Bureau of Statistics, 2001). The public school structure is divided into four main stages, following the reform implemented in the entire school system in 1968, which extended compulsory and free education from the eighth to the tenth grade: kindergarten (from age 5 to 6 years), elementary school (grades 1 through 6), middle school (grades 7 through 9), and high school (grades 10 through 12).

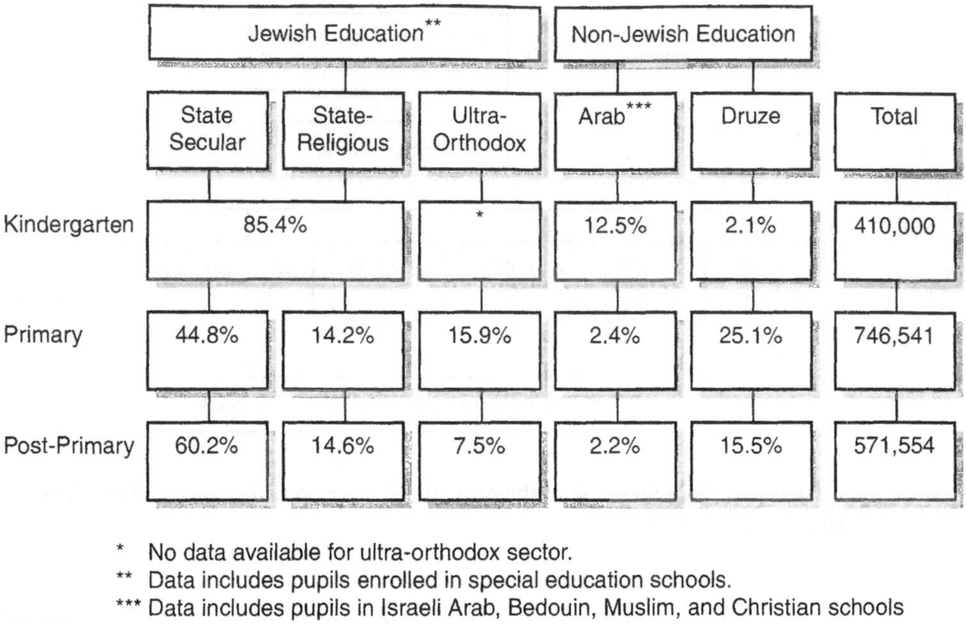
Jewish Education**
Non-Jewish Education
State Secular
State-Religious
Ultra-Orthodox
Arab***
Druze
Total
Kindergarten
85.4%
*
12.5%
2.1%
410,000
Primary
44.8%
14.2%
15.9%
2.4%
25.1%
746,541
Post-Primary
60.2%
14.6%
7.5%
2.2%
15.5%
571,554
* No data available for ultra-orthodox sector.
** Data includes pupils enrolled in special education schools.
*** Data includes pupils in Israeli Arab, Bedouin, Muslim, and Christian schools

FIGURE 7.2 A breakdown of Jewish and non-Jewish education by type of school.
Source: Adapted from Nir & Inbar (2003) and State of Israel (2001).

High schools are run either by Local Education Authorities (LEAs) or by semi-public/private nonprofit organizations. The focus of secondary schools is academic, technological/vocational, or agricultural. In rural areas, high schools are regional and serve students who live within driving distance. The annual dropout rates for pupils in upper secondary education is about 4.8 percent in Jewish education and 11.8 percent in Arab education (Central Bureau of Statistics, 2001).

More than 37,000 pupils study in special education frameworks. An additional 40,000 pupils study in general education frameworks and receive special assistance (Ministry of Education, Culture and Sport, 1998).

A Move toward Decentralization

The "Compulsory Education Law" allows parents to have their children educated according to their religious views (Bentwich, 1965). Therefore, children may enroll in one of three groups of schools, each serving a different sector of Israeli society. A school may be "official" (that is, maintained by the government and the LEAs) "recognized" (that is, supervised and supported by the government), or "exempted" (not seeking government supervision or support and in practice subjected to no government control).

LEAs are mainly responsible for issues relating to facility maintenance and for the initiation of special programs. Although great diversity exists among the different LEAs as a result of economic and political constraints and geographical location, academic standards are controlled through national matriculation examinations conducted by the MOE.

Although the initiation of a centralized structure in the Israeli educational system was meant to ensure equality and uniformity, these educational policies have limited schools' capacities to properly address the particular needs of children and to engage in activities based on local initiatives. Instead of creating educational programs that correspond with the needs of the various student populations in light of the increasing diversity in the Israeli educational system, school principals have had to confront guidelines, sanctions, and programs prepared by numerous MOE divisions and by regional inspectors (Vollansky & Bar-Elli, 1995), which in many cases have had little relevance for their schools. This increase in the discrepancy between central policies and children's needs may be understood in light of the constant growth that the Israeli educational system is facing and the increasing diversity in the educational needs of children.

Therefore, after recognizing the negative effects that strong centralization has had on the quality and adequacy of the educational processes occurring in schools, the system recently began to decentralize. Currently, a school-based policy has been introduced in elementary state and state religious schools (Nir, 2001, 2003a, 2003b) in an attempt to increase the decision-making power delegated to school principals.

Evaluation

In elementary schools, in addition to school-level efforts to track of student achievement, control is obtained through national evaluation tests. These are divided into two main categories and have undergone significant changes over the years (Levi & Nesher, 1999; Ministry of Education, Culture and Sport, 1995). The first is a National Feedback Test intended to provide decision makers with information regarding the educational system, such as basic data on inputs, processes, and outputs. However, this form of feedback focuses mainly on teaching and learning outcomes. A second feedback test is conducted at the school level and is basically a diagnostic tool intended to serve teachers and school principals in the process of learning, teaching, and other school-level activities. In its current form, this form of feedback is known as the Measure of School Effectiveness and Growth (*Meitzav*).

Teacher Training

The mass immigration and the rapid growth of the educational system focused attention on the quality of teacher education and led to the massive development of programs initially offered by postsecondary institutions called "seminars" or teaching colleges. Later, as a result of the tension between teacher education programs offered by the seminars and colleges and universities, and based on the recommendations of the Etzioni committee (a blue-ribbon committee appointed by the Minister in 1981 to improve the quality of teacher education), the seminars turned into academic institutions under the supervision of the Council for Higher Education in an attempt to promote the academization of the teaching profession and the professional status of the teachers (Etzioni, 1981). Accordingly, the majority of students in teacher education programs in Israel since the early 1990s in both seminars and the universities have been enrolled in academic programs and have graduated with a baccalaureate and a teaching diploma (Ariav & Seidenberg, 1995; Kfir & Ariav, 2004).

LOOKING FORWARD: PROBLEMS AND CHALLENGES

The Israeli public education system deals with competing identities as well as political and economic realities. Indeed, the system is under a constant state of siege as various demographic groups and goals clash with one another and compete within the marketplace. Much of the current criticism levied at the system is accurate but unavoidable as a young country tries to deal with mass immigration, wars, and economic hardships.

In this section, we attempt to describe the major challenges facing the Israeli educational system for the first quarter of the twenty-first century. To do this, we will examine three primary challenges: the ubiquitous gaps between levels of enfranchisement for different groups in Israeli society, the constant struggle between the need to achieve national unity while embracing democratic pluralism and school-level autonomy, and the crisis of teacher preparation. Each of these challenges is multifaceted in light of the inherent complexity and budgetary constraints characterizing a national system overburdened by defense costs.

The Israeli educational system must deal with major national and educational issues under the specter of severe budgetary problems. The overwhelming funds required for the absorption of immigrants as well as the perennial military threat from the Arab world (both internal and external) has impacted upon all aspects of the young nation, usurping great fiscal and human resources to keep the country physically and economically safe.

As we have stressed, Israel, by definition, is a nation of immigrants, and immigration has always, and will always, play a pivotal role in all aspects of society. The "gathering of the exiles," their modernization and molding into an informed citizenry steeped in democratic and Israeli social norms while maintaining their multicultural identity, falls primarily on the educational system.

At the same time, the fact that individuals immigrate to Israel because of a wide variety of different pull-and-push factors creates stresses that are both inescapable and exacerbated by the limited fiscal resources set aside for this purpose. The question and primary challenge of the system, therefore, involves the equitable distribution of resources in order to ensure equal opportunities for all.

The looming costs of maintaining security impacts upon, and sets the agenda for, all of Israeli society, including the educational system. The Israeli economy is reeling from years of the Intifada, massive national debt, and high rates of unemployment.

Educational Disenfranchisement

Perhaps the greatest challenge facing the educational system is the disparity between educational achievement and enfranchisement for different sectors of Israeli society. Since achieving independence, the country's leaders have repeatedly declared that a primary goal of the educational system has been to reduce the socioeconomic gaps between different segments of the population.

It is possible to examine these gaps from a myriad of economical, cultural, and legal points of view. The next section focuses primarily on educational expenditures and outcomes. The issue is examined on an interethnic level (that is, Jewish versus Arab allocations in education) and an intraethnic (*Ashkenizim* versus *mizrachim*) level.

Gaps within the Jewish Sector. Today, a significant disparity exists in educational performance among the primary Jewish groups. These gaps are visible between different socioeconomic groups; between *Ashkenazim* and *mizrachim;* between old-timers and new immigrants; and between different towns, cities, and villages as well as between Jew and Arab.

Ministers of Education over the last decade targeted the issue of high school matriculation rates, which they saw as an objective benchmark of the Israeli public education system, and set the goal of a 50 percent success rate. There has been a steady increase in the number of youngsters completing matriculation requirements for high school. In 1980, only 20 percent completed their matriculation; in 1990, 30 percent; and in 1999, 41.6 percent. In 2004, 46.8 percent all Israeli 17-year-olds passed their matriculation exams (Khromchenko, 2004; Ministry of Education, Culture and Sport, 2003; Swirsky & Atkin, 2004).

It would appear that Israel is achieving its 50 percent target. However, closer examination of these numbers and of those communities achieving degrees of success shows a disturbing trend. In 1999, only 32 of the 103 localities (31 percent) with more than 10,000 residents were able to achieve this goal. The vast majority lived in long-established or well-to-do communities in the country's center (Swirsky, 2000). In 45 out of the 103 communities, the percentage of students passing their matriculation was lower than the national average. The rate was lowest in Arab localities and development towns; 15 of the 21 were below the national average and saw high dropout rates among secondary-age students (Central Bureau of Statistics, 2000; Swirsky, 2000).

The Israeli educational system has consistently underperformed in several key areas: language arts, mathematics, and science education (National Taskforce for the Advancement of Education in Israel, 2004). Performance of Israeli students remains lower than most OECD countries for most academic areas and age groups examined (National Taskforce, 2004; OECD, 2004).

For example, an examination of Trends in International Mathematics and Science Study data (TIMSS, 2003) shows Israeli students performing well below international averages, a trend that has been developing for several years. Similarly, Progress in International Reading Literacy Study (PIRLS) data reveal a similar yet less extreme situation (Mullis, Martin, Gonzalez, & Kennedy, 2003), although Israeli youngsters underperform compared to their agemates around the world.

These diminishing results are even more vexing, as they coexist with increasing per capita expenditures. Educational expenditures in Israel are 15 percent higher per student than the average in twenty-eight developed countries in the 1990s, yet produced TIMMS test scores 8 percent lower than these same countries in 1999 (Adva Center, 1997; Khromchenko, 2004).

An examination of university acceptance requirements (National Taskforce, 2004) further negates claims of achievement implied solely by the examination of matriculation scores. It shows a substantive and widespread problem.

Acceptance to one of the six universities in the country is dependent, to a large extent, on matriculation scores weighted with psychometric evaluations. One study (Swirsky & Atkin, 2004) found that approximately 15 percent of the pupils who matriculated in 2003 were unfit and could not meet the university's minimal acceptance standards. The national committee that examined this issue pointed to several factors (National Taskforce, 2004): organizational changes that inflate the number of children entitled to a matriculation diploma; testing accommodations for pupils with learning disabilities (the same period has also seen an exponential increase in the number of students eligible for these accommodations); and an increase in the number and diversity of subjects taught in high schools. Because of this, the National Taskforce (2004) recommended not using the number of children entitled to a matriculation diploma as a measure of the system's success, but rather implied that objective benchmarks be used despite claims by the Minister of Education to the contrary (Editorial, 2004).

In summary, diminishing social gaps and increasing academic achievements are among the major challenges facing the Israeli educational system. Educational performance compared to national and international benchmarks shows that standards are lowering and schools are being asked to do more with less. To deal with this continuing problem, the MOE has enacted comprehensive regulations and standards as well as a system of high-stakes testing for all schools and all ages.

Narrowing Social Gaps. Another major challenge facing the Israeli educational system is related to decreasing social gaps and providing equal opportunities for the various social groups in Israel. Such gaps may be viewed when the amount of inputs and level of educational outputs are compared between central cities in Israel and developmental towns located in the periphery. They may also be evident between various LEAs, which differ to a great extent in their financial condition and therefore the amount of resources they allot for educational purposes. Gaps may also be evident in families' ability to purchase enrichment services for their children.

The Israeli MOE has attempted to diminish these gaps primarily by employing a differential formula for resource allocation to schools based on the socioeconomic status of the children and the communities schools serve. These efforts have not significantly decreased the existing social gaps. A prominent example may be evident when looking at the gap between the Jewish and the Arab sectors.

For the 2001–2002 school year, 1,539,600 Jewish and 374,100 Arab students were enrolled in public education in Israel. For the Jewish population, expenditures in educational infrastructure (classes, school, and personnel) have consistently exceeded expenditures for the Israeli Arab population. For instance, for the 2001–2002 academic year, the mean number of elementary school children per class for the Jewish sector was 24.24; for the Arab sector, 29.30. In middle school, this difference decreases: 30.41 versus 33.02. In high school the difference is negligible: 26.12 versus 26.91 (Ministry of Education, Culture and Sport, 2003).

Additionally, outcomes for the two sectors remain in sharp contrast. As noted, all sectors of Israeli children improved in their achievement of matriculation diplomas. However, despite gains by the Arab sector, it still consistently underperforms vis-à-vis Jewish compatriots. This difference can also be seen by examining dropout rates for the two sectors. For the 2001–2002 academic year, 4.9 percent of the Jewish sector dropped out at the legal age of 16, versus 10 percent for Israeli Arab youth (Ministry of Education, Culture and Sport, 2003).

Finding the Optimal Mix: Embracing Unity While Encouraging Multiculturalism. Israel is a country of stark dichotomies: *Ashkenazi* versus *mizrachi;* religious versus secular; immigrant versus old-timer; working class versus middle class; enfranchised versus disenfranchised; and Zionism versus multiculturalism. The nation's founders viewed these issues both as Israel's greatest strengths and greatest weaknesses. Even today, the stresses caused by these competing needs are felt by every Israeli and dominate educational decision making. The major dilemma is how to meld these different groups into a cohesive unit while maintaining each group's cultural distinctiveness.

During the early massive immigration, different subcultures entered into the largely Europeanized nascent state. Immigrants were shunted into transit camps (Hebrew: *ma'aborot*) and were homogenized into a singular identity of the "modern Israeli." This melting pot policy sought to minimize cultural distinctiveness and maximize similarities via a common Jewish identity, often cutting off immigrants from their ancestral language and customs.

This strategy, which aimed to transform newcomers into the modern Israeli ideal, has undergone a dramatic change toward pluralism following the absorption of Jews from the former Soviet Union. Despite rampant under- and unemployment, Soviet Jews had no intention of allowing Israeli society to force them to adjust to Israel; instead, they used their formidable political clout to force Israel to adjust to them. Within two or three years, labels of Israeli-made consumer goods appeared in Hebrew, Russian, and Arabic. Within eight years, Russian-language radio led to Russian-language newspapers and even a separate all-Russian television station. By the end of the 1990s, politicians had formed Russian-only political parties, had managed to place themselves in the enviable position of being king-makers, and were courted by all Israeli politicians. In the educational system, these events have also been apparent with many children attending special Russian afterschool programs that focus on academic subjects in order to "protect" them from the "inferior" Israeli educational system.

This experience was a watershed in the Israeli psyche. Today, subcultures no longer need to kowtow to the dominant Israeli cultural hegemony. Indeed, multiculturalism is now embraced and fostered. This has, however, pushed Israel into an even more factional society and with it the concomitant national struggles for unity.

The central administration of the educational system has recognized this trend and has gradually allowed individuals and communities more input in determining the educational and cultural foci of their local schools. This has led to even a greater tendency toward decentralization (Nir, 2003b) and remains one of the great challenges facing the Israeli school system. This will definitely continue to play itself out in the future.

Personnel Upgrade. Obtaining high educational outcomes is significantly contingent on the training and professional conduct of school-level educators. Therefore, a major challenge for the Israeli educational system is to build school-level educators' professional capacities and to prepare highly qualified educators who will be able to cope with the complex tasks facing Israeli schools (see National Taskforce, 2004).

It is likely that principals' professionalism will have an increasingly stronger impact on school process and outcomes. This results from the tendency toward decentralization and school autonomy, increased formal authority delegated to school principals, and high expectations for accountability and excellence.

Changes require commensurate changes in the training and preparation of school principals that will enable them to become both the pedagogical and administrative leaders of their schools. Although principals have traditionally completed a BA or a BEd and some training in educational administration, suggested guidelines now recommend that principals earn a university-level MA in educational administration followed by an internship that will facilitate the translation of theory into practice.

Transforming the professional conduct of principals is certainly not the only step required. Teacher training must also be improved if teachers are expected to effectively cope with the complex demands and increasingly heterogeneous classes characterizing a multicultural society.

Teacher training institutions in Israel operate as independent institutions under the supervision and budgeting of the Department for Educator Training at the MOE. The supervision of the training programs and curricula is in the hands of the Council for Higher Education (Greenfield, cited in Knesset Printing Office, 2003).

As shown in Table 7.1, teacher training takes place in various institutions. Besides the five general classifications of teacher colleges, teacher training is also conducted at Israel's six universities, which focus solely on the preparation of secondary school teachers. Every year about 8,000 teachers complete their studies and are entitled to teaching diplomas.

Although consistent effort has been dedicated in recent years to the development of teachers and to the promotion of their professionalism, data reveal that in Israel, as in much of the western world, approximately 50 percent of new teachers leave the profession during their first five years on the job (Gavish, 2002). Attrition results from low salaries, long hours, lack of institutional support, and pervasive school violence (Benbenishty, Zeira, & Astor, 2000; Gavish, 2002).

There can be no excellence in educational products without excellent teachers, so an improvement in teacher recruitment and training is a vital initial step. Recruitment is not only related to salaries and benefits, it is also correlated with training, the academization of the profession, and certification and licensure issues.

Recent trends in Israel toward the academization and more stringent government control of teacher training seek to do away with BEd degrees and to accept and train teachers at a university BA or BSc level. Concurrently, teacher reform also includes attempts to substantially increase teacher pay, provide merit incentives and more opportunities for advancement, and mandate longer work days for teachers. Further, in order to combat the high teacher burnout rates (Friedman, 2000), teacher mentoring programs will be implemented and evaluated. Certainly, in considering the continual and pervasive budgetary problems facing the MOE, it is unclear how these reforms will be carried out.

TABLE 7.1 Enrollment in Teacher Training Institutions in 2003

SECTOR	NUMBER OF ENROLLEES
National Secular	15,677
National Religious	5,000
Israeli Arab	2,395
Non-academic National	998
Religious Orthodox	8,876
Universities	1,000
	33,936

CONCLUSION

It is clear that educational policies, expenditures, and input have not generated the same opportunities and outcomes for all members of Israeli society. Improving the education of those living in the periphery mandates the focusing of economic and educational resources in those areas. Increased expenditures in teacher training and retention, as well as improving the physical infrastructure of the schools, should proceed concurrently with improving the local economies in all parts of the country and for all sectors of the population.

Much still needs to be accomplished. However, one cannot overlook the remarkable achievements of the Israeli educational system, which has struggled for the last fifty-five years to make social and educational dreams come true.

REFERENCES

Adva Center. (1997). Public expenditure on education as percentage of national expenditure on education: Israel and selected OECD countries. Retrieved August 24, 2004, from http://www.adva.org/ivrit/educationtt.htm

Ariav, T., & Seidenberg, A. (1995). Reform and development in teacher education in Israel. In J. J. Lane (Ed.), *Ferment in education: A look abroad, The National Society for the Study of Education* (pp. 122–147). Chicago: University of Chicago Press.

Bassok, M. (2004, August 24). On eve of 5765, population stands at 6.8m. *Haaretz*, p. 1.

Benbenishty, R., Zeira, A., & Astor, R. A. (2000). *Alimut b'ma'arechet hachinuch b'yisrael: Doch mimtsa'im mesakem [in Hebrew: Violence in the Israeli school system: Final summary report]*. Jerusalem: The Hebrew University of Jerusalem.

Bentwich, J. S. (1965). *Education in Israel*. London: Routledge & Kegan Paul.

Central Bureau of Statistics. (2000). *Examinees sitting for matriculation certificates and certificates of school completion, and degrees earned, 5758* (No. 1045). Jerusalem: Author.

Central Bureau of Statistics. (2001). *Statistical Abstract of Israel 2001*. Jerusalem: Author.

Chitrit, S. S. (2001). *Mizrachi politics in Israel: Between identification and integration to protest and alternative*. Unpublished dissertation, The Hebrew University of Jerusalem, Jerusalem.

Editorial. (2004, August 19). Serious educational crisis. *Haaretz*, p. 5.
Etzioni, A. (1981). Report of the National Committee which examined the statutes of the Teacher and the Teaching Profession [in Hebrew]. *Hed Hachinuch, 53*(18), 7–17.
Farsoun, S. K., & Zacharia, C. (1977). *Palestine and the Palestinians.* Boulder, CO: Westview Press.
Friedman, I. A. (2000). Burnout in teachers: Shattered dreams of impeccable professional performance. *Journal of Clinical Psychology, 56*(4), 595–606.
Gavish, B. (2002). *The gap between role expectations and actual role perception for beginning teachers during their first year of teaching.* Jerusalem: The Hebrew University of Jerusalem, Jerusalem.
Gaziel, H. (1996). *Politics and policy-making in Israel's education system.* Brighton, UK: Sussex.
Glasman, N. S. (1986). Funding and control linkages in education [in Hebrew]. In E. Ben-Baruch & Y. Newman (Eds.), *Educational administration and policy making: The case of Israel.* Tel Aviv: Unipress.
Gumpel, T. P., & Awartani, S. (2003). A comparison of special education in Israel and Palestine: Surface and deep structures. *Journal of Special Education, 37,* 33–48.
Israel Ministry of Foreign Affairs. (1996, January 28). *The absorption of Ethiopian immigrants in Israel: The present situation and future objectives.* Retrieved September 7, 2004, from http://www.mfa.gov.il/MFA/Archive/Communiques/1996/The%20Absorption%20of%20Ethiopian%20Immigrants%20in%20Israel%20-
Israel Ministry of Foreign Affairs. (1998, December 24). *Population of Israel: General trends and indicators.* Retrieved July 14, 2004, from http://www.mfa.gov.il/MFA/Archive/Communiques/1998/POPULATION+OF+ISRAEL-+GENERAL+TRENDS+AND+INDICATOR.htm
Israel Ministry of Foreign Affairs. (2003, April 25). *ECONOMY—Challenges and achievements.* Retrieved September 8, 2004, from http://www.mfa.gov.il/mfa/facts%20about%20israel/economy/ECONOMY-%20Challenges%20and%20Achievements
Jewish Virtual Library. (2003). Inflation in Israel. Retrieved September 7, 2004, from http://www.jewishvirtuallibrary.org/jsource/Economy/inflation.html
Kfir, D., & Ariav, T. (2004). The reform in teacher education: A partial process and its consequences [in Hebrew]. *Megamot, 43,* 170–194.
Khromchenko, Y. (2004, August 24). Matriculants don't reach university standards. *Haaretz,* p. 1.
Kleinberger, A. F. (1969). *Society, schools and progress in Israel.* New York: Pergamon Press.
Knesset Printing Office. (2003). *Center for Research and Information: Background document for discussion of teacher preparation in Israel and the structure of the curricula in teacher training institutions.* Jerusalem: Author.
Levi, A., & Nesher, P. (1999). Evaluation and feedback in the Israeli educational system [in Hebrew]. In E. Peled (Ed.), *Fifty years of Israeli education* (pp. 455–473). Jerusalem: The Ministry of Education, Culture and Sport.
Ministry of Education, Culture and Sport. (1988). *Facts and figures about education in Israel.* Jerusalem: Ministry of Education, Culture and Sport, Economics and Budgeting Administration.
Ministry of Education, Culture and Sport. (1995). *General Director's Special Memorandum #4 [in Hebrew].* Jerusalem: State of Israel, Ministry of Education.
Ministry of Education, Culture and Sport. (1996). *The educational system by the numbers [in Hebrew].* Jerusalem: Author.
Ministry of Education, Culture and Sport. (1998). *Data on matriculation examinations, 5758 (1998) [in Hebrew].* Jerusalem: Pedagogical Administration, Examinations Division.
Ministry of Education, Culture and Sport. (2003). *The educational system by the numbers [in Hebrew].* Jerusalem: Author.
Mullis, I. V. S., Martin, M. O., Gonzalez, E. J., & Kennedy, A. M. (2003). *PIRLS 2001 International Report.* Chestnut Hill, MA: PIRLS International Study Center.
National Taskforce for the Advancement of Education in Israel. (2004). *The National Plan for Education, Part I* [in Hebrew] (pp. 1–111). Jerusalem: Government Printing Office.
Nir, A. E. (2001). Planning for school-based management: The teachers' point of view. *Educational Planning, 13*(1), 19–32.
Nir, A. E. (2003a). The impact of school-based management on public schools in Israel. *Curriculum and Teaching, 18,* 65–80.
Nir, A. E. (2003b). Quasi-market: The changing context of schooling. *The International Journal of Educational Reform, 12,* 26–39.
Nir, A. E., & Inbar, D. E. (2003). School principals in the Israeli educational system: From headteachers to professional leaders. In L. E. Watson (Ed.), *Selecting and developing heads of schools: Twenty-three European perspectives* (pp. 137–148). Sheffield, England: European Forum on Educational Administration.

Organization of Economic Co-operation and Development (OECD). (2004). *OECD handbook for internationally comparative education statistics: Concepts, standards, definitions and classifications.* Paris: OECD Publications.

Shafir, G., & Peled, Y. (2003). *Being Israeli: The dynamics of multiple citizenship.* New York: Cambridge University Press.

State of Israel. (2001). *Statistical Abstracts of Israel.* Jerusalem: Government Printing Office.

Swirsky, S. (2000). *Students passing matriculation exams in 1999.* Tel Aviv: Adva Center.

Swirsky, S., & Atkin, A. (2004, June). *Eligibility for matriculation by settlement [in Hebrew].* Tel Aviv: Adva Center.

Trends in International Mathematics and Science Study (TIMSS). (2003). Retrieved August 27, 2004, from http://nces.ed.gov/timss/results.asp

Vollansky, A., & Bar-Elli, D. (1995). Moving toward equitable school-based management. *Educational Leadership, 53,* 60–62.

Yiftachel, O., & Tzfadia, E. (1999). *Policy and identity in development towns: The case of North-African immigrants, 1952–1998 [in Hebrew].* Beersheba: Negev Center for Regional Development.

Zameret, Z. (1998, July 14). Fifty years of education in the State of Israel. Retrieved September 9, 2004, from http://www.mfa.gov.il/MFA/History/Modern%20History/Israel%20at%2050/Fifty%20Years%20of%20Education%20in%20the%20State%20of%20Israel

Zucker, D. (1985). The Israeli educational system: Structure, organization, financing and patterns of action [in Hebrew]. In W. Ackerman, A. Carmon, & D. Zucker (Eds.), *Education in an evolving society: Schooling in Israel.* Jerusalem: The Van Leer Institute.

CHAPTER EIGHT

EDUCATION SYSTEMS IN AN IDEOLOGICAL STATE

Major Issues and Concerns in Pakistan

MAHNAZIR RIAZ

THE SOCIAL FABRIC

Pakistan, which means "land of the pure," emerged as an independent Muslim state on August 14, 1947, as a result of the partition of the subcontinent of South Asia into two states: Pakistan and India. Pakistan was originally comprised of two parts called East Pakistan and West Pakistan, which were separated from each other by 1,000 miles of Indian territory. The eastern part is now Bangladesh and the western part, Pakistan, stretches from the Korakoram Mountains in the northeast to the Arabian Sea in the southwest. It is home to the world's second highest peak, K2, which rises 28,245 feet above sea level. Pakistan is divided into three distinct geographical areas that generally correspond with the borders of its four provinces: the mountainous northern highlands called the North West Frontier Province (NWFP); the Indus River Valley, which includes the Punjab and Sindh provinces; and the vast Southwestern Plateau, which constitutes Baluchistan Province.

Pakistan is a mosaic of ethnic groups held together by the common religion of Islam. The major ethnic groups are Pushtuns (or Pathans), Punjabis, Sindhis, and Muhajirs (who are immigrants from India at the time of partition) and their descendants. The Punjabis and Sindhis comprise about 75 percent of the population and are subdivided into several groups.

The country has a long and colorful history dating back to the seventh century, when Muslim sailors arrived on the coast of Sindh. A series of invasions by Muslim Afghan and Turkish peoples took place during the eleventh through eighteenth centuries.

Mahnazir Riaz is former Professor and Chairperson of the Department of Psychology, University of Peshawar, NWFP, Pakistan. She was Professor at the Centre of Excellence in Psychology at the Quaid-e-Azam University, Islamabad, Pakistan. Active in numerous academic and professional organizations, her scholarly, teaching, and service contributions have been recognized through awards and distinctions. She won the Star Woman International Award (1996) and the highest national academic award—IZAZ-e-KAMAL (2002)—awarded by the president of Pakistan for her outstanding academic achievements.

This led to an increased influence of Islam on peoples of present-day Afghanistan, Pakistan, and Bangladesh. From the early thirteenth century until the beginning of British political ascendancy in the mid-1800s, Muslims ruled over the subcontinent. By 1760, the British began to exercise extensive political and military control over India. However, it took about a century to incorporate India into the British Empire. It was in 1856 that the last Mughal ruler was exiled and the British brought most of what today constitutes India and Pakistan under their rule. After ninety years of British rule, the Indian subcontinent was partitioned into India and Pakistan. The result was the formation of two independent states, on the basis of a greater concentration of Muslims in Pakistan and Hindus in India.

With the death of the first Governor General of Pakistan in 1948 and the assassination of its first Prime Minister in 1951, political instability and economic difficulty became prominent features of post-independence Pakistan. In October 1958, General Mohammad Ayub Khan assumed control of Pakistan as Chief Martial Law Administrator. He introduced reforms in the agricultural, economic, and political sectors, was elected President, and governed the country for ten years until he was compelled by numerous agitation movements to resign in March 1969. He handed over the responsibility for governing to the Commander-in-Chief of the Army, who became President and Chief Martial Law Administrator. In December 1970, elections were held that resulted in a polarization of relations between East and West Pakistan. The country was split, with neither major political party having any support in the other part of Pakistan. Negotiations to form a coalition government failed, a civil war ensued, India became involved, and the end result was East Pakistan declaring itself an independent country thereafter called Bangladesh.

Another major, and internationally even more significant, source of conflicts and instability is the disputes over the Jammu and Kashmir regions. These have been a constant source of tensions and frequent conflicts between India and Pakistan. India attacked Pakistan in September 1965, with heavy casualties on both sides. Skirmishes continued over the next three decades, and an escalating war of words led to speculations by the international media, in 2004, that a nuclear exchange between India and Pakistan might be imminent. Fortunately, continuing diplomatic negotiations have greatly reduced the level of tension.

Social and Demographic Profile

Pakistan has an estimated population of just over 161.6 million (Country faces uphill task, 2005) and is the sixth most populous country in the world. About 97 percent of Pakistanis are Muslims; the remainder includes Christians, Hindus, and other minority religions. The current rate of population growth is around 1.98 percent. About 40 percent of the population is under 14 years of age; 55.8 percent is in the age range of 15 to 64 years; 4 percent is 65 years and above. As the society is agriculturally based, around 67 percent of the population lives in rural areas.

The economic patterns and standards of living in rural areas are markedly different from the cities. Of particular significance is the fact that villages are highly underdeveloped. Most are without electricity, telephones, clean drinking water, proper sanitation, and a proper linkage of roads to the cities. In a predominantly agricultural society like Pakistan, ownership of land is a key issue in development. Despite the government's occasional efforts to introduce land reforms, landlords, tribal chiefs, and feudal and religious figures still control much of the land, and many farmers are merely sharecroppers.

Pakistani society is inegalitarian in numerous ways, with income and assets unevenly distributed among different areas, sectors, and classes. A small minority enjoys immense wealth; the great majority lives in poverty. This unequal distribution of wealth is directly related to education: The use of education facilities is directly related to income. Children of upper-income families are overrepresented among college graduates, as compared to lower-income families.

Urdu, the national language, is widely understood throughout Pakistan, but it is spoken as a first language by less than 10 percent of the population. English is still used in government offices, higher ranks of the armed forces, and as a medium of instruction in most universities, colleges, and schools.

Economic Structure

Since independence in 1947, the economic development of Pakistan has been very erratic. The economy was shattered by three wars with India (1948, 1965, and 1971); investor confidence was undermined in 1972 by the large-scale nationalization of industries and financial institutions; a massive devaluation (57 percent) of the currency took place in 1977; there was a manifold increase in oil prices in 1979; and today oil prices remain at a record highs, with crippling effects on the Pakistani economy. Another serious blow to the economy of Pakistan came in the form of fallout from the war in Afghanistan. Political uncertainty in Pakistan during 1988 to 1996 witnessed the dismissal of three elected governments and four caretaker regimes (the last one lasting only 45 days), and this created economic uncertainty. Yet, surprisingly, in view of all the adverse factors influencing development of the country, Pakistan's economy has grown more rapidly than the economies of its South Asian neighbors, including India, Bangladesh, and Sri Lanka.

Today, Pakistan's economic structure is in transition from an agricultural base to a service and manufacturing base. This is reflected in the accelerating growth in services and manufacturing as a portion of total employment and gross domestic product (GDP). Unemployment and inflation are in check, and exports are rising. Major exports of the country include cotton, textile goods, rice, hides and skins, leather items, carpets, sport goods, fruits, handicrafts, and seafood.

Of great significance is the fact that, since the end of the 1980s, Pakistan's economy has became dependent upon and dominated by the World Bank and the International Monetary Fund (IMF). These powerful agencies imposed their advisors and programs on Pakistan, and this had a profound impact on the education and economic policies of the country. In response to the influence of the World Bank and IMF, Pakistan launched a comprehensive economic revival program in 1999 to reorient the country toward a more dynamic economy characterized by limited state interference and open trade relations. This marks a new era of economic growth in Pakistan. IMF-approved government policies, bolstered by foreign assistance and renewed access to global markets since late 2001, have generated solid macroeconomic recovery. Pakistan has increased development spending from about 2 percent of GDP in the 1990s to 4.1 percent in 2003; a necessary step toward reversing the broad underdevelopment of its social sector. The country has successfully implemented IMF programs without any delay or interruption. In December 2004, Pakistan achieved the IMF's poverty reduction growth targets, marking the end of the IMF program for Pakistan. Further, real GDP growth has accelerated from 4.2 percent in 1999 to 6.4 percent in 2004, and per capita income is over $600. All these are indicators of a growing economy.

Political System

Under the 1973 Constitution of Pakistan, direct elections for 207 ordinary seats and 10 religious minority seats in the National Assembly must be held every five years. The Senate (upper house) consists of 87 indirectly elected members. The National Assembly and the Senate participate in the legislative process of the country. Both houses jointly elect a President as Head of State, and the leader of the National Assembly becomes Prime Minister and forms a cabinet. Each of the four provinces has a directly elected Provincial Assembly with a Chief Minister and Provincial Government under the overall authority of a Governor appointed by the President of Pakistan. Provincial governments are responsible for the social development of the provinces—especially education, health, agriculture, water supply, and sanitation. However, in recent years, the country continues to experience political disruptions.

The Pakistan Muslim League won the February 1997 general election with a large majority. The government was short lived, and in October 1999 the Chairman of the Joint Chiefs of Staff Committee suspended the Constitution of Pakistan. The Supreme Court of Pakistan validated the coup and granted General Musharraf executive and legislative authority for three years. He was sworn in as President of Pakistan on June 20, 2001. In a referendum held on April 30, 2002, General Musharraf's tenure as President was extended by another five years.

In this process, the structure of government changed slightly. Today, the Senate consists of 100 seats (formerly 87), and the members are indirectly elected by provincial assemblies to serve four-year terms. The National Assembly consists of 342 members (formerly 217), including 60 women and 10 members from minorities. Members of the National Assembly are elected by popular vote to serve four-year terms.

Although the international community initially condemned General Pervez Musharraf for ousting an elected government, he gained foreign acceptance after he backed the U.S. war on terror, and specifically the war in Afghanistan. After the military coup of October 12, 1999, the new Pakistani administration pursued a tough reform plan with vigor, targeting the nation's politics and the economy. In the process, Pakistan made its way back into the international community without compromising its unique political circumstances. Today, there is international recognition of the road to resurgence and stability that Pakistan has taken to play a responsible and stabilizing role in the world. Present-day Pakistan plays a pivotal role between Central Asia, West Asia, and Southeast Asia and is emerging as a force for understanding between Islam and the world's other religions, civilizations, and cultures.

The Family as a Socioeconomic Unit

Pakistan's typical family structure is patriarchal, and women usually live with their husband's family after they are married. Most households consist of kinship groups of two or more generations. Children are brought up in families where parents, grandparents, uncles, and aunts, as well as their respective families, are living and sharing the physical and the economic resources of the family.

The traditional family adheres to the norms of society, emphasizing sex role differentiation. Women are considered homemakers; men are viewed as breadwinners and represent the family to the outside world. Children are socialized according to gender from a very early age, with girls helping their mothers, staying at home, and being taught to be submissive. Boys are allowed to play more, to roam freely, and to display self-confidence and aggression. However, despite this division of labor, women play a major role in the economic life of the family. In rural areas, women often work longer hours than men in rearing livestock and in almost all farm activities, except plowing and irrigation. Most urban women contribute toward family income by seeking employment or by pursuing self-employment projects.

However, whether women are homemakers or professionals, the authority of men over women, and elders over youngsters, is strongly evident in the traditional family. The eldest man in the family makes decisions in all important family matters, including marriage.

Increasingly, urbanization, industrialization, Western-style education, and the mass media are affecting the traditional family system. Migration is scattering families. A large proportion of households, especially in towns, is now composed of nuclear families. Education for girls is becoming more popular, and increasing numbers of occupations are opening to women.

SCHOOLING

When the Muslim world started modernizing itself, it was invaded by "liberal" and "Marxist" educational, social, and political concepts. It has been easier for Muslims to resist Marxist concepts, because they are totally different from our philosophy of education. But, it has been really difficult to resist Western "liberalism." All branches of knowledge have been seriously affected by it, and Muslim scholars have not formulated Islamic concepts to replace liberal concepts. Muslim critics of "liberal education" believe that it does not guarantee in any way the continuity of past values and undermines Islamic social and educational ideals.

Islamic Philosophy of Education

Pakistan has a unique position among other countries of the world. It is not a country founded on a territorial, linguistic, ethnic, or racial basis. Rather, Pakistan is an ideological Muslim state. According to Article 31 of the Constitution of the Islamic Republic of Pakistan, our education policy has to ensure the preservation, practice, and promotion of Islamic Ideology in accordance with the Holy Qur'an and the teachings of the Holy Prophet (peace be upon him). Accordingly, the objective of education is to enable the citizens of Pakistan to lead their lives according to the teachings of Islam embodied in the Holy Qur'an and Sunnah.

However, a Muslim's faith in Islam is not a matter of blind faith; it calls for analytical reasoning of Islamic injunctions and principles to be translated and applied to one's everyday life. This antidogmatic approach is inculcated through the Quranic and the Sunnah paradigm of education. Islam demands an attitude of critical thinking and deep knowledge. There are many verses of the Holy Qur'an that refer to those who seek knowledge, who conduct research, who introspect, interpret, and reason (Al-Qur'an, 39: 9; 3: 191; 9: 122).

To achieve these principles, to educate and train the future generations of Pakistan as true practicing Muslims, our education policy lays emphasis on developing an integrated system of national education by bringing the curricula of the *Deeni Madaris* (religious educational institutions/schools) and all other formal educational institutions closer to each other. The teachings of Islam must also be made an integral part of all pre-service training programs, for example, the Pakistan Administrative Staff College, National Institute of Public Administration, Armed Force Academies, and so on.

In this, the teacher's role is crucial. A teacher must disseminate information on the fundamental principles of Islam and Holy Qur'an and must know how these can be applied to the development of an egalitarian Muslim society. Thus, extensive in-service programs are essential. Also, the curricula of pre-service teacher training must have a compulsory component of Islamic *Uswa-e-Hasana* (behavioral model set forth by the Holy Prophet Muhammad—peace be upon him—for his followers/Muslims) and *Nazira Qur'an* (reading Qur'an with translation of principles and methods of teaching Islamic courses). In other words, teachers in Pakistan must be good Muslims who are knowledgeable about the laws and ways of Islam, able to inculcate this in their students and serve as role models.

Schooling itself should aim at the balanced growth of personality through training of spirit, intellect, rational self, feelings, and bodily senses. Education must aim at growth in all aspects: that is, spiritual, intellectual, imaginative, physical, scientific, and linguistic. Both individually and collectively, it must motivate all these dimensions of human beings toward goodness and the attainment of perfection. Hence, Islamic philosophy embodies a value system that applies to all spheres of human life.

Islamic education aims at training pupils in such a manner that, in their attitudes to life, their actions, decisions, and approaches to all kinds of knowledge, they are governed by the spiritual and ethical values of Islam. Islam is not just a matter of belief. Islam is a complete code of life wherein science and technology, as well as social, economic, and cultural activities—in brief, all aspects of life—are to be guided and determined by the principles of *Hadith* and *Sunnah* (sayings and actions of our Holy Prophet Muhammad—peace be upon him) (Government of Pakistan, 1998). In this way, a student who receives Islamic education grows up peace-loving, harmonious, equable, and righteous, with faith and trust in Allah. He or she believes that all human beings are gifted with inestimable power to control and govern the universe under the authority of Allah. They know their lives will extend beyond this world, and they will be rewarded or punished for all their deeds and actions on the Day of Judgment. Such an Islamic epistemic change, at a personal level, will bring qualitative change in individual social life and remodel the cultural and economic aspects of society.

Muslim educators unanimously agree that the purpose of education is not to cram pupils' minds with facts, but rather to prepare them for a life of purity and sincerity. This total commitment to character building, based on the ideals of Islamic ethics, is the highest goal of Islamic education. The sources of knowledge, according to Islam, fall into two categories. First is Divine revelation. Allah (God) teaches that human beings cannot, on their own, discover Divine truth and life cannot be conducted in the proper manner in the absence of stable and unchangeable injunctions inspired by Allah, the Wise and the All-knowing, whose knowledge encompasses all. Second, the human intellect and its tools are in constant interaction with the physical universe on the level of observation, contemplation, experimentation, and application. Importantly, people are free to do as they please—subject to the condition that they remain fully committed to the Qur'an and the Sunnah.

Western educators have a different view, which has invaded the Muslim world. Modern Western education places an exaggerated emphasis upon reason and rationality and encourages scientific inquiry at the expense of faith. Our academically outstanding intellectuals now prefer being educated in the West. Those who pursue higher education abroad constantly get brainwashed during their stay in Western countries. After spending a few years abroad, they return to their own countries filled with ideas that contradict their traditional beliefs. Secular education and secular thinking, generated by a modern scientific approach, make people empirical in attitude and doubtful about the need to think in terms of religion. Unfortunately, religious education in Pakistani schools is not enough to provide a counterbalance, because all other books are permeated with secularist ideas emphasizing materialism.

Further undermining the values of educators to perpetuate the values of an Islamic society and education system is economic modernization through industrialization. This is gradually transforming our traditional agrarian society into a modern, intellectual, technological society. In our traditional education system, knowledge and virtue go hand in hand. Students acquire worldly knowledge while being faithful to their religion. Muslim scholars and scientists believe that by acquiring knowledge about the phenomenal world they are only strengthening their belief in the greatness and power of the Creator. Western scientific assumptions and sociological analyses of life are directly contradictory to our traditional religious assumptions. Consequently, intellectual and moral "hypocrisy" has become a public style, and anxiety is increasing.

Though religious education is compulsory in our schools, there has been no serious attempt to teach literature, fine arts, social sciences, and natural sciences from the Islamic point of view. As a result, what children are learning from religion is being contradicted by what they learn from textbooks. Such an education obviously leads to conflicts, anxieties, and tensions. There is a strong need to Islamicize the humanities and social and natural sciences by infusing basic Islamic concepts and by changing the methodology of introducing and teaching the humanities and social and natural sciences in order to create a new generation of young men and women intellectually capable of resisting the undesirable effects of secularist teaching and curricula.

The task is difficult, as Western models of secular education that are presently dominant in our education institutions follow an anthropocentric approach. They assign a central place to humanity, its needs, its wants, its likes and dislikes, and proceed to adjust their education programs accordingly. The Islamic approach, on the other hand, is theocentric. That is, God and His will, His law, His pleasure and displeasure, are the sole norms to be followed in devising and formulating education policies and programs aimed at development of an integrated personality in a harmonious manner. Such an education system encompasses the study of the Holy Qur'an as the fountainhead of all knowledge.

The activity and precepts of the Holy Prophet Muhammad (peace be upon him), that is, the *Sunnah, Fiqha,* and the spiritual disciplines and the transmission of such accumulated knowledge to guide humanity toward self-perfection and self-realization, are basic. Furthermore, education in Islam emphasizes that for comprehension of principles, articles of faith, and their implicit meanings, it is imperative that knowledge of other sciences should be acquired and applied to development strategies by scientific and technological expertise (Quddus, 1990).

To conclude, we can state that the Islamic aim of education is twofold. First, there is one ultimate aim—that is, to seek the pleasure of God in achieving a state of righteousness and in acting according to the principles of Islamic justice. Second, there are immediate aims that are not fixed but are constantly changing as a result of concrete, changing situations. Islam has set an ideal in its ultimate aim of education. It is incumbent on all Muslims to achieve the best and most noble within one's capacity. Islam lays utmost emphasis on *ama'l* or deed, putting into action what we learn. In other words, Islam accedes to the practical ends of education. Everything learned has to be acted upon, has to be translated into action (for further information, see Al-Attas, 1979; Al-Farooqi, n.d.; Kalim, 1993; Rizvi, 1986).

Tradition and Change

The education system of Pakistan has its roots in the education history of the subcontinent. Indigenous schools called *maktabs* and *madrasas* existed in India before British Rule (1857–1947). Islam lays great emphasis on acquiring knowledge. Muslims, therefore, paid great attention to learning, both worldly and spiritual. However, under the British, this tradition suffered serious setbacks. The British rulers introduced their own education system with English as the medium of instruction. To paraphrase the words of Lord Macaulay, they undertook to create a class of people Indian in blood and color, but English in tastes, in opinions, in morals, and in intellect.

As their traditional system of education was being destroyed, Muslims did not try to adjust to the new system of education. The *maktabs* and *madrasas* that had managed to survive remained exclusively devoted to religious education. The Muslim clerics teaching in the *maktabs* and *madrasas* believed the Western education system was inconsistent with their norms and values and was an implicit threat to their cultural identity.

However, during the latter half of the nineteenth century, some Muslim leaders of the subcontinent actively began to create a synthesis of the two systems. Syed Ahmad Khan worked out an education plan based on the study of modern arts and sciences along with religious education. He established a school at Aligarh that soon became a college and later developed into the well-known Muslim University Aligarh. Some Muslims and *Ulema* (religious leaders) opposed Syed Ahmad's education plans and approved only the traditional education system. However, a large majority, representing the middle-class, responded favorably to Syed Ahmad's education programs. Numerous education institutions based on similar lines were opened in the subcontinent and became the primary centers for the education of Muslims. A majority of leaders who struggled hard for the creation of a Muslim homeland were the graduates of these education institutions.

Thus, Pakistan inherited both the traditional and the Western education systems. The former was aimed at imparting mostly religious education, whereas the Western system aimed at education in modern arts and sciences. Several commissions on education have devoted considerable efforts to the integration of the two systems.

The traditional education system consists of an extensive network of Maktabs and madrasas attached to mosques, both in towns and villages. These institutions are devoted to the study of the Holy Qur'an. At the more advanced level, these institutions are called *Dar-ul-ulum* (home of knowledge), where higher education is imparted by religious scholars in *Tafsir* (commentary of the Holy Qur'an), *Hadis* (sayings and traditions of the Holy Prophet Muhammad—peace be upon him), *Fiqah* (jurisprudence), *Mantaq* (logic and philosophy), and languages (Arabic, Persian, and Urdu). Graduates of these institutions are called *Alim* or *Fazil,* depending on the field of their specialization. Their diplomas and degrees have been given equivalence with university degrees/diplomas.

Long-Range Strategies for Improving Schooling

The education system of Pakistan has undergone many changes and has greatly improved with the inception of integrated planning in the country through a series of five-year plans, starting in 1955. Such long-range planning continues, and in the last few decades education policies and five-year plans have emphasized human resources development; Universalization of Primary Education (UPE) at the earliest possible date; making curricula more relevant; reforming the examination system; expanding technical and higher education; promoting research (particularly in science and technology at the universities); and enhancing the quality of education in general.

Within these priorities, a paramount concern is to substantially increase facilities, enhance use of existent schools, and increase personnel—all with the objective of increasing access to schooling (see Table 8.1).

However, despite reforms and a substantial growth in the number of education institutions, these goals are increasingly difficult to achieve. The main obstacles are Pakistan's rapid population growth and national resource constraints. Due to ever-increasing demands for the quantitative expansion of education facilities (because of rapid school-age population growth), adequate resources cannot be found for qualitative improvement. In consequence, despite the growth of the system, education institutions continue to lack proper infrastructure, the curricula still lack relevance, and the methodology of instruction and evaluation remain far from satisfactory. Gender and rural–urban imbalances, both in availability and quality of educational facilities, remain; dropout and failure rates continue to be

TABLE 8.1 Physical Targets in Primary Education

FACILITIES /SERVICES	BENCHMARK 1996–1997	9TH PLAN TARGETS 2002–2003	POLICY TARGETS 2010	% INCREASE
New Formal Primary Schools	145,000	162,000	190,000	31%
Mosque Schools	37,000	40,000 (+3,000)	57,000 (+20,000)	54%
Double Shift in Existing Primary Schools	-	20,000	20,000	-
Non-Formal Basic Education Schools	7,177	82,177 (+75,000)	2,50,000 (+242,823)	3,485%
Upgrading of Primary Schools to Middle Level	15,000	30,000 (+15,000)	60,000 (+45,000)	200%
Recruitment of Teachers for Primary Schools	339,500	382,200 (+42,700)	527,000 (+187,500)	55%

Source: Higher Education Commission (2004).

high (see Table 8.2). Compounding these problems is the fact that the management and financing of the existing education system is highly centralized and lacks an effective system of accountability.

Structure of the Education System

The federal government, through the Ministry of Education, is responsible for policy, planning, and provision of education facilities. Provinces are responsible for policy implementation, organization, administration, and the management of public school systems. The federal government plans curricula, sets education standards, and controls a very sizable development budget. Project implementation, recruitment, supervision of personnel, and day-to-day operating budgets are the responsibilities of the provinces. Textbooks are produced by provincial governments in accordance with guidelines set by the federal Ministry of Education.

Education ministers, who are political appointees, and senior executive civil servants, called Provincial Education Secretaries, head provincial education departments. Provinces are divided into regions for administrative purposes; each is headed by a Director. These regions are further divided into districts, which are headed by District Education Officers (DEOs). In many cases, there are separate male and female DEOs. A district can encompass a population from one-half to two million people. Clearly, the system is hierarchical and all decision making and control is from the top.

TABLE 8.2 Education in Pakistan: Facts and Figures

A) ***Literacy Rate***	49%
Male	61.3%
Female	36.8%
Target Literacy Rate (2004)	60%
B) ***Elementary Education***	
Primary Education:	
• Number of Primary Schools (Including 27,000 mosque schools)	149,163
• Teachers	374,000
Male	236,000
Female	138,000
• Student–Teacher Ratio	48:1
• Children Not Attending School	5.5 million
• Net Enrollment Rate	66%
Male	82%
Female	50%
• Dropout Rate	50%
Male	44%
Female	56%
• Middle Schools	24,877
C) ***Secondary Education***	
• Secondary Schools	8,509
Secondary Vocational Institutions	580
• Higher Secondary Schools	682
D) ***Technical Education***	
1. Number of Polytechnic Institutes/Colleges of Technology	
• Public Sector	61
• Private Sector	47
2. Vocational Institutes	310
E) ***Colleges***	
Arts and Science Colleges	853
Professional Colleges	308

Source: Government of Pakistan; Federal Bureau of Statistics and AEPAM (2000–2001).

The Pakistani school system itself is three-tiered: primary, secondary, and higher education. All schools run by the government are single-sex schools, whereas some of the schools in the private sector are co-educational. In the rural areas, most of the schools are single-teacher schools, especially girls' schools. Urban schools are overcrowded and the teacher–student ratio is far from being satisfactory. Most schools do not have adequate teaching materials. They have ill-equipped laboratories and are lacking in proper facilities for drinking water and playgrounds.

As the data in Table 8.2 illustrate, Pakistan has not been able to develop an education system that can measure up to the challenges faced by our nation. Pakistan still stands far behind other nations in critical areas, having low literacy rates, high dropout rates, gender imbalance in educational achievement, and so on. The problem of inadequate facilities in rural areas has not been solved, and, above all, rapid population expansion combined with limited financial resources continue to be major constraints on achieving universal primary education and a higher literacy rate.

Primary Education

Compulsory subjects in the first five years of the primary level include Urdu, Islamiyat, Social Studies, Arithmetic, and Science. The first years are marked by an integrated approach, where two or three subjects are combined into one course. While officially the medium of instruction is supposed to be Urdu in all schools, many private institutions use English as the primary medium. Curriculum is officially standardized throughout the country, although some local variations are permissible if the schools have adequate resources. As a result of a growing demand for learning English as the language of science, technology, business, commerce, and international communication, English has been recently introduced at the primary level and adopted as one of the mediums of instruction. This phenomenon is much more prevalent at the secondary and higher levels, especially in the teaching of science subjects.

In state-funded schools, the types of courses and their content, as well as teaching methods and preparation of textbooks, are largely regulated by government polices. Efforts to expand the quantity and enhance the quality of education have resulted in a bureaucratic and centralized educational system. Private schools, on the other hand, are free to decide their own curriculum and medium of instruction, which is generally English. The quality of education in private schools is, on the whole, substantially better than in government schools, which accounts for their popularity.

Provincial governments are responsible for the establishment and management of primary schools, whereas the federal government, in consultation with the provinces, develops curriculum. A Directorate of Primary Education exists in each province. The medium of instruction in primary schools is either the national language (Urdu), the provincial language, or English. Primary education is almost free. However, Pakistan has a very low level of students participating in primary education, ranking 78th out of 87 developing countries. Low enrollment of girls is a major determinant of lower enrollment and higher illiteracy rates.

Diverse primary education projects to promote basic education facilities in the country continue to be tried. New projects have been initiated to serve as major catalysts for the improvement of the quality of instruction, along with a quantitative expansion of primary education. For example, since 1990, incentives for the private sector to open education institutions have revived the involvement of the community, mostly in urban areas. Presently, private schools account for about 14 percent of total primary enrollment and 30 percent of all urban primary enrollments. In collaboration with foreign donor agencies, concerted efforts are being made to eradicate illiteracy and promote primary education throughout Pakistan. Several projects for enhancing primary education are presently being implemented with the assistance of the World Bank; the Asian Development Bank; the United Nations Development Program (UNDP); the United Nations Education, Scientific and Cultural Organization (UNESCO); and other donor agencies.

Secondary Education

Secondary education in Pakistan is divided into three levels: three-year middle schools, two-year secondary schools, and two-year higher secondary schools. On completion of the second level, students are awarded a Secondary School Certificate (SSC).

Graduates from the two-year secondary schools may continue their studies for another two or three years in the area of technical education, specializing in science, arts, or technical and vocational studies. At the end of this period, boys and girls write examinations to be granted one of an Intermediate Certificate, a Higher Secondary School Certificate, or Diploma of Associate Engineering. Vocational secondary courses lead to a Higher Secondary School Certificate (HSSC) or a diploma in technical/vocational subjects. Polytechnics, technical and commercial institutes, and colleges offer courses at postsecondary school certificate level. They provide two- to three-year courses that lead to certificates and diplomas in commercial and technical fields.

Secondary education (IX-XII) is a crucial subsector of the educational system. It provides the middle-level work force for the economy, as well as serving as a preparatory stage for higher levels of education. However, until recently, secondary education received little attention in terms of efforts and investment for its expansion. In view of the increased emphasis on improving quality and facilitating expansion in primary education, the secondary level of education now needs to be prepared for an increased influx of students to this level. In anticipation of this, one basic problem that needs immediate attention is provision of adequate physical facilities. In addition, the number of available science and mathematics teachers is quite small compared to the need. A large number of secondary schools have vacant posts for these subjects, but teachers are in short supply. Another facet of this problem relates to the availability of science graduates for the teaching profession. Most science graduates seek employment in other technical areas and consider teaching as their last resort. There is also a gender gap; the shortage of science and mathematics teachers is more serious in girls' schools than boys' schools.

However, the curricula in science, mathematics, agro-technical, and vocational subjects have been steadily improving since the early 1990s. On a continuing basis, concepts in science are being related to the everyday observations of the learner, making them more relevant and meaningful. However, the government believes that the quality of the curricula and textbooks is still far from satisfactory. Meaningful work is being undertaken to refine a new curriculum development cycle aimed at encouraging creativity, inquiry, and analytical thinking through project-oriented and problem-solving approaches in teaching. The curricula of technical and vocational institutions are increasingly becoming related to the employment market and self-employment. New concepts of immediate importance, such as environment, education, health education, and population education, are being integrated into the school curricula. Textbooks have been revised and updated to incorporate new knowledge using graded vocabulary and a pedagogical approach compatible to the age level of the student.

Higher Education

In Pakistan, higher education refers to all levels of education above grade 12, generally corresponding with the age bracket of 17 to 23 years. The higher education system comprises universities and colleges that provide education at four stages.

University Level First Stage: Bachelor's Degree. Students study for two to four years to earn a Bachelor's degree. In arts, science, and commerce, a Bachelor's Pass degree is normally awarded after completion of two years of course work; an Honors degree requires three years. First degrees in engineering, veterinary medicine, pharmacy, and computer sciences require four years; medicine and architecture, five years.

University Level Second Stage: Master's Degree, B.Ed., and LLB. A Master's degree requires two years' study after receiving a Bachelor's Pass degree, or one year after an Honors degree. Bachelor's degrees in agriculture, engineering, and pharmacy require four years of studies. To obtain a Bachelor of Education (B.Ed.) degree, students have to study for one year after getting a Bachelor's Pass degree. The Bachelor of Law (LLB) degree is also a post-Bachelor-degree qualification. In addition, Postgraduate Diplomas are offered in many fields of studies by several universities and generally require one year of study.

University Level Third Stage: M.Phil, Ph.D. The Master of Philosophy (M.Phil) requires two years of study after obtaining a Masters degree. The course of studies is a research-based program that has a compulsory thesis component. The Doctor of Philosophy (Ph.D.) is a research degree that generally requires three years' study and research if undertaken after completing a M.Phil, or four years for candidates who hold a Masters degree.

University Level Fourth Stage: Doctor's Degree. The degrees of Doctor of Literature (D.Litt.), Doctor of Science (D.Sc.), and Doctor of Law (D.LL.) are awarded after five to seven years of study after the Bachelor level.

Universities in Pakistan are institutions that specialize in either general or professional education. While they do offer undergraduate programs, their major emphasis is on postgraduate education and research. There are 55 universities in the public sector and 45 in the private sector. In addition to universities, there are 9 Centers of Excellence, 6 Area Study Centers, and 6 Pakistan Study Centers, which deal in specialized studies.

Since 2002, higher education in Pakistan has been regulated by the Higher Education Commission (HEC). Its mandate embraces all degree-granting universities and institutions, both in the public and private sector. The scope of its authority is significant: It carries out the evaluation, improvement, and promotion of higher education, research, and development. Formulating policies, guiding principles, and priorities for higher education institutions is another area of responsibility. The HEC also prescribes conditions under which institutions may be opened and operated. As well, it supervises the planning, development, and accreditation of public- and private-sector institutions of higher education. Finally, it facilitates and coordinates the assessment of academics through external reviews by national and international experts.

Teacher Training

The quality of education is directly related to the quality of instruction in the classrooms. Recognizing the crucial role of teachers in implementing all educational reforms at the grassroots level, and remembering that a primary goal of education in Pakistan is eventually to provide access to schooling for all children, the teacher education system has quantitatively expanded to maintain a reasonable balance between demand and supply. However, in the course of rapid expansion of the education system, the qualitative aspects of teacher education have received little attention. This has resulted in increasingly larger numbers of teachers lacking adequate understanding of both the content and methodology of education.

Since independence, there has been a substantial increase in number of institutions imparting teacher training and education in Pakistan. At present, there are 90 elementary colleges and 30 high schools that offer teacher-training programs. These institutions provide pre-service training and the following certification:

Training of Pre-Primary and Primary/Basic School Teachers. A Primary Teaching Certificate (PTC) is granted to teachers seeking training after completion of ten years of schooling. The training is located in high schools and result in the awarding of a Secondary School Certificate (SSC). A Certificate in Teaching (CT) is awarded to individuals who undergo a one-year, pre-service teaching course after obtaining a Higher Secondary School Certificate (HSSC). CT teachers are eligible for teaching at the middle level.

Training of Secondary School Teachers. The Bachelor of Education (B.Ed.) is a one-year degree course in pedagogy. The minimum qualification for admission into a B.Ed. program is a Bachelor's degree in Arts or Science (B.A./B.Sc.).

The Master of Education (M.Ed.) degree is the highest degree in teaching, requiring completion of a one-year degree course after the B.Ed. There are 11 Colleges of Education, 4 Institutes of Education and Research, and 2 Departments of Education located in universities that offer programs of secondary school teacher education leading to a Bachelor's degree in education (B.Ed.). The Allama Iqbal Open University (AIOU) is also providing courses for teacher training by means of distance learning. The AIOU offers PTC, CT, B.Ed., and M.Ed. courses for teacher education. The annual training capacity of all the formal training institutions, including AIOU, is about 40,000. This is sufficient to meet the needs of the country.

Distance Higher Education

The Allama Iqbal Open University (AIOU) and thc Virtual University of Pakistan offer distance higher education. The AIOU offers a wide range of courses at different levels in Humanities, Teacher Education, Technical Education, Business Management, Commerce,

Social Science, Arabic, Pakistan Studies, Islamic Studies, Home Economics, and Women's Studies. It uses multimedia techniques such as correspondence packages, radio and television broadcasts, and tutorial instruction. The Virtual University, on the other hand, caters to the needs of students at the tertiary level in the field of computer sciences, providing online instruction throughout the country.

Evaluation

Student evaluation in Pakistan usually focuses on academic achievement, and tests and grades are used to evaluate students' learning. Teachers use the results to see whether their instruction is effective and to identify students who have difficulties in learning and are in need of additional help. Parents need these evaluations to know how well their children are doing in schools, and students can use the results to see whether their studying strategies are paying off. Progress reports also serve as a consistent mode of communication between school and home.

A formal examination system is prevalent in Pakistan. Examinations are generally held annually and are used to promote students. Students who get a minimum of 40 percent in aggregate marks, and at least 33 percent in compulsory subjects, are promoted to the next class. In the primary classes, schools conduct their own examinations. However, at the end of the fifth year, a public examination is held by the Education Department for the awarding of merit scholarships; the most competent students compete. Similarly, there is a public examination at the end of the eighth year, held by the Education Department for the award of scholarships.

The usual grading system in secondary schools ranges from A to F: A is highest on the scale; F is lowest; and E represents the Pass/Fail level. The main grading system used by higher education institutions is the following: 80 percent and above = A+; 70–79 percent = A; 60–69 percent = B; 50–59 percent = C; 40–49 percent = D; 33–39 percent = E; and below 33 percent = F (fail).

All provincial education departments hold public examinations at the end of classes X and XII. Boards of Intermediate and Secondary Education conduct these examinations; universities use the examinations for degree classes for all institutions affiliated with them. If a student fails in one or more subjects in any one of the public examinations, he or she must repeat the examination and pass in order to obtain the degree/diploma/certificate.

The present system of examinations has been severely criticized for a long time. The examination questions are mostly essay type in nature, requiring subjective assessment. A comprehensive and scientific evaluation system would make the teaching-learning process more rational and efficient. The current education policy advocates the abolition of annual examinations and wants to substitute a system of continuous evaluation. However, this policy recommendation cannot be implemented unless teachers are properly trained to assess students' academic achievement by an objective and unbiased method of evaluation.

In the meantime, professional colleges have taken another route in evaluating students. Since 1992, Pakistan's Ministry of Education has worked on the establishment of a National Educational Testing Service (NETS) for holding entry examinations to professional colleges and universities. The objective was to maintain a uniformity of scores among various examination boards, through standardized education tests. NETS came into operation in 1998; presently it is located at the Institute of Business Administration (IBA) in Karachi. Curriculum based and prepared by experts, test items in Physics, Chemistry, Mathematics, Biology, and English Language at the higher secondary level have already been prepared and implemented. Failure to qualify through a NETS test renders a student ineligible for entry into professional colleges. Gradually, admission to all higher education institutions will be made on the basis of performance on educational tests developed and standardized by the NETS.

Curriculum Reforms

The government is fully sensitive to the need for reforming the primary education curriculum. Based on baseline data, improved curriculum and instructional materials for grades I to III have already been introduced, evaluated, and refined in some districts. The development of local expertise and making the curriculum, textbooks, and learning material more relevant for the student and for the community constitute salient features of the program. Qualitative improvement of school textbooks is also receiving serious attention. Revised versions of various textbooks prepared by provincial agencies have already been reviewed, refined, and approved. The process continues as a regular exercise.

Taking cognizance of emerging realities, new global perspectives, and contemporary issues, Pakistan's education programs at other levels are also being changed. Curricula are being revised, new textbooks written, and teacher training programs redesigned to gear the education system to new challenges and new opportunities. This means not only imparting the latest knowledge and introducing the latest disciplines, it also involves preparing teachers and students to become more responsible members of their society at home and in the international community at large. New programs such as population education (to increase awareness of the alarming implications of unchecked population growth), drug education (to motivate students to fight the menace of narcotics), and environmental studies (to awaken people to the devastating effects of environmental pollution) have been initiated. A new subject, Teacher, School, and Society, has been added to teacher training programs to equip teachers with knowledge and methodology in the area of international education.

Development Strategies for Achieving Universal Primary

Pakistan has undergone serious political instability during the last four decades. Lack of a stable and persistent political structure has adversely affected the development of social and economic institutions in the country. However, past and present political leaders are aware of the significance of education for the progress of the nation. Soon after Pakistan came into being, in his inaugural address the Education Minister emphasized the need for universal, compulsory, and free education for children. All successive governments have made similar declarations and formulated policies, but achievement of full literacy and universal education remains as elusive as ever.

Starting in 1956, a succession of five-year developmental plans was implemented with only partial success. Even at this date, it is not yet possible to fully analyze the success of the 1993–1998 Five-Year Plan. However, a mid-plan review (Government of Pakistan,

1995) showed that an additional 10,477 primary and 1,860 mosque schools were established in the public sector. Some 6,656 shelterless primary schools were constructed; 3,353 mosque schools were converted into primary schools; and 8,638 new classrooms were added in overcrowded primary schools during the first three years (1993–1996). However, only 39 percent of the plan target of an additional enrollment of 3.3 million over the first three years was achieved. It was expected that the end of the Eighth Plan would achieve the enrollment targets only by 65 to 70 percent. Consequently, a project for 10,000 basic education centers/schools was launched through nongovernment organizations (NGOs) and community involvement. During 1995–1996, more than 1,100 such schools/ centers were established. By and large, the performance of primary education (except for inability to cope with increases in enrollment) was satisfactory during the 1993–1998 Five-Year Plan.

Current initiatives, like earlier policies, show the government's firm determination to reinvigorate its struggle for universal primary education by the end of this decade. Other primary objectives are the reduction of widening gender gaps and attending to urban–rural disparities in the provision of basic education facilities. Highlights of the Education Policy (1998–2010) include:

1. It is recognized that the qualifications for the primary school teaching certificate are far below the norm of other developing countries. To strengthen primary-level teacher training programs, the Education Policy (1998–2010) proposes to start a three-year Diploma in Education within secondary school certification. Through this Diploma, the teacher will study up to the Higher Secondary School Level and gain pedagogical skills for teaching at the primary level.

2. The curricula of PTC, CT, B.Ed., and M.Ed. programs will be improved by making them learner centered. Furthermore, courses will provide opportunities for prospective teachers to receive training in pedagogical skills involving creativity, problem solving, and using the project method and other innovative techniques.

3. The policy proposes to offer a separate stream of technical education at the secondary school level. Initially, existing institutions having a laboratory and a qualified teacher will offer this route. Existing B.Ed. and M.Ed. programs will be expanded to ensure a constant supply of trained technical teachers (B.Ed. Technical; M.Ed. Technical).

4. In order to achieve universal primary education in the country and to extend education facilities up to the elementary level, suitable numbers of trained teachers will be provided to disadvantaged institutions. To achieve this objective, incentives in terms of special pay, allowances, and residential facilities will be offered to teachers working in isolated rural institutions. In addition, day-care centers will be opened near these schools for children of women teachers.

5. The Academy of Educational Planning and Management (AEPAM), as the prime training institute at the national level for educating administrators, supervisors, and planners, is strained both in capacity and resources. These will be strengthened, and long-term training programs will be launched for school administrators.

In spite of the above, achieving universal primary education in Pakistan remains contingent upon several factors. For example, to establish a large number of cost-effective schools, it is imperative that curricular reforms must be implemented and awareness of parents, especially in rural areas, of the significant role of education in their and their children's mental, physical, ideological, and moral development must be heightened. However, the single most important factor in getting children to complete primary education is improving the structure of Pakistan's school system. Such a structural change requires:

1. *Decentralization of decision making.* This necessitates that the government must develop partnerships with communities, NGOs, and the private sector to delegate responsibility in order to achieve universal primary education.
2. *Demand-based education.* Replacing the supply-side orientation in education planning and implementation is a crucial implementation strategy under Education Sector Reforms (ESR). The World Bank has emphasized the expansion of access to elementary education in Pakistan by improving the quality of education in order to make coming to school—and staying in school—a more attractive option from the perspective of parents as well as children.
3. *Providing greater autonomy to schools.* Currently, principals of schools have very limited decision-making privileges. They do not have any control over major issues like curriculum, teacher appointment, discipline, and evaluation. It is highly desirable to provide opportunities for local staff development and on-site resource mobilization.
4. *Decision making.* Decisions need to be based on educational, rather than political, considerations.
5. *Research.* The information and research base on education requires expansion.

Literacy Programs

The government of Pakistan is working vigorously at both the federal and provincial levels to overcome the problem of illiteracy. As a result, the literacy rate in Pakistan, which was 16 percent in 1951, increased to 51.6 percent in 2003 (see Table 8.3).

TABLE 8.3 Literacy Rate—Population and GDP Growth from 1999 to 2003

YEAR	LITERACY RATE	CHANGE BY %	POPULATION GROWTH	GDP GROWTH
1999	45.0	1.4	2.29	4.2
2000	47.1	2.1	2.24	3.9
2001	49.0	1.9	2.22	2.4
2002	50.5	1.5	2.16	3.6
2003	51.6	1.1	2.10	5.10

Source: Government of Pakistan (2003).

Over the long run, increasing efforts to provide universal primary education, both for boys and girls, will serve as the main instrument for achieving mass literacy. Besides trying to provide universal access to schools to increase literacy, the government has been endeavoring to increase the literacy rate through direct methods. For example, a project named Eradication of Illiteracy from Selected Areas of Pakistan was launched with the goal of making 268,600 persons literate. For this purpose, 2,097 centers were established.

SUCCESSES, CHALLENGES, AND DEBATES

Despite considerable expansion in education infrastructure, over the last few decades Pakistan has continued to lag behind other countries in the region. According to the 1998 census, only 31 percent of the population (male, 32.4 percent; female, 28 percent) has studied up to the secondary school level or above. At the national level, the female literacy rate is 37 percent compared to 49 percent for males. Overall, half of the population aged 10 years and above is literate.

National Education Policy, 1998–2010

In response, the National Education Policy (1998–2010) was framed in the perspective of historical developments, modern trends in education and training, and emerging requirements of society in terms of national integrity and socioeconomic development. This education policy aimed to attain universal primary education by 2003 and then a national literacy rate of 70 percent by the year 2010. To achieve this target, the government proposed the establishment of 45,000 new primary schools and 20,000 *masjid* (mosque) schools; upgrading 45,000 primary schools to middle level; and introducing evening shifts in the existing 20,000 primary schools. Furthermore, 30,000 new secondary schools, and 305 new secondary vocational institutions were to be established. The policy proposed greater emphasis on computer education and technical training in schools, introduction of new technologies, and revised curricula in vocational institutions. It also provided for expansion of educational infrastructure both in urban and rural areas, and increased allocation for the education sector from 2.2 percent of the GNP to 4 percent by 2003.

Education Sector Reforms Action Plan 2001–2004

The Education Sector Reforms Action Plan 2001–2004 (ESR) is a short-range reform program built within the long-term perspectives of the National Education Policy (1998–2010) and the Ten Year Perspective Development Plan (2001–2011). It is an action plan to initiate a process of correcting imbalances and disparities in society and in schooling. It has among its major foci: rural areas and urban slums, girls and women, child labor and those with special needs, gypsies and riverine communities, poor and underprivileged segments of population.

Thus, ESR is a comprehensive and ongoing program aimed at increased access and enhanced equity at all levels of education. It also emphasizes improvements in the quality of education, modernization of curricula, upgrading teacher training, examination reforms, and the establishment of a National Education Assessment System. Furthermore, a National Educational Testing Service will be set up to govern admission process of professional colleges and other institutions of higher education. Another key element of the ESR is the development of partnerships between public and private sectors, and with NGOs. Thus, each education subsector—elementary, secondary/technical, higher—has included a strategic role for private sector.

To appreciate the scope and significance of the ESR Action Plan 2000–2004, eight of its major and most far-reaching programs will be briefly discussed.

1. The Comprehensive Literacy and Poverty Reduction Program

Prepared by the Pakistan Literacy Commission for disadvantaged groups of Pakistan—including nomads, refugees, working children, riverine communities, women and children in prisons and in *Darul Amans* (women's shelters)—the Comprehensive Literacy and Poverty Reduction Program included the following three projects:

- ***The Community Primary Schools Project*** had a target of making 1.02 million children (5 through 9 years of age) literate. These children were to complete primary level of education in three years through 30,000 Community Schools.
- ***The Accelerated Community Primary Schools Project*** aimed to provide primary education to 1.02 million children (10 through 14 years of age) by establishing 30,000 Community Schools.
- ***The Women's Literacy for Empowerment Project*** focused on helping 1.02 million women (15+ years of age) gain integrated functional literacy through 30,000 Community Centers.

2. Mainstreaming the Madrassas in Pakistan

Recognizing the need for a creative new system of education, *Ulemas* (clergy) in general, and *Dini Madaras* (religious educational institutions/schools) in particular, realized the need to improve and modernize their curricula. Several *Darul Ulooms* (Islamic centers of higher education) were already preparing their students for university examinations up to the Bachelor and Master levels. The Secretary General of the Pakistan Shariah Council strongly recommended a revision of the existing curricula of *Dini Madaras*—advocating the introduction of computer literacy and language courses in Arabic, English, French, and Persian to prepare graduates to project and propagate Islam internationally.

The Government of Pakistan established the Pakistan Madrassah Education Board (PMEB) in 2001. The PMEB approved revised curricula for the Model Dini Madaris, which includes English, mathematics, computer science, economics, political science, law, and Pakistan Studies for its different levels. For all practical purposes, the Higher Education Commission (HEC) considers the certificates and degrees issued by the Model Dini Madaris as equivalent to B.A. and M.A. degrees awarded by other boards and recognized universities in the formal sector of the country.

3. **Expanding Primary/Elementary Education**

Universalization of Primary Education (UPE) is the most challenging task for the Government of Pakistan. At present, 170,000 primary schools, including 27,000 mosque schools, are educating 19.6 million children in the 5 through 9 age group. The gross participation rate at the primary level is 89 percent and the dropout rate is 50 percent. To achieve UPE, about 2.4 million children needed to be enrolled between 2001 and 2004. To achieve this objective, 8,504 new primary schools need to open, and existing ones need to be upgraded by providing school buildings to shelterless schools, drinking water (56,455 schools), washrooms (79,342 schools), boundary walls (64,973 schools), and electricity (95,979 schools).

4. **Introducing Technical Streams at the Secondary Level**

The integration of technical and vocational skill development within the general stream of education has been advocated in almost every policy document since 1947. There have been many efforts to establish Technical Schools, Agro-Tech Schemes, and Vocational Institutes, but on a limited scale. At present, a Technical Schools Certificate Program is offered in ten institutions. However, this program is not only very limited in access, it is not integrated into the general stream.

In order to integrate skill development with general education, a scheme of Technical Stream at Secondary Level (classes IX–X) has been proposed. To achieve this goal, Technical Streams will be introduced in approximately 1,200 selected secondary schools, where training in one trade will be provided. Moreover, fifty-six Model Technical High Schools (MTHS) will be opened where training in three trades relevant to the needs of the area/gender will be provided. The MTHS will serve as role models, resource centers, and in-service teacher training centers for ordinary high schools where technical stream is to be introduced. These facilities are planned to provide employment skills to almost 120,000 students in classes IX and X every year.

5. **Improving Quality through Teacher Education and Training**

In order to equip elementary and secondary school teachers with the latest skills in accordance with emerging trends in the field of education, the intention is to provide better pre-service and in-service training to teachers. To provide a professional environment, the existing thirty teacher-training institutes will be converted into fully residential institutes during the first phase of the project. Additionally, a National Institute of Teacher Education and Training (NITET) will be established at federal level.

6. **Reforming Higher Education**

Three major reforms are needed in the higher education sector: improving accessibility, improving quality, and shifting to science and technological education.

At present, 2.6 percent of the relevant age group has access to higher education in Pakistan. The total enrollment in public-sector universities is about 100,000 students, which is low in comparison with other nations. At the present rate of population growth, it is estimated that Pakistan will have 25 million youth in the 17 to 23 age group by 2010. Development of human resources and attainment of development objectives demands provision of higher education opportunities to at least 10 percent of the age group by 2010. To achieve this objective, a greater differentiation and proliferation of disciplines is needed. Access to higher education opportunities in the public sector will be attained by increasing enrollments to 200,000 and by encouraging the private sector to increase enrollment to 40 percent of that total.

7. **Effecting a Major Shift toward Scientific and Technological Education**

   To achieve technological improvement and meet human resource needs, a major shift toward science and technology is being made at the secondary and higher education levels. An innovative project of video-textbooks and a library for secondary schools is being initiated in collaboration with Allama Iqbal Open University (AIOU) and the Ministry of Science and Technology. To bridge the digital divide, Information Communication Technology is being encouraged in all public-sector institutions through public–private partnerships. Computer courses at the secondary and higher secondary levels through private-sector initiatives have been introduced in three provinces of Pakistan—Punjab, Sindh, and NWFP.

8. **Strengthening the Public–Private Partnership**

   The private sector plays a significant role in the promotion of education at all levels in Pakistan. The government has introduced the concept of public–private partnerships, and identifies three key areas of activity:

   - Providing a package of incentives for private-sector involvement in all levels of education—elementary, secondary/technical, and higher education. The proposed package of incentives, particularly in rural areas and urban slums, includes provision of free land in rural areas; the assessment of utilities such as electricity, gas, and so on, at noncommercial rates; exemption from custom duties on imported educational equipment; and a 50 percent income tax exemption to private-sector institutions for faculty, management, and support staff.
   - Involving the private sector in the management of public-sector educational institutions.
   - Making Education Foundations effective bodies for providing substantial support to private-sector educational institutions. Education Foundations were established between 1990 and 1995, at both the federal and provincial levels, to provide loans and grants to private/nongovernment agencies and to encourage voluntary organizations for the development of education in the country.

Clearly, there are major changes occurring at virtually all levels of education in Pakistan. The success, significance, and consequences of these fundamental changes will take years to unfold and evaluate.

REFERENCES

Al-Attas, S. N. (1979). *Aims and objectives of Islamic education.* Jaddah: Hodder & Stroght.

Al-Farooqi, I. R. (International Institute of Islamic Thought, USA). (n.d.). *Islamization of knowledge: General principles and work plan.* Brentwood, CA: International Graphic Printing Server.

Country faces uphill task to control population. (2005, May 5). Accessed June 27, 2005, from http://www.poplibnet.org.pk/app/news/view.aspx?/newsid.40

Government of Pakistan. (1995). *Mid-plan review of eighth five-year plan of the government of Pakistan.* Islamabad: Planning Commission.
Government of Pakistan. (1998). *National Education Policy 1998–2010.* Islamabad: Planning Commission.
Government of Pakistan. (2002). *Innovation programs.* Ministry of Education, Government of Pakistan. Available on http://www.pak.gov.pk
Government of Pakistan. (2003). *Economic survey of Pakistan, 2002–2003.* Islamabad: Author.
Government of Pakistan. (n.d.) *Five-year plans (I, II, III, IV, V, VI, VII, VIII).* Islamabad: Planning Commission.
Government of Pakistan, Federal Bureau of Statistics and Academy of Educational Planning and Management (AEPAM). (2000–2001). *Economic survey of Pakistan.* Islamabad: Government of Pakistan.
Higher Education Commission. (2004). Islamabad. Available on http://www.hec.gov.pk
World Bank & UNESCO International Task Force on Higher Education and Society. (2000). *Higher Education in Developing Countries: Peril and Promise.*
ILO Revision of the Human Resources Development Recommendations. (2002). *Education Sector Reforms Action Plan 2001–2004.* Pakistan National Policies Concerning Access to Education and Training in Pakistan.
Kalim, M. S. (1993). *Studies in education.* Islamabad: National Book Foundation.
Pakistan set to launch Digital Library. http://www.Learningchannel.org
Quddus, N. J. (1990). *Problems of education in Pakistan.* Karachi: Royal Book Company.
Rizvi, S. S. (1986). *Islamic philosophy of education.* Lahore: Institute of Islamic Culture.
Seema, M. (2004). *Higher education in Pakistan: Past, present, and future.* Pakistan-Education system.
Universities in Pakistan (2004, March 8). Asiaco: The Asia Search Engine.

CHAPTER NINE

EDUCATION IN INDIA
Progress and Promise in a Land of Paradoxes

JOHN P. ANCHAN

THE SOCIAL FABRIC

The Indian Mosaic

With over a billion people—and eighteen officially recognized "principal" languages (Hindi, English, and local languages), 400 registered (distinct/unique) languages, and 1,652 dialects—India (or *Bharat,* its national name) constitutes the largest and possibly most complex democracy in the world (*The World Guide,* 2003/2004; *TIME Almanac,* 2004). Expected to exceed China in this century as the most populous nation, India "presently accounts for only 2.4 percent of the earth's surface area, yet it is home to a staggering 16.7 percent of the planet's total population" (Singh, Barkhordian, Beech, Bindloss, Derby, et al., 2003, p. 47). Jumping onto the juggernaut of the globalization train, the country has evolved into a major provider of information technology outsourcing out of Silicon Valley. Whether because of its crucial positioning as a nuclear power or its increasingly significant international economic role, India remains a complex multicultural, multiethnic, and multireligious country. As it struggles with a mix of state interventionist socialist heritage intertwined with free market entrepreneurial capitalistic dreams, India remains an enigmatic country with problems and promises that strain to make it a major economic global player.

Nurtured by very ancient civilizations, postcolonial India remains deeply influenced by its history of occupation. From Aryans to Muslim Moguls (Mughals), from the Portuguese to the British, to the more recent political landscape, India struggles between its ultra-right-wing Hindu fundamentalism and modernization, westernization, and capitalism. A country of paradox and a nation in constant flux—with its vast geographical differences, linguistic divisions, political mix, cultural diversity, and historical legacy—India

An Associate Professor of Education at the University of Winnipeg, Canada, John P. Anchan has twenty-three years of teaching experience in India, United Arab Emirates, and Canada. His areas of research interests and expertise include information technology, technology and education, cross-cultural education, global education, culture studies, and contemporary sociological issues in education.

continues to defy critics of democracy. As a mosaic with accentuated differentiation and deep divisions between rich and poor, affluent and marginalized, literate and illiterate, westernized and traditional, India remains a vibrant, perhaps even an exotic, country that seems to defy logical explanation. "India, it is often said, is not a country but a continent. From north to south and east to west, the people are diverse, the languages are varied, the customs are distinctive, the landscape is manifold" (Singh et al., 2003, p. 18).

Historical Background

The earliest records indicate the existence of the Harappan culture in the Indus Valley Civilization (circa 2500 B.C.). This was followed by the Vedic-Aryan period (circa 1500 B.C.), the era of Alexander the Great (circa 326 B.C.), and then the Mauryan, Gupta, Chola, Vijayanagar, and Mughal empires. In 1690, European colonization led to the establishment of the British East India Trading Company—the precursor to formal and extended British occupation for over 250 years. British domination ended in a relatively nonviolent manner with Mahatma Gandhi's internationally admired and successful campaigns that won India independence in 1947.

Though the liberation of India was relatively bloodless, the aftermath entailed in the partitioning of predominantly Hindu India and mostly Muslim Pakistan resulted in bloody riots that cost many lives. The long journey thereafter has seen India evolve from a largely agrarian country to an industrialized giant that has conveniently eased itself into a technology-based industrialized nation.

In 1964 India's first Prime Minister, Jawaharlal Nehru, was succeeded by his daughter, Indira Gandhi (no relation to Mahatma Gandhi). Following civil unrest and subsequent imposition of draconian "Emergency Laws," the Sikh holy Golden Temple was stormed. Gandhi was assassinated in 1984 by her Sikh bodyguards. Her son, Rajiv Gandhi, assumed the Prime Minister's position and was also assassinated, in 1991, for his involvement in the political conflict in Sri Lanka. With Narasimha Rao as the next Prime Minister, India was faced with right-wing Hindu zealots fighting Indian Muslims. The Nehru and Gandhi families had represented the more inclusive and tolerant Indian National Congress political party. In contrast, in 1998 Atal Behari Vajpayee, a moderate Hindu representing the Hindu-based Bharatiya Janata Party (Indian People's Party), became the Prime Minister of India.

The rise of Hindu nationalism, along with the ongoing slaughter of Moslems and Christians, continued until 2004, when India held the biggest free election ever in an open, multicultural, and secular society. The Bharatiya Janata Party was routed at the polls, returning the Congress party to power. But, once again, Indians were dragged into the politics of "race and religion" as they went into a frenzy in having to accept Sonia Gandhi (Rajiv Gandhi's widow), an Italian by birth and a naturalized Indian, to become the next Prime Minister of India. To many nationalists, an "Anglesi" or "white foreigner" would not rule over ancient "Hindu" India. Broad-mindedness and diversity were thrown into question. Indians debated and faced the reality of their beliefs, haunting and challenging their parochial notion of tolerance. In result, Dr. Manmohan Singh, an Oxford-educated academic who had served earlier in the 1980s as a dynamic Finance Minister who successfully revolutionized India's stagnant economy with open competition and foreign investments, became the first Sikh Prime Minister of India.

Geography

With an area of 3,287,590 square kilometers, the Indian peninsula is surrounded by the Himalayan range to the north, Myanmar to the northeast, Pakistan to the west, the Arabian Sea and the Indian Ocean to the southwest, Sri Lanka to the south, and the Bay of Bengal to the southeast. Within these boundaries lies a land of incredible geographic diversity. Extending 3,200 kilometers north to south, within India are to be found arid mountains, forests, rain forests, lake districts, fertile plains, scenic beaches, massive river valleys, and varied climates. In its greatly varied cultural regions are to be found some of the largest, most crowded, and most dynamic cities in the world. Indeed, it is more accurate to speak of "Indias" when traveling the land, rather than a single entity named India.

Demography

With a population of 1,049,799,118 people (2003, estimated), India is the second most populated country in the world. The ethnic and racial groups are varied, with 72 percent Indo-Aryan (mostly living in the north), 25 percent Dravidian (mostly in the south), and 3 percent Mongoloid and other ethnic or racial groups (mostly in northeastern regions) (*TIME Almanac,* 2004). In terms of religious diversity, 81.3 percent of Indians are Hindus, 12 percent Moslems, 2.3 percent Christians, 1.9 percent Sikhs, and 2.5 percent Buddhists and Jains. The population density in 2002 was a crowded 350.2 people per square kilometer (UN, 2002). The diversity of the vast country, along with an increasing middle class spawned by a vibrant economy, makes India a very heterogeneous country.

Economy

Until early 1991, India followed a state interventionist policy that protected it from world trade fluctuations. A more laissez-faire economic approach, promoted by then Finance Minister (now Prime Minister) Manmohan Singh, resulted in opening up a historically staid and regulated market. This quickly resulted in increased exports and imports, along with a vibrant economy that saw remarkable growth in manufacturing, banking, telecommunications, and the information technology sectors. For example, India's export earnings due to trade with the United States, its biggest trading partner, sharply increased from US$14.5 billion in 2001 to US$17.7 billion in 2002 (Singh et al., 2003).

Today, as the largest information technology outsourcing country in the world, India exports human resources and knowledge to North America. However, there is still a long way to go down the path to prosperity. The 2000 per capita income (gross national income) for India was US$450 (World Bank, 2002) and the Human Development Index (HDI), used by the United Nations Development Program (UNDP) to indicate the overall development of a country, ranked India at 115 (UNDP, 2001, cited in *The World Guide 2003/2004,* p. 59).

Culture and Politics

Dyer (2004) pointedly and insightfully describes India as a "tolerant secular democracy or a sectarian, ultra-nationalist state, with a huge chip on its shoulder" (p. A15). The country remains convinced that it should become a major international player, but there is also great ambivalence. According to some commentators, while intellectual and select activists, along with right-wing nationalists and left-wing socialists, decry the effects of globalization, the general population of India doesn't seem to mind the intrusion. During recent elections, Indian voters were not saying "Stop the globalization train, we want to get off." Rather, the tone was more like "Slow down the globalization train, and build me a better step-stool, because I want to get on" (Friedman, 2004, p. A10).

Capitalism breeds material consumerism, and India's ever-growing appetite for material goods never seems to abate. Social success and prestige are directly tied in with the acquisition of property and education. According to Nayan Chanda, the Indian-born editor of YaleGlobal online magazine, "Every time an Indian villager watches the community TV and sees an ad for soap or shampoo, what they notice are not the soap and shampoo but the lifestyle of the people using them. . . . They see a world they want access to" (Friedman, 2004, p. A10). Today, Indians seem to be keenly sensitive to the lure of capitalist materialism and recognize that the political and economic spheres are intricately connected.

Thus, despite a low national literacy rate, the Indian electorate is not unaware of the power of democratic participation. The overall population remains politically astute and relatively active. In the most recent elections, not unlike preceding elections, the Indian population voted out the government and opted for the opposing political party. Pratap Bhanu Mehta, an India professor of government, notes that "The revolt against holders of power is not a revolt of the poor against the rich: Ordinary people are far less prone to resent other people's success than intellectuals suppose. It is rather an expression of the fact that the reform of the state has not gone far enough" (Friedman, 2004, p. A10).

At the international level, India is actively lobbying for a more powerful presence on the UN Security Council. Furthermore, as a response to the arms race in the developed and developing world, India continues its ambitious rocket development research and nuclear armament program. In the development of its nuclear weapons, it has consistently refused to be audited by other powers in the West by challenging that the United States and other countries also be subject to reciprocal measures.

On the other hand, what might be a headlong rush into Western materialism and international *realpolitik* is very much tempered by India's history. With a very ancient history of culture and religion, Indian diversity goes beyond traditions and customs. As it embraces the modern and the contemporary, India does so within the paradox presented by its ancient, ritualistic, and religious roots in the past. The country that exports yoga, swamis (Hindu god-men), and New Age philosophies to eager North Americans also pines for the absurd, and the thirst for Western culture remains unquenched. In a nutshell, India refuses to be understood—both by itself and the outside world.

One particularly significant cultural and religious paradox that haunts modern Indian society is the caste system. The caste system is a historical development of social stratification involving hierarchical stratification of humans based on perceived notions of race, ethnicity, tradition, mythology, and historical superiority and inferiority. Indeed, castes and subcastes find their etymology in *Jhaathi:* separate "breeds" and "species" (Jary & Jary, 1991).

In the Hindu caste system, the five major groups (*Varna*), from the most powerful to the least, are the *Brahmins, Kshatriyas, Vaisyas, Sudras,* and *Untouchables.* It is important to remember that there are also subcastes within the larger groups; the hierarchical sorting of Indian society is very complicated and subtle. The most socially discriminated against and marginalized groups fall into a category officially called the *Scheduled Castes and Tribes* (*SC&T*), who constitute over one-quarter of the population (India at a glance, 1991). It is a disparate, detailed category about which it is hard to make accurate generalizations because it includes a very diverse group of peoples. One group is the varied peoples who historically lived in isolation: that is, mountain peoples, forest inhabitants, and communities in India's jungles. Other groups include historically transient peoples who really do not have a clearly defined formal caste affiliation. Also included are peoples who, in Western terms, could be akin to the status of aboriginals. The lowest class caste categories of Untouchables and Sudras are also included in this broad category.

While it may be possible to move between subcastes, social movement between the five major groups—either by choice or matrimony—is impossible and strictly prohibited. Not surprisingly, the upper caste Brahmin clergy wield considerable power that is based on Hindu mythological legends legitimizing their ascribed preeminence. This group usually controls the religious ritualistic rights pertaining to overall Hindu society. While the Brahmins relish in their religious privilege in dictating the lives of the "lesser" groups, the latter continue to occupy and serve in menial tasks requiring limited or minimal education. In this manner, through the caste system, wealthy and powerful social groups maintain control and prestige over marginalized groups.

Though the government has officially outlawed casteism (discriminatory actions based on caste), traditional beliefs and prejudices embedded in the culture obfuscate equality issues surrounding caste. For example, following independence in 1947, the Indian government instituted several federal laws for the protection of the SC&T—for example, The Scheduled Castes and the Scheduled Tribes (Prevention of Atrocities) Act of 1989. There are many other laws focusing on accelerating the education, training, and employment of historically marginalized groups. These laws entail affirmative action to promote equality of opportunity, institute quota systems, pertain to human rights and hate provisions, and establish special funds to facilitate the amelioration of members from the affected castes. Yet, in spite of these progressive measures, the gap between the SC&T and the rest of Indian society remains great. For example, only 18.19 percent of SC&T women are functionally literate (A review of India, 2002, cited in MKA, 2003).

The symbolism of casteism includes ritual purity, and historical antipathies influence the occupational roles allocated to individuals belonging to the various castes. This is because casteism is intricately connected to the belief in reincarnation; being born into a particular caste is directly linked to the sins or righteousness of the person during his or her previous incarnation. Being pious could facilitate a better position in the subsequent reincarnation—it is a cycle that promises either betterment or punishment. This allows a resigned acceptance of one's immutable role and position in society. Some have even argued that such an approach to life actually provides more contentment for the less privileged groups.

In any discussion of castes and casteism in India, it is important to note four caveats. First, the traditional caste system has indeed become less pronounced and obvious in larger cities. There, cosmopolitan societies have moved on to leave behind the manifestations of casteism. It is also in the urban centers that the "new" and "old" India coexist in a social dynamic that is almost incomprehensible to Western visitors. Even with homeless children, poverty, crime, holy sages, and wandering cattle on the streets—not unlike many developing countries—India has another side. BMWs and Mercedes wind through clogged streets; teenagers in blue jeans and body piercings gather around Pizza Huts and cyber cafés, iPods and text-messaging cell phones in hand, reveling to the beat of rap music; satellite television beams hundreds of channels to bring CNN, MTV, and every variety of Western media into family homes. A complex modernization process and the influence of foreign mass media and culture are two of the major forces that are significantly undermining the traditional caste system.

Second, the enduring power and prevalence of the traditional caste system in modern India must not be underestimated. Two examples—one shocking, the other bordering on the absurd—are illustrative. As Pracad (2005) reports, even the devastation of the December 2004 tsunami could not compel all Indians to pull together and put caste differences aside. "The untouchable survivors of the tsunami were thrown out of relief camps. They were reportedly barred from using makeshift toilets, and given leftover, stale food" (Pracad, 2005, n.p.). On the lighter side, Pracad (2005) also passes along an Indian news agency report about male dogs owned by Dalits (Untouchables) being forbidden to enter a particular non-Dalit village. The reason? The non-Dalit villagers were afraid that the Dalits' male dogs would mate with the non-Dalits' female dogs. This would constitute, in their eyes, a transgression of the rules of the caste system and Hinduism.

In documenting the force of casteism in manifestations that range from the petty to the profound, the literature and research on the persistence, pervasiveness, and significance of casteism in today's India is clear and compelling. It remains a fundamental Indian social dynamic; it remains a powerful rationale and vehicle for grave social inequalities and injustices.

Third, and intimately tied in to the first two caveats, is the recognition that, to this day, the resolution of issues of access and rights pertaining to the Indian Scheduled Castes and Tribes remains complex, multifaceted, and only partially resolved. Progress has been made; that is clear. However, in spite of a litany of laws and policies dealing with education, employment discrimination, and so on, the social inequality that casteism fosters remains deep and widespread.

Finally, to draw parallels with the Hindu caste system and other forms of social stratification in other nations is a tenuous exercise. To the chagrin of many sociologists, some scholars have attempted to extend the meaning of casteism to racism in Western societies. In rebuttal, it is argued that the two anomalies are distinct and drastically differ in their histories, religious/cultural/social contexts, interpretations, and politics.

SCHOOLING

History of Education

India is known for its ancient *Gurukula* system of education. This long preceded colonial introduction to Western-style academies. The *Gurukula* system entailed the young living with and serving the *Guru,* or teacher. This system of education was exhaustive, covering a host of subjects in relation to living and nature (philosophy, oral history, religion, and so on). In its more recent history, India came under the British influence and the education system in the country changed accordingly under the British colonial model. In the last fifty years, India has developed an extensive education system that has resulted in a huge pool of highly skilled academic people in scientific and technological fields.

As Gautam (2003) describes, the modern Indian education system is 140 years old. Since 1857, when the British colonizers established the first three universities—Calcutta, Madras, and Bombay—India has evolved into a vibrant and dynamic country with 242 universities and affiliated institutions. Under the Indian Constitution, Articles 36 to 51 (Part IV), the principle of free and compulsory schooling is enshrined. Furthermore, and interestingly, the issue of social inequality is explicitly linked to education in specific provisions that seek to "assure that the operation of the economic system does not result in the concentration of wealth and means of production to the detriment of the common good" (MKA, 2003, n.p).

The Education System

India has consistently been forced to deal with an inadequate supply of teachers and underfunded schools. In 1998, at the primary level, India had a pupil–teacher ratio of 1:71.9 (World Bank, 2002, cited in *The World Guide 2003/2004,* p. 31). In terms of school enrollment, the Gross Enrollment Figures (GER)—that is, the number of children enrolled at a level—primary or secondary—regardless of age, divided by the population of that age group (UNICEF, 2002)—reveal inequalities by both level and gender. The GER for primary-school-age males is 99 percent; 82 percent for females. At the secondary level, 59 percent are males; 39 percent are females (UNICEF, 2002, cited in *The World Guide 2003/2004,* p. 42).

The literacy rate increased from a 1995 estimate of 52 percent to 56 percent by 2000 (*TIME Almanac,* 2004). The latest data from the 2001 Indian census reports 64.8 percent of the population as literate. However, the large discrepancy between males and females—75.3 percent literate versus 53.7 percent—persists (Census of India, 2001). Nevertheless, while the formidable task of improving literacy rates continues, it is clear that progress has been made. "Two of every three Indians can now read and write, and the [absolute] number of illiterate people fell for the first time since independence" (*The World Guide 2003/2004,* p. 297).

Free public schooling, as has been noted, is provided for under the constitution. However, many private and for-profit schools thrive in India in the form of prestigious "English" schools. Today, even the most religious and conservative Hindus find it enamoring to spend huge amounts of money in the form of "donations"—a kind word for enormous "capitation fees"—that promise acceptance at these schools and enable their children to receive a "Western" style education. These "donations" may be a formal requirement or an informal payment to assure acceptance into these elite educational institutions on criteria other than merit. In defense, the recipient institutions argue that the money is necessary to run their operations.

Indeed, from kindergarten to professional schools—including medicine, engineering, law, teacher training, and applied sciences—India has innumerable, privately established, profit-oriented, education institutions that accept students from families who can afford to pay huge "donations." Nevertheless, many metropolitan urban public schools are relatively excellent institutions. For those who are able to achieve extremely high scores, India provides prestigious centers of excellence. Entrance to these regional centers remains highly competitive, and many graduates from the centers become a part of the brain drain to the West.

Based on data gleaned from MKA (2003), the following summative description of India's complex education structures at the elementary, secondary, and tertiary levels can be offered.

Elementary Education

The success of the Indian governments' initiatives to provide easy access to education is evident in the fact that 94 percent of the rural population in India have elementary schools within a one-kilometer radius, and 84 percent have upper primary schools within a three-kilometer radius. (*The World Guide 2003/2004.*) Under universal access for education laws and improving literacy rates, formal education remains free and compulsory for all children up to the age of 14. Still, the *net* school enrollment rate at the primary level from 1994 to 2000 was 78 percent for males, and 64 percent for females. This is because, even though mandatory measures are in place, the presence of poverty and its attendant need for child labor preclude application of federal truancy laws.

Secondary Education

Secondary education also remains free and compulsory. Besides regular public schools, India has dedicated institutions for the gifted and talented. The National Council of Educational Research and Training (NCERT), established in 1961, provides assistance in the implementation of policies and procedures governing major secondary education programs. Engaged in curriculum development, the NCERT controls the National Talent Search Scheme (NTSS) that gives out about 1,000 annual scholarship awards following written examinations. Of these, about 150 are designated for applicants from Scheduled Castes and 75 for Scheduled Tribes candidates. These awards allow students to continue education in grades 11 and 12 (pre-university education). Except for the NCERT- and CBSE-affiliated institutions, grades 11 and 12 are usually offered in community colleges and university extension centers. Hence, in the usual case, students complete grade 10 and leave school to enter pre-university education offered by community colleges or institutions affiliated to one of the universities.

Catering to the children of parents who have job assignments requiring frequent travel and relocation, government employees, diplomats, federal bureaucrats, and defense employees (army, navy, air force), the federal government has established the Central Board of Secondary Education (CBSE). CBSE schools follow a uniform school education by providing a common curriculum that addresses a cross-cultural and cross-linguistic approach spanning across provinces. The underlying idea is to promote national integration through interstate mobility of students, while helping children of transferable persons to pursue uninterrupted studies.

The Council of Boards of School Education in India (COBSE)—a voluntary association of all the Boards of Secondary Education—is responsible for providing academic assistance to its member boards and has a mandate for educational standards, planning of curriculum, evaluation of schools, and public examinations.

In 2000, 28.4 percent of the population lived in urban centers, and World Bank estimates indicate an increase to 35.9 percent by 2015 (World Bank, 2002, cited in *The World Guide 2003/2004*). Nevertheless, a majority of the population is spread across rural areas, and the government has recognized this in its mandate to address issues of literacy. Responding to the needs of children in rural areas, the government has currently established 423 *Navodaya Vidyalayas*. These institutions offer free education to talented students from grade 1 to grade 12. Currently, the Vidyalayas provide education in the streams of humanities, commerce, science, and vocational education. In general, vocational education at the secondary level has evolved into the largest program of technical and vocational education in the country.

With its vast spaces and huge populations living in inaccessible areas, India developed an early system of distance learning. These institutions, established in 1979 and called *Open Schools,* operate under the mandate of the CBSE and use print media, regular mail services, and the radio. The National Open School (NOS) was established in 1989. An autonomous educational institution, the NOS is engaged in providing distance education for school dropouts and children unable to enroll in regular schools. This program allows students to advance up to grade 12. According to one report, enrollments in 1998 reached a record high of 300,000 (MKA, 2003). With over 1,000 study centers, the NOS has an open access policy of encouraging participation from various marginalized groups.

Universities

The University Grants Commission (UGC), established under an act of Parliament in 1956, oversees the standards and implementation of higher education in India. This body also has the mandate to disburse grants to universities. There are several national research and teaching institutions that are directly under federal jurisdiction. These include the Indian Council of Philosophical Research, the Indian Institute of Advanced Studies, the Indian Council of Social Science Research, and the Indian Council of Historical Research. Provinces have their own public and private universities, but all universities are controlled by federal policies. Many universities have affiliated community colleges.

Teacher Training

The training of teachers takes place in colleges, called Bachelor of Education (B.Ed.) colleges. Each college is affiliated with a university and grants one-year after-degree certification in education. The minimum requirement for entry into a B.Ed. college is an undergraduate degree (B.Sc., B.Com., B.A., and so on.). Interestingly, India does not have a federal or provincial teacher-licensing body or provincial teacher associations to mandate salaries and benefits. Hence, except for regional centers of excellence and similar federally mandated institutions (CBSE), salary scales can be varied.

In addition to the regular B.Ed. colleges, there are four Regional College of Education (RCE) centers. Administered under the National Council for Teacher Education (NCTE), which was established in 1995, the RCE are federally regulated education training and research institutions of excellence. As is the case with other federally instituted centers of excellence, acceptance into the RCEs remains highly competitive. The Indian government has also established a federal body, the National Policy on Education (NPE), which implements an in-service program—the *Programme of Action* (POA). Similarly, the North Eastern Regional Institute of Shillong, established in 1996, provides various pre-service and in-service courses for teachers.

Distance Universities

India has had a relatively good experience with distance universities, or Open Universities. Currently, there are nine Open Universities in the country with the Indira Gandhi National Open University (IGNOU) being the second largest Open University in the world after the Television University of China. Video conferencing, along with other technology, is utilized and degree programs are offered.

Regional Institutes of Excellence

In addition to regular universities and centers, there are a number of centrally controlled regional institutes of excellence. Currently, there are seven Indian Institutes of Technology (IIT) centers and six Indian Institutes of Management (IIM) centers. These institutions provide undergraduate and graduate programs in Engineering, Science, Humanities, and Social Sciences. Besides the IIT and IIM centers, the federal government has partnered with various provinces to establish Regional Engineering Colleges (REC). Seventeen such colleges and over 300 technical institutions cater to over 65,000 students every year. Similarly, 750 polytechnic or vocational diploma institutions annually accept over 90,000 students. The doctoral programs accept over 11,000 students annually.

Adult Education

India also has an extensive and well-established adult education network that caters to a wide population. The government launched a National Literacy Mission in 1988 that addresses the needs of students in 556 districts: Sixty percent of the students are women; over 22 percent come from Scheduled Castes; and over 13 percent are from Scheduled Tribes.

Education of Women

According to government policy programs, education for women remains a high priority. Currently, the Education for Women's Equality initiative operates in 7,335 villages in 51 districts spread over eight provinces. The Women's Education Emphasis initiative deals with female enrollment, retention, and employment. This body also is responsible for curriculum issues relating to gender bias.

PROMISES AND POSSIBILITIES

Population and Competition

With over a billion people and a plethora of languages, religions, histories, cultures, and political groups, the largest democratic republic in the world has to deal with the reality that it is a very overpopulated country. One consequence of this is that the middle-income group has to compete for limited opportunities, whether in education and training or finding employment. With a quota system that in some cases allocates close to 40 percent for specific groups, the ones who fail to qualify find it extremely difficult or impossible to gain access to many institutions. This has resulted in the unrestrained sprouting of many private institutions that cater to the privileged that have the money and influence to secure positions for their children.

Credential Inflation and Competition

While education at the elementary and secondary levels is compulsory and free, not every child attends school. With the issues of poverty, child labor, and traditional farming families, many children fail to attend school. Thus the challenge of universal education, even at the elementary level, continues in India.

Nevertheless, overall, the Indian education system caters to a very high number of students. Because of the high number of graduates relative to the ability of the economy to absorb them, competition for jobs is very intense and certification in turn has become a commodity. Certificates, diplomas, and degrees are passports to gaining employment and attaining a more comfortable/better life. This in turn has created what has variously been termed "the Diploma Disease . . . the 'Paper Chase' . . . or, more pointedly, the educational rat-race. It comes to the same thing, chasing qualifications because they can pay off—in a job, an income, status and power" (Little, 1983, n.p.). With a surplus of graduates with degrees, the employment sector in India has become saturated, creating an imbalance in supply and demand. With more applicants having acquired higher qualifications (sometimes unrelated to the job), formal education gets undervalued in the employment sector. Furthermore, enormous money is expended earning degrees that simply do not provide the desired tangible returns.

In addition, some careers carry more prestige, respect, and monetary rewards (medicine, government administration, law, engineering, and some computer-based areas), while others may receive traditional respect but meager salaries (teaching school). Hence, a substantial number of promising students may never consider teaching school; this results in a lower quality of applicants for teacher education degrees. In partial compensation, Regional Colleges of Education, like the various centers of excellence in science and technology, attract qualified high-achievers, but this constitutes an insignificant number. Lack of resources, changing politics, an ongoing brain drain, and inefficient political and bureaucratic systems present a formidable challenge to dramatic reforms.

As is the case in most other areas, India does not lack resources but needs the will to make dramatic decisions. The newer generation that is connected to global changes may bring in much desired changes. In fact, some of the most ambitious and successful computer entrepreneurs in Silicon Valley are from India. In India, Internet technologies, information technology outsourcing, increasing international migration, multiple nationalities and residences, and the presence of foreign multinational corporations will influence a more educated working class that also constitutes an increasing number of consumers with disposable income. The very rich and the very poor will continue to be unaffected by dramatic changes—the rich, as always, will continue to enjoy their affluence, while the marginalized will continue to be precluded from the benefits of globalization.

With limited resources and a convoluted bureaucracy, one may seek answers to some difficult questions. Should India consider a more direct state-controlled education system based on provincial responsibility tied in with federal intervention? Would limiting the operation of for-profit private educational institutions address some of the ongoing problems? How can India address the issue of inflated credentials ("diploma disease")? What are socially positive ways to respond to changes from globalization and free trade? What measures can be instituted to address the needs of the marginalized? How can we deal with child labor without affecting traditional cultures? How can we address issues of child labor in relation to commercial industries? And, what efforts can be made to change the status of teacher training and the social and economic status of teaching as a profession?

CONCLUSION

As a dynamic and vibrant country that is much more than a regional power, India is also the largest country to outsource information technology skills to the world. With a huge population that represents a relatively vital economy, India has become a global player. Multicultural, multilingual, multireligious, and multiethnic in nature, India is an example of a very successful democracy. In spite of her many and deep problems, India has managed to survive political disruptions, economic turmoil, historical changes, religious conflicts, overpopulation, poverty, and natural disasters.

This short description of India does not purport to provide a nonbiased analysis of the country. While not always feasible, the best approach to understanding a culture is to ignore travel brochures and international committee reports and travel to live for some time within a given culture. India remains an excellent example of an enigma—a country of paradoxes. To understand some of the ambiguities, and to sort out facts from media fiction, one would have to embark on a trip that would personally engage the individual and provide that unique experience to create one's own analysis of this ancient civilization.

REFERENCES

Census of India. (2001). Retrieved February 1, 2005, from http://www.censusindia.net/t_00_006.html

Dyer, G. (2004, May 21). Gandhi's action a betrayal of trust. *Winnipeg Free Press,* p. A15.

Friedman, T. (2004, June 7). India voted for globalization. *Winnipeg Free Press,* p. A10.

Gautam, H. (2003). *University News, 38*(26), 9.

India at a glance. (1991). Retrieved February 1, 2005, from http://www.censusindia.net/scst.html

Jary, D., & Jary, J. (Eds.). (1991). *The Harper Collins dictionary of sociology.* New York: HarperPerennial.

Little, A. (1983, April). Reaching for the top. *New Internationalist, 122.* Retrieved February 1, 2005, from http://www.newint.org/issue122/reaching.htm

MKA (Malayala Manorama) Electronic Resource CD. (2003). *Manorama knowledge adventure—Manorama year book 2003.* Kottayam, India: The Malayala Manorama. Retrieved February 1, 2005, from http://www.manoramaonline.com

PocketLingo 2.0, *Houghton Mifflin Dictionary of Cultural Literacy.* (2002). New York: Houghton Mifflin.

Pracad, C. B. (2005). *Untouchability: What the tsunami couldn't wash away.* Retrieved February 1, 2005, from http://www.infochangeindia.org/analysis58.jsp

The Scheduled Castes and the Scheduled Tribes (Prevention of Atrocities) Act. (1989, September 11). Retrieved February 1, 2005, from http://ncscst.nic.in/POA%201989.htm

Singh, S., Barkhordarian, A., Beech, C., Bindloss, J., Derby, S., Ham, A., Harding, P., Hole, A., Horton, P., Pundyk, G., & Vidgen, L. (2003). *India.* Melbourne, Australia: Lonely Planet Publications.

TIME Almanac. (2004). Boston, MA: Infoplease, a Pearson Education Company.

UNDP. (2001). *Human development report.* New York: United Nations.

UNICEF. (2002). *State of the world's children.* New York: United Nations.

United Nations. (2002). *World Population Prospects: 2002 Revision.* New York: Author.

World Bank. (2002). *World Development Indicators 2002.* New York: Author.

The World Guide 2003/2004. (2004). Oxford, UK: New Internationalist Publications Ltd.

Part IV

THE NEW EUROPE

Sustaining the West; Reinventing the East

CHAPTER TEN

FRENCH EDUCATION'S DILEMMA IN THE GLOBALIZATION PROCESS

How to Accommodate Simultaneously the Objectives of Equality and Excellence?

ESTELLE ORIVEL

FRANÇOIS ORIVEL

France is one of the four western European countries that belong to the group of formerly seven (now eight) biggest economic powers (G7 and G8). Before the collapse of the communist system in central and eastern Europe, four European countries (France, Germany, Italy, and the United Kingdom) were more or less equivalent in terms of demographic importance. With the reunification of both parts of Germany (the Federal Republic of Germany and the Democratic Republic of Germany), Germany has emerged as a significantly greater power. It has more than 80 million inhabitants versus about 60 million for the three other countries.

France is divided into ninety-six Départements. The Département is a geographical entity, created after the French Revolution, that is administratively run by a Préfet, the main

Estelle Orivel started her career as Assistant Professor at the University of Burgundy and has subsequently moved to the research unit of the French Ministry of Education. She has done studies on the economics of culture and the economics of education, especially on the issue of relations between education and employment opportunities in France.

François Orivel is Senior Researcher with the Institute for Research on Education of the University of Burgundy in France. As an economist, he has worked on the cost and finance of education worldwide, as well as on the analysis of the efficiency of educational systems through comparative education. He is teaching in several master programs. He has also worked as a consultant for different international organizations.

representative of the central power at this level. The Région is a newly created geographical entity that is a set of four Départements on average. There are twenty-four Régions.

France was one of the first countries to achieve its "demographic transition." Its fertility rate began to fall as early as the beginning of the nineteenth century, immediately after the French Revolution of 1789. After having been the most populated European nation in the seventeenth century, France was passed by Russia, Germany, and the United Kingdom. Yet, the combination of a relatively high net migration surplus and a positive natural demographic growth during the twentieth century has led France to partly close its gap with other European powers during the past decades. France's fertility rate has not reached the low point of most its partners: Among the members of G8, it is 1.89, second after the United States (2.05). Its demographic prospects are in consequence slightly better than those of its partners.

Life expectancy has significantly increased in recent decades. Among the G8 countries, France ranks second after Japan. Consequently, the proportion of the retired population is increasing rapidly. This phenomenon is reinforced by the early retirement age of the population. France has the lowest participation activity rate for the 55 to 65 age group, which has raised serious problems in the financing of pensions. After having postponed the necessary reforms for a long time, France finally passed a new law in 2003 that slightly reduced the level of retirement benefits.

SOCIOECONOMIC CONTEXT

The Economy

France has the fourth largest GDP in the world, after the United States, Japan, and Germany. Its GDP per capita is close to the European Union average. After a rapid increase in the thirty years that followed the Second World War, France's slowdown during the past two decades was slightly more consequential than that of its partners.

This last period has been strongly influenced by the objective of European integration, which has forced French authorities to adopt a more rigorous monetary policy in order to fight inflation and to reduce deficits. The reduction of the public deficit is today one of our most urgent issues. The European Union introduced the common currency, the Euro, in 1999 and has made compulsory a target of 3 percent of GDP as a maximal authorized deficit. During the past three years, France has had serious difficulties in complying with this obligation and has faced acerbic criticisms from its partners.

France's unemployment rate was constantly high during the 1990s and in the years after 2000 (between 9 and 10 percent). Many economists think that this unusual level of unemployment is linked with the employers' obligation to pay a minimum salary to wage earners, associated with a high level of social contribution. In addition, there are many legal restrictions on the firing of employees, which can discourage the creation of new jobs. The cost for employers of the present level of this minimum salary, about US$1500 per month, including social contributions, is viewed as too high for the maintenance of certain jobs currently offered in other countries.

The tradition of state intervention in the economy, dating back to the seventeenth century, has made the French economy less flexible than many others. This lack of flexibility, while not necessarily a big issue during periods of slow changes, is a real handicap in periods characterized by rapid technological changes. The French population looks to state authorities for protection against the undesirable effects of progress, such as adjusting to new technologies, retraining the working population for new jobs, and competing with emerging economies worldwide.

In spite of these difficulties, the French economy is progressing and has been able to maintain good indicators in several fields. The inflation rate is at a historically low level (between 1 and 2.5 percent per year). The external trade balance is characterized by moderate surpluses, showing that the competitiveness of the economy remains good by international standards, especially in the fields of luxury products, aircraft, tourism, and automobiles.

The most important remaining problem is the lack of confidence of the French population concerning economic prospects, which leads to a tendency for entrepreneurs to underinvest and for households to underconsume. In fact, France has one of the highest saving ratios among the G8 countries: between 15 and 20 percent of the GDP.

Politics

Since the French Revolution of 1789, France has known no fewer than seventeen constitutions: from parliamentarian republics to empires, from parliamentary monarchies to the Vichy regime. However, the dominant feature of the past two centuries is the attachment of the population to the notion of republic, the present one being the Fifth Republic, born in 1958 with the return of the Général de Gaulle to power. The present republic is a bizarre mixture of a parliamentary regime, in which the Prime Minister and his or her government is dependent upon the majority in a parliament elected for five years, and a presidential regime, in which the President (originally elected for seven years, and then, since 2002, for five years) derives legitimacy from the votes of citizens. When the majority in the Parliament leans to the same side as the President, no conflict occurs between legislative and executive powers. Yet, given the fact that both elections do not necessarily coincide, the President's political affiliation may be different from that of the parliamentary majority. This situation has occurred three times since the beginning of the Fifth Republic: twice with President François Mitterrand in 1986 and 1993 and once with President Jacques Chirac in 1997. During these periods, called "cohabitations," one has a tricky situation. The President tries to preserve some decision-making powers, mainly in the fields of diplomacy and military affairs, while the bulk of executive decisions are made by the government and the Prime Minister.

The Fifth Republic emerged in a context of severe political conflicts, arising from the decolonization process. A civil war was taking place in Algeria, where about 2 million French citizens had settled and wanted to maintain Algeria within the French Republic against the wishes of indigenous movements for independence. Général de Gaulle negotiated a peace agreement in Algeria that gave independence to the country, and he organized the return to France of most French settlers from Algeria. As well, de Gaulle gave independence to former colonies located in sub-Saharan Africa.

Unlike the United Kingdom, France has maintained close ties with most of its ancient colonies. It has constantly provided financial assistance and education support, in the framework of a global "francophone" project that aims at maintaining French as a common language for enhancing cultural, political, and economic relations. This policy has known its successes and failures but, undoubtedly, the French language would have declined in importance more rapidly without this "volontarist" policy that sometimes raises a little irony in the English-speaking world.

As mentioned earlier, state intervention is deeply rooted in the French tradition. The importance of the state is not limited to economic production, but also concerns the redistribution of wealth. The "Welfare State" has been extensively developed and covers the whole social security system, which provides health care to everybody, family allowances to households with children, pensions to retired people, unemployment allowances, and free education for all, from kindergarten to university. The state also allocates subsidies to a wide range of cultural activities. The importance of the role of the state is reflected in the share of GDP captured by public taxation—as much as 45 percent. In the majority of developed countries, this share is between 30 percent and 40 percent.

The involvement of the state in socioeconomic affairs has been strongly challenged in the recent past for two reasons. The first is linked with the declining competitiveness of public management with respect to the private sector. The second is associated with the building of the European Union, which sets up new regulations to ensure fair competition within the Common Market. This movement is parallel to the worldwide tendency toward globalization and deregulation that seeks to enhance free initiative and improve competition.

As a consequence, since 1986 France has entered a phase of privatization of public enterprises. However, due to the resistance of trade unions and public opinion, this movement is less advanced than in other countries. Moreover, frequent political changes (during the last six parliamentary elections, voters have chosen alternatively the left and the right) have hampered the achievement of this privatization movement.

Religious Context

Christianity was introduced into France in the fifth century and has shaped its tradition, culture, values, and landscape. The French successfully stopped the advance of the Islamic invasion in Poitiers in the eighth century. At the time of the Lutheran Reform, France remained faithful to the Catholic affiliation and to the pope. It was then called "the elder daughter of the Church." In spite of the fact that only a minority of the French population is today practicing (about 10 percent), the vast majority still claims to belong to the Catholic Church.

Tolerance toward other religions has been uneven. At the time of the Reform, King Henry IV introduced some openness vis-à-vis the Protestants. But later on, the latter suffered from Catholic persecutions—assassinations and forced emigrations. Anti-Semitism developed during the first decades of the twentieth century and culminated under the Vichy regime when France was occupied by the Nazi army.

Yet, for a long time, France was considered as a welcoming country for foreigners and those persecuted in their own countries. It welcomed Armenians after the Turkish genocide in 1915, the Russian aristocracy after the 1917 revolution, and the Spanish republicans after the victory of Franco. Many others have been attracted by better economic prospects (Polish, Italians, Portuguese).

Since decolonization (around 1960), most new immigrants come from the South (North and sub-Saharan Africa, and Asia—in particular Vietnam, Cambodia, and China). The integration of this new wave is not as easy as previous ones. Ethnic, cultural, and religious differences are much wider, and more time is required to integrate these new immigrants.

If this integration is characterized by more conflict than in countries such as the United Kingdom, it is due in part to the fact that France pursues an objective of full assimilation of immigrants rather than of cohabitation between different communities that maintain their own traditions. One can also illustrate the French conception by its language policy. Until the nineteenth century, French was the language of the elite; the rest of the population practiced local dialects. The disappearance of most of these dialects in the past hundred years is the outcome of an affirmative policy to impose French in the educational system as early as preschool.

The Jewish community in France is presently the largest in Europe (600,000 people). It is considered well-integrated into French society. On the other hand, the integration of a growing Muslim community, mostly from North Africa, is creating problems. The present size of the Muslim community is about 4 million people, or 7 percent of the total population. The rise of the extreme right political party (Front National), led by Jean Marie Le Pen, illustrates the growing intolerance toward the Muslim community. This political party bases its political influence (about 15 percent of the electorate) on xenophobic, anti-immigrant, and anti-Islamic slogans.

Cultural Context

France is proud of its cultural achievements. During the medieval period, thousands of churches and cathedrals were built. Almost all art was religious. In the eighteenth century, French artistic values were adopted in most European royal courts. While Germany was a dominant producer in the field of music, France held for a long time the lead in fine arts. In the nineteenth century, the French "salon" of fine arts was the most important event of the year for artistic life in Europe and Northern America. Most modern tendencies, from impressionism to cubism, from art nouveau to fauvism, were born in Paris, which attracted many artists from other countries.

SCHOOLING

The French education system mirrors the main features of French society as just described. It is centralized, state oriented, and unified. It is free and egalitarian, which does not mean necessarily that it is equitable.

Structure of the System

Preschool. The availability of preschool is a well-known characteristic of the French system. Preschool is part of the primary education system; teachers have the same training and qualifications as primary teachers and can work alternatively in both levels.

Children enter preschool at age 2 for 4 years. The participation rate is 35 percent at age 2 and 99.5 percent for ages 3, 4, and 5. Preschool lasts 6 hours a day, 3 in the morning and 3 in the afternoon, and has been a powerful tool for allowing mothers to take jobs on the labor market. If necessary, children can arrive earlier and leave the school later to fit the working schedules of the parents. During these extra hours, children are not looked after by teachers, but by municipal employees.

Primary and Secondary Schools. The French education system has known three waves of expansion. The first one took place in the late nineteenth century when primary education became compulsory. The second one occurred between 1960 and 1970, when the first cycle of secondary education became *de facto* compulsory after de Gaulle's decree of January 1969 that declared school compulsory until age 16. The third wave took place from 1985 to 1995 when it was decided that 80 percent of every generation should attain the level of baccalaureate. This policy increased the percent of people reaching this level and had an immediate impact on the expansion of higher education. This is because, according to French law, every baccalaureate holder is entitled a free university seat.

The expected number of years of schooling in 2001 was 16.6 for a child of 5 years old, one of the highest within OECD countries (OECD, 1996). If preschool education were included in these data, France would likely rank first. The indicator is slightly superior for girls (16.4 versus 16.1 for boys); this is explained by the fact that girls tend to succeed better in secondary education, in particular in the baccalaureate.

The length of the school year is slightly above the OECD average (1,000 hours versus 920) and is concentrated into a lower number of school days. This last feature produces a chronic debate over the issue of school rhythms.

Upper secondary education is divided into three tracks, which lead to different types of baccalaureates. The largest and oldest track provides general education and is itself divided into three categories: sciences, humanities, and social sciences. The second track leads to the technological baccalaureate. It includes many types of technological specialties, which can be broken into industrial specialties and tertiary specialties. The third track enrolls students preparing a vocational baccalaureate. This last baccalaureate, created in 1985, was designed for upgrading the status of vocational training. Its main objective is to prepare pupils to enter the labor market, rather than pursue higher education.

The Chevènement objective of 80 percent of a generation reaching the level of the baccalaureate has never been achieved. Actually, since 1995, this percentage is stagnating at about 70 percent. The major evolution since 1995 concerns the distribution of pupils among the three tracks. The proportion of pupils following the general track (more prestigious) has declined from 37.2 in 1995 of a given generation to 32.6 in 2001. This decline has benefited the vocational track, which attracted 11.2 percent of a generation in 2001, instead of the 7.9 percent in 1995. As only 20 percent of vocational baccalaureate holders pursue higher education instead of the 100 percent for general baccalaureate holders, the rate of participation for ages 18 to 24 has declined. It was 80.2 percent at the age of 18, instead of 84.1 in 1994; 65.9 percent at the age of 19, instead of 68.6 percent in 1994.

Private Schools. Before the middle of the nineteenth century, the majority of schools were run by the Church. Since then, a struggle has developed between the state and the Catholic Church for the control of schools. In the early 1880s, a law made primary school compulsory, free, and secular. Another law then set up the separation of Church and state and confiscated Church properties for the benefit of the state. These two events transferred the main responsibility for providing education from the Church to elected public authorities. However, the Catholic Church has not disappeared from the educational scene. It was allowed to open its own schools for fees, an option used more often for secondary schools where the public supply was limited. The opening of Catholic primary schools was concentrated in certain regions with very strong Catholic traditions, especially in the west part of France.

A certain competition between Church and state persisted during most of the twentieth century, with both sides showing some level of aggressiveness toward the other. Two political events brought this fight to an end. Under Général de Gaulle's presidency, it was decided that teachers' salaries in Church schools would be paid from the state budget. In exchange, private schools had to accept the control of state authorities and follow the unified curriculum. This last condition had already applied, since the objective of Church schools was to prepare pupils for the *baccalaureate,* the final exam at the end of upper secondary education, a strong unifying goal in the French system. The change in salary structure thus has allowed Church schools to charge very low fees and to open their doors to pupils from low socioeconomic backgrounds. As a consequence, their role and image have changed. The provision of religious education has vanished, and one of their new roles is now that of giving a second chance to low achievers.

The second event took place in 1984 when the education minister, encouraged by the secular lobby, tried to restrain the public financing of private schools. This attempt became a total political failure and raised such hostility in the French population that the government withdrew its project. Analysis of public opinion at that time showed clearly that the main motivation behind this discontent was not the preservation of a Catholic system as such, but the preservation of the possibilities of a second chance and choice.

At any given time, about 20 percent of the school-age population is enrolled in private schools. However, at some point in their schooling, 37 percent of French pupils have attended a private school. At the end of the twentieth century the competition between the two systems was reduced and the cohabitation is quite peaceful. Current public opinion polls show that the French population is satisfied with the present arrangements.

Higher Education. About 50 percent of a generation enroll in higher education. After the baccalaureate, French students have six options. First, they can decide not to pursue education. In 1995, about 15 percent did this as compared to 20 percent in 2001. The proportion of this group has increased in the recent past because of the growing importance of the vocational baccalaureate.

Those who enter higher education choose between five tracks, out of which only one is not selective, the university. The universities attracted half a cohort of baccalaureate holders in 1995, but this percent declined to 40 percent in 2001. Students seem more and more to favor selective tracks.

Among the selective tracks, the most prestigious one is called *Classes préparatoires aux grandes écoles* (preparatory classes for Grandes Ecoles), which attract about 7 percent of baccalaureate holders. The network of Grandes Ecoles has developed in the last two centuries. There are presently 237 engineering schools and 257 business schools. Unlike the ninety universities, the Grandes Ecoles are structured hierarchically. For instance, among engineering schools, the best one is the *Ecole Polytechnique* run by the Ministry of Defense.

The three other selective tracks are short-term vocational education (two years). Eight percent of baccalaureate holders enter the IUTs (Technological University Institute); 20 percent enter STS (Department for Higher Technicians). Six percent enter a large variety of specialized institutes, mostly operated by the Ministry of Health and Social Affairs, that train nurses and other paramedical specialists.

Altogether, there were 2.2 million students in higher education in 2002–2003. The rate of increase of enrollments has been very rapid during the past decades up to 1995. There were only 310,000 students in 1960, 1,175,000 in 1980, and 1,700,000 in 1990. Since 1995, the evolution is more or less stagnant.

Organization and Governance. Centralized France has a centralized education system. In fact, it is sometimes said that the French Ministry of Education is the biggest world employer after the Red Army. The French system employed 1,180 million people in 2002–2003, of which 870,000 were teachers.

Most of the budget is centrally determined and most of the personnel are civil servants. Decisions concerning any aspect such as legal framework, certification, management, or the recruitment of teachers and nonteaching personnel are taken by central authorities (Parliament and government).

To facilitate the management of schools, the Ministry of Education has set up regional branches, called the *Rectorats*. Each Rectorat is headed by a rector, nominated by the Government, who represents the Minister of Education for a variety of decisions. Most rectors are replaced when a new political majority is elected. There are 27 rectors responsible for a territory called an *académie,* very close to the concept of region.

Some responsibilities are given to lower levels of administration. The maintenance of primary schools (including preschools) has always been the responsibility of municipalities. Until 1982, junior and upper secondary schools and higher education institutions were entirely managed and financed by the state budget. In 1982, a new law introduced a limited decentralization process.

The *Départements* and the *Régions* have received some responsibilities in the management of, respectively, junior and upper secondary schools. Yet, this decentralization process has not given them any authority for staff management. The Ministry of Education remains the only authority in charge of personnel. Basically, *Départements* and *Régions* build and maintain schools. However, it is clear that they cannot build a new lycée without the clearance of the central government, which will provide the relevant staff.

In 2004, the Chirac-Raffarin Government decided to extend the decentralization process to nonteaching staff of secondary schools, in spite of the strong opposition of their unions and of the left political parties. This shift concerns about 140,000 employees. The difficulties encountered in passing this law indicate that it is unlikely that the government will succeed in transferring teaching staff in the foreseeable future.

Curricula

Curricula are determined by the Ministry of Education. In the late 1980s, the Mitterrand Government set up a national think-tank in charge of curriculum reforms.

The French curriculum is often accused of being too abstract, too academic, and not enough oriented toward the acquisition of life competencies. In addition, it is divided into separate disciplines giving little space to transdisciplinary approaches.

However, when the OECD published comparative data in 1996 for the curriculum of junior secondary schools, it showed that France stands in an average position. For instance, the amount of mathematics and sciences in the curriculum, which goes from 20 percent in the Netherlands to 30 percent in New Zealand, is about 24 percent in France. Similarly, France is close to the average for the percent of reading and writing, social sciences, foreign languages, and physical education. It is slightly below the average for art and natural sciences. It does not include religious education. New technologies, in particular computer science, have some difficulties entering the curriculum.

At the upper secondary level, curricula are closely related to the objectives of the different tracks (general, technological, and vocational). Vocational curricula are often updated by commissions, including representatives of the productive world. In general education, reforms are rare, although it is often thought that the content of curricula is excessively large and should be lightened. This issue has never been addressed because of the pressure of different lobbies, each of which feels that its field is so important that it could not be reduced. It is obvious that reforming the French curriculum is a Herculean task.

At the university level, France has set up a system of national diplomas. The degree obtained by students is recognized by the French government, regardless of the university in which it was earned. As a consequence, the curriculum of each university in each discipline is controlled by ad hoc administrative units located within the Ministry of Education. In spite of the theoretical freedom left to universities to organize their curricula, central regulations have a strong homogenizing effect.

Pedagogical Theory and Practices

As in most countries, France has evolved toward less authoritarian pedagogical practices, relying less on memorization and more on the development of critical thinking. In addition, it has adopted the theory of individualization of the learning process. Yet, teachers remain entirely free to utilize any pedagogical practice and are only obliged to follow the curriculum. It is therefore difficult to ascertain the effects of modern theories on pedagogical practices.

At the university level, the theory of individualized learning has hardly penetrated. The French approach relies heavily on lectures given to large student audiences and very little on small learning groups or on the guidance of tutors.

Teacher Training

For almost a century, primary teachers (including preschool teachers) have been trained in a network of so-called "normal schools." Trainees were recruited at the end of junior high school and received their upper secondary education in the normal schools where they passed their baccalaureate. After the baccalaureate, they received some professional training, which was comprised of a significant share of practical work as teachers in close-by primary schools (application primary schools) under the supervision of experienced teachers.

This system became clearly obsolete by the end of the 1970s, and several reforms were implemented. The last one closed all normal schools and replaced them in the late 1980s with a smaller number of training institutions, called University Institutes for Teacher Training (IUFMs). These new institutions, while formally associated with universities, enjoy relative autonomy.

Two major changes have been introduced with the IUFMs. The first one is the upgrading of teacher training to the level of university training. The second change is that primary and secondary teachers are now trained in the same institution, are exposed to a similar training program, and expect similar careers and compensations.

Before the creation of IUFMs, there was no specific training for secondary teachers. Students with a university degree in mathematics or French could teach these specialties in any secondary school without any professional training. Yet, in order to become a certified civil servant, they had to pass a competitive recruitment exam. Those who were recruited as civil servants spent their first year of work as "beginners," which meant some support in the form of in-service training.

Pupil/Teacher Ratios

For primary and secondary education, French pupil/teacher ratios are close to the average for developed countries. For primary education, there are 19.3 pupils per teacher against the 17.5 average in OECD countries; for secondary education, 13.2 versus 13.8 on average.

Similar and reliable comparative data for higher education does not exist (the estimate of full-time equivalent teachers is more complicated at this level). However, it is widely known that the French higher education system is atypical from this point of view, in the sense that it has a larger number of students per teacher than other OECD countries.

These pupil/teacher ratios should therefore lead to a slightly lower percentage of education staff within the active population in France. Actually, this is not so (6.1 percent in France versus 5.5 for the OECD average) because the total number of pupils and students in the total population is comparatively higher.

Evaluation

France has not developed the tradition of standardized tests for the evaluation of pupils and students' performance because it has always been sceptical about the merits of multiple-choice exams. Rather, its tradition is based on the utilization of written essays by students. Of course, it is more difficult to give objective scores for such exercises. However, in spite of this difficulty, French pedagogues still believe that the essay approach provides more information on effective capacities and competences of students (quality of expression, capacity of structuring ideas, and so on) than multiple-choice tests.

Nevertheless, France has participated in several rounds designed by the International Education Achievement (IEA) group, as well as by OECD (PISA project). France's performances have been uneven. For reading and mathematics, the ranking of France was in the first quarter in IEA surveys; it was been only average in the PISA project.

It is probably too early to explain the decline of the French ranking in the PISA survey, but one of the likely explanations is connected with the testing philosophy. PISA has tried to evaluate cognitive competencies connected with daily life requirements, not with purely academic achievement. French pupils seem less at ease with problem-solving capacities, a problem that was regularly reflected in sciences scores, for which France's performances have been constantly below the average. Sciences as the weak point of the French education system is related to the already mentioned excessively abstract approach of the curricula.

Expenditure and Unit Costs

According to UNESCO data, public education expenditures represent 5 percent of the GDP worldwide. Within OECD countries, this percentage is slightly higher—5.1 percent. France has a tradition of higher public spending, with a percentage of 5.6. However, it is also characterized by a lower private involvement in education. While on average OECD countries allow 1.1 percent of the GDP from private sources to education, France's percentage is only half this level. Higher public expenditure compensates for lower private participation.

Unit costs usually increase with the level of education. In OECD countries, secondary education is on average 43 percent more expensive than primary education, and higher education is twice as expensive as secondary education. All levels combined, the French average unit cost is relatively close to that of OECD countries. However, the hierarchy between levels is quite different. Secondary education is more expensive than the OECD average, while higher education is significantly cheaper (50 percent less). France is the only example where university education is cheaper than upper secondary. This is due to the poor student/teacher ratio and more generally to relatively modest teaching and learning conditions at this level.

MAJOR ISSUES, CONTROVERSIES, AND PROBLEMS

Management Issues

The actual management of teaching staff has two major drawbacks. First, no care is taken to match teachers and positions (beginners are often assigned to the harshest positions). Second, there is no evaluation of the quality of the work done by teachers, and no system of promotion according to performances or merit exists.

The strong tradition of centralization has opened the door to the constitution of powerful teacher unions. Because 870,000 teachers are employed by the Ministry of Education, they represent a decisive bargaining force. This has led to an atypical system of allocation of staff, entirely driven by a set of rules designed by the unions and among which the fundamental criterion is the desire of teachers to be assigned to certain places in certain schools. These desires are not based on income differences (salary scales are determined for the whole country and based on seniority rather than on merit). They have other motivations that can be practical (to be closer to his or her spouse), contextual (a fancier city, a nicer climate), and educational (a better school, more rewarding pupils). Because the best assignments have more candidates than there are positions, the unions have set up a queueing system in which one reaches the head of the queue by accumulating points. Points are reached by seniority, the length of waiting time, the distance of spouses, time spent in harshest positions, and so on.

The main disadvantage of the system is the fact that school authorities have nothing to say about the recruitment of a teacher, and virtually nothing to say concerning his or her departure. They cannot attract teachers with specific profiles adapted to specific and local circumstances, and they cannot reject those who do not fit these circumstances. Moreover, it is unfortunate that when a position is vacant and not requested by an existing teacher, it is filled by a new teacher without experience. Vacant positions are indeed those that are considered by teachers as harsh positions; for instance, positions in difficult suburbs, in violent cities with widespread criminality problems, with large proportions of low achievers, and so on. These are hardly positions for beginners.

While it is generally recognized that the quality of the French teaching staff is good by international standards, it could be significantly improved with better staff management. Too, this average good quality does not exclude the presence of a significant minority of relatively ineffective teachers. Several evaluation studies on the determinants of school achievement have shown that after the personal characteristics of the student and his or her social background, the most important differentiating factor is the teacher. The teacher effect is much more important than all other input affecting the learning process (class size, textbooks, and other materials, time spent studying, school conditions, expenditure per pupil, and so on).

It is clear that better pupil performances could be obtained if the selection process of teachers was improved and if the management of teaching staff was based on their performances. Decentralization is not necessarily the solution if the present centralized system is simply applied at the regional level. What is important is to give more decision power to school authorities in the selection of teachers and to let school authorities have some influence on teacher's careers. The issue is therefore more a question of autonomy of schools than of decentralization.

For higher education professors, France has not initiated a system of evaluation of teaching capacities. Promotion is obtained after peer reviews based only on the academic research of the candidate. Moreover, students are not invited to give their opinions, as is the case in North America, and a bad professor can stay in a position until retirement. Similarly, a good professor is not rewarded for the efforts made vis-à-vis students.

There are some other minor problems concerning the management of teachers. One is the coexistence in secondary schools of two major categories of teachers. The first group, called *agrégé,* is selected on highly selective academic criteria and has higher monthly salaries and fewer teaching hours. The second group—*certifié*—is less severely selected, less well paid, and has more teaching hours. These differences of status are not based on actual performances or on professional competences. The higher salary offered to the *agrégés* for their entire careers is acquired before the person even starts teaching, even if he or she happens to be a bad teacher.

Having two categories of teachers could be justified, one of them being better paid, if it allowed those belonging to the lower category to be promoted under certain conditions of retraining and evaluation of effective performance. However, the French dualism does not allow for this possibility. This lack of perspective may explain why the French teaching staff tends to be conservative in its pedagogical practices. It is not open to new technologies, and external evaluation is rarely used as a means for managing the system and improving its performance.

Some observers believe that the Ministry of Education tends to be a bureaucratic monster. Its total staff, 4,000, is considered as excessive. It has a reasonably good evaluation and planning department, but, as part of the political sphere, it has not the necessary external view that could give the scientific objectivity everybody could trust.

Education Policy for Low Achievers

It is traditional that each pupil is entitled the same rights. This was translated to mean that those who face specific obstacles do not deserve specific treatments. It was a conception of equity based on equality rather than on the unequal treatment of unequals. School careers were purely determined by merit, and low achievers were excluded from the system when they did not meet its requirements.

In the 1970s, the government introduced a reform at the junior secondary level, in which the three tracks that existed were merged so that all pupils were on one track. Some differences were maintained, such as optional disciplines (Latin, Greek), but the core of the curriculum was the same for all pupils. Given that reform, the proportion of pupils leaving the school system fell from 25 percent to 8 percent at the beginning of the 1990s.

However, a plateau has been reached. The proportion of 8 percent of pupils leaving the system without qualifications has not declined further. And, for the proportion of pupils who are illiterate, it also seems to be incompressible—around 6 to 10 percent of a given cohort.

Several attempts have been made to address this issue. The most known, initiated in 1982, was called the ZEP project (*Zone d'éducation prioritaire* or Priority Education Area). A ZEP is a geographical area in which the proportion of households with a low SES is above a certain threshold. It corresponds more or less to residential areas, most of which are located in the suburbs of big cities, which face social problems (unemployment, high percentage of immigrants, criminality problems, and so on).

The measures listed in the project include three types of inputs: additional teaching and nonteaching staff (such as psychologists); additional remuneration for all staff; and an additional specific budget. This approach is thus based on a better pupil/teacher ratio with supposedly more motivated teachers, thanks to better remuneration, allowing a more individualized learning process. And, as it is assumed that part of the problem lies in the lack of social integration of certain pupils, this is addressed by special individual treatment by psychologists.

More recently, faced with the permanence of a proportion of low achievers, a debate occurred concerning the pertinence of setting up a specific track at the junior secondary level for low achievers. It was argued that a more practical curriculum oriented to more professional activities would fit better the needs of low achievers. This option is found in the small education subsector run by the Ministry of Agriculture that provides a succession of periods of schooling and periods of productive agricultural activities. It seems to work rather well.

However, the revival of a specific track for low achievers has been fiercely fought. Politically, France wants to maintain the ideal that the system works in an equitable way that ensures everybody the possibility of success at the end of junior secondary in the general track. It may be an illusion. It is obvious that a certain fraction of the pupils are reluctant to attend general classes and feel more at ease in practical streams. However, some research shows that low achievers tend to perform slightly better when they are mixed together with high achievers.

The debate on the treatment of low achievers remains quite intense, especially at the upper secondary level where the tracks cannot get rid of the image of being second-class. As well, some pupils are enrolled in this track against their wills. In spite of their low level of achievement in the general disciplines, they would prefer to stay in the general track and thus feel very badly about their orientation in the practical track. Furthermore, they often cannot choose the trade they would prefer, the system being relatively rigid. The result is that many practical classes are often inhospitable places within which are concentrated an excessively high proportion of sociopsychological problems.

We can also mention a specific problem concerning girls. The majority of them are enrolled in trades such as secretarial services and accounting. But the labor market has changed; employers do not recruit as many employees as before for these specialties, and they prefer to recruit graduates of a higher level who followed the general upper secondary track and then entered professional higher education.

The Secular Tradition of French Education and Religious Communities

The French tradition of secularism in the education system has been disputed with the growing importance of the Muslim community in France. The problem occurred when a minority of Muslim girls started to wear the scarf within the schools. This religious code was often perceived negatively by a significant proportion of teachers who support a strong secular conception of schools, rooted in a long tradition of anti-clericalism within public schools.

After September 11, 2001, the number of female students wearing the scarf increased significantly to more than 1,000—and in schools where it used to be not tolerated. Muslim students adopted a more militant attitude, refusing to withdraw the scarf. But the law concerning religious signs was unclear. It claimed that schools are secular and that religious proselytism is not allowed within school premises.

The question is: Can one interpret the wearing of a scarf as a proselytist attitude? An intense debate shook up the French population for two years. Finally, parliament passed a law in 2003 forbidding the wearing of "ostensible" religious symbols within the schools. To avoid the stigmatization of the Muslim religion, the law addresses all religious symbols: for instance, the Kippa for the Jews and big crosses for the Christians (small crosses of the size of a jewel are still allowed).

Surprisingly, female Muslim students wearing the scarf are welcomed in Catholic schools. Of course, it would be possible to create private Muslim schools where wearing the scarf would be allowed, but apparently, the demand is too low. The vast majority of the Muslim community is Westernized and does not support Muslim communitarism.

Public Finance and Equity

The tradition of free education from preschool to higher education is deeply rooted in French society. Even textbooks are free. At the beginning of every school year, the social security system allocates a lump sum per child entering school to all families below a certain level of income. This lump sum is supposed to cover family purchases linked with the new school year (school supplies, clothes).

Pupils enrolled in private schools pay modest fees to cover nonsalary expenditures. At the university level, there exist nominal fees of about 200 euros; half of it is a kind of entrance fee to the health system (this fee is far below the real cost of the health system). The other half supports part of the nonsalary expenditures of the university (about 2 percent of the unit cost). Students whose families have incomes below a certain threshold (about one-fourth of the student population) do not pay the fees and receive a scholarship to support their living expenditures. In addition, families who have children enrolled in schools benefit from a significant tax reduction up the age of 26 for their children.

Undoubtedly, free access to education in France has opened the door to education for everybody, regardless of the socioeconomic status (SES) of pupils. Children from low socioeconomic background have easy access to higher education. Nevertheless, if one puts a closer eye to equity issues within the system, it appears that the best tracks tend to be monopolized by students from high economic backgrounds. For instance, at the upper secondary level it is more likely for a pupil to enter a vocational track if he or she originates from a low SES, and it is more likely for a pupil from a high SES to enter general education. In order to have access to the elitist sector of higher education, one has to attend the best *lycées,* and within the best *lycées,* the best classes.

From this point of view, the system does not work in a fully transparent way. True, this concentration of the most able students is based mainly on merit, but only well-informed families are able to develop strategies to get access to the most promising avenues. Among these strategies are specific disciplinary options, such as a rare foreign languages (Russian, Chinese) or rare combinations (Latin and mathematics). Furthermore, in principle, families can only enroll their children in the school of their neighborhood, but in order to have access to a better school, some families cheat with their addresses. The likelihood of cheating is more frequent in better-off families.

All these strategies allow the possibility of concentrating able students in the same classroom and preparing them for the most difficult paths leading to the Grandes Ecoles. Unlike access to universities, there has not been an equalization of chances with respect to SES for the Grandes Ecoles during the past decades. On the contrary, it is likely worse. The chances for a pupil from an immigrant family to have access to the Ecole Polytechnique are lower today than they were twenty years ago, a de facto phenomenon of monopolization of the access to the best Grandes Ecoles by privileged social classes.

In addition to the fact that students from high SES enter the top schools, the inequity of the system is even more clear because per student expenditure is much higher in these best schools. The best French *lycées* in Paris that enroll the children of the elite tend to have more means and better teachers (a higher proportion of *agrégés* versus *certifiés* teachers) than less known provincial *lycées*. Comparing the two main categories of higher education institutions, the average unit cost in preparatory classes for Grandes Ecoles was about 13,220 euros in 2002, while it was about 6,850 euros in universities.

Even comparing the same type of institution, variations can be important. Recent cost studies within French universities show that one program can cost forty times as much as another within the same institution. While some of these differences are justified according to the field of study (it may be more expensive to train a future physician than a future lawyer due to differences in equipment and pedagogical devices), this factor does not explain satisfactorily the scope of unit costs variations. Similarly, concerning per student expenditure for Grandes Ecoles, the costs variations can be huge, from about 6,000 euros to 100,000 euros per year in the best schools.

The rationale for these differences in treatment have never been politically justified. The result of this situation is that pupils of low SES or low achievers tend on average to attend schools with fewer resources per pupil than those attended by students of high SES. As a consequence, taxpayers' money is allocated more generously for privileged students than for already underprivileged ones.

The democratic rules and the supposedly egalitarian treatment supporting the general organization of the system are actually strongly inequitable. This raises the question of a desirable positive discrimination in favor of underprivileged children in terms both of socioeconomic status and school achievement and of fewer public subsidies for the most privileged sectors of the education system. Such positive discrimination has recently been introduced by one of the most prestigious higher education institutions (the Paris Political Sciences Institute). Access in this school is based on a competitive exam, and the proportion of low SES students used to be negligible. To improve the equity of the access, the director decided to allocate a few seats to students educated in the poor Paris suburbs. However, this initiative is more symbolic than real and remains isolated.

Incoherent Allocation Procedures of Students in Higher Education

The baccalaureate is a sufficient but necessary key for entrance to higher education. Yet academic competencies (in terms of content and level) of baccalaureate holders are very different. Sixty-two percent of a cohort actually obtain the baccalaureate, of which 80 percent pursue higher education. In other words, about half a cohort has access to higher education.

As said earlier, the universities are the only nonselective option. They must accept any baccalaureate holder, whatever his or her characteristics. The majority of most able students tend to be enrolled in institutions that practice *numerus clauses* (or admission quotas): the Grandes Ecoles, medical studies within universities, and short-term professional education (IUT and STS). Therefore, universities attract a very heterogeneous population: a relatively small proportion of the best ones and the mass of least able students who were not accepted in the selective tracks. The least able students are relegated in university tracks that have the highest pupil/teacher ratios and the lowest level of tutorial services (law, economics, and humanities). They are not prepared for such a situation, and they fail.

This explains why the internal efficiency of French universities is low by international standards. Less than half of new entrants gain the equivalent of a bachelor degree. It is not unusual to have a passing rate at the end of an academic year of less than 20 percent. Moreover, in certain tracks, such as law, the passing rate for certain type of baccalaureate holders (technological or professional) is below 5 percent.

It would be more logical to assign students in the different institutions or tracks by optimizing their profiles with the characteristics of tracks. This principle would lead to enrolling students having a technological or a professional baccalaureate in the IUTs. Furthermore, after the end of their two-year program, IUT graduates, who belong to the group of most able students, think they should continue further higher education to reach the equivalent of a bachelor degree or more. The incoherence is huge, since they finally obtain a bachelor university degree that they could have obtained by entering from the beginning in universities. In the meantime, they have taken the places that could have been allocated to technological or vocational baccalaureate holders, who have failed in the university.

Education and the Labor Market

In the French context, the "sheepskin" role of education is important: Holding a diploma has always been a useful prerequisite for entering the labor market. This is reflected by the differences in the rates of unemployment of young French people with respect to the formal education they have received. In 2001, the rate of unemployment three years after graduation was 3 percent for Grandes Ecoles graduates, 9 percent for university leavers who did not get any diploma (a category of pupils that is not negligible), 18 percent for those who have a first professional diploma, and 26 percent for nonqualified school leavers (Céreq, 2001).

The French model illustrates particularly well the queueing theory developed by Thurow and Lucas (1972), according to whom an individual's education level determines his or her position in the queue for interesting job opportunities. This phenomenon, which can be observed in most countries, is more accentuated in France. Partly because of a rising unemployment rate, more and more education is perceived as a "sesame" for entering the labor market. This may lead to unjustified education investment. One can observe in recent years a tendency for acquiring several diplomas in the hope that it will give a better position in the queue.

The French tradition for a professional career does not rely on the idea that a new employee should begin at the bottom of the firm hierarchy with ancillary tasks and get progressively promoted. Unlike Germany and Japan where a majority of high executive positions are filled with employees who have climbed up the hierarchy ladder, most similar positions are filled in France with Grandes Ecoles graduates.

Surprisingly, a recurrent debate concerns the capacity of the education system to prepare school leavers for entering the labor market. The education system is accused of being poorly adjusted to job market requirements and is often accused of feeding unemployment.

This accusation ought to be discarded. It may be true that in certain sectors it is difficult to find some categories of manual workers, yet this has nothing to do with the operation of the education system. It is the operation of the labor market that favors white collars against blue collars and makes white-collar positions more attractive to the young generations.

Also, the lack of dialogue between the French education system and the productive world, which used to be one of the commonly denounced drawbacks of the French system, has been substantially reduced in the recent years. This issue can no longer be considered a major one.

Weaknesses in the Field of Pedagogical Innovations

The French education system tends to be conservative regarding pedagogical innovations. While this conservatism has not strongly damaged the overall effectiveness of the system, there is a problem with the wide dissemination of new information technologies (NIT). The French schooling context is not properly adapted to this evolution.

The first attempt to introduce NITs within education was decided in the mid-1980s with the famous *Plan Informatique pour Tous* (Computers for All), which aimed at providing 100,000 computers to primary and secondary schools within a two-year period. Yet the centralized and bureaucratic French tradition generated the conditions for big failure. The 100,000 computers were ordered from a state company that had developed a specific type of computer that was not compatible with any of those available on the market. The computers were delivered to the schools after a very short training (about one week) of some teachers and without the appropriate software for proper utilization. The life expectancy of these 100,000 computers was shown to be very short, not because of a lack of reliability, but because of premature obsolescence. Moreover, one of the objectives of the project, which was to support the state company in the world competition, entirely failed, since this company has disappeared from the list of significant PC producers.

After this initiative—which ended in disaster—the penetration of NITs in the French education system has been very slow. Today, all schools have Internet connections and a reasonable level of computers. But the utilization of these capacities remains modest. French schools have not recruited specialists in computers; computer utilization is left to the initiative of existing teachers, whatever their major field of competency. When a teacher uses computers, it is not in a pure computer purpose, but to enhance the capacity to learn his or her discipline. Evaluation of the effectiveness of the use of computers in this last goal has not shown yet any significant impact.

French Universities Are Badly Ranked in World Leagues

In 2004, the Jia Tong University of Shanghai published a ranking of the best 500 universities worldwide, based on five criteria. Among the top twenty, there were sixteen American universities, three British, and one Japanese. However, the data did not provide a flattering picture of French universities. The first French university (Paris 6) appears in 65th place, the second one (Paris 11) in 72nd place.

Why such a bad ranking for France? It is mostly a structural problem due to the fact that French higher education institutions are less likely to combine the characteristics that are common to most of the first 100 universities of the ranking. That is, they attract the most able students of the country, they attract the best researchers/professors of the country, and they tend to compensate their staff at a higher scale than the country's average; they have a research capacity significantly larger than the country's average higher education institutions; resources per student are significantly above the average; they tend to be multidisciplinary institutions combining natural sciences with social sciences and humanities; and they tend to be large institutions with an average of about 20,000 students and 2,000 staff members.

The dualism of the French higher education system with ninety universities and 500 Grandes Ecoles does not lead easily to the combination of these six characteristics. Some are monopolized by the Grandes Ecoles (such as the quality of students and the means per students); some are monopolized by the universities (pluridisciplinarity and critical size), and some are not developed at all (research concentration and staff selection).

The French context generates undesirable consequences. First, as the most able students are attracted by the best Grandes Ecoles, the future French elite misses two features that are elsewhere frequent: exposure to research and to a multidisciplinary environment. After five years of studies in the Grandes Ecoles, graduates' opportunities on the French labor market are at least as good as job opportunities for Ph.D. holders from the universities. Consequently, they have little incentive to enter a Ph.D. program. In this context, French researchers or academic professionals were not the most able students. It is generally thought that to increase its rate of growth, France would have to become closer to the technological frontier, but the organization of the research system and the training of the elite does not help in this goal.

Educational Science Research

For more than a century, primary teachers' training was not undertaken in university institutions, and secondary teachers' training had only a cosmetic exposure to professional training. Not surprisingly, French universities have developed education departments similar to those in other developed countries.

The recent creation of IUFMs would have developed stronger education departments. But the decision was made to recruit the existing teaching staff of previous normal schools who lacked research experience and tradition for the new IUFMs. While IUFMs also recruited university professors in different fields (mathematics professors for the training of future secondary school mathematic teachers, and so on), it was agreed that research activities of university professors would be performed in their university departments of origin and not within the IUFMs. Hence, this new context is not significantly favorable for enhancing educational research within IUFMs or within universities.

The most important institution for carrying out research on education has traditionally been the INRP (*Institut National de la Recherche Pédagogique,* National Institute for Pedagogical Research), which used to be a department of the Ministry of Education and not an academic institution. It acted under the political authority of the Minister rather than under the scientific control of peers. This status has recently changed; today it is more academically oriented, but it still employs the same staff. It is too early to evaluate the impact of this change.

This context explains why the status of educational research has remained modest in France. Moreover, the CNRS, which covers a large variety of academic fields, from physics to philosophy, has never created an education department.

The lack of education research is reflected in the political and societal approaches to education. Everybody feels authorized to have a definitive opinion on the right solution concerning educational issues. Experts who speak on French television are rarely educational experts, but physics Nobel prize winners and the like, who have undoubtedly some talents in physics and some talents as teachers, but these individual merits are of little use for the development of general solutions. Hundreds of books on educational issues are published every year, rarely based on recognized research, but on the personal intuitions of their authors. The opinions expressed are not validated by any scientific methodology. This leads to a highly ideologically biased debate on the French scene. This context gives to every political person becoming Minister of Education the feeling that personal political capacities qualify him or her for promoting a new education reform. Lack of time and lack of knowledge of the milieu and of the results of existing research do not allow the Minister of Education to go beyond cosmetic changes nor to change in depth the bureaucratic forces that run the system.

However, a certain number of universities have set up education departments in which one provides teaching on educational sciences as well as one carrying out research. The total intake of these departments in terms of students is still modest. Many students are teachers willing to improve their pedagogical practices.

THE FUTURE OF SOCIETY AND SCHOOLING

It seems more and more likely that the future of French society will take place within the framework of the construction of Europe. This evolution will accelerate the decline of the state's role, give more importance to European regulations, and very likely more responsibilities to local authorities, in particular to *Régions.*

Concerning education, the extension of decentralization will raise the issue of whether to dismantle the centralized education system of staff management. Changes will be difficult to implement. Two options are open. While the first one would transfer the responsibility of staff management to Régions, the second would give more responsibilities to school authorities. Teacher unions are opposed to both solutions. Yet, if they had to choose one of them, they would likely favor regional management, a solution that could open the door to a new co-management role. From an education efficiency point of view, it is clear that a solution that would offer schools the possibility to match more appropriately teachers' profiles and schools' needs is best. It would also give headmasters more control power concerning the motivation of the teaching staff, for they would hold some decision-making authority on recruitment and promotion, as well as on renewal of teachers' contracts. Highly incompetent teachers would probably be forced to leave the system. It is obvious that such a solution is unlikely, as illustrated by the devolution in 2004 of non-teaching staff management to *Régions.*

Europe will have also some homogenizing effect on the operation of education systems. For instance, in terms of public finance, the fact that France's past atypical behavior of increasing the share of GDP allocated to public education expenditure will no longer persist due to the necessity of ensuring a convergence of public finance and fiscal revenues between European countries. France belongs to the group of European countries that have the highest share of public expenditure within the GDP. This being a threat to the future competitiveness of the economy, French political authorities will have an incentive to design policies aimed at reducing this share.

If the expansion of the system cannot rely on additional public expenditure, there will be renewed attempts to charge fees for certain users (postcompulsory education, privileged tracks, or education programs that have high economic returns for users). These initiatives will raise intense fighting between lobbies. Part of the left may join part of the right to defend the status quo, and part of the modern left may converge with the liberal right in the promotion of new approaches.

The future role of new technologies of information in world education is still open. One cannot yet anticipate what will be the exact expansion of this role in terms of individualized learning outside the formal system. In any case, France is behind the most advanced countries in this respect (United States, Canada, Northern European countries). Yet, outside the school system, France has developed a competitive competency in the field of software development. It could use this capacity for the development of education programs. The only problem is that of creating the right incentives for teachers. This requires legal modifications concerning the delivery of diplomas and the ways of defining teachers' duties. For the time being, teachers' duties are only expressed in terms of hours of teaching. Other duties, such as private tutoring, distance tutoring and guidance, and educational software development, are presently not accounted for properly. Pedagogical innovations are not rewarded. Moreover, certification of pupils' performances is still excessively teacher referenced and rarely done through external independent evaluation procedures. This also should change.

POSTSCRIPT

The French education system is close to the end of its quantitative development. It will soon be able to concentrate its efforts on quality improvements. Past experiences concerning measures for enhancing the quality of the system have had disappointing results, and the present mood is more inclined to encourage local initiatives rather than centralized ones. The flourishing of different types of decentralized innovations should allow, after proper evaluation, the identification of the most promising innovations that could be disseminated later.

The most intense debate going on presently in the French education system concerns the situation of higher education and research, which is seen as the weakest point of the system. In particular, several reports stress the decline of French science worldwide. It is seen as both a problem of inadequate organization and management and a problem of underfunding. These problems do not have easy solutions, although they are well known: to wit, improved selection of students, higher fees for users, more competition between institutions, better integration of research institutions and universities, improved cooperation between universities and firms, and better focused incentives. All these solutions confront particular groups' interests and traditional French values, such as the ideals of equality and gratuity. In the fields of research development and of training of the elite, the compatibility of equality and excellence is hard to achieve.

REFERENCES

Céreq. (2001, December). *Génération 98: à qui a profité l'embellie économique?* Céreq Bref no. 181. Paris: Centre d'Etudes et de Recherches sur us qualifications.

Ministère de l'Education Nationale, de l'enseignement supérieur et de la recherche. (1996a). *Repères et références statistiques sur les enseignements et la formation,* Direction de l'évaluation et de la prospective. Paris: Author.

Ministère de l'Education Nationale, de l'enseignement supérieur et de la recherche. (1996b). *Le compte de l'éducation,* Direction de l'évaluation et de la prospective. Paris: Author.

Ministère de l'Education Nationale, de l'enseignement supérieur et de la recherche. (1996c). *L'état de l'école,* Direction de l'évaluation et de la prospective. Paris: Author.

OECD. (1996). *Education at a glance.* Paris: OECD.

Thurow, L. C., & Lucas R. E. B. (1972). *The American distribution of income: A structural problem.* Washington, DC: Joint Economic Committee of the United States Congress.

UNDP (1997). *Human development report.* New York: Author.

CHAPTER ELEVEN

ENGLAND

New Labour, New Schooling?

PHILIP GARNER

It is important to note that, in common with other parts of Europe, the United Kingdom's political shape has changed in recent years as a result of "devolution." In this, both Scotland and Wales now have their own statutory body—the Welsh National Assembly and the Scottish Parliament. These bodies have direct statutory control of education and social welfare, and a distinctive curricular and organizational arrangement for schools. Northern Ireland has had a similar arrangement for education over a longer period. For the sake of clarity, the present chapter focuses solely on the English system of schooling.

In an earlier commentary on the English education system (Garner, 2000), I suggested that the 1997 election of the first Labour government in nearly twenty years offered opportunities to tackle issues of long standing within education. Tony Blair's vision for New Labour was that it should have as its vanguard a progressive educational and social agenda. This was characterized by an emphasis on tackling deep-seated issues regarding social inclusion, educational failure, and access for all to a quality education service.

The climate of optimism that prevailed during those first years of the new administration forms a useful prologue to this chapter. It provides a baseline for measuring the extent to which the intentions of politicians—and the expectations of educationalists, welfare administrators, and activists, all of whom were swept up in an intense level of policy innovation—have subsequently been realized.

In the first term of New Labour's administration, pledges were made regarding education in its entirety. For the early years phase, a commitment was given to securing nursery

Philip Garner taught in English mainstream and special schools for over fifteen years. He is currently Professor of Education at Nottingham Trent University. He teaches in both master's and doctoral programs in Special and Inclusive Education. His major research interests are in the field of comparative analyses of special education policy and practice and in the education of children with perceived emotional and/or behavioral difficulties. His major recent publications include *The World Yearbook of Education* (1999, Kegan Paul), *Pupils with Problems* (1999, Trentham Books), *A Student Guide to Special Educational Needs* (2001, David Fulton Publishers) and *The Handbook of Emotional and Behavioural Difficulties* (2005, Sage).

places for all 4-year-olds; class sizes in primary schools would be reduced; and more spending on infrastructure, resources, and training would be forthcoming. Moreover, schools would see a continued devolution of financial resources from the center, enabling them to be far more proactive on local resource decisions in their schools. All of these actions have been underpinned by a signal commitment: reducing the impact of what has been an age-old tension in English education, namely, the sharp—and widening—gap between haves and have-nots, in respect to an individual's opportunity to access high-quality schooling. That gap in equality of opportunity has resulted in educational underachievement for significant numbers of the school-age population. Thus, in conclusion to that piece, I was given to remark that "The trial is beginning—the jury will remain out until beyond the millennium" (Garner, 2000, p. 111).

The new millennium is now well upon us and the present chapter provides an opportunity to return to court to continue the hearing. Whilst noting that this chapter is arranged into five sections, readers will quickly sense their mutual interdependence and overlap.

First, I will map the social fabric within which schools exist and function. From there, I will go on to identify some salient features of schooling in contemporary England. Next, the most positive aspects of current policies and schooling will be identified and elaborated upon. Immediately following will be an overview exploration of some of the key debates that are presently occurring. This section will allow for both an assessment of how well we have done and what still needs to be done. This final part of the chapter consists of concluding observations, providing a summary indication of the complexity and deep traditionalism that characterizes the provision of education in England.

THE SOCIAL FABRIC

Demographic

The population of England is approximately 48 million, with about 20 percent of this figure between the ages of 0 and 14. This population is mainly concentrated in urban or metropolitan settings, of which there are five major ones: Greater London and the Southeast, Greater Manchester, Birmingham and the West Midlands, the West Riding of Yorkshire, and the Tyne-Tees area in the Northeast. Much of these areas have undergone a period of rapid transition from industrial to service or commercial centers. What is equally clear—and an issue that has deep relevance for the provision of schooling—is that these urban spaces are characterized by diverse populations (racially, culturally, and economically) and include some of the most disadvantaged groups in the whole of the United Kingdom.

Economic

England is best summarized as a capitalist economy, one of the four most successful in Europe. It has undergone a period of rapid transition following World War II, as heavy industry has been replaced by light engineering, manufacturing, and commercial and financial services. The latter accounts for by far the largest proportion of GDP. Agriculture is intensive, highly mechanized, and efficient. There are large coal, natural gas, and oil reserves. Primary energy production accounts for about 10 percent of GDP, one of the highest shares of any industrial nation. Importantly, in terms of national economic consequences, between 1980 and 1995 successive Tory governments greatly reduced public ownership and contained the growth of social welfare programs.

As a member state of the European Union (EU), England participates in Europewide decision making via the European parliament in Brussels. However, it is not a participant in the Europewide common currency, the euro. Successive governments have deferred decisions on involvement in this, preferring instead to retain £ sterling as the unit of currency. Many of the urban and rural areas affected by changes in the profile of the English economy have been recipients of incoming EU investment. Rapid globalization has also meant investment and economic partnerships with other nations, including the United States, Japan, and emerging markets in Latin America and the former Soviet states.

Political

England is administered by a democratically elected Parliament, which comprises a House of Commons and a House of Lords. The 'Commons,' constituted of about 650 members who are elected by popular vote for five years, is the most important decision-making body. The Lords has, until recently, been occupied by 'hereditary peers.' The 'Lords' is gradually being reformed to ensure that its membership more accurately reflects English society: hitherto, it has mainly been populated by the English 'landed' classes, whose titles are hereditary. There are three principal political parties in England: the Conservative and Unionist party (Tory), the Labour party (referred to now as 'New Labour'), and the Liberal-Democrat party. The former two have separately formed every government for the last sixty years.

Local government is provided by a system of regional councils and local authorities, each comprising locally elected members. These are responsible for the direct provision and monitoring of education, welfare, health, and environment. Central government retains control over generic policy matters, including financial provision, for these services, although there has been a degree of devolution during the last decade. This is especially important in respect of schooling, where local authority controls have been sharply reduced following the Education Act of 1988.

Cultural

As with other postcolonial countries, the cultural map of England is changing rapidly. Historical divisions in society (typically referred to as the English 'class system') have increasingly become blurred, and it is now less common to refer to 'working,' 'middle,' and 'upper' classes. Nevertheless, there remains an important residue of influence from this.

One issue of importance is the net effect of a widening gap in 'social capital' within regions, and even in individual towns and cities. Thus, in spite of the economic prosperity of many, there remain large groups of people who have far less access to good housing, public transport, and recreational amenities. This is reflected in the type of schooling that often characterizes such locations. It is noteworthy, for instance, that the Child Poverty

Action Group (CPAG) has indicated that over a quarter of children in the UK are living at or below the poverty line (Flaherty, Veit-Wilson, & Dornan, 2004). Moreover, there is also something of a cultural divide between 'north' and 'south,' with significant opportunities across the human services being more accessible in the economically prosperous and influential southeast of England.

The ethnic composition of England has changed radically since 1945, and it continues to do so. Historical factors relating to England's colonial past have established the basis for a richly multicultural society. It is now estimated that well over 5 percent of the English population comprises people from so-called minority ethnic groupings. This brings with it tensions of its own, with issues of job discrimination and lack of representation of ethnic minorities in executive roles in business, the commercial sector, the public services, and government.

The spatial location of minority groups also raises important questions regarding the cultural coherence of England. About two-thirds of the minority population lives in metropolitan areas, and often in sectors of towns and cities that are viewed as less favourable for the reasons described above. Very few minority groups live in prosperous, semirural, or rural locations.

Religious

The official religion of England is Christian Protestant, or Church of England. Substantial sections of the population are Roman Catholic, with Methodist, Baptist, and, increasingly, other 'world' religions becoming numerically important. In common with other postindustrialized countries, there has been a rise in interest in new, alternative religions and groups. The rapid growth of ethnic groups has been accompanied by high levels of religious observance among Hindi, Islamic, and Sikh populations. On the other hand, a notable feature of the religious map of England is a gradual overall decline in church attendance in the last thirty or so years. Commensurately, secular morality has increased in significance. However, although it is the case that religion in general is far less important than hitherto, organized religion—especially Church of England and Roman Catholic—remains a significant stakeholder in schooling,

As with other postindustrialized nations, each of the social parameters described above impacts variously on the lives of the English population. New Labour came to office with England's economy in good health. Much of what they had inherited from the preceding four Tory administrations has been sustained into the twenty-first century. This represents a relative triumph over the negative effects of postindustrialism and postcolonialism, during which England's trading influence and industrial performance had declined considerably.

But English society, and its manifestation in education, is becoming more complex. The twin dilemmas of readjusting to an expanded role within Europe whilst redefining a world role in politics, commerce, and culture have resulted, during New Labour's period of office, in a ceaseless tide of new initiatives. Education policy and resulting provision has been the product of this emerging situation. Oppositional stances on virtually all aspects of policy and provision are commonplace.

SCHOOLING IN ENGLAND

The English system provides compulsory education from 4 to 16 years of age in the nursery, primary, and secondary age ranges. There are about 26,000 schools in England, catering to approximately 11 million pupils aged between 3 years and 18 years. In this section of the chapter I will map some of the key characteristics of schooling. This forms the canvas upon which significant and widespread changes in policy and provision are taking place. Indeed, the years that have coincided with the rise to power of the New Labour governments since 1997 have seen the rate of change increase dramatically. But, in order to understand the importance of these changes, it is necessary to give some background to the system of education that they are intended to refine. Docking (2002), Mackinnon and Statham (2000), and Gearon (2002) provide a more detailed review.

Organization and Governance of Schooling

Education in England is jointly administered by Local Education Authorities (LEAs, or what might be called 'school boards' in some countries) and by central government, via the Department for Education and Skills (DfES). LEAs represent the means by which local governance of schools is effected. There are 109 of these. This number includes 36 metropolitan boroughs and 33 Greater London boroughs. LEAs are an integral part of local government and administer education services on behalf of elected local education committees. Their specific responsibilities are for the employment and payment of teaching and non-teaching staff, the building and maintenance of schools, transportation, recreation, and provision of support services for pupils—including those who have learning difficulties or disabilities.

On a national level, the DfES is the government department responsible for education in England. It sets out the policy and broad framework for schooling, it introduces and disseminates legislation on education based on decisions of the government of the day, and it fulfills an inspectoral function. The latter is mainly carried out by the Office for Standards in Education (OfSTED).

The changes introduced into the English system as a result of the 1988 Education Act (brought in under the Tories) have impacted deeply on the way in which schools are organized and governed. That Act meant that the previously considerable powers of the LEA were diminished, and the schools themselves assumed far greater self-control. Nowhere has this been more apparent than in the respect of financial matters. Schools gained direct control over their budgets and were henceforward able to make choices about staffing matters. Some schools even chose to remove themselves from even minimal LEA control by becoming 'grant-maintained' schools (GMS), a term that was changed in 2000 to become 'foundation schools.' (Foundation schools are state schools that have a governing body that directly employs school staff and determines admission policies. As well, the school land and buildings are owned by that governing body, or by a charitable foundation.)

The governance of schooling has been in a process of virtually continuous change for the last twenty-five years, with significant alterations to the way in which schooling has been organized. Thus, the role of the LEA remains an area of acute political conflict.

Legislation, Guiding Philosophies, and Policies

The 1944 Education Act envisaged a 'balanced partnership' between central and local government in the provision of educational services (Meredith, 2002). More recent legislation threatened this relationship. The Education Act (1988) significantly reduced local powers: The Tory government of the day saw LEAs as financially reckless in their spending. Subsequently, the New Labour administrations of the 1990s and early twenty-first century have redressed this. Thus, the 1998 School Standards and Framework Act saw LEAs obtain control of a crucial aspect of education: the role of promoting standards. Nevertheless, schools themselves have retained a key self-governing role, so that the net impact of legislation has been to secure an uneasy equilibrium in the relationships between schools, local authorities, and central government.

The last Tory government summarized its policy on education by reference to 'five great themes'—quality, diversity, parental choice, greater autonomy for schools, and greater accountability (DfE, 1992). *Quality* was being secured as a result of the introduction of a standardized national curriculum, which brought with it an entitlement of all 5- to 16-year-olds to a broad and balanced range of subjects. Quality of provision was monitored by the Office for Standards in Education (OfSTED). *Diversity* was introduced by the advent of the grant-maintained schools, which are free from local authority control. Moreover, subsequent to the 1988 Education Act, schools secured the *autonomy* to select new entrants, while *parental choice* of the school their child may attend was freed from long-standing controls. New arrangements were also identified for pupils who experienced learning difficulties. All of this was also envisaged in support of greater diversity. But there was also to be far greater *accountability* via both regular school inspections and by the publication of official 'league tables' of school performance.

New Labour's policies, on their election in 1997, incorporated much of the positive rhetoric of the five themes. The first set of targets have, in the government's terms, largely been reached. Thus, no children between 5 and 7 years of age will be in classes of more than thirty. Two-thirds of 3-year-olds will have nursery places. Pupil performance, measured by Standard Attainment Tests (SATs), will be improved at both the primary and secondary level. Moreover, truancy from school would be reduced, as would the level of pupil exclusion.

Late in 2004 the government introduced a new *Five Year Strategy for Children and Learners* (DfES, 2004a). This document comprised an overview of the five key principles that government saw as underpinning its policy agenda. These are:

- Greater personalization and choice, with the needs of learners 'at center stage'
- Opening up services to new and different providers
- Freedom and independence for head teachers and 'front-line' teachers, and more streamlined funding arrangements
- Commitment to staff development
- Emphasis on partnerships with parents, employers, volunteers

But there is one overriding theme that has remained as the *leitmotiv* for New Labour policies throughout their tenure in office: that of breaking the link between social class and educational achievement. As the Five Year Strategy notes, "No society can afford to waste the talent of its children and citizens. So major challenges at each key phase of life remain" (DfES, 2004a). In the early years, therefore, greater flexibility in childcare will result in closer collaboration between education, health, and social care services. The development of 'dawn-to-dusk' schools would be a central component of policy, while greater financial and social support is to be provided to those parents who wished to stay at home with their children instead of working.

In primary schools an even greater emphasis on reading, writing, and math is foreseen, while the curriculum is to be widened. Every child will be able to learn a foreign language, play music, and participate in competitive sport. Schools will be encouraged to form supportive clusters or networks, whilst closer involvement with parents and caregivers is to be encouraged.

Secondary education would see pupils being given greater independence in their learning, and the curriculum choices available are to be made wider and more flexible. A new type of school, called 'independent specialist school,' would take the place of comprehensive schools. At the same time, the Strategy confirms that "we will never return to a system based on selection of the few and rejection of many" (DfES, 2004a). Each secondary school would be in receipt of a guaranteed budget for three years, linked to pupil numbers. Each school would also have the freedom to own its own land and buildings, and every school in the country would be systematically refurbished over fifteen years.

Perhaps the most important piece of legislation concerning schools, and one that impacts across all age ranges and school types, is the Children Bill (2004). This adventurous piece of legislation proposes to connect services for all children, thereby ensuring what the New Labour administration has referred to as "an ambitious plan for education, skills, and children's services" (DfES, 2004b).

Curricula

The introduction of a 'national curriculum' (NC) in 1988 marked the beginning of an era of close scrutiny of what is taught in English schools. Hitherto, it was very much the case that LEAs, and individual schools, decided on the precise content of each curriculum area. Whilst originally viewed with great suspicion by many education professionals, the NC has now become a substantive aspect of the education system. Its success in winning the hearts and minds of teachers was largely due to the fact that the original, very rigid format was replaced in 1993 by a more flexible approach. This, and subsequent amendments, meant that teachers secured greater flexibility, whilst still providing a curriculum that was broad, balanced, and relevant.

To date, the key changes to the national curriculum have been directed toward an even greater emphasis on literacy and numeracy, the strengthening of coverage of creative subjects (including art, drama, and music), and the introduction of new curricula for 'citizenship' and personal, social, and health education.

Subsequently, the New Labour administration has introduced a raft of new curriculum strategies. These have had the principal aim of raising the level of achievement at a time when evidence from international comparative studies (see, for example, Brooks et al., 1996, and Keys, 1996) suggested that England still lagged behind its competitors in the global 'education market.' As a response, the Labour administration embarked on three core strategies, dealing in turn with literacy (1998), numeracy (1999), and information and communication technology (1999). All three strategies are ongoing, remaining in place during the third term of New Labour administration. And, they continue to be surrounded by debates about the efficacy of centrally driven curricula (Tymms, 2004; Wyse, 2003).

Elsewhere, considerable confusion surrounds the tension at secondary level between curricula designed to meet the vocational needs of an increasingly technocratic society and the demands of curriculum traditionalists, who claim that such a focus marks a worrying dissipation in the quality of knowledge. The Report of the Working Group on 14-19 Reform has the potential to lead to a radical change to the structure and content of this phase of education in England. The next ten years is likely to see significant alterations in well-established assessment and curriculum arrangements in schools and colleges in this age phase.

Pedagogical Theory and Practice

The last twenty-five or so years have seen an increasing move toward a more balanced pedagogical approach than was previously apparent. Thus, the 1960s and 1970s were characterized by tension between professional allegiance to either so-called 'progressive' pedagogy, wherein all children, irrespective of achievement level, were educated in the same class, or to an approach based on rigid streaming based on ability. The current emphasis is upon 'differentiated pedagogy' (Burton, 2004), a process by which teachers attempt, by utilizing a variety of approaches, to enable each pupil to achieve intended learning targets. As such, the strategy is highly suited to classrooms that, increasingly during the 1990s, have become more complex on account of the diversity of learners within them.

Such an eclectic approach is also commensurate with New Labour's commitment to social justice by promoting wider access and participation in education. Nevertheless, this is a contested approach, with many schools selecting teaching groups according entirely to capability, with all of the consequences for balance and breadth of content (Ireson & Hallam, 2001).

Evaluation

Evaluation of school performance in England remains largely in the hands of OfSTED. This, as has been noted, is the statutory body responsible for standards in schools. Inspections are conducted by teams of independent inspectors, headed by a registered inspector. Teams are required to include at least one lay inspector who has no professional background in education. Each school in England now has an inspection approximately every four years. School inspection reports are public and provide information regarding the quality of education provided; the standards achieved; and the spiritual, moral, social, and cultural development of pupils—including their behavior.

Schools whose performance is deemed below a required standard are termed 'failing' schools and can be placed on a program of 'special measures' designed to remediate shortcomings. OfSTED now has the additional responsibility for inspecting local education authorities. The ongoing preoccupation with assessment of educational performance (whether of schools, teachers, or individual pupils) is directly linked to fears that England might be losing out in the competitive global marketplace.

Teacher Training

There has always been considerable scrutiny of the way that teachers are trained in England; such is the importance afforded to the role (DfEE, 1997). Until relatively recently there was a great deal of negativity directed toward the way that teachers are trained, it being implicated in such things as discipline problems and declining academic standards (Lawlor, 1990).

Subsequently, and coinciding with the election of New Labour in 1997, a new era of positive relations was forged, in which the 'profession' of teacher training entered a period characterized by trust. Prior to this, OfSTED conducted regular, systematic inspections of teacher training providers, and some of its findings—which were often challenged—had fueled the Tory quest to reform the sector (OfSTED, 1993). The Teacher Training Agency was established in 1994, and under New Labour it has become both the key regulating body for the sector as well as the focus for professional debate on a set of 'national standards' for the award of qualified teacher status (QTS). In these discussions it was a widespread view that the advent of 'lifelong learning,' information technology, and new curricular initiatives required a 'new professionalism.'

As a result of the emerging national standards for QTS (TTA, 2002) and the TTA's own corporate intention of making "teaching an evidence- and research-based profession" (TTA, 1997), the status of the teacher training community has been enhanced. Not only is it closer to the practical needs of trainees (by such nationally recognized initiatives as school-based training), but it has been able to secure a more respected position within university education itself via involvement in a variety of national research projects.

SUCCESSES

The last fifteen years have seen some significant positive outcomes for children and young people. This has in large part been a product of the education policies pursued by successive Tory, but mainly New Labour, administrations. In this subsection I will identify six areas that are indicative of this widespread success: the national curriculum, early years education, special education needs and inclusion, children's services, the professional status of teachers, and the focus on emotional health and positive behavior.

The National Curriculum

A national curriculum was introduced by the Tory government in 1988. Originally, it comprised a set of highly detailed and prescriptive requirements. This emerged as a result of a desire by politicians to make schools more accountable. As early as 1985 the DES issued *Better Schools,* which reflected a drive toward raising standards of attainment, securing breadth and balance across curriculum subjects, and making such activities relevant yet differentiated (DES, 1985). Its further origins can be found in a document by Her Majesty's Inspectors, which articulated the view that "A school's curriculum consists of all those activities designed or encouraged within its organisational framework to promote the intellectual, personal, social and physical development of its pupils" (HMI, 1988).

Despite tensions regarding the way in which the national curriculum was to be evaluated—via SATs—it is nonetheless the first time in English education that measurement of children's school performance from ages 5 through 16 was attempted. It was also viewed by many professionals, particularly those working with children with special educational needs (SEN), as a vehicle for equal opportunity. SEN pupils were seen as one of the key groups to benefit from the innovation (Stakes & Hornby, 1996). Moreover, the national curriculum placed great emphasis on continuity and progression in learning. This was accompanied by a focus upon differentiated pedagogy, which was viewed as the means by which wide-ranging learner needs could be accommodated, either within a single classroom or by grouping according to ability.

Nor has the national curriculum remained static in its original format—another significant positive feature of the initiative. In response to criticism that it was too prescriptive and heavily reliant upon bureaucracy (Basini, 1996), the NC was revised in 1995, following a period of significant consultation with teachers. Moreover, a moratorium limiting further change until 2000 was agreed upon (Docking, 2002). Even more recently, New Labour has reemphasised a commitment to 'the three Rs' (maths, reading, and writing) through a series of national strategies. At the same time, schools have been given greater freedom in what to teach outside the agreed core subjects (maths, English, science, and information technology). They were able to undertake initiatives that responded to the social, emotional and (broadly) 'citizenship' needs of children and young people (DfEE/QCA, 1999).

The process of refinement is still continuing, but the major success of the national curriculum, in providing all children with access to a 'broad, balanced, differentiated, and relevant' school experience, remains. Moreover, it has become an integral element of the professional orientation of teachers.

Early Years Education

Educational provision in England has seen dramatic changes in the field of early years education. New Labour's Early Years Policy relates not just to preschool initiatives—those that ensure that young children are socially and emotionally equipped to enter mainstream schooling. Rather, government has seen its policy in terms of a 'wrap-round,' integrated service of child welfare from 0 to 5 years. Much of its success in pursuing a change agenda in this aspect of education has been linked to New Labour's desire to ensure that the various early years initiatives are rooted at the local level in Early Years Development and Care Partnerships (EYDCPs).

A number of national initiatives, operationalized locally, are indicative of New Labour's commitment to "bring together the maintained, private and voluntary sectors in the spirit of co-operation and genuine partnership, based on existing good practice" (DfEE, 2001). 'Sure Start' and 'Early Excellence Centres' were aimed at securing integrated provision in areas of social need. These have been instrumental in tackling social exclusion, supporting families in raising children, promoting early child development, and ensuring that more children in disadvantaged settings are better equipped to begin compulsory schooling.

New initiatives in curriculum, training, and inspection supported these arrangements. A 'foundation curriculum' was developed (QCA, 1998), which is in the process of refinement. Staff training came under scrutiny, too. Previously, there was a tremendous variety in qualifications, but with the development of national vocational qualifications and the emergence of dedicated Early Years teacher training courses, a set of nationally recognized standards has been developed. Finally, the regulation of early years provision, via OfSTED inspection, has been characterized by an integrated approach, based on rigor, evidence, and respect for professionalism.

Recent initiatives, especially the *Every Child Matters* agenda (see elsewhere in this chapter) raises many questions for future Early Years policy in England. One deep-seated source of discussion has been the explanation for differential achievement levels on a European canvas. Some commentators (for example, Mills & Mills, 1998) argue that discrepancies in performance are the result of distinct preschool approaches in (for example) Switzerland, Hungary, and Belgium. Children from these countries outperform English pupils in high school in their later years.

Special Educational Needs and Inclusion

The landscape of special educational needs has been changed irrevocably as a result of policy initiatives in the last twenty years. The move away from a deficit model, via a phase where 'integration' was the vogue, through to 'inclusive practice' has been a notable success feature of government initiatives (Clough & Garner, 2003). In the latter, children and young people who experience learning difficulties are viewed as having important, undeniable rights (Knight, 1999). Such moves are consistent with global reorientations regarding the rights of all learners to access mainstream schools. These changes in policy and practice in the area of SEN have a number of constituent features, each of which hallmarks current policy as being successful.

First, a more effective, people-centered, and standardized approach to identification and assessment has been enshrined in a revised *Code of Practice* (DfES, 2001). This also sets out the organizational protocols through which SEN is dealt with. The statutory guidance it contains has done much to ensure greater equity in resourcing SEN and has also led to a dramatic raising of the status of SEN within mainstream schools. The document, for instance, establishes that all teachers have responsibility for promoting inclusion, whilst at the same time requiring that all schools have a 'Special Needs Coordinator.' The burgeoning importance of SEN has also been recognized by the fact that it is now a formal element of inspection of schools by OfSTED.

Greater involvement of parents and children, as identified by the *Code of Practice,* has also been a successful feature of policy approaches in the last few years. In this respect, they have strengthened the emphasis on parent/pupil participation highlighted in the much earlier Warnock Report (DES, 1978). Furthermore, 'parent partnership' schemes have been established in all local authorities in England, as well as the framework for arbitration and conciliation when disputes arise regarding provision for SEN.

New Labour has recently introduced a second action plan for SEN and inclusion. Entitled *Removing Barriers to Achievement* (DfES, 2004c), this sets out policy and practice imperatives for the next few years. The plan comprises actions in four key areas: early interventions, removing barriers to learning, raising expectations and achievement, and delivering improvements in partnership—all of which have been flagged at various points in this chapter.

The net effect of these policy initiatives has ensured that educational provision for children and young people who experience learning difficulties remains at the very heart of the legislative agenda. This marks a dramatic change from its marginal position a little over twenty-five years ago.

Children's Services

A concurrent success is apparent in the integration of 'services for children.' The Warnock Report (DES, 1978) recommended much closer collaboration between the various agencies involved in promoting the health, education, and social welfare of children. But progress in providing joined-up operations had, until recently, been slow (Roaf, 2002).

The New Labour government has attempted, with some success, to address the fragmentation of associated children's services. The current *Every Child Matters* agenda is at the very heart of this initiative. *Every Child Matters: Change for Children* (DfES, 2004b) is a shared program of change to improve outcomes for all children and young people. It takes forward the Government's vision of radical reform for children, young people, and families. It is premised on five outcomes which are regarded as key to well-being in childhood and later life: being healthy, staying safe, enjoying and achieving, making a positive contribution, and achieving economic well-being.

This is a wide and challenging program of change, resting on a new *Children Act* (2004). It encompasses diverse elements and enables schools to offer pupils learning that is individualized to meet their needs, as well as children and health services providing young people with increasingly *individualized* care. In a word, government has recognized that better outcomes for children depend on the integration of universal services with targeted and more specialized help and on bringing services together around the needs of the child and family.

Professional Status of Teachers

The Teacher Training Agency (TTA) in England has been at the heart of a concentrated campaign to improve the standing of teachers in the eyes of society. For some time, during the 1980s and early 1990s, teachers had been the source of much negative attention. As a professional body, they were viewed suspiciously by Tory governments who saw them as resistant to change and liberal in persuasion. Above all, teachers were implicated as being responsible for the so-called declining standards of achievement in schools (HMI, 1980). Yet, at the same time, teachers were increasingly being seen as the key to 'effective schools,' as defined in terms of academic performance (Hextall & Mahony, 1998; TTA, 1997).

The gradually improving public and professional profile of teachers is the product of a number of strategic initiatives. There is now a 'national standard' for the certification of teachers (TTA, 2002). Also, by employing a systematic process of induction, the profession has been restructured to provide financial reward to more experienced and skilled teachers who remain in the classroom. Furthermore, and importantly, the concept of 'teacher as researcher' has become core to current activity (TTA, 1997).

In addition, government has promoted the establishment of a General Teaching Council to inform policy and regulate aspects of professional conduct. It is viewed by government as a means by which teachers have a "clear professional voice, independent of government but working with us to raise standards" (DfEE, 2001).

Focus on Emotional Health and Positive Behavior

A raft of initiatives over the last three years have addressed issues of disengagement by pupils that result in behavior and attendance problems in schools. Teachers have been encouraged to recognize the importance of social, emotional, and behavioral skills (SEBS) as a core element in promoting behavior for learning. Weare and Gray (2003) have identified a range of benefits of this approach, including greater educational and work success, improvements in behavior, increased inclusion, and improvements to mental health.

Moreover, the Healthy Schools project (Department of Health, 2004) stressed that where pupils have good emotional, social, and behavioral skills, they will be able to be effective and successful learners, make and sustain friendships, and deal with and resolve conflict effectively and fairly. The notion that 'emotional intelligence' (Goleman, 1995) is a crucial element in schooling success has now become firmly embedded at policy level.

Central to this initiative is a greater involvement of children and young people in their own education. Such an approach fits comfortably with recent United Nations mandates on the rights of children. In spite of this, there remains a significant body of opinion that claims that schools allow children too great a say in what happens to them in education. Such hard-line, reactionary views will hopefully become less influential with the appointment by New Labour of a very first Minister for Children.

KEY DEBATES AND CHALLENGES

It is important to appreciate that any of the above six themes identified as points of 'success' and 'progress' within the English educational system in the previous section can also be viewed as contentious. This is because there are radically different versions of what comprises an appropriate and responsive education system for the twenty-first century. Added may be other issues of current and ongoing concern. Debate about educational policy and provision is frequently polarized and politicized; it has become a salient feature of the social discourse of the country.

I will now briefly comment on five indicative aspects of the educational debate in England—curriculum, governance, pupil behavior, educational and social inclusion, and personal and social education—in the expectation that readers will define possible links to existent tensions in other countries.

Curriculum Issues

In English state schools (i.e., those at which attendance is free and compulsory between the ages of 5 and 16 years) teachers have enthusiastically engaged with the need to provide a curriculum that is "broad, balanced, relevant and differentiated" (DES, 1985). But the imposition of a 'national' curriculum brought considerable disquiet from some teachers. While the NC has been viewed as a means of ensuring access for all children to a common curriculum, it has also meant that opportunities for curriculum innovation have diminished. Principal among pupils negatively affected by this have been those who experience special educational needs (Stakes & Hornby, 1996). At the heart of the concerns was a perceived preoccupation with testing. SATs are an integral part of NC provision, yet the limitations of the assessment format have undoubtedly diminished its positive impact and arguably have been implicit in marginalizing many pupils (Clough & Garner, 2003). Moreover, SATs have continued to be used as the chief means of identifying 'good' or 'failing' schools. As a result, some schools are less likely to want to offer places to pupils who are underperforming academically. This is especially so as SAT scores are routinely used as a means of teacher appraisal and performance management (Bartlett & Burton, 2003), as has been noted elsewhere in this chapter. The challenge facing educators will be to secure curriculum flexibility while identifying credible, but alternative, means of assessment.

The NC provides the clearest example of government's intention to control the delivery of education from the center (Avis, 1999). New Labour's education policy is best summarized by the so-called 'Third Way,' which combines neo-liberalism with state-centered socialism. Some observers have viewed this approach as a means of securing the support of the influential middle classes whilst retaining a firm grip on expenditures (Phillips, 2001). Current policy initiatives, in both primary and secondary education, demonstrate the extent to which uniformity is being acquired (for instance, the national strategies for behavior and attendance—see elsewhere in this chapter).

Such rigid control from the center brings abundant criticism. Some have argued that the net beneficiaries of the approach are those whose ideology is driven by the threefold emphasis on cost-effectiveness, efficiency, and competition. Far less obvious are the positive impacts of such centralized initiatives on individual children in school. Once more, there are suggestions that it is the pupil who experiences learning difficulty who is most adversely affected.

Governance Issues

One of the most challenging outcomes of the Education Act of 1988 is the notable decline in the power vested in LEAs. Most funding for schools now moves straight from central government directly into schools, bypassing local government. Schools are funded according to their size. Although this has undoubtedly brought the benefit of greater autonomy regarding where the money is spent, it has resulted in sharp differences in the capacity of schools to attract more qualified or experienced teachers and/or to provide an extended set of resources and facilities. Given that parents often make choices of school placement based on these issues, the situation is tailor-made for the 'rich' schools to get richer.

Pupil Behavior Issues

In 2005, OfSTED produced a report on 'challenging behavior' in schools. In spite of there being a stated large majority of schools characterized by good standards of pupil behavior, the national press chose to focus upon a reference made by school inspectors to a perceived rise in 'gang cultures.' The overall sample on which sensationalist headlines were made was minute (only three schools were viewed in negative terms). And yet, such is the level of public and professional concern about behavior in schools that calls were made for a more punitive approach to pupils who misbehave.

Major national strategies focussing on behavior, attendance, and bullying have been in place for a number of years (DfES, 2004a, 2004b, 2004c, 2004d). These are now being questioned in terms of their appropriateness, given the OfSTED findings (however tenuous their evidence base). Both New Labour and the Conservatives are planning to introduce more 'pupil referral units,' there are further signals that parents of pupils who behave badly will be held more accountable, and schools will be given greater powers to exclude pupils.

Educational and Social Inclusion Issues

All of these measures sit uncomfortably alongside notions of social and educational inclusion (Thomas & Loxley, 2001), and some commentators suggest that, in any case, such measures are little more than sticking plaster (O'Brien & Blamires, 2001). They serve only to deflect policy away from deeper causal factors that underlie pupil behavior—some of which have been referred to in this chapter. Others maintain that pupils who prevent others from learning ought not to be included in mainstream classes. Certainly, the popular media are frequently used as a means of publicizing the inherent contradictions within inclusion and infer claims of political correctness in distributing educational opportunity and resources.

Personal and Social Education Issues

The dramatic focus upon a formal, centrally determined national curriculum in England has undermined consideration of the affective element in education. Because the national curriculum comprises distinct sets of subject knowledge that is periodically assessed through SATs, teachers, parents, and pupils themselves receive both explicit and subliminal messages that these constitute most of what is important in education. Teachers are now trained mainly to 'deliver' subject knowledge—and they receive their licence to teach based predominantly upon their capacity to do so. Training providers echo this requirement in their courses.

The net result is that relatively little attention is paid to such aspects of education as emotional development, pastoral care and guidance, citizenship, and so on. Because such areas (referred to as the 'hidden' curriculum of schooling) are not formally assessed, there is less incentive for schools, teachers, or pupils to view them as important. Some argue that this state of affairs is potentially damaging—not least to the development of social cohesion and the nation-state. Thus, the English Qualifications and Curriculum Authority (QCA) suggests that attention to such affective aspects of education results in pupils having "an entitlement in schools that will empower them to participate in society effectively as active, informed and critical and responsible citizens" (QCA, 1998, p. 9). This represents a significant challenge to government and community alike—precisely during a period in which English society and its institutions are becoming more diverse.

CONCLUDING OBSERVATIONS

It is scarcely possible, within this brief chapter, to provide a comprehensive view of the changing face of the English education system—such is its complexity and ongoing nature. It may, however, be worth observing that, like other parts of the world, England has witnessed the ever-increasing effects of globalization (Coulby & Jones, 1995; Cogburn, 1998). This has been apparent in its economic, social, political, and cultural formats. But nowhere has it been more evidenced than in the education service.

Global competitiveness has resulted in deep scrutiny of standards of compulsory education in England and a committed drive to connect educational procedures with the demands of the global marketplace. It has had a corresponding impact on the curriculum, the teaching profession, and on reshaping the financing and governance of education (Coulby & Zambeta, 2005). Given that this is the case, it is unsurprising that the last decade has seen dramatic shifts in educational policy and provision. In each of the areas noted, together with others that have been omitted because of space limitations, further not insignificant developments can be expected (DfES, 2004a). To conclude by extending my original legal metaphor, there may need to be a retrial.

REFERENCES

Avis, J. (1999). Shifting identity: New conditions and the transformation of practice—teaching within post-compulsory education. *Journal of Vocational Education and Training, 51*(2), 245–264.

Bartlett, S., & Burton, D. (2003). The management of teachers as professionals. In S. Bartlett & D. Burton (Eds.), *Education studies.* London: Sage Publications.

Basini, A. (1996). The national curriculum foundation subjects. In J. Docking (Ed.), *National School Policy.* London: David Fulton Publishers.

Brooks, G., et al. (1996). *Reading performance at nine.* Slough, UK: NFER.

Burton, D. (2004). Differentiation of schooling and pedagogy. In S. Bartlett & D. Burton (Eds.), *Education studies.* London: Sage Publications.

Clough, P., & Garner, P. (2003). Special educational needs and inclusive education: Origins and current issues. In S. Bartlett & D. Burton (Eds.), *Education studies.* London: Sage Publications.

Cogburn, D. (1998). *Globalization, knowledge, education and training in the global world.* Conference paper for the InfoEthics98. Paris: UNESCO.

Coulby, D., & Jones, C. (1995). *Postmodernity and European education systems: Centralist knowledge and cultural diversity.* Stoke-on-Trent, UK: Trentham.

Coulby, D., & Zambeta, E. (Eds.). (2005). *Globalization and nationalism in education.* London: RoutledgeFalmer.

Department for Education (DfE). (1992). *Choice and diversity: A new framework for schools.* London: Author.

Department for Education and Employment (DfEE). (1997). *Teaching: High status, high standards. General teaching council: A consultation document.* London: Author.

Department for Education and Employment (DfEE). (2001). *Early years development and childcare partnerships: Planning and guidance, 2001–2002.* London: Author.

Department for Education and Employment/Qualifications & Curriculum Authority (DfEE/QCA). (1999). *The national curriculum. Handbook for primary teachers in England and handbook for secondary teachers in England.* London: Author.
Department of Education and Science (DES). (1978). *The Warnock report.* London: HMSO.
Department of Education and Science (DES). (1985). *Better schools.* London: Author.
Department for Education and Skills (DES). (2001). *Special educational needs code of practice.* London: Author.
Department for Education and Skills (DfES). (2004a). *Five-year strategy for children and learners.* London: Author.
Department for Education and Skills (DfES). (2004b). *Every child matters: Change for children.* London: Author. (http://www.everychildmatters.gov.uk/)
Department for Education and Skills (DfES). (2004c). *Removing barriers to achievement.* London: Author.
Department for Education and Skills (DfES). (2004d). *The report of the working group on 14-19 reform.* London: Author.
Department of Health. (2004). *Promoting emotional health and well-being.* London: DoH/DfES.
Docking, J. (Ed.). (2002). *New Labour's policies for schools.* London: David Fulton Publishers.
Flaherty, J., Veit-Wilson, J., & Dornan, P. (2005). *Poverty: The facts* (5th ed.). London: CPAG.
Garner, P. (2000) Vision or revision? Conflicting ideologies in the English Education system. In K. Mazurek, M. Winzer, & C. Majorek (Eds.), *Education in a global society: A comparative perspective* (pp. 95–112). Boston: Allyn and Bacon.
Gearon, L. (Ed.). (2002). *Education in the United Kingdom.* London: David Fulton Publishers.
Goleman, D. (1996). *Emotional intelligence.* London: Bloomsbury.
Her Majesty's Inspectors (HMI). (1980). *A view of the curriculum.* London: HMSO.
Her Majesty's Inspectors (HMI). (1988). *The curriculum from 5–16.* London: HMSO.
Hextall, I., & Mahony, P. (1998). Effective teachers for effective schools. In R. Slee et al. (Eds.), *Effectiveness for whom?* London: Falmer.
Ireson, J., & Hallam, S. (2001) *Ability grouping in education.* London: Paul Chapman.
Keys, W. (1996). *Third International Mathematics and Science Study (TIMSS). First national report, part 1: Achievement in mathematics and science at age 13 in England.* Slough: NFER.
Knight, B. (1999). Towards inclusion of students with special educational needs in the regular classroom. *Support for Learning, 14*(1), 3–7.
Lawlor, S. (1990). *Teachers mistaught: Training theories or education in subjects.* London: Centre for Policy Studies.
Mackinnon, D., & Statham, J. (2000). *Education in the UK.* London: Hodder & Stoughton.
Meredith, P. (2002). *Education in the United Kingdom.* London: David Fulton Publishing.
Mills, C., & Mills, D. (1998). *Despatches: The early years.* London: C4TV.
O'Brien, T., & Blamires, M. (Eds.). (2001). *Enabling inclusion: Blue skies . . . dark clouds.* London: HMSO.
Office for Standards in Education (OfSTED). (1993). *The new teacher in school.* London: HMSO.
Phillips, R. (2001). Education, the state and the politics of reform: The historical context, 1976–2001. In R. Phillips & J. Furlong (Eds.), *Education, reform and the State: Twenty-five years of politics, policy and practice.* London: Routledge/Falmer.
Qualifications and Curriculum Authority (QCA). (1998). *Education for citizenship and the teaching of democracy in schools.* London: Author.
Roaf, C. (2002). *Interagency collaboration for children and young people.* Buckingham: Open University Press.
Stakes, R., & Hornby, G. (1996). Special educational needs and the National Curriculum. In R. Andrews (Ed.), *Interpreting the new national curriculum.* London: Middlesex University Press.
Teacher Training Agency (TTA). (1997). *Annual review.* London: Author.
Teacher Training Agency (TTA). (2002). *National standards for the award of Qualified Teacher Status.* London: Author.
Thomas, G., & Loxley, A. (2001). *Deconstructing special education and constructing inclusion.* Buckingham: Open University Press.
Tymms, P. (2004). Are standards rising in English primary schools? *British Educational Research Journal, 30*(4), 477–494.
Weare, K., & Gray, G. (2003). *What works in promoting children's emotional competence.* Report for the Department for Education and Skills, London.
Wyse, D. (2003). The national literacy strategy: A critical review of empirical evidence. *British Educational Research Journal, 29*(6), 903–916.

CHAPTER TWELVE

SCHOOLING, EDUCATION REFORMS, AND POLICY SHIFTS IN THE RUSSIAN FEDERATION

JOSEPH ZAJDA

The Russian Federation came into existence in 1991, following the collapse of Soviet ideology and the breakup of the Union of Soviet Socialist Republics (USSR). During the 1980s, Mikhail Gorbachev's period of openness (*glasnost*) and restructuring (*perestroika*) was an attempt to harness the winds of change by opening up the ideologically inscribed Pandora's box of Soviet society and *Homo Sovieticus* (the Soviet man). Gorbachev was hoping that the process of genuine ideological, social, and economic renewal and transformation, both from above and below, would yield a new model of empowering socialist democracy and a new sense of liberty, equality, and the brotherhood of nations within a redefined USSR. As we now know, he was unable to control the pace of change and transformation that he had begun. By 1991, the USSR fell apart and Boris Yeltsin—a new kind of born-again democrat—deposed him.

Today, Russia occupies a land area of 17,075,000 square kilometers, making it the largest land nation in the world. The country has 11 time zones, and more than 100 languages are spoken by various nationalities. The Russian Federation consists of 89 regions and republics, divided into the following four classes: 21 republics (including Chechnya),

Dr. Joseph Zajda is Director of the Institute for International Education and Development. He teaches Research Methods in Education, Learning, and Education and Society core courses. He was presented with the *Excellence in Teaching* award in April 2004. He was Chair of the Publications Standing Committee of the World Council of Comparative and Education Societies (for the 2003–2006 period). He was elected to the Board of Directors of the Comparative and International Education Society (USA) in March 2004. He edits the following three international journals in comparative education: *World Studies in Education, Education and Society,* and *Curriculum and Teaching.* He has written and edited twenty-four books and over 100 book chapters and articles in the areas of comparative education, curriculum reforms, education policy, lifelong learning, and education reforms in Russia. His recent book publications include *Society and Enviroment; Curriculum, Culture, and Teaching;* and *Education and Society.* He is Editor of the International Handbook of *Globalisation, Education and Policy Research* (Kluwer, 2004). He is also Editor of the twelve-volume book series *Globalisation and Comparative Education* (Kluwer), and guest editor of the special issues of the *International Review of Education* (UNESCO) 52(1-2) on Education and Social Justice.

52 regions (*oblast*), 10 autonomous districts (*okrugs*), and 6 territories (*krais*). The republics are titular homelands of non-Russian minorities. Local governors administer them, most of whom were appointed by former president Boris Yeltsin, until local elections became mandatory in 1997. Autonomous *okrugs* are ethnic subdivisions of *oblast* or *krais*.

In 2004, Russia's population was 143.8 million. However, by the year 2015, the population is likely to decline to 134 million (World Development Indicators, 2004). In 2002, there were 78 million wage earners; the gross national income per capita was US$2,130 (in the United States of America, it was $35,400). This ranked Russia 99th in the world, making it hard to believe that back in 1984 the USSR was the second superpower, rivaling the United States for world dominance.

In fact, by July 1995, due to economic restructuring and the transition to a market economy, unemployment had risen to almost 14 percent. Poverty was also rising dramatically, and the World Bank estimate for 1999 indicated that 30 percent of the population was living below the national poverty line. This figure includes the 10.9 percent of the population living in extreme poverty on "below $2 a day" (*World Development Indicators,* 1999). In reality, the official 2000 figures showed that 41.2 percent of Russians (59.9 million) lived below the poverty line. Sadly, children's health and well-being became the first casualty. "It is so difficult to find a healthy child in our country," wrote one reporter. "Only 10 percent of schoolchildren are healthy. Another 40–45 percent are chronically ill, and 40–45 percent of children are ill" (*Uchitelskaia Gazeta,* 1995a, p. 2).

THE HISTORICAL AND SOCIAL FABRIC

Brief Overview of Historical, Social, and Economic Factors Affecting Education

Education as an agency for positive, progressive, social transformation has long been a significant feature of the Russian cultural heritage. This idea can be traced back to the Westernizing era of Peter the Great (1672–1725) and the reforms of the Enlightenment under Catherine the Great (1762–1796). Nevertheless, in the Tzarist period prior to 1917, primary education had been available to only 50 percent of the children in the Russian Empire (Zajda, 1992). With the Russian Revolution of 1917, the fall of the tzars, the rise of Communism, and the leadership of Lenin, education became a vital underpinning of the new regime.

The new government that assumed power after October 1917 implemented education reforms to achieve universal literacy and uniformity of academic standards, curricula, and teaching programs. The importance of education was underlined by Lenin's famous December 1919 decree, "On the Eradication of Illiteracy among the Population of the RSFSR," which directed individuals from 8 to 50 years old to become literate. In the 1920s, Lenin's decree involved the staggering task of educating some 100 million illiterates, mainly in the rural sector.

This grand design did not fail, but it was hindered by the geography of the country. The USSR covered an incomprehensibly vast area—22.4 million square kilometers, which is more than one-seventh of the world's landmass (Zajda, 1992). Education reforms had to confront the geographic isolation of some schools in the far east and the far north, where pupils had to travel a long way to school, through rivers, ice, and snow. Other problems included the size and variety of populations, nationalities, and languages. There were over 100 different nationalities in the USSR, each with its own culture, language, and customs. Newspapers, for example, were published in sixty-five different languages.

By 1921, or in less than two years after Lenin's decree, and amidst the Civil War between the Red and the White armies when the Russian government was fighting for its life, educational progress increased. Nearly 5 million people had been taught literacy (Zajda, 1980). As the USSR developed, the eradication of illiteracy continued as a major goal of government policy. By the early 1940s, the level of literacy in the 16-to-50 age group had reached 90 percent. By 1960, despite the massive setbacks due to World War II, which contributed to the loss of teachers and the total destruction of 82,000 schools, UNESCO figures claimed almost 100 percent literacy (Zajda, 1992).

In addition to the huge problem of illiteracy, the need to find a common means of communication in the new multiethnic and multiracial state presented another major problem. It was imperative to raise Russian to the status of *lingua franca* of the Soviet Union. The use of languages other than Russian was guaranteed in the law courts, local and regional governments, and in all the Union Republics and their subdivisions. But, in the schools, students had to learn Russian in addition to their mother tongues. (The existence of minorities within minorities, such as the Poles in western Ukraine or Kazakhstan, meant that in some cases students would attend Polish schools and learn Ukrainian or Kazakh—the official language of the Republic—and Russian—the official language of the USSR.)

By 1977, sixty years after the collapse of Tzarist Russia, there had been a spectacular rise in educational attainment at all levels of schooling. Ten-year schooling, corresponding to complete primary and secondary education, was free and compulsory. Compared to figures from 1914, five times as many students received secondary education; the number of students in higher education institutions had grown forty times; and the number in professional secondary colleges increased eighty-five-fold. The numbers in lifelong learning and adult education increased almost fifty-three times (Narodnoe Khoziaistvo, 1977).

In philosophical terms, the whole of Russian educational thought during the last 200 years can be seen as an ideologically unique, but totalizing, transformation; a grand narrative *par excellence.* Russian policymakers and educators, particularly during the Soviet period between 1922 and 1991, made very effective use of education and "values education" (*vospitanie*) as an agent of political and social transformation (Zajda, 1988).

Post-1991 reforms

Following the breakup of the USSR in December 1991 and given the collapse of Soviet ideology, the new post-Soviet state had to reinvent itself. In terms of education and schooling, prominent policymakers believed that the entire Soviet education system had to be restructured and transformed. For example, education reformers challenged the excessively centralized Soviet education system by introducing decentralization. Responsibilities for general education were given to the regions and local government.

The current and ongoing education reform and change in the Russian Federation is tied into the monumental and unprecedented political, economic, and social transformation between 1985 and 2003 that first began with Mikhail Gorbachev's radical policy of *glasnost* and *perestroika,* to be followed by President Yelsin's Law on Education, and continued by his successor, President Putin. The remainder of this chapter on schooling in Russia concerns the post-Soviet period from 1991 on.

SCHOOLING

The school year begins on September 1 and ends between May 30 and June 25. The first day of school in September is one of celebration throughout the Russian Federation. Children, especially preparatory and grade 1 pupils, bring flowers for their new teachers. It is a day of celebration, speech making, and community goodwill, which is difficult for Western students and teachers to comprehend.

Structure of the Education System

Preschool. Preschool education consists of nurseries for children between the ages of 6 months and 3 years, and kindergartens for children between the ages of 3 and 6. Russian kindergartens are structured and teach according to the preschool curriculum. Beyond kindergarten, general education schools *(obshchaia sredniaia shkola)* provide elementary (grades 1 to 4) and secondary (grades 5 to 11 or 12) schooling. The Russian school curriculum, unlike that in the West, is organized as a continuous program from preparatory/grade 1 to grade 11 or 12.

Elementary Education. Elementary schooling culminates with final examinations held at the end of grade 4. All elementary schools follow centrally prescribed curricula and use textbooks recommended by the Ministry of Education. The education policy and philosophy guiding the elementary school curriculum is based on the principle that schooling at that level should facilitate the development of a child's identity. Six areas of knowledge and skills are important: cognitive knowledge, communication culture, moral culture, aesthetic culture, the culture of work, and physical culture.

The elementary curriculum for grades 1 to 4 includes Russian language (3 class hours), reading (2 class hours), mathematics (4 class hours), a foreign language (2 class hours from grade 2), science (2 class hours), art/music, technology, and physical education (2 class hours each). Pupils also select electives—up to 3 hours in grade 1 (for example, English), or 8 extra hours in grade 4. New subjects introduced in the elementary curriculum from 2002 include lessons about citizenship (*Uroki Grazhdanina*) in grade 1, and a foreign language (*inostrannyi iazyk*), as well as information technology (*IKT: informatsionno-communikatsionnye tekhnologii*) in grade 2. The total class hours for a six-day (Monday to Saturday) school, which also includes local/regional courses and electives, is currently 25.

Earlier in this chapter, the way in which languages were presented during the Soviet period was pointed out. Today, the government is continuing an official policy of bilingualism. Russian, as the language of the nation, is studied in the non-Russian schools (Russian as a second language). The language of the republic also has to be taught in Russian schools situated in that republic. In other regions, where languages other than Russian are spoken, the choice of the language to be studied is decided by the local educational authority, the local community, and the school's administration.

Assessment consists of both oral and written examinations in numeracy and literacy. All pupils bring their school diaries (*dnevnik*) for every lesson, where the teacher enters the oral grade(s), if applicable, during the week. Children are marked on a scale of 1 to 5, where 5 represents excellent and 2 and 1 are unsatisfactory and very unsatisfactory.

Secondary Education

What is termed "secondary education" in Russia would be called middle or junior high school elsewhere. Secondary education covers grades 5 to 9, which enroll students between the ages of 10 and 14. All students have to sit for formal examinations in core disciplines at the end of grade 9. Approximately half of all students who successfully complete grade 9 continue with their secondary schooling by going on to upper secondary schools.

New subjects introduced in the 2004 secondary curriculum include a foreign language (such as English, French, German, or Spanish) in grade 5; biology and geography in grade 6; civics in grades 6 to 9; and IT in grades 8 and 9. While new school subjects were added, others were revised and shortened. History provides a typical example of such revisions.

The new history curriculum in secondary schools can be seen in terms of deletion (122 themes have been deleted) and additions (178 themes have been added). Among deletions were the following themes: the role of Church in the Russian empire; the people of the Russian empire; Pugachev's uprising; the conquest of Central Asia; the February 1917 revolution; the formation of totalitarianism; mass deportations; and the lessons of the Great Patriotic War (WWII). New additions include the ancient people of our country; the culture of the people (from the ancient period until the seventeenth century); Russian culture during the eighteenth century and the beginning of the nineteenth century; Soviet Russia and the USSR (1917–1991); the Constitution of 1936; the part played by the USSR in liberating Europe; Marshal G. Zhukov; Soviet culture; the events of October 1993; the new Constitution of the Russian Federation; and contemporary Russia (Boris Yelsin and Russian society and reforms, Vladimir Putin and culture and life in contemporary Russia).

Comparing the 1995 and 2004 models of the curriculum shows a decrease in Russian language and literature class hours, from 11 sessions in grade 5 in 1995 to 8 in 2004, and a slight increase in music, mathematics, and biology. In general, there has been an attempt to rationalize teaching and reduce weekly contact hours from 36 to 30. Grade 5 pupils now work according to a five-day week of 26 to 28 hours (it was a six-day week program of 32 hours in the past) structure. The most important key learning areas, judging by allotted class hours, are mathematics (25 weekly classes in grades 5–9), Russian language and literature (32 hours), and a foreign language (15 hours).

In grade 9, Russian-speaking students study Russian language and literature, a foreign language, legal studies, mathematics, chemistry, physics, geography, biology, social sciences (history, politics, and sociology), civics (*obshchestvoznanie*), IT, art/music, human movement, and labor training. In addition, they have to select electives—up to 30 weekly hours, which makes the school program very demanding.

Students in the non-Russian speaking republics or regions study in their own language. They also have to study Russian as a second language. Up to 35 weekly sessions are taken by an average grade 9 student. Schools, depending on their classification (for example, *shkola-litsei*), in addition to teaching the core, can introduce various other subjects and electives.

Upper Secondary Education

At the end of grade 9 studies, a student has three possible career paths. One is to continue with secondary education to obtain a high school certificate, which is a requirement for entering any higher education institute. Academic secondary schools offer an academically oriented curriculum. Students study a large number of compulsory school subjects, which include mathematics, physics, chemistry, biology, history, geography, literature and language, IT, and a foreign language, amounting to 36 class hours in their final year of schooling. In order to graduate from high school, Russian students have to pass mathematics and Russian and three other disciplines.

Another option is to enroll in a specialized secondary school (*tekhnikum*) that offers vocational or technical preparation combined with general education. These specialized secondary education institutions (*srednie spetsialnye uchebnye zavedeniia,* or *SSUZs*) fall into two main categories. *Tekhnikumy* train students for skilled technical occupations, whereas *uchilishcha* offer vocational training programs for a range of skilled nontechnical occupations. Courses vary in length, ranging from three to four years.

The third career path at the age of 15 is either to learn a trade in vocational/technical schools (*professionalnie-tekhnicheskie uchilishcha,* or *PTUs*), or to enter the workforce. Courses offered by PTUs are between one and two years in length in a wide variety of trades, ranging from carpentry to hairdressing.

A New Emphasis on Technical and Vocational Education

As a result of a new policy shift toward specialized schooling (*profilnoe obrazovanie*), secondary school students are now encouraged to study in specialized schools (*profilnye shkoly*). In the past, students attended general education secondary schools, known as polytechnical secondary schools. The current idea is to encourage senior high school students in grades 10 and 11 to specialize in key learning areas (KLAs) or disciplines relevant to their future careers. Students can select from the following programs: humanities, languages, science, mathematics, and performing arts. The grade 9 curriculum remains unchanged, but students will be examined by new external examination bodies (*nezavisimye mezhshlolnye komissii,* independent interschool examination boards), rather than internally, as was the case before the reform.

Special Education

Special schools offer differentiated schooling for those children who are intellectually handicapped, have other disabilities, or are gifted.

Private Schools and the Increased Differentiation of Public Schools

In recent years, diversity in Russian schooling has resulted in a proliferation of education programs and a new hierarchy of schools. The March 2001 *Tipovoe polozhenie ob obshcheobrazovatelnom uchrezhdenii* (Defining the General Educational Institution) defined, in a legal sense, and for the first time, created four different types of secondary schools in Russia: lyceums, gymnasia, special schools with intensive courses of study, and general schools.

The *shkola*—the local comprehensive school—serves most pupils. Richer parents may choose *gimnaziia, litsei,* and *kolledzh*—Russian variants of grammar schools or private schools. Another alternative is to stay home and study following the ministerial directive of May 1994, "Schooling at Home in the Russian Federation," which made it possible for children to be educated at home. A special teacher training qualification—"Home Teacher"—for teachers/tutors teaching children at home was introduced in teacher training institutions.

The term *elite* was only introduced into the Russian vocabulary in the 1990s (Darinski, 2002). Hence, the idea of elite schools is quite new in post-Soviet Russia.

Private schools are divided into private (and elite) gymnasia and lyceums, as well as the transformed and state-owned lyceums and gymnasia. From the late 1990s, in line with the policy of diversification and decentralization of the education sector, some government schools were restructured and redesignated as the new, and hopefully more prestigious, gymnasia and *litseii,* thus acquiring a higher social status.

Private schools exist in Moscow and St. Petersburg and in other major cities. Gymnasia, as in Tsarist Russia, focus on languages and humanities, whereas lyceums concentrate on mathematics and sciences and more technical disciplines. These private schools cater to the new rich, and tuition fees vary according to the school's status.

Only about 3 percent of schools are lyceums and gymnasia; they enroll 3.5 percent and 2.5 percent of students respectively (Rossiiskaia Gazeta, 2003b). At the end of the 1990s, of 21 million pupils, some 4 percent, or 800,000, were enrolled in private grammar and government *litseii.* However, numbers are growing as the state school sector is unable to compete against the more popular and much in demand gymnasia, *litseii,* and other independent schools.

Gymnasia and *litseii* use their new brand names to give themselves a higher social status and act like other similar elite schools in the West. They are popular because they follow the "fashions in education," and they care more about their "image" (*Uchitelskaia Gazeta,* 1996, p. 5) than promoting excellence and quality in school disciplines. Some of these private schools are more like finishing schools in the West. They are very selective, small, and very expensive, normally attracting the children of the new rich. One such school had only sixty students and offered individual programs for each child, including tennis, horse riding, English, and Japanese. The maximum class size was eight students, and children were brought to school in microbuses, with bodyguards (*Uchitelskaia Gazeta,* 1995b).

Higher Education

There were 600 state higher educational institutions (VUZs) in Russia in 2002. There is also a large number of private universities, some of them very dubious, operating from basements or virtual offices, charging huge fees, and offering worthless university diplomas. In fact, in 2003, when some 700 private schools and universities were inspected, it was found that 90 percent were guilty of serious breaches as they did not comply with the relevant articles of the Law on Education (*Parlamenskaia Gazeta,* 2003). Many private institutions were subsequently de-registered.

Recently, however, the largest increase—some 250 percent—in the number of first-year students was in private colleges (from 157,000 in 1994 to 384,000 in 2002). At the same time, the number of new students in state universities grew by 24 percent—from 487,100 in 1994 to 603,800 in 2002 (Sergeev, 2003).

State institutions hold some 350,000 free (non-fee) places for new students. But, under economic stress, universities prefer fee payers. By 2003, over half (53 percent) of all university students were fee-paying students. By 2008, their numbers are expected to reach 70 percent (Moskovskii Komsomolets, 2004).

It is estimated that some 80 percent of students in private and 60 to 70 percent in state higher educational institutions (VUZs) are fee-paying students. The Law on Education, which prescribes student quotas on a faculty by faculty basis, is "rarely observed" as cash-strapped universities prefer to enroll full-fee paying students (*Rossiiskaia Gazeta,* 2003b).

Private tutoring, especially preparing final year students for the VUZ entrance exam, has increased significantly during the last decade in Russia. It is estimated that 300,000 students trained by private tutors, including college academics, who are also members of the Entrance Exam Board, are admitted into the VUZ (Filipov, 2002). (Low academic salaries have forced many faculty members to seek outside work to supplement their income. In addition, young researchers are not interested in pursuing careers as academics.)

Student Assessment

The new state public examinations (*yedinssvenneyi gosudarstvennyi examen*—YGE) for the final year of secondary schooling are currently held at year 11, but Russia is gradually introducing twelve-year schooling, modeled on the West. Since 2004, Moscow final secondary school students have had to sit for five common state public exams, including two compulsory exams in algebra and language (essay), and three by choice (selected from year 10/11 curriculum). Students in special schools have to take an additional exam in their specialized subject.

The Russian language and literature exam is conducted in the traditional form. Students have a choice between an essay and oral exam, which continues to be the favored option. Finally, students select, according to their specialization, biology, chemistry, or physics. Students can sit for the mathematics exam in their schools, but their teachers are not allowed to be present. Other exams are held at the higher educational institutions.

School Texts

Contemporary Russian schools face a chronic shortage of school texts, which are produced by the Ministry of Education. In 1996, for instance, only 30 percent of the prescribed texts (the federal core curriculum) reached the schools; the rest were to come much later. Since 1996, parents have had to buy school texts, which previously were distributed free of cost.

Paying for school textbooks in a society where wages are extremely low has created a new social inequality. At the height of inflation during the mid-1990s, struggling families had a choice of paying either 40,000 rubles per set of texts per child, supplied by the school shop, or buying them privately from commercial publishers at 150,000 rubles (a teacher's fortnightly salary) or more per set. The well-known aphorism "Knowledge is power" became "Knowledge is money" in Russia during the 1990s.

School Enrollment

Education enrollment patterns have been negatively affected by Russia's low birth rate, imploding economy, and the financial hardship experienced by the average household. The gross enrollment ratio showed declining enrollments in secondary schools—from 96 percent in 1980 to 87 percent in 1996. In 1980, the USSR occupied the 5th place in the world in secondary education enrollment completion rates; by 1995 Russia had slipped to 31st place.

Similarly, enrollments in higher education had declined from 46 percent in 1980 to 41 percent in 1996, giving it 24th rank in the world (*World Development Indicators,* 1999). While other nations were experiencing a significant increase in higher education enrollments (for example, Canada from 57 percent to 90 percent, United States from 56 percent to 81 percent, and Australia from 25 percent to 76 percent in 1996), Russia showed a steady decline in enrollment in both secondary and tertiary sectors.

Some 19.2 million students attended schools in 2002 (compared with over 21 million in 1996). There were 65,665 schools, including 44,700 rural schools, compared with 67,446 schools in 1996. (*Uchitelskaia Gazeta,* 2002d, p. 36). The Ministry of Education estimates that by 2008 school enrollments will fall by 6 million to 14 million. In 2003, some 15,600 pupils did not complete primary or junior secondary school (*Parlamentskaia Gazeta,* 2004). Demographic factors, including an aging population, low birth rates, and high infant mortality rates have contributed to declining school enrollments. In 2004, about 1.3 million pupils were enrolled in grade 1 (*Parlamentskaia Gazeta,* 2004), compared with over 2.4 million in 1996. Due to demographic factors and school amalgamations in the last decade, 2,000 schools were closed. In 2002 there were still some 5,600 small rural schools with fewer than twenty pupils (*Uchitelskaia Gazeta,* 2002b).

EDUCATION REFORM AND POLICY SHIFTS

The process of post-Soviet education reform began with the Ministry of Education issuing numerous significant education policy documents that defined the structure and content of education in post-communist Russia. The pace, the extent, and the magnitude of education reform between 1992 and 2004 are unprecedented in Russia's history. In less than a decade, the entire system was transformed from its ideologically defined and dictated, and centrally controlled, educational institutions to open, diverse, and democratic schooling. Differentiation, decentralization, and flexibility in education and curricula marked a dramatic shift in education policy.

Major policy and school curricula documents, which define and regulate various aspects of modernization of education, content, and educational standards in Russia include:

- The Education Law (1992, revised January 1996). The Education Law (1996), which itself is based on the new Constitution of the Russian Federation (Article 43) guarantees the right to education and defines the content of education. A major function of the school as a social institution is to facilitate, in every way possible, the development of individual, moral, social, and normative values accepted in a contemporary democratic society.
- In 1993 provisional school curricula and programs were adopted, and revised in 1995 and 2004.
- In 1996, legislation dealing with documentation and accreditation was introduced.
- The Federal Program for Educational Development in 2000–2005 (*Federalnaia programma razvitiia obrazovaniia na 2000–2005*) defined priorities and strategies for education and the Russian Federation for the year 2010.
- The National Doctrine on Education in the Russian Federation 2000–2025 (*Natsionalnaia doktrina obrazovaniia v Rossiiskoi Federatsii do 2025*) is a significant policy document defining schooling for the twenty-first century. It was approved February 2000.
- Concepts of Modernization of Russian Education until 2010 (*Kontseptsii modernizatsii rossiiskogo obrazovaniia na period do 2010 goda*) was approved by the Russian Parliament in December 2001.
- The Program of Modernization of Teacher Education during the 2003–2010 period is directed toward improvement of teacher training.
- The revised Basic Curriculum Policy document was prepared by the Russian Academy of Education in Moscow in response to the democratization process in education during *perestroika* in the early 1990s. It was introduced to guide educational renewal of Russia's 66,400 schools with some 20,600,000 pupils during the transitional period and economic restructuring (*Uchitelskaia Gazeta,* 2002c).
- A new, and controversial for many Russians who had lived under ten-year schooling for sixty years, Basic Curriculum Plan (*Novyi bazisnyi uchebnyi plan*) for twelve-year schooling was adopted as a major policy document in 2003, with transition to twelve-year schooling in 2007. A single national examination for the final year of secondary education in the Russian Federation in 2003 proved to be the most widely discussed issue.
- Federal Core Curriculum and Standards Framework for Primary and Secondary Schools (*Federalny komponnent gosudarstvennovo standarta obshchevo obrazovaniia,* 2003) is a very significant education policy shift adopted as a policy document in March 2003. It encouraged the intensification of humanities in the curriculum. Languages other than Russian (English, French, and German) have been introduced in grade 2 and civics education is now taught in every grade, from grades 1 to 11. In grade 1, the 5-point scale of assessment has been changed to simply Pass/Fail.
- Compulsory Minimum Content of General Education (*Obiazatelny minimum soderzhaniia obshchego obrazovaniia,* 1998) defined basic offerings to be included in the curriculum.

- The State Examination (EGU or *yediny gosudarsvenny examen,* 2003), is introduced in all regions of the Russian Federation by 2006.
- Transition to intensive and specialized schooling in specific KLAs in grades 10–11 (12) (*profilnoe obrazovanie*) is introduced in 2006.

The above new documents—particularly Concepts of Modernization of Education in Russia until 2010 and the National Doctrine of Education in the Russian Federation 2000–2025—define and set the agenda for schooling in Russia for the next two decades. Affected will be the lives of some 40 million students enrolled in education institutions in the Russian Federation (*Parlamentskaia Gazeta,* 2004). Although these documents could easily be dismissed as rhetoric and political correctness, they do demonstrate Russia's incredible commitment to modernization and social change on a scale unprecedented in her history. Such grandiose and spectacular education reforms and shifts in education policy are unparalleled in the world. One could not imagine any other nation that would be able and willing to undertake such a monumental educational transformation. As Filipov (2003c) explained, "We had to achieve the revolution in the people's consciousness. We had to convince them and explain why we had to have the change [in education]. We had to make the idea of modernization more transparent and motivational" (pp. 10–12).

A report on the progress of the reforms, delivered on February 25, 2004, listed the tasks that had to be accomplished in education during 2004 and 2005. These are:

- Preparation and adoption of preschool standards.
- Introduction of the new standards in secondary education.
- Examination of the quality of school textbooks.
- Upgrading of qualifications of school administrators and teachers.
- Realization of the new mechanisms for the financing of schools.
- Adoption of the Law on the School Councils (*Obupravliaishchikh sovietakh*).
- Nationwide access of schools to the Internet.

SUCCESSES IN EDUCATION REFORMS

What are the pedagogical successes in education resulting from the education reforms in the Russian Federation during the last decade? The answer depends on what is meant by "success" and who is asking the question. Does success refer to improvements in the quality of schooling and higher standards in academic achievement, excellence, quality, and efficiency? If it does refer to all of these attributes, then we could say that there were some successes in curriculum innovation and school restructuring, particularly with the new models of school curricula, classroom pedagogy, assessment, and school-based management. Today, for the first time since the collapse of the USSR in 1991, teachers, parents, and students alike have come to terms with differentiation, decentralization, and privatization in education.

However, for many teachers, reform brought a pedagogical "culture shock." Schools were encouraged to design their own programs and teach using alternative textbooks and educational resources. Under the Soviet system, this would have been unthinkable, as the education system was one of the most centralized organizations in the world, with the Ministry of Education centrally approving and prescribing curricula, textbooks, assessment, examinations, and even lesson plans.

At a policy level, there was a shift from a quantitative ("more is better") model of growth in education to an economic view of educational planning as investment and consumption, to a more qualitative view of a "total process-planning" model in education and policy (Zajda, 2002, p. 77).

Another successful policy initiative during the 1990s was the shift toward diversity in the teaching/learning process, decentralization, and school-based management in order to give schools more autonomy and greater financial accountability. Decentralization, as a positive and potentially empowering policy shift, involved the transfer of the decision-making process from the center (Moscow) to outer or lower spheres of influence—provinces, municipalities, local councils, and school councils. The accompanying devolution of power and authority provides teachers and principals with autonomy in the decision-making process and choice.

Increasing autonomy was also linked to privatization. Private schools, unseen in Russia since 1917, began to mushroom across the country, but mainly in the capital cities such as Moscow and St. Petersburg (Leningrad).

EDUCATION REFORMS AND CHALLENGES

In any education system, and Russia is no exception, there are numerous unresolved policy issues and problems in schooling and delivery that have to do with excellence, quality in education, academic standards, assessment, academic achievement targets, resources, finances, and education outcomes. However, some issues are specifically applicable to Russia during its current transitional period. These include economic hardship and inadequate public expenditure on education, poorly paid teachers, unpaid wages, inadequately trained school administrators, inefficient use of scarce resources, shortages of textbooks and teaching resources, and poorly maintained school buildings. There are many overcrowded schools, and some schools (30 percent) are working two shifts. Problems also include uneven progress in education reforms among the various regions within the Russian Federation. Also, the education reform and policy shifts are driven by so called reform "tsars" (senior state policymakers) in Moscow (Zajda, 2005). That is, despite diversity, differentiation, and decentralization in education, schools and higher education institutions still reflect a powerful centralizing dimension of the state.

Some policy analysts (e.g., Yeroshin, 2002) are extremely critical of the major reforms during the last fifteen years and their cumulative effects on economic relations in education. They believe that unless there is a radical rethink in the economics of education, which has to take into account market forces and regional differences, the reforms, like those during the 1990s, will achieve very little. Smolin (2004) summarized the negative outcomes of reform as "downsizing, closure, and destruction." Further, Fursenko (2004) noted that although spending on education grew 5.5-fold, from 21 billion in 1999 to 117.8 billion rubles in 2004, it has not made the education system either more efficient or better.

Fursenko defined three major issues in education reforms: the content and technological dimension of education; staffing problems, including low wages, lack of growth, and inadequate training and retraining; and inadequate integration between education, the needs of industry, and the economy.

Financing of Education

The progress of educational reforms in Russia is severely affected by fiscal problems. According to the Ministry of General and Professional Education (MGPE), public spending on education declined at a rate of between 5 and 10 percent per year between 1991 and 1996. After the August 1998 devaluation of the ruble, the situation was even worse, as the GDP per capita fell to US$1,937 in 1998, which was only 60 percent of its 1991 level. Education spending in 1998 was 3 percent of GDP. There was a real danger that education reform in a time of economic crisis was likely to "increase inter-regional inequality among schools" (Canning, Moock, & Heleniak, 1999, p. 4). The increases in spending since 1999 noted in the preceding paragraph do not compensate for the precipitous decline in spending before 1999—especially with the increased demands brought on by continuing education reforms.

Education for the Job Market

Another major problem in the ongoing reform in education is the very ambitious attempt of matching schooling with students' career and work orientations (and their desires) (Zajda, 1979, p. 295). For example, the sociologist Schubkin showed that in the USSR, even in the booming 1960s, there was a mismatch between the "job pyramid" of the economy and the "desire pyramid" of pupils' career dreams and vocational aspirations (see Zajda, 1979).

Vocational-technical schools (PTUs) were originally designed to enroll vocation and trade-oriented students, rather than dropouts from secondary schools. The aim was to channel almost 60 percent of 15-year-olds who had completed grade 9 into trade-oriented PTUs. This proved to be very difficult to achieve due to the low social status of PTUs. Vocational-technical schools were, and continue to be, very unpopular with both students and parents because of their perceived low social status in the eyes of the community. Even teachers from secondary schools would at times "frighten" their students with a possible transfer to a PTU.

Indeed, the composition of a PTU student body has always been both "complex and difficult" for upbringing (moral and social development and character training) and learning. Close to 80 percent of the intake were classified as deviant—committing criminal acts, engaging in various forms of juvenile delinquency—and were labeled as "pedagogically neglected" (*pedagogicheski zapushcheny*) individuals. The police charged some 45,500 PTU students with criminal acts in 1989, and another 43,300 were charged with drunken and disorderly behavior.

It is therefore not surprising that the vocational education system is not popular among youth. By 1990, PTUs could fill only 89.5 percent of their first-year places, or approximately 1 million students, instead of 1.2 million as planned. The latest figures (2000) indicate that vocational colleges continue to remain unpopular among school leavers. Only 20 percent of grade 9 students and 15 percent of grade 11 students were enrolled in the Junior Vocational Colleges (NPO; *Nachalnoe professionalnoe obrazovanie*) sector. This created, according to the then Deputy Minister of Education, a "serious situation" that had to be "rectified" (*Uchitelskaia Gazeta,* 2002a, p. 16).

Kisiliov explained that in the latest policy document, The Conception of Modernization of Russian Education (*Konsepsiia modernizatsii Rossiiskogo obrazovaniia*), the government's top priority was given to the role of the NPO sector in the preparation of adequately trained workers for the economy. He called on the enterprises to do their "patriotic duty" and urged them to become partners with the NPO sector: "Enterprises must become the partners of the NPO, because there are only two choices—either adolescents enter the workforce or they join the criminal gangs (*uidut v kriminal*). I believe that those who know their civic and patriotic duty and who understand that the task needs to be solved, will support the interests of the government and community" (*Uchitelskaia Gazeta,* 2002a, p. 16). There were 3,893 vocational colleges in 2000, with 1,679,331 students (including 2,700 state and municipal vocational colleges and more than 150 private technical colleges that offered complete secondary education).

Differentiation and Decentralization in Education

Differentiation, decentralization, and flexibility in education and curricula, which became almost rampant in some regions of Russia, had a significant impact on access, equity, and educational outcomes, particularly academic achievement, standards, and quality (Zajda, 2005). A number of prominent policymakers and educators (e.g., Filipov, 2003a, b, d; Konstantinovski, 2000; Nikandrov, 2001) discussed the deterioration in the quality and educational standards of schooling.

One of the consequences of decentralization and privatization is a growth of disparities in education (Bray & Borevskaya, 2001). Decentralization in the spheres of governance and financing and the transfer of power to regional and local authorities (including the burden of financing schools) has resulted in significant regional differences in spending on education. For instance, of the 89 regions, only 16 spent a third more on education costs per child compared with the other 18 regions. As well, in 1998, due to decentralization, only 13 percent of the total public expenditure on schooling in the Russian Federation was allocated by the central budget; the remainder of the funding came from municipal authorities.

Pedagogy and Policy Challenges

While Russia has seen dramatic educational restructuring, some school promoters wish to place more emphasis on values education and pay more attention to orphans, students at risk, and street children. Filipov (2003c) holds that the main thrust of modernization in education should be the development of the new perspectives on personal identity and a stress on values and moral education in the classroom.

Evaluation

As some critics have argued about education reforms in general, the most controversial aspect of the genesis and impact of education policy on institutions is the resultant "moral panic" and the search for economically and politically correct remedies. Hence, influenced by the pace and direction of education reforms in the United States and Europe, Russian educators and policymakers used the metaphor of the "rising tide of mediocrity" as a politically expedient scapegoat to employ in Russia, in order to orchestrate the campaign for change in education. Like the slogan "democratization" of the late 1980s and the early 1990s, it too became a convenient political and pedagogical metaphor, with powerful ideological, emotional, and moral overtones.

The Future for Schools in the Russian Federation

Education reforms in Russia during the 1990s reflected a radical shift in policy; a departure (intended or unintended) from Russia's egalitarian-in-nature income equality.

For one thing, arguing from social change models and globalization in general, Russian policymakers were making an attempt to address the knowledge-based economy of the twenty-first century—which will affect significantly the nature of work and in turn redefine the education process. For another, if greater equality in the distribution of incomes, both nationally and internationally, were the key ideas of the New International Economic Order (NIEO) during the mid-1970s and the early 1980s in Europe then, during the 1990s, Russia was following the rest of Europe in embracing tenets of economic rationalism and abandoning income equality.

Another significant policy shift came about as a result of a changing discourse in the economics of education. In the 1960s and the 1970s neoclassical economic theory based, among other things, on the concept of investment in human capital influenced education policymakers. In the 1980s microeconomic analysis was replacing macroeconomic techniques. The perceived failure of the neoclassical economic model to deal with "realities" in the education "market," and its inability to offer effective policy recommendations prompted policymakers to focus their attention on market forces. There is no doubt that decentralization and privatization, which also led to the privatization of schools (creating a dual structure of schooling) and the dismantling of the Soviet State enterprises (perceived to be cost-inefficient) during the early 1990s were, to some extent, based on the Western model of "human capital theory" that focused more on the microeconomic analysis of education for the labor market than on students' needs.

Even as the convergence between Russian education policymakers and those in Europe can be illustrated by the similarities in the reform agenda, the fundamental question must be "What is the future for schools in Russia?" In a word, it can be said that, in general, education reform in Russia has failed to address many challenges.

Psacharopoulos (1989), in analyzing the discrepancy between educational policy goals and outcomes, argued that the reason why reforms fail is that the "intended policy was never implemented" that policies were "vaguely stated," financial implications were not worked out, and policies were based on "good will" rather than on "research-proven cause-effect relationships" (p. 179). Russia's new policy documents on education and standards, despite their symbolic and political power and the innovative platforms of selected schools and teachers, have yet to deliver the new vision of quality and excellence of schooling for the masses.

Other limitations of curriculum reforms include "teaching to the test" and combining curriculum reforms with new assessment standards. Russian teachers, as teachers in other countries, still prepare their final year students for the ubiquitous final exams in secondary school. Another problem is that the academic curriculum, with its rigorous exams, will uncover new inequalities among students, emphasizing individual, cognitive, social class (and cultural capital), racial, ethnic, and gender differences in academic achievement—particularly in examination performance.

On a similar theme, apart from "unlocking individualization," the reforms have produced a new dimension of post-Soviet social stratification and educational inequality (Zajda, 2003). Sources of educational inequality, as in the West, can be attributed to class inequality, social background, socioeconomic status, cultural capital, the family, and the school itself (Saha, 2005). The economic "meltdown" during the early 1990s has undoubtedly generated new inequalities in Russian society, partly attributable to changing material conditions of life, social and economic experiences of different social classes, and processes of social control within the family, the peer group, and the school.

Appropriate teacher preparation and effective teacher in-service education are necessary ingredients of systemic reform. This is not reflected in teacher education in Russia. At the same time, teachers' salaries are a perennial problem. Teachers in Russia, as in many other countries, earn less than tertiary-trained individuals in other professions (*Uchitelskaia Gazeta,* 2004).

CONCLUSION

It is now evident that education policymakers in the Russian Federation, in promoting the reforming zeal of the state during the 1990s, have ignored significant cultural and social variables affecting educational transformation. These are globalization, the erosion of democracy, and social inequalities. Current market-driven education reforms in the Russian Federation, designed to give a freer choice of schools to parents and pupils and offer diversity of supply in schooling, are problematic. School choice and school markets in Russia, as elsewhere, have many imperfections, including the perception that a "good" education is related to "access to the best jobs" that will confer social status, position, and privilege. The application of market principles to schooling, especially in private schools and school choice in general, seems to reflect the new trend of concentration of cultural capital and educational privilege among the children of the privileged *Novye Russkie* (new Russian bourgeoisie).

In summary, post-communist Russia's haste to reform and transform its education system after 1991, in order to shake off the hegemonic dust of the Soviet education legacy and win respect and approval from the West, may have planted new seeds of discontent in Russian education institutions and society. This effect is largely due to hastily written, poorly researched, and untested curricular models and teaching methodologies—all taking place in the climate of continuing economic hardship, growing social/economic inequality, and a moral vacuum.

By accepting the Western model of education, Russia is moving away from its previously espoused egalitarianism to a more conservative and traditional schooling that places a far greater emphasis on reproduction, stratification, and hierarchy than on equality of educational opportunity. Like all education reforms, the current market-oriented nature of schooling in Russia needs to be evaluated within the dynamics of growing social inequality and the new polarization of social classes in order to understand the social and cultural consequences that are likely to shape the future destiny of the Russian Federation.

REFERENCES

Bray, M., & Borevskaya, N. (2001). Financing education in transitional societies: Lessons from Russia and China. *Comparative Education, 3,* 345–365.

Canning, M., Moock, P., & Heleniak, T. (1999). *Reforming education in the regions of Russia.* Washington, DC: World Bank.

Darinski, A. (2002). Nuzhna li gosudarstvennaia elitarnaia shkola? (Do we need state elite schools?). *Pedagogika, 9,* 18–22.

Filipov, V. (2002, December 11). U nas pereproizvodstvo spetsialistov s vysshim obrazovaniem (We have an oversupply of specialists with higher education), an interview with Andrei Vaganov. *Nezavisimaia Gazeta* (Independent Newspaper), 266. Retrieved December 10, 2004, from http://www.edu.ru/index

Filipov, V. (2003a, April 15). Pochemu zakryvaiut selskie shkoly? (Why are the rural schools closed?) *Rossiiskaia Agrarnaia Gazeta* (Russian Rural Newspaper). Retrieved December 12, 2004, from http://www.edu.ru/index

Filipov, V. (2003b, December 9). *Tribuna.* Retrieved December 9, 2004, from http://www.edu.ru/index

Filipov, V. (2003c, December 16). Everything is changing but everything stays the same (Vsio izmeniaetsia, nichto ne ishchesaet), an interview with Irina Dimova. *Uchitelskaia Gazeta,* pp. 10–12.

Filipov, V. (2003d, December 23). Zakroesh shkolu-zakroetsa derevnia (Close the school and you close the village), an interview with Yelena Novoselova. *Rossiiskaia Agrarnaia Gazeta* (Russian Rural Newspaper). Retrieved December 10, 2004, from http://www.edu.ru/index

Fursenko, A. (2004, November 30). Educational inequality. *Parlamentskaya Gazeta.* Retrieved December 12, 2004, from http://www.edu.ru/index.php?page_id=5&topic_id=3&date=&sid=983

Konstantinovski, D. (2000). Molodiozh 90kh: Samoopredelenie v novoi realnosti (Youth during the 1990s: Self-actualisation in the new reality). Moscow: Tsentr sotsiologii obrazovaniia, RAO.

Moskovskii Komsomolets. (2004, December 2). Retrieved December 10, 2004, from http://www.edu.ru/index

Narodnoe Khoziaistvo SSR 1917–1977: Statisticheskii Ezhegodnik (1977). Moscow.

Nikandrov, N. (2001). Rossiia: Sotsializatsiia ivospitanie na rubezhe tysiachileti (Russia: Socialisation and upbringing at the crossroads of millennia). Cheboksary: Chuvash University Press.

Parlamentskaia Gazeta. (2003, 28 January). Retrieved December 8, 2004, from http://www.edu.ru/index

Parlamentskaia Gazeta. (2004, September 1). Retrieved December 9, 2004, from http://www.edu.ru/index

Psacharopoulos, G. (1989). Why educational reforms fail: A comparative analysis. *International Review of Education, 35*(2), 179–212.

Rossiiskaia Gazeta (2003a, January 9). Retrieved December 5, 2004, from http://www.edu.ru/index

Rossiiskaia Gazeta (2003b, January 30). Retrieved December 7, 2004, from http://www.edu.ru/index

Saha. (2005). Cultural and social capital in global perspective. In J. Zajda (Ed.), *International handbook on globalization, education and policy research* (pp. 745–755). Dordrecht: Springer.

Sergeev, I. (2003, April 14). Uchitsia v vuzakh smogut tolko bogachi (Only the rich can enter the VUZ). Moskovskii Komsomolets. Retrieved December 4, 2003, from http://www.edu.ru/index.php?page_id=5&topic_id=3&date=&sid=1007

Smolin, O. (2004). K doske! Mneniia (To the Blackboard! Comments). *Rossiiskaia Gazeta.* Retrieved December 12, 2004, from http://www.edu.ru/index.php?page_id=5&topic_id=3&date=&sid=1007

Uchitelskaia Gazeta (1995a, May 30), p. 10.
Uchitelskaia Gazeta (1995b, September 5), p. 13.
Uchitelskaia Gazeta (1996, October 10), p. 7.
Uchitelskaia Gazeta (2002a, July 16), p. 16.
Uchitelskaia Gazeta (2002b, August 27), p. 10.
Uchitelskaia Gazeta (2002c, August 29), p. 8.
Uchitelskaia Gazeta (2002d, December 17), p. 36.
Uchitelskaia Gazeta (2004, January 13), p. 10.
World Development Indicators. (1999). Washington, DC: World Bank.
World Development Indicators. (2004). Washington DC: World Bank.
Yeroshin, V. (2002). Problemy modernizatsii sistemy economicheskikh otnoshenii v obrazovanii (Problems of modernising the system of economic relations in education). *Pedagogika, 10,* 15–23.
Zajda, J. (1979). Education for labour in the USSR. *Comparative Education, 15*(3), 3–11.
Zajda, J. (1980). *Education in the USSR.* Oxford: Pergamon Press.
Zajda, J. (1988). The moral curriculum in the Soviet School. *Comparative Education, 24,* 389–404.
Zajda, J. (1992). *New independent states of the former Soviet Union* (NIS). Canberra: DEET.
Zajda, J. (2002). Education and policy: Changing paradigms and issues. *International Review of Education, 48,* 67–91.
Zajda, J. (2003). Educational reform and transformation in Russia. *European Education 20,* 35, 58–88.
Zajda, J. (2004). Decentralization and privatization in education: The role of the state. *International Review of Education, 50,* 1–23.
Zajda, J. (2005). The educational reform and transformation in Russia. In J. Zajda (Ed.), *International handbook of globalization and education policy research* (pp. 405–430). Dordrecht: Springer.

CHAPTER THIRTEEN

POLAND
Transformations in Society and Schooling

KAS MAZUREK

CZESLAW MAJOREK*

Since the late 1980s, Poland has been going through a difficult, but very promising, era of extensive economic and political change. That process continues to this day and has transformed post-communist Poland into a fully democratic society, with social structures and political institutions that reflect a democratic value system in form, content, and function. Education reform is one of the main vehicles for Poland's ongoing transformation. Debates and discussions at all levels of the country's political spectrum affirm education as a priority and identify how fundamental changes in education are crucial for future social and political change.

Kas Mazurek is Professor of Education at the University of Lethbridge, Canada. His research interests overlap the fields of comparative education, multiculturalism and minority group relations, the social contexts of educational ideas, policies and practices, and the logic of inquiry in education.

Czeslaw Majorek was Professor of History of Education at Krakow Pedagogical University, Poland. He was also Chair of the Commission for the Science of Education at the Krakow Branch of Polish Academy of Sciences. His research interests focused on Polish education in the eighteenth and nineteenth centuries and recent educational changes in Poland and other Central-East European nations.

In his stellar career he authored or edited seventeen scholarly books and published well over 200 refereed articles, papers, and reviews in ten different languages. He presented his research before distinguished international academic associations in dozens of nations and was recognized with numerous foreign academic fellowships and invitations for academic visits abroad and overseas. He held multiple editorial and advisory duties for international academic journals. In addition, his contributions to prestigious professional and learned societies—among them, the International Standing Conference for the History of Education, the International Society for History Didactics, the Polish Historical Society, and the Commission for the Educational Sciences of the Polish Academy of Sciences—were significant and continuing. Professor Dr. Hab. Czeslaw Majorek passed away on September 29, 2002.

*This chapter incorporates elements of Majorek, Czeslaw. (2000). A Society and Education System in Transition: Poland. In Kas Mazurek, Margret A. Winzer, & Czeslaw Majorek (Eds.), *Education in a global society: A comparative perspective.* Boston: Allyn and Bacon.

THE SOCIAL FABRIC

The evolution of the Polish education system shares many of the features and concerns of education systems in the other former Iron Curtain countries. However, the country's geography, sociopolitical framework, and history have generated some unique educational structures, issues, and problems.

Geography

Basically a plain, Poland is located between the Baltic Sea to its North and the Carpathian Mountains to its south. It is bordered by Germany on the west, Russia and Lithuania on the northeast, Belorussia and Ukraine on the east, and the Slovak Republic and Czech Republic on the south.

Poland's total area of 312,680 square kilometers is varied as a result of the belt arrangement of natural geographic regions. Lowlands stretch along the Baltic seashore, the vast northern area is a lake district, and the lowlands of central Poland form the main agricultural region and also have vast virgin forests. The uplands are highlighted by an ancient mountain range and, last, high mountains cover the south.

Demography

In terms of population, Poland is a relatively youthful country by European standards. One-quarter of Poles are under the age of 20. However, the birth rate has been declining for decades (i.e., in 1980 it was +0.96 percent; by 2003 it dropped to −0.03 percent), and this will change the situation over the next two decades (Eurybase, 2005).

In 2004, the population of Poland was 38.6 million, with a growth rate of 0.02 percent and birth rate of 10.64/1,000. Life expectancy at birth is 74.16 years overall; 70.04 for males and 78.52 for females (CIA, 2005, pp. 3–4). It is also a fairly densely populated country (12 habitants per square kilometer), and almost 62 percent of the population lives in 884 towns and cities (Eurybase, 2005).

In terms of ethnic and religious composition, Poland is a homogenous society. The population is: Polish, 96.7 percent; German, 0.4 percent; Ukrainian, 0.1 percent; Byelorussian, 0.1 percent; Roman Catholic, 95 percent (about 75 percent practicing); Eastern Orthodox, Protestant, and other, 5 percent. Poland is also a culturally developed society. The literacy rate for those aged 15 and over is 99.8 (CIA, 2005, p. 4).

Political History

World War II was one of the most tragic events in Polish history. A staggering 22 percent of the total Polish population (over half a million fighting men and women, and 6 million civilians) died. About 50 percent of these were Polish Christians and 50 percent were Polish Jews. Approximately 5,384,000, or 89.9 percent, of Polish war losses were victims of prisons, death camps, raids, executions, annihilations of ghettos, epidemics, starvation, excessive work, and ill treatment. One million war orphans and over half a million invalids were created. The country lost 38 percent of its national assets (in comparison, Britain lost 0.8 percent, France 1.5 percent) (Kasprzyk, 2004).

After the War ended, Poland found itself in the Soviet orbit of interests, its politics and economy dependent upon its big neighbor. However, increasingly frequent protests and growing social tensions eventually forced the imposed communist government to make concessions. On June 4, 1989, the first elections were conducted in which noncommunists could run for Parliament. This sparked a series of events constituting Poland's peaceful transition to democracy and a market economy. The first noncommunist government behind the Iron Curtain was appointed, and some rather chaotic economic reforms were implemented. At the same time, Poland identified memberships in the North Atlantic Treaty Organization (NATO) and the European Union (EU) as its main strategic goals. Both goals were accomplished; Poland joined NATO in 1999 and in 2004 became a member of the EU.

Structural Changes and Social Consequences under Communism

There is no doubt that structural reforms initiated under communist domination generated revolutionary social and economic changes. Increased and widespread industrialization and urbanization greatly reduced economic disparities between regions and increased horizontal social mobility. The effects of an expanded and accessible educational system and higher standards of living for rural populations reduced differences between town and village and brought about an increasingly uniform social structure. However, new social differences emerged as a result of the governing party's nepotistic practices, such as providing an elite few easier access to coveted goods.

Public Attitudes in the Communist Era

Communism also generated a new social consciousness. In the time of so-called "Real Socialism" the general social orientation was one of equal social security for every group and every citizen. The system guaranteed full employment, free health care, free schooling at all levels of the education system, and free or very inexpensive access to cultural goods, such as literature, theater, movies, sports, recreation services, and so on (Topolski, 1992).

However, on the negative side, the dictatorial communist political establishment kept individuals from developing a sense of individual responsibility. A feeling of dependency was nurtured and reinforced by state paternalism. It suggested that the "ideal citizen" always conforms to the official stance in every respect, identifying obediently with that standpoint without criticism. The state tried to instill faith that all tensions and troubles would be solved or removed by those in authority (Morody, 1993).

The Transformation to a Free Market Economy

In the communist era, Poland was an industrial-agricultural country. It was also successful; economic progress fared favorably in comparison to the average of developed countries. However, after the communist withdrawal in 1989, a radical reform of the economic system was launched. A policy of "shock therapy"—decontrolling prices, slashing subsidies, and drastically reducing import barriers—was implemented.

Almost immediately, this led to a recession—a steep decline in production characteristic of transitions from centrally run to market-based economies. The gross domestic product decreased quite dramatically, unemployment skyrocketed, and inflation reached an incredible peak of 50 percent monthly in late 1989. As a result of the lifting of state-controlled prices, prices rose by an average of 78 percent overall, and some goods and services increased by 600 percent (Government of Poland, 2005).

In spite of these hardships, the short-term goal of largely stabilizing the economy was achieved rather quickly. For example, the annual rate of inflation fell from 27.8 percent in 1995 to a mere 1.1 percent in 2003 (Eurybase, 2005). Similarly, the yearly percentage change of the gross domestic product (GDP) went from −11.5 percent in 1990, to a peak of +7 percent in 1995, remained over +4 percent until 2000 and, after dipping to just over 1 percent for the next two years (Eurybase, 2005), recovered to about 3.7 percent in 2003 (CIA, 2005, p. 7). Employment, however, stubbornly remains on the high side; in 1995 it was 14 percent, in 2003 it was 18 percent (Eurybase, 2005). However, the per capita GDP is respectable: about US$11,100 in 2003 (CIA, 2005, p. 7.).

From a relative perspective—i.e., the situations in other countries in the former Soviet bloc—the costs incurred by Polish society in making the transition to a market economy have not been too great. However, despite unquestionable economic achievements to date, Poland's road to a developed market economy is still long. Market structures and efficient techniques need time to be put in place and to function properly. A better life has now begun for some minorities, such as young educated people, new entrepreneurs, and successful businessmen living in big cities. But, for the larger sections of the population, daily life has become more difficult than it was during the last years of communist rule, and it is becoming miserable for a growing number of people now hit by unemployment and poverty.

SCHOOLING

Historical Background

The system of education now existing in Poland was formed and developed in difficult post-war conditions. As a result of World War II, Poland's infrastructure and economy were virtually destroyed. The country was also left with almost 3 million illiterate people, and a devastated school network. Over 60 percent of pre-war education buildings were in ruins, most education equipment was missing, and almost 95 percent of school library books perished. Therefore, rebuilding and development became the task of first importance. In this and other areas the communist government achieved remarkable successes.

Massive infusions of money, labor, and energy were put into the restoration and development of schooling facilities. This accomplished, the next task was to launch a general attack on illiteracy. The operation against illiteracy was carried out in the years 1949–1951. Illiterate people beyond the age of 50 were taught in courses organized in school buildings, educational centers, their places of work, and individually. Of the total 700,000 persons qualifying for literacy courses, 618,000 completed them successfully.

The next stage was to raise the general level of education up to at least grade 7. Because of the massive rebuilding effort, the whole country was already covered with a network of elementary schools, so primary education was rapidly achieved for nearly 100 percent of children. In result, secondary schools and higher learning institutions became accessible to young people from all social strata. Furthermore, schooling at all levels was tuition free, students from rural communities were ensured accommodation in boarding houses and campuses, and those with limited resources received scholarships. Thus, the school system offered a wide range of education possibilities to children, young people, and adults, especially from the lower social strata.

In the course of this rapid expansion, ideological control of the schools was firm. The communist political establishment believed that forming a new society was the task of the state, and a cornerstone of the new social order was egalitarianism. Accordingly, efforts to counterbalance the effects of being economically, socially, and culturally underprivileged were a priority. It became the central concern of schools and teachers to bring their underprivileged students up to the level of the others and to fill in gaps in their education. There were even special compensatory courses for working-class children before they started school and various supportive courses, special instruction classes, and smaller groups organized for them during their school years.

However, these efforts did not achieve the hoped-for results. By the late 1970s and early 1980s, it became apparent that the elimination of social inequalities could not be achieved by schools. Studies showed that schools had a selective effect, despite all efforts to achieve the opposite. Politicians and education leaders had to face the fact that, by the time children got to school, they showed great differences in achievement and development levels. Moreover, the differences identified at the beginning of schooling became permanent and were in very close correlation with performance in later years. Finally, it was evident that the hierarchical school system was further increasing inequality of opportunity among the various social strata (Kozakiewicz, 1990). In other words, even in a communist society, the eradication of inequalities in society and in schools was not fully accomplished.

Thus, the communist education system was unable to achieve its most cherished ideological goal, creating the conditions for egalitarianism. This coincided with another problem. Schools under communism were more or less restricted to transmitting knowledge, but that knowledge was insufficiently relevant to real-life problems. Students were not expected to question and check what was taught or to develop competence and sound judgment by discovering things for themselves.

The result was that, from the early 1980s onwards, young people started publicly criticizing schools, often from the perspective of the Roman Catholic Church. In particular, attention was drawn to education's insufficient support for creative personality development; lack of a relationship between school curricula and students' real-life experiences; absence of connections between subject matter knowledge taught and the worlds of emotion, imagination, and human ethics in general; the Communist party's monopoly on the ideological and/or religious education of young people; and the state's refusal to find compromises between conflicting individual and group interests (Kwiecinski, 1995).

The Structure of Schooling

While the ideological, curricular, and pedagogical objectives and foci of schools in Poland changed as a result of the above criticisms and the fall of communism, the actual structure of the education system had not changed significantly since 1961 (*Ustawa z 15 lipca,* 1961; *Ustawa z 7 wrzesnia,* 1991). Indeed, it would be September 1999 before a fundamental and massive reform of the Polish education system would be undertaken. The scope of the of the 1999 reform initiative is enormous. As Jakubielski (2002) summarizes, it has five major components. First, it structurally changed the entire education system from the nursery school level up to graduate studies in universities. Second, the administration and supervision of the education system was changed. Third, substantial curricular reforms and changes in teaching methods were undertaken. Fourth, external assessment and examination policies and procedures were changed. Finally, qualifications for the teaching profession were reviewed.

Implementation was gradual, and during the period of transition the old and new structures would coexist. However, even though aspects of this massive reform are still being implemented, by the 2004/05 school year the country had effectively made a transfer to the new system.

The major structural components of the Polish school system (see Figure 13.1) are discussed in the next section. (Unless otherwise noted, or specifically cited, the data below draws on a variety of sources, most notably: Bureau for Academic Recognition and International Exchange, 2005; EuryDice, 2004; Government of Poland, 2005; International Associations of Universities, 2005; Jakubielski, 2002; Karczewski, 2005; Socrates-Erasmus, 2005; Urban-Klaehn 2000a, 2000b, 2000c, personal communications with scholars in Poland; and the authors' firsthand knowledge of Poland.)

Preschool. Children aged 3 to 5 may attend preschool institutions, commonly called nursery schools in Poland. A sharp and immediate decrease in the number of children attending preschool institutions occurred during the period of political transformation after the fall of communism. For example, the number of crèches (for infants and toddlers) and kindergartens in Poland fell by over 20 percent between 1989 and 1993 (Nowicka, 2005)

The reasons for this are several. Beginning in 1990, these institutions were taken over by local councils, and preschools run by factories and industries were closed down, fees rose, and a decrease in the birth rate meant there were fewer young children (Karwowska-Struczyk, 1996). The decrease in the number of preschools is also a result of economic factors. Unemployment has reduced demands for the formal education of young children. On the supply side, there is the fact that many of these institutions simply could not afford to operate when they were taken over by local governments. When central finances and a guaranteed supply of able teachers and other professionals disappeared, many local governments were unable to keep their preschool institutions open. Finally, a continuing rise in tuition fees also reduced demand. The situation is rather critical as preschool institutions, because they are not compulsory, receive inadequate subsidies, increasingly raise fees, and fees are unaffordable for many parents. Thus many children must wait until they are eligible for free education. This now starts at the age of 6—a change as a result of the 1999 education reform; before then, compulsory schooling started at the age of 7.

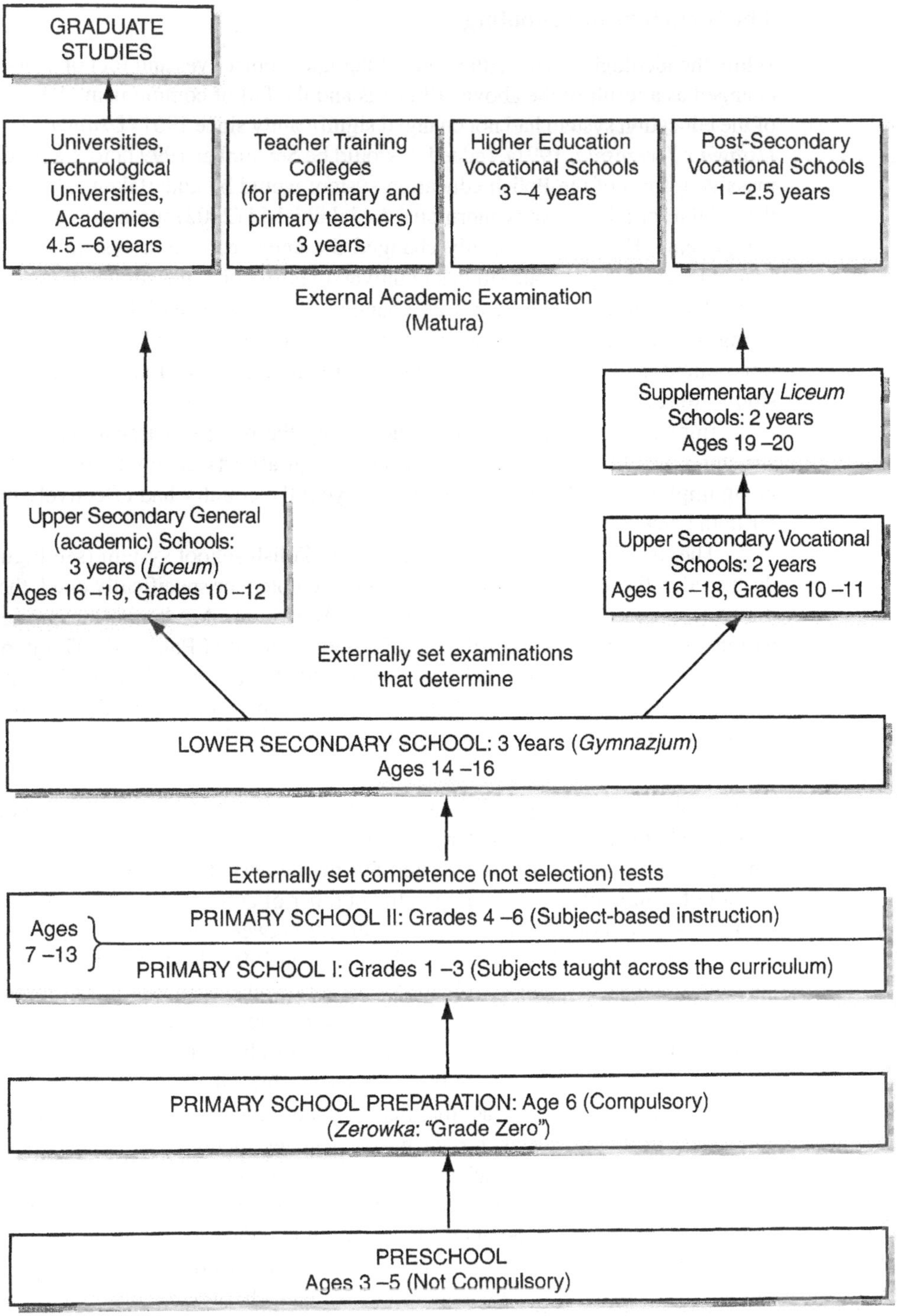

FIGURE 13.1 The school structure of Poland.

Grade Zero: Primary School Preparation. As of September 2004, compulsory schooling begins at the age of 6. It starts with a year of preparation for the first level of primary school with "grade zero" (*Zerowka*). Grade zero can be offered both in primary schools and in kindergartens. Even before it became compulsory, the option to enter grade zero was there and was well taken advantage of. For example, the year before it became compulsory, 97.7 percent of eligible children in 2003/04 were in *Zerowki* in primary schools and kindergartens (EuryDice, 2004).

Primary School I: Grades 1–3. The first three years of primary school have changed substantially as a result of the 1999 reform. Before that, a standardized curriculum was taught across the country and the structure of the school day was subject-based. Now, teachers have a lot more autonomy in organization and delivery. Teaching is integrated, subjects are taught across the curriculum, and teachers are free to adapt pedagogy to the unique characteristics of their classes. Promotion of students to the next grade is automatic.

Primary School II: Grades 4–6. The idea of integration of subjects continues, to some extent, in grades 4 to 6. The sciences, for example, are taught in a block labeled "Nature." This grouping includes biology, geography, physics, and chemistry. Similarly, music and art may be combined into one block. However, even with an emphasis on teaching across the curriculum, the division of the curriculum into discrete subjects and disciplines prevails. The core curriculum consists of Polish language, history and civics, a modern foreign language, mathematics, natural science, music, art, technology, computer sciences, physical education, and religion or ethics.

Students are promoted to the next grade on the basis of receiving a passing grade in the core subjects. There is a competency exam at the end of grade 6; however, it does not affect the ability of the student to go on to lower secondary school, nor does it stream students. All students "pass" this test as it is only for the gathering of information by Regional Examination Commissions on the degree to which national standards of education are being met. In effect since 2002, the test measures skills in five areas: reading, writing, reasoning, use of information, and practical application of knowledge. Of course, the results of these tests, although ostensibly for diagnostic purposes, in reality serve to evaluate/rank schools and teachers.

In the 2003/04 school year, there were 2,855,692 students in 15,354 primary schools (Primary I and II combined) (EuryDice, 2004). Recently, there has been a growth of primary schools offering alternative education programs. These are invariably exclusive schools located in large towns and catering to well-off families seeking educational advantages for their children. This is a new phenomenon in a country that, for half a century, experienced uniform schooling. It poses a fundamental challenge to the public school system's ideal of providing equality of educational opportunity for all children—a point that shall be returned to later in this chapter.

Lower Secondary Education. In the 2003/04 school year, there were 1,681,180 pupils in 6,927 *gymnasia* (lower secondary schools) (EuryDice, 2004). Lower secondary schools are designed to provide the final level of comprehensive schooling, but there we find three types of courses. First, there are common courses for the general student body in the usual disciplines—sciences, maths, literature, and so on. Then there are lower level courses for students who cannot achieve on a par with classmates in certain common courses. Finally, there are advanced courses for students performing exceptionally well in some or all courses (Urban-Klaehn, 2000a). The core curriculum consists of Polish language, history, civic education, a modern foreign language, mathematics, physics and astronomy, chemistry, biology, geography, fine arts and music, technology, computer studies, physical education, and religion or ethics.

Completion of lower secondary school marks the end of compulsory education. Compulsory education is defined in Poland as completion of studies in a *gymnazjum,* or until the student reaches the age of 18.

Instituted in 2002, there is now a crucial leaving exam at the end of the third year of lower secondary school. Examination results essentially determine whether the student is eligible to go on to an academic upper secondary school (*lyceum*) for three years of study or to a two-year vocational secondary school. However, the test results are not absolute, as they are blended with the school's assessment of the student's performance over the year. We now turn our attention to the two routes students can take, should they continue their studies: vocational and academic.

Vocational Schools. These offer two years of study and come in various guises, but fall into two general categories: technical and vocational upper secondary schools and basic vocational schools. Different schools have different entrance requirements and their own admission examinations. In 2003/04, there were 852,077 students in 6,376 technical and vocational schools and 203,995 students in 1,919 basic vocational schools (EuryDice, 2004). These combined numbers, as we shall see, exceed the number of students in the academic upper secondary schools.

What is common to all vocational schools is that they prepare candidates for particular occupations as skilled manual workers or specialized white-collar employees. The location of these schools, the specific programs offered, and the scale of admissions depend on the particular needs of the national and local economy at any given time. The core of a postsecondary vocational school's curriculum is a set of general vocational subjects, usually connected with one group of occupations. In addition, a large number of special courses of varying lengths to provide more focused vocational preparation are offered. Finally, some general education subjects, designed to give students a larger outlook on their future work, are included.

It is noteworthy that only about 55 percent of instruction time in basic vocational schools is spent on learning specific vocational skills. Also taught in a core curriculum are Polish language, foreign languages, history and civic education, mathematics, physics and astronomy, geography and ecology, management, physical education, and defense training.

Graduates of these schools obtain a certificate confirming that the holder possesses skills relevant for a particular trade. In the case of those who graduate into white-collar workers, their certificate confers the rank of *technician* or some other occupational title.

Interestingly, for the first time common external standardized examinations have been introduced for completion of both types of schools. In 2004, these were implemented in basic vocational schools; in 2006 in technical and vocational upper secondary schools.

The examination is in two parts. The written component evaluates student knowledge in a specific job and business activity; a practical component evaluates skill levels (EuryDice, 2004).

Supplementary Liceum Schools. While basic vocational schools are a terminal route for students wishing to enter the workforce, technical and vocational schools offer the opportunity to enter the labor market or continue studies. For those who choose to continue, there are supplementary *liceum* schools. These two-year institutions are essentially a hybrid of vocational/technical education and the three-year academic *liceum* schools discussed next. Here less than 40 percent of study time allocation is on technical and vocational skills. The remainder of the core curriculum consists of Polish language, two foreign languages, history, civic education, cultural studies, mathematics, physics and astronomy, chemistry, biology, geography, management, information technology, physical education, and defense training. This enriched academic curriculum is very important because it qualifies students for writing the all-important *Matura* examination, which is the gateway to postsecondary education institutions.

Academic Upper Secondary Schools. A *liceum* is a three-year academic school. The core curriculum is Polish language, two foreign languages, history, civic education, culture studies, mathematics, physics and astronomy, chemistry, biology, geography, management, information technology, physical education, and defense training. In 2003/04, there were 2,603 such schools, with 751,834 pupils (Eurybase, 2005). Thus, there are more students in basic vocational schools and technical and vocational upper secondary schools than in the academic schools (see above). Students in *liceum* upper secondary schools are preparing for advanced postsecondary education and must write the *Matura* examination at the end of three years to continue.

The Matura. The *Matura* is a rigorous, standardized, general examination that existed in name before the reform of 1999. A new version was introduced in 2003/04. The examination is in two parts. First, there is a written component that is designed by Poland's eight Regional Examination Commissions under the supervision of the Central Examination Commission. The second component is an oral examination prepared and evaluated by local schoolteachers (EuryDice, 2004, p. 3). Importantly, graduates of a *liceum* are not the only eligible candidates for writing the *Matura.* As noted above, graduates of supplementary *liceum* schools are also eligible to write.

Postsecondary Institutions. There are several different kinds of higher education institutions in Poland. This is a legacy of the communist era, when various faculties were separated from universities in order to create new institutions. Some institutions, like universities, pedagogical universities, economics academies, agricultural academies, and theological academies were put under the control of the Ministry of National Education. Others, such as medical academies, music academies, fine art schools, drama schools, film schools, physical education academies, military and maritime academies, fall under other ministries. Hence, the system of higher education is very fragmented. However, there is current legislation in the draft stage that would put all higher education institutions—with the exception of religious and military ones—under the overall authority of the Ministry of Education (Eurybase, 2005).

Nevertheless, in spite of diversity, there is order and logic in the current structure of postsecondary education in Poland. Institutions fall into four general categories: postsecondary vocational schools (generally 1- to 2.5-year programs); higher education vocational schools (3 to 4 years); teacher training colleges (3 years); and universities, technological universities, and academies). As our concern is with teacher training, we will forgo discussion of the full scope of higher education in Poland.

Private Schools. Since 1991 schools and other education centers are divided into public and non-public institutions. Public schools are those established, conducted, and supported by the Ministry of National Education and Sport, or other organs of government administration. Non-public schools are those established and conducted by other legal and private persons, parents, public associations, religious associations, and so on. Public schools provide free education within general educational programs. They enroll pupils according to the principle of general accessibility, employ teachers who possess specified qualifications, implement the minimum curriculum in compulsory subjects and the general education program designated for this type of school, and implement principles of evaluation, classification, and promotion of pupils set by the Ministery.

However, a non-public school may obtain public school rights, most notably the privilege to bestow national certificates or diplomas, if it implements the minimum curriculum program, applies official principles of classification and promotion of pupils, and employs fully certified teachers. Such non-public schools receive financial subsidies from the local or national budget. The amount of the subsidy varies according to a formula, but has been steadily increasing. Indeed, it is even possible to be granted 100 percent of the current expenses carried by public schools or education centers of the same type, allocated on a per pupil basis.

In 1994, there were 338 non-public preschools in Poland (*Glowny Urzad Statystyczny, 1995*). By 2002/03, the number had risen to 901, most run by religious organizations and individuals. However, the impact of privatization at the preschool level is relatively small: in the same school year, only 5 percent of children attended such institutions; the rest were in public preschools. At the primary school level, it was a mere 1 percent. Non-public lower secondary schools accounted for 1.4 percent of the total student population, and at the upper secondary general school level the proportion is about 3.5 percent. At the two types of upper secondary vocational schools, the percentage is 1.3 percent (Eurybase, 2005).

However, this completely changes at the level of higher education. By the end of 1993, 36 non-public institutions had been founded; by 1995 there were 80 (*Glowny Urzad Statystyczny,* 1996). Incredibly, by 2002/03 there were 1,828 nonpublic postsecondary institutions, enrolling 47.3 percent of the total postsecondary student population (Eurybase, 2005). The greatest numbers of these institutions are in the postsecondary and higher education vocational schools. The privatization of postsecondary education in Poland has been dramatic.

Special Needs Education. Although there is some, very limited, integration of special needs students into mainstream schools, most special needs students are educated in either specialized schools separate from the public school system or in designated classrooms in mainstream schools (EuryDice, 2004).

Adult Education. Educators and economists realize that adult and nonformal education has an increasingly important role to play in economic and cultural development (Bogard, 1992). New socioeconomic circumstances in Poland underline the significance of adult education as an important element of employment programs. Traditionally, adult education is administered within the formal education system and embraces all levels and types of education: primary, secondary, and higher. There are extramural courses that can take the form of day schooling, evening classes, correspondence courses, and university extension. Candidates must be over 17 years of age.

In recent years, nongovernmental organizations, community groups, teachers' organizations, cultural and artistic organizations, and youth organizations have initiated adult education projects. Such groups are also often involved in programs run by government agencies. New open and distance education programs are also being implemented. These include any form of learning not under the persistent or direct observation of teachers or instructors, but which nevertheless benefits from the planning and delivery of a tutorial organization. These modes include a large element of autonomous learning and hence are greatly dependent on the instructional arrangement of materials.

All these initiatives demonstrate the growing roles and different forms of contemporary adult education, training, and retraining. They are also responses to the increasing demand for education in Poland. These are radical changes in the structure and delivery of education.

Teacher Training

Since 1989, much attention has been paid to reshaping initial and in-service teacher training programs. However, fundamental or revolutionary changes have not resulted; only some innovations in content and methods have been made. Indeed, even the major reforms initiated in 1999 have yet to generate policies to significantly impact the education of teachers.

In Poland, there are three basic approaches to teacher education, and they are implemented in three types of teacher training institutions. Universities provide academically oriented programs; teacher training colleges focus on practically oriented programs; pedagogical universities offer combined programs.

Over several decades now, there has been an increasing trend to assimilate teaching training into universities. Under universities, we include both universities and higher education teacher training institutes attached to polytechnics, economics academies, agricultural academies, medical academies, and academies of music, fine arts, and physical education. To a certain degree, pedagogical universities (founded after World War II) and a new form of three-year teacher training colleges (established in the early 1990s) can be included in this sector as well (*Ministerstwo Edukacji Narodowej,* 1994). Interestingly, these diverse teacher training institutions seem increasingly to be embracing and copying the orientations of universities. As a result, the university model dominates the country's teacher training programs.

Eleven Polish universities train teachers for all subjects in the primary school curriculum and offer courses for secondary school teaching candidates in over twenty disciplines. Teacher preparation programs for preschools have also appeared in universities. University programs provide five-year, full-time, M.A. or M.Sc. courses in particular disciplines, usually combined with some education training. Students graduate with degrees that provide them with advance disciplinary knowledge in school-related subjects. such as history, mathematics, philology, geography, biology, and so on. Concurrently, they obtain teaching qualifications for both elementary and secondary school levels.

This approach to teacher training has been under attack for some time now. For example, a 1992 Ministry of Education report lamented that "The role of universities in training fully qualified teachers is declining . . . as some of them completely abandon pedagogical training and others reduce the amount of time spent on it. They no longer comply with the specified minimum hours for teacher training subjects" (Republic, 1992, p. 57). To understand why this is the case, it must be appreciated that in the Polish academic tradition the accent is on subject expertise. Therefore, students, including teachers in training, until recently were required to take just one discipline over five years of university studies. It was not until 2004 that the Ministry of Education decreed that students beginning a teacher training program in September of that year must be competent to teach two subjects, not just one; in addition, new students are now required to take increased hours of professional training, gain competence in information technology, and master a foreign language (EuryDice, 2004).

In response, at the beginning of the 1990s, three-year teacher training colleges were established to promote a skill-based and more practically directed approach to teacher education. One of the core innovations in the college arrangement is the emphasis placed on practical training. This includes lesson preparation, questioning, interpersonal communication, classroom management, and evaluation skills. It is argued that carefully planned, arranged, and supervised teaching practice is the most fundamental qualification of a fully prepared teacher. These institutions are still a novelty in the system, though in recent years they have come to be regarded as the best models for training elementary school teachers, especially those in the early grades.

The third form of teacher education is offered by nine state-maintained pedagogical universities, established in the last fifty years. As time went on these institutions, called *higher pedagogical schools,* became more and more similar to universities. They obtained full academic rights and, like universities, offered undergraduate, graduate, and postgraduate courses. They run five-year courses in both single-subject areas and in groups of disciplines associated with broader education studies.

However, in contrast to universities, pedagogical universities have harmonized education studies with academic subject areas. In consequence, there is a balance between professional training and single-subject academic knowledge. Pedagogical universities organize practical experiences for prospective teachers in the regular classrooms of public schools and, at the same time, strong support and guidance exists within the program. However, in spite of intentions, this combination of theoretical studies and practical training often lacks coherent and well-thought-through education objectives and is inclined to emphasize and accredit narrow teaching competencies. Ultimately, such a narrow professional focus is inconsistent with the wider roles teachers and schools are called upon to play in Poland's rapidly changing society.

Teacher Certification, Titles, and Ranks

To teach at the primary and preprimary level, one can take university-type higher studies of three or five years in length. Alternately, a teacher training college can be studied at for three years. Lower secondary schools have the same certification requirements. Upper secondary schools require five years of university-type studies. The degree of *Licencjat* is awarded for three years of university-type studies; five years earns a *Majister* degree; teacher training colleges award diplomas.

In addition to differential qualifications to teach at the upper secondary level, there are also clear differences in status in the teaching profession. As of 2004, there are four categories of teachers: trainee teacher, contract teacher, appointed teacher, and chartered teacher. Additionally, chartered teachers who have outstanding records may be awarded, upon rare occasion, the title "honorary school education professor" (Socrates-Erasmus, 2005). One begins a career as a trainee teacher, which lasts for one year. Upon successful promotion to contract teacher, another successful tenure of almost three years is required for promotion to appointed teacher. However, beyond that, promotion becomes very difficult. Chartered teachers have evaluation and mentoring responsibilities and are recognized as not only senior but also expert teachers (Eurybase, 2005).

Furthermore, parents' councils are not only involved in, but literally determine, promotions. There are also substantial differences in salary. The average salary of a trainee teacher equals 82 percent of a stipulated and annually updated basic salary for state employees. Contract teachers receive 125 percent, appointed teachers receive 175 percent, and chartered teachers receive 225 percent of the average salary of a trainee teacher. In the 2002/03 school year, 5.5 percent of teachers in Poland were trainee teachers; 14 percent contract teachers; 72.4 percent appointed teachers, and 7.4 percent chartered teachers (leaving .5 percent in an "other" category) (Eurybase, 2005). Clearly, in Poland, all teachers are not created equal.

SUCCESSES, CHALLENGES, AND DEBATES

Poland is a nation that has undergone profound transformations since 1939. A cultured and proud nation was, as noted above, literally turned into a pile of rubble through the tragic events of WWII; an entire generation lost both its infrastructure and its schooling. The subjugation to communism saw both a complete reversal of culture and ideology, as well as a frantic effort to rebuild and re-educate. Next came consolidation; a new social consciousness had to be shaped by communist ideology; its antithetical predecessor had to be eradicated from an entire nation. Then, the task half completed, the Marxist era ended and Poland had to rediscover herself. The task was profoundly complicated by an economic catastrophe that still leaves scars today. Now reforms are everywhere and, with membership in the EU, are guaranteed to continue into the indefinite future.

The turmoil was and is such that it is difficult to break this section into three distinct categories. The categories overlap. What is seen as success by some is a huge blunder to others and a topic of profound debate; what are challenges to some are merely the effects of an unwise retreat from the successes of the past and fodder for heated debate about the future. Judging the past, present, and future is a matter of perspective. Accordingly, the issues brought up below will be discussed under one encompassing category.

Education Reforms and Social Transformation

Education reform, in the shape of important changes in education policies, objectives, and structures, is an internal part of social transformation; it has repercussions beyond the education system itself. In other words, the idea of education reform is linked to broader ideas of societal change.

The changing education system in Poland is part of a more complex and long-term transition in politics, economy, and culture, as well as in social structure and public attitudes. The withdrawal of the socialist system cannot be considered as "a simple transition" but rather as "an inversion of the whole system: from a totalitarian, self-referential society to a democratic and open society providing the widest political, economic and social freedom for all individuals" (Wichmann, 1996, p. 1).

Two elements have particularly important roles in the transformation of an education system: redefining education objectives and creating new education policies and administrative structures to implement the new objectives.

Redefining Education Objectives. Today, school objectives focus on shaping virtues such as initiative, the ability to take risks, responsibility, creativity, imagination, self-sufficiency, and so on. Before, during the communist era, the centralized school system hardly reacted to new situations and challenges created by scientific, technological, and economic changes. An old-fashioned concept prevailed in the post-war period: The ideal of political leaders and factory managers was the obedient and faithful worker.

Another fundamental change in education objectives after the communist withdrawal was a shift in emphasis that involved accepting the principle of individualization; a recognition of differences in students' personal, intellectual, emotional, and practical skills according to their physical and psychological development. The previous dogmatic collectivism, ready to sacrifice the unfolding of the individual in the name of an abstract common personality, was rejected.

Yet another major change is rejection of the ideological uniformity and official indoctrination that had been imposed on schools during the communist period. This is expressed in the idea that public schools ought to be neutral or objective in matters concerning ideology and attitudes. However, in Poland this principle remains unrealized. Since the communist withdrawal, public schools have become an arena of religious inculcation. As early as 1990, the government introduced religion classes in all elementary and secondary schools. Thus (although the rights of religious minorities were legally protected), public education became *de facto* denominational with the granting of special status to Roman Catholicism.

Following the official sanction of religion classes in public schools, the Roman Catholic Church has become more active in debates on education philosophy. Officially,

Catholics (strongly supported by the Church) call for "critical independent thinking and free choice," an "active involvement in a democratically reformed Poland which promotes responsible social participation by the individual," and "an education system founded on philosophy which advances individualism, self-education and continuing education" (Nowak-Fabrykowski & Sosnowski, 1995, p. 57). In reality, however, they represent conservative and dogmatic modes of reasoning on education matters and tend to dominate the whole system.

Another recent main development is the efforts directed toward rebuilding national autonomy and national identity. The education system is viewed as an important instrument in preserving the nation's cultural unity. In official education documents, it is clearly advocated that the provision of knowledge and skills in schools, as well as the development of students' intellectual abilities, emotional responsiveness, and ethical civic values, should be based on national values.

Finally, tolerance is advocated. While internationalism, equity among individuals, and solidarity with oppressed people and those fighting for their freedom were ideological cornerstones of education in the former socialist model of education, in fact, racial, religious, national, and ethnic biases and prejudices did not diminish. On the contrary: They remained sharp. Ironically, today—as the economic conditions of the country rebound from the deteriorated conditions of the 1990s and early 2000s, these biases and prejudices are becoming accentuated. Great divides—economic, educational, and cultural—characterize Polish society. The progress down the path of equality of opportunity made under the Soviet regime has been reversed.

Creating New Education Policies and Administrative Structures. With the fall of communism, the Polish state's monopoly on establishing and running schools was broken. Non-state schools were opened at various levels of the system and with various specializations. At the end of 1980s, there were only ten non-public (that is, not run by the state) schools, compared to 25,000 public schools. In 1995 the number of non-public schools reached 1,300 (OECD, 1995). Today, as noted above, while the percentage of students in non-public schools is low, postsecondary schooling has been appropriated by non-public institutions.

With regard to the management and administration of education, post-communist governments pursue a policy of decentralization. For almost half century, the system of education in Poland was strongly centralized. The decision-making center, moreover, was placed outside the Ministry of National Education; that is, in the Central Committee of the governing communist party. The Ministry, as well as lower divisions of education administration, was only expected to implement directives coming from that center. At the local levels of the formal education structure, there were almost no decisions made on school management or curricula. The result was curricular stagnation. Extreme uniformity killed teachers' curricular and methodological initiatives and at the same time lowered the quality of education.

Thus, elimination of excessive administrative control and supervision became an essential task. Hierarchical management structures were abandoned in favor of horizontal ones. All schools of a given type are no longer required to apply precisely the same curriculum, work in exactly the same organizational conditions, and use only one textbook.

This means fewer directives from above and more cooperation at the grassroots level. Most decision making has been delegated to education councils (school, local, and national), which are composed of representatives of teachers, parents, students, and local communities. In 1996 the responsibility for running pre-primary, primary, and certain secondary schools was transferred from the government administration to local self-governments. At the same time, higher education institutions were granted extensive autonomy with regard to both curricula and organizational arrangements. The reforms of 1999 continue this trend.

However, these changes must not be interpreted as a full, radical decentralization of schooling in Poland. The new education regulations have also established a new hierarchy of decision making and responsibility. The Ministry of National Education and Sports coordinates and implements state education policy, supervises local education superintendents, and decides on every regional education program. This power is exercised through control of the purse strings—local initiatives are financed at the discretion of the Ministry. Thus, the system of educational management remains centralized but allows some modifications to reward and encourage local participation.

When we turn to reforms that have been centrally initiated, we find changes in methods, means, and organization of education. However, the most important change has been an attitudinal one. In sharp contrast to the orientation of the communist era, central and local educational authorities, as well as educational researchers, are in agreement that schools should provide students with an education corresponding as much as possible to their individual abilities and interests.

Teaching Democracy and Teaching about Democracy

Developing democratic competencies and democratic behavior is considered an indispensable primary task of contemporary Polish formal education. The phrase *teaching democracy* is frequently understood as providing opportunities for self-education during which students can develop and organize their personal experiences, acquire specific competencies, and gain knowledge about the possible implementation of democratic procedures in future professional activities. The emphasis placed on the development of these competencies is a result of the view that democracy is a dynamic process, and thus a democratic society is process oriented. Social, institutional, and government changes occur in democratic societies faster than in other societies. Accordingly, it is not the task of schools to inculcate students with static prescriptions for behavior. Rather, it is to help them learn how to cope with change and to develop adaptive strategies.

Curricular Innovation

Two major, but antithetical, perspectives underlie recent moves to elaborate new curricula for both elementary and secondary schools. The first emphasizes an unlimited autonomy for teachers and school administrators; the second advocates a precise specification of subject matter and lessons in every subject and period of teaching. These two opposing perspectives can be found in all debates on education policy in post-communist countries.

As early as 1990, alternative teaching programs, consistent with the state core curriculum, became permitted. That was a prologue to major changes in the whole education system. Under the former, overly centralized decision-making system, the teacher's task was content transmission. The curriculum drawn up at the central level was the same for the entire country. With the successive introduction of alternative teaching programs by post-communist governments, a systemic school reform has been initiated.

However, with diversity, it then became necessary to devise mechanisms for ensuring equivalency in the new curricula. Such a guarantee is contained in the core curriculum, established centrally by the Ministry of Education. This takes the form of curriculum guidelines, which serve as education canons in general education. In other words, the Ministry rejected a detailed central curriculum, but at the same time deemed the core curriculum indispensable—and is enforcing its teaching through newly devised and revised standardized tests.

Gender, Schooling, and Jobs

In the last few decades, vocational schools at all levels have been rapidly expanded. However, the student population is predominantly male because of the historically deep-rooted social convention that technical or artisan occupations are appropriate for boys, while girls are better served by studies for clerical, medical (nursing), teaching, commercial, and similar professions. The ironic side effect of that assumption is a considerable increase in higher education opportunities for females. While males numerically dominate upper secondary vocational schools; females are predominant in the upper secondary general school population.

That social phenomenon was not predicted by policymakers; they had unconsciously created a condition for overcoming schooling gender discrimination resulting from traditional sex role stereotyping in Polish society. Figures show that women are surpassing men, at least at the level of attaining a university education. But, this is not reflected in terms of jobs. Entrance to higher positions is still much more difficult for women than for men. Thus, there is a pressing need for action (including legislation) that will diminish discrimination against women in the workplace and in vocational training at the upper secondary and higher education levels.

The Market Economy and Vocational and Higher Education

The objectives of vocational training clearly represent a shift from serving the requirements of a centrally planned economy to serving a market economy. Upper secondary vocational schools are now viewed as instruments for implementing professional training that emphasizes an ability to transfer core skills to new situations, an ability to adjust to a rapidly changing occupational environment, competence in occupational skills, and habits that complement work, community expectations, and adult life. Thus, there is a conscious tendency to form a bridge between general and vocational education. The result is that today there is a basis for building a competitive national economy and developing a high standard of production technologies and expert services. In terms of both national business development and international economic relations, it is only logical that attention is being focused on preparing highly skilled and professional technical managerial staff.

However, this takes money—money of which Poland does not have sufficient quantities. In particular, schools at all levels need to sufficiently equipped with modern teaching aids. The present inadequate supply of computers, electronic books, journals, and so on, must be overcome. Special emphasis needs be placed on preparing the young for the information society, new technologies, and a scientific environment.

CONCLUDING COMMENTS

Today, perhaps for the first time in the modern history of Poland, neither a strong sense of national identity nor a pervasive ideology/religion are being emphasized in official state documents on education. Hence, it can cautiously be said that recent education guidelines are free of overt ideological content. However, as emphasized earlier, it must be remembered that Catholic fundamentalism continues to play a very significant role in the country's education system.

Polish educators and education policymakers and planners recognize that Poland is a rapidly changing society and that education reforms have serious social implications for the future. Yet, what OECD inspectors advised a decade ago still holds today: "A reformed educational system will form the surest base on which the new Polish social order may be built" (OECD, 1996, p. 2). As noted above, the reforms of 1999 have almost found their way into full implementation. Little is left to be done; all Poles can do is allow the next decade to document whether the right choices were made.

REFERENCES

Bogard, G. (1992). *For a socializing type of adult education: Report.* Strasbourg: Council for Cultural Cooperation.

Bureau for Academic Recognition and International Exchange. (2005). The Polish System of Education. Online. Accessed February 4, 2005, from http://www.buwiwm.edu.pl/educ/educ.htm#primary

CIA. (2005, February 10). *The world factbook: Poland.* Online. Accessed February 4, 2005, from http://www.odci.gov/cia/publications/factbook/print/pl.html

Eurybase: The Information DataBase on Education Systems in Europe. (2005). *The education system in Poland (2002/2003).* Online. Accessed February 4, 2005, from http://www.eurydice.org/Eurybase/Application/frameset.asp?country=PL&language=EN

EuryDice. (2004, December). *Summary sheets on education systems in Europe: Poland.* Online. Accessed February 4, 2005, from http://www.eurydice.org/Documents/Fiches_nationales/en/frameset_EN.html

Glowny Urzad Statystyczny (1995). *Rocznik statystyczny GUS* (Polish statistical yearbook). LV. Warszawa: GUS.

Government of Poland, Ministry of Foreign Affairs. (2005). Online. Accessed February 4, 2005, from http://www.poland.gov.pl/?document=1627

International Associations of Universities. (2005). Online. Accessed February 4, 2005, from http://www.euroeducation.net/prof/polaco.htm

Jakubielski, L. (2002). *Reform in a changing society: The case of Poland.* Online. Accessed February 4, 2005, from http://www.umich.edu/~iinet/crees/outreach/jakubielski.htm

Karczewski, J. (2005). *Education and the economy.* Online. Accessed February 4, 2005, from http://www.masterpage.com.pl/outlook/lms.html

Karwowska-Struczyk, M. (1996). *Who is caring for young children in Poland?* Online. Accessed June 24, 1996, from http://biz.map.com/polfined.html

Kasprzyk, M. (2004). *The history of Poland.* Online. Accessed February 4, 2005, from http://www.kasprzyk.demon.co.uk/www/HistoryPolska.html

Kozakiewicz, M. (1990). Educational research and Polish perestroika. *Prospects, 20,* 41–48.

Kwiecinski, Z. (1995). *The sociopathology of education.* Torun: Edytor.

Ministerstwo Edukacji Narodowej. (1994). *Glowne kierunki doskonalenia systemu edukacji w Polsce* (Main directions of Polish education system improvement). Warszawa: MEN.

Morody, M. (1993). *Spoleczenstwo polskie w procesie przemian* (Polish society in the process of transformation). In M. Grabowska & A. Sutek (Eds.), *Polska 1989–1992. Fragmenty pejzazu* (Poland in 1989–1992. Fragments of the social and political landscape). Warszawa: IFiS PAN.

Nowak-Fabrykowski, K., & Sosnowski, A. (1995). Education in transition: Changes in the Polish school system. *Canadian and International Education, 24,* 55–64.

Nowicka, W. (2005). *Factors affecting women's health in eastern and central Europe with particular emphasis on infectious diseases, mental, environmental and reproductive health.* Online. Accessed February 4, 2005, from http://www.un.org/womenwatch/daw/csw/factors.htm

Organization for Economic Cooperation and Development (OECD). (1995). *Raport na temat polityki edukacyjnej w Polsce. Raport i pytania wizytatorow* (Report on education policy in Poland. Report and questions of the OECD examiners). Warszawa. (Manuscript in the author's collection.)

Organization for Economic Cooperation and Development (OECD). (1996). *Review of education policy in Poland: Examiners' report and questions.* Paris. (Manuscript in the author's collection.)

Republic of Poland, Ministry of National Education. (1992). *The development of education in Poland in 1990–1991.* Warsaw: MEN.

Socrates-Erasmus Programme in Poland. (2005). *The education system in Poland.* Online. Accessed February 4, 2005, from http://www.socrates.org.pl/erasmus/en/education_system.html

Topolski, J. (1992). *Historia Polski* (History of Poland). Warszawa-Krakow: Poloczek.

Urban-Klaehn, J. (2000a). *Changes in education system in Poland (III).* Online. Accessed February 4, 2005, from http://www.bellaonline.com/Article.asp?id=622

Urban-Klaehn, J. (2000b). *Education system in Poland—overview—Maturity Exam (I).* Online. Accessed February 4, 2005, from http://www.bellaonline.com/Article.asp?id=618

Urban-Klaehn, J. (2000c). *Reforms in education system in Poland–public or private? (II).* Online. Accessed February 4, 2005, from http://www.bellaonline.com/Article.asp?id=621

Ustawa z 15 lipca 1961 o rozwoju systemu oswiaty i wychowania (Act of July 15, 1961, on the development of the system of education). *Dziennik Ustaw Polskiej Rzeczypospolitej Ludowej, 32.*

Ustawa z 7 wrzesnia 1991 o systemie oswiaty (Act of the Education System of September 7, 1991). *Dziennik Ustaw Rzeczypospolitej Polskiej, 95,* point 425.

Wichmann, J. (1996, October). *The transformation of educational systems in central and eastern Europe: Prospects and problems.* Paper presented at the 17th CESE Conference, Athens.

Part V

NORTH AMERICAN NEIGHBORS

Worlds Apart

CHAPTER FOURTEEN

MEXICAN EDUCATION

A Melding of History, Cultural Roots, and Reforms

ALINA GAMBOA

CAROLINE LINSE

THE SOCIAL FABRIC

Modern Mexico is made up of 31 states and the Federal District, which is the capital, better known as Mexico City. The population of Mexico, estimated at 100 million, is mostly *mestizo.* This is a mixed ethnicity of European and indigenous heritage, with some of its members mostly European and some mostly indigenous. A roughly estimated 10 percent of the population is made up of 56 different ethnic groups, many of whom still speak their own indigenous languages (Vargas, 1995).

Mexico has a geographic area of 1.97 million square kilometers (1.25 million square miles) with 11,000 kilometers (6,800 miles) of coastline. The terrain is very diverse and encompasses breathtaking landscapes. In addition to well-known beaches, there are deserts, tropical areas, forests, and lakes. There are many mountainous areas with elevations up to 5,000 meters (15,000 feet). Mexico is blessed with plenty of rainfall and fertile soil for

Alina Gamboa is currently a Ph.D. student the Department of Politics and International Studies at the University of Warwick. Her doctoral research is examining the creation of microregions in Mexico and Central America, with a special emphasis on the role of education in development. She holds a master's in International Political Economy, where she focused on the impact of education on Mexico's development and social inequality. Prior to postgraduate study, she worked as the press attaché for the British Embassy in Mexico City, where she had extensive contact with several Mexican Government Ministries, including the Ministry of Public Education (SEP).

An Associate Professor at Sook Myung University in Seoul, Korea, Dr. Caroline Linse has over twenty-five years of teaching and research experience in the United States, Mexico, American Samoa, the Baltics, Belarus, and Korea. She has worked with learners of all ages from preschool through graduate school. As the author of a wide range of both academic and practical publications, she is especially interested in helping teachers tailor educational experiences to build upon their local cultural context. She has recently finished conducting a study in Belarus entitled "The Power of English Teachers: The Women Who Bridge the East with the West."

agriculture. There are abundant natural resources, such as the metals and minerals that attracted its colonial conquerors, crude oil and natural gas, as well as materials used in construction.

Mexico's geographic diversity, combined with a lack of infrastructure in many regions, has brought disparity in the development of its different regions, particularly in remote areas inhabited by indigenous peoples (Aguirre, 2002). At the same time, Mexico's geographical location between the United States and Central America offers both advantages and disadvantages. The U.S.–Mexico border region extends more than 3,100 kilometers (2,000 miles) from the Gulf of Mexico to the Pacific Ocean, and 100 kilometers (62.5 miles) on each side of the international border. This large border allows for extensive trade to take place between the two nations, notwithstanding the problems that are also attributed to this area.

There are numerous immigrants from Central America who have settled in Mexico or traveled through to reach the United States. This is in addition to the emigrants who leave Mexico and enter the United States both legally and illegally. The numerous points of entry between the two nations aggravate the drug trafficking problem between Mexico and the United States.

The Mexican economy is closely linked to the United States through trade. Since the implementation of the North American Free Trade Agreement (NAFTA) in 1994, the Mexican economy has converged with the U.S. business cycle. Trade has become the motor of growth, but has made Mexico vulnerable to U.S. downturns. Exports to the United States (89 percent of all exports) account for nearly 25 percent of GDP.

Mexico entered into the twenty-first century as the tenth largest economy in the world. Nevertheless, 32 percent of the population lives in extreme poverty, subsisting on less than $2 dollars per day. There is 9.57 percent rate of illiteracy, and there exist high levels of inequality (Cuetara, 2001). Inequality, combined with periods of economic instability and a growing debt, are some of the factors that keep Mexico in the category of 'developing nation' or 'emerging economy.'

Indigenous groups are the most affected by the poverty cycle. Most of the indigenous population has been left out of the mainstream Mexican economy. In fact, more than 80 percent of members of indigenous groups in Mexico live in poverty in comparison to less than 20 percent of members of nonindigenous groups (Iglesias, 1998). The extreme marginalization of the indigenous population has been brought to international attention through the emergence of insurgent groups such as the Zapatista National Liberation Army and the Popular Revolutionary Army, which claim to look after the interests of the indigenous people forgotten by government.

Brief History of Mexico

To understand the complicated and complex education system of Mexico and the pervasive influence of institutions such as the Catholic Church and the Secretariat of Public Education (SEP), it is necessary to make a brief excursion along the bookshelf of time. Contemporary Mexican education should be viewed in terms of the melding of its history, cultural roots, and education reforms.

The first name of the country was the Viceroyalty of New Spain. During a 300-year colonial period, the flavors of the pre-Columbian cultures merged with those of the European continent. Today, visitors can see evidence of Mexico's indigenous and European history as great pre-Columbian pyramids stand next to colonial buildings throughout the central and southern areas.

It was in the early sixteenth century that the Spaniards began to colonize Mexico. In 1519, five priests joined Hernan Cortes as he conquered the Aztecs. Within six years, both the Franciscans and Jesuits had arrived in an attempt to convert the indigenous peoples to Catholicism (Grayson, 1992). The pre-Reformation version of Catholicism that arrived in Mexico with the Spanish Conquistadores was highly elitist and intent on imposing the Spanish language and beliefs on the conquered people. Many of the orders, particularly the Jesuits, established schools that functioned to spread the scope of the Catholic Church in Mexico, help individuals maintain an allegiance to Spain, and generate profit.

When Mexico claimed its independence in 1821, it was double the size of the United States of America and reached all the way up to the California–Oregon border (Anna, 1998). Independence in 1821 and the first attempts toward government engendered a struggle for power between conservatives and liberals. The conservatives, backed by the Church, were intent on establishing a monarchical system and keeping close ties with Europe. The meddling of the Church during this period brought about the installment of Iturbide as emperor in 1821, who was toppled within a year by the liberal government officials.

In the costly U.S.-Mexico War that lasted from 1846 to 1848, over one-third of Mexican territory was lost to the United States. Santa Anna, the president of Mexico at the time, first agreed to give up territory in the peace treaty of Guadalupe Hidalgo that ended the war; he then agreed to sell further territories. This loss of land heightened the debate between liberals and conservatives.

Ten years later, the Church, in conjunction with France and backed by the conservative faction, installed Maximillian of Austria as emperor in Mexico. In 1857, the liberal president, Benito Juarez, restored the republic. In 1859, President Juarez declared the separation of Church and state. The Church was not allowed to own property, clergy was not allowed to wear religious clothing in public or be involved in public education, and the Church was to remain completely out of politics. If Church leaders violated, or rather were caught violating, any of these laws, they would lose their tax-free status.

The ongoing struggle for political stability turned into a thirty-year dictatorship from 1876 to 1911 with Porfirio Diaz at its head. During the regime, social inequality and injustice prevailed even as investment and modernization were encouraged. Railroads were built and industry grew in urban areas. In the rural areas, land was concentrated in large plantation-like *haciendas.*

The 1910 Revolution designed to overthrow the dictator Porfirio Diaz was also intended to attain land reform by bringing about regime change. Although regime change was attained, the redistribution of land was only partially achieved and revolutionary leader Emiliano Zapata openly attacked the new government's land reform as being conformist and not equal throughout the country.

After the Revolution, however, a process of reconstruction began, even while lacking agrarian reform. A new Constitution was drafted in 1917. From 1920 until the 1950s, the amount of funding allocated to the military declined to prevent the military from becoming an important political player (Cothran, 1994).

Prior to the 1910 Revolution, the illiteracy rate was estimated to be 68 to 78 percent (Vaughan, 1990). Certainly, during the nineteenth century, primary education was not reserved just for the wealthy elite; many children who were considered to be poor attended school (Vaughan, 1990). Nevertheless, in the late nineteenth and early twentieth centuries, the purpose of education for indigenous peoples was to make them "civilized" (Hatfield, 1998).

The 1917 Constitution decreed that education would be secular, national, and free of charge. Following that lead, the Secretariat of Public Education (SEP) was established in 1922 with the stated objective of confronting the unequal distribution of education in the country and the marginalization of the indigenous population. It is important to note that the term *Secretariat* was used instead of the term *Minister of Education* as in many other countries because those in power wanted to make sure that there was not the slightest possible link between the government and the Catholic Church.

In 1930, popular President Lazaro Cardenas brought unity with his strong stance against property, nationalizing railroads, oil wells, and other industries. His successor solidified the system and strengthened his political party; it would become the National Institutional Party (PRI) that remained in power until the year 2000.

The PRI political party was said to maintain power through coercion, corruption, and eliminating any real opposition, instead of through popular support. For example, the PRI exerted its power into the classrooms in many different ways. PRI officials were often SEP officials as well. The teachers' union was also closely aligned with the PRI party and the membership even carried out party political activities in the regions (Cortina, 1992).

Over the following decades, the Mexican system developed into a highly centralized government. It maintained political power, wealth, and industry close to Mexico City, the capital, which grew and developed disproportionately compared to the rest of the nation. During this period, the country withstood two economic crises, a massive devaluation of the currency, spiraling inflation, several structural adjustment plans, an increasing foreign debt, and political assassinations (Newell & Rubio, 1998). At the same time, the SEP evolved into a huge highly centralized and bureaucratic machine. By the early 1980s, the SEP was an unwieldy bureaucracy with three quarters of a million staff (Morales-Gomez & Torres, 1990).

Well into the 1980s, the Mexican government followed policies of protectionism and industrialization financed through foreign borrowing and oil revenues. This brought on a debt crisis in 1982, when Mexico threatened to default on its foreign debt. There began several years of austerity and large budget cuts due to a structural adjustment plan imposed on Mexico by the International Monetary Fund. The government began to restructure the economy by opening up trade and selling off government-owned companies.

Nevertheless, in 1983 an education revolution was promoted. The main reform was made to the SEP itself. By 1985, much of the budget and resources had been decentralized, and the process to revert control back to the states and municipalities had begun.

The seventy-year rule of the PRI ended with the election of PAN candidate Vicente Fox in the year 2000. President Fox promised to place the eradication of poverty, economic growth, and education reform at the top of his agenda. By the end of his six-year term, he had made some progress in decentralizing the system and increasing support to the most vulnerable. But, according to many, the steps taken have barely begun to address the fundamental problems of the country.

SCHOOLING SYSTEM IN MEXICO

Mexico is a land of cultural fusion. It is a diverse nation, a kaleidoscope of natural resources, history, culture, and politics. Education in Mexico, as in many other countries, is a product of its geography, demographic makeup, cultural heritage, and history, as well as the underlying economic differences between and within the different regions and social groups.

The modern education system in Mexico is governed by the SEP. The SEP has very strict guidelines that must be adhered to by schools providing instruction to children in preschool through ninth grade. It is not uncommon for one or more persons to be employed by a school with their only work responsibility being to make sure that all of the SEP regulations are followed. This work also includes maintaining records for both staff and students.

In Mexico, school is supposedly free. School-age and preschool-age learners do not have to pay tuition, and primary school students are given textbooks free of charge. Nevertheless, some families can't send their children to school because they need their children to work to help out the family. For other families, extra costs are more than they can afford; consequently, they do not send their children to school, or their children's attendance is irregular. For example, in addition to the required uniforms, teachers generally send home school supply lists and students are usually asked to purchase the exact items on the list. One teacher might require all the students to purchase a specific type of notebook because it will be easier to grade the notebooks if they are all the same. However, frequently the supplies demanded by individual teachers are not the ones that are on sale in the larger stores.

There have been some monetary education grants set up as part of the PROGRESA poverty alleviation program given to the neediest families so that they can cope with the expense of sending children to school. Average monthly benefits currently make up about 22 percent of total income for beneficiary families (Coady & Walker, 2004). However, these programs do not meet the demand and also require that children fulfill a minimum attendance and have passing grades.

Preschool (*Prescolar*)

Mexico has paid attention to the widely held belief in international education circles that children who receive preschool education are more successful academically later on and has decided to make preschool education compulsory for children. In the year 2004–2005, preschool was made compulsory for 5-year-olds. In the year 2005–2006, it became compulsory for 4-year-olds; in the year 2007–2008, it will become mandated for 3-year-olds. Mexico is also very forward thinking with regard to the training of preschool teachers. Preschool teachers are gradually being required to not only possess university education degrees but also degrees in early childhood education.

There are both federal (national level) and state (local) public kindergartens. In small and scattered rural areas, community preschools and indigenous preschools cater to 5-year-olds and are tended to by members of the community. Instruction is often provided to children in their home languages.

Because there are too few public preschools to meet the demand, many private preschools have emerged. Previously, only preschools that were incorporated into the SEP followed the SEP program. But, as this level became compulsory in 2002, the SEP began to set the standards for private preschools, causing some confusion.

During these first years, private schools are having to adjust to the SEP curriculum and school calendar. Private preschools are also grappling with the implementation of the new regulations for qualified teachers. The problem is that the SEP wants all teachers working at the compulsory levels to possess a degree from an accredited early childhood higher education institution. Because of these new regulations, there are some very fine private preschools that have been forced to close their doors since their teachers (who might hold a BA in another subject) do not meet the stringent requirements set forth by SEP.

Primary School (*Escuela primaria*)

Primary school begins for children at the age of 6 and lasts for six years, until the age of 12. Primary school is compulsory and schools must comply with the official SEP-mandated curriculum and the official 200-day calendar. Children who successfully complete the six-year program receive a *Certificado de Primaria,* which is essential for employment.

Primary schools are divided into public and private schools. There are four categories within the public sector of government-funded schools. General schools (95 percent of the total) have a school director and in most cases a minimum of one teacher per grade. There are also bilingual/bicultural indigenous schools (about 3.5 percent) that are frequently run by the National Council for Educational Development and the National Indigenous Institute, specialized alternative agencies within the SEP. In unitary schools (about 1 percent) there is a single teacher for several grades. The final category is the special needs schools (about 0.5 percent).

Middle School (*Secundaria*)

Middle school is compulsory. It lasts approximately three years and usually caters to young people aged 12 to 15 or 16. Just as for primary school, the SEP provides a very strict curriculum that must be followed. Within the public school system, there exist several options for middle school.

General middle school accepts the majority of students who complete primary school. These will complete their course by fulfilling the minimum levels required for finishing school or for continuing into high school.

The technical or vocational middle school also equips students with the middle school graduation standards necessary to enter high school. However, students who attend these schools receive an additional skills certificate in areas such as industry, agriculture, fishing, and/or forestry. Approximately 27 percent of middle school students opt for this type of education.

The Workers' Middle School (*Secundaria para trabajadores*), occasionally referred to as Night School, is aimed at older learners and is usually arranged by employers with large numbers of employees. The education programs provide workers with specific technical skills necessary to do their jobs and also with literacy and numeracy skills.

High School (*Preparatoria*)

High School is three years in length and can consist of academic classes and, in some cases, vocational courses. The ages of learners range from 16 to 19 years. Those who wish to continue into higher education can choose from three different types of education: general, academic pre-professional qualifications, or vocational schools that give technical training that prepares students for the labor market. Some "two-pronged" senior high schools prepare students for entering into higher education and also provide graduates with technical training coupled with the diploma of a "skilled technician."

There are also special polytechnic high schools. These public government-funded schools provide students with specialized instruction in math and science and computers; even, in some places, instruction in tourism. The educational programs offered in the polytechnic high schools usually feed into polytechnic or technological universities (public or private) that focus on math and sciences.

In addition, there are public and private high schools that are affiliated with tertiary institutions. Like the polytechnic high schools, these schools serve as feeder institutions to higher education establishments. Although it is not guaranteed that high school graduates will be admitted to an affiliated university, it is often considered a more efficient way to prepare to enter a specific higher education institution.

Private Schools

According to the SEP, as of the year 2000, 8 percent of students in grades 1 to 12 were enrolled in private schools. All private schools must follow the SEP curriculum for school-age learners. At the middle school level, a few select private schools are allowed to opt out of following the SEP program and students then can "revalidate" their studies by taking exams and obtaining a *Certificado de Secundaria* (middle school) for fulfilling the required standards at the level.

There are numerous types of private schools. Catholic schools are more common than any other kind, in spite of conscious efforts to minimize the Catholic Church's role in educational affairs. Throughout Mexico, there are also bilingual schools that offer instruction in English and Spanish with a wide range of time spent in the study of English each week. In Mexico City, a parent can send a child to a bilingual school where the child will learn in English and in another language such as German or French. As well, schools in different parts of Mexico are accredited to offer the International Baccalaureate Program in Spanish and other languages.

Private school education is not just limited to the wealthy; individuals from a variety of socioeconomic backgrounds choose to enroll their children in private schools (Martin, 2003). Many reasons underlie this choice. First, we could consider the couple who has a 4-year-old daughter and lives in Guadalajara. The mother works as a housekeeper in the mornings and the father works six days a week as a laborer. There are not any openings in the public preschool that is close to the couple's Guadalajara apartment, and the couple comes from a small town and doesn't have any relatives who can look after their child. Although the price of tuition is only a little less than what the mother earns, the parents feel that they are getting their daughter off to a good start by sending her to a private school. At the other end of the spectrum is a family where both parents are physicians. They hope that their 3-year-old son will pass the entrance exam so that he can attend a very expensive elite bilingual (English-Spanish) school. In between are middle-class families who scrimp and save so that they can send their children to the best school that they can afford. Unfortunately, there are situations where a child may start in a private school but will have to drop out because the family's financial situation has changed or the tuition has been raised to such a level that it is no longer within the family's reach.

Targeted Groups of Learners

Mexico has recognized that there are specific groups of learners who could be identified as at risk for not reaching their potential. The government, and in some cases private entities, are trying to meet the needs of these learners.

Street Children. With an estimated 1 million street children worldwide (UNESCO, 2003), this is a global problem, not just confined to Mexico. However, according to the 2001 SEP report, there are approximately 130,000 street children in Mexico (although NGOs such as Caza Alianza estimate up to 15 percent more).

In Mexico, street children are especially visible in large cities. They are often found begging or doing stunts at major intersections while motorists wait for the light to change from red to green. For example, a boy may jump out in the middle of the street and juggle balls or lie on broken glass. They jump up and then bang on the windows of the cars for coins. Some of these children often turn to glue or solvent sniffing in a desperate attempt to lessen their pain.

Both private and public agencies are trying to address the needs of these children. For example, some groups have set up centers where children can come for tortillas and soup and are often given free clothes. Christian groups of Mexican as well as foreign missionaries have set up innovative education programs, working with children on the street as well as trying to get them off the streets.

It is not uncommon for children to have dropped out of schools because of learning disabilities or embarrassment because they are behind their peers and are placed in groups with children up to four years younger. Many are unable to attend because they work during school hours and, if they were to go to school, they would be turned away from most schools that require them to provide a permanent address, basic materials, uniforms, and a parent/guardian. Missionaries provide help to these children, many of whom have special needs with basic literacy instruction.

The 2001–2006 Education Plan for Mexico recognizes the problem of street children's access to education and is designing a program that can be carried out on the streets. Taking into account studies that show how difficult it is for street children to be mainstreamed into a regular classroom, which they often find boring or irrelevant to their street life, this program would have to appeal to children on the streets. The main objective is to provide street children with basic literacy skills as well as life skills necessary for their survival, including health, hygiene, and technical skills. The program has not yet been put into practice, so it cannot be evaluated at this time.

Children with Special Needs. Mexico recognizes its obligation to learners with special needs and has had an office in the SEP responsible for programs for these students since the 1970s (Backhoff, Larrazolo, & Romano, 1995). It is estimated, however, that there are 190,000 disabled or special needs children who have little access to the system as it stands. The problem of providing special needs education is twofold: first, working with parents of children with severe needs to convince them that their children would benefit from an education, and second, having classrooms and teachers equipped for special learning needs.

There is a concentrated effort to make sure that, beginning in preschool, children receive specialized services. For those in the larger cities, it is not uncommon for special education services, including physical therapy in a designated room, to be provided in kindergarten. But like other educational programs and services, these are not uniformly available in every region of the country. In some places, especially Mexico City, the services to individuals with special needs are far more sophisticated than they are in other parts of the country.

There is a great deal of room for improvement in the area of special education. The majority of school buildings (public or private) in Mexico are not handicap accessible. Nor are all teachers provided with the training necessary to address the education needs of children with exceptionalities.

Programs for Indigenous Learners. When people mention the term *bilingual education,* English/Spanish and French/English programs often come to mind. However, in Mexico bilingual and bicultural education is aimed at members of indigenous groups who do not speak Spanish as their primary language.

Mexican education has designed bilingual and bicultural programs to meet the needs of these learners. One of the objectives of the government is to increase dramatically the number of bilingual and bicultural schools aimed at indigenous communities throughout Mexico. The main difficulty of these programs is finding trained teachers whose mother tongue is an indigenous language.

In addition to increasing the number of bilingual programs for children entering the school system, the nature of the programs is changing. In the past, programs were designed only as a bridge to Spanish. Now, however, the philosophical orientation is more enlightened and the hope is also to help children maintain linguistic skills in their home languages. In order to meet this objective, bilingual education is moving into middle schools. This will hopefully help to preserve the indigenous languages of Mexico before they are lost. This is also significant because it shows a formal effort to honor the linguistic heritage of indigenous people in Mexico.

Programs in Rural Areas. The number of students who complete primary basic education in Mexico has been lower in rural areas (especially in the southeast) than in other parts of Mexico (Bracho, 1999). The SEP, constantly examining and reexamining ways to address the needs of students residing in rural areas, has created special programs to meet the needs of these learners.

The *Telesecundaria,* or middle school by satellite television, caters to the needs of learners in small isolated communities where it would otherwise be impossible to provide further than primary education. The Telesecundaria is often the continuation to unitary schools where the satellite is hooked up in the same building used by primary-school-age learners following a request from parents to the local authorities. This request is granted as long as there is a minimum of fifteen students who have completed elementary school (K-6) and who do not have access to a local middle school (Duran, 2001). Books (usually two per subject) to accompany the Telesecundaria are provided to learners free of charge, though these must be returned in good condition. The Telesecundaria facilities are also used, in some cases, to provide distance in-service to teachers working in rural areas.

Since its first trial classes in 1967, the Telescundaria has helped fill a need for learners who wish to go beyond primary education and do not have access to a local school. Unfortunately, not all of the equipment is adequately maintained and sometimes it is placed in villages that have interrupted power supplies.

The National Council for the Encouragement of Education (CONAFE), an alternative arm of the Secretary of Public Education, searches for other innovative ways to improve the scope of education to rural areas in Mexico. Special one-room schoolhouses have been set up in 30,000 extremely rural communities (Zehr, 2002). These alternative schools serve children in the primary grades.

The majority of these schools are in communities with fewer than 100 residents. The residents could send their children up to several kilometers in order to attend the regular public schools. In mountain communities with roads frequently washed out during the rainy season, the one-room schools are often far more accessible to young learners.

Teachers in these programs must have completed at least a ninth-grade education. In exchange for a minimum of one year of service as a teacher, the teacher receives funds for up to six years of education. The Secretary of Public Education provides periodic teacher in-service training for the teachers; the community must provide food and lodging.

Learners with Incomplete Schooling: The Open System. Many individuals in Mexico have failed to complete primary school, middle school, and high school. Some students who have completed at least four grades of primary school and who are legally classified as being literate are, in reality, functionally illiterate. To meet the needs of these learners, Mexico has created a very responsive program known as the Open System (*Sistema abierto*). It is appropriate for students who, for whatever reason, were unable to complete their studies. Many adults who decide to continue their education find this system to be accessible as it can be combined with work and family responsibilities.

The system is based on self-study: Students learn on their own through modules but also have access to teachers when they need help. At the end of the process, learners sign up to take examinations in secure, supervised settings with other students. Successful candidates can obtain the equivalent of a primary school diploma (*Certificado de Primaria*), middle school diploma (*Certificado de Secundaria*), and high school diploma (*Certificado de Bachillerato*). It can be hard for students to stick with the program since there is not regular direct contact with teachers as in more traditional programs. In spite of this drawback, the Open System has been very successful.

Tertiary Education (*Educacion superior*)

In 2002, there were 1,550 institutions of higher education consisting of 606 public institutions and 944 private institutions. The public tertiary institutions are divided into a subsystem of public universities, technological institutions, technological universities, and teacher training colleges. Some programs are coordinated by the federal government; others are decentralized institutions belonging to each state government.

Probably the best known school in Mexico is the public Mexican Autonomous University, known as UNAM, with over 130,000 undergraduates and 13,000 graduates. Although UNAM is autonomous and is not affiliated directly with the government or the Church, it evolved from the Royal and Pontifical University of Mexico, which was established in the mid-sixteenth century and was the first significant university in the Americas (Lanning, 1940). Among other subjects, students at UNAM can study the humanities, the sciences, medicine, law, and engineering. In addition to being known for producing outstanding graduates in past years, UNAM is also known for major riots in 1968 and a strike against the implementation of fees that began in 1999 and closed the university's doors for many months.

To obtain a higher education degree, a student must complete the required course work, complete a thesis or project, fulfill a certain amount of hours of social service, and also take a professional examination. Students who fulfill the required coursework but have not completed the rest of the requirements are considered *pasantes.*

University students attending public institutions are charged nominal tuition, but they must absorb other costs such as textbooks and supplies. Too often, students must choose between working for survival and attending school.

Private tertiary institutions include universities, institutes, and education centers. To be officially recognized, courses leading to a degree must have the Official Recognition for the Validity of Studies (*Reconocimiento de Validez Oficial de Estudios*) from the SEP or the individual state governments.

Private school higher education can be very costly, yet an increasing number of students are seeking private rather than public education. Thirty-eight percent of university students are enrolled in private institutions. Many students find Catholic universities to be an appealing option for higher education (Grayson, 1992). Other families, especially those who have sent their children to private high schools, are often willing to pay for private higher education in part because they see it as an alternative to the ills that have plagued public tertiary institutions (Kent & Ramirez, 1999).

Postgraduate Education

About 13 percent of university graduates continue into postgraduate study, a very small proportion of the total number of graduates. Although some private institutions are promoting and improving their postgraduate programs, a large proportion of postgraduate studies take place in public institutions, mainly in the Mexican National Autonomous University (UNAM).

The fact that there are so few postgraduate students explains why most university faculty members do not possess advanced university degrees. Moreover, many of the students who earn advanced degrees do so mainly in medicine and are not intending to enter teaching or research. However, current trends are increasingly demanding doctoral degrees for academic positions in good universities, where previously a master's degree would have been sufficient.

The Teaching Force

It is very difficult to establish new requirements for teachers in Mexico because of the different institutions that provide training for teachers. In addition, the highly politicized and powerful national teachers' union is always very vocal when changes are being made for students as well as for teachers. For example, the teachers' unions have influenced the number of students allowed in each class and the voice that teachers have in the administration of public schools. It should be pointed out that the widespread organization and uprisings of teacher unions, especially in poorer regions of Mexico (Chiapas and Oaxaca) helped bring about dramatic positive change for teachers (Cook, 1996).

One of the aims of Plan 2001–2006 is to have clearly articulated goals and objectives for teacher education programs. The plan intends to set standards for acquiring the Teacher's University Degree (the equivalent of a bachelor's degree) by having the program externally evaluated.

There are also new areas of specialization that will provide seven additional options for teacher education candidates: preschool, primary, secondary, special education, physical education, art, and indigenous education. In 2006, 30 percent of all teachers are required to have these qualifications. In addition, current teachers now need to take a minimum of two in-service courses each year to keep up with new teaching methods.

SUCCESSES IN MEXICAN EDUCATION

As we showed in the brief history that opened this chapter, Mexico's complicated history played a large role in the evolution of the Mexican educational system. Over the 300 years when Mexico was ruled by Spain, society was clearly divided by class, ethnicity, and language. Colonial governments maintained education at an elite level for those of Spanish descent. Wealthy male landowners were most likely to get an education. With independence in 1821, efforts to provide education to broader segments of the population appeared.

However, it was after 1950 that really concerted efforts to improve public education for students throughout Mexico were seen. Of the many different initiatives designed to improve conditions for teachers and students, probably one of the most dramatic emerged when President Salinas launched the 1992 Reform that led to the 1993 General Law on Education. This was transformed into a revised basic education and a new curriculum to boost reading, writing, and mathematics. This Law also caused the number of years of compulsory schooling to be increased from six to nine (to include middle school). As well, the school year for students in grades 1 to 6 was increased to 200 days from the previous 180 days. Subsequently, the length of the school year for middle school learners was also increased to 200 days.

The lengthening of the primary school calendar to 200 days was ill received. Some observers felt that the number of days was increased so that Mexico would become more competitive with Japan, a country that has traditionally had a greater number of days for school-age learners; others believed that the school year was lengthened so that young children would be supervised for a greater number of days. Teachers were not given a significantly higher salary, and they were not given additional materials for the extra days of instruction that they were to provide for learners.

Another tangible improvement in education has been the quality of free textbooks. The government provides books free of charge that fit in with the official curriculum for all children, regardless of their attendance in public or private schools. But in the 1960s and 1970s the paper was so thin that if a child wrote something and then erased it, the paper would probably tear in half. The colors in the books looked like the colors found in dirty stained glass windows. Even after the 1992 curriculum reform, the actual books had to be recalled after publishing due to errors, and the history books were criticized for changing their slant. Nowadays, free textbooks look more professional and are more attractive to students than their predecessors. They are produced using higher quality paper, ink, and printing processes.

The 1992 reform also changed the qualifications necessary for teachers. Prior to 1992, teachers were only required to obtain a normal school specialized teacher training diploma, not considered a higher education degree. However, in 1993 teachers were required to earn a higher education degree equivalent to a bachelor's degree.

The latest reforms spelled out in President Fox's National Education Plan 2001–2006 are designed to improve a number of different aspects of education, including teacher education and education for targeted groups of learners. Educational programs are being strengthened for specific groups of students, including preschoolers, street children, indigenous students, students with special needs, and students with incomplete educations. The Plan is still, at the time of this writing, in the process of being implemented, and there are a number of details that are being worked out by the SEP. Worth mentioning also is the decrease in pupil–teacher ratio at both the preschool and primary levels. The student–teacher ratio has essentially been cut in half.

As we have already mentioned, innovative education programs, in conjunction with the government program *De la Calle a la Vida* (from streets to life) launched in 2002, are being designed and implemented for the estimated 130,000 street children who work instead of attending school. The number of bilingual-bicultural programs targeting indigenous children is being doubled. Education programs for learners with special needs are being improved and expanded since Mexico now formally accepts the responsibility to educate all school-age students. Mexico is also striving to help learners complete their education.

In order to prevent lower income learners from attending school on empty stomachs, placing them at a disadvantage from other learners, a program to serve nutritious subsidized breakfasts was introduced seventy-five years ago. Run by the Integral Family Development (DIF), these school breakfasts now reach 5.2 million preschool and primary school children daily, providing them with 30 percent of estimated nutritional requirements at a cost of 0.35 to 0.65 pesos per breakfast (3 to 5 U.S. cents), with concessions to the poorest families. Though falling short of the 7.6 million–children target, the program has been a pillar for the DIF's social development programs. Since 1995, it has been run on a state level, instead of on a national level (Morales, 2004).

CHALLENGES FACING MEXICAN EDUCATION

Probably the biggest challenge facing the Mexican education system is the adequate allocation of resources for education. Money is needed for facilities, textbooks, teacher salaries, and the infrastructure.

Lack of Proper Facilities

Most public schools have two shifts on the same premises to try and accommodate the ever-growing demand. In many cases, there are two different schools using the same building, where students from the second shift are not able to use the same equipment or resources as those from the first shift. Many of those who attend the second shift have to do "paid work" in the morning, so by the time they get to school they are too tired to pay attention to their studies.

Many of the public schools are also in very poor repair. Although in the higher elevation regions of Mexico it is very cold at night and in the morning, school buildings are not heated. There isn't always money to repair windows when they break or to repaint buildings on a regular basis.

In 1989, under the "Solidarity" social development scheme, a program called *Escuela Digna* (dignified schools) was designed to bring school buildings up to a minimum functional standard. In order to qualify for the scheme, parents needed to put forth an application to the municipal authorities detailing what was needed in the school in order to qualify for federal funds. Parents needed to be involved in the process, and the funds could not be used to build new schools, but to "dignify" existing schools that had unsafe buildings, lacked drinking water, lacked functional desks or chairs, and had unhygienic toilets or an unsafe playground. Since the program began, over 2 million projects have been financed.

There has also been an effort to make new schools more earthquake resistant since the devastating earthquake in Mexico City in 1985. Simultaneously, there is a thrust to repair older schools so that they are more earthquake resistant.

In the light of new technologies and a more integrated world, schools are trying to keep up with the times in terms of computer use and language teaching. However, during the election campaign in 2000, one candidate promised to ensure computer literacy and the teaching of English in all public schools. At the time, it seemed to the Mexican people (particularly the press, who made a joke out of it) that focusing on computers and teaching English was ludicrous, considering that some students didn't have access to a proper school or teachers even to fulfill the basic curriculum. However, some public schools do have computers and access to other technological learning tools. They may have obtained these from large companies or private schools renewing their equipment, as a donation from an NGO, or from a foreign embassy.

Classroom Instruction

The required curriculum provided by the SEP for preschool and primary is generally well rounded and age-appropriate. In middle school, this is not necessarily the case. The lack of art, music, and other creative programs that fill the day in schools that have more materials and in private schools are sometimes replaced with numerous school assemblies. Although the SEP requires having school assemblies every Monday for honoring the flag and singing the national anthem, some schools do this daily, taking up to an hour out of classroom instruction time.

Teachers' Salaries

The conditions for teachers have improved over the years. For example, until 1992, teachers were federal employees rather than state or regional employees.

Although the pay is very low for public school teachers, proportionately it is getting better than it was in the past. However, the requirements for teachers have greatly increased, and teachers need to spend more time in the classroom themselves as learners before they can assume the role of teacher.

The lack of teachers and low salaries has forced some public school teachers to teach in both morning and evening shifts, usually at different schools. In order to attract the best possible teacher education candidates, teachers' salaries must be improved. Teachers should be compensated for the number of days that they deliver instruction.

Equal Opportunities for All Learners

Creating equal educational opportunities across Mexico, especially in rural areas, and those where there are indigenous populations, requires financial and human resources. Mexico has been very ambitious in its attempt to extend the classroom walls to a greater number of learners for a greater period of time. The regulations exist to ensure that every child from preschool through ninth grade can get an education, but the financial resources do not exist to carry out this goal. In some rural schools, classes are only offered for students up to the fourth grade because of lack of facilities and teachers. To meet needs, the expenditures for education must be drastically improved.

The SEP

The educational bureaucracy, SEP, is in many ways a reflection of the monolithic bureaucracy of the Mexican government. After sixty years of existence, it had become highly centralized and bureaucratic. In 1982 the SEP had close to 800,000 staff and 10,000 civil servants (Morales-Gomez & Torres, 1990). By 1985, much of the budget and resources had been decentralized, and the process to devolve control back to the states and municipalities had begun.

The SEP had always played the role of a buffer between the strengths and weaknesses of the state education system, including finances. However, in the 1992 Agreement on Educational Modernization, basic education and teacher training previously managed at a national level were transferred to the states, except that of the Federal District. Further restructuring continued in 1992, but it was not until October of 2004 when the Mexico City education budget was devolved that resources stopped being controlled centrally. The SEP still regulates course content, official school calendar, official ceremonies, and continues to design and publish free compulsory textbooks.

CONCLUSION

Mexico is a country with a vibrant history and the potential to be a developed country, and not to continue at the developing stage. Currently, as a developing country with an emerging economy, Mexico is attempting to meet the needs of all its learners. The government recognizes that education is the key toward development and has placed it at the center of its political agenda.

Mexico offers a wide variety of educational options for students of different ages, different means, and different backgrounds. Unfortunately, the quality is not consistent for every student throughout the Republic. Although there are many positive aspects to Mexican education, more work still needs to be done to make sure that every learner has equal access to quality education.

REFERENCES

Aguirre R. C. (2002). *Chiapas en Perspectiva Historica.* Novagrafik: SA Espana.

Anna, T. (1998). *Forging Mexico: 1821–1835.* Lincoln: University of Nebraska Press.

Backhoff, E., Larrazolo, N., & Romano, H. (1995). Children with learning disabilities in Mexico: The behavioral approach. In A. J. Artiles & D. P. Hallahan (Eds.), *Special education in Latin America: Experiences and issues.* Westport, CT: Praeger.

Bracho, T. (1999). Basic education in Mexico: An overview. In J. B. Anderson (Ed.), *Schooling for success: Preventing repetition and dropout in Latin America in Latin American primary schools.* New York: Sharpe.

Coady, D., & Walker, S. (2004). Cost-effectiveness analysis of demand and supply-side educational interventions: The case of PROGRESA in Mexico. *Review of Development Economics, 8*(3), 440–451.

Cook, M. L. (1996). *Organizing dissent: Unions, the state, and the democratic teachers' movement in Mexico.* University Park: Pennsylvania State University Press.

Cortina, R. (1992). Mexico. In S. Cooper & T. Kerchner (Eds.), *Labor relations in education: An international perspective.* Westport, CT: Greenwood Press.

Cothran, D. (1994). *Political stability and democracy in Mexico: "The perfect dictatorship"* Westport, CT: Praeger.

Cuetara, C. (2001). Gender, higher education, and social development in Mexico. *International Journal of Sociology and Social Policy, 21*(1/2), 143–159.

Duran, J. (2001). The Mexican Telesecundaria: Diversification, internationalization, change and update. *Open Learning, 16*(2), 170–177.

Grayson, G. (1992). *The church in contemporary Mexico.* Washington, DC: The Center for Strategic and International Studies.

Hatfield, S. B. (1998). *Chasing shadows: Indians along the United States Mexico border, 1876–1911.* Albuquerque: University of New Mexico Press.

Iglesias, E. (1998). Income distribution and sustainable growth: A Latin American perspective. In V. Tanzi & K. Chu (Eds.), *Income distribution and high-quality growth* (pp. 5–21). Cambridge, MA: MIT Press.

Kent, R., & Ramirez, R. (1999). Private education in Mexico: Growth and differentiation. In P. Altbach (Ed.), *Private Prometheus: Private higher education development in the 21st century.* Westport, CT: Greenwood Press.

Lanning, J. T. (1940). *Academic culture in the Spanish colonies.* Oxford, UK: Oxford University Press.

Martin, C., with Solorzano, C. (2003). Mass education, privatization, compensation and diversification: Issues on the future of public education in Mexico. *Compare, 3*(1), 15–29.

Morales, A. (2004, November 4). *Harán censo nutricional* de niños. *El Universal,* Nación.

Morales-Gomez, D., & Torres, C. A. (1990). *The state, corporatist politics, and educational policy making in Mexico.* New York: Praeger.

Newell, R. G., & Rubio, L. F. (1998). *Mexico's dilemma: The political origins of economic crisis.* Boulder, CO: Westview Press.

United Nations Educational Scientific and Cultural Organization (UNESCO). (2003). http://www.unesco.org

Vargas, L. (1995). *Social uses and radio practices: The use of participatory radio by ethnic minorities in Mexico.* Boulder, CO: Westview Press.

Vaughan, M. K. (1990). Primary education and literacy in nineteenth-century Mexico: Research trends, 1968–1988. *Latin American Research Review, 25,* 31–56.

Zehr, M. A. (2002). Mexican schools give new meaning to student-teaching. *Education Week, 21,* p. 8.

CHAPTER FIFTEEN

SCHOOLING IN THE UNITED STATES

Democratic and Market-Based Approaches

TIMOTHY E. JESTER

Educators and policymakers in the United States face a central question: How do you educate a diverse population in a democratic society? Two contrasting themes play out in response to this question.

One theme emphasizes access and equity in education, on the principle that these reflect democratic ideals. For instance, during the past fifty years, schools have been called upon to advance democratic principles by providing high-quality, personally relevant education to all students. In this perspective, the United States—as a pluralistic, multicultural, and democratic society—must have public schools that reflect its great social diversity and democratic political foundations.

The second theme stems from a market-based orientation, focusing upon competition and economic outcomes. Policymakers, politicians, and business leaders rooted in this orientation have made concerted efforts since the 1980s to define schools as a medium that promotes economic competitiveness in a global marketplace. This group has also advanced a market-based model for the structure, governance, and practices of schools that applies business concepts such as performance standards, competition, and high-stakes accountability (McNeil, 2002; Wells, Slayton, & Scott, 2002).

Timothy E. Jester works as Assistant Professor of Elementary Education at the University of Alaska–Anchorage. Prior to beginning his university appointment, he taught in elementary schools for eleven years, five of which were in a Yup'ik village in rural Alaska. His scholarly interests include education reform, Alaska Native schooling, postcolonial/neocolonial education, and teacher identity. He holds a doctorate in International Education Development from Teachers College, Columbia University.

Acknowledgments

The author would like to thank Thomas Sileo for his helpful editorial advice and Donald Shackelford for his insightful feedback on an earlier draft of this chapter.

Somewhat complicating matters is the fact that the rhetoric and vocabulary of these two contrasting orientations often overlap. That is (as will be evidenced in this chapter), promoters of market-based schooling often include the very same language of equality in their reform initiatives as do advocates whose primary focus is access and equity.

This chapter examines schooling in the United States as an arena in which the above principles—those of a market economy and those of a democracy—coexist and interact. Throughout, it is recognized that schools function within the nation's broader sociocultural context. The major forces and events that shape the contemporary social milieu are identified and discussed. Also addressed are central aspects of education in the United States, with particular attention to recent education reforms. Finally, the chapter examines key successes, challenges, and debates relevant to schooling in the United States.

THE SOCIAL FABRIC: SCHOOLS' SOCIOCULTURAL CONTEXT

In order to understand schools and schooling, it is necessary to recognize the broader sociocultural context of the society in which they are situated. Thus, in this section, three features of the United States' sociocultural context are discussed: (1) diverse demographics, (2) settler society, and (3) democratic society.

Diverse Demographics and Inequalities

The United States is increasingly becoming racially, ethnically, and linguistically diverse. Immigration rates almost tripled from 1970 to 2000, and by 2050, Asian and Hispanic populations are expected to increase by 213 and 187 percent, respectively. During the same period, the White population is expected to grow by only 32 percent (National Center for Education Statistics [NCES], 2004a; U.S. Census Bureau, 2004). The Census Bureau's racial and ethnic categories fail to capture the vast cultural diversity that exists within the United States. For example, "Asian" includes people with origins from many Asian countries, including such countries as China, Japan, Korea, and India. Each of these Asian groups living in America signifies unique cultural and linguistic backgrounds (Grieco & Cassidy, 2001).

The number of people who speak a language other than English at home is also increasing in the United States. For example, the number of non-English-language speakers more than doubled between the years 1980 and 2000, increasing from 23 million to 47 million (Shin, 2003). The Census Bureau has identified four major groups of languages other than English that are spoken in the United States: (1) Spanish; (2) other Indo-European languages (e.g., Germanic, Scandinavian, Romance, and Indic languages); (3) Asian and Pacific Island languages (e.g., Chinese, Dravidian languages, and Polynesian languages); and (4) all other languages (e.g., Uralic, American Indian, and Alaska Native languages) (Shin, 2003).

It is important to appreciate the educational and economic disparities that exist between racial and ethnic groups in the United States. For instance, 50 percent of Asians and 30 percent of Whites held a bachelor's degree or higher in 2000. Yet only 17 percent of

Blacks and 11 percent of Hispanics had reached this level of educational attainment (Stoops, 2004). Regarding economic disparities, between 1995 and 2001 Whites' net worth (i.e., assets minus debt) increased 37 percent, while minority populations' net worth decreased 7 percent—Whites' average net worth grew from $88,500 to $120,900 while minority populations' fell from $18,300 to $17,100. In addition, the median yearly income for Whites in 2001 was almost $20,000 more than for minority populations; Whites earned $45,200, and minority populations made $25,700 per year (Leondar-Wright, 2003).

Settler Society

The sociohistorical context of the United States as a settler society is rooted in the colonization of America beginning in the late fifteenth century, when Europeans invaded and occupied land that had been inhabited by indigenous peoples for thousands of years. The invaders attempted to dominate Native Americans through physical force and hegemonic practices. In this chapter, "Native American" refers to American Indians and Alaska Natives, defined by the 2000 census as "people having origins in any of the original peoples of North and South America" (U.S. Census Bureau, 2001, p. 2). In addition, "indigenous people" is used interchangeably with "Native American." It is recognized that distinct tribal affiliations exist within the general categories Native American, American Indians, Alaska Natives, and indigenous people (e.g., Navajo and Yup'ik).

By the mid-1800s, European Americans often relied on the theory of Social Darwinism to rationalize and justify their invasion and occupation of the land (Adams, 1995). Social Darwinism transferred the principles of biological evolution to social phenomena and ranked societies, cultures, and races on a continuum from savage to civilized. Accordingly, White European societies had reached the apex of civilization while Native Americans remained in the savage stage of social, cultural, and racial development (Adams, 1995). Social Darwinism enabled European Americans to justify their presence and practices in the United States as natural extensions and consequences of social evolution.

During the nineteenth century, politicians and policymakers embarked on an agenda to civilize the Native in an attempt to create Natives who would facilitate rather than disrupt the expansion of the United States into the western regions of the new nation (Adams, 1988). The core premise of the civilization agenda was that Natives must break away from their ties with tribal ways of life and replace their tribal identity with a civilized American identity.

Schools played a central role in the civilization agenda through three primary strategies: first, removing Native children from their savage, tribal homes and placing them in boarding schools where they would be immersed in civilization; second, providing a comprehensive, Eurocentric curriculum that de-emphasized academics and focused on values, behaviors, and technical skills necessary to live a civilized life; and third, indoctrinating Native children in the civilization-savagism paradigm so they would accept White Americans' superiority, and, conversely, their inferiority to White Americans (Adams, 1995). The civilization agenda attempted to eradicate Native Americans' identities and assimilate them into the dominant society. The education programs of boarding schools, Eurocentric curriculum, and indoctrination promoted the realization of this agenda.

The United States emerged from this sociohistorical context as a settler society similar to Canada, Australia, and New Zealand (Hickling-Hudson & Ahlquist, 2003). Unlike locations where European nations established colonial empires and eventually withdrew (e.g., India, Algeria, Zambia), in a settler society the colonists took up residence and established a new nation in the land inhabited by indigenous peoples. This historical event has resulted in complex dynamic relationships between Native Americans and invaders that continue to manifest and create effects in today's sociocultural milieu (Smith, 1999).

Assumptions and practices reflective of a settler society are evidenced in contemporary schooling in the United States. Indeed, to this day, the ideologies and practices related to the United States as a settler society are reflected in the nation's broader social and schooling contexts where stakeholders attempt to educate a diverse student population. Educational researchers have found that in many schools with Native American students, educators continue to implement a Eurocentric curriculum that is culturally irrelevant and, in effect, promotes an assimilation agenda (e.g., Hickling-Hudson & Ahlquist, 2003; Jester, 2002; Lipka, Mohatt, & Ciulistet Group, 1998). Some scholars argue that this curricular approach results in Native American students' educational failure, as well as social, psychological, and/or economic challenges (Hickling-Hudson & Ahlquist, 2003; Kawagley, 1995). As Lomawaima and McCarty (2002) have noted, "focusing on American Indian education—the enterprise charged with remaking and standardizing Indigenous people as 'Americans'—forces us all to confront the fault lines in the topography of the American democracy" (p. 281). Thus, the United States as a settler society provides the sociohistorical background for understanding current schooling in a diverse and democratic society.

Democratic Society

Several significant issues related to the meaning, form, and effects of democracy shed light on the sociopolitical context of the nation's society and schools. In the United States, democracy and capitalism are commonly promoted as interrelated, symbiotic paradigms in which democracy cannot exist without the capitalist free market—or vice versa (Held, 1987). However, a Marxist orientation argues that democracy and capitalism are contradictory paradigms because democracy promotes social equity, while capitalism promotes competition that results in social stratification where some people win and others lose (Carnoy & Levin, 1985; Held, 1987).

To understand the relationship and dynamics of capitalism and democracy, and to comprehend the United States as a democratic society, requires explication of different democratic models. There is no unitary meaning of democracy in the United States and, as such, groups and individuals use the word "democracy" to mean vastly different concepts and outcomes. Although it is clear that the English word *democracy* is derived from the Greek word *demokratia* and may be translated as "rule by the people," debates, misunderstandings, and conflicts center around two key questions: What does "rule by the people" mean? and What form of government best reflects "rule by the people"?

Two models of democracy, relevant to U.S. sociopolitical context, respond to these questions in different ways: representative democracy and participatory democracy (Held, 1987).

Representative Democracy. Representative democracy connotes a limited role for the government in private and civil affairs. At the same time, it promotes individual liberties and relies on market forces to facilitate the common good (Held, 1987; Wells, Slayton, & Scott, 2002). In this form of democracy, citizens elect representatives to pass laws that both protect their individual freedoms and facilitate operation of a free market. A system of governmental checks and balances, as well as the voting constituency, hold elected representatives accountable for their actions (Held, 1987). It is assumed that the state operates according to a rational, consensus-based process within legally recognized governmental structures, and the market follows objective principles, such as supply and demand. Accordingly, in the context of such a "neutral" state and market, a meritocracy is established where an individual is provided equal opportunity to pursue life, liberty, and happiness and can ultimately achieve whatever social status he or she is capable of reaching.

Since the 1970s, influential politicians, known as the "New Right," have extended representative democracy in a neoliberal paradigm that aims to further reduce the role of government in social affairs, curtail citizens' dependency on governmental assistance such as social welfare programs, and diminish the power of certain interest groups such as trade unions (Held, 1987). The goal to increase "the market to more and more areas of life" (Held, 1987, p. 243) is central to the New Right's neoliberal approach. This has resulted in significant effects in the sociopolitical arena. For instance, according to some social theorists, democracy and capitalism have become so intertwined in America's sociopolitical discourse that democracy is now equated with an economic concept rather than a political one. This, for example, is evidenced in President George W. Bush's post–September 11 speech when he urged Americans to display their freedom by "going shopping" (Wells, Slayton, & Scott, 2002). In addition, policymakers often apply the neoliberal paradigm to the structure and operation of social institutions, including schools (Lubienski, 2001; Wells, Slayton, & Scott, 2002). This phenomenon is discussed in the section on standards-based education.

Participatory Democracy. Although representative democracy features prominently in America's sociocultural milieu, a second model of democracy—participatory democracy—also plays a significant role in the United States. Participatory democracy has historical links with Marxist theory. It challenges a core premise of the representative democracy paradigm by proposing that neither the state nor the market is neutral. Rather, in a capitalist society, government and other social institutions function to perpetuate social structures, norms, and practices that benefit society's economic elite under the symbolic notions of equal opportunity and a free market (Feinberg & Soltis, 2004).

From a Marxist perspective, rather than achieving social status within a "neutral" social system, a person's ascribed social class determines opportunities for success in society (Feinberg & Soltis, 2004; Held, 1987). For example, children from educated, wealthy families are more likely to succeed educationally and economically than are children from families of poverty (Nieto, 2004; Strickland, 1997). Based on this critique of representative democracy, proponents of participatory democracy promote social equity and call on citizens to participate directly in the regulation and function of social institutions, rather than deferring this role to representatives (Held, 1987).

In recent times, Marx's focus on capitalism, social class, and determinism has been modified by neo-Marxists to include other ideological systems and social phenomena, such as sexism, racism, and heterosexism (Feinberg & Soltis, 2004). For example, in a patriarchal society, feminists argue that social institutions tend to perpetuate structures, norms, and practices that benefit males while marginalizing females. The work of feminist-oriented advocates and policymakers has resulted in laws that address issues of gender discrimination in United States, such as the passage of Title IX of the Educational Amendment Act in 1972 that outlawed sex discrimination in educational programs.

In sum, democracy in the United States has divergent meanings that often create conflicting expectations for social institutions and individual citizens. Currently, the representative model, with its emphasis on individual liberties, free market, and limited role of government, appears to hold prominence in the United States. However, the participatory democracy model that calls for citizens to actively participate in political life is also rooted in the nation's social fabric. Thus, a key feature of the United States as a democratic society is the interplay and tension between representative democracy and participatory democracy, the dynamics of which are reflected in U.S. schooling.

SCHOOLING IN THE UNITED STATES

The previous discussion considered the sociocultural context in which schools are situated in the United States—a context characterized by diverse demographics, a settler society, and a democratic society. In light of this context, this section describes the basic structure of U.S. public schools and teacher and student demographics. In addition, two educational reforms that have entered the educational arena during the past three decades are discussed: multicultural education and standards-based education.

Overview of the Public School System

The Constitution of the United States does not address education, and, therefore, the federal government ostensibly plays a limited role in the nation's school system. Currently, only about 8 percent of states' educational resources are received from the federal government (National Education Association, 2004b). However, the federal government provides funds for states to address national issues such as teacher shortages, poverty, and global economic competitiveness (Spring, 1998). When states and school districts receive these funds, they must implement accompanying federal guidelines and regulations. For example, the federal government provides funds to schools that educate students from low-income families, and schools that receive these funds must follow the federal government's standardized testing requirements.

In general, individual state governments play the central role in regulating U.S. public schools with the following public officials and government entities serving key policymaking and regulatory functions: governor, state legislature, commissioner or superintendent, state department of education, and state board of education. Joel Spring (1998) has identified seven primary educational functions of state governments: establishing academic standards for pupil promotion and graduation; licensing teachers; establishing academic standards and curriculum guidelines for local school districts; passing laws regulating the content of instruction (these laws vary with some states requiring the teaching of patriotism, free enterprise, driver's education, and other educational topics); providing for statewide testing of students; financing of local schools; and governing state higher educational systems (p. 197).

Local school districts within each state prepare curricula and educational programs that meet state and federal guidelines, while also responding to local needs and issues. School districts typically consist of a board of education and central office administration, such as a superintendent and curriculum director. At the local school level, administrators, teachers, and support staff, such as a school counselor and paraprofessionals, implement curricula and educational programs.

Demographics: Teachers and Students. Almost 3 million teachers work in U.S. elementary and secondary public schools, 90 percent of whom are White and 75 percent are female (National Education Association [NEA], 2004b, 2004c). A teacher's average salary in 2002–2003 was $46,000, ranging from $56,000 in California to $35,000 in Mississippi. Teachers are typically contracted to teach 181 days in the classroom and spend about 50 hours per week on school-related tasks, including out-of-class preparation (NEA, 2004b).

Students in U.S. schools represent a diverse population. For instance, in 2000, minority populations constituted 39 percent of the students enrolled in public schools, up from 22 percent in 1972 (NCES, 2002). Hispanics were the fastest growing minority student population between the years of 1972 and 2000, increasing from 6 to 17 percent of the total school-age population (NCES, 2002). According to Villegas and Lucas (2002), "By 2050, so-called minorities will collectively account for nearly 57 percent of the student population" (p. 3).

Students who speak languages other than English are increasing in the nation's schools. Between 1991 and 2002, Limited English Proficient (LEP) students enrolled in public schools increased 95 percent, from 2.4 million to 4.7 million students (National Clearinghouse for English Language Acquisition [NCELA], 2002). Although Spanish is most widely spoken by language minority students, other languages commonly represented in public schools include Vietnamese, Hmong, Haitian Creole, Korean, Arabic, Chinese (Cantonese, Mandarin, and unspecified), Russian, Tagalong, Navajo, Khmer, Portuguese, Urdu, Serbo-Croatian, Lao, and Japanese (NCELA, 2002).

There are striking educational and economic-related disparities between minority and White students. For example, in 2001 the dropout rate for Whites between the ages of 16 and 24 was 7 percent, while 11 percent of Blacks and 27 percent of Hispanics in this age group dropped out of school (NCES, 2003b). In addition, minority students are more likely than White students to come from low-income families. For example, using students' eligibility for the government funded free or reduced-price lunch program to identify students from low-income families, 40 percent of fourth-grade students were eligible for the program in 2003. Of the eligible students, only 23 percent were White. In addition, in 2001 significantly higher numbers of minority students attended high-poverty schools—that is, schools with more than 75 percent of the students eligible for the free or reduced-price lunch program. Only 5 percent of White students attended high-poverty schools, while 47 percent of Black students and 51 percent of Hispanic students attended such schools (NCES, 2004b).

MULTICULTURAL EDUCATION

With historical links to ethnic studies in the late nineteenth and early twentieth centuries, as well as to the 1960s civil rights movement, multicultural education emerged in the 1970s as an educational reform movement that has influenced discourse and practices at all levels of the U.S. educational system (Banks, 2004). The following discussion addresses the definitions and aims of multicultural education in public schools and examines curriculum as an example of schools' structural dimensions where these approaches are implemented.

Definition and Aims

Scholars and educators have developed multiple theories to explain and implement multicultural education (Banks, 2004; Sleeter & Bernal, 2004). Consequently, it eludes a single, unitary definition. However, according to Banks' (2004) review of scholarly literature, consensus exists around three aims regarding multicultural education:

- Reform the schools and other educational institutions so that students from diverse racial, ethnic, and social-class groups will experience educational equity.
- Give male and female students an equal chance to experience success and mobility.
- Understand how the interaction of race, class, and gender influences education. (p. 3)

Multicultural education, as articulated in these aims, can be defined as a school reform movement that promotes educational and social equity by addressing multiple prejudices and discrimination and providing all students equal opportunity for academic and social success. In essence, multicultural education reflects the democratic imperatives of access and equity that were discussed above.

Although the aims and definition incorporate notions of access and equity, a significant group within the field of education has argued that much of what occurs beneath the umbrella of multicultural education does little to critique power issues that create and perpetuate discrimination and social inequities in the United States (e.g., Nieto, 2004; Sleeter & Bernal, 2004; Villegas & Lucas, 2002). This group, reflective of the participatory democratic tradition, promotes critical multiculturalism (Sleeter & Bernal, 2004, p. 241) in which students are taught to critically analyze the underlying causes of social inequities with the aim of taking action to change schools and social structures in ways that advance social justice. For example, rather than simply identifying or defining racism, a critical multicultural approach probes beneath the surface to examine questions such as: How does racism function in U.S. society? What groups benefit from racism? How is racism perpetuated in society? What actions can be taken to reduce racism and its effects?

Proponents of critical multiculturalism argue that, when educators exclude critical analysis of power and privilege issues that underlie social inequities, students are not equipped to understand or respond effectively to racism or other forms of prejudices and discrimination. As a result, basic power structures remain unchallenged and social inequities perpetuate (Villegas & Lucas, 2002).

Multicultural Education and Curriculum

Multicultural education, as a systemic reform, is intended to impact all aspects of schooling in ways that promote educational and social equity. Schools' structural dimensions, the ways schools are organized, and their concomitant discourses and practices are fundamental aspects of schooling that promote or preclude the realization of the democratic ideals of equity and access. According to Nieto (2004), examples of schools' structural dimensions include physical structures; disciplinary policies; roles of students, teachers, and families; pedagogical practices; retention policies; tracking; standardized testing; and curriculum. In this section, curriculum as a structural dimension of schools is discussed.

A school's formal curriculum includes the knowledge, skills, and values that have been identified officially as what students should learn in school through a school district's curriculum guide and/or textbooks. Although the "hidden curriculum"—the knowledge/skills/values that students learn through the "organizational features and routines of school life" (Feinberg & Soltis, 1998, p. 21)—is a significant aspect of a school's curriculum, the following discussion focuses on the formal curriculum.

Curricula in U.S. schools, according to proponents of multicultural education, typically reflect Eurocentric knowledge and values. As a result, schools' curricula are irrelevant to many minority students, contribute to their limited educational success, and/or perpetuate social inequities (Banks, 2004; Nieto, 2004). In addition, a monocultural curriculum presents a limited, narrow view of the world that fails to provide all students, including White students, the opportunity to examine and understand issues and events from multiple perspectives (Nieto, 2004). Proponents of multicultural education, therefore, call upon schools to develop and implement a multicultural curriculum that is relevant to all students, presents multiple perspectives, and critically analyzes social phenomena (Banks, 2004; Nieto, 2004).

How teachers can put these principles into classroom practice is well articulated by James Banks. Banks (2004) describes and explains four levels of, and approaches to, multicultural curriculum design as follows:

- Level 1: *The Contributions Approach:* The focus is on heroes, holidays, and discrete cultural elements.
- Level 2: *The Additive Approach:* Content, concepts, themes, and perspectives are added to the curriculum without changing its structure.
- Level 3: *The Transformational Approach:* The structure of the curriculum is changed to enable students to view concepts, issues, events, and themes from the perspective of diverse ethnic and cultural groups.
- Level 4: *The Social Action Approach:* Students make decisions on important social issues and take action to help solve them. (p. 15)

The approaches help to illustrate how a multicultural approach can be implemented in a school's curriculum. The contributions and additive approaches provide limited inclusion of multicultural examples in the curriculum; for instance, teaching a lesson that simply identifies Dr. Martin Luther King as an African American hero. Although the contributions and additive approaches include content outside a Eurocentric perspective, neither approach changes the basic structure of the curriculum and, thus, multicultural education remains separate from the regular curriculum.

The transformational and social action approaches, on the other hand, attempt to alter the structure of the curriculum and make multicultural education pervasive throughout the curriculum. For instance, it is common in schools' curricula to present Western Expansion as the historical movement of European Americans from the Atlantic seaboard toward the Pacific coast. According to a Eurocentric perspective, White Americans brought civilization to an empty wilderness and savage Natives (Banks, 2004; Lowen, 1995). This Eurocentric version of Western Expansion resonates with neocolonial and racist ideologies as it positions White Americans as the central point of reference. Thus, American history is articulated as White Americans' settling the West and elides the fact that the land was not an empty wilderness. Native Americans had inhabited and were settled in the land prior to the arrival of European Americans. In addition, the Eurocentric Western Expansion narrative fails to incorporate Native Americans' potential counternarratives that emphasize an invasion and occupation of their land.

In the above example, a teacher implementing the transformational multicultural approach could use the regular curriculum as a springboard for challenging students to consider the Western Expansion narrative from multiple perspectives. For example, a teacher could ask students to think about how Native Americans might have viewed and/or currently view the movement of White Americans into their land. Application of the transformational approach in this example enables a teacher to create a forum for students to consider alternative perspectives and potentially connect in culturally relevant ways to students from communities that do not hold a Eurocentric perspective of Western Expansion.

Banks's social action approach, reflective of critical multiculturalism, would take this curricular example to a different level by facilitating students' critical understanding of Western Expansion and consideration of actions that might disrupt racists' notions embedded in the Eurocentric narrative. For example, a teacher applying the social action approach might engage students in critical questions similar to the following: What does the Eurocentric narrative tell us about the United States as a settler society regarding power relationships between Whites and indigenous peoples? What does the narrative reveal about the broader sociocultural context related to issues of power, privilege, and social inequities? What actions can we take to reveal and challenge the Eurocentric narrative and its potential negative effects? In addition to exploring critical questions, a teacher could engage students in a learning activity through which students take action that reveals and challenges the Eurocentric Western Expansion narrative. For example, students might write a children's book in which the Eurocentric narrative is presented in juxtaposition to a counter-explanation.

In sum, multicultural education promotes the democratic themes of equal access and social equity. The approach challenges a Eurocentric curriculum that has resulted in marginalizing many students through cultural irrelevancy and academic failure while perpetuating the sociopolitical status quo. In addition, multicultural education assumes that the best way to educate a diverse population in a democratic society is to create a curriculum that is culturally relevant, provides multiple perspectives on social phenomena, and promotes educational and social equity.

STANDARDS-BASED EDUCATION

At the other end of the educational reform spectrum in the United States—at odds with, and in contrast, to multicultural education—is standards-based education. Standards-based educational reform has swept the U.S. educational landscape during the past two decades; its significance cannot be overstated. Currently, virtually every state has developed and implemented some version of standards-based education (Sandholtz, Ogawa, & Scribner, 2004). This section outlines the background of the standards-based reform movement, describes its features, and examines the links between standards-based education and a market-oriented approach to schooling.

Background

Standards-based educational reform emerged after the National Commission on Excellence in Education published *A Nation at Risk* in 1983. The Commission, established by then U.S. Secretary of Education T. H. Bell, conducted an eighteen-month study of the quality of U.S. education. *A Nation at Risk* contained the Commission's findings and recommendations. A primary feature of the report is its scathing indictment of the U.S. educational system. The report argued that the nation's economy, and its "intellectual, moral, and spiritual strengths" (National Commission on Excellence in Education, 1983, p. 2), were in grave peril due to an ineffective educational system. In the words of the Commission:

> [T]he educational foundations of our society are presently being eroded by a rising tide of mediocrity that threatens our very future as a Nation and a people. . . . If an unfriendly foreign power had attempted to impose on America the mediocre educational performance that exists today, we might well have viewed it as an act of war. (p. 1)

In response to the national crisis described in the very strong language above, the Commission called for fundamental changes to the education system. The central theme of the Commission's recommendations was a call for educational institutions to "adopt more rigorous and measurable standards, and higher expectations, for academic performance and student conduct" (National Commission on Excellence in Education, 1983, p. 3). Embedded in this recommendation for higher academic standards was an emphasis on using standardized achievement tests for determining students' attainment of academic standards and identifying students who need either "remedial intervention" or "the opportunity for advanced or accelerated work" (p. 3).

Following *A Nation at Risk,* the federal government earnestly began to promote standards-based educational reform. For instance, during the 1990s, *Goals 2000* legislation offered financial incentives to states that developed and mandated content and performance standards, with accompanying standardized tests to hold school districts, administrators, teachers, and students accountable (Ravitch, 1997; U.S. Department of Education, 1998). The standards-based reform movement was ostensibly advanced with President Bush's signing into law the *No Child Left Behind Act of 2001,* a comprehensive educational law that discursively promotes high academic standards (U.S. Department of Education, 2004).

Standards-based reform has also found support outside the formal policymaking arena from many business leaders and parents, as well as key segments of the educational community. For instance, the Business Roundtable's (2000) *Essential Components of a Successful Education System* includes standards as the first of nine components necessary for successful educational reform. The public's support for higher academic standards is indicated on the United States Department of Education's *No Child Left Behind* website, where it is reported that 88 percent of the "public says schools should raise standards" (U.S. Department of Education, 2002). And the education community's support for standards-based education is illustrated by endorsement from the American Federation of Teachers and the National Education Association, the two largest teacher unions in the United States (American Federation of Teachers, 2004; National Educational Association, 2004a).

Features of Standards-Based Education

A variety of standards-based models have been developed and implemented throughout the United States. Within these, two basic orientations are dominant: standards-based education that aims for systemic change and standards-based education for high-stakes accountability (Darling-Hammond, 2004). The following discussion considers these orientations.

Standards-Based Education and Systemic Change. Standards-based education, according to one line of reform discourse, functions as the framework for creating systemic school change that improves teaching and learning. Two related features of standards-based education especially relevant to the systemic change orientation are academic standards and assessments.

Academic standards. During the 1990s, policymakers, business leaders, and school reformers called for states and school districts to develop rigorous academic standards for all students as a way to promote student learning, better teaching, and educational equity (Cohen, 1996; Darling-Hammond, 2004). Turning first to student learning: Standards-based reformers, in an effort to improve student learning, have promoted a departure from a basic knowledge and skills curriculum to one that focuses on students' higher level cognitive processes and conceptual understanding of academic content (Cohen, 1996). Cohen (1996) described the application of rigorous standards in classroom practice as follows: "Teachers should help students understand mathematical concepts, to interpret serious literature, to write creatively about their ideas and experiences, and to converse thoughtfully about history and social science" (p. 99).

Second, proponents of standards-based education argue that rigorous academic standards will improve teaching. This is because the model requires teachers to have a thorough grounding in content and learning theory, as well as skills in implementing pedagogical strategies that facilitate students' thinking and conceptual understanding (Cohen, 1996; Darling-Hammond, 2004). According to Linda Darling-Hammond (1997), "the fundamental premise of today's standards-based reform is that challenging education goals and contemporary knowledge about how people learn can be incorporated into practice when standards guide decisions about curriculum, teaching, and assessments" (p. 212). Thus, from this perspective of standards-based education, the quality of teaching will improve as teachers gain in content knowledge, understanding of learning theory, and pedagogical skills necessary to teach students effectively in a rigorous academic environment (Darling-Hammond, 2004; Thompson, 2001).

The third major rationale for developing rigorous academic standards is that such standards will promote educational equity for students from marginalized, disadvantaged, backgrounds. Darling-Hammond (1997) explained that standards, when aligned with appropriate assessments, "can be used to identify and address inequalities in access to learning opportunities" (p. 191). Smith, Fuhrman, and O'Day (1994) have proposed that "common, challenging standards and high expectations could serve equity well . . . [when] accompanied by measures to ensure equal opportunity to learn" (p. 23). In addition, Albert Shanker, former president of the American Federation of Teachers, viewed performance standards as "the only assurance that disadvantaged children will receive the knowledge they need to succeed" (as cited in Mosle, 1996, p. 56).

By way of implementation, states and/or school districts have developed two types of academic standards in an attempt to explicitly identify what students should know and be able to do: content standards and performance standards. Content standards indicate the knowledge students are expected to learn; performance standards identify how students should demonstrate their knowledge and skills. For instance, a math content standard in Alaska states that students "should understand and be able to select and use a variety of problem-solving strategies" (Alaska Department of Education and Early Development, 2000, p. 13). A performance standard for math problem solving for Alaska's students ages 11–14 indicates that they should "select, modify, and apply a variety of problem-solving strategies including graphing, inductive and deductive reasoning, Venn diagrams, and spreadsheets" (p. 70).

Assessments. Proponents of a systemic change approach argue that assessments linked to academic standards serve as a window into seeing what students know and are able to do. For instance, Darling-Hammond and Falk (1997) conceptualized the role of assessments in standards-based education as follows: "Assessments tied to standards can provide important information to students, families, and communities about how students are progressing in their learning" (p. 191). In addition, data gleaned from assessments can guide teachers' practices related to curriculum and pedagogy. The end result should be improved teaching and student learning (Darling-Hammond, 1997; Darling-Hammond & Falk, 1997; Kornhaber, 2004).

Three types of assessment instruments have become part of the standards-based environment: (1) standardized achievement tests, (2) criterion-referenced tests, and (3) performance-based assessments (Elmore, Abelmann, & Fuhrman, 1996). Standardized achievement tests are norm-referenced exams that commonly consist of multiple-choice questions intended to measure a student's knowledge and/or skills in various academic content areas. A student's individual score is then compared to a national sample of students who are the same age and grade level (Darling-Hammond, Ancess, & Falk, 1995; Popham, 1999).

The second form of assessment common in standards-based reform is the criterion-referenced test. Although a criterion-referenced test may be standardized in the sense that a state develops one test used in all public schools, a key difference between it and standardized achievement tests is that the criterion-referenced tests link exam items to specific learning objectives or outcomes. Many states have designed criterion-referenced tests that are aligned to the state's content and/or performance standards (Elmore, Abelmann, & Fuhrman, 1996).

Performance-based assessments are a third type of assessment promoted by some standards-based reformers. Performance-based assessments are intended to serve as comprehensive measures of students' knowledge and skills application (Elmore, Abelmann, & Fuhrman, 1996). Sometimes referred to as authentic assessments, performance-based assessments engage students in real-world tasks that can "provide a broad range of continuous, qualitative data that can be used by teachers to inform and shape instruction" (Darling-Hammond, Ancess, & Falk, 1995, p. 10). Examples of performance-based assessments include portfolios, oral presentations, and collections of students' work over time (Darling-Hammond, Ancess, & Falk, 1995; Herman, Aschbacher, & Winters, 1992).

Standards-based educational reform that focuses on systemic change views standards as an essential component for creating an educational system that improves teaching and learning. In this orientation, assessments aligned to rigorous academic standards help facilitate an educational environment that enhances all students' academic achievement.

Standards-Based Education and High-Stakes Accountability. A second reform orientation in U.S. schools promotes standards-based education as a mechanism for holding schools, teachers, and students accountable. This theme has recently gained momentum as policymakers increasingly emphasize high-stakes accountability (Darling-Hammond, 2004; Diamond & Spillane, 2004; Thompson, 2001). Although the high-stakes accountability reformers include academic standards and assessments in their reform model, these features primarily serve an accountability purpose, rather than a systemic change function. Granting rewards to recognize schools, educators, and/or students who meet specified standards, and applying sanctions to those who fall short of the standards, are common practices in the high-stakes accountability approach (Elmore, Abelmann, & Fuhrman, 1996).

Students' test scores on norm-referenced and/or criterion-referenced exams have become the central accountability mechanism. For instance, school systems routinely use test scores as a basis for making decisions regarding tracking, retention, and/or graduation (Darling-Hammond, 2004; Elmore, Abelmann, & Fuhrman, 1996; Heubert & Hauser, 1999). States and/or school districts increasingly are using students' exam scores to determine schools' and teachers' effectiveness. They are also linking test scores with financial rewards and sanctions that include school funding and administrators' and teachers' compensation (Elmore, Abelmann, & Fuhrman, 1996; Holt, 2001)

Standards-Based Education: Links to the Market Paradigm. As noted previously, during the past two decades many policymakers and business leaders have conceptualized schools as primarily serving economic outcomes (Apple, 1996). The purpose of schools, from this perspective, is to ensure the nation's economic competitive advantage in the global marketplace. Teachers are "viewed as economic actors" (Welmond, 2002, p. 41) whose primary responsibility is to produce students with skills and knowledge required for the nation's economic success.

In addition to promoting economic advantage, the standards-based model reflects the market orientation themes of efficiency, accountability, and competition. Efficiency characterizes the standards-based model in numerous ways. First, the notion that the educational system needs to be tightly aligned to standards assumes that the goal of schooling is to reach performance outcomes in an efficient manner. Second, the assumption that policy-makers and/or educators should determine what students should know and accomplish in advance of knowing the specific needs and/or background of the students represents attempts to promote an efficient system. Finally, standardized achievement test scores are an efficient way to collect quantitative data regarding students' learning and hold schools, teachers, and students accountable for their behavior.

The accountability theme of the high-stakes movement is another example of the market-based approach to schooling. The underlying assumption reflected in a high-stakes environment is that teachers and/or students are motivated to improve their performance when their behaviors are linked to standards and consequences. Thus, teachers and students are rewarded or punished, as in business world where the bottom line is based on high performance measures, such as quantifiable profits.

Another key element of the standards-based model's accountability focus is the promotion of competition among schools. The high-stakes accountability approach generally, and the competition emphasis specifically, have been institutionalized further in the educational system with passage of the *No Child Behind Act of 2001*. For instance, under *No Child Left Behind* guidelines, if a school does not demonstrate Adequate Yearly Progress (AYP) based on students' test scores, parents may elect to transfer their children to a school that has met AYP guidelines. The effect is that the failing school loses the funds that are attached to the students who transfer to another school. This policy is based on a market-oriented paradigm that assumes competition among schools will force failing schools to improve.

Although standards-based education is closely akin to a market-based approach, the former's reform discourse also contains references to equality of opportunity. The *No Child Left Behind* (2001) legislation stresses high academic achievement for all students. Proponents of standards-based reform, as a systemic change approach, contend that setting high academic standards facilitates equality of opportunity for all students. Two points related to the market-based orientation appear significant in this context.

First, coupling equality of opportunity with a market-based approach reflects representative democracy, in which democracy and the market operate in a symbiotic relationship in U.S. democratic capitalist society. Second, standards-based education is rooted in the assumption that, if educators offer all students a rigorous academic curriculum, then motivated and capable teachers and students will rise to the occasion and meet the demands of the standards. This approach illustrates the idea of a meritocracy in which individuals are provided opportunities to succeed and then are judged based on their performance.

SUCCESSES, CHALLENGES, AND DEBATES

Schooling in the United States may be viewed as an arena in which the principles of the market and democracy occur simultaneously. Concomitantly, two salient school reform movements in the United States reflect market-based and democratic orientations: standards-based education as an example of a market-based approach to schooling and multicultural education as a reflection of democracy. In this final section, I draw from the preceding discussion of U.S. sociocultural and schooling contexts to explore educational successes, challenges, and debates.

Successes

Multicultural educational reform holds promise for improving the educational experience of all children in the diverse and democratic U.S. society. First, multicultural education provides a useful framework for developing and implementing relevant curricula that connect to students' experiences and foster all students' academic achievement. Second, in theory and practice, multicultural education represents the democratic ideals of equal access as well as social and educational equity. Specifically, the critical multicultural model has potential to promote a vision of democracy that facilitates citizens' active participation in the political process in ways that can uncover roots of social inequities and facilitate social change.

Standards-based educational reform requires establishing high academic expectations and holding stakeholders accountable for their actions. However, current implementation of standards-based reform and high-stakes accountability has potential negative ramifications that overshadow a simple endorsement of the model. Although there are concerns regarding standards-based reform, the increased focus on academic expectations, students' achievement, and teacher quality represents a potential positive outcome. For instance, the standards-based movement has brought attention to disparities between racial and ethnic groups' school performance. This may serve as a catalyst to probe underlying social and educational issues that have marginalized certain groups of students, such as minorities. Examination of, and participation in, dialogue about these issues could create opportunities for new educational changes that may perhaps simultaneously facilitate improved teaching and learning, *and* social equity.

Challenges

There are a number of challenges associated with implementing multicultural education and standards-based reform. These challenges are addressed throughout the remainder of this chapter.

Although multicultural educational reform represents a promising model for promoting educational and social equity, two formidable challenges relative to implementing this educational approach are evident. First, multicultural education, as an example of participatory democracy, contradicts the representative democracy paradigm, which appears dominant in the U.S. sociopolitical and educational arenas. Therefore, it may be challenging in this context to create the policy and structural supports needed to institutionalize multicultural education in schools.

A second challenge for implementing multicultural education relates to teacher education. The tenets of multicultural education call for educators to examine their beliefs about and positions in the social structure, the sociopolitical connections between school and society, and the role of curriculum and pedagogy in promoting social and educational equity (Garmon, 2004; Villegas & Lucas, 2002). In the absence of these opportunities, three outcomes are likely to occur that contradict the intent of multicultural education.

First, multicultural education may function as a superficial add-on without fundamentally changing the school's curriculum or teacher's pedagogy (Banks, 2004). Second, teachers may maintain and articulate damaging stereotypes and generalizations about certain racial, ethnic, and/or social class groups (Nieto, 2004). Third, sociopolitical ideologies and structures that contribute to social inequities may remain in place (Villegas & Lucas, 2002). Therefore, universities, colleges, and school districts are challenged to design preservice and inservice programs that provide opportunities for educators to develop the knowledge, skills, and dispositions necessary to implement multicultural education.

Debates: Effects of Standards-Based Education

Currently, a central debate in the U.S. education arena stems from the following question: What are the effects of standards-based education? Proponents of standards-based education point to a number of positive effects to justify their support for the model. First, standards-based education brings coherence to the various layers of the educational system as the state, school district, school, and classroom teacher are focused on the same goals (Ravitch, 1995). Second, standards allow teachers and students, respectively, to know the academic content they should teach and learn, and how students must demonstrate learning (Schmoker & Marzano, 1999). Third, standards provide equality of opportunity for students from marginalized, disadvantaged backgrounds (Darling-Hammond, 1997; Smith, Fuhrman, & O'Day, 1994). Finally, standards and their accompanying assessments effectively hold students, teachers, and schools accountable for teaching and learning (Elmore, Abelmann, & Fuhrman, 1996).

Although the standards-based model has become embedded in U.S. schools, contestation regarding the effects of standards-based education is also occurring. A central argument in opposition to standards-based reform is that the reform model creates a standardized high-stakes environment that limits both students' educational experiences and teachers' curricular and pedagogical options (McNeil, 2000). Thus, from this opposing perspective, the positive effects noted above are seen as factors that create negative and challenging situations for students and teachers. These challenging effects relate to two potential outcomes of standards-based reform: It narrows curriculum and limits pedagogy, and it promotes an assimilation agenda.

Narrows Curriculum and Limits Pedagogy. Standards-based reformers argue that their model will improve teaching and learning. However, recent research indicates that standards-based education, coupled with high-stakes testing, actually narrows the curriculum and limits pedagogical options for teachers. Teachers are increasingly driven to focus on basic content knowledge and lower level cognitive skills (Darling-Hammond, 2004). For instance, Linda McNeil (2000) found that a standards-based, high-stakes environment in Houston, Texas, had created a "standardization [that] reduces the quality and quantity of what is taught and learned in schools" (p. 3). This limiting curricular and pedagogical effect relates to two central aspects of standards-based reform: mandated content and performance standards that teachers are expected to teach and assessments that are aligned to academic standards and serve high-stakes accountability purposes.

First, teachers are expected to teach a curriculum based on standards that are mandated by policymakers. One effect of this expectation is that teachers' curricular options are limited because they are required to focus on prescribed standards.

Second, in the current accountability environment, assessments are aligned to academic standards and function as high-stakes accountability mechanisms. Teachers are expected to prepare students to pass the exam, which often results in a "teach to the test" approach (Darling-Hammond, 2004; McNeil, 2000). In addition, recent research has found that, in the context of high-stakes accountability, tracking and retention practices are becoming more common, as well as an increase in dropout rates (Darling-Hammond, 2004). These effects are especially prominent in schools with high concentrations of minority students and/or students from low socioeconomic backgrounds. Thus, although proponents of standards-based reform promote the model as providing equality of opportunity for minority students, in effect, it appears to limit students' educational opportunities.

Promotes an Assimilation Agenda. Some critics of standards-based education argue that the model functions as a mechanism for assimilating minority students into dominant society by promoting Eurocentric knowledge and norms, while at the same time excluding alternative epistemologies and forms of knowledge (Bigelow, 2003). The following questions are significant in light of the U.S. evolutionary context, discussed at the beginning of this chapter, as a settler society: Should schools aim to assimilate all students into the dominant culture as a way to facilitate a common culture and social cohesion? Or, should schools reflect and promote the demographic reality represented in the nation's society and schools: the reality of diverse perspectives and knowledge?

Three additional essential questions are embedded in the assimilation issue associated with standards-based education: What/whose knowledge is included in the curriculum? What counts as a legitimate way of demonstrating having learned it? Who asks and answers these questions?

One response to these questions is that dominant social groups, such as policymakers, should control the development process and form of standards-based reform policies. To the extent that standards-based reformers create standards reflective of the values and norms of dominant society, minority students are marginalized and expected to assimilate into the mainstream of U.S. society. Berlak (1999) explained the situation as follows: "[L]inking standards and curriculum to high-stakes testing is a powerful way to ensure the continued hegemony of the dominant culture" (p. 11).

On the other hand, the case can be made that all students should have access to a common body of knowledge to ensure equal opportunity for success in the United States. From this perspective, standards-based education provides a systematic way to develop curriculum and hold students, teachers, and schools accountable for meeting rigorous academic standards that open doors of opportunities.

CONCLUSION

This chapter opened with a crucial question that policymakers and educators face in the United States: How do you educate a diverse population in a democratic society? Two basic responses to this question currently play out in the U.S. educational arena: promote the democratic ideals of access and social equity by providing a culturally relevant education to all students, and apply the principles of the market through standards-based education and thereby provide all students equality of opportunity for success in school and society. The successes, challenges, and debates discussed in this chapter reflect issues with which many educators and other stakeholders grapple as democratic and market-based approaches are simultaneously advocated for U.S. public schools.

The issues and tensions that arise in schools are reflections of the broader U.S. social and cultural context—where divergent views of democracy and capitalism compete and interact. As such, schools in the United States provide a window through which the uneasy interplay of democratic ideals and market-based principles can be viewed and examined.

REFERENCES

Adams, D. W. (1988). Fundamental considerations: The deep meaning of Native American schooling, 1880–1900. *Harvard Educational Review, 58*(1), 1–28.

Adams, D. W. (1995). *Education for extinction: American Indians and the boarding school experience, 1875–1928.* Lawrence: University Press of Kansas.

Alaska Department of Education and Early Development. (2000). *Alaska standards: Content and performance standards for Alaska students.* Juneau, AK: Author.

American Federation of Teachers. (2004). *Standards-based reform.* Retrieved August 1, 2004, from http://www.aft.org/topics/sbr/index.htm

Apple, M. W. (1996). *Cultural politics and education.* New York: Teachers College Press.

Banks, J. A. (2004). Multicultural education: Historical development, dimensions, and practice. In J. A. Banks & C. A. McGee Banks (Eds.), *Handbook of research on multicultural education* (2nd ed., pp. 3–29). San Francisco: Jossey-Bass.

Berlak, H. (1999). Standards and the control of knowledge. *Rethinking Schools, 13*(3), 1–2.

Bigelow, B. (2003). Standards and multiculturalism. In L. Christensen & S. Karp (Eds.), *Rethinking school reform: Views from the classroom* (pp. 231–239). Milwaukee, WI: Rethinking Schools.

Business Roundtable. (2000). *Essential components of a successful educational system.* Retrieved August 1, 2004, from http://www.businessroundtable.org/taskForces/index.aspx

Carnoy, M., & Levin, H. M. (1985). *Schooling and work in the democratic state.* Stanford, CA: Stanford University Press.

Cohen, D. K. (1996). Standards-based school reform: Policy, practice, and performance. In H. F. Ladd (Ed.), *Holding schools accountable: Performance-based reform in education* (pp. 99–127). Washington, DC: The Brookings Institute.

Darling-Hammond, L. (1997). *The right to learn: A blueprint for creating schools that work.* San Francisco: Jossey-Bass.

Darling-Hammond, L. (2004). Standards, accountability, and school reform. *Teachers College Record, 106*(6), 1047–1085.

Darling-Hammond, L., Ancess, J., & Falk, B. (1995). *Authentic assessment in action: Studies of schools and students at work.* New York: Teachers College Press.

Darling-Hammond, L., & Falk, B. (1997). Using standards and assessments to support student learning. *Phi Delta Kappan, 79*(3), 190–199.

Diamond, J. B., & Spillane, J. P. (2004). High stakes accountability in urban elementary schools: Challenging or reproducing inequality? *Teachers College Record, 106*(6), 1145–1176.

Elmore, R. F., Abelmann, C. H., & Fuhrman, S. H. (1996). The accountability in state education reform: From process to performance. In H. F. Ladd (Ed.), *Holding schools accountable: Performance-based reform in education* (pp. 65–98). Washington, DC: The Brookings Institute.

Feinberg, W., & Soltis, J. F. (1998). *School and society* (3rd ed.). New York: Teachers College Press.

Feinberg, W., & Soltis, J. F. (2004). *School and society* (4th ed.). New York: Teachers College Press.

Garmon, M. A. (2004). Changing preservice teachers' attitudes/beliefs about diversity: What are the critical factors? *Journal of Teacher Education, 55*(3), 201–213.

Grieco, E. M., & Cassidy, R. C. (2001). Overview of race and Hispanic origin. *Overview of race and Hispanic origin: Census 2000 Brief.* Retrieved October 15, 2004, from http://www.census.gov/population/www/cen2000/briefs.html

Held, D. (1987). *Models of democracy.* Stanford, CA: Stanford University Press.

Herman, J. L., Aschbacher, P. R., & Winters, L. (1992). *A practical guide to alternative assessment.* Alexandria, VA: Association for Supervision and Curriculum Development.

Heubert, J. P., & Hauser, R. M. (Eds.). (1999). *High stakes: Testing for tracking, promotion, and graduation.* Washington, DC: National Academy Press.

Hickling-Hudson, A., & Ahlquist, R. (2003). Contesting the curriculum in the schooling of indigenous children in Australia and the United States: From Eurocentrism to culturally powerful pedagogies. *Comparative Education Review, 47*(1), 64–89.

Holt, M. (2001). Performance pay for teachers: The standards movement's last stand? *Phi Delta Kappan, 83*(4), 312–317.

Jester, T. E. (2002). Healing the "unhealthy Native": Encounters with standards-based education in rural Alaska. *Journal of American Indian Education, 41*(3), 1–21.

Kawagley, O. A. (1995). *A Yupiaq worldview: A pathway to ecology and spirit.* Prospect Heights, IL: Waveland Press.

Kornhaber, M. L. (2004). Assessment, standards, and equity. In J. A. Banks & C. A. McGee Banks (Eds.), *Handbook of research on multicultural education* (2nd ed., pp. 91–109). San Francisco: Jossey-Bass.

Leondar-Wright, B. (2003). *News from the Federal Reserve's Survey of Consumer Finances: Racial wealth has widened.* Retrieved October 26, 2004, from http://www.faireconomy.org/econ/RWG/SCF_Race_2003.html

Lipka, J., Mohatt, G. V., & Ciulistet Group. (1998). *Transforming the culture of schools: Yup'ik Eskimo examples.* Mahwah, NJ: Lawrence Erlbaum Associates.

Lomawaima, K. T., & McCarty, T. L. (2002). When tribal sovereignty challenges democracy: American Indian education and the democratic ideal. *American Educational Research Journal, 39*(2), 279–305.

Lowen, J. W. (1995). *Lies my teacher told me: Everything your American History textbook got wrong.* New York: Touchstone.

Lubienski, C. (2001). Redefining "public" education: Charter schools, common schools, and the rhetoric of reform. *Teachers College Press, 103*(4), 634–666.

McNeil, L. M. (2000). *Contradictions of school reform: Educational costs of standardized testing.* New York: Routledge.

McNeil, L. M. (2002). Private asset or public good: Education and democracy at the crossroads. *American Educational Research Journal, 39*(2), 243–248.

Mosle, S. (1996, October 27). The answer is national standards. *The New York Times Magazine,* 45–68.

National Center for Education Statistics (NCES). (2002). *The condition of education 2002: Racial/ethnic distribution of public school students.* Retrieved October 21, 2004, from http://www.nces.ed.gov//programs/coe/2002/section1/indicator03.asp

National Center for Education Statistics (NCES). (2003a). *The condition of education 2003: Indicator 4: Language minority students* (NCES Publication No. 2003–067). Washington, DC: U.S. Government Printing Office.

National Center for Education Statistics (NCES). (2003b). *The condition of education 2003: Indicator 17: Status dropout rates, by race/ethnicity* (NCES Publication No. 2003–067). Washington, DC: U.S. Government Printing Office.

National Center for Education Statistics (NCES). (2004a). *The condition of education 2004: Past and projected elementary and secondary school enrollments.* Retrieved October 21, 2004, from http://www.nces.ed.gov//programs/coe/2004/section1/indicator04.asp

National Center for Education Statistics (NCES). (2004b). *The condition of education 2004: Concentration of enrollment by race/ethnicity and poverty.* Retrieved October 21, 2004, from http://www.nces.ed.gov//programs/coe/2004/section1/indicator05.asp

National Clearinghouse for English Language Acquisition (NCELA). (2002). *The growing number of limited English proficient students* (Poster No. Poster_v3.qxd). Retrieved October 20, 2004, from http://www.ncela.gwu.edu

National Commission on Excellence in Education. (1983). *A nation at risk: The imperative for education reform: A report to the nation and the Secretary of Education, United States Department of Education.* Washington, DC: U.S. Government Printing Office.

National Education Association (NEA). (2004a). *Accountability and testing.* Retrieved July 21, 2004, from http://www.nea.org/accountability/index.html

National Education Association (NEA). (2004b). *Rankings and estimates: Rankings of the states 2003 and estimates of school statistics 2004.* Washington, DC: Author.

National Education Association (NEA). (2004c). *Status of the American public school teacher 2000–2001.* Washington, DC: Author.

Nieto, S. (2004). *Affirming diversity: The sociopolitical context of multicultural education* (3rd ed.). Boston: Pearson.

Popham, W. J. (1999). Why standardized tests don't measure educational quality. *Educational Leadership, 56*(6), 8–15.

Ravitch, D. (1995). *National standards in American education: A citizen's guide.* Washington, DC: The Brookings Institute.

Sandholtz, J. H., Ogawa, R. T., & Scribner, S. P. (2004). Standards gaps: Unintended consequences of local standards-based reform. *Teachers College Record, 106*(6), 1177–1202.

Schmoker, M., & Marzano, R. (1999). Realizing the promise of standards-based education. *Educational Leadership, 56*(6), 17–21.

Shin, H. B. (2003). *Language use and English-speaking ability: 2000.* Census 2000 Brief. Retrieved October 14, 2004, from http:www.census.gov/population/www/cen2000/briefs.html

Sleeter, C. E., & Bernal, D. D. (2004). Critical pedagogy, critical race theory, and antiracist education: Implications for multicultural education. In J. A. Banks & C. A. McGee Banks (Eds.), *Handbook of research on multicultural education* (2nd ed., pp. 240–258). San Francisco: Jossey-Bass.

Smith, L. T. (1999). *Decolonizing methodologies: Research and indigenous peoples.* London: Zed Books.

Smith, M., Fuhrman, S., & O'Day, J. (1994). National standards: Are they desirable and feasible? *Association for Supervision and Curriculum Development: 1994 Yearbook,* 12–29.

Spring, J. (1998). *American education* (8th ed.). Boston: McGraw Hill.

Stoops, N. (2004). *Educational attainment in the United States: 2003. Population Characteristics.* Retrieved October 14, 2004, from http://www.census.gov/population/www/socdemo/educ-attn.html

Strickland, J. (1997). *Sociology: Discovering society.* Belmont, CA: Wadsworth.

Thompson, S. (2001). The authentic standards movement and its evil twin. *Phi Delta Kappan, 82*(5), 358–362.

U. S. Census Bureau. (2001). *Overview of race and Hispanic origin.* Retrieved October 1, 2004, from http://www.census.gov/population/www/socdemo/race.html

U. S. Census Bureau. (2004). *U.S. interim projections by age, sex, race, and Hispanic origin.* Retrieved October 21, 2004, from http://www.census.gov/ipc/www/usinterimproj

U. S. Department of Education. (1998). *Goals 2000: Reforming education to improve student achievement—April 30, 1998.* Retrieved June 14, 2004, from http://www.ed.gov/pubs/G2KReforming/g2exec.html

U. S. Department of Education. (2002). *Facts about state standards.* Retrieved June 14, 2004, from http://www.ed.gov/nclb/accountability/standards/standards.html

U. S. Department of Education. (2004). *No Child Left Behind* homepage. Retrieved June 14, 2004, from http://www.ed.gov/nclb/landing.jhtml

Villegas, A. M., & Lucas, T. (2002). *Educating culturally responsive teachers: A coherent approach.* Albany: State University of New York Press.

Wells, A. S., Slayton, J., & Scott, J. (2002). Defining democracy in the neoliberal age: Charter schools and educational consumption. *American Educational Research Journal, 39*(2), 337–361.

Welmond, M. (2002). Globalization viewed from the periphery: The dynamics of teacher identity in the Republic of Benin. *Comparative Education Review, 46*(1), 37–65.

Part VI

SNAPSHOTS FROM TWO SOUTHERN CONTINENTS

Repair and Reconstruction; Learning from Experience

CHAPTER SIXTEEN

POST-APARTHEID POLICY AND PRACTICE

Education Reform in South Africa

DAVID GILMOUR

CRAIN SOUDIEN

DAVID DONALD

David Gilmour teaches in the School of Education at the University of Cape Town. He began his career in the Department of Public Administration at UCT and has taught in a variety of institutions since then, including the University of Fort Hare and Rhodes University. Since joining the School of Education in 1987 he has developed interests in policy and planning in education, the sociology of education, and the evaluation of educational projects. He has worked on a number of national commissions in the reconstruction of education in South Africa, including recent evaluations of learner performance in mathematics and literacy.

Crain A. Soudien is Professor and Head of the Department of the School of Education at the University of Cape Town and teaches in the fields of Sociology and History of Education. His research interests include race, culture and identity, school and socialization, youth, teacher identity, school effectiveness, and urban history. He has published over sixty articles and book chapters in the areas of race, culture, educational policy, educational change, public history, and popular culture. He is also the co-editor of two books on District Six, Cape Town, and is actively involved in a number of social and educational projects including the Iziko Museums of Cape Town and the District Six Museum, which he and colleagues established in 1989; the Cape Town Festival; and the Independent Examinations Board. He has also undertaken a number of educational and cultural initiatives in the city and in the country. He was educated at the Universities of Cape Town, South Africa, and holds a Ph.D. from the State University of New York at Buffalo.

David R. Donald is Professor of Educational Psychology at the University of Cape Town. He has taught in schools, has practised as an educational psychologist, and has been involved in training teachers, special educationists, and educational psychologists in South Africa over a number of years. As the author of several books, chapters in books, and a range of articles, his research and publication have focused extensively, although not exclusively, on issues affecting the delivery of education support services in developing contexts, especially in southern Africa.

When the *apartheid* government came into power in South Africa in 1948, it saw the schooling system as the major vehicle for the propagation of its beliefs. For the period of apartheid's duration, schools were one of the system's most stark symbols. Today, as a new and democratic government seeks to repair and reconstruct the fabric of South Africa's ravaged past, it is to the schooling system that much attention has turned.

THE SOCIAL FABRIC

In May 1994, after almost fifty years of *apartheid,* South Africa became a formal democracy. Nelson Mandela became the first freely elected president of the country and the African National Congress (ANC), which was banned in 1962, assumed the reins of power in the new Government of National Unity (GNU). The heritage that confronted this new government was complex. As a result of history, South Africa was (and still) remains a country in which the inscriptions that divide race, class, culture, and religion run deep.

Apartheid

A central tenet of the National Party government that was in power in 1948 was that the South African population consisted of discrete groups that were racially and culturally distinct. Based on this philosophy, four identifiable groups were defined: Whites, Africans, Indians, and Coloreds. Their places in society, according to *apartheid,* were unique and demanded political, social, and cultural arrangements that would enable them to fulfill their distinct destinies. It was therefore necessary, went the argument, that they lived in their own separate social and political spheres. African people, and indeed other people of color, had no rights or entitlements in the world of White people. Rigid and impermeable barriers were thus created between people presumed to be of different racial backgrounds.

Overlaying these boundaries of race and color, there were (and still are) boundaries of class. Such class-bound divisions have served to separate the majority of the working and nonworking poor, consisting largely of people of color, from a relatively small middle class, which is largely White.

As part of its policy of *apartheid,* the National Party government attempted to resettle African people in ethnically distinct homelands out of the major urban areas. The homelands were human dumping grounds where people were literally forcibly resettled from "White" areas. They were generally located in the most desolate and underprovided parts of the country that offered their inhabitants little prospect of development. As is well known, these policies bred a spirit of defiance and resistance among people of color and produced what came to be known as *the struggle* for equal rights and democracy.

Economy

As a result of a combination of international sanctions against South Africa and poor management of the economy, the country spun into a reverse growth phase in the mid-1980s. By the time the new government assumed power in 1994, the capacity of the economy to support the new democracy had been severely cut back.

Equally, the country is characterized by uneven growth, with much of the development occurring in the dense urban areas, especially the Witwatersrand, Durban, and Cape Town. This is significant in that 72 percent of all schools are classified as nonurban and much of the resourcing has clearly not flowed into these areas.

Unemployment remains relatively high—27.8 percent in 2004. An expanded definition, which includes those who are not actively seeking work, puts this figure at 42 percent in 2003 (Statistics South Africa, 2004). This clearly places pressure on the education system both in a curricular and a political sense.

Demography and Diversity

In 1994, when Nelson Mandela came into office, the country had a population of 40,648,574 (South African Institute of Race Relations, 1996). By 2004, Statistics South Africa estimated that the population had grown to approximately 46.6 million. African people were in the majority (nearly 37 million), constituting 79.3 percent of the total South African population. The number of White people was estimated to be 4.4 million, Colored people 4.1 million, and Asian people 1.1 million (Statistics South Africa, 2004). The country has substantial Jewish, Muslim, and Hindu communities, each with its own unique cultural visions, although the majority of its people belong to a variety of Christian denominations (Moosa, 1997). Fifty-one percent (approximately 23.6 million) of the population is female.

Two more characteristics about the profile of the present South African population have a bearing on education and its provision. First, in 1993, 37.3 percent of this population was in the 0-to-14 age group category (South African Institute of Race Relations, 1996). Ten years later, these proportions remain the same. Second, it was estimated that the HIV-positive population in 2004 stood at approximately 3.83 million people, with an HIV prevalence rate of 15.2 percent within the adult population. The accumulated AIDS deaths up to 2004 were estimated to be 1.49 million (Statistics South Africa, 2004).

SCHOOLING

In the past, the structure for education in South Africa was marked by the central principle of *apartheid,* namely separate schooling infrastructures for separate groups. In terms of the *apartheid* principle, nineteen education departments were established so that each designated ethnic group had its own educational infrastructure. Theoretically, and to some degree in practice, there was a central coordinating department called the Department of National Education. The Department of Education and Training (DET) administered education for African people outside of the homelands. Each of the homelands, ten in number, had its own separate and "autonomous" education department. Out of the House of Assembly came the Department of Education and Culture for whites with four provincial departments. The House of Representatives for Coloreds and the House of Delegates for Asians likewise had their own Departments of Education and Culture.

When the new government came into power in 1994, one of its first acts was to dissolve the nineteen education departments and to bring them under a centrally constituted

Department of Education. This national department was given the responsibility for formulating national policy. The nine new provinces that came into being as a result of the new dispensation were each entrusted with the responsibility of administering the new system. The new provinces are Eastern Cape, Free State, Gauteng, KwaZulu Natal, Mpumalanga, Northern Cape, Northern (now Limpopo) Province, North West Province, and Western Cape.

The Structure of Schooling

The South African schooling system is essentially organized into two major sectors, primary and secondary. At the primary level, African schools tend to be organized into junior and higher primary schools. Where schools are organized into junior and higher primary subdivisions, the former takes students up to the third grade, and the latter span grades 4 to 7.

The division in the rest of the system is simply between that of primary and secondary, where the terminal grade is the equivalent of the seventh grade. Primary schooling thus consists of seven years. Secondary schooling begins at the eighth grade and is made up of five years of which the last three constitute preparation for the end of school matriculation examinations. On completion of twelve years of schooling—eligible students may enter tertiary and continuing education tracks.

In 2001, there was a total of 11,738,126 pupils in South African schools. There were 6,286,723 primary pupils; 3,475,418 secondary pupils; and 1,975,985 pupils in combined, intermediate, and middle schools. These children were served in a total of 27,258 schools, divided as 17,184 primary schools, 5,670 secondary schools, and 4,604 combined primary/secondary schools. At the same time, there were 178,829 primary teachers, 111,523 secondary teachers, and 62,849 teachers in the other schools—353,201 teachers in all (Department of Education, 2003).

Of significance for understanding the system is that a large number of teachers continue to be underqualified. The Department of Education's national director of teacher development said that a 2001 audit showed that of about 350,000 teachers, 58,000 were underqualified. Half of these had upgraded their qualifications or were in the process of having them upgraded (*Sunday Times,* 2004). This has implications for the abilities of teachers to carry out the complicated curricular reforms that have been mooted and also impacts on resources for retraining.

On the question of resources, an urban bias in the distribution of resources creates considerable difficulties in the equalization of resources. Keep in mind that 72 percent of all schools are classified as nonurban (Arnott & Chabane, 1995; Edusource Data News, 1996).

Higher Education

Until 1998, the higher education sector consisted of 21 universities, 15 *technikons* (a South African variant of polytechnics), and 140 single-discipline vocational colleges (education, nursing, and agriculture), all previously divided along racial lines. The sector was considerably reconfigured after 2001 when the Department of Education released its *National Plan for Higher Education* (Department of Education, 2001b). In terms of this plan, the higher education sector was reduced from 36 institutions to 21 through a national process of mergers. Concurrent with this development, vocational colleges have all but disappeared and have been subsumed into new large amalgamated Further Education and Training colleges.

As the work of Jansen (2002) has shown, the merger process (which continues) has been difficult and has been characterized by struggles between merging institutions bringing with them very different histories and experiences of funding, participation rates, staff/student ratios, throughput rates, and quality. Articulation between different levels of institutions under the *apartheid* system was weak. The question of articulation was addressed through the development of a National Qualifications Framework, which sought to facilitate opportunity for more movement between different kinds of institutions.

Curriculum

Curriculum development in South African education during the period of *apartheid* was controlled tightly from the center. While, theoretically at least, each separate department had its own curriculum development mechanisms and protocols, in reality curriculum formation in South Africa was dominated by committees attached to the White House of Assembly. These committees invariably determined the core content of what was taught in all the other departments (see NEPI Framework Report, 1992). So prescriptive was this system, abetted on the one hand by a network of inspectors and subject advisors, and on the other, as can be seen below, by several generations of poorly qualified teachers, that authoritarianism, rote learning, and corporal punishment were the rule. These conditions were exacerbated in the impoverished environments of schools for children of color. Examinations were profoundly important in entrenching these conservative pedagogical approaches. Examination criteria and procedures allowed teachers very little latitude to determine standards and interpret the work of their students; they were also instrumental in promoting the political perspectives of those in power.

This approach was authorized as the official educational philosophy of the South African educational system. It brought to education deeply authoritarian and intolerant values and practices. Other approaches, furthermore, were declared unscientific and invalid. The consequence of this approach was that the curriculum was perceived, particularly by the disenfranchised, as being oppressive and exclusionary. It came to be seen as the transmission belt for the system's hidden and explicit racism.

As discussed below, a new curriculum has been introduced. The purpose of this new curriculum is to address issues of progression, portability, and skills development and to reform the exclusionary nature of the old apartheid approach to schooling.

Governance and Financing

Under *apartheid,* the system was structured so that control of the most important administrative and pedagogical tasks lay in the hands of the government. The state determined at the central level what salaries were to be paid; the guidelines for appointments, which individual departments were expected to implement; and, as was discussed above, the norms and standards for syllabus and curriculum development.

This state of affairs, particularly in embattled Black schools, was fiercely resisted. Wide-sweeping changes have been initiated by the new government to deal with these difficulties. It is important to spell out the more formative steps the government has taken.

One major achievement of the process of reform, as was explained above, has been the establishment of a single ministry of education. Another was the passing of the South African Schools Act in 1996. This Act established the right of every person to basic education and equal access; the right to be instructed in a language of choice (where practicable); the right to the freedoms of conscience, belief, expression, and association; and the right to establish education institutions based on a common language, culture, and religion. With respect to funding, the Act permitted schools to levy school fees, but simultaneously prohibited schools from denying entry to individuals who were unable to pay such fees. Other developments have included the redesigning of the curriculum, the rationalization of a complex of different types of schools into two forms only (from eight different categories of public school)—state and private schools—and the introduction of strong parental participation in school governance.

The impact of these developments has had far-reaching implications for teachers and is being felt differently in the diverse schools of the country. Having consolidated the fractured education system, the first challenge that confronted the authorities was that of equalizing per capita expenditure and resource commitment within it.

One measure that the state adopted was that of diverting emergency funds to schools for physical upgrading. Schools in bad repair in the black townships were awarded sums of money for the restoration of their structural fabric. Another measure, much more controversial, was to address the differences in teacher/pupil ratios between, particularly, White schools and African schools. This represented not only a pedagogical redistribution but, of course, a financial one. Ratios as low as 1:20 had been achieved in the former, while in the latter they had escalated to highs of 1:80. To bring uniformity, two standards were developed for the entire system: For high schools a ratio of 1:35 was developed, while primary schools were set a target of 1:40. The immediate consequence of the measure was to initiate the process of redistributing funding from schools that were highly subsidized to those that were poorly subsidized, and schools that were perceived to be overendowed were required to reduce their expenditure on staff. These measures, as we indicate below, were not without their own disabling difficulties.

MAJOR ISSUES, CONTROVERSIES, AND PROBLEMS

Prior to the democratic elections of 1994, the ANC had already clarified its educational priorities and reform agenda. The key policy initiatives for the next five years were to be the following: reconstruction of the bureaucracy, governance, and management; the integration of education and training; restructuring of the format of school education; changing the curriculum; paying attention to early childhood care, adult basic education, and special education; changes in the preparation of teachers; restructuring higher education; and restoring buildings and physical resources (African National Congress, 1994)

Following the above, three key issues are discussed in the following section. The first area of focus is the curriculum; the second is inclusive education and the problem of special needs education. The final section reviews the efforts by the state to deal with inequalities in the schools.

Curriculum Reform

Curriculum change in the new era began almost as soon as the new Education Minister took office. Within months of the historic elections of 1994, an announcement was made by the Department of Education that it was undertaking a process of purging the *apartheid* syllabi of their more offensive content. An elaborate series of committees was appointed to review texts and curricula materials.

This development occurred while other curriculum debates were taking place elsewhere. A particularly important debate had been begun in the early 1990s in which business, government, trade unions, educationists, and a variety of other groups participated. The interests brought to this debate were varied, ranging from concerns with a curriculum that would prepare a productive labor force, to concerns about a curriculum that would promote quality in learning, to concerns about the curriculum having as its *raison d'être* the development of equity and equality. Joined in a common purpose were business leaders, educationists, and political groups. Business people were dissatisfied with the previous curriculum, which they described as irrelevant and inadequate in terms of providing young people with the knowledge and the skills to make productive contributions in a modern economy. Educationists and political groups, for their part, were unhappy about the *apartheid* bias of the curriculum.

Through several years of discussion, which involved consultations with experts in countries such as the United Kingdom and New Zealand, agreement was reached around the development of a National Qualifications Framework (NQF) as the rubric within which the new curriculum could be structured. At the level of the school, a new curriculum was unveiled called Curriculum 2005, consisting of two parts, a first compulsory phase called the General Education and Training (GET) phase made up of grades 1 to 9, and a second post-compulsory phase called the Further Education and Training (FET) phase consisting of grades 10 to 12. Central to these developments was the idea of putting in place a learning environment and framework that would promote lifelong learning, integrate education and training, recognize learning gained outside of formal institutions, and allow for flexible, portable credits and qualifications.

In terms of Curriculum 2005, nationally agreed-upon learning outcomes for grades 1 to 8 (described as the General Education and Training Phase) were formulated, together with assessment criteria to assist the educator in determining whether the outcomes had been achieved. Outcomes were formulated around nationally agreed-upon unit standards in terms of which a learner was expected to demonstrate competence through both understanding and application.

For grades 1 to 8, the curriculum itself was developed around eight Learning Areas. These were language, literacy, and communication; mathematical literacy, mathematics, and mathematical sciences; human and social sciences; natural sciences; technology; arts and culture; economic and management sciences; and life orientation.

The significance of this curriculum change was great, but did not, as might be expected, unfold without criticism. While the development was welcomed as a step forward from the authoritarian and content-based curricula of *apartheid,* anxieties were expressed about the speed of the implementation of the innovation, the underrepresentation of important stakeholders in both the conception and implementation phases of the initiative and, most importantly, the underemphasis in the curriculum on subject content.

At the heart of the debate was the accusation that the new curriculum model contained a tension between an interest in the development of competence and the more immediate demonstration or performance of particular skills that made it unviable (see Muller, 1996). More practical concerns were also expressed about the obfuscating language that was used to define the curriculum and the poor guidance provided to teachers in implementing it. A consequence of these concerns was a decision on the part of the Department of Education to revise the curriculum and to introduce a more streamlined and simplified version, generally referred to as the Revised National Curriculum Statements in 2001. Significantly, the essentially outcomes-based orientation of the curriculum was kept in place and was introduced into the FET phase of schooling for 2005. The FET is to be offered in three sites—at a school level as indicated before, at the vocational college level, and through learnerships where industries work in partnerships with vocational colleges.

Special Education

With the adoption of the new Constitution and Bill of Rights in 1996, South Africa committed itself to a rights-based and broadly inclusive approach to education. However, a particular challenge arises in relation to those with special educational needs. Here, inclusion specifically implies that, wherever possible and practicable, a child's special needs will be met in the normal, mainstream school, classroom, and curriculum. A primary assumption in this is that the mainstream itself is sufficiently resourced and is an optimally facilitative environment for meeting the developmental needs—special or not—of all children. In South Africa, this is still far from the reality.

Recognizing this reality, the state's policy on inclusion includes two major thrusts (Department of Education, 2001a). The first is directed at transforming the mainstream, including the curriculum, to one where differences in individual learning needs are more explicitly acknowledged, identified, and accommodated. Inherent in this thrust is the notion of prevention—particularly of the many factors that exacerbate special educational needs through lack of recognition for what they are (Donald, Lazarus, & Lolwana, 2002). Inevitably, the success of this thrust is bound up with the challenges facing curricular reform as a whole.

The second thrust is more explicitly aimed at developing district support services for those with special educational needs in the mainstream and for their teachers. Within this, existing special schools are required to become resource centers and sources of support to local mainstream schools, while still addressing the needs of those with the most severe disabilities. However, the demands in meeting the requirements of this thrust, both fiscal and human, have been severe, particularly given the broader demands of transformation.

What remains certain is that the challenge of achieving effective inclusive education in South Africa will be a long-term process. Ultimately, it is inseparable from the other broader issues and challenges that have been outlined in this chapter.

Equity in Education

One of the key focus areas of reform since 1994 has been the linked issues of equity, equality, and redress. Given the disparities created by the previous regime, these issues not only have educational but also political significance as the new government attempts to generate visible signs of change. Space permits only a brief discussion of equity in this chapter. However, the noted overlap of equity, equality, and redress means that light will also be shed on the latter two.

While the issue of equity is multifaceted, we will limit ourselves to discussion of two main mechanisms that have been employed to achieve it. The first relates to input-based fiscal reallocations to provinces based on the pupil–teacher ratios (PTRs) referred to earlier (40:1 in the primary school and 35:1 in the secondary school). In this plan, equal spending between provinces on a pupil-per-capita basis was to be phased in by the year 2000. Given the consequences for staffing levels in "overstocked" provinces, the process is also referred to as a form of "right-sizing" or "rationalization" (*Cape Argus,* June 12, 1996).

We may illustrate the process with the example of the first round of fiscal reallocations for 1995/1996 of grants to the provinces. A scenario emerged where two provinces were to receive substantial cutbacks in expenditure. In the Western Cape, the projected decrease was 4.2 percent and in Gauteng the decrease was 1.8 percent. In human terms, this meant that the Western Cape was scheduled to shed 6,000 teachers in 1996 and a further 6,000 in 1997 (35 percent of total establishment), while Gauteng was to shed 6,800 by 1997 (14.2 percent of the total establishment) (Edusource, 1996). This was in the face of an overall budgetary increase of 7.76 percent (Provincial Budget Guidelines, 1996). Despite these measures, there is still differential per capita spending, with the poorest provinces having the lowest pupil expenditures. These gaps are, however, narrowing (Department of Education, 2002).

The second mechanism for achieving equity is the school-by-school right-sizing that is to occur within *all* provinces irrespective of the total allocation to the province. This is also referred to as "redeployment," an attempt to ameliorate right-sizing. An exemplar of this is KwaZulu Natal, where although there was an overall shortage of 2,200 teachers, some 3,000 had to be redeployed to understaffed schools (presumably in either rural or less desirable areas) (Edusource, 1996). At this level, principals are to guide the process through rationalization or right-sizing committees.

In respect of this mechanism, the policy means that not only is the burden of responsibility for deciding who should go and who should stay placed on individuals/schools, but that even in schools where there was/is disadvantage, educators there too are eligible for voluntary severance/retrenchment packages. This latter anomaly derives from teacher union pressure to apply rationalization to all schools on grounds of fairness.

Other important aspects of the rationalization process are that a condition of taking the package is that those leaving are not permitted to re-enter the school system and, as indicated, it is hoped that those who are in danger of being retrenched will voluntarily redeploy themselves in provinces or regions where there are teacher shortages. In this way, it was hoped that an equitable distribution of teachers would occur without having to retrench people.

Such a mechanism obviously relies on the willingness and ability to move on the part of teachers. Thus, for this plan to be feasible, accurate information about teacher numbers and their teaching subjects, pupil distribution data, reasonably accurate demographic forecasting counts, as well as the release of posts in provinces where there were shortages is needed. Few of these conditions were/are present.

Finally, the policy also requires changes in the nature of the supply of teachers from teacher training institutions. The 1994 stock of teachers was 341,903, of whom 61 percent were primary and 39 percent secondary teachers. If the aims for PTRs were achieved by 2000, the National Teacher Audit estimated that there would be a decline of ±6,000 primary school teachers (2.8 percent) and an increase of ±49,500 secondary teachers (38 percent) by 2004 (Hofmeyr & Hall, 1996). This would seem to indicate a shift in provision from the colleges that produce mainly nongraduate primary school teachers (and which account for ±80 percent of trainee teacher enrollments) to universities and technikons that produce mainly secondary school teachers.

The consequences of these approaches soon became obvious. First, the process of retrenchment divided schools, generated pupil protests, created a political furore, and placed intolerable burdens on principals who have to oversee the process. In the Western Cape, for example, 25 percent of principals themselves took the packages (*Cape Argus,* September 9, 1996). The effect on teacher morale and the ability of schools to take up the challenges of reconstruction cannot be underestimated.

Second, with some 12,000 teachers having taken the voluntary severance packages (*Mail & Guardian,* January 10–16, 1997), there has been a stripping of expertise from the system, both at the managerial level and at the level of classroom specialization. This was because there is no restriction on the eligibility of those who may wish to leave. A further irony is that the Minister is now contemplating hiring Cuban teachers in areas of skills shortage, namely mathematics and science (*Mail & Guardian,* March 7–13, 1997), at the same time as volunteer teachers from Ghana, Sri Lanka, and India in these subjects are being expelled from rural Eastern Cape schools (*Weekend Argus,* 1/2 March, 1997a).

Although the Department is unclear as to which subject areas have been affected by the retrenchments (*Mail & Guardian,* January 31/February 6, 1997), the impact on quality has been severe and is reflected (albeit by proxy) in the final-year, grade 12 matriculation examination results. From 1994 to 1999, the results showed a marked decline from a 58 percent to a 49 percent pass rate, with only 12 percent of the candidates qualifying for university entrance in 1999. There has been a largely unexplained and controversial increase since then to a pass rate of 73 percent in 2003 and a 19 percent university entrance pass (Mukwevho, Khosa, & Kgobe, 2004; Taylor, Muller, & Vinjevold, 2003). This increase is unexplained in the sense that that there is little systemic evidence to show why this has been the case. The overall effect, however, was that by 2003 there was a decline in candidates presenting themselves for the grade 12 examination from 495,408 in 1994 to 440,267 in 2003, a decline of 55,141 or 11 percent (Mukwevho et al., 2004). Importantly, the burden of these declining results have largely fallen on African and poor students.

Third, and compounding the above, has been the financial crises in the provinces caused by the implementation. The first difficulty in terms of funding the retrenchments has been that funds for this were only allocated to the provinces designated as "over-funded"

(Northern Cape and Free State were added to Western Cape and Gauteng), while, as indicated, all teachers could apply for the package. Second, with the reorganization of the various departments, funds that could previously have been squeezed from other departments, such as Public Works, now have to be found within education budgets. This has meant an immediate shortfall in moneys available for capital expenditure. Third, and equally serious, the spending excesses in the last days of *apartheid* have left several new provinces, particularly those that took over the former homelands, with deficit budgets to begin with (particularly Mpumalanga and Eastern Cape). The overall consequence was that all provinces faced immediate deficit budgets.

The response of provinces was predictable. In almost all cases, nonteaching professional services (such as counseling and special education) were cut. Building maintenance declined; and importantly, textbook ordering was reduced as provinces sought to cut in soft areas. While this was partly due to administrative chaos, it was also a consequence of deficit budgeting. Current policy aims to correct this to an 85:15 division of personnel and other budget items (Department of Education, 2002).

Other targets for cuts have been in teacher colleges and teacher training. Currently, the funding of Colleges of Education is a provincial affair without any restriction on where the graduates have to teach—which obviously means that some provinces subsidize others in terms of providing teachers. In a situation of tight fiscal constraint, the response has been to respond to provincial rather than national demand for teachers, which has meant the closure of colleges in at least two provinces (Western Cape and Northern Province) in line with the general re-organization described above. At the same time in these provinces, bursary offers to teaching students have been dropped.

These short-term measures, combined with a general uncertainty about the profession, have had knock-on effects of declining education student enrollments, particularly at university levels where considerable training of secondary teachers and in-service work takes place. Overall, and in combination with the HIV/AIDS pandemic, it is predicted that there will be a "yearly deficit of 12,000 teachers between 2011 an 2015" (Hofmeyr & Lee, 2004, p. 168). The impact on quality of these shortages is likely to be very problematic.

The public and media reaction to, and the political fallout from, such a situation was predictable. Indeed, the acting secretary-general of the ANC, in an unprecedented action, in January 1997 issued a "friendly word of criticism" to the Minister about the unintended consequences of the policy (*Eastern Province Herald,* 1997). In February, it was revealed that the Western Cape, having traumatically shed 6,000 teachers, would need to hire ±3,000 teachers to meet shortfalls due to miscounts and an influx of pupils from other provinces (*Cape Times,* 1997). By the end of the first week of February, the Minister called for a "thorough rethink of the structure, specifically of the severance packages" (*Mail & Guardian,* January 31/February 6, 1997).

The ANC-aligned teacher union, the South African Democratic Teachers' Union (SADTU), having originally supported the changes, now blamed the National Teacher Audit for having produced inaccurate figures about teacher–pupil ratios and demanded a rethink on the ratios. This has led to renegotiation with the Education Labour Relations Council, and the whole redeployment program has now been halted pending the outcome of negotiations. However, as of 2004, the ratios referred to above remain the basis for funding within schools.

THE FUTURE OF SOCIETY AND SCHOOLING

The future of schooling in South Africa is clearly indistinguishable from the larger social, political, and economic circumstances that are playing themselves out. There are historical roots and tensions that perhaps have tended to compromise the reforms of the state. While these may partly relate to the exigencies of power, the compromises also reflect the scope of reform and the lack of conceptual clarity attendant upon (an understandable) haste.

The Minister's response to this situation at the time was illuminating and indicates just how far conceptions of equity and equality had shifted and how far the process of compromise had reached. In a full-length interview in March 1997 (*Weekend Argus,* 1997b), the Minister stated that "Equity was not related to affirmative action. . . . All that equity says is that we reduce the budgets of the provinces that were funded above average and increase the budgets of those that were funded below average" (p. 22). He further explained that *redress* is perceived of as the redeployment of teachers to understaffed schools and that *affirmative action* is the promotion of African teachers. (The unwillingness of non-African teachers to shift to the African schools and take demotion is perceived as racism.) These are very different conceptions from the original ideals, and the question is how these shifts are to be interpreted and what influence they will have on the shape of education.

In general, though, the system has settled from the massive policy changes it has had to absorb on all fronts—administrative, financial, curricular, and political. The state and the provinces have come to recognize the significance of outcomes as key measures of performance in particular and equity in general. And so, while the first steps to equity may have lain through equality and consequent input-related measures, there is an important recognition now that equity really does rely on attention to the processes and outputs of education.

This recognition of the equity–equality distinction set apart the early democratic movement discourse from that of the *apartheid* state but has seemingly been lost in the pressure to reorganize. The problem for the state now is how to recapture these aims within the context of its own policy-practice without losing sight of those whom the system has yet to serve.

REFERENCES

African National Congress. (1994). *A policy framework for education and training.* Braamfontein: Author.

Arnott, A., & Chabane, S. (1995). *Teacher demand, supply, utilisation and costs: Report for the National Teacher Education Audit.* Craighall: Edusource.

Cape Argus. (June 12, 1996). Right-sizing of education. Message from Professor Sibusiso Bengu, Minister of Education. p. 25.

Cape Argus. (September 9, 1996). 1 in 4 school heads to quit, p. 1.

Cape Times. (February 4, 1997). Teacher shortage after cuts bungle, p. 1.

Department of Education. (2001a). *White paper on special needs education: Building an inclusive education and training system.* Pretoria: Government Printer.

Department of Education. (2001b). *The restructuring of the higher education system in South Africa—A report of the National Working Group to the Minister of Education.* Pretoria: Author.

Department of Education. (2002). *Education for all status report 2002. South Africa incorporating country plans for 2002–2015.* Pretoria: Author.

Department of Education. (2003). *Education statistics in South Africa at a glance in 2001.* Pretoria: Author.

Donald, D., Lazarus, S., & Lolwana, P. (2002). *Educational psychology in social context* (2nd ed.). Cape Town: Oxford University Press.

Eastern Province Herald. (January 24, 1997). ANC slams education plan, p. 4.

Edusource Data News. (1996). *A brief overview of education.* 1995, No. 12/April 1996.

Hofmeyr, J., & Hall, J. (1996). *The National Teacher Education Audit. Synthesis report.* Johannesburg: Centre for Education Policy Development, Edupol (NBI).

Hofmeyr, J., & Lee, S. (2004). The new face of private schooling. In L. Chisholm (Ed.), *Changing class: Education and social change in post-apartheid South Africa.* Cape Town: HSRC Press.

Jansen, J. (2002). *Mergers in higher education: Lessons learned in transitional contexts.* Pretoria: University of South Africa.

Mail & Guardian. (January 10–16, 1997). Officials and unions urge rethink over redundancies, p. 10.

Mail & Guardian. (January 31–February 6, 1997). Rethink on teacher severance, p. 8.

Mail & Guardian. (March 7–13, 1997). SA's plan to hire Cuban teachers, p. 4.

Moosa, E. (1997, March). Tensions in legal and religious values in the 1996 South African constitution. Paper presented at the Cultural Transformations Conference in Africa, University of Cape Town.

Mukwevho, T., Khosa, V. R., & Kgobe, M. (2004). An analysis of trends in matric results. *Quarterly Review of Education and Training in South Africa, 11,* 19–23.

Muller, J. (1996, October). A harmonized qualifications framework and the well-tempered learner: Pedagogic models, teacher education and the NQF. Paper presented at the conference "Lev Vygotsky, 1896–1996: A cultural historical approach: Progress in human sciences and education." Moscow, Russia.

National Education Policy Investigation (NEPI). (1992). *Support services.* Cape Town: Oxford University Press/NECC.

Provincial Budget Guidelines: 1994/95–1995/6 Budget Comparisons. (1996). Parliamentary briefing paper for the Education Standing Committee, Provincial Legislature (Western Province).

South African Institute of Race Relations. (1996). *Race relations survey, 1995/1996.* Johannesburg: South African Institute of Race Relations.

Statistics South Africa. (2004). http://www.statssa.gov.za/keyindicators/ifs.asp; http://www.statssa.gov.za/keyindicators/-mye.asp

Strauss, J. P., Plekker, S. J., Strauss, J. W. W., & van der Linde, H. J. (1995). *Education and manpower development 1995, No 16.* Bloemfontein: Research Institute for Education Planning, University of the Orange Free State.

The Sunday Times. (February 8, 2004). http://www.sundaytimes.co.za/2004/02/08/news/news01.asp

Taylor, N., Muller, J., & Vinjevold, P. (2003). *Getting schools working. Research and systemic school reform in South Africa.* Cape Town: Pearson Education South Africa.

Weekend Argus. (March 1/2, 1997a). Gestapo-style crackdown on expat teachers, p. 8.

Weekend Argus. (March 1/2, 1997b). Teacher row hots up as Bengu hits back, p. 1.

CHAPTER SEVENTEEN

BRAZIL

The Quest for Quality

CANDIDO ALBERTO GOMES

CLÉLIA CAPANEMA

JACIRA CÂMARA

THE SOCIAL FABRIC

Brazil is a country of continental dimensions, with 8.512 million square kilometers (5,313 square miles). It occupies the central-eastern part of South America. Brazil's population was estimated at 155.8 million in 1995, with the projection of 184.2 million for the year 2010. This places Brazil among the nine developing countries of highest population in the world—Brazil, People's Republic of China, Mexico, India, Pakistan, Bangladesh, Egypt, Nigeria, and Indonesia.

Candido Gomes received a Ph.D. in Education from UCLA. He is Professor of Education at Brasília Catholic University and has been a consultant for several international organizations. His previous position was of advisor for educational affairs to the Federal Senate and the National Constituent Assembly. Author of over 150 publications in nine languages, his academic interests are educational policy and management, as well as educational finance and comparative education.

Clélia F. Capanema is Professor of Education at the Catholic University of Brasília, Brazil, and was previously a Professor at the University of Brasília, from which she retired recently. Her B.A. in pedagogy and her M.Sc. in educational administration and planning, as well as her Ph.D. in international and multicultural education, were taken at the University of Southern California in the United States. From 1985 to 1986 she was in a postdoctoral program in comparative education at the Institute of Education, University of London. She was a visiting fellow at the same institution in 1996. Her main research interests include educational policies and management. She has published in books and in academic journals in Brazil and in the United States.

Jacira Câmara earned a Ph.D. in Education from the George Peabody College of Vanderbilt University and was a postdoctoral fellow at the University of London Institute of Education. She is now Director of the Graduate Program in Education and Professor of Education at Brasília Catholic University. Her numerous publications in Brazil and abroad focus on curriculum issues and comparative education. She has also occupied leading positions in national and international academic organizations.

Historical Developments

Brazil was one of the greatest jewels of the Portuguese colonial empire. Early Brazilian colonial society was elitist and ornamental. The rich cities of the time were marked by the flourishing of the baroque style adapted to Brazilian environment. However, society was based on slave labor. All the schools were religious, thanks to the association between the Portuguese Crown and the Catholic Church, but educational opportunities were in general scarce. Women of European origin did not receive any education, and it was nonexistent for the slaves.

According to the customs of the families of the great plantation owners, the first son inherited the land and the slaves, the second was destined to become a priest, and the third would be "lettered." This last one, in general, went to a Portuguese or French university to take a course, such as law, which had, in principle, no practical usage in the colony.

At first, sugar was important, but the seventeenth century saw the decline of the sugar economy in the Brazilian Northeast and the end of the monopoly shared by the Portuguese and Dutch. The beginning of the eighteenth century saw the discovery of gold and diamonds in the central region, and the mining economy opened opportunities for free labor and an urban society. However, the decline of mining in the last quarter of the eighteenth century led to a disassociation of interests between the colony and its colonial power.

A political pact in 1822 brought separation from Portugal. Despite national integration (which took a little longer than one century), the country was marked by acute regional and social disparities, the latter in great part resulting from the tardy legal abolition of slavery (1888). As well, there was particular negligence toward primary and teacher education, precisely those levels that could have been of benefit to those of lower socioeconomic group status.

Modern Brazil

It was in the early 1800s that Brazil's economy began to shift to the exportation of coffee, a product whose market had greatly expanded in the United States and Europe with the Industrial Revolution. The coffee economy was only displaced by the Great Depression of 1929. Not being able to generate foreign exchange credit, a vigorous process of industrialization to substitute imported goods was undertaken in Brazil. As in other Latin American countries, the industrial era counted on the incentive of the state as a planner and investor.

This continued into the 1970s. But the country started facing problems of stagnation: It had a closed economy, regulated by the state, and was not competitive internationally. Therefore, a crisis of external debt that affected the developing countries in the 1980s found Brazil with an economy that was commercially introverted and financially extroverted. The fiscal crisis and the elevated inflation that followed made public services unstable, including education.

Modern Brazil discusses and implements the adoption of fiscal, administrative, and social security reforms, among others, and many plans of economic stabilization have been put into practice and are continuing. For example, in 1994 the introduction of a new currency, the Real, was successful. A new general law of education and new mechanisms for financing it (1996) aimed at elevating the efficiency, the quality, and the equity of education, mainly in the historically neglected primary level.

SCHOOLING

Recent decades have witnessed a rapid quantitative expansion of education and the establishment of many islands of excellence in higher education. As well, the deceleration of demographic growth opens up new perspectives for educational improvement, since the country will now be able to shift priority from quantitative expansion to the improvement of quality and equity.

On the down side, the problems faced by Brazilian education—the country's large territory, sizable population, and an economy riddled with problems—have not changed much in the last decades. There are also problems concerning representative democracy, since Brazil is a federative republic with three levels of government—the federal, the state, and the municipal. The responsibilities falling on each of these three levels need to be better defined so that more efficient mechanisms for reducing inequalities within and among regions can be devised.

Basic Tenets for National Education

The General Education Act includes some innovative points. In summary, these are:

- *Decentralization and autonomy for educational systems.* The Act states that the educational system must be organized in terms of collaboration among the union, the states, and the municipalities. It also determines what role will be played by each administrative entity.
- *Enhancing the teaching profession.* The Act establishes higher standards of teacher training than those currently accepted, requiring "the association of theory and practice." It stresses the participation of teachers in the drafting up and implementation of the schools' teaching programs. It also establishes some mechanisms to assist the enhancement of education professionals.
- *Decentralization and autonomy for schools.* Primary and secondary educational institutions can exercise autonomy; they are henceforth responsible for drafting up and implementing their pedagogic proposals and managing their personnel, materials, and financial resources. Teachers have the freedom to carry out their work plans, to make use of appropriate methods to help students, and to work more closely with families and communities.
- *Decentralization and autonomy for universities.* The Act puts forward concepts concerning the rights of universities to autonomy and decentralization. However, certain conditions are laid down—the authorization and the recognition of courses, as well as the certification of higher education institutions, will be given only for specific periods of time. Periodic renewal will be contingent upon a regular evaluation process.

Organization and Structure of the Education System

The Brazilian education system is organized in two levels: basic education, including preschool education, primary, and secondary education; and higher education. Basic education is compulsory for children from 7 to 14 years of age. It seeks the development of the student, aiming at the acquisition of skills that are indispensable to the exercise of citizenship, to insertion into the job market, and to progress toward higher studies.

Basic education can be organized in diverse ways, depending on what the interest of the learning process recommends. These include annual grades, semester periods, cycles, alternating regular study periods, non-grade groups, or groups based on age, competence, or other criteria.

A general overview of the Brazilian education system is shown in Figure 17.1.

Preschool

Preschool education seeks the integral development of children under 6 years of age and can be offered in day-care centers and preschools. Evaluation at this level is made through observation of the children and records of their development, not aiming at promotion, not even for access to primary education.

Primary Education

Primary education is compulsory for 7-year-old children and optional for 6-year-olds. Its objective is the basic education of a citizen through the development of the capacity to learn, aiming at the acquisition of knowledge and abilities, as well as of attitudes and values. This is demonstrated by a full command of reading, writing, and arithmetic; an understanding of the natural and social environment, of the political system, of technology, of the arts, and of the values upon which society is founded; and the strengthening of ties of family, of human solidarity, and of mutual tolerance.

Regular primary education is given in Portuguese. However, indigenous communities are allowed to use their own languages and learning processes.

Secondary Education

Secondary education is the final stage of basic education, lasting three or four years, the last one being optional. Its goals are the consolidation and deepening of the knowledge acquired in primary education, making the continuation of studies possible. Secondary school also seeks to provide basic preparation for work and for the exercise of citizenship, as well as the refinement of the student as a person. This includes the development of ethical behavior, intellectual autonomy, and critical thinking.

The secondary education curriculum highlights basic technological education; an understanding of the meaning of science, of literature, and of the arts; the historical process of social and cultural transformation; the Portuguese language as a tool for communication and access to knowledge; and the exercise of citizenship. Besides the requirement of one foreign language, the inclusion of another optional language is suggested.

Secondary education has a flexible organization in order to respond to the different needs of the students. All the courses of secondary education have legal equivalence and qualify the student to further his or her studies. Preparation for work may be developed in the secondary education institutions themselves or in cooperation with other institutions specialized in vocational training.

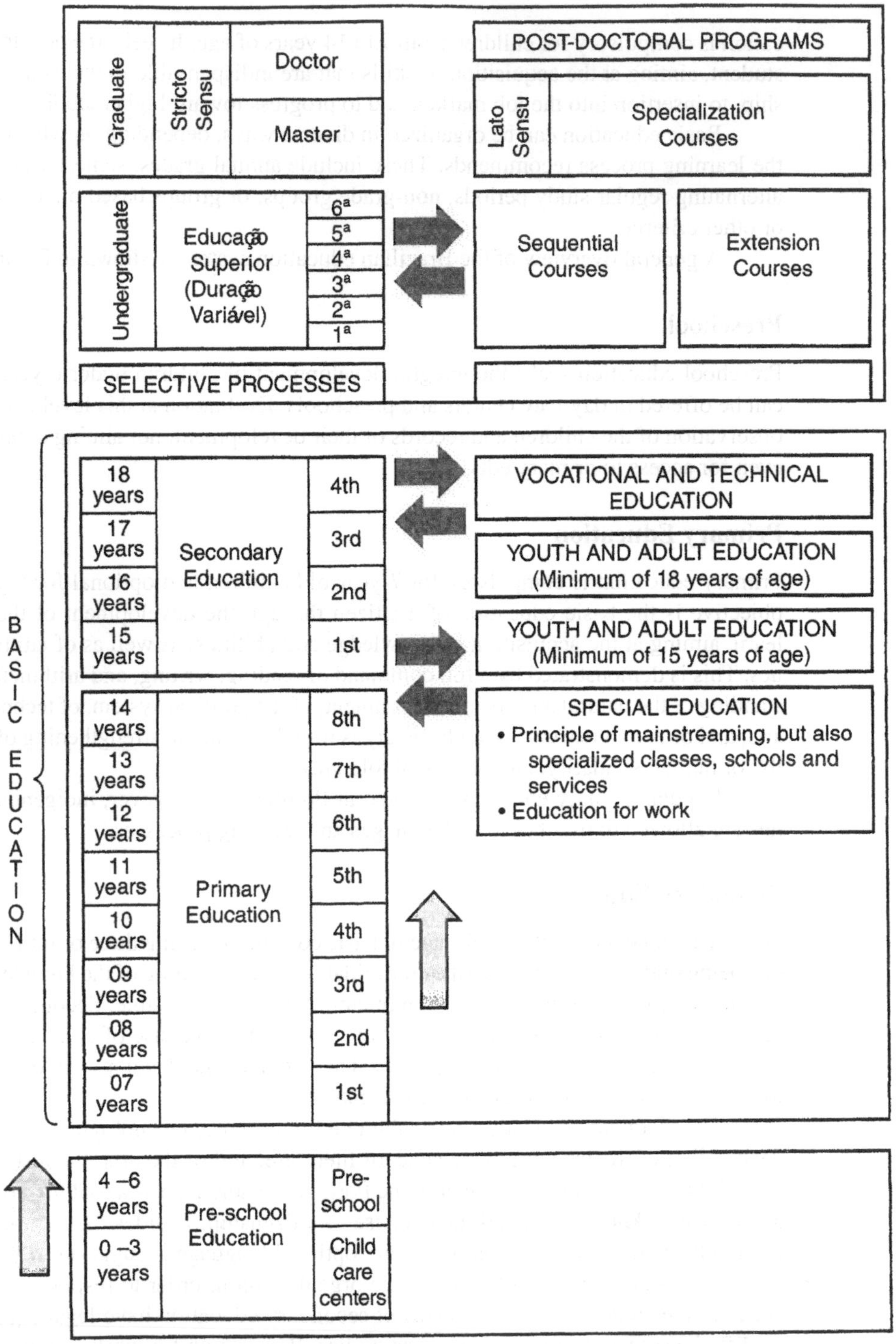

FIGURE 17.1 Organization and structure of the Brazilian education system.

Higher Education

The objectives of higher education are to stimulate cultural creativity and to develop a scientific spirit and analytical thought; to train students in the different fields of knowledge; and to make them capable of participating in the development of Brazilian society. Higher education also aims at stimulating research and scientific investigation; at promoting the dissemination of cultural, scientific, and technical knowledge; at fostering knowledge of national, regional, and contemporary world issues; at rendering community service and establishing a reciprocal relationship with that community; and expanding educational opportunities to all citizens by promoting adequate forms of cultural extension. Higher education includes short careers in different areas.

Undergraduate courses are open to candidates who have finished secondary school. Graduate courses provide deeper command of a specialization area, including improvement and extension courses.

Youth and Adult Education

Youth and adult education was designed for those who have not attended or finished regular schools at the appropriate age. The educational systems offer courses on the subjects prescribed in the national curriculum. Learning is assessed by exams, according to the different levels of schooling and to the different age groups. The students who graduate can then carry on their regular studies.

Technical and Vocational Education

Technical and vocational education aims at the permanent development of the capacity for a productive life. It is integrated as different forms of education, work, science, and technology and is offered either within regular education or through different strategies of continuing education. It can take place either in specialized institutions or in the workplace.

Vocational and technical schools, in addition to their regular courses, offer special courses open to the community. Enrollment in these courses is conditional on the capacity of the individual to benefit from it, not necessarily on the student's level of schooling.

Special Education

Special education, understood as the modality of school education for students with special needs, is offered preferably in the regular school system. It begins with the age group from zero to 6 years of age. The educational systems ensure specific assistance by modifying curricula, methods, techniques, educational resources, and organization for students with special needs.

The introduction of inclusive policy is currently one of the great challenges facing Brazilian education. This policy of including students with special needs in the regular school system goes well beyond their physical permanence in the schools' premises. It represents a daring attempt to review notions and paradigms in order to develop these students' potential, respecting their differences, and attending to their needs. Among the major obstacles to introducing this policy are the need to intensify, both in quantitative and in qualitative terms, the training of human resources; obtaining financial resources; and the provision of specialized pedagogical services capable of ensuring the educational development of students.

Management of the Educational System

Early childhood and primary education are predominantly the responsibility of the municipalities. The states are in charge of secondary and, partially, higher education.

The private sector is free to participate at all levels of education, depending on approval and evaluation by the government. Autarchic (para-state organizations that receive public resources, add private money from several sources, and are managed by businessmen/women of the respective sector) systems provide TVET (agriculture, manufacture, commerce and services, transportation).

SUCCESSES

Innovative Solutions for Access and Management

Brazil has attained significant gains in access to education. To a lesser degree, there are gains in efficiency. One example is illiteracy among the population aged 15 and older. The rates have declined from 39.6 percent in 1960 to 20.1 percent in 1991 and 11.8 percent in 2002. But in spite of the significant decrease of the total number of illiterate people, during the last decade, there was still a concentration in the older age brackets. By 2000, however, the illiteracy rate of the 20-to-24 age bracket fell to 6.7 percent, an amount not too different from the residual rates of some developed countries.

Pointing to a general expansion of the system are examples of the increase in access and coverage and the rise of the average number of years of schooling. Between 1992 and 2002, this amount rose from 5.2 to 6.5 years among the population aged 15 and older.

The net primary schooling rate rose from 86.6 percent in 1992 to 96.9 percent in 2002. The same indicator for secondary education rose from 18.2 percent in 1992 to 40.7 percent ten years later. In higher education, the rate went from 4.6 percent to 9.7 percent in 1992 to 2002.

Simultaneously, the number of students who are older than the official school age decreased, although slowly. Primary school students with age–grade distortions amounted to 47.2 percent of total number in 1998 and 3.9 percent in 2003. In secondary school, these proportions dropped from 53.9 percent to 49.3 percent in the same period. Although not as fast as could be desired, student flows are being corrected, leading to a reduction of costs and the liberation of an internal source of funding for the educational system.

These changes, as well as the quest for quality in basic education, were based on a number of factors. Chiefly, these were advances in terms of financing, decentralization of school administration, and improved inputs.

The Primary Education Fund

This fund, established in 1996, consists of a tax reform for education, passed as a constitutional amendment. This equalization fund consists of the earmarked use of 15 percent of state and municipal selected taxes, divided up according to the number of students and deposited in a bank account, usually controlled by the Secretary of Education. The fund provides for complementary federal funds in regions where the average expenditure per student does not reach the standard minimum.

The fund targets the lack of priority to primary education and the great differences in the use of funds among the states and municipalities. Evaluation of the immediate impact was very positive. There was an increase in resources, especially in the poorer municipalities. The net schooling rate improved faster in the states receiving complementary funds from the federal government.

The teaching profession benefited almost immediately, especially in poorer areas. The salaries of full-time teachers increased by 29.6 percent (59.6 percent in the poorest region) between June 2000 and December 1997, which caused an increase in their level of schooling (Brazil, 1999; Gomes, 2002; World Bank, 2003). Yet, in some areas at least, teachers' salaries are not maintained (Verhine & Rosa, 2003).

School Improvement Project: *Fundescola*

Another relevant change occurred in the use of international resources. One program, funded with a total of US$1.3 billion from the federal government and from credit operations involving the World Bank, encompasses nineteen states in the North, Northeast, and Central-West regions and about 400 municipalities in priority areas. It emphasizes the development of initiatives for strengthening school management and the teaching-learning process. The use of strategic planning in schools through School Development Plans (PDE) is one of the crucial components of this project.

External evaluation demonstrated that, although there were no statistically significant gains in the performance of students attending the schools served, there was a decrease in dropout and grade repetition rates. Absenteeism levels, formerly high, dropped considerably, and there was a modest but significant effect on income earnings. Thus, although there were no notable advances in the performance in Portuguese and mathematics, the significant increase in the number of students being promoted in schools that have School Development Plans may ultimately be more important to the future economic success of these students than higher grades in academic performance.

Training of Unlicensed Teachers for Primary Education: *Proformação*

This program consists of a distance education system that combines self-study, school-based practice, local biweekly meetings among tutors and trainees, and a support communication system. Communication includes assistance to tutors and trainees in each state provided by training agencies and the establishment of permanent communication channels among the participants.

One of *Proformação*'s noticeable characteristics is its management and control strategy. Because the program was developed through a partnership involving the Ministry of Education, states, and municipalities, each of these levels performs specific functions in the program's implementation. The program is supervised and monitored by a central team and must undergo an external evaluation. Slightly over one-third of funding comes from federal sources; the rest is shared by participating states and municipalities.

Results have been encouraging so far. For one thing, in spite of its efficiency, the program is far from expensive, considering the fact that training a teacher for two years has an average cost of US$1,100. Second, pass rates are significantly high in relation to distance education standards: Of the 27,392 teachers who started the course in 2000, 86 percent accomplished it. Finally, external evaluation showed that teaching practices improved after the course. Teachers started planning classes and adopted new teaching and management practices. They demonstrated improvement in attitudes toward students with greater expectations of the students' learning capacity and performance levels. And, most importantly, in many cases there was a significant improvement in the self-esteem of graduates.

National Schoolbook Program, School Libraries, and School Meals

The expansion of several ongoing programs combined with the establishment of new initiatives have contributed to the increase of schooling rates in Brazil. The National Schoolbook Program has been broadened in scope the most.

In the mid-1990s, following an evaluation process, the Ministry of Education established rules for the purchase processes and the choice of books to be bought and distributed to primary schools.

Changes meant that over the last few years there was an intense renovation and expansion of the collection of textbooks available to schools. Resources increased fourfold in terms of nominal figures. The numbers grew from 56.9 million books for 5.5 million students in 1995, to 80.3 million books for 31.9 million students in 2001. In 2001, the program covered 90.5 percent of the population enrolled.

Simultaneously, the Ministry is developing another important activity: the National School Library Program. With resources amounting to US$20 million, almost 8 million collections have been distributed to nearly all primary schools and also to youth and adult education institutions over the past few years. The number of schools served grew from 20,000 in 1998 to 139,000 in 2001.

The National School Meal Program should also be considered, as it has attained a great level of decentralization of resources. The number of students served increased from 33.2 million in 1995 to 37.1 million in 2001.

Likewise, federal resources that were previously distributed according to political criteria were decentralized under the Money Straight to the Schools programs. Funds, now transferred directly to schools, are used to meet current expenses (with the exception of expenses of staff and small investments), with the participation of the community (Brazil,

2002). Since the new government took office in 2003, per pupil resources have gradually increased.

The decentralization of funding to the schools received very positive evaluations. The main difficulty was the loss of funding from other sources. Another problem centered on the low level of community participation in management, which, more often than not, was left to the principals.

School Attendance Scholarship: *Bolsa-Escola*

Sending children to school may be a burden to poor families in which child labor is a source of income. For that reason, income transference programs tied to school attendance were experiments within several areas of Brazil in the early 1990s and were expanded to full scale in 2001 by the federal government. An evaluation of the program conducted in the country's capital city indicated that, in four years, it had served 25,680 families and 50,673 children. The total cost of the program was equivalent to 1 percent of the total annual budget.

Evaluations (e.g., Abramovay, Andrade, & Waiselfisz, 1998; Aguiar & Araújo, 2002; World Bank, 2001b) pointed to good results, as well as the fiscal affordability of the program. School attendance increased and grade repetition and dropout rates significantly diminished; so too did age–grade discrepancies. Cash transfers to mothers contributed to empowering women and increasing the responsibility assumed by the family. The *Bolsa Escola* also contributed to breaking down mechanisms traditionally used by schools to exclude poorer students. However, evidence of improved learning outcomes was much weaker.

While the *Bolsa Escola* was predominantly developed in metropolitan areas, the Program for the Eradication of Child Labor (PETI), considered an experience unique in all the world, focused on nonurban areas, especially in rural zones. The evaluation of the five years of program implementation, carried out by the World Bank (World Bank, 2001a), yielded very positive results. The total percentage of working children went down from 20 percent in 1992 to 15 percent in 1999. In three states in the country's poorest region, child labor decreased by 15 percent, 5 percent, and 10 percent, respectively.

Accelerated Learning Programs

Accelerated learning programs target students with age–grade discrepancies who have lagged behind and need to make up for the time lost. Learning conditions are simple and basic and in keeping with good practice as defined by the best education manuals. As they gain access to special teaching-learning conditions, students' self-esteem also improves. The total enrollment in acceleration classes was 1,072,648, corresponding to 3.1 percent of the total primary education enrolment.

Acelera Brasil is the main and probably the most comprehensive of these programs. Some of its requisites are a maximum number of students per class, abundant educational materials, in-service teacher training and supervision, and political commitment on the part of the authorities of related policy areas.

External evaluations (Gomes, 2004) indicate that considerable progress has been made by students, and that resources have been saved, compensating for the cost of the program.

Academic achievement, in general, is equivalent to that of students who attend regular schools. Self-esteem is lower among the students who did not participate in the program, although the differences observed were not significant. Some difficulties were found in terms of the reinsertion of students into regular education, since a similar treatment was not provided.

CHALLENGES

Recent years have seen gains both in access and in the efficiency of Brazil's educational systems. However, there remain many challenges in terms of quality, of equity, and of social and regional inequality.

Because of these challenges, there is lingering disappointment with the modest results of the education policies adopted in the last decades. These include reforms aimed at the reformulation of both the theory and the practice of curriculum; the modernization of the administrative systems by means of decentralization; and the administration of units according to a democratic view based on participation and school autonomy.

Although Brazil has not yet overcome the challenges regarding access, the main problems faced by the country's education refer to quality and equity. This is demonstrated clearly in the modest academic performance of its students, international evaluations, and the inequality of educational conditions and achievement according to regions and social classes. For example, a biennial assessment of quality rates, measured by the Basic Education Evaluation System (SAEB) between 1995 and 2003, shows a decline in the performance curves for students of primary and secondary schools, although not statistically significant in several instances. Moreover, there are recurrent and conspicuous inequalities in school achievement among different social groups and across regions of the country.

Next, we discuss these challenges.

Illiteracy

Data on illiteracy indicate that, in many cases, schools produce functionally illiterate adults. One research study suggests that only 23 percent of Brazilian youths and adults, university students included, are capable of solving a problem involving proportional calculations (percentages). This same study found that only 29 percent of Brazilians have mathematical skills for reading numbers expressing prices, timetables, telephone numbers, measurement instruments, calendars, and mathematical representations such as tables and graphics (Delgado, 2004).

The most recent literacy program, *Brasil Alfabetizado* (Literate Brazil), is a 2004 initiative of the Ministry of Education. Aimed at reaching out to 1.6 million youths and adults, the program was adopted by 23 states and 370 municipalities, as well as 59 public-interest civil society organizations and universities. Approximately US$56 million was earmarked for literacy training and close to US$143.6 million to the youth and adult education that forms a prong of the program.

Access

As in nearly all Latin American countries, Brazil has a growing reliance on education systems more efficiently adapted to the new social, political, and market realities of a sophisticated knowledge society within a globalized world. Economic and educational reforms are an attempt to build capacity to compete.

Brazil's challenge consists not only in broadening access to quality education at the secondary and tertiary levels, but also improving quality in the primary schools. Although elementary access is now virtually universal, it is still deficient in terms of practical effects due to high rates of school dropouts, grade repetition, and poor achievement.

There has been a significant expansion of enrollment in secondary education. In 1996, 1.3 million students were enrolled; this number increased to 2.2 million students in 2002 (Brazil, 2002). Yet, this is not being followed by improved quality. Neither is it changing the encyclopedic nature of secondary education learning, which is viewed merely as a preparation for higher education.

Early Childhood Education

Whenever resources are scarce, good-quality early childhood education should focus on the more vulnerable social groups. Hence, the demand for good-quality early childhood education is growing continuously and becoming more urgent, posing the challenge of prioritizing the provision of services for the more vulnerable groups. For example, there have been strong pressures to provide childcare centers and preschools in urban environments where working mothers exist in greater numbers.

Attempts to provide nonformal education have yielded inadequate results, with poor services being offered to those in need of good early childhood education. The expansion goals of the ten-year National Plan of Education clash with the limited financial capacity of municipalities and also with the priority conferred to compulsory primary education. If the expansion goals are pursued, in the poorer regions the average spending per child per year would total less than a hundred dollars.

Solutions are politically difficult. They involve a regime of subsidiary cooperation among the state and federal levels that would provide for successive needs, and, perhaps, also the establishment of a basic education fund.

Grading, Retention, and Promotion

The repetition rate in the early grades of primary education is still 6.9 percent;10.8 percent in the last grades; and 9.0 percent in secondary education. Legislation has encouraged alternative experiments, such as the creation of cycles, age groups, and progressive advancement.

According to an evaluation of basic education conducted in 2001, the effects of grades and cycles upon student achievement are virtually the same. In view of the low average performance, it could be said that both systems appear as equally inadequate, or that neither has significant effects on school achievement. However, the automatic promotion of students in the cycle system disregards the social pact upon which the school is founded and frustrates all school actors. When students are unconditionally promoted without a corresponding degree of achievement, it is harmful mainly to the socially underprivileged.

Higher Education

Issues relevant to higher education pose daunting challenges to policymakers and educational managers. The first is the debate on the importance of evaluation as a natural consequence of quality, joined to the paramount role of research in higher education, an activity that should take place inside the universities. The second is the problem of financing in relation to school autonomy, viewed as an indispensable requisite for the promotion of quality.

Universities in general, and public universities in particular, were asked to perform research in order to generate knowledge, stimulate creativity, and promote innovation and change by combining education, science, and technology. The aim was to lead the development of the country and create an intellectual elite. Besides demanding a highly qualified staff, these roles demand monitoring by efficient evaluation.

Another issue is the close relation between funding and autonomy. The costs of tertiary education are high, both in private and in public institutions. The expansion of the public university system places a heavy burden on the state. The high price of tuition in the private sector makes it increasingly unaffordable to the students who belong to the less privileged segments of society, since they have to work all day and take night courses. That is the ugly face of social injustice. This picture is very upsetting to policymakers, to academics, and, of course, to the university students themselves.

Since their founding, public institutions have always provided education free of charge. Every once in a while, however, the possibility of public universities charging tuition is raised, based on the argument that their students belong to the higher social classes and can afford to pay for their studies. The debates on the issue are invariably heated and charged with an emotional tone because they carry a strong ideological component.

It is true that higher education has significantly expanded: Enrollment grew from 1.5 to 3.5 million between 1992 and 2002. The private sector was responsible for 59 percent of the total enrollment in 1992 and increased its participation to 70 percent ten years later. Such growth, however, did nothing to change the fact that Brazil is one of the Latin American countries with the lowest rates of provision of higher education to the population, far behind Chile and closer to Mexico. Neither did this expansion result in the inclusion of minorities or the underprivileged social classes, or in greater equality among regions in terms of the quality of the education provided.

Numbers that describe higher education in Brazil reflect the magnitude of the effort that must be undertaken in order to offer higher education to all Brazilian youth. Only 9 percent of all Brazilians aged between 18 and 24 gain access to public institutions of higher education. Of every 10 students who do obtain a place, 7.5 eventually graduate: that is, a percentage of 75 percent, with a 25 percent loss. In private institutions, this number falls to 5 graduates for each 10 students who enroll: that is, a loss of 50 percent, often the result of a lack of capacity to afford tuition (Delgado, 2004).

To minimize the sharp inequalities in educational opportunities currently existing in higher education, the Ministry of Education is proposing affirmative action by means of social quotas, both in public and private universities. This measure, however, does not seem to be enough to solve the problem of the access of underprivileged students.

The problem that can be anticipated from start is that, in broadening its scope of service to include this specific population, universities will be receiving students who had very deficient primary and secondary education and who will need specialized training to catch up with their colleagues.

A much more efficient mechanism would be the improvement of the public primary and secondary schools systems so that they would be able to qualify students to pass the entrance examinations to public universities. This measure might be accepted on a provisional basis, provided great care is taken not to jeopardize the quality standards of higher education institutions.

Another response is the University for All Program (PROUNI), launched by the federal government. It is an ambitious, complex, and polemic project. The object is for private institutions, by means of scholarships, to receive 300,000 low-income students within a period of four years, starting in 2004. Opposing voices argue that public resources should be channeled only to public universities and that PROUNI will render official an absurd situation—sizable public resources will be invested in private institutions. The majority of the academic community are in this camp and view PROUNI as a misguided policy. They would prefer that resources be directed to the expansion and improvement of public institutions.

The criticism coming from the private institutions points in a different direction. They argue that the mandatory nature of the provision of full scholarships will reduce the total number of students who receive scholarships of other kinds. The program, therefore, will result in more exclusion than the one existing at present. Government responses to these criticisms contend that this initiative deals with the issue on an emergency basis. They say that urgent and incisive action is needed in order to launch a policy of social justice in education.

Running parallel to the PROUNI, a system of quotas for Blacks, Indians, and underprivileged students graduating from basic education public schools has already been implemented. Most critics say that it is better to invest in educational quality so as to prepare all ethnic groups for furthering their studies, as it is doubtful that students who have gained admission to the universities based on criteria other than merit and competition will ever attain educational success.

DEBATES AND CONTROVERSIES

A New Evaluation System for Higher Education

Private universities, with some exceptions such as community colleges or universities of confessional denominations, are sharply criticized. They are taken to task first for being much more interested in financial profits than in education, and second, for being businesslike institutions that offer only low-cost courses, such as business administration, law, fine arts, and pedagogy, which do not demand expensive premises and equipment, such as laboratories, and, by and large, do not hire a highly qualified staff (Demo, 1993).

This situation is likely to improve since the new Supplementary Law of Guidelines and Basic Principles prescribes an external evaluation to be conducted every five years as a requisite for renewing the authorization for the functioning of each higher education course. The courses that do not meet the official requirement of minimal standards of effectiveness must be closed down.

Legitimization of the performance of universities leads to the issue of evaluation—one that is highly complex and subject to much controversy. Evaluating higher education in Brazil means dealing with a multifarious set of institutions, ranking from excellence at the top to mediocrity at the bottom. A great deal of the criticism addressed to higher education is rooted in the fact that legislation and policies give homogeneous treatment to sharply heterogeneous entities (Castro, 1994).

While evaluation is an all-pervading issue, the approaches to it are divergent. From the government's standpoint, the cost-benefit argument prevails. For the academic community, evaluation should have an educational, critical, and emancipatory orientation. It is doubtful that these two rival views will some day be reconciled (Figueiredo & Sobreira, 1996).

Educational Management

In recent decades, the concepts of education and school management have undergone significant mutations all over the world. The same is true for Brazil. Democratic management and the autonomy of public schools and universities are key words in the Brazilian education ideology, starting from the terminology used in the Constitution and in supplementary legislation.

After the enactment of the new Constitution, an atmosphere of political liberalization pervaded the country, and the application of democratic principles to the educational sphere was a natural consequence. Brazilian educators are now able to put into practice a long-cherished ideology that links together school effectiveness, school improvement, and school-based management. The Ministry of Education leads a program of resource allocation for supporting public schools as a starting point to autonomy. This means autonomy to decide on pedagogic and administrative issues, calling for greater responsibility on the part of the schools' personnel, the parents and teachers associations, and the communities within which the schools are located, particularly through the action of a school council. The fact that democratic management, as well as a reasonable amount of research, is being established all over the country, gives rise to great optimism among education professionals, and many of the outcomes are in fact very positive and promising (Wittman & Jarbas, 1993).

However, scholars, researchers, and practitioners must probe deeper into the subject in order to improve democratic management in the public schools and in the education system as a whole. Valuable contributions can be obtained from the international experience. Countries such as Australia, New Zealand, Canada, England and Wales, and the United States have useful information to share, contained in a number of studies carried out with a view to a better understanding of the effects of school-based management from a multinational perspective, represented by a variety of models, based on empirical research.

The most significant question to ask refers to the association between school-based management and the quality of the curriculum and of the teaching and learning processes. As far as Brazil is concerned, numerous successful experiences of democratic management with the intense participation of the community are under way. Democracy in school life is being disseminated at all levels, and school autonomy, though difficult to implement, is the most cherished principle among educators.

Resource Increase versus Better Allocation

One of the excuses presented to explain the allocation of fewer resources to the social sectors, education included, is that these resources tend to be misused due to the deficiencies of bureaucracies, to patrimonialism, and to waste. The same is never said of other equally inefficient sectors, a point relevant to the ideological bias of fiscal austerity.

Bureaucracies certainly do devour resources and teachers, and students may be poorly distributed across the school system. There is indeed an excessive number of underpaid teachers and, above all, a large number of nonteaching employees. Conservation of materials is often deficient, and administrative activities tend to receive greater attention than target activities.

However, Brazil needs not only to dramatically improve the allocation of educational resources, but also to expand these resources and to improve their distribution among the different levels of government. In 1999, the average annual cost per student in preschool was US$509 dollars; in primary education, US$609; in higher education, US$5,376. These levels not only are very low compared to other countries, particularly those of OECD, but there is a vast gap between the education provided to the people and the education of the elite.

A constitutional proposal for the establishment of a basic education fund is presently under discussion in Brazil and is seen as a route to improve both efficiency and equity. The most serious obstacle is how to add new money in order to gradually reduce regional disparities.

Education and Social Equity

To pursue this theme, the most recurring topic is the relation between education and social equity. As a systemic phenomenon, social equity cannot be addressed within the sphere of education only. The social system as a whole must be transformed so that educational policies aiming at social inclusion can succeed, and education can fulfill the goals to which the Brazilian State is committed: that is, the full development of the person, his or her preparedness for the exercise of citizenship, and his or her qualification for work. In other words, the self-realization of each and every Brazilian, who should all be treated as equals.

This conception of equality, full political citizenship, and the qualifications for economic competition imply a national project. This is outlined in the Constitution, which seeks the development of national virtues such as democratic behavior, respect for the cultural diversity characteristic of the plurality of the Brazilian people, and social solidarity.

The left-wing government that took office in January 2003 has highlighted programs such as the fight against hunger, minimum income, universities for all, and suchlike. Although the launching of these programs has often been rather chaotic, they are all inspired by the principles of justice, inclusion, and equal opportunities. It is hoped that implementation flaws will not result in the abortion of worthy ideas as has happened on past occasions and administrations.

Presence and Role of the Third Sector

An important issue is the presence of the so-called "Third Sector"—organizations that are nongovernmental and nonprofit, a fairly recent phenomenon. These nongovernmental organizations (NGOs)—a name conferred by the World Bank and the United Nations—are not new in Brazil. Membership consists of socially active professionals and technicians, as well as religious groups. The NGOs have had a strong presence in the education sector, usually in the development of adult literacy activities.

There are simultaneously social movements that are playing a part in Brazilian day-to-day politics. Numerous and differentiated groups such as women, senior citizens, blacks, children, and homosexuals are demanding participation in the decision-making processes, especially those that affect their lives and confer on them the right to have their distinctiveness respected by the state and by society at large.

Political representation is no longer enough. They are trying to create alternative political spaces other than the Parliament and are opening up new fields of political participation. Instead of relying on the work of conventional instances of political representation, these groups go to the streets and cry out their demands, concerns, and interests.

An eloquent example of a powerful social movement is the *Sem Terra* (the Landless), a large group of rural workers who demand the right to own a piece of land to cultivate and to live on. As a grassroots movement, *Sem Terra* demonstrates the potential for agrarian reform in Brazil. Participants have loud voices, fair demands, and can count on strong political support from prestigious organizations such as the Catholic Church, political parties, and several civil organizations. Recently, when thousands marched upon Brasilia in a peaceful demonstration for agrarian reform, they were met by unanimous support from the Government, the Congress, the media, several nongovernmental organizations, and from the population in general.

But even as Brazil is convinced of the urgent need to promote agrarian reform, some segments of society disagree with the methods employed by the Landless Movement. They cannot condone the way the movement has occupied farms all over the country in order to force the government to meet its demands.

POSTSCRIPT

Over the last two decades, education in Brazil has gone through both quantitative expansion and qualitative development.

The most sensible attitude, in the face of the many complex problems of Brazilian education, would be not to discard any initiative offhand. The future of society and of the educational system will depend on the nation's capacity to learn from experience, to be innovative, and to promote desirable changes.

REFERENCES

Abramovay, M., Andrade, C., & Waiselfisz, J. J. (1998). *Bolsa Escola: melhoria educacional e redução da pobreza (School attendance scholarship—Educational improvement and reduction of poverty).* Brasília: UNESCO.

Aguiar, M., & Araújo, C. H. (2002). *Bolsa-escola: educação para enfrentar a pobreza (School attendance scholarship—Education to fight poverty).* Brasília: UNESCO.

Brazil, Ministry of Education. (1999). *Avaliação do Programa de Complementação de Recursos do Fundo de Manutenção e Desenvolvimento do Ensino Fundamental e de Valorização do Magistério (FUNDEF) (Evaluation of the Supplementary Resources Program for the Fund for Primary Education Maintenance and Development and for the Valorization of Teachers—FUNDEF).* Brasília: MEC, SEF, INEP.

Brazil, Ministry of Education. (2002). *Fundo Nacional de Desenvolvimento da Educação (National Fund for the Development of Education).* Brasília: MEC/FNDE.

Castro, C. de M. (1994). *Educação brasileira: consertos e remendos (Brazilian education: Repairs and mendings).* Rio de Janeiro: Rocco.

Delgado, M. (2004, September 19). *Jornal de Brasília,* p. 14.

Demo, P. (1993). *Desafios modernos da educação* (Modern challenges in education). Petrópolis, RJ: Vozes.

Figueiredo, M. C. M., & Sobreira, M. I. F. (1996). The evaluation of higher education system in Brazil. In R. Cowen, D. Coulby, & C. Jones (Eds.), *The evaluation of higher education systems.* World Yearbook of Education (pp. 34–50). London: Kegan Paul.

Gomes, C. A. (2002). *The challenge of educational equity: Evaluation of a fund in Brazil.* Paper presented at the Annual Meeting of the International Cultural Research Network. Brasília: Brasília Catholic University.

Gomes, C. A. (2004). Quinze anos de ciclos no ensino fundamental: um balanço das pesquisas sobre a sua implantação *(15 years implementing ungrading in primary education: A research review). Revista Brasileira de Educaçãol, 25,* 39–52.

Offe, C. (1983). A democracia partidária competitiva e o Welfare State keynesiano: fatores da estabilidade e desorganização (Competitive party democracy and the Keynesian welfare state: Factors of stability and disorganization) *Dados - Ciências Sociais, 26,* 29–51.

Oliveira, R. P. de. (2003). A municipalização cumpriu suas promessas de democratização da gestão educacional? Um balanço crítico (Has municipalization fulfilled its promises of democracy in school administration?). *Gestão em Ação, 6,* 99–106.

Verhine, R. E., & Rosa, D. L. (2003). Fundef no Estado da Bahia (Primary education fund in Bahia state). *Gestão em Ação, 6,* 107–118.

Wittman, L. C., & Jarbas, J. C. (Eds.) (1993). *Gestão compartilhada na escola pública: o especialista na construção do fazer saber fazer* (Shared management in the public school: The specialist in the construction of making and knowing how to make). Florianópolis: AAESC:ANPAE/SUL.

World Bank. (2001a). *O combate à pobreza no Brasil (The fight against proverty in Brazil).* Washington, DC: Author.

World Bank. (2001b). *Eradicating child labor in Brazil.* Washington, DC: Author.

World Bank. (2001c). *Brazil: An assessment of the Bolsa Escola Programs.* Washington, DC: Author.

World Bank. (2003). *Brasil: educação municipal no Brasil (Municipal education in Brazil).* Washington, DC: Author.

AUTHOR INDEX

Abelmann, C. H., 316, 317, 320
Abu-Libdeh, H., 129, 130, 131, 132, 133, 134
Abu-Shokor, A., 126
Adams, D. W., 306
Aguirre, R. C., 288
Ahlquist, R., 307
Al-Attas, S. N., 175
Al-Faroogi, I. R., 175
Al-Nimer, K., 127, 137
Althbach, P. G., 98
Anabtawi, S., 130
Ancess, J., 316, 317
Anna, T., 289
Apple, M. W., 317
Ariav, T., 160
Arimoto, A., 81
Arnott, A., 330
Aschbacher, P. R., 317
Ashman, A. F., 113
Astor, R. A., 164
Atkin, A., 161, 162
Austin, A. G., 108
Avis, J., 242
Awartani, S., 149

Back, H. K., 62, 65
Backhoff, E., 295
Badran, N. S. A., 137
Bahr, N., 112
Balla, J., 113
Ballantyn, S., 126
Banks, J. A., 311, 312, 313, 319
Bar-Elli, D., 159
Barkhordian, A., 192
Barnes, C., 131
Bartlett, L., 106
Bartlett, R., 111
Basini, A., 238
Bassok, M., 150
Beck, H. K., 62, 65
Beech, C., 192
Benbenishta, R., 164
Benevenisti, M., 126
Bentwich, J. S., 158
Berlak, H., 321
Bernal, D. D., 311
Bigelow, B., 321
Bindloss, J., 192
Blamires, M., 243
Bogard, G., 275
Borevskaya, N., 259
Bracho, T., 295
Bray, M., 259
Bredekamp, S., 139
Brooks, G., 235
Burton, D., 236, 242

Campbell, J., 112
Canning, M., 258
Carnoy, M., 307
Carrington, V., 112
Cassidy, F., 116
Cassidy, R. C., 305
Castles, S., 107
Castro, C. de M., 354
Chabane, S., 330
Chen, D. Y., 80
Chen, Z. L., 82, 86
Cheng, L., 92, 94
Cheng, S. H., 84
Cheng, Y., 95
Ciulistet Group, 307
Clough, P., 239, 242
Coady, D., 291
Cobbold, T., 114
Cohen, D. K., 315
Cook, M. L., 298
Cope, W., 107
Cortina, R., 290
Cothran, D., 290
Cuetara, C., 288
Cui, C. Y., 79, 87, 88, 89
Cuskally, M., 112

Darinksi, A., 252
Darling-Hammond, L., 315, 316, 317, 320, 321
Davis, G., 115, 116
Deibes, I., 132
Delgado, M., 350, 352
Demo, P., 354
Dempsey, L., 113
Deng, X. P., 69, 74
Derby, S., 192
Diamond, J. B., 317
Docking, J., 233, 238
Donald, D., 334
Dornan, P., 232
Dukmak, S., 140, 142, 145
Duran, J., 296
Dyer, G., 194

Elmore, R. F., 316, 317, 320
Etzioni, A., 159

Falk, B., 316
Farsoun, S. K., 151, 153
Feinberg, W., 308, 309, 312
Feng, D. H., 94
Figueiredo, M. C. M., 354
Filipov, V., 253, 256, 259
Flaherty, J., 232
Forlin, C., 113
Forlin, P., 113
Foreman, P., 113
Freedman, D., 110
Freire, P., 142
Friedman, I. A., 164
Friedman, T., 195
Fuhrman, S., 316
Fuhrman, S. H., 316, 317, 320
Fursenko, A., 257

Garmon, M. A., 319
Garner, P., 229, 230, 239, 242
Gary, G., 241
Gautman, H., 198
Gavish, B., 164
Gaziel, H., 156
Gearon, L., 233
Ghali, M., 131, 143, 144

Giacaman, R., 132
Gilmore, L., 112
Givner, C. C., 113
Glasman, N. S., 156
Goertz, M., 110
Goleman, D., 241
Gomes, C. A., 347, 349
Gong, F., 95
Gonzalez, E. J., 161
Gow, L., 113
Grace, N., 111
Gray, G., 241
Grayson, G., 289, 297
Green, W., 108
Grieco, E. M., 305
Gronn, P., 115
Gu, R. F., 75
Gumpel, T. P., 149
Guo, X. M., 78, 79

Hall, J., 336
Hallam, S., 236
Han, K. U., 63, 64
Harmon, K., 80
Hatfield, S. B., 290
Hauser, R. M., 317
Held, D., 307, 308
Heleniak, T., 258
Henderson, E., 142
Henry, M., 111
Herchell, G., 111
Herman, J. L., 317
Heubert, J. P., 317
Hextall, I., 240
Hickling-Hudson, A., 307
Ho, A. K., 74
Hofmeyr, J., 336, 337
Hommous, N. A., 129
Hornby, G., 238, 242
Hu, J. T., 74
Hu, R. W., 76
Hunter, L., 112

Iglesias, E., 288
Inbar, D. E., 158
Ireson, J., 236

Jakubielski, L., 269
Jansen, J., 331
Jarbas, J. C., 354
Jary, D., 195
Jary, J., 195
Jester, T. E., 307
Jiang, Z. M., 93
Jung, D. V., 113
Jung, D. Y., 63, 64, 65, 66
Jupp, J., 107, 116, 117

Kalantzis, M., 107
Kalim, M. S., 175
Kamal, S., 141, 142
Kanawati, R., 140
Kang, C. D., 63
Kang, M. S., 64
Kapitzke, C., 112
Karczewski, J., 269
Karwowska-Struczyk, M., 269
Kasprzyk, M., 266
Kawagley, G. A., 307
Ke, Z., 79
Kennedy, A. M., 161
Kent, R., 297
Keys, W., 235
Kfir, D., 160
Kgobe, M., 336
Khosa, V. R., 336
Khromchenko, Y., 161
Kleinberger, A. F., 154
Knight, B., 239
Knight, J., 106
Kodomo, Katie S., 37, 45
Konstantinovski, D., 259
Kornhaber, M. L., 316
Kozakiewicz, M., 268
Kwiecinski, Z., 268
Kyoiku, G. S., 48

Lahav, H., 136, 137
Land, J., 113
Land, R., 111
Lanning, J. T., 297
Larrazolo, N., 295
Law, W. W., 77, 79, 80
Lawlor, S., 237
Lazarus, S., 334
Lee, S., 337
Lee, W. O., 75
Leondar-Wright, B., 306
Levi, A., 159
Levin, H. M., 307
Li, J. W., 70
Li, X. L., 84
Lian, Y. M., 71
Liang, W. G., 84
Lin, Y. G., 79
Lingard, B., 106, 111, 114
Lipka, J., 307
Little, A., 202
Liu, L., 95
Liu, N., 87, 92
Liu, N. C., 95
Lolwana, P., 334
Lomawaima, K. T., 307
Lovat, T. J., 110
Lowen, J. W., 313
Loxley, A., 243
Lu, Z. Y., 70
Lubienski, C., 308
Lucas, R. E. B., 223
Lucas, T., 310, 311, 319, 320
Lui, S. J., 70, 71
Luke, A., 111, 112

Maari, S. K., 124, 126, 127, 133, 137
Maas, L., 134, 142
Mackinnon, D., 233
Mahony, P., 240
Malin, M., 116, 117
Martin, C., 293
Martin, M. O., 161
Marzano, R., 320
Masubuchi, Y., 43
Matters, G., 111
Mayer, D., 112
Mccarty, T. L., 307
Mcconkey, R., 131, 145
Mcneil, L. M., 304, 320, 321
Meadmore, P., 110, 114, 115
Meek, V. L., 80
Meredith, P., 234
Meyer, L. H., 113
Mills, C., 239
Mills, D., 239
Mitchell, J., 112
Mittler, P., 145
Mohatt, G. V., 323
Moock, P., 258

Moosa, E., 329
Morales, A., 299
Morales-Gomez, D., 290, 301
Moreton-Robinson, A., 117
Morody, M., 266
Morrissey, M., 107
Mosle, S., 316
Mukwevho, T., 336
Muller, J., 334, 336
Mullis, I. V. S., 161
Murata, Y., 38
Murray, S., 112

Nasku, F., 146
Nesher, P., 159
Newell, R. G., 290
Nieto, S., 308, 311, 312, 319
Nikandrov, N., 259
Nir, A. E., 158, 159, 163
Nowak-Fabrykowski, K., 279
Nowicka, W., 269
Numata, H., 43, 45, 46

O'brien, T., 243
Ochiai, T., 113
O'day, J., 316, 320
Ogawa, R. T., 314
Ogi, N., 40, 43, 45
Oliver, M., 131, 145
Onoda, M., 44

Park, H. C., 113
Pascoe, S., 114
Pearson, N., 117
Peled, Y., 152, 153
Pendergast, D., 112
Phillips, R., 242
Pan, Y. G., 87, 88, 89
Popham, W. J., 316
Porter, P., 106
Postman, N., 45
Praced, C. V., 197
Psacharopoulos, G., 260

Quddus, N. J., 175

Ramirez, R., 297
Ravitch, D., 314, 320
Rigby, A., 138, 143, 144, 146
Rizvi, F., 111
Rizvi, S. S., 175
Roaf, C., 240
Romano, H., 295
Rosa, D. L., 347
Rubio, L. F., 290

Saha, 261
Sandholtz. J. H., 314
Saunders, C. A., 132
Schmoker, M., 320
Scott, J., 304, 308
Scribner, S. P., 314
Seidenberg, A., 160
Sergeev, I., 253
Shafir, G., 152, 153
Shalabi, F., 130
Shen, J. L., 88
Shimbun, A., 31, 34, 37, 38, 43, 45, 47
Shin, H. B., 305
Singh, S., 192, 193, 194
Slayton, J., 304, 308
Sleeter, C. E., 311
Smith, D. L., 110, 111
Smith, L. T., 307
Smith, M., 316, 320
Smolin, O., 257
Snow, D., 113
Soboh, N., 134, 142
Sobreira, M. I. F., 354
Soltis, J. F., 308, 309, 312
Sosnowski, A., 279
Spillane, J. P., 317
Spring, J., 309
Stakes, R., 238, 242
Stevens, L., 112
Stewart, F., 68
Stoops, N., 306
Stratham. J., 233
Strickland, J., 308
Swirsky, S., 161, 162

Takak, S., 38
Taylor, N., 336
Taylor, S., 111
Thomas, G., 243
Thompson, S., 316, 317
Thurow, L. C., 223
Topolski, J., 266
Torres, C. A., 290, 301
Trow, M., 81
Tymms, P., 236
Tzfadia, E., 153

Urban-Klaehn, J., 269, 272

Vargas, L., 287
Vaughan, M. K., 290
Veit-Wilson, J., 232
Verhine, R. E., 347
Villegas, A. M., 310, 311, 319, 320
Vinjevold, P., 336
Vollansky, A., 156

Walker, S., 291
Wang, S. H., 88, 89
Wang, X., 90
Wang, X. X., 84
Ward, J., 113
Weare, K., 241
Wei, Y., 94, 95
Wells, A. S., 304, 308
Welmond, M., 317
Western, M., 115
Westwood, P., 113
Wichmann, J., 278
Winters, L., 317
Wittman, L. C., 354
Wu, B. W., 84
Wu, D. S., 87, 89
Wu, W. S., 90
Wu, Y. W., 87
Wyse, D., 236

Xiao, Y. B., 87, 89
Xu, M., 90, 98

Yan, K., 88, 89
Yeroshin, V., 257
Yiftachel, O., 153
Yu, B. Y., 90
Yuan, G. R., 93

Zacharia, C., 151, 153
Zajda, J., 247, 248, 257, 258, 259, 261
Zameret, Z., 154

Zehr, M. A., 296
Zeira, A., 164
Zhang, Y., 83, 84
Zhang, Z. M., 83, 84
Zhoa, W. H., 95
Zhou, T., 90, 96
Zhou, Y. Q., 93
Zhu, K. X., 93
Zhu, R. J., 70
Zucker, D., 156
Zughby, S., 141

SUBJECT INDEX

Academic *versus* vocational/technical focus, 14, 16, 19, 20, 22, 23, 25, 26, 27. *See also* School types/categories—technical and university; and brain drain/gain
Accountability, decentralizing, downsizing, 14, 15, 16, 17, 18, 19, 20, 22, 23, 25, 26, 74, 79, 155, 159, 163, 164, 186, 214, 226, 227, 230, 233, 248, 257, 259, 260, 279, 280, 290, 301, 315, 317, 318, 321, 343, 349, 355. *See also* Privatization
Administration, policies, regulations, 14, 16, 17, 18, 19, 25, 26, 38, 55, 72, 108–110, 128, 129, 177, 214–215, 233, 242, 279, 291, 331–332, 343
At-risk children, *see* Children at risk

Bilingual education, 249–250, 295, 299
Brain drain/gain, 14, 15, 19, 20, 22, 26, 81, 91–92, 96, 174, 199. *See also* Academic *versus* vocational/technical focus.
Bullying, 35, 43, 243

Caste system, 195–197
Children at risk, 15 17, 18, 20, 21, 23, 25, 26, 146, 187, 219–220, 258, 259, 294–295, 299
Class size, 37, 65, 136, 162, 178, 198, 216, 217, 299, 332
Comparative studies
  approaches to, 7
  component of teacher education, 4
  types of, 4
  value and utility of, 4–5, 11–13, 149
Compulsory education, 36, 41, 60-61, 76, 88, 109, 155, 158, 184, 198, 199, 212, 213, 233, 244, 248, 269, 271, 291, 292, 298
Curriculum, 6, 15, 16, 20, 25, 26, 27, 38, 65, 105, 110–112, 118, 131, 133, 142–143, 157, 184, 199, 215, 235–236, 237–238, 242, 243, 244, 249–251, 255, 261, 271–273, 280–281, 298, 331, 332, 333–334
  content, 37, 56, 77–79, 82, 111, 137, 158, 173, 179, 180, 183, 188, 200, 235, 249, 250–251, 268, 271, 272, 273, 333–334, 345
  defined, 312
  goals, 35, 36, 54–55, 56, 77–78, 173, 174, 175, 238, 278, 279, 280, 311–313, 345–346

Decentralization, *see* Accountability, downsizing, decentralization
Development education, 4
Diagnostic tools, 6, 145, 316
Distance education, *see* School types/categories—distance
Downsizing education bureaucracy, *see* Accountability, downsizing, decentralization
Dropouts, 35, 42, 43, 136, 158, 163, 176, 178, 179, 189, 200, 219, 310, 321
  defined, 43

Early childhood education, *see* School types/categories—preschool/kindergarten
English as a second language, 58, 82, 83, 97, 98, 179, 293
Essential learnings, *see* Curriculum content, goals
Evaluation, 38, 72, 83, 85–87, 112, 118, 130, 131, 159, 161, 183, 216–217, 227, 236–237, 238, 250, 253, 256, 260, 261, 271, 272, 273, 314, 316–317, 331, 336, 354
Examinations, *see* Evaluation
Expansion of education, 14, 15, 16, 17, 18, 20, 21, 23, 25, 74, 76, 80, 81, 157, 176, 179, 182, 185, 187, 189, 212, 342, 352

Financial constraints, *see* Funding
Foreign language education, *see* English as a second language, Bilingual education
Funding, 14, 16, 17, 18, 19, 20, 21, 22, 23, 25, 26, 55, 83, 108, 113, 114, 115, 116, 131, 136, 161, 179, 217, 221, 222, 230, 257, 258, 259, 274, 300, 309, 330, 332, 335–337, 352, 355

Gender equality/inequality, 15, 16, 17, 18, 20, 21, 22, 23, 24, 64, 134, 142, 143, 172, 176, 178, 179, 180, 187, 196, 198, 199, 201, 212, 220, 281, 304
Globalization, defined, 19
Grade retention, 321, 352

Higher education, *see* School types/categories—university, and technical

Indigenous peoples, 106, 108, 109, 116–117, 287, 288, 290, 295, 299, 301, 307
  defined 306
Intelligentsia, 7, 12
International education, 4, 184

Juvenile delinquency, 64, 90, 258

Kibbutz movement, 154

Lifelong learning, 17, 62–63, 201, 248, 275, 293, 296, 346
Literacy/illiteracy, 16, 18, 21, 22, 61, 66, 75–76, 130, 132, 134, 142, 178, 179, 180, 186, 187, 188, 198, 200, 201, 219, 248, 265, 267–268, 290, 296, 350

Meiji Restoration, 32, 33, 35, 40, 41, 42, 46, 48, 49
Middle schools, *see* School types/categories—middle
Migrant children, 72, 81, 87–91, 97, 105, 106, 107, 152
Multiculturalism/multicultural education, 17, 22, 23, 24, 117–118, 304, 311–313, 314, 319

No Child Left Behind, 314, 315, 318
Nongovernment organizations (NGOs), 127, 129, 141, 180, 185, 186, 275, 294, 348, 356

Pedagogy, 5, 26, 97, 139–140, 144, 215, 224, 236, 256–257
Population
  aging, 16, 34, 53, 63, 208, 254
  description of, 31, 69, 107, 108, 125, 126, 150, 168, 169, 194, 211, 232, 248, 265, 287, 305, 328, 329
  numbers, 8, 31, 53, 69, 105, 124, 125, 126, 150, 151, 169, 192, 207, 230, 247, 265, 287, 329, 336
  youthful, 17, 230, 265
Primary schools, *see* School types/categories—elementary
Privatization, 14, 18, 19, 20, 21, 22, 23, 25, 210, 257, 259, 260, 274. *See also* Accountability, decentralizing, downsizing
Pupil-teacher ratio, see Class size

Refugees, 105, 126, 135, 188
Religious studies/religious education, 143, 173, 174, 175, 176, 278
Research initiatives, 5, 60, 80, 94, 112, 145–146, 176, 186, 225–226, 227

School types/categories
  cram, 65, 66, 84, 86–87, 253
  distance, 109, 182–183, 200, 201, 296, 347–348
  elementary, 36–37, 58, 75–76, 109–110, 130, 178, 199, 212, 235, 249, 268, 271, 292, 330, 345, 351
  foundation, 233, 234
  home, 252
  indigenous, 175–176
  Juku, 32, 34, 37, 49, 50
  middle, 58, 112, 250, 292
  preschool/kindergarten, 36, 56, 58, 65, 130, 136, 212, 230, 238–239, 249, 269, 274, 291–292, 343, 351
  private, 22, 46, 64–65, 66, 90–91, 106, 109–110, 114–115, 141, 157, 158, 179, 189, 198, 202, 213, 221, 252–253, 271, 274, 292, 293–294, 297, 332, 353
  religious, *see* Religious studies/religious education
  secondary, 37, 59, 130, 158, 178, 199, 214, 235, 236, 248, 250–251, 271–272, 330, 343, 351
  special education, 36, 59, 132, 145, 251, 275
  technical, 37, 38, 55, 63, 76, 77, 128, 129, 130, 178, 180, 185, 187, 189, 201, 212, 251, 258–259, 272–273, 281–282, 292, 293, 331, 345
  university, 45–46, 59, 115–116, 130, 178, 181–182, 200, 213–214, 215, 221, 222–223, 227, 248, 252–253, 273–274, 297–298, 330–331, 343, 345, 352–353
  underground, 84, 87–89, 138–139
Settler society, 107, 118, 306, 307, 321
Special education, special needs, inclusion, 15, 18, 19, 59, 60, 66, 112–113, 128, 131–132, 134–135, 144–145, 158, 239–240, 243, 251, 275, 293, 295, 333, 334, 337, 345–346. *See also* School types/categories—special education
  defined, 113
  special needs individuals, 64, 66, 128, 130, 134, 162, 199, 200, 238, 242, 295, 299
Standards testing, *see* Evaluation
Street children, *see* Children at risk

Teachers
  as *intelligentsia,* 7, 12
  attrition, 25, 26, 116, 164
  education, certification, programs, 4, 14, 18, 20, 25–26, 40, 60, 63, 65–66, 132, 136–137, 144, 159–160, 164, 182, 184, 185, 189, 200–201, 202, 216, 237, 243, 255, 261, 274, 275–277, 291, 298, 299, 319–320, 342
  gender, 116, 132–133, 178, 310
  numbers, 72, 116, 130, 164, 178, 217, 310, 330, 337
  shortages, 25, 26
  status, 39–40, 217–219, 240–241, 277
  stress, 25, 26
  workload, 44–45
Teacher training, *see* Teachers—education, certification, programs
Teaching strategies, *see* Pedagogy
Technology, 14, 15, 19, 20, 23, 26, 82, 189, 224, 227, 300
Tertiary education, *see* School type/categories—universities
Textbooks, 56, 181, 184, 221, 249, 253–254, 291, 299, 348–349
Themes of the text, 14–27

Unemployment, 34, 71, 92, 125, 153, 163, 208, 223, 247, 267, 269, 329
Universities, *see* School types/categories—university
international rankings, 95–96, 98, 224–225

Urban/rural differences and inequalities, 15, 17, 18, 20, 21, 23, 25, 71, 72, 83, 94, 97, 105, 162, 169, 176, 179, 266, 295, 296, 301

Violence in schools, 35, 43, 164

Vocational education, *see* Academic vs vocational/technical focus, School type/categories—technical